Cruising the
CHESAPEAKE

A GUNKHOLER'S GUIDE

WILLIAM H. SHELLENBERGER

THIRD EDITION

INTERNATIONAL MARINE / McGRAW-HILL
Camden, Maine • New York • Chicago • San Francisco
• Lisbon • London • Madrid • Mexico City
• Milan • New Delhi • San Juan • Seoul
• Singapore • Sydney • Toronto

International Marine

A Division of The McGraw-Hill Companies

10 9 8 7 6 5 4 3 2 1
Copyright ©1990, 1993, 2001 International Marine
All rights reserved. The publisher takes no responsibility for the use of any of the materials or methods described in this book, nor for the products thereof. The name "International Marine" and the International Marine logo are trademarks of The McGraw-Hill Companies. Printed in the United States of America.

Cataloging-in-Publication Data is on file with the Library of Congress

Questions regarding the content of this book should be addressed to
International Marine
P.O. Box 220
Camden, ME 04843
www.internationalmarine.com

Questions regarding the ordering of this book should be addressed to
The McGraw-Hill Companies
Customer Service Department
P.O. Box 547
Blacklick, OH 43004
Retail customers: 1-800-262-4729
Bookstores: 1-800-722-4726

Printed by R. R. Donelley on 60# Finch.
Design by dcdesign
Edited by Jonathan Eaton and Joanne S. Allen
All photos by the author unless otherwise noted.
Regions 1–7 maps by Alex Wallach. Maps pages xv, 56 and Regions 8–11 by Paul Mirto.

CONTENTS

Region 1

Region 6

POTOMAC RIVER TO WOLF TRAP LIGHT 299

Region 6

THE ATLANTIC COAST & THE DELAWARE BAY & RIVER

ACKNOWLEDGMENTS

NO ONE WRITES A BOOK of this type without a great deal of help from many others, and my case is no different. I would like to express my appreciation to many of those people without whose help or forbearance this book and its subsequent editions would not have been possible.

First and foremost, I thank my immediate family and cruising companions, my wife, Judy, and my two daughters, Juliet and Lauren, who helped research material contained in this book and put up with me during the writing of the first edition and during revisions. Judy, in particular, was instrumental in locating potential photographs for the cover.

I am still grateful to Wayne and Sherrill Bower, Stew and Diana Kauffman, Bill and Ann Milne, and Don Wood and his late wife, Lynne, all of whom provided the benefit of their experience in reviewing cruising regions of the first edition for accuracy, completeness, and clarity. In the same vein, I would like to thank my late mother, Virginia, a former English and reading teacher, who proofread the draft text of the first edition and pointed out several areas that needed work. Lessons learned then helped in subsequent editions.

For much of the information on land-based sights and for many of the photographs used throughout the book, particular thanks go to the following: Gary Holloway, Samuel Britten, and Jim Pottie, Aberdeen Proving Grounds; Jane White, Baltimore Office of Promotion & Tourism; Herman Schieke, Annapolis Chamber of Commerce; Paula Johnston, Calvert Marine Museum; Peter McClintock, Virginia Natural Resources Commission; Lee Ann Sink, Virginia Peninsula Tourism & Conference Bureau; Deborah Padgett, Jamestown Festival Park; Elaine Justice, College of William and Mary University Relations; and James Resolute, City of Portsmouth Department of Economic Development. For many of the photographs used in the third edition, especially the new regions 8 to 11, a great deal of credit goes to Darrell Luskin; Steve Anderson; Christof Spieler; Tom McGuire (www.tommcguire.com); Freda Gandy; Capt. Robert Glover, Kalmar Nyckel Foundation; Rita Rock, Chesapeake Bay Bridge & Tunnel District; Christina Claggett, St. Clements Island–Potomac River Museum; Sheila Brennan, Navy Museum; and Tracy Mosa, Baltimore Area Convention & Visitors Association.

Many thanks also go to numerous people who sent me much information without even including their names. For that reason, my thanks go to the Kent County Chamber of Commerce, the Dorchester County Chamber of Commerce, the Somerset County Chamber of Commerce, the Crisfield Area Chamber of Commerce, the Isle of Wight/Smithfield Chamber of Commerce, the Norfolk Chamber of Commerce, the Maryland Department of Natural Resources, the National Park Service, the Maryland Forest, Park & Wildlife Service, the Williamsburg Area Convention & Visitor's Center, the Chesapeake Bay Foundation, the Virginia Division of Tourism, the Eastern Shore of Virginia Tourism Commission, and the Chesapeake Bay Estuary Program of the U.S. Fish & Wildlife Service.

My sincere appreciation goes also to the many friends and acquaintances, especially those in the Arundel Yacht Club and others too numerous to name individually, who have provided not only information but invaluable encouragement for all three editions.

PREFACE

The captain takes the seadogs ashore for their constitutional.

T HINGS CHANGE! OUR lives progress. Children grow up and leave home. Dogs and other pets age and pass on, to be replaced by others. Technology changes at a fantastic pace. Even the waters upon which we cruise and the land bordering them change. Sometimes it is for the better; sometimes it is for the worse; sometimes it is simply different.

This book is the culmination of a love affair of more than 30 years with the Chesapeake Bay and nearby waters. The "we" that recurs often in these pages is not editorial. "We" have always sailed the Bay as a family from the time of our first boat, a 14-foot runabout, through three others, to our present 31-foot Westerly twin-keeled sloop. Recently, our crew composition changed. Our daughters, now grown, still join us occasionally for cruises, but most of the time the human crew consists of my wife, Judy, and myself. Our "trademark" Scottish and West Highland white terriers have passed on, and now we have a pair of unique Tibetan terriers, who also make great boat dogs. When our daughters join us, they bring a Scotty and a West Highland white terrier to augment the canine crew. These latter crew members may explain my apparent preoccupation with beaches and convenient places to land.

With more than 3,000 miles of shoreline, the Chesapeake Bay offers one of the best cruising areas in the world. The harbors, creeks, rivers, bays, and bights offer plentiful opportunities for relaxed cruising, with surroundings ranging from cosmopolitan to provincial to pristine; yet nowhere in the Bay are you more than a short distance from a safe, protected harbor. Whether you prefer a slip at a busy marina in the middle of a city like Baltimore or a quiet gunkhole where your only neighbors are wildlife on the shore or surface-feeding fish, you will find what you seek in the Chesapeake.

This book addresses the entire Chesapeake Bay, from the Chesapeake and Delaware Canal to the north all the way to Cape Henry and the Atlantic Ocean to the south, as well as the Delaware Bay and River and the Atlantic coast harbors from New York City to Cape Henry. No one can expect to visit every inch of these waters in his or her lifetime, which is precisely what makes cruising this area so fascinating. We've gleaned information from literally hundreds of sources. Although as much of the information in this book as possible has been personally verified, things do change with time and so not all the information can be up-to-the-minute. We welcome comments, corrections, or suggestions for future editions.

Although it is *our* primary interest, this book is not limited to gunkholing. Those of you unfamiliar with the terms *gunkhole* and *gunkholer* needn't bother to look for them in a dictionary: they are common only in the lexicon of the inveterate cruiser. *Gunkhole* generally refers to a small, quiet, out-of-the-way body of water seldom frequented by the boating fraternity because it is difficult to find or enter, or at least it is perceived to be. This natural exclusivity is the gunkhole's primary appeal. To our minds, it is part of what places gunkholes among the best anchorages.

A *gunkholer* is a breed of power or sail cruiser who finds his or her way into gunkholes of all sizes and descriptions, both for the satisfaction of doing so and in search of serenity.

Anytime two or more cruising types get together, the conversation inevitably turns to anchorages, especially if at least one of them has recently visited a new place and acquired new "local knowledge." We have all had such conversations, and they seem to follow a standard script. Everyone wants to know what the "expert" has learned. Six topics dominate these gams:

1. *Location.* Where is the area relative to better-known harbors and reference points?

2. *Recommended approach.* What landmarks and ranges can be used for entering an anchorage? Are there shoals to beware of? Which side of the channel should be favored in which portion of the approach?

3. *Recommended anchorage.* How enthusiastically is this harbor recommended, and why? Where is the best anchorage? Is the anchor-

age snug, or is it open for a fetch of a mile or more in any direction? What is the range of water depth inside, and what is the controlling depth in the entrance? Is it peaceful or disturbed by traffic, congestion, or water-skiers? Is there a time of year to avoid it? Why? When is it likely to be crowded?

4. *The surrounding area.* What is there to see? Is there a beach? Are there islands or other places to explore? Can you go ashore or is the whole area private property? Is swimming possible? Why or why not?

5. *Facilities.* Are restaurants, marinas, self-service laundries, or stores readily accessible? Where are they, and what are they like? Are there any pumpout stations in the area?

6. *Special-interest items.* Are there any historic landmarks or museums nearby? Is there wildlife activity or anything else worth noting?

Remember that negative information is just as valuable as positive, sometimes more so. For example, what areas should be avoided, why, and when?

While we're on the subject of negative information, although the focus of this book is not the ecology of the Bay but the enjoyment of its waters, we have watched the Bay change over time—for many years for the worse but recently for the better.

The rockfish became very scarce for a while, but following a moratorium on catching them, they have fully rebounded and now share the Bay with bluefish, vying for the eagerly sought catch of today. The famous Chesapeake Bay oysters have been decimated by a bacterial disease, exacerbated by siltation, that has denuded once heavily populated beds and threatens to wipe out the oystering industry completely. The Bay will be a far poorer place economically and aesthetically if the working skipjacks and tongers are lost.

But there is light on the horizon! For example, early in our cruising days we saw the once plentiful osprey become an endangered species. So much so that in the late 1960s the construction of a radio tower on Bodkin Point, at the mouth of the Patapsco River, was halted permanently, and a new tower erected, when an osprey built a nest on the unfinished tower. Now, with a ban on the DDT that nearly wiped them out, ospreys have made such a comeback that it is rare to find a daymark or other navigational beacon in the Bay that does not have an osprey nest on it. That unfinished radio tower stood for many years on Bodkin Point as a monument to this dramatic turnaround. Eagles, too, have rebounded, and it is not uncommon to sight one or two of these majestic birds in many areas of the Bay.

The seaweed and sea grass in the Bay were once so common that they interfered with anyone trying to swim ashore from a boat or wade near the shore in water more than knee deep. Over the years this plant life disappeared from the waters—a visible indicator, along with huge algae blooms, of the progressive deterioration of the Bay's health. Recently seaweed has started to come back in many places due to active replanting and the increasing use of pollu-

tion controls. Even the algae blooms in the northern Bay, while still present, have decreased markedly.

Several organizations are working actively to save and restore the Bay. In 1983 the governors of Maryland, Pennsylvania, and Virginia joined with the mayor of Washington, D.C., and the administrator of the Environmental Protection Agency to establish a joint program to clean and protect the Chesapeake estuary.

If the programs are to work in the long run, the public must continue to be vigilant about the problems facing the Chesapeake Bay. It took more than 10,000 years for the rising sea to create the Bay as we know it, and it will take both time and effort to correct the damage done in the last 300 years of use and neglect. The Chesapeake Bay and its bounty will endure only so long as we who live, work, and play in its environs remain constantly alert and active in its preservation and protection.

HOW TO USE THIS BOOK

THE INTRODUCTION CONTAINS general information about the Chesapeake, the Delaware, and the Atlantic Coast, including sections on references, weather, hazards to navigation, and restricted areas. We suggest you read this information first.

THE REGIONS

We have divided the Bay into seven regions, and the Atlantic Coast and Delaware Bay and River into four more regions (see page xviii for more on those regions). Within each region of the Chesapeake, a typical sailboat (traveling at a speed of 5 knots) can reach all the points mentioned in an easy, one-day cruise. Powerboats, of course, are not constrained by time in quite the same way, but the same range generally applies to them due to their need to refuel. This

guideline breaks down in the cases of some of the longer rivers, such as the 90-mile Potomac, but even then there are plenty of intermediate anchorages. Partly by design and partly by coincidence, the cruising characteristics described at the beginning of each chapter tend to be relatively homogeneous.

Anchorages are grouped in geographical order, trending from the head of the Bay (at the Chesapeake and Delaware Canal) to its mouth. Within each region, first the Eastern and then the Western Shore of the Bay is covered. Most people cruise the Bay predominantly on one side or the other, regardless of region, since the trip across the Bay is generally long compared with harbor hopping on the same side.

The north–south trend is frequently interrupted, however, by the same complicated geography that makes the Bay a 22 paradise. One glance at a chart of the Choptank River, for ex-

REGIONS OF THE CHESAPEAKE BAY

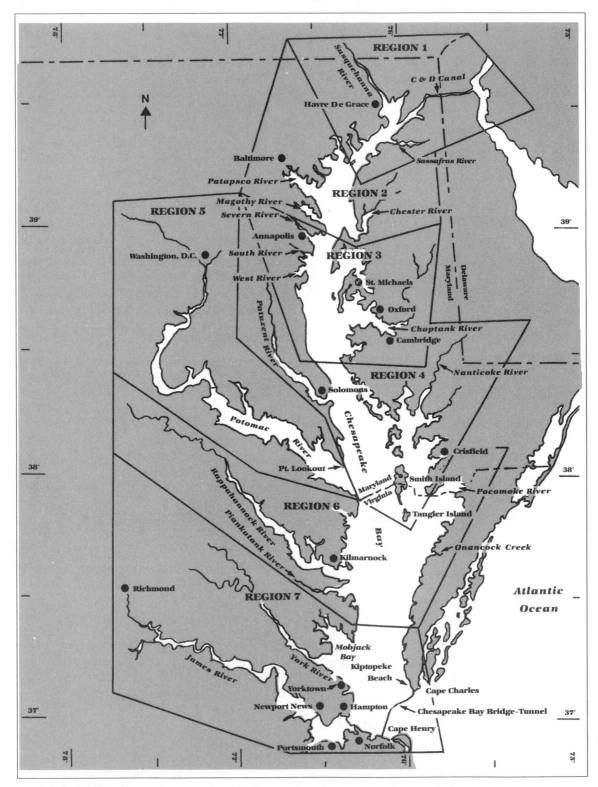

REGION 1

Susquehanna River

C & D Canal

Havre De Grace

Sassafras River

Baltimore

Patapsco River

REGION 2

Magothy River

Severn River

Chester River

REGION 5

Annapolis

REGION 3

Washington, D.C.

South River

St. Michaels

Delaware
Maryland

West River

Oxford

Patuxent River

Choptank River

Cambridge

REGION 4

Nanticoke River

Solomons

Chesapeake

Potomac

Crisfield

River

Pt. Lookout

Smith Island

Maryland
Virginia

Pocomoke River

Rappahannock River

REGION 6

Tangier Island

Bay

Onancock Creek

Piankatank River

Kilmarnock

Richmond

REGION 7

Atlantic
Ocean

Mobjack
Bay

York River

Kiptopeke
Beach

James River

Yorktown

Cape Charles

Newport News

Hampton

Chesapeake Bay Bridge-Tunnel

Cape Henry

Portsmouth

Norfolk

REGIONS OF THE MID-ATLANTIC COAST

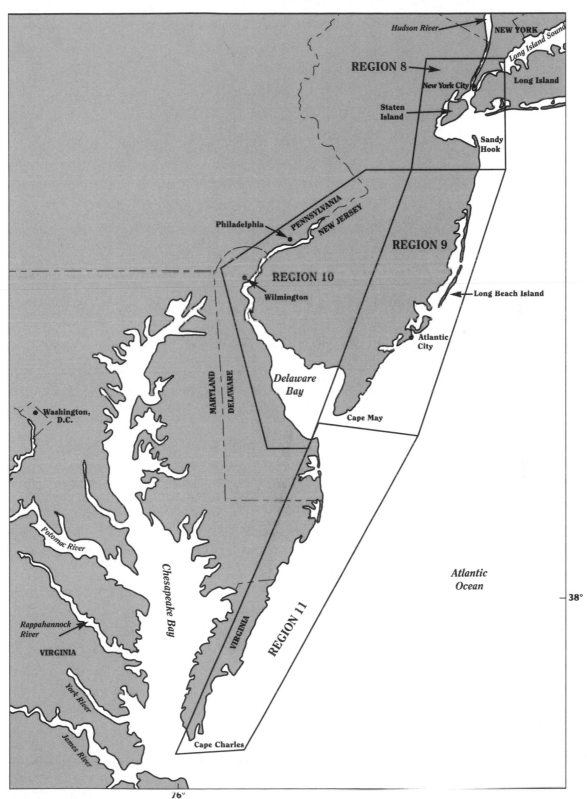

Hudson River   NEW YORK

Long Island Sound

REGION 8

New York City

Long Island

Staten Island

Sandy Hook

PENNSYLVANIA

Philadelphia

NEW JERSEY

REGION 9

REGION 10

Wilmington

Long Beach Island

MARYLAND   DELAWARE

Delaware Bay

Atlantic City

Washington, D.C.

Cape May

Potomac River

Chesapeake Bay

Atlantic Ocean

— 38°

Rappahannock River

VIRGINIA

VIRGINIA

REGION 11

York River

James River

Cape Charles

76°

ample, will show the futility of attempting to impose a rigid north-to-south consistency on anchorage groupings. Instead, for tributaries of the Bay large enough to contain several or perhaps even dozens of tributaries and anchorages, we begin at the mouth and proceed upstream.

This book is designed primarily for those who are cruising the Bay, not those who are passing through on the way to somewhere else. (This is not quite true, of course, in the case of the regions addressing the harbors of the Atlantic coast.) For this reason the detailed description of the Chesapeake and Delaware (C&D) Canal, for example, appears under region 1, not under region 10, the Delaware Bay and River. I am a hard-core gunkholer, and this book is organized in the spirit of gunkholing.

The division of the Atlantic coast and the Delaware Bay and River into four regions follows a logical, north-to-south clustering for the Atlantic coast regions and upstream from the mouth of Delaware Bay for the Delaware Bay and River region. No attempt has been made to group the regions into possible single-day cruises. Travel in these regions is more closely akin to passage making than to laid-back cruising. The harbors are described and rated in the same way as those in the Chesapeake are. However, this part of the book is designed primarily for those who are passing through on the way to somewhere else, unlike the part devoted to the regions of the Chesapeake, where safe and interesting harbors abound and cruising is an end in itself.

Other than that, everything that is said about the anchorages, ratings, and sketch maps for the Chesapeake Bay also applies to these regions.

To show how this works in practice, let's take a closer look at the Choptank River, which is introduced in region 3 (see pages 185–206) with the typeface used for a body of water containing two to two dozen anchorages, as follows:

> ## CHOPTANK RIVER
> Charts: 12263, 12266, **12268**, 12270

Beginning at the mouth of the river, we look first at Knapps Narrows, which connects the river mouth with the Bay proper north of Tilghman Island. Note: The chart number listed in boldface type is the preferred chart for the area; the others listed also cover the area but may not have as much detail or full coverage. Since Knapps Narrows offers marinas and restaurants, as well as a shortcut to the Bay, it's introduced in the style used for individual anchorages, as follows:

> ### Knapps Narrows
>
>
> Charts: 12263, **12266**, 12268, 12270

Next upriver on the Choptank we encounter Harris Creek, which is not an anchorage but a complicated tributary containing many anchorages. It is introduced as follows:

> ### Choptank River, Harris Creek
> Charts: 12263, **12266**, 12270

and under it come such anchorages as Dun Cove, Waterhole Cove, and Briary Cove.

> ### Harris Creek, Dun Cove
> *No facilities*
> Charts: 12263, **12266**, 12270

And so it goes, clockwise around the basin of the lower Choptank (with a long excursion up the Tred Avon) before we venture up into the upper Choptank toward the town of Choptank.

Ratings and facility listings (see below) are given only with individual anchorages (not with the larger bodies of water containing more than one tributary or discrete anchorage area), and individual anchorages are introduced in the style used above for Knapps Narrows or Dun Cove, depending on its place in the hierarchy. The hierarchical classification breaks down in some places—indeed, no rigid structure could embrace the Chesapeake without exceptions—and author and publisher beg your forgiveness, but the Choptank is as complicated as it gets. If you can follow us here, you can follow us anywhere in the Bay.

ANCHORAGES

Anchorages are listed in geographical order from the head of the Bay to its mouth, starting at Cabin John Creek. To find a specific spot, check the index or use the header running along the lower right edge of each right-hand page. These will lead you to the immediate geographical vicinity and in many cases to the anchorage itself. As an additional guide, anchorages along rivers or embankments that don't empty directly into the Chesapeake Bay itself are designated by the tributary name as well as the anchorage name. Thus, "Harris Creek, Dun Cove" tells you that Dun Cove is in Harris Creek and that Harris Creek does not empty directly into the Chesapeake. The header at the bottom of page 188 tells you that Harris Creek empties into the Choptank River.

RATINGS

Anchorages suitable for use as an overnight stay, either anchored or renting a slip at a marina, are rated in accordance with three categories: beauty and interest, protection from weather, and availability of facilities for the cruiser. (Due to the rapid changes in the availability of dockside sewage pumpout facilities, pumpouts are not necessarily found at anchorages listed as having all facilities. See appendix 5.) It is worth noting that these ratings are made from the perspective of the transient cruiser, not the permanent resident.

BEAUTY AND INTEREST

 Both beautiful and interesting. Not to be missed.

 Very attractive or interesting. Definitely worth a visit.

 Attractive or interesting.

 Nothing special, but OK.

 Not very attractive.

PROTECTION

 Hurricane hole. May be uncomfortably hot in the summer months.

 Well protected from all directions.

 Well protected from waves, open to wind from one or more directions.

 Exposed for a mile or more in at least one direction. Use in settled conditions or as a day stop only.

 No protection.

FACILITIES

 Fuel (gas and diesel)

 Fuel (gas only)

 Fuel (diesel only)

 Water

 Ice

Repairs

Slips and/or moorings

Groceries within walking distance

Laundromat

Marine supplies or hardware available

Shower

 Restaurant nearby

 Pumpout

SKETCH MAPS

Sketch maps or chart segments are included where appropriate to help you navigate a tricky channel or passage, identify anchorage and moorings areas, or locate shoreside services.

CAVEAT YACHTSMAN

In preparing this book every effort has been made to provide information that is accurate and up-to-date, but it is impossible to guarantee complete accuracy, and there is no substitute for experience and prudent seamanship. This guide should be used as a supplement to official U.S. government charts and other publications. The author and publisher disclaim any liability for loss or damage to persons or property that may occur as a result of the use or interpretation of any information in this book.

Introduction

INTRODUCTION

A BIT ABOUT THE CHESAPEAKE

*"a faire bay encompassed but for the mouth
with fruitful and delightsome land."*

— Captain John Smith

THE CHESAPEAKE BAY IS the largest inland tidal body of water on the Atlantic seacoast of the United States. It ranges 170 nautical miles from its northern point (head-waters) at the Chesapeake and Delaware Canal to its southern opening between Cape Charles and Cape Henry. Its width ranges from about 3½ miles in the northern portion to about 23 miles in the south. Not counting the myriad tributary rivers and creeks, 48 rivers flow into the Bay. Because of this flow of freshwater, the character of the Bay changes as you proceed north from its mouth—from salty, near-ocean conditions, through brackish water, to fresh-water in the extreme northern Bay and well up-stream on some of the longer rivers.

Formed about 10,000 years ago, when melt-ing glacial ice caused a corresponding rise in the ocean level, the Chesapeake Bay is actually the drowned valley of the Susquehanna River. To be more precise, the Bay is an estuary. A bay is defined as a body of water partially enclosed by land but with a wide opening to the sea (or other parent body of water). An estuary, liter-ally "boiling tide," has both tidal flow from the ocean and a large influx of freshwater from rivers, producing a whole series of ecosystems. The action of the tides and river currents pro-duces diverse chemical and physical character-istics that permit the growth of a vast and varied collection of both animal and plant life. Thus, an estuary is the most productive habitat in nature.

Forty-eight rivers with more than 100 trib-utaries flow into the Chesapeake. The Susque-hanna River, which originates about 400 miles to the north, in the middle of New York State, is known as the mother of the Bay because it pro-vides half of all the freshwater flowing into the Chesapeake—typically 60,000 to 80,000 gallons per second. Even with this steady flow, were the Bay suddenly emptied of all its water, it would take a year to refill it!

Naturally, the water in the Bay is saltier to the south than it is to the north, but because salt water is heavier than freshwater, the Bay's water is also saltier at the bottom than at the top. This creates an interesting phenomenon. The salty water coming in from the ocean has a net movement up the Bay on the bottom, while the freshwater from the rivers has a net move-ment down the Bay on the top.

The combination of tidal and freshwater cur-rents produces an ebb that is stronger and longer than the Bay's flood current, running a good half-hour longer than the flood current in most of the Bay.

Another factor affecting salinity and, to some extent, currents is the amount of rainfall.

With heavy rain, more freshwater flows into the Bay than during a dry season, with the resulting cyclic change in salinity. This change in salinity sets up a nontidal circulation. When the salinity is high, saltier water is forced along the bottom up the Bay and into the tributaries, and bottom water is flushed from the tributaries back into the Bay. This movement reverses when the Bay's salinity is low. Normally, the Chesapeake is saltier in the late summer and fall than in the winter and spring.

ESTUARY CYCLES

Estuaries are born, live, and die with the ebb and flow of ice ages. As glacial ice melts and the sea rises, estuaries are born. As the land rises and the water basin fills with sediment, estuaries die.

It took about 10,000 years for the Chesapeake Bay as we know it today to be formed. From 15,000 to 5,000 years ago the sea level rose more than three feet each century, encroaching farther and farther up the continental shelf and into the wide valley of the Susquehanna River. Ten thousand years ago there was no Bay as such. The sea had just reached the level of what is the present mouth of the Chesapeake. Five thousand years ago the head of the Bay was near present-day Annapolis. Then, 3,000 years ago the Bay stopped growing. What was once a river valley wending its way to the sea was now a great estuary. Its shape was much like it is today. The water was clear and deep, and the shores and tributaries were covered with dense vegetation.

With the cessation of the Bay's growth, the sedimentation process began. Never again would the Chesapeake be as deep and clear as it was 3,000 years ago. Sediment from the rivers began to fill up the headwaters and the deltas of each tributary, an inevitable process in the life of any estuary. If things followed their natural course, the Bay would cease to exist in 10,000 to 20,000 years.

Sedimentation is an estuary's natural weapon against the inroads of the rising sea. From a human perspective, it is a slow process. But as long as the rivers that feed the Bay continue to flow, land will be eroded and sediment will be deposited at the margins of the Bay and its tributaries. The resulting broad flats of silt eventually are colonized by grasses and become marshes. The buildup of silt continues until the marsh becomes part of the new shoreline.

Many factors influence the speed of the sedimentation process—weather, currents, the composition of the land that is affected, tides, winds, and human activity. Within the last 350 years human activity has greatly accelerated this process. Giving little thought to soil erosion, colonists cleared thousands of acres of land, stripping the soil of its protective vegetation. The amount of sediment carried to the Bay since colonial times is estimated to be four to eight times what it was in precolonial times. Recent construction has increased even this accelerated pace to hundreds of times the "natural" rate of sedimentation. The result is that sedimentation has significantly altered the Bay's coastline, causing colonial seaports such as Joppatown and Port Tobacco, Maryland, to become landlocked. And the clear Bay waters of the 1600s have become brown, with visibility now measured in inches instead of in tens of feet.

RESPECT FOR THE ENVIRONMENT

Pressure on the Bay environment increases constantly. Twelve to fourteen million people now live within what could be called Chesapeake Bay country, with more and more arriving every year.

Industries have dumped toxic chemicals into the Bay; improperly treated sewage from overloaded processing plants and leaky septic systems still ends up in the water. Even runoff from farmland hundreds of miles away ends up in the Bay.

A little bit of fertilizer is good: it provides nutrients for the microscopic plant life upon which the entire food chain depends. Too much of a good thing, however, can be disastrous. Algae blooms alternate with massive die-offs, making the levels of dissolved oxygen in the water too low to support marine life, and so more death results. Carried to the extreme, this could turn the beautiful Chesapeake into a foul-smelling, liquid desert.

Advocacy Groups. Fortunately, there is hope for a better future. Several organizations are working actively to save and restore the Bay. Most notable of these is the Chesapeake Bay Foundation (CBF), the original "Save the Bay" organization, founded in 1966. The goal of the CBF is to promote and contribute to the orderly management of the Chesapeake, with a special emphasis on maintaining a level of water quality that is capable of supporting the Bay's diverse aquatic species. The CBF has programs that include in-the-field instruction in estuarine ecology; scientific investigation and legal representation for conservation and management of estuarine resources; preservation and management of significant Bay land; and research in and demonstration of agricultural practices with a low chemical input. Not only does the CBF serve as an advocate for the Bay and ensure that its best interests are represented in the public forum but it actively preserves and manages some 4,000 acres of land in the Bay area, holding it in its natural state and using it for educational purposes.

The CBF has three offices: 162 Prince George Street, Annapolis, MD 21401, phone 410-268-8816; Suite 815, Heritage Building, 1001 East Main Street, Richmond, VA 23219, phone 804-780-1392; and 214 State Street, Harrisburg, PA 17101, phone 717-234-5550.

The government has been doing its part as well. In 1983 the governors of Virginia, Maryland, and Pennsylvania; the administrator of the Federal Environmental Protection Agency; the mayor of Washington, D.C.; and the chairman of the tristate legislative Chesapeake Bay Commission met to establish a joint program to clean and protect the Chesapeake. Four years later they met again and signed the 1987 Chesapeake Bay Agreement, which was revitalized in a subsequent meeting on 5 January 1989 to endorse cooperative efforts "to eliminate all toxic discharges into the Bay, protect tidal and nontidal wetlands, remove blockages to migratory fish passages, increase public access, and formulate water quality and habitat guidelines for living resources." In 2000 the agreement was reviewed, and a new accord was signed, reflecting to some extent what has and has not worked and which areas require increased emphasis.

Estuaries support a diversity of wildlife. Here black ducks and mallards mingle with pintails and whistling swans.

Luther C. Goldman/Sport Fisheries & Wildlife

Estuary waters support a diversity of life—plants, fish, birds, waterfowl, and marine and nonmarine mammals. The nation's prime steward in this type of broad-based protection is the U.S. Fish & Wildlife Service (FWS). The FWS's Chesapeake Bay Estuary Program is committed to reversing damage already done to the Bay, arresting further degradation, and restoring the Bay as nearly to its former productivity as time, technology, and resources allow. In addition to its work in habitat and wetlands protection, research, technical assistance, and species conservation and protection, the FWS manages the National Wildlife Refuges and National Fish Hatcheries in the Bay area and across the nation. The FWS produces a variety of publications, including the Chesapeake Species of Special Emphasis Series, that help educate the public regarding the living resource that the Chesapeake Bay is and what role each person can play in its restoration. Write to the service at U.S. Fish & Wildlife Service, 1825 Virginia Ave., Annapolis, MD 21401, phone 410-269-5448.

A great deal of progress has been made. Never before have there been three state governors determined to clean up the estuary, a cadre of world-renowned environmental scientists working to unlock the Bay's many mysteries, and a well-organized and capable network of environmental advocacy organizations and citizens dedicated to the preservation and reclamation of the Chesapeake. Many programs have been implemented, and many more are to come.

Although progress is evident, the work is far from done. If the programs are to work for the long run, we who live, work, and play in the Bay environment will have to do our part. The health and bounty of the Chesapeake Bay relies on our vigilance and activity for its protection—not only in public advocacy and pressure but in our personal actions and habits.

Boaters' Responsibility. Boatowners have a special responsibility to the Bay. The Chesapeake Bay Foundation says it this way: "While the effect of a single boat on the Bay may seem insignificant, multiply it by the nearly 400,000 boats that use the Bay and such effects become both significant and increasingly apparent."

Common sense and prudence can go a long way toward combining the joy of boating on the Bay with the need to safeguard the quality of the Bay environment for the future.

The booklet *Your Boat and the Bay,* from the CBF Homeowner Series, addresses specific ways that individual boaters can join the movement to save the Bay. A list of some of the ways to minimize the impact of your boat follows; write to the CBF for your own copy of this booklet, which has more good advice on the subject.

- If you have a Type I or II marine sanitation device (MSD), always flush your system in open water that is at least 20 feet deep. This aids the rapid dispersal of waste materials and reduces damage to the shellfish beds, which are in shallow waters.
- If you have a Type III MSD, check the location of pumpout facilities on your route or near your destination and use them. (See appendix 5 for a list of dockside sewage pumpout facilities.)
- Use onshore bathhouse facilities whenever you are docked. This minimizes the need to discharge your system.
- Use a nonphosphate detergent and a scrub brush when you clean teak, hull sides, and deck while in the water. Specialty cleaners usually have high levels of a variety of toxic substances.
- Be careful with engine oil. Wipe up all spills, no matter how minor, when changing or adding oil. Consider using a bilge "pillow" (oil-absorbing sponge) so that bilge water pumped into the Bay will be oil-free.
- Dispose of old antifreeze onshore, and if possible, use propylene glycol-based antifreeze, which is less toxic than ethylene glycol-based varieties.
- Avoid topping off your fuel tank. This often causes fuel to be spilled from overflow vents, creating miniature toxic slicks.
- Watch your wake. Boat wakes contribute to shoreline erosion, especially in the smaller creeks and coves that gunkholers love. Wakes also stir up sediment, which reduces

the amount of essential light that reaches submerged aquatic vegetation, the start of many food chains in the estuary.

CRUISING THE BAY

The Chesapeake Bay Bridges, near Annapolis, serve as a dividing line in the Bay in more than a topographic sense. As you pass the bridges, the very character of the Bay undergoes subtle changes. The water becomes noticeably less salty as you proceed farther north, as mentioned above. The wave action changes, becoming choppier, with lower wave heights and far fewer of the long rollers often encountered well south in the widest part of the Bay. The harbors become fewer and more crowded. Some, such as Worton Creek, are so full of moorings that there is hardly room enough to swing a cat, let alone a boat at anchor.

As may be said of any place, there are some drawbacks to cruising in the Chesapeake, chief among them being the hot, humid weather and summer calms in July and August. No one should cruise the Chesapeake without power, and in the summer the knowledgeable will have a good awning to provide shade and screening for protection from insects. Spring and fall are the ideal cruising times. Then the air and water are usually pleasant and comfortable, the flying insects are seldom in evidence, and the sea nettles either have not yet appeared or have gone.

But it is all the Chesapeake Bay, one of the best cruising grounds in the country. From the southern near-ocean conditions to the northern freshwater, the Bay has countless harbors and anchorages that are high on the "must visit" list of the serious cruiser.

HELPFUL PUBLICATIONS

All those who cruise the Chesapeake need several publications, some for navigation and some to add to the enjoyment of the cruise. Here are the ones I consider to be most useful.

NOAA Charts. A complete list of the navigation charts available from the National Oceanic & Atmospheric Administration (NOAA) is presented in the *Nautical Chart Catalog 1*, available from most marine stores or from the Distribution Division (N/ACC 3), National Ocean Service,

Riverdale, MD 20737-1199 (www.noaa.gov/), at no charge. Telephone orders may be placed at 301-436-6990 or 800-638-8972. More than 35 charts cover the Chesapeake Bay and its tributaries, not counting those for the Atlantic seaboard from New York to the Chesapeake Bay entrance and the Delaware Bay and River. If you normally only cruise one area, your best bet may be to buy the two or three full-size NOAA charts that cover your area of interest. This list includes better alternatives if you tend to cruise a large portion of the Bay or beyond.

Maptech Chart Kit 4: Chesapeake & Delaware Bays. Maptech apparently has replaced or bought out the previous Better Boating Association Chart Kits. They now publish a series of chart kits that are authorized reproductions of the NOAA charts. These are far less expensive than a full set of government charts, and they're easier to store and handle. The 17-by-22-inch charts are spiral-bound for easy use; the kit contains Loran-C plots, as well as the latitude and longitude markings. Many of the significant buoys or markers also have their latitude and longitude indicated. The kit you want covers both the Chesapeake and Delaware Bays (chart kit 4) as well as the Atlantic Coast of the Delmarva peninsula. This kit is probably the best bet if you plan to cruise a large portion of this area. A vinyl cover is available to protect the chart kit from weather while leaving the particular chart of interest visible. Kits are available from most marine stores and mail-order houses for approximately $100.

Guide for Cruising Maryland Waters. This is a marine atlas published by the Maryland Department of Natural Resources that covers the tidal waters of Maryland, including the Potomac River. Adequate for cruising the Bay itself, it lacks the detail (e.g., water depth soundings) needed for gunkholing into the tributaries. The 10-by-14-inch book provides charts containing more than 200 courses, with magnetic-compass directions and distances, which have been laid between buoys to most of the boating centers. Unfortunately, the guide no longer includes the NOAA tidal-current charts for the upper Chesapeake Bay. The guide is available in most regional marine stores or directly from the Department of Natural Resources, Tawes State Office Building, Annapolis, MD 21402 (www.dnr.state.md.us/index.html). The price is about $25.

ADC's *Waterproof Chartbook of the Chesapeake Bay.*

A collection of waterproof reproductions of NOAA charts, this approximately 11-by-16-inch book covers the tidal waters of both Maryland and Virginia. It is published by ADC, "The Map People," Alexandria, VA (www.adcmap.com). It is very useful for those who want a more compact set of charts that address the waters of both states around the Chesapeake Bay. While weak as a guide for gunkholing, it does address the entire navigable length of the James River, a shortfall in many other chart kits. The book first came on the market in 1988 and is available from most area marine stores and mail-order houses. Priced at about $35, it is a good buy.

Mid-Atlantic Waterway Guide.

Available from Intertec Publishing, this volume of their series of chart kits/cruising guides (approximately 8½ by 11 inches) covers from the C&D Canal on the Chesapeake Bay down the ICW to the Florida border, including the Delmarva Atlantic coast. Obviously aimed primarily at those making the north–south passage, it does provide an adequate set of charts for cruising the Chesapeake, but these charts tend to lack sufficient detail for gunkholing off the main Bay. However, it does provide the location and facilities of the majority of marinas along the way. It is available at most area marine stores and mail-order houses for under $40.

The Boating Almanac, volume 4.

One of the most useful and compact reference sources for cruising the Chesapeake Bay and its tributaries, this 5½-by-9-inch book was published annually by Boating Almanac Company, Inc., Severna Park, MD 21146. Unfortunately, it is now out of print, but if you can get your hands on an old copy, there is a wealth of still useful information contained in its pages, particularly the location and facilities of marinas in the area. Published in four volumes covering the Eastern seaboard from Maine through Virginia, it contains just about everything that you need to know for either extended cruising or short trips. Volume 4 covers the Chesapeake Bay, Delaware, Maryland, Washington, D.C., and Virginia. It contains information on marina facilities and locations, launch-ramp locations, area charts (not for navigation except in a pinch), the *NOAA Nautical Chart Catalog,* and much more. I was quite unhappy to see this useful tome go out of print. I know of nothing comparable to it.

USCG *Local Notice to Mariners.*

This weekly publication notifies all mariners, be they on large ships or cockleshells, about anything affecting safe navigation on the waters in each district. For the Chesapeake Bay area, this publication may be obtained free of charge simply by writing to Commander, Fifth Coast Guard District, Aids to Navigation Branch, Federal Building, 431 Crawford Street, Portsmouth, VA 23704-5004; or you can download printable files from a link at the USCG Navigation Center's Web site, www.navcen.uscg.mil/.

The Fifth Coast Guard District includes the coastal and inland waters of New Jersey, Maryland, Delaware, Virginia, and North Carolina. The *Notice* includes announcements of such things as closures of locks on the Intracoastal Waterway (ICW), channel closures, and so on; discrepancies in aids to navigation, missing markers, extinguished lights, and so on; changes to charts and chart corrections; dredging operations; the condition and operability of bridges across navigable waterways; date, time, and place of regattas; proposed projects that may affect mariners; and more.

If you plan to cruise or use a boat in any part of the covered area, get on this publication's mailing list.

Reed's Nautical Almanac and *Reed's Nautical Companion.*

Anyone who does even a minimal amount of navigation on the water will prize this publication. These two volumes, sold separately, provide virtually all information, exclusive of nautical charts, necessary for navigation anywhere within its area of coverage. The nautical almanac is published annually and contains the information that changes annually, such as sun, moon, stars, tide and current tables as well as selected current charts and harbor chartlets. The companion contains permanent information such as conversion tables, distance tables, and navigation calculation tables and instructions.

For the part of the world covered by this cruising guide, use the *Reed's Nautical Almanac, North American East Coast Edition* for the current year and add a copy of the *Reed's Nautical Companion, North American Edition* to your boat library. With an appropriate set of charts and these books (plus, of course, this cruising guide), you have all the information needed to navigate safely and efficiently. Even if you never travel out of sight of land and related landmarks, the set of current tables and charts alone are worth the annual price of the almanac.

Each volume costs less than $30, less at discount, and once you have the "companion," you have a permanent reference.

Eldridge Tide and Pilot Book. For those primarily interested in the Atlantic coast tide and current tables, including the Delaware Bay and the Chesapeake and Delaware Canal, Eldridge provides that information at about half the cost of *Reed's Nautical Almanac.* However, it contains little or no tidal or current data for the Chesapeake Bay. For a coastal trip, it's fine. If you're only cruising the Chesapeake Bay, don't bother with this book.

The following books are just a few of the ones that might add to your general enjoyment of a Chesapeake cruise; more are listed in the bibliography.

Fodor's Chesapeake. Fodor's practical guide, which is updated yearly, offers a smattering of historical background and lots of useful information on hotels and motels, restaurants and eateries, and things to do. A basic tourist's guidebook, it is available at most bookstores at a cost of about $9. Cruisers intending to spend a lot of time ashore in the southernmost regions of the Bay and the James River area will want to get *Fodor's Virginia* too.

This Was Chesapeake Bay. This informative publication includes excerpts from ship logs, historical photographs, and the personal recollections of the author, Robert H. Burgess. It covers a wide range of subjects, from the Bay in the Miocene period to colonial settlements, from steamboating to naval warfare, from soft-shell clamming to dredging for oysters. Each chapter stands alone, so that you can benefit from reading only those sections that interest you. Burgess's *Chesapeake Circle* uses the same anecdotal format. Both books are published by Cornell Maritime Press of Centreville, Maryland.

Chesapeake Bay: A Pictorial Maritime History. This book, also published by Cornell Maritime Press, is a compilation of pictures of events, objects, and vessels on and around the Bay. Written by M. V. Brewington, the collection is held together with a brief text that takes the reader from the time of the European settlements to the present.

Chesapeake. This entertaining novel by James A. Michener is a story of the Bay and its wildlife. It is also the author's tribute to the Bay's watermen, whom he sees as quiet heroes living and working in the beautiful yet unforgiving waters of the Chesapeake.

NAVIGATING THE BAY

WINDS & WAVES

The Chesapeake Bay is considered "semiprotected waters." Although most of the tributaries are well sheltered, when the wind pipes up from the right direction (or perhaps the wrong direction, depending on your viewpoint), the waters of the Bay can get rough enough to command your full attention. Due to the relative shallowness of the water over most of the Bay, waves tend to peak in sharp points spaced rather closely together (trochoidal), instead of the big, widely spaced rollers common in the ocean. As a result, the waves don't have to get very high before you have your hands full, particularly if you happen to be heading into them.

One of the nicest features of cruising the Chesapeake—if you are not in a hurry to get to a particular spot—is the abundance of good harbors on both shores, so that you rarely need to fight your way into a strong wind to reach shelter. If the wind begins to "dust up," there usually is an alternate harbor where you can take refuge until it dies down.

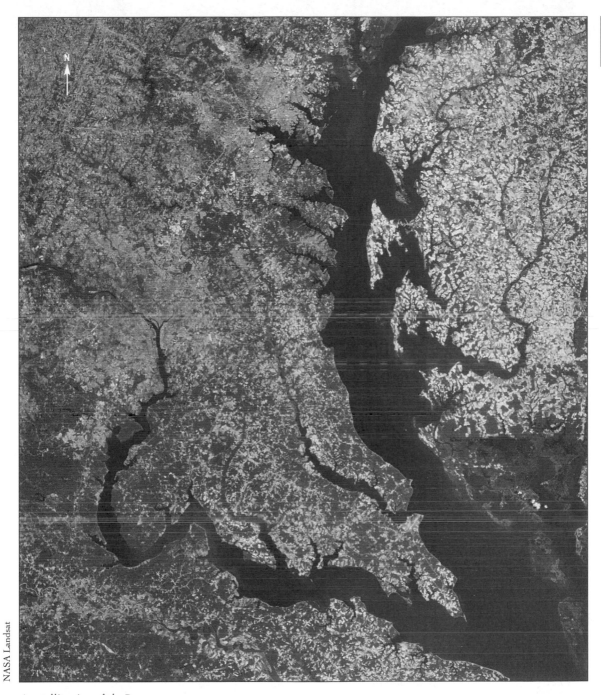

A satellite view of the Bay.

The prevailing winds seem to alternate, blowing up and then down the Bay, with northerly winds predominating in the late fall and southerly breezes more frequent in the late spring and summer. Spring and fall winds usually have higher average velocities than do summer winds. Flat calms or light breezes tend to be the norm in July and August, especially at night and in the morning. At this time of year the sailor's most useful sail is the "iron topsail."

Conditions in the southern Bay differ from those in the north in that the harbors are farther apart, particularly between the Choptank and Potomac Rivers. The water is generally deeper, and below the Patuxent River the waves are generally, but not always, more like the round swells of the ocean, although they are still closer together than in the deep ocean waters. The main difference is that they don't have the sharp peaks of the trochoidal wave, so that they are easier to handle even though they may be bigger than the waves up the Bay. More than once we have surfed down the Bay under working jib alone, watching the rollers chase us. This is an exhilarating experience, but I wouldn't care to be going in the other direction! Fortunately, wind direction in the Chesapeake is such that if you can afford to lay over a day when the winds are adverse, they are likely to change direction, force, or both.

Bottom Conditions & Shoaling. There are very few rocks in the Chesapeake except near the mouth of the Susquehanna River and the famous White Rocks in the mouth of Rock Creek on the Patapsco River. Although the seas can be steep enough to be a challenge, there is no big surf crashing on the shore to destroy a grounded boat. Running aground in the Chesapeake is very much a "so-what" affair. In fact, if you don't run aground here a few times a year, you just aren't adventurous enough!

Running aground in the Chesapeake is so commonplace that the Bay may seem little more than a series of shoals connected by channels, but nothing could be further from the truth. A glance at the charts shows plenty of shoals and a considerable number of small creeks but also a far greater number of navigable rivers, creeks, and harbors that boats carrying a draft of 6 feet or more can follow nearly to the headwaters. For boats with 5 feet of draft or less, the number of available harbors increases dramatically. The next large jump comes at water depths of about 3 feet, accommodating shallow drafts such as on medium-size to smaller powerboats.

Even so, Chesapeake Bay cruisers are more likely to run aground than those who cruise other waters. Since going aground here usually damages one's dignity and rarely one's boat (the exception being the planing inboard powerboat, on which the prop is the lowest part of the hull), I suspect that Bay cruisers tend to be more careless. Even when care is exercised, it is easy to hit one of the many unmarked shoals when exploring small creeks and coves. Many dredged channels and harbors are constantly filling in and being dredged again, so that charts are rarely up-to-date regarding the latest controlling depths.

The judicious use of a depth-sounder—or better yet, a sounding pole—will permit you to poke into many a fascinating small creek that could never be attempted in other areas. The lack of rocks and the 2-foot tidal range make safe adventuring more possible here than anywhere else. Since the bottom is usually soft mud or hard sand, you need only a little effort to release your boat. (Marine insurers say that the Chesapeake is one of the least expensive places to keep a boat because of the forgiving soft bottom.)

The small range of tide also can be a liability if you do go aground. A falling tide won't leave you very dry, but you might have to wait some time before the tide rises enough to get you off when you are really hard aground. Take heart: unless you have an "aptitude" for it, you will rarely get stuck so hard that you can't get off in just a few minutes, often by using powerboat swells.

Temperature. The summers on the Chesapeake tend to be hot and humid, especially in August. As pointed out earlier, the best times for cruising are spring and fall, from early April to mid-June and from mid-September to mid-November. As a general rule, the weather tends to be mild, but fall cruising, in particular, requires that you be prepared for a wide range of temperatures. While it can be on the chilly side in April and November, the temperature varies considerably. We have sailed in subfreezing temperatures in mid-October and in shirtsleeves in November.

The accompanying climatological table may provide a better "feel" for the ranges to be expected. This table is based on records for Baltimore, but it is representative of the entire Bay. The table includes both the normal maximum and minimum ranges of temperature and the extremes recorded for the area.

Storms. To call a Chesapeake Bay line squall "just a thunderstorm" is akin to calling a tor-

Table 1. Climatological Table for Baltimore (in °F)

| | AVERAGE | | | EXTREME | |
	DAILY MAX.	DAILY MIN.	MONTHLY	RECORD HIGH	RECORD LOW
April	65.8	42.6	54.2	94	20
May	75.9	52.8	64.4	98	32
June	83.5	61.4	72.5	100	42
July	87.2	66.4	76.8	102	52
Aug.	85.0	65.0	75.0	102	48
Sept.	78.6	57.6	68.1	99	35
Oct.	68.4	45.6	57.0	92	18
Nov.	56.5	34.4	45.5	83	13

nado "a bit of wind." Although technically a thunderstorm, a line squall tends to be far more impressive when you are out on the water; its potential for damage is enormous. You have to experience the violence of one of these storms to put it in proper perspective.

The storms usually approach from the west or northwest. They can jump on you unbelievably quickly if you ignore the warning signs. The wind can go from almost still to 70 to 90 mph in seconds, whipping the waves into a froth and dumping buckets of water on your head. Lightning cracks and crashes; visibility drops to mere feet. Waves don't usually cause too much trouble; the wind blows their tops right off.

Don't let this or other accounts alarm you unduly. These storms don't sneak up on you. They give visible warning signs hours beforehand. Large black or gray cumulus clouds gather to the west and northwest, and often you see lightning or hear thunder. Sometimes the storms are preceded by a copper-colored haze. If you keep your eyes open, you will have plenty of time to prepare for a line squall. If a squall is en route and you don't have enough time to reach shelter, prepare to anchor or use your engine to hold your position until it is over. *(Sailors should drop all sails.)* Don't try to make any progress through the storm; lack of visibility makes this too risky. These storms rarely last

more than 15 minutes or so; they just seem to last longer when you are in one.

Although squalls can occur at other times, they are most common from mid-June to mid-September, generally during hot, humid weather. They rarely come before 4:00 P.M. and are most common just before sundown. A single storm generally covers a relatively narrow path, but storms often come in clusters. Once we were caught out as one passed to our right and another passed to our left without affecting us. However, we were so busy watching these two that a third caught us unawares, hitting us squarely. We had a rather busy few minutes as a result!

You can never be sure what a squall will amount to before it hits. It may look really fierce and amount to little more than a rainstorm, or it can blow hard enough to knock over a large port cargo crane, as happened in Baltimore in 1980. When you see signs of a squall, lower your sails and secure them well and then prepare to anchor, run before the squall, or hold position under engine. Get into a good shelter early, making sure you are well protected to the west and northwest. Assume that the storm will be bad and play it safe.

Once a squall has passed, the wind generally drops to near zero for 15 to 20 minutes—often longer—leaving you sitting in a flat calm wishing for breeze.

PREDICTING WEATHER IN THE CHESAPEAKE

Starting on this topic gave me some pause. Who among us has not made the weatherman the butt of numerous jokes? He who attempts to predict the weather, be he a modern-day meteorologist with access to satellite pictures and computer reports or a layman making his guess based on the current signs around him (no, no—not the entrails of a rooster!), is likely to be a subject of ridicule, rarely reverence. In fact, our family has a standing joke that has become a "classic" for reasons better not discussed: "Think it'll rain today?" "Naw! The wind's in the wrong direction." These lines are normally delivered in a pouring rain, in the total absence of any measurable wind at all and heavy, black, cloud cover, or both.

With that preface, I'll make the rash statement that there are three ways of obtaining information on what weather lies in the immediate future (12 hours to two days). The first two are relatively conventional: listen to the TV or radio weather reports or tune into the VHF-FM WE-1 or WE-2 NOAA weather radio stations for broadcasts by professional (and often wrong) meteorologists. The third is to do it yourself using a decent barometer and tracking the wind direction.

No joke! If you learn how to use a barometer and learn the historical weather patterns associated with barometric pressure trends and wind direction, you actually stand a better chance of accurately predicting the weather *in your location* than if you simply listen to broadcast weather predictions, which necessarily cover a far larger geographical area than the one in which you are interested.

First, a short word about instrumentation. You generally get what you pay for! Forget the cheap barometers that cost well under $20—they make a nice wall decoration. For the accuracy and reliability you need, you'll have to pay at least $70. If you are really serious, look into the purchase of a barograph; this device records the changing pressure on a piece of graph paper with the use of a clockwork mechanism. Be forewarned that a barograph costs several hundred

dollars. Whichever instrument you choose, you probably will have to calibrate it to a sea-level reading with the adjustment screw in the back. The simplest procedure is to listen to a *recent* weather report and correct the instrument to the reported pressure, assuming that conditions are not changing rapidly. Repeat this calibration several times until you are confident that your instrument gives reasonably accurate readings.

You also need a wind-direction indicator. For the purpose of weather prediction, you can rely on a compass and a wet finger or spend several hundred dollars on instruments. Here's how the less elaborate system works: Wet your finger and hold it up in the wind. The coldest side indicates the direction from which the wind is blowing. Now look at your compass to see what that direction is. The nearest 45 degrees normally is close enough.

For starters, forget the words *rain, change,* and *fair* usually found on the face of a barometer. They are meaningless save as reminders of the probable significance of a trend or direction and rate of change in the barometer reading. Since the trend is usually more important than the current pressure reading, a single reading is useless for prediction purposes. You need a series of readings, taken about once an hour for a minimum of three hours and preferably for six hours, to establish the trend in barometric pressure.

Due to the influence of the sun and, to a lesser degree, the moon, there are cyclic daily variations in the pressure readings, which need to be corrected for accuracy. In the latitude of the Chesapeake Bay there is a peak-to-peak variation of about 0.04 inch of mercury (the units of pressure used) twice a day. Using daylight saving time as your reference, correct your reading by subtracting 0.01 inch for every hour past 5:00 A.M. until 9:00 A.M. For every hour past 11:00 A.M. until 3:00 P.M., add 0.01 inch. Then subtract 0.01 inch for every hour past 5:00 P.M. until 9:00 P.M. and (if you're a night owl) add 0.01 inch for every hour past 11:00 P.M. until 3:00 A.M. the next morning.

Table 2. Predicting Bay Weather

BAROMETER	WIND DIRECTION	PROBABLE WEATHER
29.8 or less falling rapidly	N to E	gale warning; heavy rain imminent
29.8 or less falling rapidly	E to S	storm warning! clearing in 24 hours
30.0 or less falling rapidly	NE to SE	high wind and rain; clearing in 36 hours
30.0 or less falling slowly	NE to SE	rain, continuing up to 2 days
30.0 or less rising slowly	S to SW	clearing in hours, fair for days
30.1 & above falling rapidly	NE to E	rain in 12–24 hours, increasing wind
30.1 & above falling slowly	NE to E	with light wind, rain in a few days
30.1 to 30.2 falling rapidly	NE to S	increasing wind and rain in 12 hours
30.1 to 30.2 falling slowly	NE to SE	rain in 12–18 hours, wind steady
30.1 to 30.2 falling slowly	SE to S	rain in 24 hours, wind steady
30.1 to 30.2 rising rapidly	SW to NW	fair, rain in 2 days or less
30.1 to 30.2 steady	SW to NW	fair, no change for 1–2 days
Above 30.2 steady	SW to NW	continued fair, no change in sight
Above 30.2 falling slowly	SW to NW	fair for 2 days; temperature rising slowly

Having completed that exacting exercise, if you are less diligent, you can forget the fine corrections as long as you will accept a gray area in the definition of a "slow" change. A "slow" change is defined as a change of from 0.02 inch to 0.10 inch in either direction over a six-hour period. A "fast" change is defined as a change greater than 0.10 inch over a six-hour period.

Once you have established your set of readings for the current wind direction, the current pressure trend, and the current value, corrected for sea level, you are ready to attempt to "predict" the weather *in your immediate vicinity* for the next 12 to 24 hours by applying these readings to the climatological table. May you have better success than your "local" weatherman!

Tides & Currents. The range of tide in the Chesapeake is not great. In the northern Bay it runs from 1 to 1½ feet, while in the southern Bay, well below the mouth of the Potomac River, it may run as high as 2½ feet.

The direction, strength, and duration of the wind have a far greater effect on water level, causing drops of 3 feet or more below the normal range or adding a couple of feet to the normal high. Strong northerlies tend to "dry out" the Bay, whereas southerlies tend to "fill it up." To produce extreme effects, the wind has to blow from the same direction for a few days. Except in a few marginal creeks, dredged channels, and harbors you can ignore the tide for the most part unless you expect a strong northerly wind.

Tidal currents, although relatively mild in most of the Bay, are another matter. The maximum currents range between 1 knot and 1½ knots, with the higher velocities on the ebb. The wind can increase these currents by roughly half a knot, particularly a north wind on an ebb current.

It is sometimes possible to minimize the effect of a foul current by hugging the shore. However, this works only if the shoreline is concave, such as in the region between Cove Point and the Patuxent River on the Western Shore. As a rule, you are better off simply scheduling your course to take advantage of aiding currents and avoiding foul currents. A set of current tables for the year is a must, and, for cruising in the north, from Elk River to the Patuxent River, a set of *Tidal Current Charts, Upper Chesapeake Bay,* compiled by NOAA, is invaluable. Currents in the southern Bay are not charted at present, but they follow the general guidelines given here. Current charts and tables are also included in *Reed's Nautical Almanac* and in the *Eldridge Tide and Pilot Book.*

In a few areas the Bay's currents can be substantial. The current directly under the Bay Bridges sometimes reaches 2 knots and can exceed that speed at the Chesapeake Bay Bridge-Tunnel in the mouth of the Bay. In the Kent Narrows, the "shortcut" between the Chester River and the eastern Bay, the current reaches an impressive speed; here we have encountered a current well in excess of 3 knots directly in the chute under the drawbridge. Fortunately, this is only a short distance. Once you are clear of the bridge, the current falls off rapidly.

The Chesapeake and Delaware Canal is probably the only other area where tidal currents may present a significant problem. The peak current through the 16-mile-long canal is between 2 and 2½ knots, with currents reaching and exceeding 3 knots not uncommon. Some of the locals claim that currents of 6 knots are possible. Stating the obvious: If you plan to transit the canal, pick your time carefully.

ATLANTIC COASTAL REGION & APPROACHES TO THE CHESAPEAKE

It may seem a little strange that a body of water as large as the Chesapeake Bay is considered to be a part of the Intracoastal Waterway, but it is. The ICW stretches from New York to Florida along the Eastern seaboard of the United States. The stretch through New Jersey is, for all practical purposes, nonexistent for any vessels other than shallow-draft powerboats due to the number of fixed bridges with inadequate clearance (a considerable number having only 35 feet of clearance) and shoal depth (frequent controlling depths may be 3 feet or even less).

In spite of this, most consider the relatively protected coastal route south to start at City Island, at the western end of Long Island Sound. From there your course will take you through the East River into the rather busy New York Harbor and out the Hudson River to Sandy Hook Bay. Here there are several harbors offering protected stopovers where you can lie overnight before starting down the coast or to await favorable weather.

Most cruising boats heading south, especially sailboats, must make the Atlantic passage from Sandy Hook, at the mouth of the Hudson River, to Cape May, with a few possible inlets in between in which they may seek shelter or rest. Deep-draft powerboats and sailboats with fixed keels or masts more than 35 feet above the waterline should watch the weather and select favorable conditions to make the outside passage between Sandy Hook and Cape May. Convenient stopover points, to break up the trip or for refuge in the event of conditions changing for the worse, are Manasquan, Barnegat, and Absecon (Atlantic City) Inlets. There are others, but these are the most hospitable in terms of access from the sea. Small craft that are unsuitable for open waters or shoal-draft powerboats should opt for the protected route of the ICW. Note that the New Jersey portion of the ICW starts at Manasquan. From Sandy Hook to Manasquan Inlet there is no choice but to go "outside" along the coast, a distance of about 25 miles.

The true inside route to Florida from the north really starts at Cape May, New Jersey. From there the southbound cruiser has two choices: the outside route down the Atlantic coast of the Delmarva Peninsula to the mouth of the Chesapeake and the harbors in the Norfolk area or the inside route up the Delaware Bay, through the Chesapeake & Delaware Canal, and down the Chesapeake Bay to Norfolk. At Norfolk there is again a choice, between the outside route around Cape Hatteras and one of the two inside routes of the ICW, which start from the Elizabeth River at Norfolk and rejoin in Albemarle Sound, North Carolina, by Roanoke Island.

For those "snowbirds" headed back north in the spring, the reverse is, of course, true.

To be strictly correct, there is only one "northern" approach to the Chesapeake Bay, the inside route up the Delaware Bay, through the C&D Canal, and into the Elk River at the extreme northern end of the Bay. From there the entire expanse of the Chesapeake with its hundreds of harbors and points of interest lies before you. The outside route down the Delmarva Peninsula really bypasses the entire Chesapeake, and even if you enter the mouth of the Bay, you will miss most of the better cruising grounds.

Prevailing Wind & Weather

As for any offshore or coastal passage, the primary controlling factors are the weather and sea conditions. The coastal region from the Hudson River to the mouth of the Chesapeake Bay, far to the south, is no exception. Not surprisingly, conditions vary with the time of year, so the season should be taken into account when planning any coastal cruise.

No one willingly braves any part of the North Atlantic in the winter. Conditions then can be quite severe, and even when the weather is relatively mild, they can deteriorate rather suddenly.

In the spring and fall, strong frontal systems regularly move across the coast, bringing strong winds, usually nor'westers, that can keep you locked into port for days. Fog is not uncommon in the spring and early summer, although it usually burns off by noon. The prudent mariner will carefully watch the weather patterns and await favorable conditions before venturing out for an ocean passage.

The summer is normally the best time for passage making along the Atlantic coast. The prevailing winds are southerlies. Any early morning fog usually is relatively light and burns off early. The high-pressure systems common at this time of year generally bring moderate to light northerly winds and fair weather, allowing sailboats to select favorable winds for a northerly or southerly passage.

Between June and November there is always the possibility of a tropical storm or even a hurricane reaching this far north. If one of these storms is in the offing, everyone, not just the mariner, needs to take appropriate precautions.

Early fall—September and early October—is perhaps the best time for an extended passage south. From late October to early November the cold fronts begin to come in frequently, usually followed by strong easterly winds and high seas, which make most of the coastal inlets dangerous if not completely impassable.

In short, be aware of the weather conditions and plan your passage accordingly. You won't always find a combination of wind, wave, and weather in your favor, so be sure to allow for a layover day or two (or three) somewhere along the route.

The Fine Art of Running Inlets

The running of inlets is not usually fun, especially for low-powered and slow vessels, such as sailboats. The approach from seaward is substantially more hazardous than departing since in the latter case the vessel is on the safe side of the inlet and the skipper usually has the option of staying there or turning back if the conditions demonstrate that to be the prudent action. In addition, dangerous areas are far easier to spot from the inside, and a boat heading into the surf is much more easily controlled than one running with the waves. For that reason, this section concentrates on entering an inlet. If you can make the correct judgments for entering, your exit decisions will be relatively easy.

Even under benign conditions negotiating an inlet demands respect and caution. Unless the sea is completely flat, a fairly rare condition, the offshore swells will rapidly build up in height and steepness as they approach the shore because of the resistance created by the bottom as the water depth becomes increasingly shallower. Most natural inlets unprotected by breakwaters, and many with breakwaters, tend to erect a bar across their mouths. When an ocean swell reaches the bar, it rapidly changes from a roller to a short, steep-sided wave, which may break where the water is shallowest.

Even a short distance offshore the sea may be relatively smooth, and the inlet, from seaward, may not look as bad as it actually is. When approaching from seaward, you should take this annoying little fact into consideration. As the swells build offshore, they may create breakers that extend across the entire mouth of an inlet, even in a buoyed channel.

Speaking of buoys, keep in mind that in many inlets the shoals shift so rapidly and frequently that buoys may not actually indicate the best water or even the correct channel. This is a case in which the vaunted "local knowledge" may be extremely important. If you are not sure where the actual channel lies, it may be wise to hold off until you can get local advice or are able to follow a local boat into the inlet. You may find that locals ignore the buoyed channel and pick their way in by observing the appearance of the sea, judging the best depth by the smoothest surface and the absence of breakers. In rough conditions it may be advisable to remain offshore until conditions moderate or to abort to a more hospitable inlet rather than risk running in through breakers.

If there is any significant sea running, *do not enter the inlet during the ebb current* if you can avoid it. You certainly should avoid entering during the peak ebb-current times under most conditions. An ebb current builds up a far worse sea at the shallow points than otherwise would be the case, due to the rush of the water out against and under the incoming groundswell and other waves. Flood current works the other way around, cutting water away from the bottom of the waves and smoothing them out.

However, a strong flood current may push you through the inlet a bit too fast, making it hard to negotiate your way around any obstacles or obstructions. Optimal times for negotiation of an inlet would then appear to be the relatively short periods following the slack after the ebb current or just prior to the slack after the flood current. (Elsewhere in this book are a few tales of what happened when I failed to follow my own advice.)

If you do make the decision to enter under less than benign conditions, in addition to picking the times of slack water or flood current, there are several things that you can do to make your entrance safer and more comfortable (or at least less uncomfortable).

Don't rush in. Take your time standing off, well offshore of any bar, to watch the action of the waves and see where and how they pile up at the shallower, more critical parts of the channel. Use this information to pick your entrance route. Waves usually come in groups of three, sometimes more, but always at least three. There is something to be said about the seventh wave being larger than others, but it's not a general rule. However, the last wave in a group will be bigger than the rest, and by careful observation it may be picked out of the successive groups.

When you feel that you are prepared to enter the inlet, stand off until a big wave comes along, then run in behind it. Here's where things can get dicey! Watch the waves both ahead of and particularly *behind* your vessel. Match your speed to that of the waves and try to hold your position behind the wave you have chosen to follow. You do not want to overtake the wave ahead or to let the wave behind catch up to you if you can help it. This is where low-powered and slow vessels are at a big disadvantage, as they may not be able to hold position relative to the waves. An overtaking breaker will make control difficult and present the very real danger of causing a broach (where the boat yaws so badly that it is thrown broadside into the trough of the wave, out of effective control). If that should happen, you are in real trouble.

As always, it's the responsibility of the skipper to determine whether his or her skill and vessel are up to negotiating an inlet under the existing conditions. May your judgment always be correct, or at least err on the side of caution.

DISTANCES

As always, responsibility for planning appropriate passages lies with the skipper. He or she will have to take into account many factors, including the size and capability of the vessel, the current and predicted weather conditions, the courses, and the time or distance involved in each leg. The nomographs in this section are intended as a planning aid. The distances are calculated from inlet entrance to inlet entrance and do not take into account the additional distances through the inlets to marinas or anchorages inside.

Table 3. City Island to Atlantic Highlands Distances (nautical miles)

CITY ISLAND								
7	RIKERS ISLAND, EAST END							
10	3	HELL GATE BRIDGE						
17	10	7	THE BATTERY					
23	16	13	6	FORT HAMILTON, THE NARROWS				
26	19	16	9	3	GRAVESEND BAY MARINE BASIN			
31	24	21	14	8	8	GREAT KILLS, STATEN ISLAND		
34	27	24	17	11	10	9	SANDY HOOK (HORSESHOE COVE)	
34	27	24	17	12	10	9	2	ATLANTIC HIGHLANDS YACHT BASIN

FOR EXAMPLE, THE DISTANCE BETWEEN THE BATTERY AND GREAT KILLS, STATEN ISLAND, IS 14 NM.

Table 4. New Jersey Coastal Distances (nautical miles)

GREAT KILLS, STATEN ISLAND															
11	ROCKAWAY INLET, LONG ISLAND														
9	8	SANDY HOOK (HORSESHOE COVE)													
9	9	2	ATLANTIC HIGHLANDS YACHT BASIN												
24	22	24	27	SHARK RIVER INLET											
30	28	30	33	6	MANASQUAN INLET										
54	51	54	56	29	24	BARNEGAT INLET									
72	69	71	74	47	41	18	BEACH HAVEN INLET								
76	71	76	76	49	43	22	2	LITTLE EGG INLET							
79	74	79	79	52	47	25	4	3	BRIGANTINE INLET						
83	81	83	86	59	53	29	12	9	7	ABSECON INLET					
89	87	89	93	65	59	35	18	16	15	8	GREAT EGG INLET				
97	95	97	101	73	67	43	26	24	23	16	8	CORSON INLET			
103	101	103	107	79	73	49	32	30	29	22	14	6	TOWNSENDS INLET		
111	109	111	115	87	81	57	40	38	37	30	22	14	8	HEREFORD INLET	
118	113	118	112	91	85	65	46	45	42	36	28	20	15	7	CAPE MAY INLET

Table 5. Delmarva Coastal Distances (nautical miles)

CAPE MAY INLET								
17	BREAKWATER HARBOR (LEWES, DE)							
30	13	INDIAN RIVER INLET						
48	31	18	OCEAN CITY INLET					
84	67	54	36	CHINCOTEAGUE INLET				
110	93	80	61	26	WACHAPREAGUE INLET			
125	108	95	76	41	15	GREAT MACHAPONGO INLET		
132	115	102	83	38	22	7	SAND INLET (COBB BAY)	
156	139	126	107	73	47	34	24	BAY BRIDGE-TUNNEL (CTR)

Table 6. Delaware Bay Distances (nautical miles)

CAPE MAY CANAL R "8"								
17	BREAKWATER LIGHT (LEWES)							
7	11	BRANDYWINE SHOAL LIGHT						
15	21	10	MIAH MAULL SHOAL LIGHT					
20	26	14	4	CROSSLEDGE LIGHT				
30	35	24	14	10	SHIP JOHN SHOAL LIGHT			
33	37	26	15	11	2	COHANSEY RIVER ENTRANCE		
44	48	37	27	22	13	12	ARTIFICIAL ISLAND R "3B"	
50	55	44	34	29	20	19	6	REEDY POINT C&D CANAL
80	85	77	67	62	53	52	39	33	PHILADELPHIA

HAZARDS TO NAVIGATION

Running aground on one of the numerous shoals, which I discussed on page 10, is not the only thing to watch out for in the Bay. The cruiser needs to be aware of other hazards, many of which are unique to the Chesapeake.

CRAB TRAPS

Crabbing is one of the major industries on the Bay. Blue crabs abound in these waters, as evidenced by the unbelievable number of crab-trap floats scattered throughout the Bay. In some areas, trap floats are so thick that it is difficult to navigate a boat without hitting several. Floats range from those made commercially to bleach bottles and almost anything else that floats well.

The floats themselves are no problem to boats; they are usually soft, smooth, and easily pushed aside by the bow wave. The problem is the line that fastens the float to the heavy wire crab trap on the bottom. This line can become trapped in the propeller or around the rudderpost of a boat, lifting the trap off the bottom and producing a fantastic amount of drag. There have been instances of line being wound up around the propeller until the heavy trap slammed against the hull, sometimes puncturing it. The line also can work into the propeller shaft housing, scoring the shaft and destroying the bearing.

Keep a careful watch and steer clear of trap floats. Freeing a trap line with a boathook or similar device from on deck or in a dinghy alongside is a rare bit of luck. Usually you have to dive over the side and try to work it loose. Make every effort to free the line *without cutting it*. What is a nuisance to you is the waterman's livelihood. When you cut a line, he loses that trap and any income it might have produced.

Even cruisers with the best intentions accidentally foul a pot from time to time. If you hit a trap line while under power, immediately take the engine out of gear to reduce the chance of wrapping the line around the prop, cross your fingers, and watch for the float to reappear in your wake. If it doesn't, you have no choice but to do whatever is necessary to free it before proceeding.

We once picked up a trap in mid-Bay while under sail in more than 25 knots of wind. There was nothing we could do but drag it to where we could anchor in the partial shelter of a point of land before diving over the side and cutting it free. With the heavy drag, we couldn't control the boat well enough to negotiate any harbor entrances. It was an experience we would rather not repeat, and one that I hope you won't repeat either! (See Crabbing, Traps & Trotlines, page 43, for more about crab traps.)

Fish Traps

Fish traps consist of a long line of stakes, some stretching 200 yards or more, that are used to string nets and channel fish into them. The ends of these lines are supposed to be marked with both day and night signals. In practice, they rarely seem to be lit, or if they are, the light is dim. Daymarkers generally consist of a small bush or tree branch of a tree lashed to the stake at either end of the line. These are easily visible and can be used to navigate around the line of stakes. In some areas fish traps are so thick that they present a real maze through which you must thread your way. Navigation can be difficult in the daytime, and at night or in one of the rare fogs it is nearly impossible. The boundaries of fish-trap areas are plainly marked on the NOAA charts; in conditions of poor visibility,

lay a course around these areas, if possible. There are fairways in many of the river channels and harbor entrances, but some of them will require careful navigation if the area is heavily populated with traps.

The areas most heavily populated with fish traps are south of the Potomac River mouth, with a real maze off Mobjack Bay. However, fish traps can be found throughout the main body of the Bay. Both working fish traps and abandoned stakes may be found miles off the Western Shore. If you neglect your navigation, they can show up all of a sudden; a dense thicket of them may prove a real test of skill to negotiate.

Restricted Areas

A quick study of the charts reveals areas where access is restricted but does not reveal just what the restrictions are. Except for the area near Aberdeen Proving Grounds, in the northern Bay, and the Navy bombing ranges near Tilghman Island, in the southern Bay, these restricted areas don't seriously interfere with cruising. There are a couple of other restricted areas in the Potomac River, but they are rarely in use anymore.

These ranges are patrolled by the Coast Guard or other range-associated craft. You will be warned if you happen to stray into an active target-practice area.

Duck Blinds

Duck blinds are usually located in shallow water, which you ought to avoid in any case. (They can warn of shoals in relatively unmarked areas.) However, duck blinds can be mistaken for navigational aids or beacons from a distance, so they do present a small hazard. Other than that, they are just part of the scenery.

Shipping

The skippers, pilots, and crew of the large ships that negotiate the Bay would undoubtedly take exception to being labeled a hazard to navigation. To them, the plethora of small boats scattered throughout the Bay are the real navigational hazard. In a sense, they are right. Large ships negotiating the Bay are restricted to narrow shipping channels and are infinitely less maneuverable than the small boats that buzz around them like flies. They have nowhere else to go to avoid a small craft in one of those channels, and it takes them more than a mile to stop even in an emergency. The prudent small-boat operator must stay alert and keep well out of the way of these ships. In fact, Rule 9 (the Narrow Channel Rule) of the *Inland–International Rules of the Road* clearly states that no vessel, sail or power, shall cross a narrow channel or fairway if such crossing impedes the passage of a vessel that can safely navigate only in that channel or fairway.

This conduct holds true in encounters with smaller commercial vessels, especially tugs with tows. Many times a tug will tow a barge some distance behind it on a cable that could tear apart a small boat. Never attempt to pass between a tug and its tow; you won't make it. Be especially careful when sailing at night because it is hard to distinguish a barge being towed behind a tug just by looking.

FISHING BOATS AND RIGHT-OF-WAY

The Inland–International Rules of the Road, commonsense conventions of right-of-way between vessels on potential collision courses, are essential to the safe operation of all kinds of boats, from sailboards to giant ships. These conventions determine actions that will be taken to prevent such a collision. These "rights" are based upon each vessel's relative ability to maneuver. The less maneuverable vessel usually (but not always) has right-of-way over the more maneuverable one. If both parties involved in a "meeting" situation know, understand, and abide by the Rules of the Road, there is rarely any problem. It is when the rules are ignored or misunderstood that life on the water quickly becomes difficult.

One of the primary misconceptions concerns the rights of vessels engaged in fishing, especially private powerboats that are trolling. The rules state that "fishing vessels" have the right-of-way over powerboats and sailboats. However, this only applies to vessels using nets, lines, trawls, or other gear that severely restricts the maneuverability of the vessel in responding to the presence of another vessel on an intercept course. In addition, "fishing" vessels are supposed to display the proper dayshapes during the day and lights at night. If all of these conditions are not satisfied, the vessel does not meet the legal requirements for a "fishing" vessel for right-of-way purposes! In practice, Chesapeake Bay commercial fishing vessels 20 or more meters in length rarely, if ever, display the "proper dayshape" while they are working; operators of these vessels seem to feel that their identification is so obvious during the day that dayshapes would be redundant. Here tradition takes precedence over the rules: most boats display sufficient prudence around these fishing vessels to prevent any problems.

Do trolling boats have the right-of-way over sailboats and other powerboats because they are engaged in fishing? Absolutely not! According to the *Inland–International Rules of the Road*, both of which specifically exclude trolling boats from the definition of fishing vessels, boats trolling a line or lines while under way have no special rights over other vessels other than the Rules of the Road for the relative vessels themselves. This misunderstanding rears its ugly head again and again, fanning the flames of antagonism between powerboaters and sailboaters. There really is no need for it. Understanding and adherence to the Rules of the Road, plus common courtesy, would easily avoid any problems and the resultant antagonism. My crew and I go well out of our way, even under sail hard on the wind, to stay clear of any boats that are obviously involved in fishing of any type, including trollers. Wouldn't it be nice if these actions were reciprocated?

Last, but by no means least, there is the General Prudential Rule. In brief, this means that no matter who is supposed to have the right-of-way, the skipper of a boat is required to take whatever action is necessary to avoid a collision. How's that for common sense?

GENERAL HAZARDS

SEA NETTLES

The sea nettle, or medusa jellyfish (*Chrysaora quinquecirrha*), is probably the single biggest nuisance in the Chesapeake Bay, at least for those who like to swim or cool off in the water.

The nettles usually start to appear in June, showing up first in the lower Bay and working their way north as the season progresses. Both the density of the nettle population and the rate and maximum distance that they travel up the Bay is determined largely by the amount of rainfall in the spring and early summer. The more rain, the fewer the nettles and the slower their spread. This is probably due to both the decrease in salinity of the Bay waters and the rate of nontidal flow of water out of the Bay. Those who like to swim tend to cruise toward the southern part of the Bay in the early part of the year. Then as the nettles move up the Bay, swimmers cruise toward the head of the Bay as the summer progresses. Even in the worst years for nettles the Susquehanna and Sassafras Rivers provide nettle-free swimming, as do the upper reaches of many of the longer rivers.

The nettle appears to be little more than a translucent, bell-shaped dome of jelly with tentacles as long as 4 feet underneath. These tentacles are covered with stinging cells that are used to paralyze fish so that they can be eaten. When touched, each cell fires a microscopic "dart" filled with venom. The venom is a complex protein that causes a burning sensation on human skin. The usual result is a thin red line or welt that remains about 15 to 30 minutes in most cases. An unfortunate few may be hypersensitive to the venom and experience shortness of breath and severe pains that may last for days. There are innumerable "remedies" for relief from these stings (see the Chesapeake Bay Jellyfish sidebar, pages 119–20), most of which seem to have their greatest effect in the mind of the believer. We have found removing any remaining cells and applying straight ammonia liberally to the affected area to be most effective in stopping the stinging. Do not apply alcohol, as this will cause any unfired cells to discharge immediately.

Don't look for the elimination of these Bay devils. Sea nettles have no known natural enemies save a certain variety of sea slug, called a *nudibranch*, which feeds on the nettles during their polyp stage. Nets have occasionally been used at some beaches, but the results have not been very satisfactory. Coating your body with oils or petroleum jelly is effective for a short time, but I would rather chance getting stung. The best solution for those who like to swim is

to head for the far northern portion of the Bay or well up some of the longer rivers, where the nettles rarely penetrate.

INSECTS & DEFENSE TACTICS

Entomologists classify insects into thousands upon thousands of categories and subcategories. Those of us outside of that profession tend to use much looser terminology, the politest of which is probably *bugs*. Those who cruise the Chesapeake Bay are likely to become concerned only with the flying, biting insects. For the purposes of this book, I will divide these beasties into three categories based on the defense tactics required and refer to them in terms that will probably make an entomologist scream: *flies, mosquitoes,* and *biting gnats* or *no-see-ums.*

The main line of defense against all three is a set of close-meshed, well-fitted screens on all ports, hatches, and other openings into the cabin of a boat. If you can keep them out of the cabin, you'll have a haven of refuge where you can relax and at least sleep in peace. This refuge can be extended by screening in the cockpit of a cruiser or sailboat.

Making this screening sounds more difficult than it really is unless you are a neatness nut. For a cabin cruiser it is easy. Simply make a set of screens that you can put up in place of the canvas cockpit cover. Leave plenty of material to hang loose around the snaps to aid in sealing little gaps and openings (see next page).

Screening in a sailboat is a little more difficult. The easiest way is to combine screening with a sun awning. Velcro strips fastened to the top edge of the awning will permit ready attachment of the screen and still preserve the flexibility needed for adjustment of the awning and movement around and outside of the cockpit. You will need to devise a means of fastening the bottom of the screen. If enough material is left at the bottom to allow several folds to drape, this can be done with judicious placement of weights and tying off to stanchions or other fittings. Closure of the screens around stays, lines, or the boom can also easily be done with Velcro. Just be sure to leave enough screen material beyond the Velcro strip to fill in the inevitable gaps (see next page). This screen permits you to sit out in the cockpit well after twilight in cer-

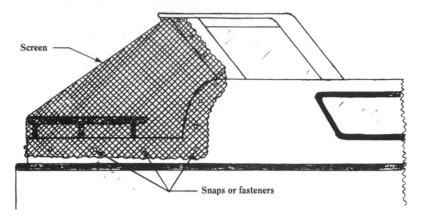

Screening the cockpit of a cabin cruiser.

Screen

Snaps or fasteners

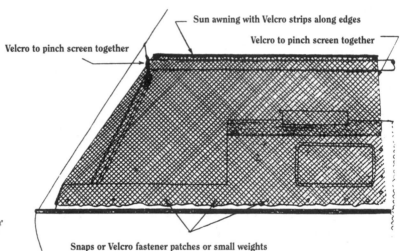

Screening the cockpit of a sailboat.

Sun awning with Velcro strips along edges

Velcro to pinch screen together

Velcro to pinch screen together

Snaps or Velcro fastener patches or small weights

tain buggy anchorages without immersing yourself in repellent or being eaten alive.

From here on, the defense tactics vary depending on which insect is "bugging" you. Please notice that I am ignoring the wide assortment of flying insects that are pesky but do not bite. The methods used to deter their nastier cousins usually handle these offenders too.

Flies. This category covers all of the larger biting flies that show up at almost any time, anywhere, even miles offshore—horseflies, deerflies, green flies, and so on, down to ordinary houseflies. All are easily kept out of the cabin by screens but can be a problem for the crew when you are under way. The majority are not deterred by insect repellents, not even the fly dopes usually found in stores that cater to campers and fishermen. Fear of their bite can be more devastating than the bite itself since even the ominous buzz of the circling fly can render its intended victim senseless.

On the Bay, we usually don't bother with fly dope. The most effective device I have found for keeping all sorts of flies under control, both at anchor and underway, is the time-honored flyswatter—likely one of man's first attempts at insect repellent. (Have you ever noticed how flies seem to disappear at the first appearance of a flyswatter?) The Bay's flies tend to be at their worst after a day or so of rain. The rest of the time they are comparatively sparse; a keen eye and an accurate flyswatter can prevent them from being much of a nuisance. Of course, from time to time you will have to dispose of all the little carcasses littering the deck.

Mosquitoes. Even though there are hundreds of different types of mosquitoes, all we care about is that they bite and the bites itch! After that we only care to avoid an encounter with any mosquito, regardless of its type. Different types of mosquitoes are active at different times of day, 24 hours a day. Although when viewed as a group they seem to have no time constraint, they do have limits. Mosquitoes do not venture more than half a mile offshore except in freak cases, and even at anchor they are rarely a problem when a good breeze is blowing. These bloodsuckers are at their worst a few hours after sundown.

Mosquitoes are easily kept out of a cabin by screens, but there is always the "Lone Ranger" that sneaks into the boat prior to dark, before you have fastened the screens. Once in, it finds a dark recess and lies in wait until you fasten the screens and relax your vigilance. Then it begins its maddening whine as it seeks you out.

What attracts mosquitoes? Researchers are still trying to pin that down, but so far they have determined that these insects seek heat and humidity; they are more attracted to people with higher skin temperatures and higher rates of moisture transpiration. This means that if you have a sunburn or are simply hot and sweaty from exertion, you are a mosquito meal waiting to happen. Studies have also shown that mosquitoes perk up in a stream of carbon dioxide, which means that the same exertion that makes you hot and sweaty could cause you to exhale too much and too frequently to allow these beasties to pass you by. Lastly, human skin has varying degrees of attractive chemicals; so far only lactic acid has been pinpointed as a possible lure. It seems that we are their natural prey. I have been unable to find any scientific research to buttress this claim, but personal research has shown that mosquitoes like dark clothing, especially blue. Try to avoid

wearing blue denim when you plan to do some hard work.

Repellent lotions and sprays are quite effective against these minuscule monsters, but different kinds of repellent seem to have varying degrees of effectiveness for each individual, probably something that harkens back to skin chemistry. A trial-and-error process will help you find the one that works best for you. Many cruisers swear by Skin-So-Soft bath oil, an Avon product, but the Letterman Army Institute of Research in San Francisco tested it and found that while it had some repellency, standard repellents on the market were 30 times as effective. There are also the traditional botanical repellent oils, pennyroyal and citronella. These seem to work only when the bugs aren't bad, and they have to be reapplied often to keep up the repellency. Some families use them on children because they are not as toxic as the most effective repellent to date, DEET, or N,N-diethyl-*meta*-toluamide. Any repellent with DEET is a good start to stopping mosquitoes and no-see-ums (more on them soon). DEET is an irritant and a solvent for plastics—don't push up your sunglasses right after you apply repellent—so you will need to try several varieties of repellent to discover which one has the right percentage of DEET, enough to repel insects but not so much that you develop a rash.

The latest round of research at the U.S. Department of Agriculture's (USDA) Insects Affecting Man and Animals Research Laboratory in Gainesville, Florida, has uncovered a new type of insect combatant. Permethrin is technically a contact toxicant, not a repellent, but it still gets rid of the bugs. This chemical doesn't work when applied to your skin, but it is deadly to insects when it is sprayed on clothing. Any mosquito or other insect that lands on treated clothes dies after a few seconds. Used in combination with a DEET-based repellent, permethrin packs quite a one-two punch. Bugs will stay away from exposed skin and die when they land on treated clothes. Right now, permethrin is licensed for sale in 29 states as an aerosol spray, Permanone Tick Repellent. It was developed as protection from Lyme disease and Rocky Mountain spotted fever, both carried by ticks. It is too early to tell what impact such a toxicant might have on the food chain and whether it

23

will be licensed for sale in the remaining states. It sounds like it would be terrific when used on screening around the cabin, but I will wait until all of the results are in.

Biting Gnats & No-See-Ums. Gnats are a more insidious insect, primarily because of their minute size. The Chesapeake is home to a host of biting gnats, the worst of which is the nearly invisible monster known as a no-see-um. Gnats are active during daylight hours and until well after dark, with a peak of activity in the late afternoon and evening. In most cases they do not venture more than 100 yards offshore, but if you are anchored within their range and are unprepared, they can drive you to tears.

Like mosquitoes, gnats are less bothersome when a stiff breeze is blowing. Unlike mosquitoes, they are not deterred by screens alone but can squeeze right through the mesh! Your best line of defense is to anchor out of range and use repellents (6-12 is my repellent of choice for gnats). Whatever your brand, it must cover every inch of exposed skin because gnats will simply concentrate on the untreated areas. Be sure to cover the small of your back if your shirt rides up when you bend over. Gnats will home in on even an occasional exposure of untreated skin, and the bites can itch for a long time. Although you have to be zealous in your application of repellent, be careful about applying it to your face; if it gets in your eyes, it will burn severely, whatever the brand.

I don't want to paint too black a picture. The only times we have serious problems with gnats is when we go ashore in some of the more remote areas. We have been in only one anchorage where we were bothered while we were aboard; that was in a small gunkhole off the Tred Avon River during an evening calm in late May.

In summary, if you take my advice and prepare for summer "air raids" with screening, effective repellents, and a trusty flyswatter, you should be able to go or anchor almost anywhere and feed only the occasional bug that penetrates your defenses. You may have to put up with a little good-natured ribbing about your paranoia concerning flying insects, but notice who is and isn't scratching an itch the following morning. Last evening's paranoia will be the morning's common sense.

AN ABBREVIATED CHESAPEAKE ROMANCE

THE FIRST INHABITANTS

Although the nearest glacial ice sheets were 200 miles north of Maryland, the area that is now the Chesapeake Bay was "open" but much cooler than it is today. As the climate warmed and the ice melted, creating the Bay (see pages 2–3), the early inhabitants had to adapt their lifestyle to meet the changing conditions. The region's grasslands became forests; where once the natives hunted mammoth, mastodon, and other large game, they now relied on rabbits and deer as well as roots, nuts, and berries. The flooding of the Susquehanna River valley created a holding tank for a readily available marine diet of fish, oysters, and clams.

By 1000 B.C. the native population began to settle. The pattern of wandering after game and gathering vegetation on the way shifted to more efficient hunting with the creation of the bow and arrow (about A.D. 500) and the cultivation of corn, beans, and squash (about A.D. 800). As farming increased, permanent settlements or villages were established. The villages were collections of rectangular bark houses encircled by a post stockade, usually with one entrance or exit that could be closed to hostile intruders. Post mold patterns (marks left in the ground from a post or piling that has decayed and the resultant hole fills with dirt and debris, resembling a mold) have shown up at several village excavations, such as the one at the Biggs Ford Village site in Frederick County, Maryland. This time of settlement, known as the Woodland Period, lasted until the arrival of Old World explorers and settlers in the 1600s.

NATIVE AMERICANS OF THE CHESAPEAKE

At the time of European contact there were two distinct families, or confederations, of tribes in the vicinity of the Chesapeake. Most belonged to a large family of tribes known as Algonquins. The other tribe, one branch of the very large Iroquois Nation, the Susquehannocks, lived along the Susquehanna River, mainly in the vicinity of what is now the Pennsylvania–Maryland border. The warlike Susquehannocks claimed the hunting grounds as far south

"Powhattan held this state and fashion when Captain Smith was delivered to him a prisoner, 1607."

as the Patuxent River on the Western Shore and to the Choptank River on the Eastern Shore. They strengthened that claim with sporadic raids on the Algonquin tribes to the south. The more peaceful Algonquins were distributed around the shores of the Bay and its tributaries from the Patuxent River to Cape Henry and on most of the Eastern Shore.

The Algonquins of the Chesapeake were roughly divided geographically into three major tribes, each comprising a number of smaller tribes. Those living south of the Potomac River were known as Powhatans. The tribes known collectively as Piscataways were distributed south of the Patuxent River, in the region between the Potomac River and the Chesapeake Bay. The remaining family, the Nanticokes, dwelt on the Eastern Shore, primarily south of the Choptank River.

It was the Powhatans that the Jamestown settlers encountered when they established their colony on the shore of the James River in 1609. The Native Americans gave them a friendly reception, and in spite of a substantial number of bloody incidents, relations remained peaceful. Without that peace the colony could not have survived. By the third year the number of colonists had dwindled as a result of disease and starvation. A Native American attack could easily have wiped them out. The reason for this continued peace is not fully understood even today, but it undoubtedly rested mainly with the chief of the tribe, Wahunsonacock (called King

Powhatan by the colonists). Wahunsonacock had developed a grudging respect for the doughty Captain John Smith, who headed the colony during its establishment, and probably believed that he could gain an advantage over other tribes through trade goods obtained from the colonists. (Surely everyone has heard the story of how Pocahontas, the chief's daughter, saved Captain Smith's life and later married a colonist, John Rolfe.)

The Jamestown colony not only survived but prospered. More and more colonists arrived and settled on more and more Native American land, resulting in not infrequent bloodshed between the colonists and the Native Americans. Even so, the shaky peace lasted until 1622, four years after the death of Chief Wahunsonacock and the assumption of the chieftainship by his brother Opechancanough.

The shaky peace crumbled when the colonists hanged a Native American for the *suspected* murder of a white trader. Opechancanough assembled a war party, and on 22 March 1622 the Powhatan warriors attacked, killing 347 colonists—men, women, and children. The war was on.

For 10 years battles and skirmishes continued, with considerable losses on both sides, until a peace treaty was agreed upon in 1632. This peace, as shaky as the previous one, lasted for 12 years. The colonists kept arriving, swelling their number to nearly 8,000. Then, in April 1644 warriors under Opechancanough attacked again, killing nearly 500 colonists. The colonists retaliated, and fighting continued for another two years, until Opechancanough was killed and another shaky peace treaty was made.

The Powhatans were not the only natives to feel the pressure of European colonization. Colonists arrived in Maryland in 1634 and established their colony at St. Marys City. There the Piscataway tribes were the ones involved. Later, as both colonies continued to grow and expanded to the Eastern Shore, the Nanticokes and, finally, the Susquehannocks began to feel the pressure.

There was a ready and lucrative market in Europe for the tobacco grown in the colonies. Colonists continued to arrive in boatload after boatload. More and more land was needed, and taken from the Native Americans. In early en-

Typical Susquehannock attire at the time of the Jamestown settlement, from Captain John Smith's map.

counters the Native Americans generally reacted with curiosity, generosity, and the offer of friendship. Friendly contact exposed the Native Americans to European germs, and many natives were decimated by disease. Repeated betrayal, trickery, and treaty violations on the part of the whites worked to create a pattern of periods of fighting followed by shaky peace between the colonists and the Native Americans.

Under this pressure and repeated raids by the Susquehannocks, most of the Piscataway tribes left Maryland, moving well into the wilds of Virginia, as did the Powhatans. The Nanticokes of the Eastern Shore first were established in a reservation near the junction of Chicone Creek and the Nanticoke River, but that didn't solve any of the problems and they eventually left for areas well to the north, vanishing into history. The Susquehannocks later went on the warpath against the colonists, only to be badly defeated by combined forces from the Virginia and Maryland colonies and driven back to Pennsylvania.

By the latter part of the 18th century few Native Americans remained in the Chesapeake Bay area, and their numbers continued to dwindle over the next hundred years. Today a few descendants of the Nanticoke and Piscataway tribes remain on the Eastern Shore and in southern Maryland.

The Native Americans may be gone, but they left behind their names to label many of the rivers, creeks, and a few other places where they once dwelt. These names and a scant few traces in the shell mounds on beaches and occasional arrowheads found on the sites of old encampments are reminders that the Bay cradled people and cultures before written history.

COLONIAL ERA

The English under Captain John Smith were not the first Europeans to settle on the shores of the Chesapeake. They were, however, the first to survive and remain there.

In 1526, not far from the site of Jamestown, on the James River, the Spanish attempted to establish a settlement called San Miguel de Gualdape. Between (mostly internal) fighting and rampant disease, it was soon abandoned. Repeated settlement efforts in the 1570s all failed. During this period Spaniards circumnavigated the Bay under Vincente Gonzales, but the expedition produced no charts and was soon forgotten.

The Chesapeake Bay was rediscovered in 1585, this time by an Englishman, Sir Ralph Lane, from the Roanoke Island Colony in North Carolina, established by Sir Walter Raleigh. Even so, it was more than 30 years before the English capitalized on this find.

Then in May 1607 three little ships sailed into the Chesapeake, landed briefly just inside Cape Henry (where a cross now stands to commemorate the event—the Cape Henry Memorial), and then sailed 32 miles up the James River to found the settlement of Jamestown. More ships were to follow, but the *Susan Constant*, *Godspeed*, and *Discovery* were the first, preceding the *Mayflower* by more than a decade. (Replicas of these three ships are at the Jamestown Festival Park, just above the site of the original settlement on the James River.)

The following year, Captain John Smith set out with a small party to explore the Bay. They spent two months gunkholing an estimated 3,000 miles of the Chesapeake, in search of the elusive Northwest Passage to the Indies. Of course, they didn't find it, but they did produce the first reasonably accurate map of the Bay and its rivers, sending it to England for publication.

Despite the knowledge gained through exploration and the bounty of the Bay and its tidewaters, Jamestown almost ended in disaster.

The first summer had been hard; the 105 colonists were unprepared for the Virginia heat, and bad food caused a lot of sickness. Even Smith became ill, but fortunately he recovered. The settlers had many unfriendly encounters with Native Americans. Ironically, it was the capture of Smith by the Powhatans that saved the weakened colonists. While he was being held by the Native Americans, Smith befriended Pocahontas, the chief's daughter. She not only intervened to save his life but, after his release, brought substantial gifts of food to the colonists every four or five days. Pocahontas alerted Smith to a planned attack by the Powhatans, foiling her father's plans.

Severely injured in an accident, Smith returned to England in October 1609. With his departure, the colonists lost any goodwill on the part of the Native Americans. During that winter many starved to death, and the 32 weakened survivors prepared to abandon the settlement in the spring. The timely arrival of Baron De La Warr, known as Lord Delaware, in June 1610 brought the supplies and new colonists necessary to save Jamestown. The colony eventually prospered, establishing the English in the Chesapeake Bay.

The Bay and its multitude of rivers turned into a watery road to riches, thanks to the cultivation of tobacco and a ready market for it in Europe. (It does seem odd that a plant now considered harmful and noxious played a major role in the founding and building of this country.) Plantation fields were cleared in the tidewater region, and each plantation had a wharf where ships could load tobacco. Later, lumber, flour, and grain replaced tobacco as the prime cargo for ships visiting the upper Bay. Small tidal streams provided waterways for small boats taking crops to market, and safe

Captain John Smith's map of the Chesapeake Bay, the earliest accurate map on record.

harbors abounded for watermen who caught fish and shellfish to sell in local markets.

The Bay and its waterways also provided easy access for invaders and raiders for more than two centuries after the founding of Jamestown, notably the British during the American Revolution and the War of 1812, as well as a wide assortment of pirates and privateers. In fact, it was the failure of the British to control the lower Chesapeake, due to the intervention of the French fleet off the Virginia capes, that forced Lord Cornwallis to surrender at Yorktown, effectively ending the Revolutionary War in the colonists' favor.

PIRATES

Piracy came to the Chesapeake with the colonists. Shortly before the arrival of Lord Delaware in June 1610, a party of about 30 desperate colonists from Jamestown stole the *Swallow*, the larger of the colony's two remaining ships, in order to go a-pirating. Although the ship's ultimate fate is unknown, its theft marked the beginning of a 200-year plague of pirates, pickaroons, privateers, and assorted raiders in and around the Bay.

In 1634 the *Ark* and the *Dove* arrived in the Chesapeake with the settlers who would establish the new colony of Maryland at St. Marys City, under Lord Baltimore's charter. The Maryland and Virginia royal charters conflicted, which set the scene for the strife that was to follow.

William Claiborne and his company had established a trading station in 1631 at Kent Island, three-quarters of the way up the Bay, under the Virginia charter. Claiborne insisted on sole trading rights with all the Native American tribes in the Bay. In the spring of 1635 a small Maryland pinnace attempted to trade with the Native Americans and was captured by Claiborne's men near what is now Garrett Island, in the Susquehanna River. This act, dubbed piracy by the Marylanders, sparked a series of ship seizures and battles between the contending parties. The matter was resolved only when the forces of Maryland's Governor Calvert captured Kent Island. The Maryland Assembly charged Claiborne with murder and piracy and returned him to England. When Claiborne lost his petition to the Lords Commissioners of Plantations, the governor of Virginia withdrew his support. Kent Island and several other islands in the northern Bay now formally belonged to Maryland. The charter conflict was resolved.

The next stage of piracy was a result of the English civil war between the Royalists (or Cavaliers), who supported King Charles, and the Roundheads, of Parliament, who supported Oliver Cromwell.

King Charles had just sent orders to Maryland to seize any Parliament ships and their goods when Captain Richard Ingle, who had plied the Virginia trade for more than a decade, put his pinnace, *Reformation*, in at St. Marys City in January 1644. He was arrested upon his arrival, accused of supporting Parliament and uttering treasonous words against the king. He shortly managed an incredible escape, reclaimed his ship, and sailed off.

Angered at his arrest and the subsequent warrant for what he felt were unjust charges of treason, Ingle attacked, captured, and looted several vessels anchored in St. Georges Creek, at the mouth of the St. Marys River. Charges of piracy, mutiny, and "trespass" were upheld by the court. With the return to England of Ingle and the *Reformation*, the matter was, quite erroneously, considered closed.

Captain Ingle was now fully committed to the cause of Parliament. In October 1644 he managed to obtain for the *Reformation* one of the first letters of marque issued by the Lord High Admiral of England to seize all ships hostile to Parliament, along with their goods. Armed with that, he again set sail for Maryland, ostensibly to deliver a cargo but evidently bent on revenge. While in Virginia, he prepared his crew to "go up to Maryland to plunder the Papists."

In February 1645 Ingle sailed into the St. Marys River, took the small fort at St. Inigoes Creek virtually unopposed, and captured the Dutch ship *Speagle*. Installing his mate as commander of the *Speagle*, he then attacked the capital, St. Marys City. The city fell virtually without a fight; Ingle was in command of Maryland.

A reign of terror ensued for the Catholics of Maryland. Plantation after plantation was plundered, justified by supposed loyalty to Parliament and the Roundheads. Although Captain Ingle remained in Maryland waters only 14 weeks before returning to England, his followers continued the depredations for some time. Colonists were forced to flee their homes and seek refuge elsewhere. The population plummeted from 400 settlers to 100.

Maryland was left without a government until late 1646, when Governor Calvert raised a force to retake the colony and did so totally unresisted. Nearly two years of anarchy finally came to an end.

From 1662 to 1666 Dutch privateers raided throughout the Bay area. Before the end of hostilities these privateers had captured 13 or more ships and burned 6 others, including the British guardship HMS *Elizabeth*, assigned to protect the Chesapeake.

In 1684 Virginia's new governor, Francis Howard, issued a proclamation prohibiting all trade with pirates and privateers by the local inhabitants. Not only did settlers continue the forbidden commerce but many of them tried their own hand at pirating. In fact, local pirates were instrumental in establishing the College of William and Mary.

In the summer of 1688 Captain Simon Rowe, commander of the Chesapeake guardship *Dumbarton*, stopped a small shallop manned by four men for a routine check. An investigation produced three large sea chests full of gold, silver, and other valuables. The four buccaneers—Peter Cloise (a black slave), Edward Davis, Lionel Delawater, and John Hinson—were instantly arrested on suspicion of piracy. Thus began several years of charges, countercharges, petitions, and trials that culminated in an interesting deal, the result of a petition that the accused submitted to King Charles. The king's final decree on the matter in 1693 resulted in the release of the prisoners with most of their treasure, provided that a fourth part of it be used to establish a "Free School or College in Virginia." The College of William and Mary's first endowment was obtained from pirate booty!

Peace in Sight. In early 1700 the destruction of the pirate vessel *La Paix* (Peace) by Captain

BALTIMORE CLIPPERS

Baltimore clippers were built for speed in an era when speed on the high seas was synonymous with survival. They won the respect of the maritime nations of the world and helped establish the reputation of the port of Baltimore. In fact, in the 1790s Baltimore was the undisputed leader of the shipbuilding industry on the Chesapeake Bay.

During and immediately following the American War of Independence the United States had little navy to speak of. As a result, the small American merchant marine had no protection on the high seas and quickly became the prey of pirates and foreign naval ships. Speed became the best survival insurance that an American vessel could have. Chesapeake Bay shipbuilders were the first to respond to this need and created one of the fastest vessels afloat in its day.

During the War of 1812, President James Madison attempted to overcome the lack of a navy by issuing "letters of marque and reprisal," which allowed private shipowners to arm their vessels and seize the commercial cargo of vessels of hostile nations. Such a vessel was known as a privateer. Baltimore clippers were ideally suited to operate as privateers, and American privateers captured or sank some 1,700 British merchant vessels during the war. This activity was a major factor in the British decision to attack the city of Baltimore in 1814. The ensuing American victory at Fort McHenry was described by Francis Scott Key in the words that became our national anthem, "The Star-Spangled Banner."

In the years following the War of 1812 the very characteristic that made the sleek Baltimore clipper fast, the slim hull design, contributed to its ultimate demise. The limited space for cargo made the boats unprofitable for their owners. As a result, the Baltimore clipper gave way to enlarged variations of the original clipper, which eventually led to the development of the large cargo-carrying Yankee clippers of the 1850s.

William Passenger, commander of the warship HMS *Shorham,* marked the start of a 15-year period of relatively untroubled waters, save for the occasional harassment by privateers during the War of Spanish Succession. At the close of that war privateers of all nationalities were suddenly unemployed and so turned to piracy. Fortunately for the Chesapeake, the treasure ships of the West Indies and South America were far more lucrative targets for pirates than the Bay area's tobacco trade.

This was the time that spawned the most fearsome pirate in history, Captain Edmund Teach, better known as Blackbeard. Although it is doubtful that Blackbeard actually conducted operations in the Bay itself, his legend is of such stature that he is often included in apocryphal stories of the Chesapeake Bay.

The period of relative peace lasted until the spring of 1741. The War of Austrian Succession had broken out in Europe in 1740, and its effects were soon felt in the New World. Spanish and then French privateers began to harass the Virginia coast. This lasted until 1748, when hostilities ceased in Europe. The tidewater then remained relatively free from attack.

Patriots & Picaroons. The American Revolution swept the Maryland and Virginia tidewater into a conflict more destructive than the early charter incidents. For almost eight years settlers dwelling along the shores of the Bay, including its myriad rivers, creeks, islands, and marshes, were subjected to repeated raids by land and sea. Neither patriot nor Tory was spared in the high passions of that conflict, for in the Chesapeake tidewater area the war was fought on two planes: one was a fairly conventional conflict between opposing armies and navies; the other was an especially nasty guerrilla war, initially conducted by Tories against the patriot populace and the merchant marine in the Bay, that frequently degenerated into acts of revenge and even piracy against both sides.

One of the notorious Tory sea raiders, or picaroons, was Joseph Wheland, whose raids on the Eastern Shore infused local Tory strongholds with the urge to rise up and create some disorder on their own.

Wheland and his crew were captured off Holland Straits in late July 1776 by a detachment of 30 patriots. He remained in jail for five years before finally managing to secure his release. Once free, he returned to raiding with such a vengeance that his excesses were deplored by Tories and patriots alike. Following Wheland's capture, few picaroons were active on the Chesapeake until the spring of 1779 — thanks to the efforts of the Virginia and Maryland state navies.

In the summer of 1780, however, picaroons and pirates seemed to be everywhere in the lower Bay. More than 25 vessels were active in outright piracy, raiding and robbing at will. By August, shipping had come to a standstill. The raiders soon took to attacking the homes and businesses of citizens along the shores of St. Marys County. By September local picaroons and New York raiders were in control of the middle Bay region and began to focus their attacks on the Eastern Shore. Matters got worse in October 1780, when a British fleet under General Alexander Leslie arrived to attack Richmond and Petersburg, an event that galvanized even lukewarm picaroons into action.

One year later these greedy opportunists were plundering fellow Tories as well as patriots, having degenerated into base piracy. Leaders on both sides of the Revolutionary conflict were disgusted with the picaroons, pirates, and other privateers in the Bay. Lord Cornwallis, commander of the British troops at Portsmouth, Virginia, complained to his commander in chief that this activity was hardening the resolve of the patriots and even driving some Tories from the crown. The French navy soon took control of the Bay, resulting not only in the surrender of Cornwallis at Yorktown on 19 October 1781 but also in a much-longed-for respite from lawless plunder.

This respite was brief. Diehard picaroons from the Eastern Shore, assorted privateers from New York, and Royal Navy deserters continued attacks on ships and shore for another 18 months. The combined efforts of the French navy and armed barges from both Virginia and Maryland proved insufficient to capture or destroy enough of the raiders to quiet the Bay. Peace returned only when news of the formal cessation of hostilities between England and the American colonies reached Annapolis on 29 March 1783: the war was over.

The days of the Whelands, the Teaches, and the Ingles were gone. That these were the last of the Chesapeake Bay pirates was particularly fortunate because the Bay was about to become a major site in the conflict that became known as the War of 1812. References to this event are scattered throughout this book in the various areas where some of the action took place.

SHELLFISHING

OYSTERING

Oysters have been harvested on the Chesapeake Bay for several thousand years. Archaeologists have discovered evidence of Native American shell mounds dating to 5,500 B.C. at various sites around the Bay. Even so, no one can look at an oyster on the half shell without wondering about the courage—or foolhardiness—of the person who ate the first one millennia ago! The first colonists were aware of the oyster, and some left written notes containing references to the huge quantity and individual size of these shellfish. One writer, comparing the Chesapeake oyster with those in England, claimed that the New World oysters were often four times the size of those he had known.

In spite of that, the colonists did not consider oysters a prime source of food and would only eat them in any quantity when little else was available. Commercial harvesting of oysters did not begin until the early 1800s, and even that was a result of New Englanders' traveling to the Chesapeake for oysters because their own oyster beds were exhausted.

More people have made their living from the oyster in Maryland than in any other state. The industry not only boomed, it got out of control. When it reached a peak in 1885 with a harvest of about 15 million bushels, the competition was so fierce that it started the "oyster wars." This was not a friendly commercial rivalry. As one wag said, "If all the bullets fired in the oyster wars were recovered, they would satisfy the market for fishing sinkers for near a century!"

CHESAPEAKE BAY OYSTERS

The famous Chesapeake Bay oyster (*Crassostrea virginica*) is not really limited to the Chesapeake Bay. This gastronomical delight is widely distributed along the eastern coast of North America, from the Gulf of St. Lawrence to the Gulf of Mexico. Although there is much rivalry over the supposed superiority of oysters from a particular region, presumably because of the special flavor imparted to the creature from the waters in which it grows, they are all the same animal.

In the more southerly waters of the United States oysters may be found in clusters right up to the tide line. In the Chesapeake, however, they cannot tolerate the freezing temperatures found in extremely shallow waters. Therefore, they are found in waters 8 to 25 feet deep. These oyster beds, or bars, are located throughout the Chesapeake. Oysters seem to thrive best in the mid-Bay region; there the waters are salty enough to suit the oysters but too brackish for many of their predators.

Oysters can survive on a wide variety of hard bottoms, but the soft, silty bottom found in much of the Bay would smother them. For that reason, the beds tend to be clustered in areas where there are suitable hard anchorages for the oysters. These beds are charted and well known (by name, even) to the commercial oystermen and the Natural Resources Police who regulate them. The state creates many bars by dumping old oyster shells in clusters to form new bars. These old shells are obtained from two sources: "fresh" shell is obtained from Bay area oyster-shucking houses; "fossil" shell by dredging old, nonproducing beds. A frequent sight in the Bay is one or more barges loaded with heaps of shells being moved to a new location, where the shells are blasted over the side by powerful streams of water from turret-mounted hoses.

Oyster tonging remains the most common form of oystering in the Bay.

(For more on the oyster wars, see the Oyster Wars sidebar, page 249.)

Today most oystering in Virginia is done on privately leased bars regulated by the state. This approach worked well until the combination of MSX (a one-celled protozoan parasite that debilitates oysters) and overfishing nearly destroyed the oystering industry in the southern Bay; it still hasn't fully recovered.

Oystering in Maryland works on the principle that the bottoms of the Bay are public. Anyone can oyster in the Maryland Bay waters at his or her own financial risk; it is not necessary to work for someone who holds a lease on a particular oyster bed. The beds are maintained and policed by the state for use by licensed watermen. This has resulted in a fiercely independent

breed of watermen. It is a hard life and certainly not one to make watermen rich, but watermen run their own lives as they see fit, subject only to regulation by weather and state laws. Only? The law sets regulations on when they can fish, where they can fish, and the minimum size of oysters that they can keep. Still, watermen are a rugged breed, perhaps among the last of the traditional American rugged individualists, possibly an endangered species.

Besides the relatively recent practice of diving for oysters with underwater breathing gear, oysters are harvested on the Bay by using an assortment of tongs or by dredging. Currently, tongers and divers are allowed to oyster from 15 September to 30 March; dredgers are restricted to the slightly shorter period from 1 November to 15 March. In addition, oystering is permitted only six days a week, Monday through Saturday, from sunrise to sunset. Any oyster smaller than 3 inches must be returned to the bed for continued growth; only larger ones may be kept and sold. These regulations are rigidly enforced by Maryland's Natural Resources Police.

As a result of gear restrictions imposed by the state, the tongs and dredges used today are little different from those used more than a century ago. The main improvement has been the use of power winches to replace manual effort in all except hand tonging.

Robert de Gast

In deeper Bay waters oystermen use patent and hydraulic tongs.

Tongs. Other than in details of the design of the metal "basket," hand tongs haven't changed since their first known use in 1701. In their simplest form tongs resemble a pair of garden rakes hinged together with a "basket" attached to the back of the head of each "rake." The handles vary in length from about 12 feet to as much as 30 feet, depending upon the depth of the water to be worked.

Taking oysters by tonging demands considerable physical strength and a remarkably good sense of balance. It obviously is confined to relatively shallow water. Oysters are so scarce, and this method is so inefficient, that the tonger rarely reaches the 25-bushel daily limit. Even so,

hand tonging remains the Bay's most common form of oystering, and there are sound economic reasons as well as other advantages to this seemingly perverse and old-fashioned preference.

Unlike for either power tonging or dredging, the initial equipment investment is small; repairs are few and inexpensive when needed. The lightweight, small equipment permits the tonger to use a skiff or other small boat and to work near home in creeks or rivers where dredgers and power tongers are prohibited from operating. This, in turn, reduces fuel expenses.

Oyster tonging is not a business for any but the strong, hardy, and fiercely independent. Tongers must stand by the boat's gunwale, lower the tongs to the bottom, pull the handles apart, then bring the handles back together to rake oysters into the basket part of the tongs. (How tongers can tell whether they have oysters in the tongs as opposed to debris I don't know, but many claim that they can "feel" oysters on the bottom through the handles of the tongs.) When the tonger thinks that he has a good haul, or "jag," he raises the tongs, hand over hand, until he can swing the head aboard over a culling board to dump his catch. The assembly, complete with catch, can weigh as much as 70 pounds! This process is repeated until a good haul is sitting on the culling board; then the tonger turns to cull the catch. If there is a helper to cull, the tonger does not stop tonging until regulations force him to or until the boat is in danger of sinking, whichever comes first.

In 1887 a Patuxent River blacksmith, Charles L. Marsh, devised a set of tongs that operated remotely by lines attached to a winch. He promptly patented the mechanism, which became known as "patent tongs." This mechanism allowed watermen to reach oysters in depths not previously accessible, and they could work faster and with far less physical effort than they could using hand tongs. The first patent tongs operated by a hand winch, frequently mounted on a mast with a boom that swung out to drop the patent tongs over the side or back to drop the catch inboard. These winches were power driven as soon as appropriate engines became available.

In 1958 another Calvert County waterman, William Barrett, and a local blacksmith, T. Rayner Wilson, modified the patent tong with a hydraulic mechanism. This new design could be run by one person and operated twice as fast as the earlier version.

The hydraulic tongs were so efficient that they supplanted the earlier version, virtually driving those oystermen who did not invest in them out of business, and caused a change in the law. As a result of a court case in 1971, hydraulic tong use is currently limited to the Bay proper and a few other areas (such as the mouth of the Patuxent River) where the water is too deep to be worked using shaft tongs.

Dredging. Many different types of sailing craft have been designed for use on the Chesa-

peake Bay, ranging from the early dugout canoes to the skipjack, which was the last of the commercial sailing craft to be developed. There is no single design for the skipjack. It started out as a fairly small craft in the 1890s, based on the V-bottom crabbing skiff commonly used to run trotlines in shoal waters of the Bay. Called *bateaux*, and in some locales *dead-rise*, they all had the wide beam, low freeboard, shallow draft, and V-shaped bottom so suitable to oyster dredging, or "drudging," as the watermen say. The jib-headed, leg o'mutton mainsail sloop rig with a clipper bow makes the skipjack readily recognizable from a distance.

The early skipjacks stayed close to home and sold their catch either locally or to "buy" boats from the cities. Within 10 years, the skipjack had become large enough to carry its catch to whatever Bay destination the captain wished.

Maryland has the only remaining sail-powered oyster-dredging fleet in North America. The main reason for its continued existence is the 1865 law restricting oyster dredging to sail-powered boats. Amended in 1967 to permit the use of gasoline-powered "push boats" on Monday and Tuesday of each week, this law is still enforced. There are now only 15 to 20 working skipjacks left on the Chesapeake, a drastic drop from the hundreds that plied its waters after the turn of the century.

The rough-and-tumble tactics used by dredger captains back then are long gone, and good riddance to them. Today's captain is a businessman as well as a skipper. He must find oysters, keep a good crew throughout the season, and make enough money to stay in operation. Which of these tasks is the hardest to accomplish is debatable, but one thing is certain: the success or failure of an oyster-dredging operation rests squarely on the captain.

The best chance to see one of these graceful, fascinating boats is at Chesapeake Appreciation Day, held the Saturday before 15 November, when skipjack races are held off Sandy Point, near the Bay Bridges. At this time the boats are in the area anyway for the start of the Bay's oystering season, traditionally begun near Annapolis. Most cruisers rarely see a skipjack in operation, let alone dredging for oysters. These boats work when most cruising boats

S H E L L F I S H I N G

Maryland has the only remaining sail-powered oyster-dredging fleet in North America. This skipjack is berthed in Wenona, Deal Island.

Oyster dredge and winch on the deck of a skipjack at the Calvert Marine Museum, Solomons.

have given up for the season. Skipjacks dredge all winter, being limited only by storms and ice.

Dragging a dredge over an oyster bar is by far the most efficient oyster-harvesting method ever used on the Bay—too efficient, some say. The dredge has a roughly triangular metal frame with a toothed raking bar along its lower leading edge, which loosens oysters as the device is dragged along the bottom. The bar's width cannot exceed 44 inches. Some larger ones can be found, but these were built to be operated only over leased beds by local oyster companies and therefore were not subject to state regulation. Most boats carry three or four pairs of dredges with raking bars of different designs for use on different types of bottoms. To the rear of the dredge frame is the collecting basket, or "dredge bag," whose bottom half is usually made of iron links or chains joined with S hooks and whose top half is made of mesh cording. The dredge bag collects the oysters plus assorted debris broken free by the raking bar.

The dredge is lowered over the side of the boat, and its line is let out until the captain judges the lead of the line to be right for the depth of the oyster bar. Usually, two dredges operate at the same time, one on each side of the boat. The dredges are towed until the captain judges that the dredge bags are full or that no more oysters can be gathered at that site. Then, one at a time, the dredges are brought to the surface and raised aboard with a winder (a winch designed for this purpose) and their contents dumped on the deck.

The crew lowers the dredges over the side again, and dredging continues while they cull the catch to select the oysters that are at least 3 inches long. As oysters are culled, the "keepers" are tossed into four piles, two piles forward and two aft. This keeps the boat in trim and leaves a clear working space in the middle. Then the crew dumps everything else back overboard.

This process is repeated all day long. The boat makes pass after pass, each parallel to the previous one, until the bar is exhausted or (with luck) the harvest limit is reached. Then the watermen either off-load their catch onto a buy boat or return to port to off-load and return home. Those who have traveled far to reach their working area may elect to stay overnight

in a sheltered creek or river near their dredging grounds. The next day, they repeat the process.

Diving. In recent years younger watermen have tried using underwater breathing apparatus for oyster harvesting. At first the traditionalist watermen felt that this approach was "unfair," that divers would take all of the "good" oysters from the beds. Cooler heads soon prevailed, helped by government regulations to restrict where the divers could operate and the realization that the murky Bay waters forced a diver to rely on "feel" rather than on easy visual selection.

Oyster divers cannot work the beds used by tongers, with a few minor exceptions. They must dive on beds in the main Bay or in some of the larger river mouth areas, all of which are clearly and carefully defined on maps produced by the Department of Natural Resources; these areas are policed diligently. The restrictions, combined with the frigid winter waters (which make diving a cold operation even with the protection of a wet suit), make it highly unlikely that divers will dominate the oystering industry.

A few divers use scuba gear, but most operate with an air pump in the boat, which provides air through a long hose attached to a full face mask. This allows the diver to stay down longer and eliminates the need to recharge and carry bulky air tanks on board. In addition, divers have a ready guide to the boat above.

A diver's boat is manned by at least two oystermen. One dives and gathers oysters into a basket; the other tends the air pump, controls the boat, and hauls the basket of oysters aboard when signaled by the diver. Presumably, the initial culling is done by the diver on the bottom and finished by his partner.

The Inland Navigation Rules Act of 1980 requires a vessel engaged in diving operations to display the international code flag Alpha, a blue-and-white, swallow-tailed flag. Rarely does anyone other than a commercial salvage diver display this flag. Instead, most fly the traditional "diver down" flag, a rectangular red flag with a white diagonal stripe. If you see either of these flags, you are required to keep well clear.

Like tongers, divers operate from small, relatively open boats, generally the same skiffs used for crabbing, oyster tonging, or clam dredging. There is no real need for cabin accommodations other than as protection from the weather. And divers, like tongers, return home every evening.

CLAMMING

Two kinds of clams of commercial interest are found in the Chesapeake Bay: the hard clam and the soft-shell clam, better known as manninose. Both are harvested and sold commercially, but few people not involved in the business have a clear understanding of how they are taken or with what kind of equipment, even though these clammers, especially those harvesting the soft-shell clams, are among the Bay's more unusual sights.

Hard Clams. The hard clam has a thick, heart-shaped shell. This is the clam the Ameri-can Native Americans called *quahog* and used for wampum. Quahogs are categorized by size: the young, small ones are *littlenecks* and *cherrystones;* the large ones are called *chowders.* The first two are eaten raw on the half shell. Chowders are tougher and are usually cooked, as their name suggests. The name *littleneck* refers to two small siphons that can be seen just below the cut muscle on freshly shucked clams. Their shortness means that hard clams cannot burrow deeply. The hard clams (*Mercenaria mercenaria*) require relatively high salinity (at least 15 parts salt per 1,000 parts water), which restricts their growth to the lower Bay waters. The heaviest concentrations are found from the lower James River to the lower York River on the western side of Virginia's portion of the Bay and on the lower portion of Virginia's Eastern Shore. Strangely enough, cherrystone clams are not limited to the vicinity of Cherrystone

TRY YOUR HAND AT SHELLFISHING

While I encourage you to try clamming and oystering, get to know the rules covering these activities so that your experiences will be legal.

Neither Virginia nor Maryland requires a fee or a license if you are **clamming** for personal consumption. If you are interested in small-scale clamming for market, you will need a gear license, the fees for which vary according to the type of equipment you use. In Virginia, for example, hand-tong or hand-rake fees run $15 per year for residents. Nonresidents must pay a $350 annual fee in addition to the gear-licensing fee. Clamming for personal consumption must be done with a hand rake in Maryland; using any other equipment puts you in the commercial clamming category. This applies to divers as well as surface clammers.

Clamming in both states is restricted to "Clean Areas," which are marked by signs. If you have any doubts about an area where you want to clam, call the Virginia Marine Resources Law Enforcement Division at 757-247-2200; this office will help you contact the Marine Patrol officer operating nearest you (there are 80 officers patrolling the Virginia waters of the Bay). In Maryland contact the Department of Natural Resources at 410-974-3216.

Maryland restricts one's clamming take to one bushel a day; Virginia has no size or quantity limits.

In Maryland the restrictions for clamming apply to **oystering** for personal consumption or recreation. You are limited to one bushel a day, and you must stick to the Clean Areas, which are marked by signs. There are no fees.

The Virginia Public Oyster Grounds are open only from October to March, limiting the appeal of this "sport" for cruisers. In addition, the laws governing oystering in Virginia waters are incredibly complex. You will need to read the Virginia Code Book and familiarize yourself with additional regulations and orders. For those who must know, contact Stephanie Averson, Statistic Program Director for Fisheries, Virginia Marine Resources, 2600 Washington Avenue, 3rd floor, Newport News, VA 23607; 757-247-2203.

A hydraulic clam dredge in operation.

Joan B. Machinchick

Inlet on the Eastern Shore, though these succulent clams are traditionally bountiful at that location.

Harvesting of hard clams is done in one of two ways. On the lower Eastern Shore the tidal flats are so extensive that even the small range of tide exposes enough of the flats to permit gathering clams by the traditional method of wading the flats with bucket and clam rake to rake through the mud, picking up the clams exposed by the process. The method is effective but messy.

The other technique uses tongs that are much like oyster tongs but have a finer mesh on the basket. These are used from a boat anchored over a clam bed. Since clams normally live between the tide line and where the water is about 20 feet deep, this method is also quite effective.

Manninose (Soft-Shell) Clams. The soft-shell clam has a thin shell that is easily broken. It is elongated, not as round as the hard clam. The siphons of the soft-shell clam are long and retractable, but they cannot be completely withdrawn into the shell. These long siphons enable

soft-shell clams to burrow much deeper than hard clams. The manninose (*Mya arenaria*) are best prepared steamed, fried, or in chowders. They are found throughout the Bay, except near the headwaters, where the water is close to being fresh. They live in all types of bottoms (except soft mud) and in shallow waters (up to 20 feet deep). They burrow into the hard mud, using a long "snout" to take in water, from which they filter out their food. Unlike oysters, clams can move, mostly vertically, in the mud, which allows them to survive in silting conditions that would smother oysters.

Most of the clams harvested in the Chesapeake Bay area are not eaten locally. The majority are shipped out, save those bought by watermen for use as eel bait. For some reason, an appreciation for the taste of these clams has never taken hold in the region.

Clamming is a relatively young industry in the Chesapeake. It developed as the result of a shortage of New England clams in the 1950s, caused by overfishing and disease, and as the result of the invention in 1950 of a clam dredge, by Fletcher Hanks, of Oxford, Maryland, which was put into commercial use in 1952. Because of the high demand from New England and the availability of efficient dredging equipment, clamming in the Chesapeake moved into high gear. Hanks's clam dredge accounts for the entire commercial harvest in Maryland; its use is prohibited in Virginia's waters.

The clamming boom was short-lived, however. Catches started falling off, and the state imposed a maximum catch limit of 40 bushels a day for a boat and restricted the maximum working depth of the dredges to 15 feet. Combined with the effects of Hurricane Agnes in June 1972, which devastated the crop, this nearly killed the industry. It still survives, but the harvest has yet to reach pre-Agnes levels.

For obvious reasons, the Department of Natural Resources designates clamming areas that are distinctly separate from oyster beds, and the laws against clam dredging in unauthorized areas are strictly enforced.

In operation, the clam dredger's conveyor is mounted on the starboard side of the boat and rigged to hinge at the rear so that the front end, with its hydraulic jets, can be lowered to the bottom. Then the conveyor belt and water pump are started. The boat moves slowly forward while the high-pressure jets, just forward of the lower end of the conveyor belt, blast clams loose from the mud. The clams are forced back onto the chain-mesh conveyor belt, where they are carried up to the side of the boat. As the clams and other debris pass by him, the waterman picks out the "keepers" (legal clams must be at least 2 inches long) and allows everything else to continue on to drop off the end of the belt, back into the water behind the boat.

The original systems needed three engines: one to operate the boat, one to drive the belt, and one to drive the high-pressure water pump. Today most boats are diesel powered, and the main boat engine is used to drive everything on the rig except the water pump. A second engine is used solely for the pump.

Most clamming operations take place in the spring, after the oystering season and before the crabs really start to run. Frequently the waterman uses the same boat for oystering, clamming, and crabbing. After tonging oysters in the winter, he mounts the dredge for clamming in the spring and then removes the rig to crab throughout the summer and fall, until he can resume tonging for oysters again, completing the circle.

CRABBING

The Beginning. Although crabs have been caught and eaten since long before recorded history, commercial crabbing did not become significant in the Bay until the late 1870s. The first recorded shipment of soft-shell crabs was from Crisfield to Philadelphia sometime in 1873 (give or take a year). Suddenly the crabbing industry leapt into being, reaching a peak take of 50 million pounds in 1920. The current take from the Chesapeake Bay ranges from 25 million to 40 million pounds annually. Since it takes about 1¾ "typical sized" crabs to make 1 pound, the sheer number of crabs caught and sold each year boggles the mind. And this doesn't include the take by amateurs.

Well, then, what about the blue crab and crabbing? No one should cruise the Bay without knowing something about the creature itself, the industry based on it, and how anyone on or near the Bay can take advantage of this bounty.

Blue Crabs. The blue crab (*Callinectes sapidus*, meaning "savory, beautiful swimmer") is widely distributed along the East Coast of the United States down into the Gulf of Mexico. While obviously not unique to the Chesapeake Bay, it is extraordinarily abundant there, so much so that it is simply referred to as "the crab," and everyone knows exactly what animal is meant.

The crab is an aggressive creature found throughout the Bay, from the salty, oceanlike waters of the mouth of the Bay to the almost fresh waters of the head of the Bay. It feeds on virtually anything that it can catch, including recently deceased fish, plant materials, oysters, and the soft-shell stage of its own kind. While predominantly a bottom feeder, the crab is an excellent and very active swimmer. The paddlelike fifth pair of legs, called *swimmerets*, allow it to move far more swiftly through the water than its relatively awkward appearance would lead one to expect.

The front pair of its five sets of legs are armed with claws that can really catch your attention if you handle the crab carelessly. (The only safe place to grab a crab is in back of the carapace.) The middle three pairs of legs are used for walking, the traditional sideways scuttle with which the crab on land moves with surprising speed.

The first set of legs gives the blue crab its name. The claws are really largely blue. The rest of the crab is a dull green. It is only when it is cooked (steamed or boiled, depending on your preference) that it turns the bright orange-red one sees just before devouring them in gustatorial delight.

Until they reach the adult stage, crabs are preyed upon by virtually every other marine creature. The adult blue crab has only one serious predator—people. From the casual, amateur crabber with his baited line and net to the commercial crabber with his trotline or dozens of traps, it seems that every man is out to "get" the blue crab. There are times when the crab traps in the Bay are so thick that you would swear there was no space between them for any crabs to pass. Even with catches that number well into the millions of crabs every year, the crab population seems undiminished. Harvests steadily increased from the 1930s to the 1970s. Then the crab catch suffered a 10-year decline. Since 1980, catches have been on the rise again. One Smith Island crabber claimed that if it weren't for the crabbers catching so many, those crabs would multiply so fast that they might just take over the world.

While most people today are at least aware of the appearance of the hard crab (even if they have never eaten one), few would recognize the soft crab, a hard crab that has just shed its shell. Before reaching full size, a crab sheds its shell, or molts, 18 to 20 times, increasing its size by one-quarter to one-third each time. Only the last couple of molts produce what we call the soft-shell crab. Until then, the crab is too small to be gastronomically interesting.

The molting process itself has several stages. In the first stage, when the crab is called a *peeler*, a hard crab has a fully formed soft shell under the hard shell and is ready to start the molting process. In the next stage, during which the crab is called a *buster*, the crab cracks its old shell just before shedding it. These first two stages are what commercial crabbers carefully look for when they catch crabs. Peelers and busters are sorted out and placed in peeler

pounds (special holding pens) to be harvested as soft crabs when they shed their shells.

As soon as the old shell is shed, the creature is called a *soft crab*, or *soft shell*. At this stage, the crab is totally defenseless and virtually immobilized. This period, before the shell starts to harden, lasts about 9 hours, unless arrested by man. During the first 2 hours the crab rapidly absorbs water to increase its size to the maximum for its next stage. It is during this period that the soft-shell crab is harvested and packed in ice to prevent further development (and bring the maximum price).

For 9 to 12 hours after shedding the crab is called a *paper shell*. During this period, when the shell is beginning to harden, it is papery to leathery in texture, thus its name. At this stage it still has commercial value as a soft-shell crab, although not as much as in the true soft-crab stage.

For the next 12 hours, before the shell becomes truly hard, the crab is a *buckram*. During this stage the shell is stiff and brittle. Crabs in this stage are left alone by watermen, who simply wait until their shells harden to add them to a hard-crab catch.

In order to sound like a true crab expert, you need to know a few more names for the crab. Young females are referred to as *sally crabs*, and adult female crabs are called *sooks*. The names mentioned above also apply at different stages of a sook's life, so she can be a paper shell, for instance. A female carrying eggs is equally referred to as a *busted sook*, a *sponge crab*, or less often, a *berry crab*. The adult male is called a *jimmy* or a *channeler*.

Each summer, the sook is either already in or migrates to the saltier waters of the lower Bay, where the fertilized eggs, which she is carrying as a result of her mating the previous summer, will hatch. She extrudes 1 million to 2 million eggs; these form a large mass, or *sponge*, which attaches to her abdomen. They develop as she migrates to the saltier waters of the lower Bay, turning darker in color as they develop, from the orange or yellow of newly deposited eggs to the dark brown of those almost ready to hatch. This is the reason that the sponges of sooks caught in the middle or upper regions of the Bay are noticeably lighter in color than those caught in the lower, saltier part of the Bay. Most of the sooks will produce a second sponge of eggs in the same summer, and a few will even produce a third.

After the last set of eggs hatch, the sook usually dies. A rare few may survive for another season, but they will be barren, neither mating again nor producing any more eggs.

When the eggs hatch, they bear no resemblance to anything we might recognize as a crab. The larvae, or *zoeae,* are microscopic in size; they join the surface plankton to feed and be fed upon. The zoea molts several times, making noticeable changes in shape each time.

With the last molt as a zoea, the larva metamorphoses drastically into a new form called a *megalops.* This stage is the first one that is large enough to be seen without significant magnification. For the first time the creature has claws. It resembles a cross between a crab and a lobster. It can swim, although somewhat *erratically,* but it is still at the mercy of any significant currents, frequently being washed out to sea. The incursion of the so-called water fleas, which cause bathers at the beaches near the mouth of the Bay some degree of skin irritation and itching, is actually the incursion of the megalops. Those claws may be tiny, but they can already be felt.

The megalops stage usually lasts for only about 12 days, but under unfavorable conditions this stage can last as long as three months, or until the megalops can find its way back to less salty water to continue on to the next stage.

With its next molt, the surviving megalops again goes through a metamorphosis. Although less than 1/16 inch in size, the BB-size animal is now recognizable as a blue crab. Save for reproductive organs, it is now complete and can perform all of the activities of the crab as we know it. It is now secure from most of its enemies and can concentrate on feeding and growing as it begins its long journey up the Bay or up any of the several larger rivers toward the brackish water that it prefers.

By late fall the crabs are as much as 2 inches across, having molted every 10 to 15 days, or as many as eight times. Now the water is beginning to get really cold, and the little crabs move to deep water and bury themselves in the mud to wait out the winter.

By the late summer of their second year the crabs have reached their adult size of 4 to 6 inches and undergo one more change, that of attaining sexual maturity. Only in the female is there any external sign of this change: the Y-shaped abdominal apron changes to a nearly circular one. It is only during this molt that the female can be fertilized by the male.

The process starts with an elaborate courtship ritual. The male approaches a receptive female well before her actual molt starts and begins his courtship dance, a series of postures and movements. If the female is really ready, she will back toward him, waving her claws in and out. The male will grab her and try to put her in the proper cradle-carry position, with her underneath him and surrounded by his walking legs as if in a cage. She soon settles down and allows herself to be carried.

The cradle carry lasts from two days to as long as a week before the female molts. This is the stage of the "doubler," when the male may be seen paddling near the surface with the female contentedly riding in her cradle. This process has two great biological advantages: it provides protection for the female during her vulnerable and difficult last molt, and it ensures that a suitable male will be present during the very brief time that the female is capable of accepting him.

When the female's molt begins, the male stands over her, enclosing her in the cage of his walking legs. On completion of the molt, a process of several hours, the male helps the female, now a soft shell, to turn on her back in a face-to-face position under him. When ready, the female opens her abdomen, now nearly circular in shape, to expose her two genital pores, into which the male inserts his two genital organs. She then extends her abdomen over the male's back, a position they maintain for 5 to 12 hours.

The male continues to cradle-carry the female for another two days, while her shell hardens and her muscles recover. Upon release, the sook, for that is what she now is, starts her migration back down to the salty waters of the lower Bay to wait out the winter buried in the mud. The sperm is not utilized until the following spring, when the life cycle starts all over again with the fertilized eggs of the sook. The male remains behind, where he may molt a few more times and mate again with a female the next summer.

Now that we have gone through its terminology and life cycle, let's move on to the business of catching, cooking, and—of most interest to us—eating the Chesapeake Bay blue crab.

Of course, before they can be cooked and eaten, they first have to be caught. There are four basic ways to catch hard crabs: Amateurs, or "chickenneckers," generally catch hard crabs with handlines and dip net or scoop them with a hand net from the bow of a moving boat; professionals use either crab pots or trotlines. Soft-shell crabs are different. Amateurs tend to skim soft-shell crabs from the shallows, flats, or pilings where they seek shelter during this vulnerable phase. Professionals keep peelers or buckrams in pens until they shed their shells, as described above.

Only hard crabs that measure at least 5 inches from point to point on their carapace may be legally kept; all others must be returned to the water. In addition, in Maryland waters all females carrying eggs (sponge sooks), regardless of size, must be released.

In Virginia, a substantial winter crabbing industry dredges for hibernating crabs, using dredges not unlike those used for oyster dredging. In fact, about 60 percent of all of the crabs provided on the Eastern seaboard during the winter and early spring months come from winter crab dredging in Virginia. Since most of the crabs in the southern Bay are sooks with eggs,

this seems at odds with sensible conservation measures.

Workboats. There is probably no such thing as a standard workboat design for crabbing. However, while details and deck plans may vary, the workboats used by commercial watermen have several common features, all based on practicality and utility. Everything said here about crabbing boats holds true for oyster-tonging and clam-dredging craft since watermen generally engage in all these seasonal activities in order to be employed year-round, and most use just one boat.

First and perhaps foremost, the boats have to be stable and have a low freeboard. These boats are taken out in all kinds of weather, and the waterman, frequently alone, has to lean over the side to snag a float and haul up his trap. Just think about doing that in a boat that rolls with every ripple!

Virtually every workboat we have seen has a set of controls located amidships, on the starboard side. There are a few "lefties," but these are rare. A large wooden lever is the traditional means of steering, although a few have more conventional helmsman stations. Everything is set up to allow a single waterman to perfectly control his boat without ever having to leave the station where he works his pots, even if he has a crew to help out.

SHELLFISHING

Joan B. Machinchick

42   *A waterman works his trotline in the Wye River.*

Of course, the boat has to be big enough to securely carry enough bushelbaskets to hold the crabs the waterman expects (or hopes) to catch and still allow room for him to work and sort the catch as it comes in. This usually means a boat of 30 to 40 feet LOA. Smaller boats are used, but they quickly become self-limiting.

Once these basic requirements are met, details begin to vary. Some boats have a small cabin forward to protect the operator when he is not actively working the set of pots. Some are comparatively open to weather, with only a small windshield for protection from spray. Some have a structure over the deck to provide shade and to carry part of the large collection of traps when initially setting the string or picking it up to move it elsewhere; some have nothing. Each design has evolved over time to meet the needs of these hardy watermen.

Traps & Trotlines. The most common sight on the Chesapeake Bay, at least from late spring until well into the fall, is of literally acres of floating, tethered objects—bleach bottles, cork floats, small buoys—of every shape and color. These are the most visible sign of the magnitude of the crabbing industry's mainstay, the crab pot.

Usually rectangular, about 2 by 2 by 3 feet, and made of heavy-gauge chicken wire and reinforcing rods with a weighted bottom to help keep the trap upright, the crab trap, or pot, is a very simple but quite effective device. One side (sometimes two sides, and sometimes all four) has a circular hole with a truncated cone of the same wire leading into the pot. Bait—usually salt eel because of its durability, but sometimes fishheads—is secured near the middle of the trap. (There isn't a real waterman alive who will admit to using chicken necks.) A float of the crabber's choosing and marked with his designated color code is attached to the top of the trap by a stout line approximately 20 feet long. Pots are usually placed in 10 to 20 feet of water, the most common place to find hard crabs during the main season.

A hungry crab attracted by the bait searches around the pot until it finds the opening and enters the trap through the cone. Once inside, it will attempt to get away, not the same way it came in but by swimming up through one of the two holes into the area known as the "church," from which it rarely escapes. Apparently, it is baffled by the shape and placement of the smaller aperture of the cone. The hapless crab remains in the "church," along with as many of

NAVIGATIONAL HAZARD OR LIVELIHOOD AT RISK?

Skippers, please take note: The floats at each end of the trotline are usually relatively large, measuring a foot or more in diameter, and colored bright red or orange. This isn't for the waterman's benefit—he knows exactly where his line is—it's to warn other boats, especially pleasure craft, where the end of his line lies to allow them to steer clear of it and not interfere with his efforts to work it. It certainly seems reasonable for passing boats to pass far enough behind him to avoid both the boat and the trotline. One jostle of the trotline, and all the crabs on it may drop off, at least for that pass. Surely we all can afford to give the working waterman this simple courtesy.

Trotlines and crab pots are navigational hazards, but they also represent the waterman's livelihood. Watermen already have to adjust their work time to accommodate pressures from pleasure boaters; weekend hours get shorter every year as the number of cruisers increases. They also must compete for water space: marina development reduces workable water bottom because of the poor water quality around marinas. And few marinas rent to watermen because their boats are noisy and messy. The slip shortage forces watermen to travel farther and farther to reach workable shellfish beds. The waterman can ill afford the time and money ($25 or more apiece) to replace traps that cruisers destroy through carelessness.

its relatives as manage to make the same bad decision, until the crabber returns, hauls up the pot, and retrieves all the legal-size crabs in it. Undersize crabs, less than 5 inches across the back, are thrown back, and then the trap is re-baited and set back into the water to await its next victim(s).

Maryland law states that no crab pots are to be set in tributaries of the Bay. In Virginia, it is unlawful to place crab pots within navigable channels that are marked with aids approved by any agency of the government. This essentially has the same result.

Since there are plenty of crabs in the rivers and creeks off the Bay, a different, albeit less productive, means of commercial crabbing has developed: trotlining. In reality, this is simply an adaptation of the old English fishing practice called "longlining" to make it suitable for catching crabs. Bait, predominantly salt eel pieces, is tied every few feet to several hundred feet of heavy cord or line, with weights attached to each end. The line is then carefully flaked into tubs of brine to preserve the bait and ready the trotline for use.

The boats used for trotlining range in size from a rowboat to 30- and 40-footers. No matter what the size of the boat, all have one thing in common: a roller mechanism mounted outboard of the starboard gunwale.

To deploy his trotline, the waterman selects a likely area in one of the rivers or creeks off the main Bay. A buoy with enough line to reach the bottom is attached to the weight at each end of the trotline. Then one buoy and its corresponding weighted end of the trotline are dropped into the water, and the waterman proceeds in a straight line, paying out the trotline as he goes, until the other end with its float passes over the side. The trotline is now deployed. Some watermen, usually those with the bigger boats and a helper, will deploy two or more trotlines to increase their catch. The next step is to catch the crabs attracted to the bait.

Catching crabs on a trotline is simple in principle. Putting it into practice effectively takes a fair amount of skill, learned only by experience. To work the deployed trotline, the crabber lifts one end of the line (remember that buoy?), places it over the roller mounted outboard of his gunwale, and proceeds slowly along the line to-

ward the float at its other end. As the line passes over the roller, it gently lifts the bait from the bottom and brings it to the surface, where the crabber, hoping to find a crab stubbornly attached, waits with a metal mesh dip net.

As soon as a crab can be seen, the waterman deftly scoops it up with his net, swings all "keepers" aboard and into a temporary basket, then turns back to the water to watch for the next crab on the line to appear. The whole process takes just seconds for the experienced professional. If the crabber is alone, he stops periodically to cull the crabs, keeping the legal ones and sorting them into bushelbaskets for sale. All others are returned to the water.

If he feels that the crabs aren't "running" well in the area he has chosen, the waterman may pick up and redeploy his line elsewhere, sometimes many times in a day.

Chickenneckers. *Chickenneckers* is the not-exactly-complimentary moniker watermen use to refer to the assortment of amateur crabbers who use individually baited lines to catch crabs. Somehow this name does not seem inappropriate since chicken necks are, or at least were, the traditional crab bait used by amateurs. Today, whether the amateur is using chicken necks, salt eel, or filet mignon for crab bait, in the Bay he or she is and forevermore a chickennecker.

If we don't count the semiprofessional crabber who sets a string of pots or runs a trotline,

Lauren Shellenberger chickennecking with some friends.

amateur crabbers normally use either a hand-line and dip net or a hand trap to catch crabs for their own use. How you prepare any crabs you catch is a matter of personal choice. There are as many recipes as there are people who cook them.

Handline & Dip Net. This is the original, basic method used by chickenneckers to catch crabs from time immemorial. With a dip net, some cord, a few weights, and bait, you are fully equipped to catch crabs (some assembly required). Of course, something to hold any crabs that you may catch is a rather good idea too; allowing angry, aggressive blue crabs to run around your feet can be somewhat disconcerting. A basket, a bucket, or an empty ice chest (some ice isn't a bad idea either) will do just fine. Water in the holding container is a bad idea as the crabs will soon deplete the oxygen in the water and suffocate. Crabs can last a day or more out of the water, provided they are protected from the sun. Uncooked, dead crabs spoil with amazing speed and should never be cooked and eaten.

So how do you go about catching crabs with this exotic equipment? First, the required assembly: (1) Cut to lengths of about 20 feet as many pieces of cord as you think you will be able to tend or have room to place with minimum danger of tangling together. (2) Tie a weight to one end of each 20-foot cord. It need not be very heavy, just enough to keep the bait

on the bottom; a couple of large metal washers, a nut, or anything comparable will do just fine. It is important that it weigh less than 1 ounce so that you can "feel" the crab on the line. (3) Make a small slipknot in the cord right next to the weight, slide a piece of bait into the loop, and pull it tight. The handline assembly is now complete, and you are ready to go.

Now, where do you go? That's easy: nearly anyplace in the saline waters of the Bay where the water is between 6 and 20 feet deep and you can find a place to both stand and tie the free (unbaited) end of your handline. Of course, your spot also needs to be close enough to the water to allow you to reach 1 to 2 feet below the surface with your dip net. This tends to rule out bridges, but docks and most boats are ideal. Before you set up, make sure that you have permission to crab there if you don't own the place!

Boats give you more freedom concerning where you crab, but there are a few practical restrictions, most of which are related to unwanted motion of the boat. Once a crab grabs the bait, you need to draw it to the surface gently. Any sudden tugs, and the crab will probably drop off. This obviously means that, aside from the discomfort to the crew, you don't want to try crabbing by handline in an area subject to frequent waves or wakes. By the same token, if your boat tends to "sail" at anchor (swinging widely back and forth), you should either find a more protected spot or put

TRY YOUR HAND AT CRABBING

In 1993 Virginia enacted legislation requiring recreational crabbers who want to set more than two traps to obtain a license from Marine Commission agents for $5. Maryland only requires a noncommercial license for recreational crabbers who want to set more than ten traps. For unlicensed crabbers, Virginia sets a limit of two pots or traps per person; Maryland allows up to ten traps per person. Both states limit the catch to one bushel per day per person (but no more than two bushels per boat), and both limit the size of each crab to 5 inches spine to spine (or tip to tip; the spine is the tip of the spike). All

waters in both states are open to crabbing from 1 April to 30 November.

Crabbing regulations for the two states differ in one respect. Maryland prohibits the taking of sponge crabs (female crabs with an egg mass). Virginia holds that any crab, including a berried female or sponge crab, is fair game as long as it meets the size requirements. While you can keep a sponge crab, it is better for the future of crabbing to toss it back. As an added incentive, the meat of the sponge crab is of lower quality than meat from other stages.

down a second anchor to steady you. Aside from the danger of tangling the crab line in your propeller or twisting the lines together, you would be moving the bait around, which would reduce the probability of catching anything.

Once you have a stable platform, tie the free end of each line to something and drop the baited end into the water. Each line should be long enough to reach the bottom with a little slack. Separate the lines enough that they won't interfere with one another. Then wait and watch the lines.

Any lines that start to move away from the others probably are being dragged by a crab. Gently try lifting each line in turn. If a crab is on the bait, you will feel it tugging through the line. Slowly and gently start pulling up the line, preferably with someone else standing by with the dip net. If you are alone, you will have to bring up the line hand over hand while your third hand holds the net! As the bait nears the surface, lower the net below the surface a couple of feet away from where the line breaks the surface. When you can see the crab, swing the net underneath it and raise it smoothly and swiftly up under the crab, bait and all. There is a knack to doing this, learned only through practice. Many a crab will escape during the learning process—and thereafter, for that matter.

Once you have your crab, check to see whether it is legal (5 inches across the back). If it is not, throw it back. (You probably will see it again before long.) If it is legal, dump it from your net into your holding container. (Note: A metal mesh net is easier to empty than a twine net. The points, legs, and claws of the crab tend to get stuck in the twine mesh, and you may have to risk fingers to extract it.)

To pick up a live crab bare-handed, grab it just behind the carapace. It is easy to do, but watermen wear gloves and just let the crab bite. We take the chicken's way out and use a pair of tongs, which you'll need anyway if you choose to cook the crabs on board.

Hand Trap. Catching crabs with a hand trap is something like using a handline with a dip net. The typical trap is a metal mesh cube, usually measuring about a foot in each dimension. (Yes, I know that some are pyramid-shaped, but the

Once the crab is in the dip net, the trick is to get it out.

cube is most common and easier to make and store.) Most hand traps fold flat for storage. When assembled, the trap has a fixed mesh panel on the top and bottom. Four lines, joined a little above the top of the trap, are attached in such a way that when the trap is resting on the bottom and the line to the trap is slack, all four sides hinge out and lie flat, leaving it wide open. Bait is suspended from the top of the trap to lure a crab inside.

The idea is that a crab will be occupied trying to pull the bait loose or attempting to eat it in place; when the crabber periodically pulls up each trap to check it, the sides of the trap will slam shut with the crab inside. It does get a little tricky if a big, feisty crab is inside when you

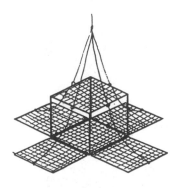

A crab hand trap.

DISMANTLING A CRAB

Now that you have your crabs and they are ready to eat (never mind whether you caught and cooked them yourself or bought them in that condition), what do you do? This bright-colored critter sitting in front of you is armor plated and bristling with sharp points. How do you get past these defenses and obtain that succulent crabmeat?

There are numerous variations on the crab-dismantling theme, and I will probably provoke the ire of various "experts" by outlining my method, but here goes.

First, make sure that you are armed with the traditional crab mallet, a 6-inch-long hammer with a wooden head about 1 inch in diameter and 2 to 3 inches long. This is not to subdue the aggressive crab—boiling or steaming will have accomplished that. Use the hammer to crack the claws and front legs so you can get at the meat. A collection of newspapers spread out to absorb the juices and debris from the process is also a good idea unless you plan to hose down the area (and yourself) afterward.

Break off the claws at the joint with the carapace. Set them aside to crack open at your leisure. That's the easy part.

Then break off and discard the rest of the legs. Turn the body over, abdomen up, and use a thumb or knifepoint to pry up and lift off the apron flap. Discard the flap.

With thumb or knifepoint, lift off the top shell and discard it. This will expose the tube-like gills (dead man's fingers) and the soft yellow "mustard." Tear or scrape off the gray gills and the yellow "mustard," exposing the semitransparent membrane that covers the edible crabmeat. Hold onto both sides of the crab and break it apart at the centerline.

The meat under the membrane cover in each half of the crab can be exposed by removing the cover with a knife or by slicing halfway through the center of each half. Either approach exposes the large chunks of meat, which can then be removed fairly easily with fingers or knifepoint.

Crack open the claws with the mallet and you are ready to feast on the succulent crabmeat. Handle it according to your desires or individual preference, but enjoy!

---

try to empty the trap. Consider trying to keep all four sides together with one hand, holding up the trap with the other hand, and opening only the side you want the crab to fall from while balancing the whole assembly over your crab container!

Other than that, the main disadvantage of this technique is that the only way to tell whether a crab is in the trap is to haul it up and look. It also requires investing a little more in equipment and space to store it. On the other hand, you don't need a dip net, and you can use this method from a bridge. For whatever reason, even when we were using both methods at the same time, we have yet to catch a single crab with the two hand traps we carry aboard, while we have had great success with the hand-lines and dip net. Explain that one—I can't!

FISHING

FISH, FISHERMEN, & THE BAY

In the early days of this country, fish were so numerous that the early colonists, once they learned how from the Native Americans, were able to catch remarkable quantities of fish from the bountiful waters of the Bay even with their comparatively primitive methods, usually haul seines. In fact, salted herring, which could be preserved for months, remained a staple for settlers and residents in the tidewater region well into the 20th century. Although the quantities of fish have been greatly reduced in recent years for a variety of reasons, the Bay can still be called nothing less than bountiful.

Today, the range of fishing activities on the Bay is enormous, probably unsurpassed anywhere else in the world. More than 200 species of fish live in the Chesapeake Bay and its tributaries.

Sport fishing, with fly or hook and line, is done using every conceivable means, from the hoary bamboo pole and worm bait dangled off a dock or bank, to rowboats in the rivers and creeks, to gold-plated powerboats rigged with an impressive array of trolling gear. There are even "surf-casters" who fish off the Bay beaches, although I am sure that they operate somewhat differently than surf-casters on ocean beaches, if only because real surf is lacking in most parts of the Bay. Most obvious to the cruiser are the charter "head boats" drifting with the wind or current, loaded with crowds of fishermen standing shoulder to shoulder along the sides of the boat, and the private powerboats moving around in loops dragging trolling lines behind them. The latter are often a source of conflict with sailboats, as well as some cruising powerboats, over the right of way. (See Fishing Boats and Right-of-Way, page 20.)

CHESAPEAKE SPORT FISH & FISHING

Although there are more than 200 species of fish living in the tidal waters of the Chesapeake Bay, only a relative few of these species are sought after by sport fishermen. These include bluefish, flounder (fluke), white and yellow perch, spot, wahoo, dolphin, albacore, catfish, sea trout (gray trout, weakfish), hickory and American shad, kingfish, shark, black drum, red drum (channel bass), striped bass, mackerel, speckled trout (spotted sea trout), and cobia.

Once, striped bass (rockfish) and American shad were popular targets of sport and commercial fishermen alike. Then, during the 1970s and 1980s, the population decline of these fish caused enough concern for them to be placed on the endangered-species list in Maryland, and all harvesting halted. By 1989 the population had increased to healthier levels, thanks to the reversal of degraded water quality in the Bay and stocking with hatchery production. A restricted rockfish season is still in place in both Virginia and Maryland, with stringent limits on both the maximum and minimum size and number of fish that each individual hook-and-line fisherman may keep.

48

STRIPED BASS (ROCKFISH)

FLOUNDER (FLUKE)

COBIA (BONITA)

SEA TROUT (GREY TROUT, WEAKFISH)

BLUEFISH

SPECKLED TROUT (SPOTTED SEA TROUT)

BLACK DRUM

RED DRUM (CHANNEL BASS)

Edible fish of the Chesapeake Bay.

Virginia Marine Resources Commission

Table 7. Where They're Biting

FISH	AREA OF BAY (UPPER TO LOWER)	WHEN
STRIPED BASS	Choptank River	May to December
	Susquehanna River (to dam) and Flats	end of May to mid-October
	Lower Patuxent River	May to October
	Potomac River (to D.C.; Rte. 301 to mouth)	best from May to October
	Magothy River (mouth)	spring and fall
	Severn and South Rivers (mouths)	occasional runs in spring and fall
SHAD (both Hickory and American)	Susquehanna River	early April to July (Hickory); mid-May to late June (Am.)
	Potomac River (especially Port Tobacco River area)	May to June
	Pocomoke River (mouth)	May to June
SEA TROUT	Lower Patuxent River (guides at Benedict and Solomons)	May to October
	Tangier Sound, mouths of Nanticoke, Wicomico, and Manokin Rivers	mid-July through fall
BLUEFISH	Lower Patuxent River	May to October
	Pocomoke River	occasionally
COBIA	Potomac River, especially Smith Creek area (guides near Wayne)	August to late October

Not all species are found throughout the Bay, and there are some that do not remain in any particular region of the Bay at all times. Beyond some very rough geographical areas (see table 7), I make no guarantees regarding where they may be found. All species are known to be in the following areas of the upper Bay: the Bay Bridges area, Turkey Point, Spesutie Island, Battery Point, Pooler Island, Worton Point, Tea Kettle Shoals, Eastern Neck Island, Hickory Thicket, and Love Point. In the middle Bay, fishermen frequent Dolly's Lumps, Brick House Bar, Bloody Point, Eastern Bay, Poplar Island, Holland Point, and Tilghman Island with success. Hot spots in the lower Bay include Sharps Island, Winter Goose, James Island, Round Ragged Point, Little Choptank River (mouth), Taylors Island, and Cove Point. If you really want to find fish, you should go out with a guide or an experienced Bay fisherman, either private or charter. At the least, talk to bait-and-tackle shopkeepers. The annual periodical *Fishing in Maryland* can be found in most tackle shops and many marine stores in the Bay area (Virginia used to have a similar publication but no longer does). It covers the types of sport fish to be found in different areas of the Bay at different times of the year, but you need to have some Bay fishing experience—some of the vaunted "local knowledge" so valuable anywhere—to make effective use of this information. Most of the newspapers in the Bay area run a column on fishing during the main season.

Bluefish (a fairly recent denizen of the Chesapeake in significant numbers) are migratory, traveling over great distances to a variety of locations, and their schools are sizable. The striped bass (rockfish) also follow a migratory pattern, although their schools never approach the size of bluefish schools.

Perch are usually found in many of the tributaries off the main Bay, especially in the north. Most fishermen bottomfish for them at the mouths of these tributaries and sometimes out in the Bay itself.

Flounder, spot, sea trout (weakfish), and catfish are found in both Maryland and Virginia waters, while red drum (channel bass), black drum, and cobia are generally found only in the southern Bay, where the salt content of the water is higher.

Both Maryland and Virginia have instituted laws requiring sport fishermen in the tidal waters of the Chesapeake Bay or its tributaries to obtain fishing licenses. Those fishing the tidal Potomac can obtain a Potomac River Fisheries license for the Potomac and its tributaries or either a Maryland or Virginia saltwater license. A boatowner can obtain either a personal license or a boat license that covers him or her and any guests on board. The two states and the Potomac River Fisheries Commission have reciprocal agreements, and each honors all licenses. Costs are: Maryland individual license, $5, and boat license, $25; Virginia and Potomac River Fisheries individual license, $7.50 (Virginia also has a 10-day permit for $5, boat license for boats under 27 feet, $30, and license for boats 27 feet and over, $60). Each state has its own regulations, and they are subject to change. For the most recent information, contact: Maryland Department of Natural Resources, Tawes State Office Building, Annapolis, MD 21401, 410-974-3216; and/or Virginia Marine Resources Commission, 2600 Washington Ave., Newport News, VA 23607, 757-247-2200.

Sport fishing is a subject about which volumes have already been written, and it is beyond my personal ken anyway. Suffice it to say that there are multitudes of charter "head boats" available for fishermen interested in that sort of fishing, and even more private powerboats bottomfish or troll in all areas of the Bay.

While the type of fish caught varies with the seasons and the movements of the various species of fish, commercial fishing today is a year-round activity. Commercial fishing in the Bay is roughly divided into two basic categories by the type of equipment used. Fish traps are used to catch eels and, to a lesser degree, catfish. Everything else is caught with nets. Although there are several types of nets, three types predominate in commercial use: purse seines, gill nets, and pound nets. These are the only ones the cruiser is likely to notice, even if he or she doesn't know what they are.

EELING

Did you ever wonder about the source for all the eels used in the multitudes of crab pots and trotlines? It turns out that eeling is a substantial industry on the Bay, carried on right under our noses, so to speak. In the spring, at least, many of the floats that we see, especially those in the Bay's tributaries, are not attached to crab pots, as most of us probably assume; they are attached to eel pots, a different device altogether.

In spite of its snakelike appearance, the eel (*Anguilla rostrata*) is a true fish, with scales, fins, and gills. But they are unlike other species in behavior as well as appearance.

Through various articles and TV programs, most of us are aware of the habits of anadromous species, such as the salmon, which live most of their life in the ocean waters but return to freshwater creeks and streams where they were originally hatched to spawn. Eels do something similar, but with a backward twist. Eels spend most of their lives in the brackish waters of the Bay and its tributaries, leaving those waters to head out into the blue Atlantic, especially the Sargasso Sea, to spawn.

When the young hatch, they begin a truly amazing journey from the far reaches of the Atlantic between Bermuda and the West Indies to the waters of the Bay and its tributaries, a trip that can take up to two years. Considering that the tiny young, or *elvers*, are only 2 to 3 inches long by the time they reach the Bay, such a journey is remarkable. They continue on their way back to the rivers, streams, and ponds from which their parents came. That they can find their way back to a place that only their parents, not the elvers themselves, have seen is even more remarkable than the return of the salmon to their birthplace!

While eels are considered a delicacy in many other parts of the world, most Americans don't eat them, probably because of their appearance. They are harvested in the Bay solely for export (predominantly to Belgium and the Netherlands, where they are prized as gourmet fare) and for use as bait, mostly for crabs.

Eels destined for exportation are kept alive, first in special boxes in the waterman's boat, then in large tanks with circulating water onshore. They can remain alive for a week or more in the large tanks, until an export company collects them and ships them to their final destination. The rest of the catch is salted down to be sold (or used by the eeler himself) for crab bait.

Most commercial eeling takes place in the spring, as soon as the water temperature rises enough to awaken the eels from their winter hibernation in the mud on the river bottom. In the summer and fall, eeling activity falls off rapidly as the watermen switch their efforts to crabbing, but it does continue sporadically into the late fall.

The first commercial eel pots were based on designs used by the Native Americans and made from white-oak splints woven, just like a basket, around a cylindrical mold. Although the materials have changed over the years, in general the pot's basic design has varied only slightly. Today most eel pots are made from a galvanized wire mesh. The pots are typically about 2 feet long with a diameter of 7 to 9 inches. Internal funnels, which allow the eel to enter easily but rarely to escape, are made of a variety of modern materials, such as wire, solid metal, and synthetic netting. Some watermen use cube-shaped pots that look like crab pots but are usually smaller and made from a much finer mesh.

The eel pots are baited with crushed softshell clams, horseshoe crabs, or both; nearly any *fresh* bait can be used. (There is a pattern evident here: soft-shell clams not used for people food are used for eel bait; eels caught with the clams, not exported for food, are used for crab bait; and crabs caught with eels are *all* eaten by people.)

The eeler sets his eel pots on the bottom, preferably with the open end facing down-stream, attached to a buoyed line long enough to reach the surface with a little slack. Eels, attracted to the bait, swim into the pot through the funnel(s), and there they remain, unable to find their way back out.

The pots are hauled just like crab pots. The buoy line is hooked and the pot hauled to the surface. Lifting it on board, the eeler opens the end, dumps the eels into his "live tank," rebaits the pot, resets it, then moves on to the next buoy in line and repeats the process. This continues until his tank is full or darkness falls, whichever comes first. Then he heads home to transfer his catch to the large "live tank" onshore or to start salting those eels intended for bait.

There are other methods of catching eels, such as spearing and using unbaited "fyke" nets, or baited-and-hooked long lines (like the trotlines used for crabbing, but with the whole line buoyed with small floats), but none is used commercially.

THE MENHADEN FLEET (PURSE SEINING)

Purse seining is a method used by the menhaden fleet based near the town of Reedville, Virginia, on Cockrell Creek, off the Great Wicomico River. At present only one company, Zapata Haynie, still engages in the business of catching and processing fish for products used for animal feed, fertilizer, and making paint and cosmetics. The boney, oily, and unappetizing menhaden are almost exclusively the fish used for this purpose. They are likely the fish Native Americans taught settlers to plant with their corn seed, since the Native American name, *munnawhatteaug*, means "that which manures."

The menhaden (*Brevoortia tyrannus*), a species of herring, is a seagoing fish that frequently visits tidal estuaries like the Chesapeake Bay. Although they spawn at sea, the juveniles and, with fair frequency, the adults will move into brackish or even fresh water of estuaries to find food and to escape from voracious bluefish.

Although the adult menhaden is only about a foot long and weighs only about a pound, by sheer numbers the menhaden are the most common fish in the sea. Scientists estimate that the poundage of menhaden swimming the seas is greater than that of any other species! They cluster together in vast schools that literally cover acres and, unlike most other species, they do not scatter when attacked by other fish or stressed. Instead, they cluster closer together and remain near the surface, which makes them especially easy to net.

The menhaden itself is not sought by sport fishermen, but as the schools are followed by predatory fish, such as bluefish, which are of considerable interest to these fishermen, menhaden schools are watched for and quickly recognized by them. The menhaden are so oily that a school actually leaves a slick on the water surface as it passes, making sighting these fish fairly easy.

Menhaden, or pogies, often sicken and die in great numbers in the Bay in the summer months. The cause of their death is not well understood, but this "fish kill," as it is commonly called, apparently has little or nothing to do with pollution or any other clearly identifiable man-made problem, in spite of media hype to the contrary.

Purse-seining operations are prohibited in Maryland waters of the Bay, but you can hardly fail to see at least a few of the seiners in Virginia waters. They also operate in the Atlantic Ocean off the Carolina capes and as far north as Maine. Once dependent on sightings of menhaden schools from towers mounted on the fishing seiners, the menhaden fleet now uses light planes as spotters. When a spotter locates a large school of fish, the seiners head for the location as fast as they can. On arrival, they launch smaller boats that carry the end of the purse net out from the main boat, around the school of fish, and back to the main boat. Then the net is closed at the bottom and drawn in, or pursed, until the fish are compacted together close to the seiner.

The closely packed menhaden are then taken on board with a giant suction pump, which is something like an oversize vacuum cleaner. The size of the catch is measured by how long it takes to pump the fish aboard.

When the operation is complete and the holds of the seiner are full, the ship returns to port to off-load its catch at the processing plant, where the fish are cooked and the oil pressed out.

The oil is used in making paints and soaps. Also produced from this fish oil is nitroglycerine, as well as other more stable explosives. A large portion of the munitions consumed in World Wars I and II were derived from the humble pogie. The fish meal remaining after the oil is removed is dried and used in cattle feed and for fertilizer.

POUND NETS

To the uninitiated, among the more puzzling sights in the Bay are the lines of stakes with a cluster of similar sticks at one end, seemingly at peculiar locations. Those who give them a casual glance and attempt to pass between any of these stakes may be in for an unsettling time. Strung between these stakes is a pound net, a method used by generations of watermen and local farmers to catch fish. While the net can foul your propeller or other underwater parts of a boat, resulting in a great deal of trouble for you, your course can cause a lot more trouble for the pound netter since these nets are his livelihood.

The nets are supposed to be marked at each end with a white light placed at least six feet above high water and strong enough to be visible for a mile. (Unfortunately, the lights we have encountered have tended to be rather dim or extinguished.) Usually the pound netters place a bush or a basket on the same poles to make them readily visible in the daytime. However, should you enter an area peppered with nets, you may find yourself in a maze that can drive you into a state of gibbering. For this reason, those regions marked on the chart as fish-trap areas are best avoided by a wide margin.

The principle of the pound net is fairly simple; the implementation and use takes a bit of skill and not a little effort. They range in size

A pound net on the Bay. The actual pound is in the background. The stakes in the foreground mark and support the leader net.

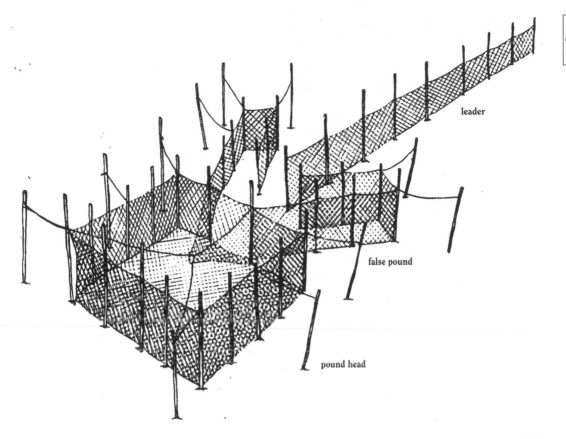

A pound net of the type used on the Bay. The actual pound net is to the left. The leader and false pound channel fish into the pound.

from relatively small nets placed close inshore to extensive rigs (we have seen some that appeared to be a hundred yards long) placed a good distance offshore.

Normally, the nets are placed perpendicular to the shoreline, or at least to the flow of the tidal current, in water 10 to 20 feet deep, with the trap portion, or *pound,* located on the side of the net toward deeper water. As schools of fish swim along the shore or some other path that "channels" them, they encounter the *leader,* the portion of the net strung across their path. Their natural instinct leads them to turn toward deeper water, where another set of nets is strung to direct them into the main pound net, where they are trapped in a smaller net, or *pocket.*

The net may be left in position for months at a time, but it is checked daily at each slack current. This net with its catch is normally too heavy to be hauled aboard the fisherman's boat, so it is raised toward the surface by working around the pound, lifting each side until the fish are gathered together near the surface. Then the fish are scooped out of the water with large dip nets and dumped into a holding receptacle, which varies with the size of the boat. After the fish have been removed, the net is reset, and the cycle resumes.

Pound nets are rare in the northern Bay these days, and they are becoming less common in the southern Bay as diminishing catches and increasing government restrictions combine to make their operation less and less profitable. They are being replaced by the less expensive and more easily maintained gill nets or are being abandoned altogether. (The stakes from an abandoned pound net are supposed to be removed, but frequently they are not.)

GILL NETS

A gill net is very much what its name implies, a net with a mesh designed to trap a fish by its

53

gills. The mesh allows the head and gills to pass through but is too small for the rest of the fish's body. When the fish attempts to back out, its gills (actually its gill covers) become caught in the net, and the fish is held securely until the fisherman collects it.

In the past, gill nets were much less prevalent than either pound nets or haul seines. (A haul seine is the simplest and most ancient form of seining. The seine has two wings and a *bunt*, or bag. One end is held onshore while the net is laid from a boat. The other end is then landed, surrounding a semicircle of water, and the two ends are hauled up on the beaches.) Today, haul seines are virtually nonexistent and pound nets are in decline. The use of gill nets is on the rise because they are less expensive to buy and maintain than other nets, small enough to be worked by one person, and more selective (a function of net gauge), making compliance with government regulations easier.

The Department of Natural Resources regulates both the gillnetting season and the mesh size of the net to protect specific declining species of fish (such as rockfish). As of 1 November 1984 the mesh size was restricted to a range of 4 to 6 inches. This size prevents larger fish, such as rockfish preparing to spawn, from being "gilled" and permits smaller fish to swim through the net.

Gill nets are usually deployed in a straight line across the anticipated path of schooling fish, normally in water depths of 6 to 10 feet, supported by stakes driven into the bottom. These are the lines of stakes that you see stretching for as much as 100 yards. They are marked at each end with a light and there is usually a bush attached to the top of the stake at each end of the line to make the setup, especially the ends of it, more visible by day.

The net is fastened to the stakes and may or may not also have intermediate floats attached to the top of the net. Weights secured to the lower edge of the net keep it on the bottom. It is important in both making and setting the net that it hang straight in the water so that the fish cannot easily see it. Most nets today are made of twisted nylon netting (and increasingly, of nearly invisible monofilament), which is not only cheaper than the cotton or linen netting used in the past but also more durable and harder for the fish to see.

As in the case of pound nets described earlier, *under no circumstances should you attempt to pass between these stakes.* Not only will you foul the net, getting assorted parts of your boat entangled in it, but you will damage the net, for which you will be financially responsible (an average gill net runs about $200 per 300-foot length).

Gill nets are sometimes deployed in two other configurations: as anchor or drift nets. Neither is especially apparent to the casual cruiser, but it is a good idea to be aware of them, especially in the mouths of the larger rivers of the southern Bay and near the shore and shoals. Occasionally they show up in the northern Bay. Once, a gill net sprang up "overnight" in the mouth of the Patapsco River, where one had never been seen before. We were sailing at night and nearly came a cropper on it! Fortunately, we saw it in time and veered off.

Anchored gill nets are usually set in water deeper than 10 feet and have buoyed anchors at each end securing the net in place on the bottom. As in the case of the staked gill net, weights keep the lower edge of the net on the bottom, while floats suspend the upper edge to hold the net vertically in the water. The top edge of the net is an indeterminate distance below the surface, deep enough, one hopes, that boats passing over it can clear it.

Drift gill nets are buoyed at the top so that the top edge of the net is at or near the surface, while weights keep the bottom down so that the net is vertical. These nets usually have a large float at one end, with the other end attached to a boat. A rare few may be left to drift with the tide, but that seems like a really risky operation for the fisherman as well as a hazard to other boats. In any event, should you see a commercial fishing boat moving in an apparently inexplicable manner, especially in the southern Bay, watch out for a drift net behind it!

SUGGESTED CRUISES

THIS SECTION IS INTENDED primarily to aid the novice cruiser, or one who is unfamiliar with the Chesapeake Bay, in planning a cruise on the Bay. It is not intended to dictate the "best" itinerary for cruising the various parts of the Bay for different lengths of time. I suggest that you use the itineraries given here as a starting point, modifying them to suit your schedule and interests.

Any cruise plan must take into account a considerable number of factors that will influence where, how far, when, and for how long the cruise is planned. For starters, you need to take into account the size and fitting out of the vessel and its seaworthiness, the experience and capability of crew and captain, and the predicted weather. If you must adhere to a schedule, as most of us do, be sure to allow for contingencies in your planning, especially your ports of call at the tail end of the cruise. You want to be in a location that will enable you to return to your final destination on schedule, especially if you are chartering. Having to cross the Chesapeake Bay or travel a long distance in relatively unprotected waters during a blow or in the face of an approaching thunderstorm or line squall is definitely not a good idea.

With that in mind, I have divided the Chesapeake into three parts: the northern Bay, the central Bay, and the southern Bay. For each part I offer a set of itineraries based on cruises of three days (i.e., a long weekend), nine days (i.e., a week, counting both weekends), and sixteen days (i.e., two weeks, counting the weekends on either end). There is nothing sacred about this division. Obviously, cruise areas can overlap, and the cruise durations may vary. Destinations may also change with your interests, the weather, or any of several other factors. These itineraries are meant to serve as frameworks for cruises; I do not expect them to be followed slavishly. With the exception of a couple of recommended layovers for the longer cruises in the central and southern Chesapeake Bay, no allowance has been made in these itineraries for layovers due to inclement weather or a desire to stay put for a day or even more. Such layovers definitely need to be considered. You really don't want to be on the go every day, in spite of what these itineraries suggest.

Although I've selected a major boating center for the start of each itinerary, at least for the longer cruises you obviously can start at any segment of the suggested cruise and continue on around the "loop" to return to your starting point. Note that each itinerary sets areas, not specific anchorages, as destinations. Thus, distances mentioned are only approximate distances, intended as a rough guide to the probable duration of particular legs. For example, if your boat can maintain an average speed of 5 knots, a 40-mile leg will take about 8 hours. If

55

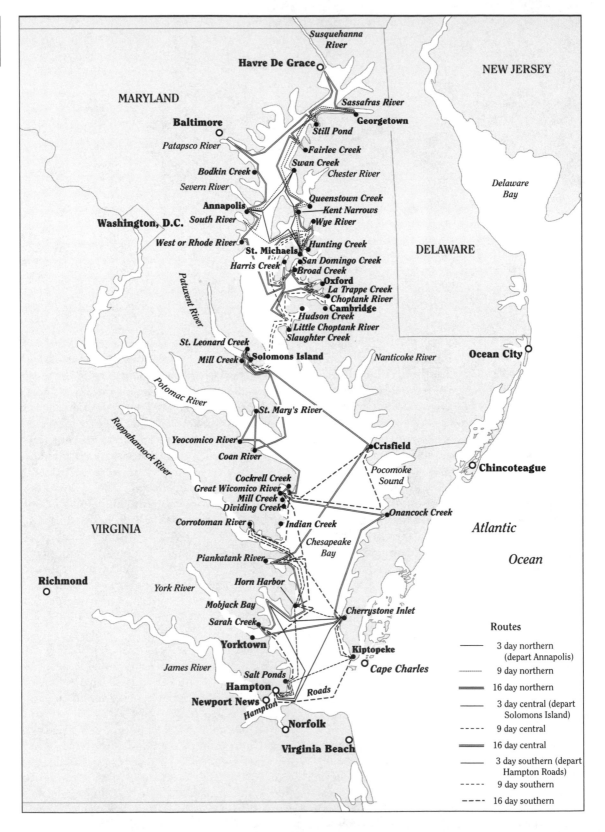

Havre De Grace

Susquehanna River

NEW JERSEY

MARYLAND

Baltimore

Patapsco River

Sassafras River

Georgetown

Still Pond

Fairlee Creek

Swan Creek

Chester River

Bodkin Creek

Severn River

Delaware Bay

Queenstown Creek

Kent Narrows

Wye River

Annapolis

Washington, D.C.

South River

West or Rhode River

Hunting Creek

DELAWARE

St. Michaels

San Domingo Creek

Harris Creek

Broad Creek

Oxford

La Trappe Creek

Choptank River

Cambridge

Hudson Creek

Little Choptank River

Slaughter Creek

Patuxent River

St. Leonard Creek

Mill Creek

Solomons Island

Nanticoke River

Ocean City

Potomac River

St. Mary's River

Rappahannock River

Yeocomico River

Coan River

Crisfield

Chincoteague

Pocomoke Sound

Cockrell Creek

Great Wicomico River

Mill Creek

Dividing Creek

Onancock Creek

Corrotoman River

Indian Creek

Chesapeake Bay

VIRGINIA

Piankatank River

Atlantic

Ocean

Horn Harbor

Richmond

York River

Mobjack Bay

Sarah Creek

Cherrystone Inlet

Yorktown

Kiptopeke

James River

Salt Ponds

Cape Charles

Hampton

Roads

Newport News

Hampton

Norfolk

Virginia Beach

Routes

———	3 day northern (depart Annapolis)
··········	9 day northern
═══	16 day northern
———	3 day central (depart Solomons Island)
- - - -	9 day central
═══	16 day central
———	3 day southern (depart Hampton Roads)
- - - -	9 day southern
– – –	16 day southern

you plan to sail at a lower speed, a shorter maximum leg distance is strongly recommended. Likewise, a faster boat may do well with a longer leg. For that reason, a 40-mile leg is the maximum length I'll suggest. Other than that, it's your choice.

Exactly where you choose to anchor or tie up each night is, of course, up to you. Use this book as a guide for selecting your specific destination for the night. In many cases the choices are too varied for me to even suggest where you should anchor or tie up for the night. I have attempted to suggest destinations that offer a variety of harbor types, from relatively bucolic to cosmopolitan. In fact, some of the suggested

destinations will offer both, depending on the exact location within the destination area that you choose. For example, the St. Michaels area, in the northern Chesapeake Bay, offers the marinas, restaurants, and other amenities of the town of St. Michaels, while a short run across the Miles River from St. Michaels will take you into Leeds Creek, where you may anchor with little in sight on the shore but trees. In other areas the choice may not be as wide, but wherever possible, the destinations will be ones where you will be permitted to anchor rather than required to rent a slip, although in most cases that will be an option.

SUMMARY OF SUGGESTED CRUISES

NORTHERN CHESAPEAKE BAY (p. 58)
Three-Day Cruise (70 nm): Annapolis–St. Michaels–Swan Creek–Annapolis

Nine-Day Cruise (160 nm): Annapolis–Swan Creek–Still Pond–Georgetown–Fairlee Creek–Queenstown Creek–St. Michaels–Wye River–South River–Annapolis

Sixteen-Day Cruise (291 nm): Annapolis–Bodkin Creek–Baltimore–Still Pond–Havre de Grace–Georgetown–Fairlee Creek–Queenstown Creek–Wye River–St. Michaels–Broad Creek–Oxford–La Trappe Creek–Little Choptank River–Harris Creek–West or Rhode River–Annapolis

CENTRAL CHESAPEAKE BAY (p. 67)
Three-Day Cruise (20 nm): Solomons Island–St. Leonard Creek–Mill Creek–Solomons Island

Nine-Day Cruise (183 nm): Solomons Island–Little Choptank River–Wye River–St. Michaels and Hunting Creek–Kent Narrows–San Domingo Creek–Oxford–Cambridge and La Trappe Creek–Slaughter Creek–Solomons Island

Sixteen-Day Cruise (358 nm): Solomons Island–Crisfield–Piankatank River–Mobjack Bay–Sarah Creek–Cherrystone Inlet–Onancock Creek–Mill Creek (Great Wicomico River)–Cockrell Creek–Yeocomico River–St. Marys River–Coan River–Mill Creek (Patuxent River)–St. Leonard Creek–Solomons Island

SOUTHERN CHESAPEAKE BAY (p. 76)
Three-Day Cruise (95 nm): Hampton Roads–Cherrystone Inlet–Mobjack Bay–Hampton Roads

Nine-Day Cruise (205 nm): Hampton Roads–Sarah Creek–Horn Harbor–Piankatank River–Corrotoman River–Horn Harbor–Cherrystone Inlet–Kiptopeke–Salt Ponds–Hampton Roads

Sixteen-Day Cruise (338 nm): Hampton Roads–Kiptopeke–Cherrystone Inlet–Piankatank River–Corrotoman River–Dividing Creek–Cockrell Creek–Onancock Creek–Crisfield–Mill Creek (Great Wicomico River)–Indian Creek–Piankatank River–Horn Harbor–Sarah Creek–Salt Ponds–Hampton Roads

NORTHERN CHESAPEAKE BAY

The northern Chesapeake Bay is probably the best place for a first-timer or the less experienced to begin cruising. Virtually no place in this part of the Bay is very far from a sheltered harbor. There is no need for any long passages unless you specifically choose to make them. You can pick up any of the suggested itineraries at any point along the way and complete the loop with easy legs each day. The same is not quite true of the central and southern Chesapeake Bay, where the legs tend to be somewhat longer.

There is another advantage to cruising the northern Bay from early July to at least mid-September. It is only in the northern Bay that you can swim, wade, or just take a dip to cool off without running afoul of the notorious sea nettle. As you proceed north of the Bay Bridges, the water becomes less and less salty, until at the level of Pooles Island it is nearly fresh. At the same time, the sea nettles decrease in number, with virtually none found at or north of Pooles Island. The same is true as you proceed well up many of the rivers and creeks branching off the Bay in this area (i.e., the Chester River).

I chose Annapolis as the origin of this set of cruises since it is a centrally located, major yachting center with several marinas and charter companies. I could just as well have picked Kent Narrows, Baltimore, or Rock Hall. If you are chartering in hot weather, you might consider starting your cruise from one of the more northerly locations, even Havre de Grace, on the Susquehanna River, or Georgetown, on the Sassafras River. Should you choose one of the latter two starting points for a short cruise, see the sixteen-day-cruise suggestions for aid in selecting routes and destinations from those locations.

* * * * * *

THREE-DAY CRUISE (chart p. 59)

Day 1: Annapolis–St. Michaels, 25 nm.

The St. Michaels area makes a very good destination for any cruise (see region 3, pages 180–83). The town of St. Michaels offers marinas, restaurants, groceries, and, of course, the famous St. Michaels Maritime Museum on Navy Point. There is some room to anchor to the north and east of Navy Point, or you can find a slip at one of the marinas in the basin south of Navy Point.

After your tour of the town or museum, you can find more bucolic surroundings just across the Miles River in Leeds Creek or a couple of miles upstream in Hunting Creek.

Day 2: St. Michaels–Swan Creek via Kent Narrows, 25 nm.

Heading up to Swan Creek through Kent Narrows is an interesting experience in its own right (see region 2, pages 120–22 and 125–28). There are several restaurants both north and south of the bridges where you can tie up for a meal before continuing on, and there are two marinas north of the bridges where you can obtain fuel, water, and marine supplies. The drawbridge opens every half-hour, and the new channel on the Chester River side makes the passage much easier than it was only a few years ago.

As you pass out of the Chester River on your way to Swan Creek, remain at least ¾ mile offshore of Eastern Neck Island as a long, wide shoal protrudes from the island toward C"3" in the Chester River. Either watch your depthsounder carefully or honor C"3" before turning to head between Swan Point Bar and the mainland toward the entrance to Swan Creek. You will also find at least one fish trap in this vicinity. Beware of it, especially if you are traveling under conditions of reduced visibility.

Swan Creek offers the amenities of several marinas and an extensive anchorage area. It's a popular anchorage in prime boating season, so you certainly won't lack for company. If you land at any of the marinas, it is about a 1-mile walk to the town of Rock Hall with its restaurants and other facilities.

Day 3: Swan Creek–Annapolis, 20 nm.

Once clear of Swan Point Bar, you will encounter few hazards on your trip to Annapolis, the self-proclaimed sailing capital of the world (see region 3, pages 209–13). (I don't count the Bay Bridges as a hazard. They are obvious.)

Northern Bay Three-Day Cruise

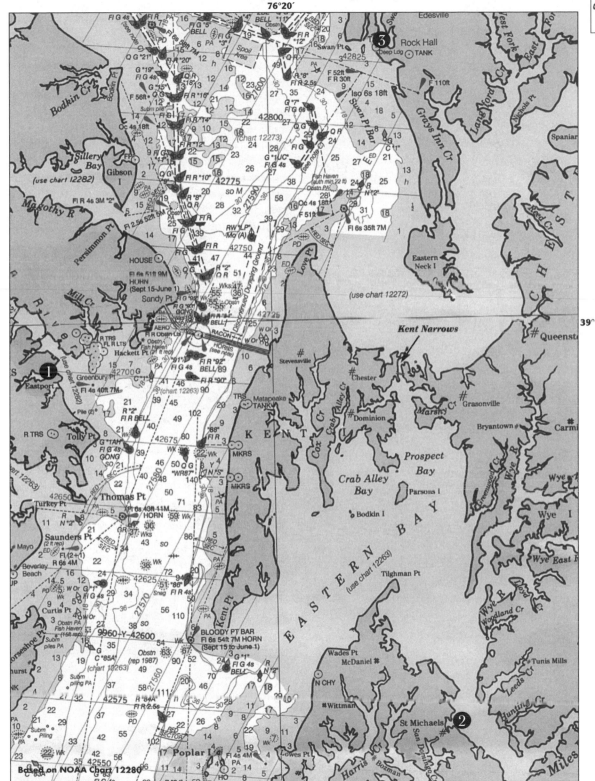

SCALE **1:223,077**

NINE-DAY CRUISE (chart p. 61)

Day 1: Annapolis–Swan Creek, 20 nm.

The leg from Annapolis to Swan Creek is relatively free of hazards (see region 2, pages 120–22). Even Swan Point Bar isn't much of a hazard unless your vessel draws six feet or more. Although crossing this bar is normally not much of a problem, when you are approaching from the south the prudent course is between the bar and the mainland.

Swan Creek offers the amenities of several marinas and an extensive anchorage area. It's a popular anchorage in prime boating season. If you land at any of the marinas, it is about a 1-mile walk to the town of Rock Hall with its restaurants and other facilities.

Day 2: Swan Creek–Still Pond, 25 nm.

If you draw 5 feet or less, you can easily cut across Swan Point Bar to cut considerable distance from the leg to Still Pond (see region 1, pages 100–101). Head south from the Swan Creek entrance until you pass C"5" near Rock Hall. Then swing gently west until you are on a course just north of the large, white front range marker, heading due west. Remain on this course until the tip of Swan Point is past your beam or until the water depth begins to reach 8 feet or more before swinging to a northerly course for Still Pond.

Still Pond is a lovely anchorage, although it can get crowded on weekends during the prime boating season. There are no marine facilities here, but there is a nice, sandy beach, as well as the famous Churn Creek "Chute Ride." The anchorage is exposed to the north-northwest, so if there is going to be any significant wind from that direction, consider proceeding into the shelter of Stillpond Creek, which has a narrow but well-marked entrance.

Day 3: Still Pond–Georgetown, Sassafras River, 15 nm.

Although it is quite feasible to anchor in several locations on the Sassafras River on your way to Georgetown (see region 1, pages 98–99), the wakes from the considerable number of large power cruisers roaring up and down the river in prime boating season can make it a bit uncomfortable at times. The no-wake speed limit in the vicinity of

Georgetown eliminates this annoyance, and there are several marinas that offer slips, moorings, and all the other amenities you may desire.

If you don't want to rent a slip or mooring and can't find room to anchor among the moorings, simply proceed past the drawbridge (which opens on demand) and anchor just about anywhere above the bridge. There are several restaurants in Georgetown (or Fredericktown), and a walk into Galena, a mile away, will take you to a supermarket, a pharmacy, and several other stores that you may find of interest.

This is a very pretty, freshwater river well worth the trip regardless of where you choose to stop.

Day 4: Georgetown–Fairlee Creek, 20 nm.

As you head down the coast from the Sassafras River, it's a straight shot from the tip of Worton Point to the entrance to Fairlee Creek (see region 1, pages 102–3). Although the Fairlee Creek entrance has a reputation for being a little tricky, it really is quite easy thanks to the string of green private markers placed there by Great Oak Landing. Just honor the buoys, swing around the point into the main part of the creek, and anchor just about anywhere you choose.

Alternatively, you may choose to take a slip at Great Oak Landing Marina, to the east immediately inside the creek entrance. Even if you don't tie up there, be sure to take a meal at the Great Oak Landing Restaurant. It's not cheap, but the food is great.

Day 5: Fairlee Creek–Queenstown Creek, 25 nm.

Queenstown Creek is at the far end of the "umbrella handle" in the Chester River formed by Eastern Neck Island (see region 2, pages 128–30). Pay attention to the entrance instructions to this creek or you may have to get out and walk. The channel is narrow, and the sides rise abruptly. However, the instructions are easy to follow. If you take it slowly, you should enter with no problems.

Once you are inside, the area to the north opens out into a lovely anchorage. There are a couple of protruding shoals, but follow the directions in the section on Queenstown Creek, pages 128–30, and you will easily avoid them. Just pick a spot and drop your hook.

Northern Bay Nine-Day Cruise

76°20′ 76°

39°20′

39°

Kent Narrows

Based on NOAA Chart 12280

SCALE **1:532,000**

There are no marine facilities here, but if you must find a place to eat out or need some incidental groceries, head into the south part of the creek. There you may be able to tie up your boat at the town dock long enough to walk into Queenstown or up to Route 3 to the grocery-carryout store there. If someone beats you to the town dock and there is no room for you, simply anchor in the basin, avoiding the stakes where the workboats tie up, and land by dinghy. Don't plan to spend the night there; instead, return to the north basin before dark to anchor for the night.

Day 6: Queenstown Creek–St. Michaels via Kent Narrows, 20 nm.
As you leave Queenstown Creek, head for the Chester River green "9." On clearing green "9," do not head directly for the outer channel marker to Kent Narrows. Swing well to the west to avoid the broad shoal that extends to the north of the Narrows channel until you can head due south to the first channel-entrance marker, red "2K." (See region 3, pages 180–83, and region 2, pages 125–28.)

There are several restaurants both north and south of the bridges in Kent Narrows proper where you can tie up for a meal before continuing on, and there are two marinas north of the bridges where you can obtain fuel, water, and marine supplies. The drawbridge opens every half-hour, and the new channel on the Chester River side makes the passage much easier than it was only a few years ago.

The St. Michaels area makes a very good destination for any cruise. The town of St. Michaels offers marinas, restaurants, groceries and, of course, the famous St. Michaels Maritime Museum on Navy Point. There is some room to anchor to the north and east of Navy Point, or you can find a slip at one of the marinas in the basin south of Navy Point.

After your tour of the town or museum, you can find more bucolic surroundings just across the Miles River in Leeds Creek or a couple of miles upstream in Hunting Creek.

Day 7: St. Michaels–Wye River, 5 nm.
Following a visit to the bustling metropolis of St. Michaels, the Wye River offers the opposite extreme (see region 3, pages 170–78). With the marginal exception of Wye Landing, near the junction of the Wye East River and Skipton Creek, there are no marine facilities and no towns as such in either fork of the Wye River. Here you are on your own.

Whether you choose to anchor in the wide expanse of Shaw Bay, near the entrance to the Wye, or proceed well up either fork to the plethora of well-protected anchorages on this river, you simply can't go wrong by making a visit to the Wye River. If this is your first trip to the Wye River, be sure to visit Skipton Creek, if only to see the herd of black sheep that keeps the lawn of Wye Plantation well trimmed.

Day 8: Wye River–South River, 20 nm.
As you exit Eastern Bay and cross the main Chesapeake, if you just look for the famous Thomas Point Lighthouse, near the Western Shore, and leave it to the north, you will find the entrance to South River (see region 3, pages 218–24).

South River is another area that offers a choice of full marina facilities in Selby Bay and a few other locations or bucolic anchorages where you can swing at anchor in well-protected harbors. Be sure to select an anchorage sheltered from powerboat wakes in the main river.

Day 9: South River–Annapolis, 10 nm.
As you exit the South River, once again use the Thomas Point Lighthouse as a guide. Leave it to port and swing around it until you come to a course due north. Hold this course until Tolly Point comes abeam to avoid the shoal extending for a surprising distance to the east of the point. Then swing and head for the mouth of the Severn River and your point of origin in the Annapolis area (see region 3, pages 209–13).

Sixteen-Day Cruise (chart p. 63)
Day 1: Annapolis, Severn River–Bodkin Creek, 15 nm.
Bodkin Creek, near the mouth of the Patapsco River, offers an excellent jumping-off point for a cruise to anywhere in the northern Bay (see region 2, pages 141–42). You can anchor nearly anywhere in this creek, although the best anchorage is in Jubb Cove, about a mile into Main Creek. Here the speed limit provides protection from the powerboat wakes that frequently disturb anchorages closer

Northern Bay Sixteen-Day Cruise

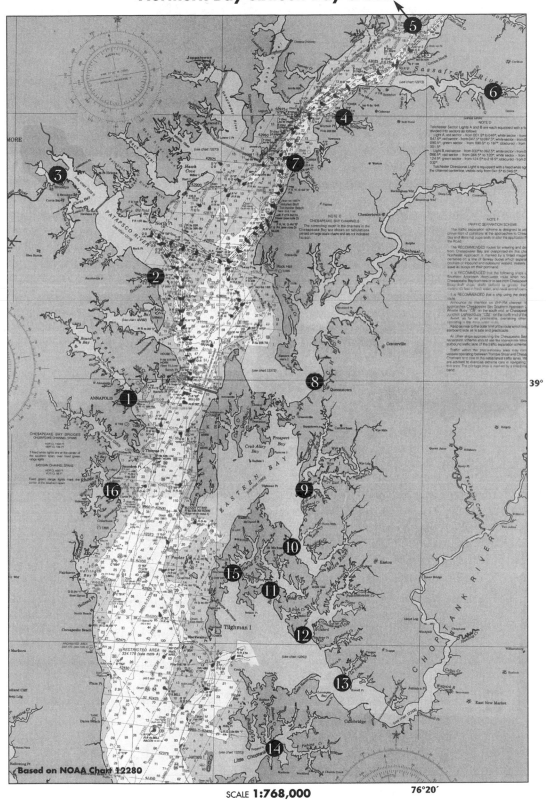

Based on NOAA Chart 12280

SCALE 1:768,000

76°20′

39°

to the creek entrance. Swimming is good here, as it tends to be free of nettles all summer.

Ventnor Marina, just inside the mouth of Main Creek, offers fuel, water, and some marine supplies. If you are looking for a restaurant, the only one on the Bodkin is The Cheshire Crab near the headwaters of Main Creek at Pleasure Cove Marina.

Day 2: Bodkin Creek–Baltimore, Patapsco River, 15 nm.
If you are cruising anywhere in the area, a visit to Baltimore at least once is a real must (see region 2, pages 144–52). Although anchorages are in short supply, there are plenty of marinas where you can take a slip, or you can tie up at the sea wall in the Inner Harbor or in Fells Point.

From any of these locations you can take a water taxi to virtually any other place in the Baltimore harbor area, including Fort McHenry, Canton, Fells Point, and several locations around the Inner Harbor. Baltimore's harbor has something for everyone.

Day 3: Baltimore–Still Pond, 25 nm.
As you exit the Patapsco River, give North Point a wide berth before coming onto a course toward the south end of Pooles Island. Pass to the east of Pooles Island and head for a point about ½ mile west of the entrance to Still Pond to keep clear of the shoals between Worton Point and the entrance to Still Pond. Time your passage carefully as currents in this part of the Bay can often exceed 1½ knots.

Still Pond is a lovely anchorage, although it can get crowded on weekends in the prime boating season. There are no marine facilities here, but there is a nice, sandy beach, as well as the famous Churn Creek "Chute Ride." The anchorage is exposed to the north-northwest, so if there is going to be any significant wind from that direction, consider proceeding into the shelter of Stillpond Creek, which has a narrow but well-marked entrance.

Day 4: Still Pond–Havre de Grace, Susquehanna River, 20 nm.
Havre de Grace is at the end of a long but well-marked channel leading into the Susquehanna River mouth (see region 1, pages 105–8). There are several marinas where you may obtain fuel, water, and marine supplies, the most easily accessible of which is Tidewater Marina, about ¼ mile before you reach the first railroad bridge. You can take a slip, rent a mooring, or anchor in this area to visit the town or other points of interest, such as Concord Point Lighthouse or the Decoy Museum, not to mention a wide assortment of restaurants.

If you can pass under the railroad bridge (52 feet clearance MHW), better-protected anchorages are available upstream. The water here is essentially fresh, and the swimming is good throughout the summer. An added advantage is that if you remain here for any time, the salt water fouling on your vessel's bottom will be killed and tend to drop off.

This is a very pretty, freshwater river well worth the trip regardless of where you choose to stop.

Day 5: Havre de Grace–Georgetown, Sassafras River, 25 nm.
Although it is quite feasible to anchor in several locations on the Sassafras River on your way to Georgetown (see region 1, pages 98–99), the wakes from the many large power cruisers that roar up and down the river in the prime boating season can make it a bit uncomfortable at times. The no-wake speed limit in the vicinity of Georgetown eliminates this annoyance and there are several marinas that offer slips, moorings, and other amenities.

If you can't find room to anchor among the moorings, simply proceed past the drawbridge, which opens on demand, and anchor just about anywhere above the bridge. There are several restaurants in Georgetown (or Fredericktown), and Galena, which is a mile away, has a supermarket, a pharmacy, and several other stores.

Day 6: Georgetown–Fairlee Creek, 20 nm.
As you head down the coast from the Sassafras River, it's a straight shot from the tip of Worton Point to the entrance to Fairlee Creek (see region 1, pages 102–3). Although it is reputed to have a somewhat tricky entrance, the set of private green markers installed by Great Oak Landing makes the approach fairly easy. As you swing around the point at the entrance, the creek opens up and you can anchor just about anywhere you choose.

Great Oak Landing, to the east immediately inside the creek, offers slips, some moorings, and an excellent restaurant. Even if you choose to anchor out, a meal at the Great Oak Landing Restaurant is highly recommended. It isn't cheap, but the food is great.

Day 7: Fairlee Creek–Queenstown Creek, 25 nm.
Queenstown Creek is at the far end of the "umbrella handle" in the Chester River formed by Eastern Neck Island (see region 2, pages 128–30). Pay attention to the entrance instructions to this creek unless you plan to get out and walk. The channel is narrow, and the sides rise abruptly. However, the instructions are easy to follow, and if you take it slow, you should enter with no problems.

Inside, the area to the north opens out into a lovely anchorage. There are a couple of protruding shoals, but read the section on Queenstown Creek in this book and you will easily avoid them. Just pick your spot and drop the hook.

There are no marine facilities here, but for a place to eat out or some incidental groceries you can head into the southern part of the creek. There you may be able to tie your boat to the town dock long enough to walk into Queenstown or up to Route 3 to the grocery-carryout store there. If someone beats you to the town dock, simply anchor in the basin, avoiding the stakes where the workboats tie up, and land by dinghy. Don't plan to spend the night there. Return to the north basin to anchor before dark.

Day 8: Queenstown Creek–Wye River via Kent Narrows, 20 nm.
As you leave Queenstown Creek, head for the Chester River green "9" buoy. On clearing green "9," do not head directly for the outer channel marker to Kent Narrows. Swing well to the west to avoid the broad shoal that extends to the north of the Narrows channel until you can head due south to the first channel entrance marker, red "2K." (See region 3, pages 170–78, and region 2, pages 125–28).

There are several restaurants both north and south of the bridges in Kent Narrows proper where you can tie up for a meal before continuing on, and two marinas north of the bridges offer fuel, water, and marine supplies. The drawbridge opens every half-hour, and the new channel on the Chester River side makes the passage much easier than it was only a few years ago.

With the marginal exception of Wye Landing near the junction of Wye Narrows, the Wye East River, and Skipton Creek, there are no marine facilities and no towns as such anywhere in either fork of the Wye River. Here you are on your own.

Whether you choose to anchor in the wide expanse of Shaw Bay, near the entrance to the Wye, or proceed well up either fork to the plethora of well-protected anchorages on this river, you simply can't go wrong by making a visit to the Wye River. If this is your first trip to the Wye River, be sure to visit Skipton Creek, if only to see the herd of black sheep that keep the lawn of Wye Plantation well trimmed.

Day 9: Wye River–St. Michaels, 5 nm.
The St. Michaels area makes a very good destination for any cruise (see region 3, pages 180–83). The town of St. Michaels offers marinas, restaurants, groceries, and, of course, the famous St. Michaels Maritime Museum on Navy Point. There is some room to anchor to the north and east of Navy Point, or you can find a slip at one of the marinas in the basin south of Navy Point.

After your tour of the town or the museum, you can find more bucolic surroundings just across the Miles River in Leeds Creek or a couple of miles upstream in Hunting Creek.

Day 10: St. Michaels–Broad Creek via Knapps Narrows, 25 nm.
If you draw 6 feet or more, it would be highly advisable to pass Poplar Island on the Bay side, as you may bump passing between the islands and the mainland. Similarly, deep-draft vessels would be wiser to round the southern tip of Tilghman Island to enter the Choptank River rather than take the shortcut through Knapps Narrows. Otherwise, the passage inside Poplar Island and through Knapps Narrows can save a great deal of time and distance traveled when entering the Choptank River from the north. (See region 3, pages 189–91 and 185–87.)

Proceed slowly and carefully on entering the narrows. The channel on the Bay side is quite narrow and subject to shoaling from storms. Hold close to the markers, monitoring your depth-sounder at all times, and make sure you know which way to turn if the depth suddenly decreases. On rounding the second red marker, red "4," head for the middle of the entrance to the narrows proper and you will enter with no problems. Several restaurants in the narrows make good lunch stops, and fuel is available. Do not plan to overnight in the narrows; continue through to the Choptank.

Broad Creek offers many well-protected anchorages but no marine facilities. If you anchor in San Domingo Creek, you can land and walk into St. Michaels via the little-known "back door." See the section on San Domingo Creek in this book for details.

Day 11: Broad Creek–Oxford, Tred Avon River, 10 nm.
A cruise of the Choptank River is not complete without a visit to Oxford (see region 3, pages 192–95). Pull into Town Creek, where you can anchor or take a slip at the one of the many marinas there or tie up at the Schooner Restaurant for a meal. Take a walk around the quaint little town to visit the shops and/or restaurants there. Although it is rapidly becoming a bit "touristy," it still is very much like going back in time to the mid-20th century.

When you have had your fill of the town, you may simply head across the Tred Avon River and anchor in Plaindealing Creek or the unnamed creek to its west. In fact, you could anchor there in the first place and take your dinghy across or ride the fascinating Oxford-Bellevue ferry to visit Oxford without entering Town Creek at all. There are many other anchorages off the Tred Avon River, but these are the most convenient if you want to see Oxford.

Day 12: Oxford–La Trappe Creek, 6 nm.
La Trappe Creek is one of the prettiest bodies of water in this area (see region 3, pages 198–99). The entrance is easy, and anchorages abound. The most popular anchorage is in the little basin to port immediately inside the entrance. Unfortunately, most of the shore is now posted with "No Trespassing" signs. No matter. Simply head farther upstream and anchor anywhere that takes your fancy. It's all attractive and well protected.

In fact, a run upstream past the huge estates bordering the creek to near the headwaters at the Dickerson Boat Yard is a unique experience. You run through overhanging trees forming almost a tunnel on smooth, chocolate-colored water. The feeling is slightly otherworldly. Try it.

Day 13: La Trappe Creek–Little Choptank River, 25 nm.
The Little Choptank River has several creeks, most of which are well worth exploring (see region 3, pages 201–6). It is frequently used as a jumping-off point for cruises to the southern Bay or as a stopover point on the return leg.

A pleasant little marina in Slaughter Creek has fuel and water, and there is another, somewhat less accessible one in Madison Bay. Other than those, you are in anchoring country, and pleasant anchorages abound. The most popular one is in the mouth of Hudson Creek.

Day 14: Little Choptank–Harris Creek, 20 nm.
The anchorages on Harris Creek are normally used as stopover points on the way to somewhere else (see region 3, pages 187–89). The most popular anchorage is in Dun Cove, the first opening to the west as you enter Harris Creek. Other anchorages are a little less protected or at least farther up the creek.

There are no marine facilities anywhere in Harris Creek. For fuel, water, or anything else in this area, you will have to enter Knapps Narrows.

Day 15: Harris Creek–West or Rhode River, 25 nm.
Unless you have a draft of 6 feet or more, the usual route to the West and Rhode Rivers is through Knapps Narrows (see region 3, pages 224–25). Pick up the first in the line of green markers leading into the narrows, remaining a boat length or more to the north of the markers outside of the narrows proper as the channel does not run right up to them. Beware of the narrow channel exiting into the main Bay by holding within about a boat's length from red "4" as you swing around it into the channel toward the green "1" marker. From there, proceed south of Poplar Island and well into the Bay before turning to your northwest course toward the entrance to the West River. Be sure to honor the green "1A" in the mouth of

the West River, rounding it before you head for the middle of the entrance.

If you are looking for marinas and restaurants, head for Galesville, on the West River. If you are looking for an anchorage, the Rhode River offers better choices, although wakes from powerboats and water-skiers can be a problem during the day. The southeast fork of the West River provides a quieter anchorage than does the Rhode River, but it is a bit more exposed to weather, and the only place to land is at the Galesville marinas, as the shore is all private property.

Day 16: West River–Annapolis, Severn River, 10 nm. The short trip back to the Annapolis area is easy (see region 3, pages 209–13). Just honor the markers as you exit the West River. Leave Thomas Point Lighthouse to port and stay ¾ mile off Tolly Point as you round it to enter the mouth of the Severn River. You really should honor Green "1AH" off Tolly Point but you can cut inside of it if you hold to within 100 yards of it.

This gives you an easy, relaxed final day of cruising with time to enjoy Annapolis should its bustle tempt you.

* * * * * *

CENTRAL CHESAPEAKE BAY

The central Chesapeake Bay is a mix of harbors on the Western Shore, the Eastern Shore, and the Potomac River. I have selected Solomons Island, the major yachting center in this part of the Bay, as the starting point for cruises of the central Bay area, although cruising to the north will overlap the northern Bay area and cruising to the south will overlap many cruise destinations in the southern Bay area.

For a cruise of only a few days, the Patuxent River offers a variety of excellent and interesting harbors, all of which are within only a short sail of one another. If your time is short, it is hard to beat a relaxed cruise on the Patuxent River.

To go to any harbors south of the Patuxent River requires a leg of about 40 miles either across the Bay to Crisfield or south around

Point Lookout into the Potomac River. If you head north to the Little Choptank River, it's a shorter leg of about 25 nm.

If you start from somewhere on the Potomac or Virginia's Western Shore, all of the legs will be more reasonable since the majority of harbors in this part of the Bay are located there. The longer legs across or along the Bay are more suitable for cruisers with a bit more experience.

For those reasons, I have chosen to confine the suggested three-day cruise itinerary strictly to the Patuxent River and the week-long (nine-day) cruise to the northerly cruising grounds of the Choptank River area, reserving the routes with longer legs to the extended, sixteen-day cruise, which allows you time to choose your weather on both leaving and returning to the Patuxent River.

THREE-DAY CRUISE (chart p. 68)

Day 1: Solomons Island–St. Leonard Creek, 10 nm. One of the nice things about a leisurely, relaxed cruise on the Patuxent River is that you have the luxury of taking your time and looking the area over instead of having to make a beeline to your destination (see region 4, pages 258–60). You may want to continue upriver to take a look into Battle Creek, Island Creek, or the upper part of the Patuxent River before turning back to enter St. Leonard Creek. Because of the short distances involved, the same holds true for the other two legs of this cruise of the Patuxent.

Once you enter St. Leonard Creek, you can anchor just about anywhere that strikes your fancy. Coves and small bights abound, most of

Central Bay Three-Day Cruise

76°20

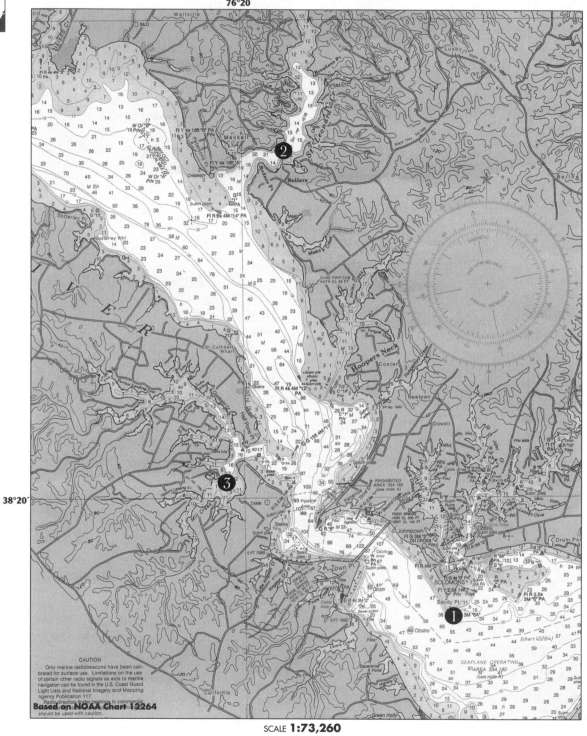

Based on NOAA Chart 12264

SCALE 1:73,260

which are quiet and protected. Should you need fuel or want to try a unique restaurant, head upstream to the intersection of Johns and St. Leonard Creeks, where you will find Vera's White Sands Marina and Restaurant. If you want a unique experience, give it a try.

Day 2: St. Leonard Creek–Mill Creek via Sotterly Plantation, 5 nm.

As you depart St. Leonard Creek, Sotterly Plantation lies directly across the Patuxent River (see region 4, pages 258–60 and 260–61). You will see a pier in front of a small white shed. To the right (north) of this pier is the entrance to a small basin where you can tie up your boat and walk up the dirt road lined with raspberry bushes that leads to the plantation. You can take a guided tour, visit the gift shop, or simply wander around on your own. By all means pay it a visit.

Mill and Cuckold Creeks share a common entrance. As you pass between the two points at the entrance, Cuckold Creek bears off to the right, Mill Creek to the left. The former is almost fully developed, and the shore is lined with private homes. Mill Creek is more open, with interesting cliffs on the north side. Unfortunately, a water-skiing course is frequently set up in this vicinity, marked by a string of buoys. You may want to anchor some distance from this if it is active.

Day 3: Mill Creek–Solomons Island, 5 nm.

Given the short run back to Solomons from Mill Creek, in decent weather you may want to continue past Solomons to visit the section of Calvert Cliffs on the north side of the mouth of the Patuxent (see region 4, pages 253–56). There you can anchor within 100 yards of the beach. Stroll along the beach at the base of the cliffs and try your luck at finding fossils that have tumbled down from the eroding cliffs. It's a bad day if someone in your party doesn't find some shark teeth at the very least.

The run back to Solomons harbor is short and easy. Here you will find virtually every facility, from marinas and restaurants to the fascinating Calvert Marine Museum. Don't miss the museum.

NINE-DAY CRUISE (chart p. 70)

Day 1: Solomons Island, Patuxent River–Little Choptank River, 25 nm.

The Little Choptank River has several creeks, most of which are well worth exploring (see region 3, pages 201–6). It is frequently used as a jumping-off point for cruises to the southern Bay or as a stopover point on the return leg.

A pleasant little marina in Slaughter Creek has fuel and water, and there is another, somewhat less accessible marina in Madison Bay. Otherwise, you are in anchoring country, and pleasant anchorages abound. For this leg, I suggest anchoring in the mouth of Hudson Creek.

Day 2: Little Choptank River–Wye River, 32 nm.

This run will take you through Poplar Narrows, between Poplar Island and the mainland, unless you draw 6 feet or more (see region 3, pages 170–78). In the latter case, pass Poplar Island on the Bay side. Even if you choose not to honor the red buoys off Tilghman Point, don't stray too far inshore of them because of the shoal off the point. As you head for the entrance to the Wye River, stay well south of the tip of Bennet Point at the entrance and honor the green C"3" can before heading into the mouth of the Wye.

With the marginal exception of Wye Landing, near the junction of Wye Narrows, the Wye East River, and Skipton Creek, there are no marine facilities and no towns as such in either fork of the Wye River. Here you are on your own.

Whether you choose to anchor in the wide expanse of Shaw Bay, near the entrance to the Wye, or proceed well up either fork to the plethora of well-protected anchorages on this river, you simply can't go wrong in making a visit to the Wye River. If this is your first trip to the Wye River, be sure to visit Skipton Creek, if only to see the herd of black sheep that keep the lawn of Wye Plantation well trimmed.

Day 3: Wye River–St. Michaels and Hunting Creek, 10 nm.

The St. Michaels area makes a very good destination for any cruise (see region 3, pages 180–83). The town of St. Michaels offers marinas, restaurants, groceries, and, of course, the famous St. Michaels

Central Bay Nine-Day Cruise

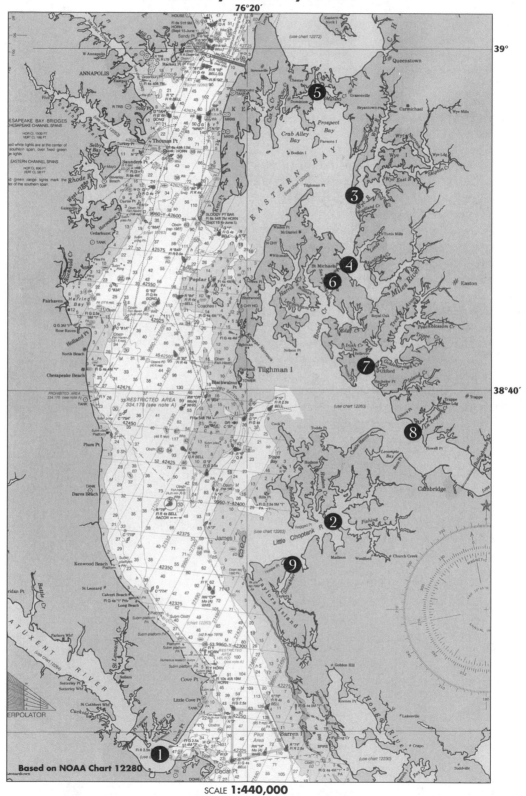

Based on NOAA Chart 12280

SCALE **1:440,000**

Maritime Museum on Navy Point. There is some room to anchor to the north and east of Navy Point, or you can find a slip at one of the marinas in the basin south of Navy Point.

Following your tour of the town or museum, you can find more bucolic surroundings a couple of miles upstream in Hunting Creek. Be sure to give the first green marker in the entrance to Hunting Creek a wide berth as the shoal has a tendency to encroach beyond it. Thereafter anchor anywhere that suits your fancy. The island on one side is uninhabited, and the scattered homes on the mainland are unobtrusive. There's little traffic in this quiet and peaceful area.

Day 4: Hunting Creek–Kent Narrows, 15 nm.

There are several restaurants both north and south of the bridges in Kent Narrows proper where you can tie up for a meal before continuing on, and two marinas north of the bridges offer fuel, water, and marine supplies (see region 2, pages 125–28). The drawbridge opens every half-hour, but unless you need marina facilities there is no need to negotiate the bridge.

Kirwan Creek offers a very nice anchorage within dinghy distance of the restaurants on the south side of the narrows. The entrance, however, must be very carefully negotiated. Start your approach about two-thirds of the way from the southern narrows channel entrance to the green "1" light near Hog Island. Then simply hold about 75 yards off Hog Island as you swing around it to enter Kirwan Creek. Anchor wherever you like, but stay out of the middle as there will be some local traffic here, some of it after dark.

Day 5: Kent Narrows–San Domingo Creek, Broad Creek, 28 nm.

If you draw less than 6 feet, you can use Knapps Narrows as a shortcut into the Choptank River (see region 3, pages 189–91). Then head for the entrance to Broad Creek. Swing to the east toward San Domingo Creek and give the first green marker a wide berth for the usual shoaling reasons. From there on you can anchor anywhere along the uninhabited Hambleton Islands or farther up the creek.

If you want to take advantage of the "back door" into St. Michaels, anchor near the head-

waters of San Domingo Creek and take your dinghy to the pier in the last little cove to the east. From there it's about a 1-mile walk to the center of town.

Day 6: San Domingo Creek–Oxford, Tred Avon River, 12 nm.

A cruise of the Choptank River is not complete without a visit to Oxford (see region 3, pages 192–95). Pull into Town Creek, where you can anchor, take a slip at one of the many marinas there or tie up at the Schooner Restaurant for a meal. Take a walk around the quaint little town to visit the shops and restaurants there. Although it is rapidly becoming a bit "touristy," it still is very much like going back in time to the mid-20th century.

When you have had your fill of the town, you may simply head across the Tred Avon River and anchor in Plaindealing Creek or the unnamed creek to its west. In fact, you could anchor there in the first place and take your dinghy across or ride the fascinating Oxford-Bellevue ferry to visit Oxford without entering Town Creek at all. There are many other anchorages off the Tred Avon River, but these are the most convenient if you want to visit Oxford.

Day 7: Oxford–Cambridge and La Trappe Creek, 12 + 6 nm.

Leaving Oxford, you can either head directly for the bucolic splendors of La Trappe Creek or go into Cambridge for a lunch stop, before partially retracing your path to La Trappe Creek for the night (see region 3, pages 199–200). At Cambridge you can either tie up in the Municipal Boat Basin, in the river a little short of the bridge, or you can head into Cambridge Creek. Inside the creek you can anchor in the basin where the creek widens. Alternatively, you can tie up at the sole restaurant by the edge of the water or at the gas station a bit beyond the restaurant. There is no good reason to remain here after your lunch stop and perhaps a bit of shopping, so head back out toward La Trappe Creek.

La Trappe Creek is one of the prettiest bodies of water in this area. The entrance is easy, and anchorages abound. The most popular anchorage is in the little basin to port immediately inside the entrance. Unfortunately, most of the shore is now posted with "No Trespassing" signs. No matter. If you want to land, simply head farther upstream and anchor anywhere that takes your fancy. It's all attractive and well protected.

In fact, a run upstream past the huge estates bordering the creek to near the headwaters at the Dickerson Boat Yard is a unique experience. The run through overhanging trees forming almost a tunnel on smooth, chocolate-colored water seems almost otherworldly. Try it.

Day 8: La Trappe Creek–Slaughter Creek, Little Choptank River, 20 nm.

From La Trappe Creek it's an easy run to the Little Choptank River, which is the best place to prepare for the run down the Bay to Solomons (see region 3, pages 201–3). Although most of the creeks off the Little Choptank provide attractive anchorages, Slaughter Creek offers anchoring in near-pristine surroundings and there's a little marina, just short of the bridge, if you need fuel or water or if you want to experience an Eastern Shore snack bar.

The entrance to this creek has been dredged and re-marked recently, providing a far easier entrance than that of only a few years ago. Even so, follow the markers carefully until you are well inside the entrance. Thereafter, there is plenty of water nearly from shore to shore, although it does shoal considerably along the sides of the creek. Anchor where you wish.

Day 9: Slaughter Creek–Solomons, 23 nm.

The run down the Bay to the yachting facilities of Solomons should be a pleasant one (see region 4, pages 253–56). Stay at least ½ mile off of Johns Island as you round it to enter the Bay. The water shoals a long way offshore.

Consider stopping by the part of the Calvert Cliffs just at the entrance to the Patuxent River before returning to Solomons. In mild weather you can anchor within 100 yards of the beach, then land to search for fossils that continuously fall from the cliffs. It's a bad day when someone in your party cannot at least find some fossil shark teeth.

SIXTEEN-DAY CRUISE (chart p. 73)

Day 1: Solomons Island, Patuxent River–Crisfield, 40 nm.

The run from Solomons to Crisfield is a fairly lengthy one (see region 4, pages 242–43). The navigation is easy, but be sure to check the weather before departing since you'll be in the open Bay for quite a while.

Crisfield is one of the bright spots on the Eastern Shore in this area. There is some room to anchor by the Coast Guard station in Somers Cove, but we highly recommend taking a slip at the excellent Somers Cove Marina. In addition to other marina amenities, it has a good restaurant and a nice swimming pool, a welcome item in hot weather, when the sea nettles are in. It is only a short walk to town, where you will find shops, restaurants, and ferries to Smith and Tangier Islands. Plan a layover day to take full advantage of this location.

Day 2: Layover at Crisfield, visit Smith Island by ferry.

We highly recommend a visit to Smith Island or Tangier Island while you are in this area. Although you can easily take your own boat to either island, you may find some difficulty finding a place to tie up. If only for that reason, lay over in Crisfield and visit the islands via one of the ferries that depart from the docks at Crisfield.

This way, you can have a no-hassle visit to the islands and return to the amenities of the town and marina knowing that your boat has been safe and secure the entire time.

Day 3: Crisfield–Piankatank River, 40 nm.

This is another longish run, although somewhat shorter than the indicated 40 miles, depending upon where in the Piankatank you choose to stop (see region 6, pages 322–27). The Piankatank offers a range of options. There are plenty of full-service marinas in Jackson Creek, Milford Haven, and Fishing Bay, if that's what you are looking for.

Virtually everywhere on the tributaries of the Piankatank are excellent, quiet anchorages with protection ranging from the hurricane hole of Wilton Creek to the open, hot-weather anchorage in Fishing Bay. I think that the Piankatank epitomizes some of the prime reasons we go cruising.

SUGGESTED CRUISES

Central Bay Sixteen-Day Cruise

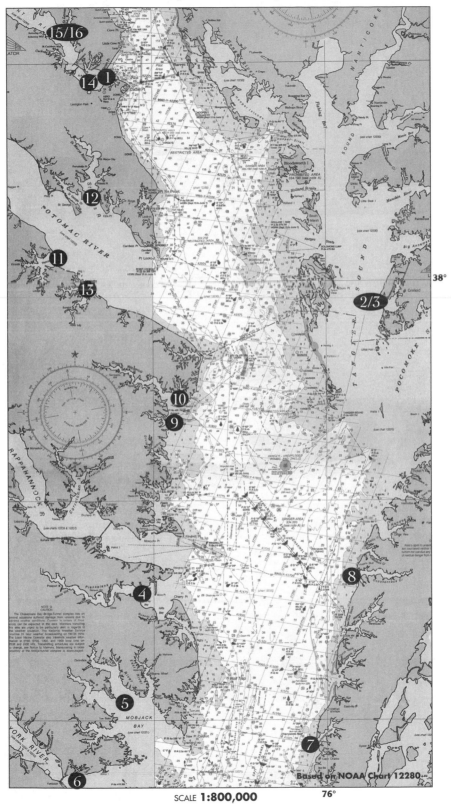

SCALE **1:800,000**

Day 4: Piankatank River–Mobjack Bay, 35 nm.
I hesitated before selecting Mobjack Bay as a destination for this leg. It's great if you are looking for secluded anchorages, but if you want to visit the Yorktown area, it may be wiser to bypass Mobjack Bay and head directly for Sarah Creek in the York River, planning to lay over the next day.

The rivers and creeks off Mobjack Bay offer numerous attractive anchorages, and some even offer limited marina facilities, notably fuel and water. The Severn River probably offers the nicest set of anchorages, especially for the first-time visitor. (See region 7, pages 335–41.)

Day 5: Mobjack Bay–Sarah Creek, York River, 20 nm.
Together with the James River, the York River forms one of the borders of the famous Gloucester Peninsula, where you will find the historic towns of Yorktown, Williamsburg, and Jamestown, not to mention Newport News at its tip (see region 7, pages 344–45). In Yorktown there is an information center where you can arrange for tours of Yorktown, as well as more extensive excursions to Jamestown and Williamsburg.

There is no place to tie up in Yorktown. However, in good weather it is possible to anchor for the day just above the bridge, near the Waterman's Museum, and land on the beach downstream of the museum to visit Yorktown.

A better bet is to put in to Sarah Creek, across the York River from Yorktown, and anchor or take a slip at one of the marinas there. You can then either walk the 2 miles across the bridge to visit Yorktown or arrange for transportation at one of the marinas to visit Yorktown, Williamsburg, or Jamestown.

Day 6: Sarah Creek–Cherrystone Inlet, 30 nm.
Almost directly across the Chesapeake from the York River lies the triad of Cape Charles Harbor, Kings Creek, and Cherrystone Inlet, all of which share the same entrance (see region 7, pages 330–32). Marina facilities are available in both Cape Charles Harbor and Kings Creek. For a quiet, beautiful anchorage go to Cherrystone Inlet.

A glance at the chart may give you a little pause, as there are few navigation buoys in Cherrystone Inlet. However, negotiating the entrance and finding a good place to anchor is quite easy. Should you err, the bottom is soft and forgiving. This is also the location of the Cherrystone Aqua Farms, which you can probably visit if you ask nicely.

Day 7: Cherrystone Inlet–Onancock Creek, 35 nm.
The town of Onancock lies up a long and winding channel from the Bay (see region 6, pages 305–6). This is a pretty little Eastern Shore town that we have enjoyed visiting several times. It's like stepping back in time to about the mid-20th century. The Town Dock, near the Hopkins Brothers Store, offers free dockage for a couple of hours and a reasonable fee for tying up overnight.

Just a short distance downstream, in sight of the Town Dock, is a nice, well-protected anchorage in good holding. There's little traffic, and you will find it peaceful.

Day 8: Onancock Creek–Mill Creek (Great Wicomico River), 35 nm.
Straight across the Bay from Onancock Creek is the mouth of the Great Wicomico River, which has many attractive anchorages (see region 6, page 313). One of the prettiest of these lies in Mill Creek, immediately to the south of the main entrance. You may sight a pod of dolphin as you enter the Great Wicomico.

Mill Creek offers miles of river cruising through mostly wooded terrain with only a few houses in sight. You may anchor anywhere here, but the best anchorage is near the mouth of the creek, where it makes its first sharp bend to the west. You can anchor off a beach of white sand in good holding with a nice breeze while fully protected from waves.

Day 9: Mill Creek–Cockrell Creek (Great Wicomico River), 5 nm.
A short run out of Mill Creek and across the entrance to the Great Wicomico will take you into Cockrell Creek (see region 6, pages 309–11). Here you will probably pass a pod of dolphin that seem to have taken up a semi-residence.

Anchor in either fork of the creek. The left (west) fork is a more attractive anchorage, but the east fork provides access to a marina with fuel, water, and a restaurant, as well as to the town of Reedville. You can land at the Reedville

SUGGESTED CRUISES

Marine Railway to start your tour. Visiting Reedville, a town included in the Virginia Historic Register, is like taking a trip back in time. The only street in town is lined with homes from the end of the 19th century, the oldest dating to 1875. Partway down the street is a monument to Elijah W. Reed, the town's founder. The Reedville Fisherman's Museum is located on Main Street, about ½ mile inland of the Reedville Marine Railway. The town also has a couple of very good restaurants.

Day 10: Cockrell Creek–Yeocomico River (Potomac River), 38 nm.
Swing around Smith Point Lighthouse and maintain about that distance offshore until you are well into the Potomac River to avoid the shoal that extends a long way out from Smith Point (see region 5, pages 273–74). Proceeding up the Potomac, it would be prudent to remain almost as far out until you can pick up the buoy at the entrance to the Yeocomico River.

There are three forks to the Yeocomico, and all three have marina facilities. It's a case of personal preference which fork you enter. We have always preferred the middle branch (West Yeocomico River) for two reasons: there are several sandy beaches where you can land, and the restaurant at the Port Kinsale Marina, just inside the branch entrance, is one of our favorites.

Day 11: Yeocomico River–St. Marys River, 15 nm.
Across the Potomac from the Yeocomico River is the beautiful St. Marys River (see region 5, pages 267–72). There is only one marina on this river, in Carthagena Creek. If you don't need fuel, water, or ice, continue up the main river to St. Marys City to anchor either in the bight where you can usually see the reproduction of the *Dove*, which brought the first colonists to Maryland in 1634, or past Church Point and the docks of St. Marys College. You may tie up at the college docks for a while, but the college would prefer that you not remain there overnight.

While there, don't miss a visit to Historic St. Marys City, where costumed players act the part of the seventeenth-century colonists among reproductions of the buildings of that era. You can also tour the *Dove*.

Day 12: St. Marys River–Coan River (Potomac River), 15 nm.

Back across the Potomac are the three branches of the Coan River (see region 5, pages 272–73). This is really waterman's country, but there is one marina in Kingscote Creek where you can get fuel, water, ice, and possibly a slip. Otherwise, pick your spot in any of the branches for a lovely and serene anchorage, well protected from wind and wave.

Day 13: Coan River–Mill Creek (Patuxent River), 35 nm.
Following your run up the Bay and into the Patuxent River, continue past the Governor Johnson Bridge to your chosen anchorage in Mill Creek (see region 4, pages 257–58). (Note: this is not the Mill Creek in Solomons Harbor.) Mill Creek and Cuckold Creek share a common entrance.

As you pass between the two points at the entrance, Cuckold Creek bears off to the right, and Mill Creek to the left. The former is almost fully developed, and its shore is lined with private homes. Mill Creek is more open, and there are interesting cliffs on the north side. Unfortunately, a water-skiing course is frequently set up in this vicinity, marked by a string of buoys. You may want to anchor some distance from this if it is active.

Day 14: Mill Creek–St. Leonard Creek, with a visit to Sotterly Plantation, 5 nm.
Once you enter St. Leonard Creek, you can anchor just about anywhere that strikes your fancy (see region 4, pages 258–61). Coves and small bights abound, most of them quiet and protected. Should you need fuel or want to try a unique restaurant, head upstream to the intersection of Johns and St. Leonard Creeks. Here you will find Vera's White Sands Marina and Restaurant, which promises a unique experience.

On your way to St. Leonard Creek, by all means visit Sotterly Plantation, which lies directly across the Patuxent River from the mouth of St. Leonard Creek. You will see a pier in front of a small white shed. To the right (north) of this pier is the entrance to a small basin where you can tie up your boat and walk up the dirt road lined with raspberry bushes to visit the plantation. You can take a guided tour, visit the gift shop, or simply wander around on your own. By all means pay it a visit.

Day 15: Layover in St. Leonard Creek.

By now you may want to take a day to simply kick back and relax (see region 4, pages 258–60). Otherwise you may want to explore some of the upper reaches of the Patuxent River, including Island or Battle Creeks, or to explore the Patuxent River as far upstream as the bridge. Perhaps just taking a run out to enjoy going nowhere in particular before returning to anchor in St. Leonard Creek will seem appealing.

After all the running around you have done on this cruise, this "leg" provides a built-in contingency day in case of a delay somewhere along the route due to inclement weather or simply some "down time" to invest in the hard job of doing nothing.

Day 16: St. Leonard Creek–Solomons Island, 10 nm.

Because the run back to Solomons from St. Leonard Creek is short (see region 4, pages 253–56), in decent weather you may want to continue past Solomons to visit the section of Calvert Cliffs on the north side of the mouth of the Patuxent. You can anchor within 100 yards of the beach. Stroll along the beach at the base of the cliffs and try your luck at finding fossils that have tumbled down from the eroding cliffs. It's a bad day if someone in your party doesn't find some shark teeth at the very least.

The run back to Solomons harbor is not only short but easy. Here you will find just about any facility, from marinas and restaurants to the fascinating Calvert Marine Museum. Be sure not to miss the museum.

* * * * * *

SOUTHERN CHESAPEAKE BAY

In the southern Chesapeake Bay, nearly all of the harbors are on the Western Shore or up the major rivers in the area. There are, of course, a couple of notable exceptions that can easily be included in a cruise. All of the legs between harbors are relatively short; however, you may elect to make some long legs by skipping harbors.

If you remain on the Western Shore, you will always be close to a secure harbor in the event of sudden inclement weather, much like in the northern Bay area. Of course, cruising from the Norfolk area for a longer period of time will allow you to include several of the harbors mentioned in the sixteen-day cruise suggested for the central Bay. For that reason, you may find some overlap between the points of

call mentioned here and those mentioned in the itinerary for that cruise.

The assumption here is that you are most likely to begin a cruise from the Hampton Roads or Norfolk vicinity. I chose the Hampton Roads area as the point of origin because this is the only major yachting center in the southern Bay, with Norfolk on the southern side of the James River mouth and Hampton on the northern side. Once again, you can pick up the suggested one- and two-week cruises at any point and complete the loop with equal facility from just about any point in it. You may note some redundancy in the suggested harbors within a single cruise. The reason for that is simply to keep what would otherwise be a rather long leg to a more reasonable distance for laid-back cruising.

THREE-DAY CRUISE (chart p. 77)

Day 1: Hampton Roads–Cherrystone Inlet, 30 nm.

Almost directly across the Chesapeake from the York River lies the triad of Cape Charles Harbor, Kings Creek, and Cherrystone Inlet, all of which share the same entrance (see region 7, pages 330–32). Marina facilities are

available in both Cape Charles Harbor and Kings Creek, but for a quiet, beautiful anchorage go to Cherrystone Inlet.

A glance at the chart may give you a little pause as there are few navigation buoys in Cherrystone Inlet. However, negotiating the entrance and finding a good place to anchor is quite easy. Should you err, the bottom is soft

Southern Bay Three-Day Cruise

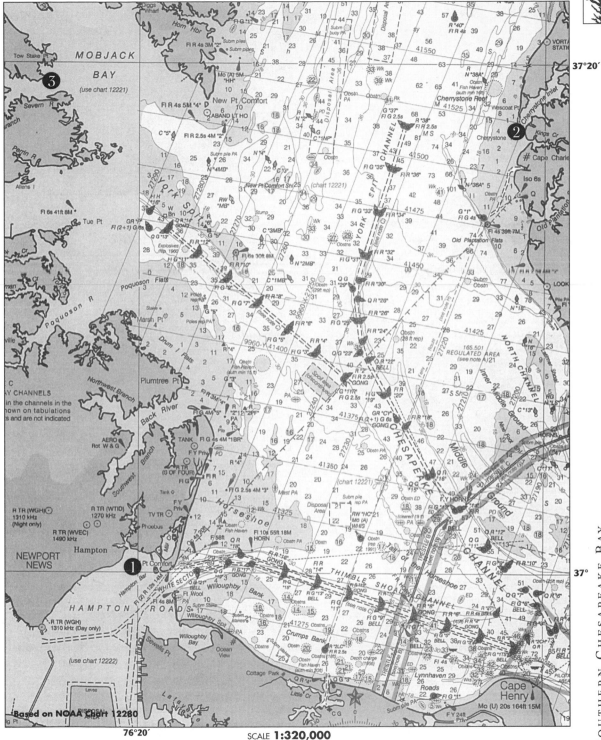

SCALE **1:320,000**

Based on NOAA Chart 12280

and forgiving. This is also the location of the Cherrystone Aqua Farms, which you can probably visit if you ask nicely.

Day 2: Cherrystone Inlet–Mobjack Bay, 30 nm.

The rivers and creeks off Mobjack Bay offer numerous attractive anchorages, and some even offer limited marina facilities, notably fuel and water (see region 7, pages 335–41). The Severn River probably offers the nicest set of anchorages, especially for the first-time visitor.

If you are looking for a full set of marina facilities, you may want to bypass Mobjack Bay entirely and put in to Sarah Creek in the York River. The distance from Cherrystone Inlet to Sarah Creek is just about the same as to Mobjack Bay harbors and possibly a little shorter.

Day 3: Mobjack Bay–Hampton Roads, 35 nm.

As you head out of the York River, follow the marked channel at least until you have passed the mouth of the Poquoson River (see region 7, pages 352–54). Thereafter, remain at least 2 miles offshore to stay clear of the shoal that extends almost that far. Continue to stay that distance from shore until you can turn and head into Hampton Roads at about the level of Salt Ponds.

From there on, navigation is easy. All you have to worry about is avoiding the shipping traffic as you return to your starting point.

NINE-DAY CRUISE (chart p. 79)

Day 1: Hampton Roads – Sarah Creek, York River, 35 nm.

As you depart Hampton Roads, set a course that will take you about 2 miles offshore by the time you pass Salt Ponds. Hold that distance until you pick up the marked channel into the York River. (See region 7, pages 344–45.)

Together with the James River, the York River forms one of the borders of the famous Gloucester Peninsula, where you will find the historic towns of Yorktown, Williamsburg, and Jamestown, not to mention Newport News at its tip. In Yorktown there is an information center where you can arrange for tours of Yorktown, as well as more extensive excursions to Jamestown and Williamsburg.

There is no place to tie up in Yorktown. However, in good weather it is possible to anchor for the day just above the bridge near the Waterman's Museum and land on the beach downstream of the museum to visit Yorktown.

A better bet is to enter Sarah Creek, across the York River from Yorktown, and anchor or take a slip at one of the marinas there. You can then either walk the 2 miles across the bridge to visit Yorktown or arrange for transportation at one of the marinas to visit Yorktown, Williamsburg, or Jamestown.

Day 2: Sarah Creek–Horn Harbor, 20 nm.

This is not the same Horn Harbor as the snug little hurricane hole near the headwaters of the Great Wicomico River. This Horn Harbor is about 3 miles north of New Point Comfort, on the north side of the entrance to Mobjack Bay. (See region 7, pages 334–35.)

Once you pass the red "4" daymark, you can anchor nearly anywhere in the creek or continue on past the next two bends to visit Horn Harbor Marina, where you will find gas, diesel fuel, ice, and some limited hardware (mostly for powerboats). Shortly beyond the marina the water quickly thins. Near the marina is a good place to anchor in a blow.

This is not the greatest harbor around. It is included as a stopover simply to break up what would otherwise be a rather long leg.

Day 3: Horn Harbor–Piankatank River, 25 nm.

The Piankatank is another area that offers a range of options (see region 6, pages 322–27). There are a number of full-service marinas in Jackson Creek, Milford Haven, and Fishing Bay.

Virtually everywhere on the tributaries of the Piankatank there are excellent, quiet anchorages with protection, ranging from the hurricane hole of Wilton Creek to the open, hot-weather anchorage in Fishing Bay. I think that the Piankatank epitomizes some of the prime reasons we go cruising.

Day 4: Piankatank River–Corrotoman River (Rappahannock River), 30 nm.

About 3 miles past the Rappahannock River bridge, the Corrotoman River offers peaceful

SUGGESTED CRUISES

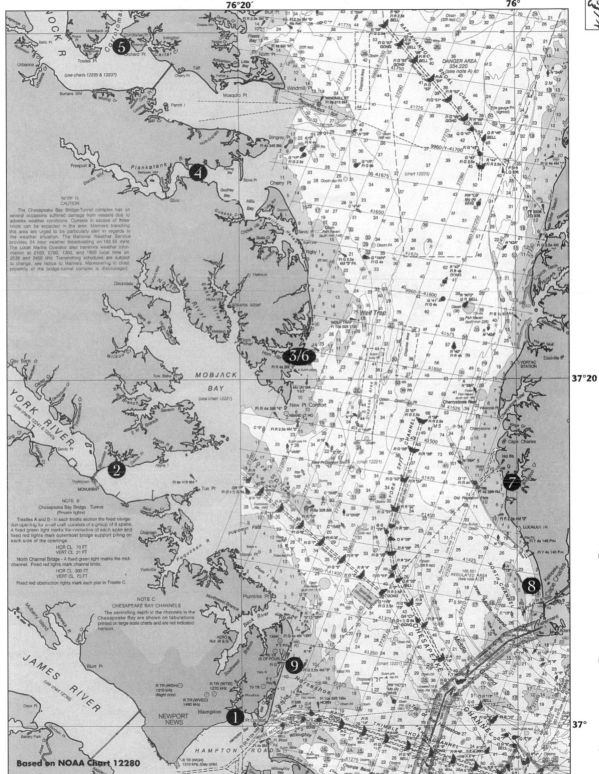

Based on NOAA Chart 12280

SCALE **1:566,666**

SOUTHERN CHESAPEAKE BAY

cruising grounds where you easily could spend several days exploring or simply enjoying its relatively unspoiled, thickly wooded shoreline. Poke around all parts of the Corrotoman to take in the scenery. The few protruding shoals are well marked. (See region 6, pages 318–19.)

Myer Creek lays claim to having the only marina on the Corrotoman River, Yankee Point Sailboat Marina, just inside the north fork of the creek. The marina has some limited marine supplies and a dockside sewage pumpout facility for holding tanks. At the marina you should be able to arrange for transportation to a nearby store for other supplies.

Day 5: Corrotoman River–Horn Harbor, 35 nm.
Unless you count the extremely narrow, shallow, and twisting entrance to Winter Harbor (which nearly all sizable cruising boats should avoid) a couple of miles to its north, Horn Harbor is the first acceptable harbor in a long stretch of the Western Shore of the Chesapeake as you head south from the vicinity of the Piankatank (see region 7, pages 334–35). For that reason, Horn Harbor appears twice in this suggested cruise itinerary even though it is not exactly a four-star harbor.

The only alternatives are to continue another 15 miles to Sarah Creek, to one of the anchorages off Mobjack Bay, or to make the long run across the Bay to Kings Creek or Cherrystone Inlet.

Day 6: Horn Harbor–Cherrystone Inlet, 20 nm.
Almost directly across the Chesapeake from the York River lies the triad of Cape Charles Harbor, Kings Creek, and Cherrystone Inlet, all of which share the same entrance (see region 7, pages 330–32). Marina facilities are available in both Cape Charles Harbor and Kings Creek, but for a quiet, beautiful anchorage go to Cherrystone Inlet.

A glance at the chart may give you pause as there are few navigation buoys in Cherrystone Inlet. However, negotiating the entrance and finding a good place to anchor is quite easy. Should you err, the bottom is soft and forgiving. This is also the location of the Cherrystone Aqua Farms, which you can probably visit if you ask nicely.

Day 7: Cherrystone Inlet–Kiptopeke, 10 nm.
A sail across the Bay to the Eastern Shore

a little north of the northern terminus of the Chesapeake Bay Bridge-Tunnel leads to Kiptopeke (see region 7, pages 332–33). Kiptopeke was the terminal used by the Cape Charles ferry until the Chesapeake Bay Bridge-Tunnel replaced it. The old ferry slip is protected by a breakwater constructed by sinking nine World War II–surplus ferrocement ships between the slip and the Bay. You really should see this at least once.

Kiptopeke is now a Virginia State Park, complete with a boat-launching ramp and a fishing pier. You will have to land by dinghy, but fresh water and showers are available. This unique anchorage is quite popular with many cruisers from the Hampton Roads area.

Day 8: Kiptopeke–Salt Ponds, 15 nm.
It is a straight run across the Bay to Salt Ponds (see region 7, page 352). The entrance to Salt Ponds is through a mile-long, well-marked channel into the basin, where a sharp turn to the south will take you to the excellent Salt Ponds Marina. There is room for a few boats to anchor at the south end of the basin, but taking a slip here will be a pleasant experience. The marina offers floating docks, a pool, a restaurant, a great beach, and a great view of the Bay, on the other side of the basin.

A canal to the west leads to a residential community. Don't enter the canal, and don't anchor where you might block the entrance.

Day 9: Salt Ponds–Hampton Roads, 15 nm.
On exiting Salt Ponds, follow the marked channel all the way to the end, about a mile, before turning south and heading for the entrance to Hampton Roads (see region 7, pages 352–54).

Once you are in Hampton Roads, navigation is easy, except for dodging shipping traffic, as you return to your point of origin.

SIXTEEN-DAY CRUISE (chart p. 81)

Day 1: Hampton Roads–Kiptopeke, 25 nm.
A sail across the Bay to the Eastern Shore a little north of the northern terminus of the Chesapeake Bay Bridge-Tunnel leads to Kiptopeke (see region 7, pages 332–33). Kiptopeke was the terminal used by the Cape Charles

Southern Bay Sixteen-Day Cruise

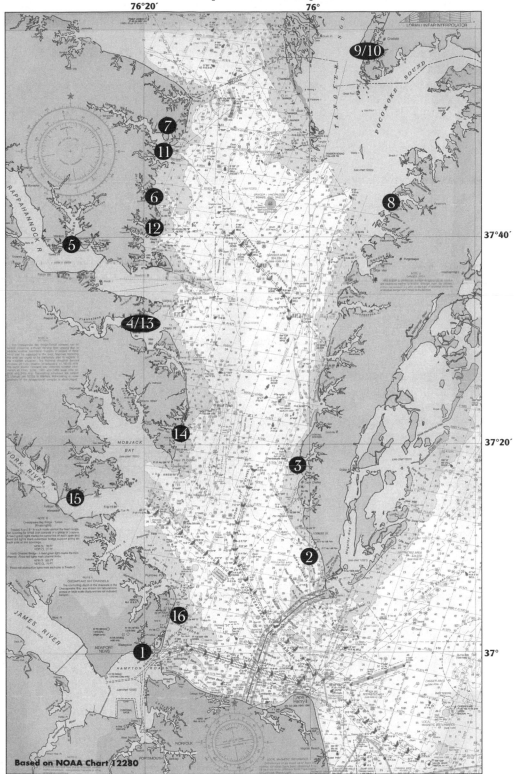

76°20′

76°

37°40′

37°20′

37°

Based on NOAA Chart 12280

SCALE **1:971,428**

ferry until the Chesapeake Bay Bridge-Tunnel replaced it. The old ferry slip is protected by a breakwater constructed by sinking nine World War II–surplus ferrocement ships between the slip and the Bay.

Kiptopeke is now a Virginia State Park, complete with a boat-launching ramp and a fishing pier. You will have to land by dinghy, but fresh water and showers are available. This unique anchorage is quite popular with many cruisers from the Hampton Roads area.

Day 2: Kiptopeke–Cherrystone Inlet, 10 nm.

A short run northward along the Eastern Shore leads to the triad of Cape Charles Harbor, Kings Creek, and Cherrystone Inlet, all of which share the same entrance (see region 7, pages 330–32). Marina facilities are available in both Cape Charles Harbor and Kings Creek. For a quiet, beautiful anchorage, go to Cherrystone Inlet.

A glance at the chart may give you pause, as there are few navigation buoys in Cherrystone Inlet. However, negotiating the entrance and finding a good place to anchor is quite easy. Should you err, the bottom is soft and forgiving. This is also the location of the Cherrystone Aqua Farms, which you can probably visit if you ask nicely.

Day 3: Cherrystone Inlet–Piankatank River, 35 nm.

The Piankatank offers a range of options (see region 6, pages 322–27). There are many full-service marinas in Jackson Creek, Milford Haven, and Fishing Bay.

Virtually everywhere on the tributaries of the Piankatank there are excellent, quiet anchorages with protection, ranging from the hurricane hole of Wilton Creek to the open, hot-weather anchorage in Fishing Bay. I think that the Piankatank epitomizes some of the prime reasons we go cruising.

Day 4: Piankatank River–Corrotoman River, Rappahannock River, 30 nm.

About 3 miles past the Rappahannock River bridge, the Corrotoman River offers peaceful cruising grounds where you easily could spend several days exploring or simply enjoying its relatively unspoiled and thickly wooded shoreline (see region 6, pages 318–19). Poke around all

parts of the Corrotoman to take in the scenery. The few protruding shoals are well marked.

Myer Creek lays claim to having the only marina on the Corrotoman River, Yankee Point Sailboat Marina, just inside the north fork of the creek. In addition to fuel and water, the marina has some limited marine supplies and a dockside sewage pumpout facility for holding tanks. At the marina you should be able to arrange for transportation to a nearby store for other supplies.

Day 5: Corrotoman River–Dividing Creek, 30 nm.

Although exposed to the southeast for most of its length, Dividing Creek offers some secure anchorages in its tributaries (see region 6, page 313). There are no facilities here, so most of the people you encounter will be locals or cruisers looking for an out-of-the-way anchorage.

The approach is easy. Simply pick up the first marker, a lighted green "3" (there is no "1" marker), and follow the markers to the northwest into the mouth of the creek. Beware of the unmarked shoals off Kent Point and the point north of Prentice Creek. See page 313 for multiple anchorages on this creek.

Day 6: Dividing Creek–Cockrell Creek (Great Wicomico River), 15 nm.

As you enter the Great Wicomico River, you probably will see at least some of the dolphins that are semi-resident there (see region 6, pages 309–11). Immediately, you will have to decide where to go to spend the night. To the south is Mill Creek and relative solitude. To the north is Cockrell Creek with the town of Reedville and its marinas and restaurants. To the west is the rest of the Great Wicomico with numerous creeks and anchorages, including the hurricane hole of Horn Harbor and, just short of the bridge, another marina.

Since Mill Creek is suggested as the destination following Crisfield on this cruise, I suggest that you enter Cockrell Creek. Anchor in the west fork for the night, but visit the east fork if you need marina facilities or want to land at the Reedville Marine Railway to visit Reedville, with its restaurants and the interesting Fisherman's Museum.

Day 7: Great Wicomico River–Onancock Creek, 30 nm. The town of Onancock lies up a long and winding channel from the Bay (see region 6, pages 305–6). This is a pretty little Eastern Shore town that we have enjoyed visiting several times. It's like a step back in time to about the mid-20th century. The Town Dock, near the Hopkins Brothers Store, offers free dockage for a couple of hours and a reasonable fee for tying up overnight.

Just a short distance downstream is a nice, well-protected anchorage in good holding in sight of the Town Dock. There's little traffic, and you will find it peaceful.

Day 8: Onancock Creek–Crisfield, 23 nm. Crisfield is one of the bright spots on the Eastern Shore in this area (see region 4, pages 242–43). Although there is some room to anchor by the Coast Guard station in Somers Cove, we highly recommend taking a slip at the excellent Somers Cove Marina. In addition to the other marina amenities, it has a good restaurant and a nice swimming pool, a welcome item in hot weather, when the sea nettles are in.

It is only a short walk to town with its shops, restaurants, and ferries to Smith and Tangier Islands. Plan a layover to take advantage of the amenities of this area.

Day 9: Layover at Crisfield, visit to Smith or Tangier Island by ferry. We recommend a visit to Smith or Tangier Island while you are in the area (see region 4, pages 243–49). Although you can easily take your own boat to either island, you may have some difficulty finding a place to tie up there. If only for that reason, I recommend a layover in Crisfield and a visit to the islands on one of the ferries that depart from the docks at Crisfield.

After a no-hassle visit to the island(s), you will return to your safe, secure boat with time to enjoy the amenities of the town or the marina.

Day 10: Crisfield–Mill Creek, Great Wicomico River, 30 nm. Immediately after entering the mouth of the Great Wicomico River, swing to the south to enter Mill Creek (see region 6, page 313). There are no marine facilities anywhere on this creek, but by now you are probably interested in a little solitude.

This is perhaps one of the prettiest bodies of water in the area. Mill Creek offers miles of river cruising through mostly wooded terrain with only a few houses in sight. Although you may anchor anywhere here, the best anchorage is near the mouth of the creek, where it makes its first sharp bend to the west. Here you can anchor off a beach of white sand in good holding ground with a nice breeze while fully protected from waves.

Day 11: Great Wicomico River–Indian Creek, 15 nm. Like Dividing Creek, Indian Creek is easily entered (see region 6, page 314). It is also exposed to the southeast for more than two-thirds of its length, and anchorages are to be found only in tributaries and in the last third of the main creek. Indian Creek has some excellent marine facilities and is much more built up than Dividing Creek. Even so, Indian Creek is pretty cruising ground.

The small marina at Kilmarnock Wharf is nicely laid out and has some transient slips, ice, gas, and diesel fuel. The marina also has a small marine store. There is also a gift shop. The town of Kilmarnock lies about 2 miles down Wharf Road from the marina. Transportation to town can usually be arranged at the marina.

Day 12: Indian Creek–Piankatank River, 20 nm. While this is the second visit to this area on this cruise, the Piankatank offers a considerable range of options (see region 6, pages 322–27). Just pick a different location than on your previous visit, and it will be brand new.

There are plenty of marinas in Jackson Creek, Milford Haven, and Fishing Bay. Virtually everywhere on the tributaries of the Piankatank you can find excellent, quiet anchorages with protection ranging from the hurricane hole of Wilton Creek to the open, hot-weather anchorage in Fishing Bay. I think that the Piankatank epitomizes some of the prime reasons we go cruising.

Day 13: Piankatank River–Horn Harbor, 20 nm. Unless you count the extremely narrow, shallow, and twisting entrance to Winter Harbor (which nearly all sizable cruising boats should avoid) a couple of miles to its north, Horn Harbor is the first acceptable har-

83

bor in a long stretch of the Western Shore of the Chesapeake as you head south from the vicinity of the Piankatank (see region 7, pages 334–35). The only alternative is to continue another 15 miles to Sarah Creek, to one of the anchorages off Mobjack Bay, or to make the long run across the Bay to Kings Creek or Cherrystone Inlet.

This is not the same Horn Harbor as the snug little hurricane hole near the headwaters of the Great Wicomico River. This Horn Harbor is about 3 miles north of New Point Comfort, on the north side of the entrance to Mobjack Bay.

Once you pass the red "4" daymark, you can anchor nearly anywhere in the creek or continue on past the next two bends to visit Horn Harbor Marina, where you will find gas, diesel fuel, ice, and some limited hardware (mostly for powerboats). Shortly beyond the marina the water quickly thins. Near the marina is a good place to anchor in a blow.

Day 14: Horn Harbor–Sarah Creek, York River, 20 nm.

Together with the James River, the York River forms one of the borders of the famous Gloucester Peninsula, where you will find the historic towns of Yorktown, Williamsburg, and Jamestown, not to mention Newport News at its tip (see region 7, pages 344–45). In Yorktown there is an information center where you can arrange for tours of Yorktown, as well as more extensive excursions to Jamestown and Williamsburg.

There is no place to tie up in Yorktown, but in good weather it is possible to anchor for the day just above the bridge near the Waterman's Museum and land on the beach downstream of the museum to visit Yorktown.

A better bet is to enter Sarah Creek, across the York River from Yorktown, and anchor or take a slip at one of the marinas there. You can then either walk the 2 miles across the bridge to visit Yorktown or arrange for transportation at one of the marinas to visit Yorktown, Williamsburg, or Jamestown.

Day 15: Sarah Creek–Salt Ponds (marina reservation recommended), 25 nm.

The entrance to Salt Ponds is through a mile-long, well-marked channel into the basin, where a sharp turn to the south will take you to the excellent Salt Ponds Marina (see region 7, page 352). There is some room for a few boats to anchor in the south end of the basin, but taking a slip here will be a pleasant experience. The marina offers floating docks, a pool, a restaurant, a great beach, and a great view of the Bay, on the other side of the basin.

A canal to the west leads to a residential community. Don't enter the canal, and certainly don't anchor where you might block the entrance.

Day 16: Salt Ponds–Hampton Roads, 10 nm.

On exiting Salt Ponds, follow the marked channel all the way to the end, about a mile, before turning south and heading for the entrance to Hampton Roads (see region 7, pages 352–54).

Once you are in Hampton Roads, navigation is easy, except for dodging shipping traffic, as you return to your point of origin.

Region 1

HEAD OF BAY TO POOLES ISLAND

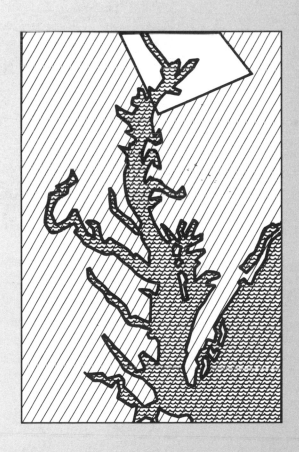

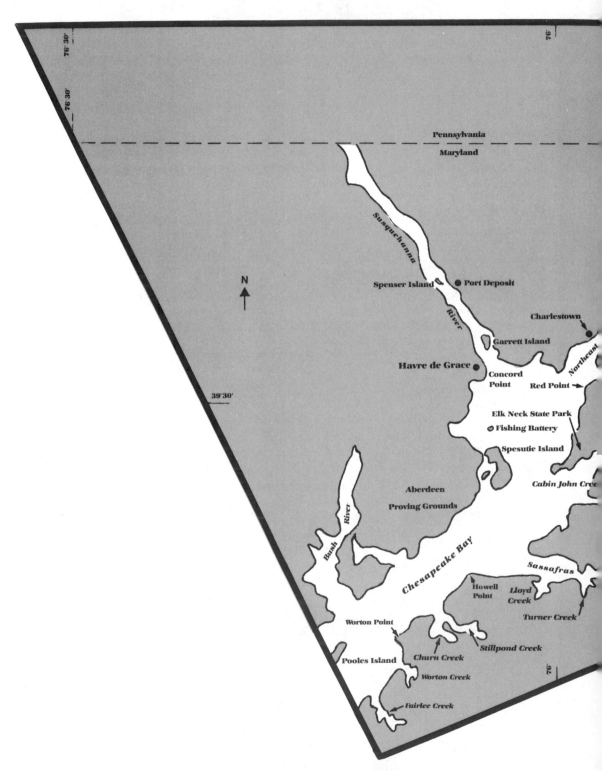

76° 30'

76°

76° 30'

Pennsylvania

Maryland

Susquehanna

N

Spenser Island • Port Deposit

River

Charlestown

Garrett Island

Havre de Grace •

Northeast

Concord
Point

Red Point

39° 30'

Elk Neck State Park

Fishing Battery

Spesutie Island

Cabin John Creek

Aberdeen
Proving Grounds

Sassafras

Bush River

Chesapeake Bay

Howell
Point

*Lloyd
Creek*

Worton Point

Turner Creek

Pooles Island

Churn Creek

Stillpond Creek

Worton Creek

76°

Fairlee Creek

SCALE **1**″ = **5.7** NAUT. MILES

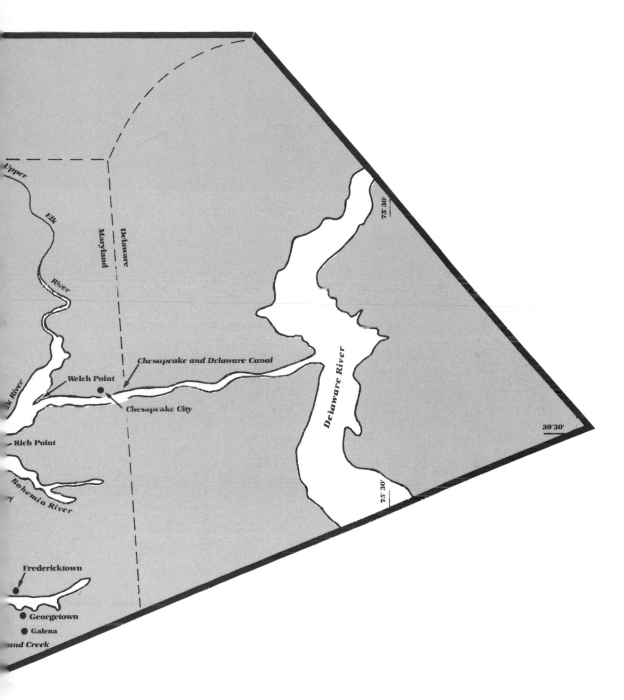

Region 1

Upper

Elk

River

Maryland

Delaware

Chesapeake and Delaware Canal

Welch Point

Chesapeake City

Rich Point

Bohemia River

Fredericktown

Georgetown

Galena

and Creek

Delaware River

75°30'

39°30'

75°30'

HEAD OF BAY TO POOLES ISLAND

THE EXTREME NORTHERN part of the Chesapeake Bay is more closely akin to a large freshwater river than to a tidal estuary. The water in the upper Bay is only lightly brackish, and as you proceed up most of the tributaries it becomes fresh. Crabs and oysters are relatively rare, and sea nettles seldom, if ever, penetrate. The area is scenic and thinly settled, at least in comparison with areas near Baltimore, farther south.

Like the tines of a pitchfork, the head of the Bay is split into four forks by the Susquehanna, Northeast, Elk, and Sassafras Rivers. The Bohemia River and the Chesapeake and Delaware Canal—or C&D Canal—form additional forks off the Elk River. All offer secure and interesting harbors to the visiting yachtsman, with all the facilities needed for resupply or repairs. Farther to the south, Pooles Island and Worton and Fairlee Creeks form a transition area where the water changes from the nearly fresh water of the head of the Bay to the more brackish waters of the main part of the northern Bay.

Most of the Western Shore, between the Susquehanna River and Pooles Island, is a restricted area belonging to the Aberdeen Proving Grounds. Landing there is strictly prohibited at all times; this includes swimming or touching the bottom, shore, or a pier. The entire restricted area is closed Monday through Friday from 7:30 A.M. to 5:00 P.M., except on national holidays. Additional closed times are announced over broadcast and VHF-FM radios. When actual firing is in progress on the range, patrol boats warn the unwary out of the area. When the area is open, boats may navigate through it, fishing or crabbing is allowed, and water-skiing is permitted up to within 200 meters (220 yards) of the shore. For specific information, call 410-278-2250, VHF-FM Radio channel 16, or CB channel 12. A detailed map is also available from APG Public Affairs, Aberdeen Proving Grounds, MD 21005.

As a direct result of the above, the approximately 15 miles of Western Shore associated with the proving grounds, except for the U.S. Army Ordnance Museum on the main part of the post, is not discussed in detail here.

EASTERN SHORE

ELK RIVER

Charts: 12273, **12274**

Many consider Turkey Point, at the mouth of the Elk River, to be the true "top of the Bay." Near here, the Elk, Sassafras, Susquehanna, and Northeast Rivers all join forces with the Bay. The Elk River itself offers little of direct interest to the cruiser except for a few potential day stops along Elk Neck State Park. In colonial times there was a major port at the headwaters that was burned out by the British forces during the War of 1812. Now it is silted in and pretty much forgotten, save for a mark on the charts showing Old Frenchtown Wharf. The Elk River connects the C&D Canal and the Bohemia River with the rest of the Bay. How-

ever, there are still quite a few harbors and points of interest worth mentioning here.

Cabin John Creek

  No facilities

Charts: 12273, **12274**

Approaches. Less than 2 miles up the Elk River from Turkey Point, Cabin John Creek lies on the east shore. Although a little shallow (5 feet mean low water [MLW]), this creek is a popular anchorage with shallow-draft vessels for swimming and a convenient "duck-in" shelter for some occasions. Unfortunately, you cannot proceed very far into the creek, and it is exposed to the northwest, the most common direction for a "blow." Not unexpectedly, there are no moorings or marine facilities. A good beach on the south side of the creek lends itself to swimming, wading, and beachcombing.

Anchorage. Except right in the mouth of the creek, there is little room to anchor because the water shoals rather quickly as you proceed into the creek. You can anchor in at least 5 feet of water within about ¼ mile from the entrance, but watch your depth carefully as the shoaling tends to increase each year.

Elk Neck State Park

  No facilities

Charts: 12273, **12274**

Approaches. To port as you proceed up the Elk River, most of the land is part of Elk Neck State Park. Comprising more than 1,700 acres, the park has a quite varied topography, ranging from sandy beaches to marshlands to woodlands that are more than 100 feet above sea level. It is a wildlife sanctuary. There is no "approach" as such. Just pick a likely looking spot as you proceed up the Elk River and pull over, making sure you are well away from the commercial channel, and monitor the depth as you approach shore. Holding is good in sand and mud, but the wind blowing up and down the river is essentially unrestricted.

Anchorages. Although anchoring off any of several beaches is possible, there is little or no protection from either the elements or the wakes from boat and ship traffic. There are facilities for boat launching and rental in Rogues Harbor, about 1½ miles above Turkey Point and directly across the Elk River from a large housing development with look-alike white houses placed cheek by jowl. The launching facility is designed for small powerboats or day sailers. Other trailerables with a draft well under 3 feet also can make use of the facility. Trailers and cars can be parked at a separate area just up the hill.

You can anchor off this cove, but the shallow water and lack of protection from weather and ship wakes make it less than a desirable anchorage. For just putting a small boat in for the day or even windsurfing it is a good spot.

Bohemia River

Charts: 12273, **12274**

Approaches. Slightly more than 3 miles up the Elk River from Turkey Point lies the mouth of the Bohemia River. It is nearly a mile wide with depths of 7 to 10 feet, so no buoyage is necessary, but give Town Point a wide berth if you are approaching from the north. The Bohemia frequently serves as a stopover point for boats planning to transit the C&D Canal, 4 miles to the north.

Anchorages. The first and probably best anchorage within the river is Veasey Cove, 1 mile to starboard from the river's entrance. Exposed to the northwest, it is otherwise well protected. In calm weather or with southerly winds, many local boaters prefer to anchor closer to the river mouth, by the bluffs that extend from Ford Landing to Veasey Cove, in order to make use of the gradually sloping beach and nice sandy bottom. The only problem may be an occasional wash from shipping traffic in the Elk River. If the weather is threatening, you would be better off moving farther upstream. Although a good number of boats will be found anchored in Veasey Cove on summer weekends, the number dwindles rapidly in the evening as the "locals" up anchor and go home.

Marinas & Provisions. If you are looking for marine facilities or prefer to tie up at a marina overnight, there are plenty of facilities upstream. There are three marinas on the north shore, just inside Rich Point, all of which have dockside facilities for sewage pumpout. The Bohemia Bay Yacht Harbor (410-885-2706) is the only marina that offers diesel fuel. It also has a marine store and a laundromat. There are three more marinas on the south shore farther upstream, just before the bridge. Both Hacks Point Marina (410-275-8168) and Long Point Marina (410-275-8181) also have dockside sewage pumpout facilities. Among these marinas, you can to find just about any facilities you want or need. For groceries, you will have to go to Hacks Point General Store, near the bridge.

Head of Bay

Region 1

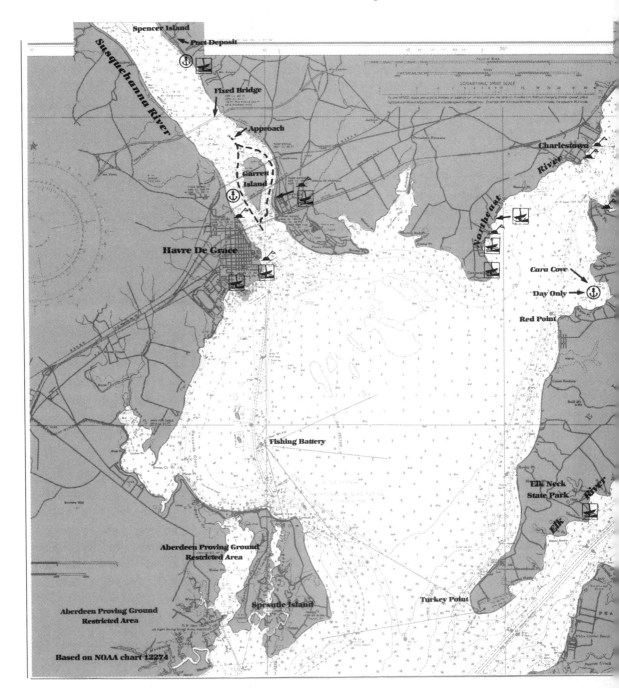

Spencer Island

Port Deposit

Susquehanna River

Fixed Bridge

Approach

Charlestown River

Garrett Island

Northeast

Cara Cove

Day Only

Red Point

Havre De Grace

Fishing Battery

Elk Neck State Park

Elk River

Aberdeen Proving Ground Restricted Area

Spesutie Island

Turkey Point

Aberdeen Proving Ground Restricted Area

Based on NOAA chart 12274

 SCALE **1"** = **1.56** NAUT. MILES **Good anchoring** **Marina** **Launching site**

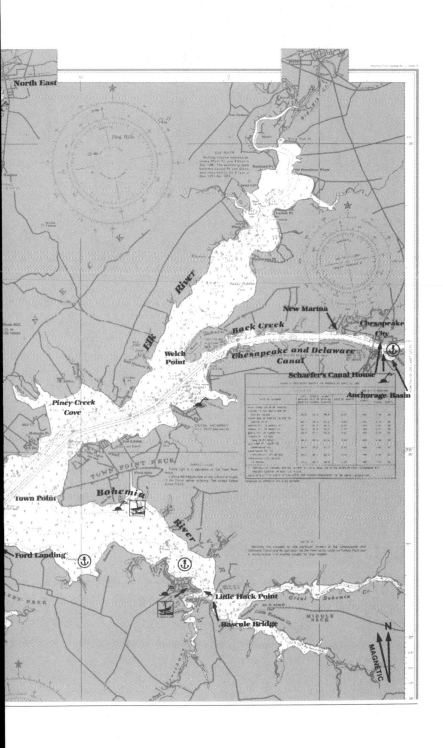

National Geodetic Survey

92   *Chesapeake entrance to the C&D Canal with Chesapeake City at the bottom. View is looking west from Elk River toward entrance of C&D Canal .*

Although there are several homes on the river, most are hidden by trees. This presents cruisers with an unspoiled, wooded shoreline, which greatly adds to this river's appeal.

The bridge over the river is fixed, in spite of what some charts may say, with a vertical clearance of less than 10 feet. This, of course, bars passage to all sailboats and most powerboats. It is probably not worth the trouble to go above the bridge because the channel there is narrow, winding, sometimes shoaling, and virtually unmarked. This is really runabout country; in warm weather there are usually quite a few shallow-draft boats zipping around, with or without skiers in tow. Hard-core gunkholers may want to give it a try anyway.

If you wish to explore the river above the bridge, we recommend that you do so by dinghy. As long as you stay in the channel, you will find 7- to 10-foot depths for 1½ to 2 miles beyond the bridge in both Little and Great Bohemia Creeks. Don't expect to find a spot to anchor where you won't be in danger of bumping a shoal should the wind change direction.

Upper Elk River

Charts: 12273, **12274**

Anchorages. Above the Bohemia, there is little to recommend on the Elk River. Piney Creek Cove, on the west shore, opposite Old Town Point Wharf, is a possible anchorage for those with drafts less than 4 feet. Personally, I wouldn't recommend it because of its lack of protection from weather and ship wakes.

Marinas. This leaves Harbor North Marina as the only place to stay overnight before entering the C&D Canal. It is about ½ mile up a dredged channel northeast of Courthouse Point. This marina, which claims to hold 10 slips available for transients, monitors VHF-FM channels 16 and 6. I suggest contacting them in advance by radio or by phone at 410-885-5656 if you intend to use their facilities.

Above the entrance to the canal, the Elk River shoals and should be left to boats with less than a 3-foot draft. There are at least four fair-sized marinas in the area between Henderson, Locust, and Plum Points, all of which cater to powerboats. If you have the draft to allow it, a short cruise up this region of the Elk promises to be a scenic trip to take at least once. Repeated trips are best left to the resident boats.

Chesapeake & Delaware Canal

Charts: 12274, **12277**

History. Originally opened on 4 July 1829, the canal has been modified three times to improve and expand its capability. Originally a 22-foot-wide barge canal, the C&D was purchased by the U.S. government in 1919 and converted to a sea-level waterway with a width of 46 feet and a depth of 12 feet. In 1938, it was widened to more than 200 feet, and its depth was increased to more than 25 feet. Finally, it was widened to more than 400 feet with a depth in excess of 40 feet to accommodate modern ships. As a sea-level link between the northern Chesapeake Bay and the Delaware Bay, the canal is heavily used by commercial shipping and is a vital part of the Intracoastal Waterway.

At least on the Maryland portion of charts, the C&D Canal seems to have two names—Chesapeake & Delaware Canal and Back Creek. The reason for this is simple: Back Creek was transformed into the C&D Canal.

Approaches. Although it appears tranquil on the surface, the canal demands constant attention. In addition to commercial traffic—freighters and tugs with barges (and their wakes)—cruisers need to watch the water for frequent debris, washed in from the Delaware. Most of all, pay attention to the current. Official publications list the peak current around 2 to 2.6 knots. However, currents frequently are well in excess of 2 to 3 knots. According to some of the locals, it can reach close to 6 knots at times! It is extremely important to pick your transit times so that the current is either slack or aiding your progress. In addition, if you are attempting to dock or pass structures, such as the bridge at Chesapeake City, beware of dangerous eddies. It is always safer to err on the side of caution.

The canal is under the supervision of the

District Engineer, Army Corps of Engineers, Philadelphia, which enforces certain restrictions for canal transit. This control of the canal extends from Welch Point on the Maryland side to Reedy Point on the Delaware side. Between these points water-skiing and transiting under sail are prohibited. All small pleasure craft in the canal must relinquish the right-of-way to deeper-draft vessels with limited maneuvering room (a prudent procedure in any case). Other than that, all vessels proceeding with the current have the right-of-way over vessels heading in the other direction. Smart cruisers stay out of the center of the canal, just in case. A large ship probably will not be able to stop for or maneuver around an incapacitated small craft in midchannel.

Located at Old Town Point Wharf, on Town Point Neck, just north of the Bohemia River, and at Reedy Point, Delaware, are red and green traffic-control lights. Red indicates that the canal is closed to traffic, green that it is open. TV cameras located at these two points monitor traffic through the canal. In case of emergency, the dispatcher at Chesapeake City also monitors channel 16 on VHF-FM radio in addition to the normal working channel, 13. Although no clearance is required for pleasure craft, it is a good idea to check in with the dispatcher on channel 13 prior to transit, if only to obtain information on any expected shipping traffic in the canal.

The canal is well marked with buoys and lights throughout its length. Be advised that the colors of the buoyage system reverse at the Chesapeake City bridge. As you enter from the Elk River on the Maryland side, the red lights and even-numbered markers are on the south side of the canal. Past the bridge, they reverse, so that between the bridge and Delaware Bay the red lights and even-numbered markers are on the north side. At night the canal is lighted with mercury vapor lights, positioned roughly 140 feet back from the edge of the channel and 250 feet apart on both banks.

Anchorages, Marinas, & Provisions. Summit North Marina (302-836-1800), located about 7½ miles from the Delaware River entrance to the canal in an offshoot to the north,

Pay attention to the current in the C&D Canal, especially because of dangerous eddies near structures such as the Route 213 bridge at Chesapeake City.

Anchorage at Chesapeake City, on the south side of the C&D Canal.

has some transient slips and a T dock that can accommodate larger craft. In addition to diesel and gas, they have a marine store, groceries, and virtually any facilities you might need. They claim a minimum depth of 8 feet of water up to the fuel dock, but I have not verified this. If you plan to stop there overnight, reservations are highly recommended.

Within the 16-mile length of the canal there is really only one place where you can anchor, Chesapeake City. Anywhere else would be downright risky, not to mention foolhardy! Here you will find an anchorage, possibly a slip or two, fuel, some marine supplies, and restaurants. Chesapeake City is where ships transfer between Delaware and Chesapeake pilots. A small pilot boat pulls alongside the moving ship, and the pilots climb up or down a ladder along the ship's side. If you happen to be having dinner at Schaefer's Canal House at this time, you will hear the maître d' announce the name of the ship, as well as its tonnage, cargo, and ports of call.

On the north side of the canal you can tie up at Schaefer's Marina (410-885-2204) for a meal or to spend the night. Be sure to provide adequate bumpers to protect your vessel, and beware of the current as you approach the dock. There is no charge if you tie up for dinner. If you remain overnight, there is a charge. Fuel,

ice, marine supplies, some groceries, and other necessities are also available. Privacy at the dock is minimal, as diners tend to stroll up and down the dock inspecting the boats as if they were on display.

Many pleasure craft that spend the night in the canal prefer to anchor in the anchorage basin on the south side of the canal (South Chesapeake City). The basin has been dredged to a depth of 15 feet. You are supposed to get permission from the Army Corps of Engineers dispatcher to anchor overnight, but it is unlikely that anyone will bother you if you don't. There is a marina with haul-out facilities as well as a restaurant in the basin. The preferred anchorage is in the eastern half of the basin. On the west side of the basin is the Chesapeake Inn Restaurant and Marina (410-885-2040), which has 35 transient slips, a small marine store, a pumpout, and, of course, an excellent restaurant.

What to See & Do. South Chesapeake City is the location of the C&D Canal Museum, housed in the gray stone pumphouse built before 1829 for one of the old canal locks. The museum is open Monday through Saturday and on major nonreligious holidays between 8:00 A.M. and 4:15 P.M.; Easter and Sundays through Thanksgiving, between 10:00 A.M. and 5:30 P.M. Most of the exhibits are in the old boiler room,

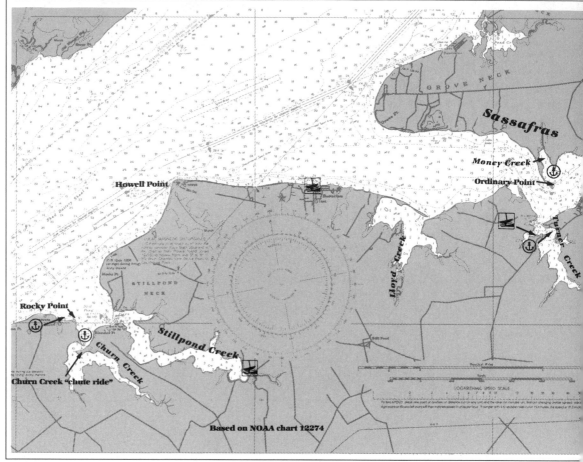

Howell Point

Rocky Point

Churn Creek "chute ride"

Money Creek

Ordinary Point

Stillpond Creek

Based on NOAA chart 12274

SCALE **1″** = **1.56** NAUT. MILES ⚓ **Good anchoring** ⚓ **Mooring area** ⛵ **Launching site**

where the steam power to operate the old pumping engine was once generated. The museum's slide show covers the 150-year history of the canal; in addition to dioramas, ship models, and assorted exhibits, there is a moving model that shows how the old locks worked. If you stop at Chesapeake City, make a point to visit the C&D Canal Museum. Admission is free.

SASSAFRAS RIVER
Charts: 12273, **12274**

When Captain John Smith first explored this river in 1607, he named it the Tockwogh, in reference to the edible plant we call sassafras, which was used by the Indians living along the banks to make bread and for a variety of other purposes. Shortly after the arrival of the

Calverts, in 1634, Tockwogh yielded to Sassafras as the river's official name. The name remains, and it is still one of the loveliest rivers on the Bay.

Wildlife abounds along the shores; in the early morning you may see deer coming down to the water to drink (yes, it is fresh). In some places the banks bordering the river rise gently to meet wheat fields, barely visible beyond the camouflage of lush trees. Elsewhere the banks soar to 80 feet above the river. High on these bluffs or nestled below are several beautiful old mansions, which can sometimes be glimpsed behind the deep foliage. The Sassafras has an immense estuary. A couple of miles upstream it narrows, becoming much like a succession of small, landlocked lakes. It provides endless variety and opportunity to explore.

Lloyd Creek is definitely not an anchorage in any sense of the word. Twenty-five years ago it was barely possible for a boat with less than a 4-foot draft to enter the mouth of this creek. Even then there was no place to go and little room to consider anchoring. Since then shoaling has done its work to the point that no one, save a few shallow-draft runabouts, even thinks about it.

Turner Creek

3   3   *No facilities*

Charts: 12273, **12274**

Approaches. The first possible anchorage as you proceed upstream is in Turner Creek, which has at least 6 feet of water in a narrow channel that continues about halfway to the head of the creek and is well protected from weather in all directions. Homes line its banks, making it less pastoral than other creeks along this river. Turner Creek also is decidedly more difficult to negotiate: the entrance channel is narrow and winding, presenting a bit of a challenge even though it is well marked. Enter cautiously!

Anchorages. About ½ mile in from can "1," at the end of the creek entrance channel, is the Turner Creek Public Landing, on the point off the southwest side of the creek, directly ahead. There is a fair amount of room to anchor once you have cleared the entrance channel, although the creek shoals quickly a little past the point with the public landing. There are a few private moorings here but no marine facilities of any kind. Just inland from the public landing is the Kent Museum, open between 10:00 A.M. and 4:00 P.M. on the first and third Saturday of each month. Near the museum is the huge colonial mansion known as Knock's Folly.

There may be prettier anchorages on the Sassafras, but this one is by far the best protected from wind and wakes until you reach Georgetown.

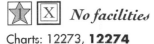

Still Pond

The approach is one of the easiest on the Bay. There is deep water all the way to the Route 213 bridge, and the channel is well marked. You can run aground, but if you follow the buoys you probably won't. Anchorages abound.

Lloyd Creek

★   X   *No facilities*

Charts: 12273, **12274**

Ordinary Point

  No facilities

Charts: 12273, **12274**

Anchorages. The next anchorage, on the north side of the Sassafras, just east of Ordinary Point, is a good one. Stay well out from the mouth of Money Creek since the water shoals rapidly as you head north from the tip of Ordinary Point. This area has one of the nicest sandy beaches on the river. Unfortunately, it is open to passing traffic, which is heavy with power cruisers (which make large wakes) on most summer weekends. A frequently used tactic for minimizing the effects of the wakes is to drop your main anchor off the bow and carry out a stern anchor to hold the bow pointed toward the channel.

Ordinary Point was so named because it had a colonial tavern, or *ordinary*, that served travelers using the ferry that was also located here. Today there are no signs of either the ordinary or the ferry docks. There is a pair of stone steps on the point, but whether they had anything to do with the tavern is not known.

Back Creek

 No facilities

Charts: 12273, **12274**

Approaches. About 1½ miles upstream from Ordinary Point is Back Creek, which has a narrow entrance channel. Favor the north side of the creek for the first ½ mile in from the entrance, holding about 200 yards off the north shore. After clearing the northern tip of Knight Island, head southeast across the creek until you are close to the southeast shore. This is the shallowest portion of the entire creek and should not be attempted if you carry more than a 4-foot draft. From this point, continue upstream along this shore; the water will stay between 5 and 15 feet deep.

Anchorages. This part of the creek is well protected on all sides and is usually very peaceful unless water-skiers take it into their heads that they own the place. Stay out of McGill and Dowdel Creeks, near the head of Back Creek; both have less than 2 feet of water. A good anchorage would be across from McGill Creek in the 11-foot spot.

Woodland Creek

 No facilities

Charts: 12273, **12274**

Another popular anchorage is in the mouth of Woodland Creek, about 3 miles above Ordinary Point and 2 miles from the excellent marinas and restaurants in Georgetown. This is a fairly well protected anchorage with several small, sandy beaches and all of Daffodil Island to explore.

Boats drawing more than 4 feet should proceed with caution because the depths drop to 4 feet or less as you approach Daffodil Island. Only runabouts or dinghys should proceed beyond Daffodil Island because the water becomes extremely shallow; in fact, it may be easier to wade. The bottom is hard sand.

Georgetown–Fredericktown

All facilities

Charts: 12273, **12274**

Fredericktown is on the north shore of the Sassafras, just short of the Route 213 bridge. Georgetown is on the south side of the bridge. For convenience, in all further references I'll simply call it *Georgetown*. Here you can find an assortment of fine marinas and all the facilities that you are likely to need or want.

Anchorages. Anchoring space is scarce among all the moorings, but you can either rent a slip or mooring for the night or move a short distance downstream or above the Route 213 bridge to anchor.

Restaurants. Georgetown has at least two excellent restaurants: the Kitty Knight House, on a hill overlooking the Georgetown Yacht Basin, and The Granary, on the other side of the river next to the Georgetown Yacht Club. (The Granary burned in 1985 and has been completely rebuilt.) The Sassafras Harbor Marina has a small sandwich-type restaurant. (Note: At the beginning of 2000 the Kitty Knight House was closed and up for sale. Its fate is still unknown.)

History. The Kitty Knight House, by the way, has an interesting history. During the War of 1812 it reportedly was the only house in Georgetown not burned by the British. Two days after they burned Havre de Grace, a contingent of British marines and sailors in several small boats made their way up the river, accompanied by the notorious Admiral Cockburn. Ignoring the British warning not to resist, the local militia opened fire. The poorly trained militia could not stand up to the British regulars and was forced to retreat. In retaliation for being fired upon, the British promptly began to set fire to all of the houses in Georgetown and Fredericktown. The strong-willed and salty-tongued Catherine (Kitty) Knight, then in her late thirties, wasn't about to tolerate such an indignity and beat the fire out with her broom. Admiral Cockburn was so impressed with Kitty's courage that he called off his men, saving the house. More than 175 years later, the Kitty Knight House still stands on the hill looking down the length of the Sassafras River.

Marinas & Provisions. The six marinas in Georgetown provide just about every service a yachtsman could desire, including complete hull, rigging, and engine repair. If you can't find what you need at one of the marinas or shops here, one of them can probably get it for you. Georgetown Yacht Basin has a sail loft and rigging shop, and it can arrange a rental car for you. Skipjack Cove Marina has sailboats of various sizes for charter. All of the marinas have heads, showers, pumpouts, and marine supplies. There are also at least four laundromats. Otwell's Market (410-648-5111) provides both grocery delivery and taxi service if you need such amenities.

What to See & Do. From Georgetown Yacht Basin it is about a mile south on Route 213 into the town of Galena. Formerly called Downs Cross Roads, it was renamed for the variety of silver discovered in 1813 and mined near the town. (The mine was closed during the War of 1812 to prevent the British from using it.) Here you will find several interesting old shops, including a tiny but well-stocked pharmacy and a supermarket.

About two-thirds of the way into Galena you pass Twinny's Place, an unimposing little restaurant reminiscent of a turn-of-the-century diner. There are only about nine tables and five stools at the counter in the dining room. The menu is posted in several locations on the walls, but you have to look for them. It's a friendly lit-

tle place with a down-home atmosphere and great food. I don't know where they get their ice cream, but we have never tasted better. (Of course, a walk along a road in the heat of a Maryland summer greatly enhances the flavor of anything cold.) An apocryphal sign over the kitchen area reads: "This is not Burger King. You can't have it your way." Not true! Don't miss a visit to Twinny's.

Upper Sassafras River

Charts: 12273, **12274**

Approaches. It is possible to navigate beyond the Route 213 bridge (12-foot vertical clearance, closed) at Georgetown, although not many take the trouble to do so. The bridge opens between sunrise and sunset Monday through Friday and at any hour on Saturday and Sunday between 30 May and 30 September. At other times advance notice to the Coast Guard is required. We are told that it will soon be manned 24 hours a day year-round, but we have not confirmed any change to the previous schedule.

The river is navigable for another 2 miles above the bridge, where it passes by high, wooded banks with an occasional herd of cows on the north shore. It is certainly far less traveled and more secluded than the lower part of the river. To us, that is an attraction in itself. An additional advantage is the lack of frequent wakes from large power cruisers from the marinas below the bridge.

Marinas. The Gregg Neck Boatyard on the south side, just before Swantown Creek, takes pains to blend into the wooded surroundings. It offers both gasoline and diesel fuel and also has a dockside sewage pumpout facility. The boatyard reportedly no longer caters to transients, but it won't hurt to ask. (If the owners take a liking to you, you might overnight for nothing!) It is a small, family-run yard reminiscent of the Bay marinas of two or more decades ago, and the owners obviously like their work.

Anchorages. Probably the best anchorage above the bridge is in the mouth of Swantown Creek in 5 to 9 feet of water. Don't proceed into the mouth of the creek beyond about level with the mooring area of the marina as it shoals quickly.

If you want to get away from the hustle and bustle and wakes of powerboat traffic, try this area!

HOWELL POINT TO FAIRLEE CREEK

Charts: 12273, **12274, 12278**

South of the Sassafras River, three anchorages open directly off the Eastern Shore of region 1.

During the summer months, Still Pond is one of the more popular anchorages in the northern Bay. Rumor has it that the name is a corruption of the Elizabethan English name Steel's Pone, meaning Steel's favorite. Another version has it that the name originally was Steel's Pond.

Located roughly midway between Howell Point, at the mouth of the Sassafras River, and Worton Point, this area is far enough north that sea nettles are rarely, if ever, a problem and far enough south to be readily accessible from the more populated areas near the Bay Bridges.

Worton and Fairlee Creeks are good intermediate stopovers for gunkholing and relaxed cruising between the extreme northern Bay and the region of the Bay Bridges. Although they are not well suited for a large number of transient boats, either one is a pleasant one-day stopover for the solitary cruiser.

Still Pond

   No facilities

Charts: 12273, **12274**

Approach & Anchorages. This anchorage is well protected from all directions but the northwest. When there is a blow from this direction, knowledgeable cruisers get out in a hurry, push as close as possible to the western side of the anchorage, or work their way into Stillpond Creek. If you have a choice, pass into Stillpond Creek. The entrance is well marked, and if you don't have a draft over 5 feet, you shouldn't have any trouble (barring the possibility of recent shoaling at the entrance). Entering at the change of tide is not

for the timid as there is a substantial current. Once past the bar, you have 5 to 9 feet of water for well over a mile from the entrance. To port just inside the entrance is a U.S. Coast Guard station, established in 1969. This station is the base for search-and-rescue operations for the entire upper Chesapeake.

The first bend in the river past the Coast Guard station may present some problem to boats with more than a 3-foot draft; the channel is now well marked but still presents a bit of a white-knuckle entry for deeper-draft boats. However, by hugging the shore to starboard just past the bend (almost close enough to touch some of the tree branches), a vessel with a 5-foot draft can get through at even very low tide. You will need to feel out the channel cautiously the first time. (To find it the first time, before the channel markers were installed, I got out and walked!) For this reason, and because of the lack of reasonable anchorage room near the Coast Guard station, larger vessels should be careful if the weather looks threatening.

I don't recommend trying to enter Churn Creek in anything larger than a dinghy or a small outboard. Although the water is deeper than the 2 feet indicated on a chart, there is no marked channel and very little room to maneuver. If you do manage to get inside, there are depths of 3 to 10 feet for about a mile. (A couple of small sailboats are permanently moored in here, so entry is possible.) More important, when the tide is turning, there is a very strong current, possibly as much as 5 knots at the peak, through the entrance. You don't want to buck this flow or be driven ahead of it in anything big and heavy.

What to See & Do. On the other hand, it is this very current that makes the mouth of Churn Creek one of the more fascinating aspects of visiting Still Pond in the summer months. On a falling tide, if you take a cushion, raft, or dinghy and launch yourself from the sand spit into the current, you will experience an exhilarating ride through and beyond that chute. If you watch the swirls in the water, you can take advantage of the eddys on the eastern side to return almost to the starting point and then take that ride over and over again with relatively little effort on your part. Go to the left, and the current will carry you over the 1- to 2-

foot-deep shoal most of the way to where boats anchor. Unfortunately, the incoming current isn't nearly as exciting.

In the main part of Still Pond tranquillity is the norm except when there is a strong northwest wind. Along the western and southern shores are several nice, sandy beaches. A long, wide shoal extending well out from the south and southwest shore prevents anchoring closer than about 200 yards. This shoal makes for a long walk—that's right, walk—ashore if you choose to stop here. There are other, equally attractive beaches along the western shore, and you can anchor much closer to them.

Rocky Point, on the western shore, comes by its name honestly. There is a large outcropping of sandstone here. The waves have washed out small caverns under these rocks, which thrum and gurgle as the water washes into them. Children find them fascinating! Off these rocks the water is about 2 feet deep for a distance of about 50 yards. The only drawback is that the bottom is covered in round stones 6 to 10 inches in size, which make walking in the water a little difficult—they roll under your feet.

If you proceed past the point toward the Bay, you'll come to perhaps one of the prettiest sandy beaches in the Bay. The beach slopes gently into the water and continues to deepen gradually. You can anchor to within less than 50 yards of the beach. It is a nice spot to be during the heat of a midsummer day, but I don't recommend overnight anchoring here. Holding seems to be good, but you are exposed to the entire sweep of the Bay to the north and west. Should the wind decide to blow during the night, you could get uncomfortable fast.

On summer weekends Still Pond tends to be a bit crowded for our taste. Boats line the entire length of the shore and fill the southern portion on the Churn Creek side. Swimming, fishing, crabbing, and other typical Bay activities are in process all the time then. If you shun crowds and plan to visit Still Pond in summer, do so on a weekday.

Worton Creek

  All facilities

Charts: 12273, **12278**

Worton Creek is due east of the northern tip of Pooles Island. It is completely sheltered beyond the narrow entrance channel, providing a snug haven to wait out inclement weather. Space to anchor is scarce, except for a small area to the west of the junction of Worton and Mill Creeks that was cleared of moorings in the late 1980s. However, moorings are usually available for the transient yacht (at least those drawing less than 4 feet). The shoreside facilities are readily available, but you will need a dinghy since there is no launch service.

Approaches. When approaching the entrance to Worton Creek, stay far enough to the north side of the estuary to permit approaching the red nun "2" buoy from the northwest, thereby avoiding the shoal off Handys Point. Swing wide around nun "2" and head due south so that you don't come too close to green can "3" until after it comes abeam, then turn to port and pass close to it. After passing can "3" and can "5" just beyond it, head toward the center of the opening between Green Point Wharf and the sandspit opposite. Although there is a shoal to the north of this sandspit, you can pass very close to the eastern side of the spit because the depth there drops sharply to about 8 feet within 6 feet of the shore.

Marinas. From here to Worton Creek Marina, at Buck Neck Landing, you have only to follow the channel between the rows of moored boats on either side. There is at least 6 feet of water all the way to the gas dock, where you can lie alongside long enough to arrange for a mooring at the office, refuel, or pick up ice or sundry supplies. If you carry much more than a 5-foot draft, do not approach any of the other piers because you will stand an excellent chance of grounding at low water.

What to See & Do. Once on your mooring or (if you are lucky and a little more adventurous) at anchor, you have several options for recreation. With the possible exception of late August, both swimming and beachcombing are excellent along the northeast end of Handys Point, especially off the sandspit you passed on the way in. You can dive off this spit into deep water, but watch out for passing boats. Unfortunately, in late August the bottom often purges, making the water look dirty and uninviting. We have been told that there is an old

Indian mound on the northern portion of Handys Point, near the small pond; we have never searched for it.

Marinas & Provisions. Two marinas just inside the entrance, Green Point Marina and The Wharf at Handys Point, both welcome transients and offer fuel, ice, and small marine stores. The Wharf also has a laundromat and a dockside sewage pumpout facility.

At the head of the creek, Worton Creek Marina, in addition to the usual marine engine and hull repair facilities, has a limited hardware and grocery selection, ice, soft drinks, beer, and a laundromat. It also has a dockside sewage pumpout system. A shower and head facility is located halfway up the slope of the hill overlooking the marina.

At the top of the hill above the marina is the Harbor House Restaurant, where we have often had superior meals at reasonable prices in a quiet, relaxing atmosphere. There is a pleasant view of the anchorage from most tables.

Anchorages. If you don't care for the congestion in Worton Creek, can't get a mooring or slip, are unable to find room to anchor in adequate depth, or simply are more adventurous, Tims Creek could be your alternative. This is a gunkholer's delight. The entrance is tricky, quite difficult to find and negotiate. Tims Creek branches to the northeast three-quarters of the way through the entrance channel to Worton Creek. However, the entrance channel is extremely narrow and very close to the east shore. It is unmarked and definitely not for the timid! Don't try it at low tide or if your draft approaches 5 feet unless you enjoy dredging new channels. In fact, if you draw 6 feet or more, you would be wise to pass up both Tims and Worton Creeks altogether.

If you do manage to make it into Tims Creek, the only anchorage is in the bight made by the sandbar extending to the southeast from the sandspit at the mouth of the creek. You can anchor in good holding ground with at least 5 feet of water at low tide, well sheltered from the weather, in comparative isolation, off a good, sandy swimming beach. You still will be within easy dinghy range of all of the Worton Creek facilities. Don't try to proceed much farther upstream; it gets progressively shallower.

Fairlee Creek

★3 ☐3 *All facilities*

Charts: 12273, **12278**

Approach. The entrance to Fairlee Creek lies directly to the east of the southern tip of Pooles Island, less than 2 miles from the well-marked shipping channel. While it's an easy approach to the first of the creek entrance markers, the red "2" lighted buoy, the entrance itself is "interesting": you must follow the markers carefully, even though a couple of them may be hard to believe.

From red "2," steer a course of 182 degrees, which will take you between the next pair of red and green buoys. Red "4" is practically on the beach, but the entire approach was dredged to a depth of 8 feet in the fall of 1992, widening the channel to about 75 feet. As you pass red "4" a line of green cans guides you in. You can pass close enough to the beach to almost shake hands with someone ashore. If you need reassurance, use the private marker labeled "7A" on the shore directly ahead as an aiming point. Turn sharply around the end of the sandspit to starboard to enter the creek. Be careful! When the tide is running, and in the summer season, this can be tricky. *Don't* try this under sail.

Once through the narrow inlet, you can relax; the water runs about 7 feet deep. Past the huge collection of piers and slips belonging to Great Oak Landing to port, the water depth decreases to 5 feet (near the center of the creek) for most of the distance to the headwaters, shoaling rapidly toward the sides.

What to See & Do. Great Oak Landing was a private club until 1976, when it was opened to the public. In 1980 it changed hands, and additional slips were added; more slips have been added over the past several years. This resort has every facility and amenity; its airport, however, has been closed. Dockage is free for guests while they are at the restaurant. There is launch service for anchored or moored boats (sound your horn twice).

Great Oak Landing, as big as it is, occupies only one cove on the creek. Across the creek from Great Oak Landing, the sandspit that you cleared on the way in provides an excellent sheltered harbor and beach for swimming. There is a 7-foot water depth to within a few feet of the shore, and you will often find sizable boats with their bows on the sand and their stems in deep water. Unfortunately, the entire sandspit is heavily posted "No Trespassing" because of past problems with fires and littering. People still go ashore, to be periodically chased off by the sheriff. During the peak boating season this area tends to be crowded, so if you have a draft of less than 5 feet, you may want to head farther upstream.

Anchorages. Upstream you can anchor almost anywhere without worrying about traffic and, once away from the creek entrance, in relative seclusion. There are several other sandy beaches along the shores—none as nice as the one at the entrance—but the shoals stretch for a long way off the beaches.

This is a lovely location any time of year. However, due to the shallowness of the water, in the very hot weather of July and August the water may be uncomfortably warm. As a result, your cabin could be hotter at night than you would expect, even when the air temperature drops to a comfortable level.

WESTERN SHORE

NORTHEAST RIVER
Charts: 12273, **12274**

As you approach Turkey Point on the way into the Northeast River, give it a good berth and start looking for red "2," just over 2½ miles ahead. Once you reach red "2," stay close to the buoys. To port lies the Susquehanna Flats, an area notorious for craft running aground.

The scenery here is magnificent. The 100-foot-high, wooded bluffs of Elk Neck State Park rise to starboard above sandy beaches. Although Elk Neck to starboard and the Susquehanna Flats to port cause most people to believe that the river begins at Turkey Point, officially you are still in the Chesapeake Bay!

The Northeast River begins at red "6" off Red Point. You should only enter the Northeast River with the intent to remain overnight if you plan to visit one of the clusters of marinas here; this river offers no good, secure anchorages to entice the cruiser. Elk Neck, however, has several nice beaches that warrant a day stop, and the high, wooded bluffs provide some beautiful scenery. Elk Neck used to be inhabited by a tribe of the Iroquois Nation, the Susquehannocks, so many people search the beaches here for Indian artifacts. Literally thousands of items have already been found.

Cara Cove
  No facilities

Charts: 12273, **12274**

About 5 miles above Turkey Point, Cara Cove opens to starboard, providing a partially sheltered anchorage for boats with less than a 4-foot draft. Totally exposed from the southwest through the northwest, it does offer some possibilities. A pretty spot with a beach under the high, wooded cliffs, it should serve as only a day stop if there is any possibility of bad weather.

Hance Point Creek

Charts: 12273, **12274**

Just past Hance Point, roughly 7 miles above Turkey Point, Hance Point Creek opens up to display a pair of extensive marinas and the Hance Point Yacht Club.

Marinas. Right inside the point is Sheltered Cove Yacht Basin (410-287-9400). The fuel dock is immediately ahead as you pass through the protecting bulkhead at the en-

Region 1

trance. Here you will find a self-service laundry and the Jackson Marine Store, which is about 100 yards inland from the docks.

The next marina, Bay Boat Works (410-287-8113), is equally extensive. Judging from the size of a couple of sailboats there, the marina must have at least 5 feet of water in the entrance and at the piers.

Both marinas cater primarily to powerboats, and both offer slips to transients. There is no anchorage here. To spend the night, you'll have to take a slip.

Charlestown

Charts: 12273, **12274**

History. Across the Northeast River from Hance Point is Charlestown. This town began about the same time as Baltimore, in 1742, and the two were rivals for shipping interests until the Revolutionary War. Baltimore had the edge in both facilities and location, and Charlestown began to decline. In 1780 the county seat was moved from Charlestown to Elkton; then the hurricane of 1786 provided the coup de grâce when it cut a channel that made Havre de Grace the more easily accessible port. Today Charlestown is a small country town with a cluster of marinas.

Marinas & Restaurants. The first and largest of the marinas, Charlestown Marina, has a long causeway on its south side; this blocks waves from the otherwise wide open exposure to the main Bay, a nicety that also protects the three marinas to the north. An outer steel bulkhead protects the other piers from the easterly direction. Gas, pumpout, and marine supplies are available here. A short walk into town enables you to try out the Market Street Cafe, which was once a general store and is now a restaurant with a display of antiques.

Charlestown has no anchorage. To spend the night you'll have to take a slip at one of the marinas.

North East

Charts: 12273, **12274**

Located at the head of the Northeast River, the town of North East was founded in 1658. One of the oldest buildings still remaining is the St. Mary Anne's Episcopal Church, established in 1706 as North Elk Parish. The present building was built in 1742. The rest of the town offers plenty of stores for shopping, but it is a fair walk from the waterfront.

Anchorages, Marinas, & Restaurants. Tucked away in the northeast corner of the Northeast River, east of where the river necks down to a relatively small stream, is an anchorage basin. Although relatively shallow, there is plenty of water for any boat with a draft of 4 feet or less. In the east corner is the Anchor Marina (410-287-6000), catering primarily to powerboats. To the immediate west of the marina is the Harbor House restaurant, which sports multiple piers that seem designed to accommodate many small- to medium-size powerboats. Those dining at the restaurant may tie up free of charge.

What to See & Do. To the west of the restaurant is a large public park with pavilions, a playground, ball fields, and a picnic area. Here you will also find the Upper Bay Museum, which is dedicated to preserving the heritage of the commercial and recreational hunter and houses an extensive collection of hunting, boating, and fishing artifacts native to the upper Chesapeake. The museum is sponsored by the Cecil-Harford Hunters Association, dedicated to the propagation and conservation of waterfowl and upland game and to improving their environment. The museum is open 9:00 A.M. to 4:00 P.M. on Sundays between Memorial Day and Labor Day.

Each year on a weekend in mid-July the town of North East holds a Water Festival in the anchorage basin off the park. There are lots of water events, including a Bay-craft boat parade, various boating skills contests, a water-ski show, and the hilarious bathtub race. Information on the schedule for the year can be obtained from the Administrative/Park Office, 300 Cherry Street, North East, MD 21901.

NORTHEAST RIVER

SUSQUEHANNA RIVER

Charts: 12273, **12274**

The Susquehanna River alone is responsible for about half of the entire supply of freshwater to the Bay. Stay here for a couple of days, and your boat bottom will be the cleanest it has been since it was launched freshly painted! The freshwater kills off all the marine organisms, including slime, that have been growing on your hull in spite of the antifouling paint. If only for this reason, the trip here is worth it. The most interesting portion of the Susquehanna River, the region from Havre de Grace to Port Deposit, lies to the northwest of the Susquehanna Flats.

The takeoff for cruising the Susquehanna is the red-green "A" midchannel buoy between Spesutie Island and Turkey Point. (Note: many of the main Bay buoys are being renumbered, and this may be one of them. However, it is the only one there.) The channel from here is well marked and considerably more forgiving than it may appear on the chart. However, do not stray far from the channel because a few additional feet can shift you from 10 feet of water to hard aground rather suddenly.

From red-green "A," a course of 343 degrees magnetic takes you past can "1" to nun "2," a distance of 2 miles. From nun "2" the channel veers a few degrees to port. You should be able to see can "3," which is less than a mile away. As you leave can "3" to port, you will see a cluster of red and green buoys about ½ mile ahead. They are a little difficult to make out until you get closer, but be sure that you head between nun "6" and can "5" before swinging to starboard to pass between nun "8" and can "7." From here on, follow the buoys. Don't be misled by Fishing Battery Light, a white lighthouse located on one of a cluster of little islands in this area. If you head directly for the lighthouse, you will run aground.

The islands to the west of the channel are the result of past channel dredging. Held in place by brush, they offer very nice, sandy beaches for swimming, sunbathing, or camping. In calm weather during the summer many small boats cluster around these islands. The swimming is great, and you are never bothered by sea nettles. Watch the depth carefully as you approach because these islands are surrounded by exten-

sive, shallow shoals. Anchor within 100 yards or less of the channel if you have a draft over 1 foot. Do not spend the night here—it is totally exposed and can get nasty in a storm.

Region 1

Havre de Grace

  All facilities

Charts: 12273, **12274**

History. The town of Havre de Grace owes its name to General Lafayette. As the story goes, Lafayette came to America in 1782 to visit General Washington. During that time he traveled from Washington's home at Mount Vernon to attend a meeting of the Continental Congress in Philadelphia. His route took him through a town then known as Lower Susquehanna Ferry. As he was admiring the beauty of the place, he was informed that a countryman of his, on first sight of the place, was heard to exclaim, "C'est Le Havre de Grace!" General Lafayette reputedly replied, "It is, indeed, much like Le Havre. In this new free country, it may fittingly be called Le Havre de Grace." Three years later, Lower Susquehanna Ferry was officially given the name Havre de Grace, meaning "harbor of mercy."

As you approach Havre de Grace, you see the white Concord Point Lighthouse with its black top. This lighthouse, built in 1827, was in continuous operation for more than 150 years. No longer in service, the light is still a useful landmark. It has now been restored and is open for visitors from 1:00 to 5:00 P.M. on Sundays, May through October. A small, floating dock in front of the lighthouse makes it easy to anchor off and visit the site by dinghy.

During the War of 1812 the British, under Rear Admiral Cockburn, attacked the town of Havre de Grace. The few militia in town fled, and the British burned the town to the ground, unimpeded except by one man. Close by the Concord Point Lighthouse there is a cannon-surmounted monument to John O'Neil bearing a bronze plate inscribed as follows:

"This Cannon of the War of 1812 marks the site of the battery on Concord Point where John O'Neil served the guns single-handed during the British attack upon Havre de Grace, May 3, 1813, until disabled and captured. He

Mouth of Susquehanna River

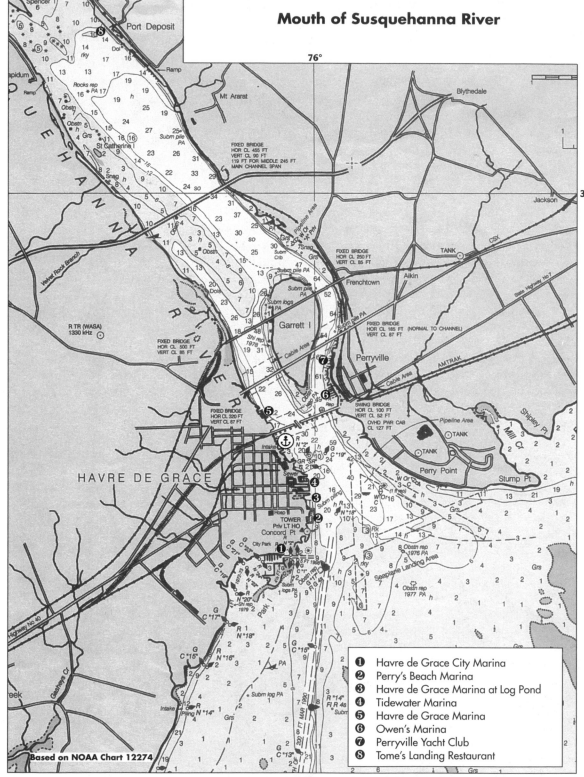

❶ Havre de Grace City Marina
❷ Perry's Beach Marina
❸ Havre de Grace Marina at Log Pond
❹ Tidewater Marina
❺ Havre de Grace Marina
❻ Owen's Marina
❼ Perryville Yacht Club
❽ Tome's Landing Restaurant

Based on NOAA Chart 12274

SUSQUEHANNA RIVER

SCALE **1.807" = 1** NAUT. MILE   ⚓ **Good anchoring**   ⚓ **Marina**   🚤 **Launching site**

SUSQUEHANNA RIVER

Mouth of the Susquehanna River. Havre de Grace (left), Garrett Island, and Perryville (right).

Concord Point Lighthouse and monument, Havre de Grace.

was relieved from the British Frigate *Maidstone* through the intercession of his young daughter, Matilda, to whom Admiral Cockburn gave his gold-mounted snuff box in token of her heroism. As a tribute to the gallant conduct of her Father, the citizens of Philadelphia presented a handsome sword."

Anchorage, Marinas, Restaurants, & Provisions. There are five marinas in Havre de Grace, but only two, Havre de Grace Marina at Log Pond (410-939-2161) and Tidewater Marina (800-960-8433), offer transient facilities. Only Tidewater offers transient moor-

The swing railroad bridge at Havre de Grace. Garrett Island is in the background.

SUSQUEHANNA RIVER

ings. Both have full marine facilities, including a marine store, diesel/gasoline, and pumpout facilities. All are within walking distance of the center of town.

Just past Tidewater Marina is a small basin where you may anchor just off the Tidewater Grill Restaurant. You can land at a small beach here (if you can make it through the weeds in the water) to walk into town for groceries, stores, and so many restaurants that you may never have to go to the same place twice. Everyone we have met in Havre de Grace has been unfailingly polite, courteous, and as helpful as possible. There are facilities here to satisfy virtually any cruising need.

What to See & Do. Past Concord Point Lighthouse, follow the redbrick walk to the stairs leading to the Havre de Grace Decoy Museum (410-939-3739). The museum, which opened in November 1986, is dedicated to the art of making decoys and contains four primary points of interest: the decoy exhibit of master carvers, the Life-Like Display of R. Madison Mitchell (master carver), a panorama, and a display of various types of gunning boxes. Admission is free.

Between the lighthouse and the Decoy Museum is the Havre de Grace Maritime Museum (410-939-4800), intended to showcase the area's nautical heritage and the local interest in wooden boats.

On the Fourth of July the town puts on a terrific parade, much larger and longer than you would expect given the size of the town. If you're in the area at this time, don't miss it.

Garrett Island Area

Charts: 12273, **12274**

Approaches. As you proceed upstream, the first obstacle that you encounter is a railroad bridge. It has a closed vertical clearance of 52 feet at mean high water (MHW). If you are in a sailboat, be sure that you know your maximum mast height, including any radio antennas. Actually, only the biggest boats, those in excess of 35 feet LOA, will have any trouble. Even these can pass if they really want to do so, but they must notify Conrail Railroad Company in Philadelphia 24 hours in advance. The phone is 215-596-2876; you might need to let it ring.

Once past the first bridge, pay careful attention to your chart and particularly to the navigation aids on the river. Look sharp: there are big rocks here, not the usual sand or mud found in other parts of the Chesapeake Bay.

The easiest route upstream is to pass to the west of Garrett Island, where there is deep water all the way. If you should choose the east route past the island, swing hard to starboard as soon as you pass through the first bridge. Then parallel the bridge, maintaining a distance of between 25 to 50 yards from it until you are well past the tip of Garrett Island. This takes you clear of the shoal extending toward the bridge from the island, keeping you in at least 9 feet of water. Regardless of which side of the island you pass, the remaining bridges present no problem. The lowest of them has an 86-foot clearance.

Anchorages. On the western route past the island the first good anchorage is to port,

anywhere along the western shore just past the Route 40 bridge (the second bridge). Pull in until you get a sounding of 10 to 15 feet and drop the hook. The holding is excellent, and the densely wooded banks under the high hills in the background make for a well-protected, secluded anchorage except in a blow from the northwest. Even then, the bridges upstream provide a surprising amount of protection. There are rarely many, if any, other boats here even in midsummer. (The trains crossing the two railroad bridges do make a bit of a racket, but we seldom hear them much once we go below deck for the night.) Stay close to Garrett Island as you proceed upstream, but don't try to anchor near it on the western side: the water is too deep (30 feet or more) to anchor comfortably; you will be in the mainstream of any traffic, and rocks all along the shore make landing difficult. Past the third bridge, the deep water runs along the east side of the river.

If you choose the eastern route past the island, it is possible to anchor to the east of it. The shore on this side of the island is appeal-

MIGRATING WATERFOWL: DUCKS, GEESE, AND SWANS

One of the more fascinating sights on the Bay occurs every fall, when hundreds of thousands, perhaps millions, of Canada geese, snow geese, tundra swans, and assorted species of ducks arrive in the Chesapeake either on their way farther south or to spend the winter. They literally blanket the water in some creeks and bays or crowd wing to wing in fields to glean grain missed in harvesting. It is a sight that many cruisers go out of their way to observe. And the noise these birds create "talking" to each other is nothing short of phenomenal!

Most of the waterfowl using the Bay summer (and reproduce) near the Arctic Circle in Canada, with some in Alaska and others in Greenland. Some, such as the canvasback duck, summer in the North American prairie. When the weather starts to cool and the days grow shorter, heralding winter and its harsh conditions, these birds gather in flocks, often

extended families, to migrate south to more benign conditions. This migration follows well-established routes that combine to form the continent's four major flyways: the Atlantic, the Mississippi, the Central, and the Pacific. The Atlantic flyway is the one that channels waterfowl to the Chesapeake.

The Atlantic flyway stretches from Alaska and the Northwest Territories to the western shores of Greenland, tightening to a narrow band on the Atlantic coast somewhere between New Jersey and Virginia. This tightening accounts for the spectacular quality of this migration in the Bay. Of the estimated 100,000 whistling swans on the North American continent, half winter in the Chesapeake Bay–Currituck Sound area!

Species of ducks frequenting the Atlantic flyway include the American black duck, the *(continued next page)* mallard, the American widgeon, the northern pintail, the green-winged teal, the blue-winged teal, the northern shoveler, and the gadwall. (Canvasbacks and redheads follow this route, though not in such large numbers.) The species reach peak migration at slightly different times in the fall. For instance, whistling (tundra) swans and canvasback ducks seem to consistently arrive in the Bay at about the same time.

Historically, Bay waterfowl were present in large numbers during the winter and were hunted vigorously. Market gunners killed thousands of ducks, geese, and swans and sold them to commercial markets in Baltimore, Philadelphia, and New York. Market gunning was an honorable and respected profession back then, meeting the needs of a hungry nation. And these hunters were incredibly efficient. Huge guns, often multibarreled, killed dozens of waterfowl with a single shot. Many market gunners became outlaw gunners when this commercially approved slaughter was banned after the Migratory Bird Treaty Act

(1916), which established hunting seasons and bag limits. The legal bans and changing national appetites gradually reduced the number of birds killed.

The 1916 treaty between the United States and Canada, along with successive agreements with Mexico in 1936, Japan in 1972, and the Soviet Union in 1976, certainly saved many species of birds from extinction and have allowed some waterfowl to rebuild their numbers. In fact, recovery of the Bay waterfowl populations in the last half of the 20th century was remarkable.

Even so, many species continue to decline in number. In the early 1980s, more than 600,000 Canada geese wintered in Maryland. By the late 1990s, winter counts estimated that from 312,000 to 377,000 Canada geese used the area—the lowest count in 20 years. Between 1954 and 1985 the canvasback population plummeted from 400,000 to 50,000, and black duck counts dropped from 220,000 to 41,000.

Habitat disruption is one of the big reasons for this decline. Water pollution from municipal waste, industrial discharge, and agricultural and residential runoff has killed aquatic plants and insects on which the birds feed. Some birds suffer from the long-term effects of pesticides on their ability to reproduce. Then, too, development of the shores and wetlands to meet human desires for marinas, homes, and recreation spots has reduced the amount of available habitat. For wary breeds, such as the black duck, the mere increase in human presence can cause birds to abandon an area.

It will take continued commitment from residents, vacationers, industry, and government agencies to reverse the damage already done and to restore the Bay estuary, as far as possible, to its previous viability and variety. This area is so rich that it is difficult for those who have not witnessed its decline to appreciate the damage that has been done. It supports swans, geese, and ducks even in the summer, and the mass migrations in the fall impress all who see it. Every fall the Chesapeake is alive with the flapping and calling of thousands of waterfowl, a sight we never tire of watching and at which we marvel annually.

U.S. Fish & Wildlife Service

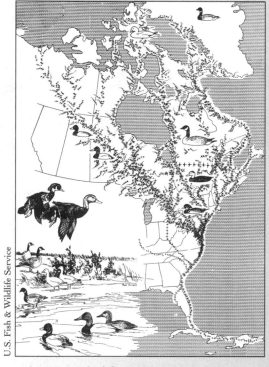

Atlantic waterfowl flyway of North America.

ing, with several small sandy beaches frequented by campers. Other than campers, the island is uninhabited (although my wife has regaled our offspring with tales of the "madman who lives in the woods of Garrett Island," a story whose source I have never been able to determine). However, those used to anchoring in most tributaries of the Chesapeake should prepare for some problems. The water is 50 to 60 feet deep.

Marinas. There is a marina and a yacht club in Perryville, on the east bank of the river opposite Garrett Island, which offer gasoline, and Havre de Grace Marina, on the west bank, offers a small marine store and both gasoline and diesel. However, only the Perryville Yacht Club formally offers any transient facilities, and it has only one transient slip.

Garrett Island to Port Deposit

Charts: 12273, **12274**

Anchorages. From the north end of Garrett Island it is just over 2 miles to Port Deposit. Above the I-95 bridge anchorages are in short supply. If you intend to remain overnight, retreat below two or three of the bridges to anchor or take a slip unless the weather is expected to remain mild. (Who believes the weatherman?)

Approaches. Above Garrett Island, remain in the northern half of the river to avoid the long shoal extending from can "21" all the way upstream in the southern half. As you reach the I-95 bridge, stay clear of the northern three spans to proceed beyond it. On the upstream side, about 100 yards past the bridge, there is at least one piling—and probably more—just at or below the surface, ready to snag the unwary.

Once you are clear of the bridge, there is 25 to 30 feet of water in the north half of the river until you reach Port Deposit.

Above Port Deposit the river begins to shoal quickly. Cruising boats should not proceed much beyond the downstream tip of Spencer Island, a short distance past Tome's Landing.

If you look upstream, the reason becomes obvious. These are big rocks, not the forgiving mud bottoms of the main Bay. Clearly visible beyond the jumble of rocks are the huge Conowingo Dam and its hydroelectric plant. Beyond the dam is a lake 1 mile wide and 14 miles long, but you cannot get to it by boat.

Marinas & Restaurants. A condominium complex and marina (Tome's Landing) have been built in Port Deposit. Access to the restaurant there, as well as several others in town, is provided by a long, bent-finger pier on the upstream side of Tome's Landing. You can tie up there long enough to stop at the marina or the marina restaurant. Be warned that there is an electronically locked gate at the end of the pier. You'll need to get the combination from the restaurant to get back to your boat.

In the summer, trailers line the shore below town. At one time gas for smaller powerboats was available at the floating dock of a little restaurant there. In the summer of 1988 we were anchored a little south of Port Deposit when my youngest awoke us in the wee hours of the morning to "Come look! You have to see this!" Grumbling a bit, we arose. Sure enough, there was something to see: the little restaurant to the west of the line of trailers was on fire. And a spectacular fire it was! The flames were leaping well over 100 feet into the sky. The propane tanks for the stoves must have been feeding the flames. Fire engines arrived, but all they could do was keep the fire from spreading. By morning the little restaurant was ash. It has never been rebuilt.

SPESUTIE ISLAND TO POOLES ISLAND

Charts: 12273, **12274**

South of the Susquehanna along the Western Shore, the coast from Spesutie Island to Pooles Island is dominated by the Aberdeen Proving Grounds (APG), which is not a cruising area. In fact, it is surrounded by a restricted water area that is closed to navigation from 7:30 A.M. to 5:00 P.M. daily except Saturday, Sunday, and national holidays. During periods of active firing the area is patrolled by boats from APG's "navy" to prevent anyone from straying into the

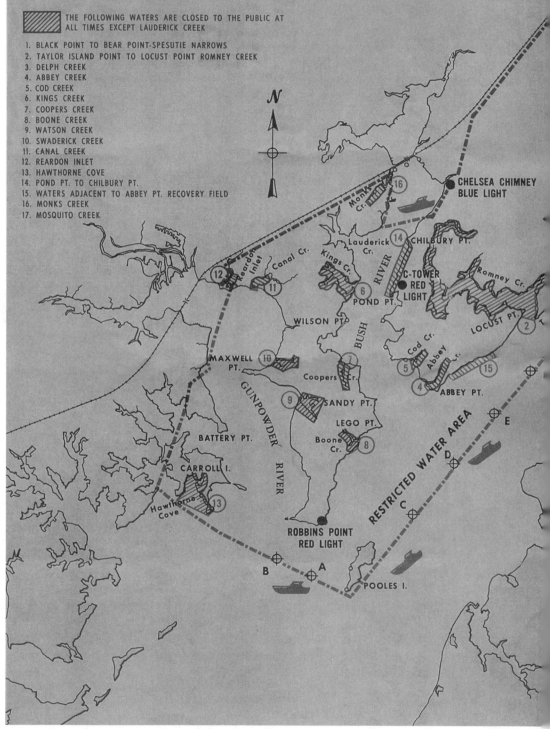

THE FOLLOWING WATERS ARE CLOSED TO THE PUBLIC AT ALL TIMES EXCEPT LAUDERICK CREEK

1. BLACK POINT TO BEAR POINT-SPESUTIE NARROWS
2. TAYLOR ISLAND POINT TO LOCUST POINT ROMNEY CREEK
3. DELPH CREEK
4. ABBEY CREEK
5. COD CREEK
6. KINGS CREEK
7. COOPERS CREEK
8. BOONE CREEK
9. WATSON CREEK
10. SWADERICK CREEK
11. CANAL CREEK
12. REARDON INLET
13. HAWTHORNE COVE
14. POND PT. TO CHILBURY PT.
15. WATERS ADJACENT TO ABBEY PT. RECOVERY FIELD
16. MONKS CREEK
17. MOSQUITO CREEK

Aberdeen restricted area.

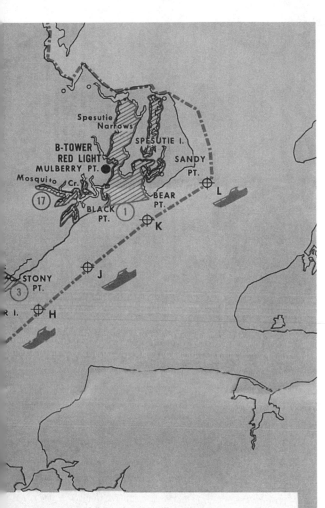

area at an "inopportune moment." APG is included here because it is an area that we consider a point of high interest, well worth visiting if the opportunity presents itself.

Unfortunately, there is no harbor or public docking facility to permit boaters to visit the Aberdeen Proving Grounds directly by water. In addition, the entire shoreline is restricted; no one is permitted to land on the shore or even to approach within 200 meters at any time. The reason is obvious if you stop to think about it. The waters, shorelines, and islands within the installation are used in weapons and ammunition testing and research. Hitting a "dud" shell or some other form of ordnance could set it off and really ruin your day!

However, APG's fascinating U.S. Army Ordnance Museum and many outside collections of historical and modern weaponry make it worth docking in Havre de Grace and finding some form of transportation (taxi, rental car, friendly local, etc.) to get there.

Each year APG holds one open house, usually on Armed Forces Day, the third Saturday in May. The highlight of the day is a firepower

IMPORTANT NOTICE TO BOATERS

The adjoining map illustrates the waters, shorelines, and islands within Aberdeen Proving Ground's restricted water zone. Normally, these restricted waters are closed from 7:30 a.m. to 5 p.m. daily except on Saturday, Sunday, and national holidays.

However, the shaded areas on the map which are listed above are closed to the public at all times.

Opening of the restricted water zone is granted for navigational and fishing purposes only.

Navigation includes anchoring a boat within the restricted waters or using the restricted waters for water skiing provided that no boat or person touches any land (either dry land or underwater land) within the Proving Ground reservation and that no water skier comes closer than 200 meters to any shoreline.

Persons outside of any vessel for any purpose, including, but not limited to, swimming (except for purposes of water skiing as outlined above), scuba diving, or any other purpose are considered in violation of navigation. Violators are subject to prosecution under 18 U.S.C., section 1382, and other applicable statutes.

Landing of boats or personnel on the shorelines or islands within the restricted zone is prohibited at all times.

Entrance into the restricted waters for navigational purposes during periods of firings can be made only by securing a clearance from either the installation's B-Tower Control by telephoning 278-2250/3971, personal or radio contact on ship-shore FM channel 16 and citizen band channel 12 with range control (call letters AAAA) or B-Tower AAAA-1, Worton Point AAAA-2, and Meeks Point AAAA-3. Loud speakers and flashing red or blue lights as warning signals are installed on all patrol boats.

⊕ **ABERDEEN RESTRICTED AREA BUOY-** Can Buoy, yellow with letters. **Maintained June 5 to October 1.**

The U.S. Army Ordnance Museum at Aberdeen Proving Grounds has an outstanding collection of weaponry. It is worth docking at Havre de Grace and finding transportation in order to visit it.

demonstration using some of the heavier and more impressive weapons systems. We still remember one demonstration of a post–Civil War Gatling gun and a modern 20 mm Vulcan cannon, which were set up to fire the exact same number of rounds, 500 shots. The vintage weapon took nearly two minutes to complete firing, whereas the Vulcan exhausted its ammunition in seconds! During the open house the visitor can see more than 50 displays and exhibits detailing the mission of nearly every agency at APG. The day's events conclude at 5:00 P.M. with the traditional retreat ceremony, the sounding of taps and lowering of the flag to signify the end of the day. All events are free, and large groups can be accommodated.

The U.S. Army Ordnance Museum on APG is open to the public year-round. Its collection policy is to maintain significant items in the evolution of the various types of ordnance equipment, both U.S. and foreign, resulting in the most complete collection of weapons in the world. In addition to providing instruction to army personnel, the museum accommodates more than 200,000 visitors each year. Photographing exhibits is permitted. The museum is open Tuesday through Friday from 12:00 to 4:45 P.M. and Saturday and Sunday from 10:00 A.M. to 5:00 P.M.; it is closed on Mondays, Christmas, and Thanksgiving.

Bush River

Charts: 12273, **12274**

This whole area has remained relatively isolated because of the barriers of the Aberdeen Proving Grounds and a low bridge on the Bush River. It will probably stay that way for the foreseeable future. Nearly two-thirds of the Bush River, from its mouth to just below the railroad bridge close to the headwaters, lies within the restricted area of the APG. There are no anchorages below the bridge, and the water shoals to 3 to 6 feet in the region above the bridge. The bridge itself has a vertical clearance of 12 feet for a width of 35 feet and does *not* open on demand. Those who need to have the bridge opened in order to pass through and have a strong desire to do so must make arrangements through the Bush River Yacht Club, Long Bar Road, Abington, MD 21009.

Approaches. While official restrictions prohibit passage through the restricted area from 7:30 A.M. to 5:00 P.M. Monday through Friday, locals claim that in practice passage up or down the river is allowed except when firing is in progress. At those times, they say, an APG patrol boat is stationed near Chilbury Point, at the upper part of the restricted area of the river,

THE BALD EAGLE

The national emblem of the United States, the bald eagle (*Halideetus leucocephalus*, or "white-headed sea eagle"), is truly a magnificent creature. A large bird, it weighs from 7 to 14 pounds, measures 2½ to 3½ feet long, and has a wingspan of 6 to 8 feet, impressive talons and beak, and a fierce, stately appearance. (The females are larger than the males.) The white head and tail, which appear when the adult is 4 or 5 years old, make it one of the most easily identified raptors.

The bald eagle subsists primarily on fish, although it is not above eating ducks, geese, small mammals, rodents, snakes, and turtles.

Even stranger, while it is quite capable of catching live, healthy prey, it seems to prefer to feed on dead or dying fish, a habit that caused Benjamin Franklin to withdraw his support of it as the national symbol. Unlike the osprey, which will dive from a considerable height, plunging into the water to capture a fish, the eagle flies along just above the surface of the water, reaching with a taloned leg to grab an unwary fish swimming close to the surface. This is not as effective as the osprey's dive-bombing technique. Perhaps this is why the eagle often plays robber baron, stealing the legitimate prey from other birds, especially osprey. Larger and faster, the eagle will harass an osprey with repeated passes until the terrified opponent drops its fish. Then the eagle dives to reclaim its prize, usually before it hits the water.

An eagle's nest, or *aerie*, is usually a massive structure, growing 6 to 8 feet in width and as deep as 10 feet. The aerie is an untidy collection of sizable sticks and branches that are jammed into place to form a platform. This platform is then lined with assorted materials, such as broom sedge, pine needles, and other soft material. At least one theory holds that the whole mass is really held together by layer after layer of guano!

Eagles mate for life, and a pair will return to the same nest again and again, adding to it each year. Most eagle pairs maintain two or more nests in an area, alternating between them from year to year. Apparently, they guard even the unused nests, driving off other birds that attempt to use them.

While the bald eagles' winter population is densest in the Blackwater Wildlife Refuge, they can be found throughout the Bay. Populations

Bald eagle concentration areas.

shift seasonally. Bald eagles also winter in the areas of the Pocomoke, the Rappahannock (Virginia), and the Mason Neck National Wildlife Refuge. In the summer they congregate in Hopewell and in Caledon State Park (both in Virginia). But you will have the best chance of sighting a bald eagle near the Aberdeen Proving Grounds, where this raptor spends time in both summer and winter.

The eagle is definitely making a comeback in the Chesapeake Bay area! Seeing one of these great birds on the wing is always an impressive sight, one that with luck and some care we will continue to see well into the future.

Craig Koppous, Fish & Wildlife Service

Bald eagle chick.

and another one is stationed in the main Bay near the river mouth, to stop traffic. Reportedly, traffic is usually delayed for only about ½ hour. Of course, if you have any doubts, official restrictions have the right-of-way.

In any event, if you do choose to make the 7-mile passage up the river and proceed past the railroad bridge, the Bush River opens out, looking more like a landlocked lake than a tributary of the Chesapeake Bay. The water has the Bay's typical milk-chocolate color rather than the clearer waters of a lake.

Anchorages & Marinas. There are some sailboats here, but this is really powerboat country. Past the bridge there is a host of marinas, primarily on the shores of Otter Point Creek, with two more on opposite shores of the upper Bush River itself. Otter Point Creek has a depth of 3 feet for a distance of just under a mile from its entrance. In the Bush River, where it proceeds toward Church Creek, the water is 3 to 5 feet deep as far as Church Point. You can anchor in either of these two branches if your draft permits you to get there at all. The considerable runabout and small powerboat traffic in the region creates an uncomfortable chop for an anchored boat during most of the daylight hours. Of course, if you happen to be in one of those small powerboats, this is an ideal location. The waters are protected, and there are plenty of launching ramps and facilities catering to powerboat activity.

Pooles Island

 No facilities

Charts: 12273, **12278**

This mile-long, wooded island holds down the southeast corner of the Aberdeen Proving Grounds restricted area. The attractive island, with its sandy beaches, may tempt you to explore, but it is all U.S. Government property—landing on the island is strictly prohibited. If there is any doubt in your mind, simply read any of the several signs posted around the is-

land, which state: "U.S. ARMY PROPERTY, NO TRESPASSING, (DANGER) UNEXPLODED SHELLS, KEEP OFF."

The island was first named Powells Island by Captain John Smith, for one of his companions, during his exploration of the Chesapeake in 1608. By the time the map of his voyage was published in 1612, the name had become Powels Isles. By the time of the publication of the famous Augustine Herman map of Maryland, in 1659, it had somehow become Pooles Island.

During the American Revolution the island had an area of 255 acres and was owned by John Bordley, a patriot. He donated all of the livestock from the island to the Continental Army, and he also raised crops on the island and donated them to the army for the duration of the war.

Pooles Island was one of many Chesapeake islands occupied by the British during the War of 1812. The British plundered everything on the island and set up a gun battery to cut off trade in the upper Bay. How effective this battery really was remains unknown.

Still standing but no longer operational is a lighthouse on the northwest corner of the island. Built in 1855, it was in continuous operation until 1939. Like the rest of the island, the lighthouse is off-limits.

From 1873 until the island was taken over by the Aberdeen Proving Grounds in 1917, a peach orchard on the island reputedly produced peaches of superior flavor. Virtually all Pooles Island peaches were sold in nearby Baltimore.

Today, the island is quiet, uninhabited except by wildlife. There is a herd of deer, which occasionally may be glimpsed from passing boats, as well as a sizable great blue heron rookery. Bald eagles are occasionally seen in the area and may be nesting on the island.

The island is now about 190 acres in size, indicating a loss of only about 65 acres in the last 200 years, which is pretty good by Bay standards. (The much larger Sharps Island in mid-Bay completely disappeared during the same time.) This particular Bay landmark should be around for some time to come.

POOLES ISLAND
TO BAY BRIDGES

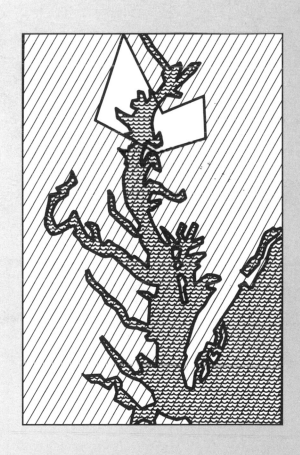

SCALE **1"** = **10.1** NAUT. MILES

Pooles island, near Fairlee Creek, and the Chesapeake Bay Bridges serve as dividing lines in the bay in more than a topographical sense. As you pass each of these points the very character of the bay begins to change subtly. As you proceed north from below the bridges, the water becomes less and less salty; the wave action changes, becoming more choppy, with lower wave heights and far fewer of the long rollers often encountered below the bridges. Even the shoreline changes, although that may be more in the mind's eye than in actuality. The harbors become fewer, more crowded, and, some say, not as attractive as those farther south. The change as you head north past Pooles Island is not quite as evident. The main difference is that the water rapidly loses salinity, becoming more fresh. The sea nettles rarely penetrate north of this island, making it an excellent area for swimming throughout the summer.

Regardless of changes, it is all Chesapeake Bay country—one of the best cruising grounds in the United States. Many harbors and anchorages here belong on the "must visit" list of the serious cruiser.

CHESAPEAKE BAY JELLYFISH

Three basic types of jellyfish are found in the Chesapeake Bay: the infamous sea nettle, the winter jellyfish, and comb jellies. The first two have long tentacles covered with stinging cells, which make them rather unpopular with people who like to go into the water. The last type comprises different kinds, all harmless to anything but plankton.

The **sea nettle** (*Chrysaora quinquecirrha*) is the best known of all of the Chesapeake Bay jellyfish, perhaps better known than any other form of marine life, and for good reason. The adults, or *medusae*, invade the middle and lower Bay in such numbers during the summer months that you can't enter the water without getting stung unless you cover your skin with full protective clothing.

Jellyfish are capable of limited propulsion by the repeated contraction and expansion of the bell of the medusa. However, they are mostly carried by tidal and other currents, so their areas of concentration change, usually in a matter of hours.

Sea nettles are saltwater creatures. They cannot survive in freshwater or water with low salinity. As a result, they are rarely seen north of Pooles Island and Fairlee Creek; their density as far south as the Little Choptank River fluctuates based on the spring rainfall—more rain means fewer nettles.

A minor brush with the tentacles can cause inflammation and a stinging sensation that usually disappears after 15 to 30 minutes. Normally the sting can be treated by first removing any remaining tentacles, scraping or rubbing the affected area with sand, then applying calamine, witch hazel, ammonia, or vinegar. *Do not* apply alcohol.

Severe, multiple stings can be dangerous to a person who is especially sensitive to the venom. Emergency treatment in this case is the same as for bee stings in an allergic person. Should the victim begin to wheeze or feel faint, apply ice packs and promptly seek professional medical care. Antihistamines can also help.

The adult stage of the **winter jellyfish** (*Cyanea capillata*) occurs only during the winter and early spring months (late November to early June). As a result, it is not nearly as well known as the sea nettle, although sometimes it can be as plentiful. Winter jellyfish cannot reproduce in water with low salinity and are rarely seen in great numbers much farther north than the Little Choptank River, although we have seen them in the Chester River at times.

In the spring the adults are sometimes mistaken for sea nettles that have somehow wintered over, surviving due to a mild winter. They

(continued next page)

(continued from previous page)

can easily be distinguished from the colorless sea nettle, for they are a brownish orange and their tentacles are not nearly as long, even though the bells are similar in size. Their sting is comparatively weak.

Two species of **comb jellyfish** are found in the Bay: the pink comb jelly (*Beroe ovata*) and the sea walnut (*Mnemiopsis leidyi*). Although comb jellies are far more numerous than sea nettles in the Bay, we rarely notice them because they are virtually invisible in the water and don't bother us. They are also quite small, seldom much over 4 inches long.

They are present year-round, but their population begins to rise sharply in the spring, reaching a peak in the late summer. They feed exclusively on plankton and have no stinging cells. The sea walnut is found almost throughout the Bay, as far north as the vicinity of Pooles Island, where the salinity is so low that even the sea nettle is rare. The pink comb jelly is not as tolerant of low salinity and is rarely found much above the Bay Bridges.

EASTERN SHORE

TOLCHESTER BEACH, SWAN CREEK, & ROCK HALL

Charts: **12272**, 12273, 12278

Until you reach Rock Hall and the Chester River region, this section of the Eastern Shore has few offerings. While Tolchester serves as a harbor of refuge, only Swan Creek has an anchorage.

Tolchester

  All facilities

Charts: **12272**, 12273, 12278

About midway between Fairlee Creek and Swan Point is Tolchester Marina, in an artificial harbor just south of Tolchester Beach. This is the only harbor of refuge on that 10-mile stretch on the Eastern Shore. Here you will find all the facilities you are likely to need, including a laundromat, which is a real find on any extended cruise.

Approach & Dockage. To enter, simply go between the jetty pilings until you are within the dredged basin inside. Pull up to the fuel dock to get information about where you can stay. You have to take a slip at the marina to stay here; this is not an anchorage. Only two transient slips are available, and they are assigned on a first-come basis. No reservations are taken.

Swan Creek

  All facilities

Charts: **12272**, 12273, **12278**

Approaches. Swan Creek is approximately 6 miles north-northeast of the northern tip of Kent Island. The approach to the creek is interrupted by Swan Point Bar, which extends about 2½ miles south-southeast from Swan Point. Although the bar is not really much of a barrier for shoal-draft boats, use caution when crossing it if you have a draft approaching 4 feet. Those with drafts exceeding 4 feet should round can "3," marking the southern limit of Swan Point Bar, even though it is a little longer. If you approach Swan Creek from the south or from the mouth of the Chester River, the bar will present no problem because you will be running parallel to it.

Once you're inside Swan Point Bar, the approach is easy. Pick up Huntingfield Point Light "4" (N39° 07.30' W76° 15.62'), a single piling that is hard to see until you are within a mile of it. Come to within 100 yards of this light before turning to head due magnetic north, past can "5" to nun "6," at the mouth of Swan Creek. From there simply keep near the center of the creek until you reach the prime anchorage opposite The Haven, a baylike appendage extend-

Eastern Shore with Chester River

Region 2

SCALE **1"** = **2.62** NAUT. MILES   ⚓ **Good anchoring**   ⚓ **Marina**   🖼 **Launching site**

TOLCHESTER BEACH, SWAN CREEK, & ROCK HALL

121

ing southeast of the main creek. Hold close to the red "8" daymark in the 1-foot spot at the mouth of The Haven to avoid the unmarked shoal on the north shore of the creek, opposite the daymark.

Don't be intimidated by the Swan Creek Marina moorings that extend out into the channel. Hold close to them. Stay out of The Haven unless you are in a shallow-draft boat or are headed for a marina there. Outside of its dredged channel The Haven is very shallow, effectively negating it as an anchorage.

Anchorages. Up to a mile past the red "8" daymark, most of the north-south portion of the creek is suitable anchorage. Almost any type of anchor holds well in the soft mud bottom. While this portion of the creek is completely protected from wave action, the surrounding land is so low that it offers little protection from the wind. On a hot summer night, when any breeze is welcome, this is a prime anchorage. The water depth ranges from 7 feet to almost nothing, depending on how close to shore you drop the hook. It remains reasonably deep to within about 50 yards of the western shore, but the eastern side shoals farther out. Water-skiers have not been a problem, but the anchorage is often crowded, especially on summer weekends.

At other than high water, there are some sandy beaches on the eastern shore, backed by dense stands of trees. Except for scattered farms and the town of Gratitude, the area is relatively uninhabited. The swimming is generally good even late into the jellyfish season, although you should inspect the water for these beasties in late July and August. Mosquitoes can be a bit of a problem on breezeless summer nights, so be sure to have netting and repellents on hand.

Marinas. For those who prefer to tie up, the two marinas at the mouth of the creek often have transient slips available; one of them, Swan Creek Marina, also has moorings available.

Gratitude Marina is located on the bay side of Gratitude, right in the mouth of Swan Creek, to starboard on entering. Although the marina is exposed to the bay, its slips are completely protected by large wooden breakwaters surrounding its piers, creating a small artificial harbor.

Swan Creek Marina is located just around the point, in a little cove called Deep Landing.

This marina now comprises two yards, one on each arm of the cove. In the past few years its growth has been phenomenal. Its character has also changed. Years ago, it was full of powerboats, with a few sailboats on moorings. Now it has mostly sailboats, with a sprinkling of powerboats.

Located well back in The Haven are the Haven Harbor Marina and the Osprey Point Marina and Yacht Club. There you will find several transient slips, a dockside sewage pumpout station, and facilities for complete engine and hull repairs. There are a number of good-sized sailboats here to support the claim that the depths in the channel and the marina hold at about 6 feet MLW. From here, it's only about a mile walk into Rock Hall.

Tavern Creek
Charts: **12272**, 12273, 12278
Tavern Creek, just west of the mouth of Swan Creek, is inaccessible due to shoaling to about 1 foot across all the approaches. If there is any way into this 4-foot-deep creek, I don't know it. By the same token, I don't consider it cruising territory even for a gunkholer.

Rock Hall

 All facilities

Charts: **12272**, 12273, 12278
Approaches. About a mile south of the entrance to Swan Creek, you can easily see the entrance jetties to Rock Hall Harbor. To approach Rock Hall, follow the instructions for entering Swan Creek until you reach the flashing red "4" off Huntingfield Point. Then swing to starboard to can "1" near the dredged approach to the jetty entrance. Once you pass between the green "3" and red "4" lights, head directly for the jetty entrance. Then simply follow the markers. You can either follow them north around the perimeter of the harbor or take the passage straight across. (The northern course is a little easier to follow.) In either case, you'll be in about 9 feet of water all the way to Sailing Emporium, the large marina in the southeastern corner of the harbor. You must retrace your course to get back out because the channel does not complete the circle along the southern shore.

Marinas, Restaurants, & Provisions.
Rock Hall's look has changed radically in recent years. Once a shallow harbor used exclusively by watermen and their powerboats, the entire harbor area has been enhanced to make it more attractive to yachtsmen while continuing to serve the commercial watermen who have fished there for generations. Now marinas, marine stores, restaurants, and grocery stores, as well as a sprinkling of arts-and-craft shops have sprung up along Rock Hall's Main Street. Be sure to stop at Durding's Store, at the intersection of Sharp and Main Streets, for a return to the 1930s, including a fantastic soda fountain.

Three restaurants right on the harbor offer free dockage for patrons while they dine: Masons Ribs and Crabs, Waterman's Crab House Restaurant (30 slips), and Dockside Café.

Fuel is available only at the Sailing Emporium (410-778-1342), at the end of the harbor. It also has a pool, a good-size marine store with limited groceries, and virtually any other marine facilities you may need. The only problem is that it is a longish walk from there to the main part of Rock Hall. Keep in mind that many of the restaurants offer free shuttle service to and from the marinas. The marina also offers complimentary bicycles and mopeds.

History. An early ferry that reputedly was used by George Washington on eight separate occasions once crossed the Bay here, but no trace of the landing now remains. It was here that Colonel Trench Tilghman began his ride to carry word of Cornwallis's surrender at Yorktown to the Continental Congress in Philadelphia.

What to See & Do. Speaking of the American Revolution, the old-fashioned Fourth of July celebration in Rock Hall has become something of a major event in the area. The Rock Hall Volunteer Fire Company holds a fish fry that draws quite a crowd; the menu includes such delicacies as fried eels, baked beans, oven-baked fresh bread, and a large assortment of other tasty fare. A boat-docking contest between watermen at the public docks on Bayside Avenue is followed by a seafood bash that includes traditional fried clams, crabcakes, and all the fixings. On the Fourth itself there is a parade, complete with theme floats and other entries. Other events include a whistling contest, a sack race, a turtle

race, a tug of war, bluegrass music, and the traditional flea market and craft tables. It is crowded, so if you go by boat, go into Swan Creek and walk over to Rock Hall from there.

Be sure to stop by the museum in the basement of the Municipal Building, on South Main Street. Many of the museum's displays relate to the ferry lines that used to visit Rock Hall, shuttling passengers between the Eastern and Western Shores. Many other displays provide a sense of what this little bayside community was, and is, all about.

In 2000 the Rock Hall Trolley Company opened, establishing a regularly scheduled shuttle service to transport visitors and local residents from residences, marina areas, and bed-and-breakfast accommodations to Rock Hall attractions. It makes a complete loop approximately every 45 minutes. Riders may ride the shuttle as often as they wish for $1 a day. Call 410-639-7996 for more information.

CHESTER RIVER

Charts: 12263, 12270, **12272**, 12273, 12278

Resembling a J-shaped umbrella handle, the broad sweep of the lower part of the Chester River starts at Love Point Light, at the northern tip of Kent Island, and hooks around Eastern Neck Island to swing to the north for a distance of about 5 miles. Then it turns to the northeast, splintering into a spray of interesting creeks with an assortment of excellent, well-protected anchorages. While the main Chester River winds its way from here into the heart of the Eastern Shore for another 15 to 20 miles, the cruiser need look no further for some of the best anchorages on the river.

Eastern Neck Island is a 2,285-acre wildlife refuge established in 1962 by the U.S. Fish & Wildlife Service. It is also the site of many Woodland Indian artifact discoveries dating back 2,700 years. The island has no harbors suitable for cruising boats. However, the Ingleside Recreation Area, on the northwest side, is frequently used by those who like to wade the bay "flats" in search of soft crabs. The area also has crabbing and car-top boat-launching facilities, wildlife trails, a boardwalk, and a bayside observation

CHESTER RIVER

123

deck. (For more information on the refuge, write to: Eastern Neck National Wildlife Refuge, Route 2, Box 225, Rock Hall, MD 21661.)

As you enter the Chester River from the Chesapeake Bay, follow a compass course of 162 degrees from Love Point Light until you pick up can "3" (you need not honor can "3"; there is plenty of water all around it). From can "3," come to a course of 150 degrees until you reach can "7" if you plan to head upriver. If you are heading south through the narrows, assume a course of 170 degrees to the R"2K" quick-flashing buoy at the entrance to the Kent Narrows Channel. The compass courses are helpful as the buoys cannot be seen until you are within a mile or less from them. For the upriver course, head 130 degrees from can "7" to the flashing 4-second can "9." Stay at least ¾ mile off Eastern Neck Island at all times as the shoal extends a surprising distance offshore and has some nasty lumps in it. (One dark night we "located" a log there by tacking in a little too close.)

If you enter the Chester River from Kent Narrows, can "9" is easily visible as you clear the last daymarks on the way out of the Kent Narrows Channel.

A course of 55 degrees from can "9" takes you past can "11" to the lighted red "12" between Hail Point and Tilghman Creek. (Note: this is not the Tilghman Creek off the Miles River; this one is not navigable.) Both can "11" and the red "12" buoys are difficult to see even with binoculars until you are less than a mile from them.

Can "11" is directly off Hail Point, where in colonial days ships were hailed and inspected before going farther upriver.

For all practical purposes, once you have cleared can "11" off Hail Point, you can head due north, ignoring nun "14" but staying well off Piney Point to starboard until you pick up either can "1" off the mouth of Grays Inn Creek or the green-red "LC" buoy about a mile southwest of Nichols Point, off the entrance to Langford Creek. The green-red "LC" buoy marks the outer point of the shoal extending from Nichols Point, where Langford Creek splits off from the main Chester River.

From here you can either continue on upriver or head into the Corsica River, to starboard. Any shoals in the main river are well

marked, and navigation presents no problem until you reach the Route 213 bridge at Chestertown.

Once you pass Comegys Bight, the river narrows and begins to resemble many of its tributaries. There are no proper anchorages, although you could anchor anywhere out of the mainstream of traffic in perfect security. There are several small creeks that look interesting, but stay out of them: all are shallow.

Castle Harbour

Charts: 12263, 12270, **12272**, 12273

Castle Harbour is actually an artificial harbor located on Kent Island, about 3½ miles upriver from Love Point Light. This is the first place on the Chester River where you can find refuge or supplies. The next place is Kent Narrows, the channel to which is approximately 1½ miles farther upriver.

Marina & Restaurant. This harbor opened several years ago under the name Castle Marina. It was a dredged yacht basin whose entrance silted in fairly rapidly. Since then it has changed hands and been renamed Kent Haven Yacht Harbour, then Castle Harbour Marina. The entrance channel has been dredged. The present ownership plans to maintain a minimum of 5 feet in the channel at low tide. Castle Harbour Marina is a condominium marina, but transients are welcome. A swimming pool and restroom and shower facilities are close to the harbor, and a restaurant with bar (the Yachtsman's Inn) is located in an old mansion a short walk from the water. To stay here, you'll have to take a slip; there is no anchorage.

Approach. The easiest way to approach this harbor is to run to the flashing red "6" buoy located in the Chester River southwest of Eastern Neck Island. From red "6" a course of 240 degrees takes you directly to the marina entrance, a distance of about 2 miles. You can, of course, chart a more direct course, but this approach is easy and neatly avoids all of the shoals; it makes the entrance unmistakable. (An alternative course is 185 degrees from Love Point Light.) The entrance channel is marked by a pair of flashing lights, green "1" and red "2." From them, follow the double row of privately maintained markers into the yacht basin. The fuel dock is directly ahead.

Kent Narrows

  3 *All facilities*

Charts: 12263, 12270, **12272**, 12273

For those traveling to the Miles River area from the north or to the Chester River from the south, Kent Narrows provides a shortcut that is several miles less than the route around Kent Island. However, it is not a passage for the timid, and sailboats above the dinghy class should not attempt it without auxiliary power. The channel is well marked and quite easy to follow, at least since it has been relocated. The substantial current during tide changes is strongest directly under the Route 50 drawbridge, where it has been known to exceed 2 knots. During the prime boating season, especially on holiday weekends, the traffic can be very heavy. Be sure to keep an extra sharp watch if you negotiate the narrows at these times.

The passage through the narrows is used extensively and is well worth the bit of extra effort. With a little foresight and planning, nearly all of the complications can be minimized or eliminated through proper selection of your transit time.

A number of documents can assist you in planning for the easiest passage through Kent Narrows. The most important are a large-scale chart of the Chester River with an inset showing Kent Narrows in detail (such as NOAA chart 12272, Chester River — Kent Island Narrows and Rock Hall Harbor), a current copy of the tide and current tables for this area (Fort McHenry and Sandy Point, respectively), and a set of the Tidal Current Charts for the upper Chesapeake Bay. Plan your arrival time at Kent Narrows for high tide and slack water, or at least water with a favorable current.

The buoyage system is referenced to Kent Narrows at the bridges. That is, if you are entering Kent Narrows from the Chester River (i.e., heading south), keep all red markers to starboard (right) and all green markers to port until you pass the bridges. At the bridges, the buoyage system reverses, and you must keep the red markers to port and the green markers to starboard until you exit the narrows channel.

The area of the Kent Narrows bridges is known to have a peak current of 2 knots and sometimes much more during changes of the tide.

CHESTER RIVER

125

Kent Island Narrows

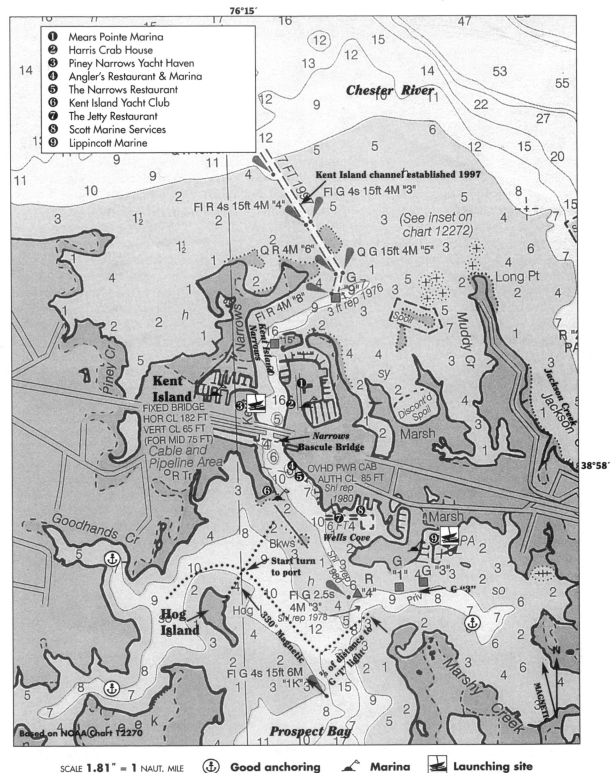

Region 2

1. Mears Pointe Marina
2. Harris Crab House
3. Piney Narrows Yacht Haven
4. Angler's Restaurant & Marina
5. The Narrows Restaurant
6. Kent Island Yacht Club
7. The Jetty Restaurant
8. Scott Marine Services
9. Lippincott Marine

76°15´

Chester River

Kent Island channel established 1997
Fl G 4s 15ft 4M "3"

Fl R 4s 15ft 4M "4"

(See inset on chart 12272)

Q R 4M "6"   Q G 15ft 4M "5"

G "9" 3 ft rep 1976

Fl R 4M "8"

Spoil

Long Pt

Muddy Cr

Jackson Creek

Kent Island

FIXED BRIDGE
HOR CL 182 FT
VERT CL 65 FT
(FOR MID 75 FT)
Cable and
Pipeline Area

Narrows
Bascule Bridge

Discont'd
Spoil

Marsh

OVHD PWR CAB
AUTH CL 85 FT
Shl rep
1980

Wells Cove

Marsh

Goodhands Cr

Bkws

Start turn
to port

330° Magnetic

Hog
Island

Hog

Fl G 2.5s
4M "3"
Shl rep 1978

⅓ of distance to G "1" light

Marshy Creek

N

MAGNETIC

Fl G 4s 15ft 6M
"1K"

Prospect Bay

Based on NOAA Chart 12270

CHESTER RIVER

SCALE **1.81" = 1** NAUT. MILE   ⚓ **Good anchoring**   ⛵ **Marina**   🚤 **Launching site**

The new Kent Narrows northern channel was established in 1997.

Of course, it is the other way around if you are headed north toward the Chester River.

Approaches. When approaching Kent Narrows from the mouth of the Chester River, the simplest course is to take a heading of 165 degrees from Love Point Light to bring you to the red "6" buoy in the Chester River. As you reach this buoy the Kent Narrows bridge will be visible to starboard. From R"6" a course of 180 degrees magnetic will take you directly to the Q Fl R"2" light at the entrance to the channel into Kent Narrows (N38° 59.21′ W76° 14.77′). A green C"2" can conveniently defines the boundaries of the entrance channel. From there, simply follow the markers into the narrows. (Note: The channel was completely changed well to the west in the late 1990s. If you have a chart that shows the entrance channel leading from the northeast to the southwest into a couple of doglegs, *it is wrong!*)

If you are approaching from the upstream part of the Chester River, it is not advisable to head directly from Fl G 4s G"9" (N38° 59.58′ W76° 12.73′), off the southern tip of Eastern Neck Island, toward R"2" at the channel entrance. A long, wide shoal stretching out from the vicinity of the narrows may cause deeper-draft boats some problems. A course of 175 degrees magnetic from G"9" will take you clear of the shoal. (This is 15 degrees to the west of a direct course to the narrows entrance marker.) Hold this course until R"2" at the narrows channel entrance is roughly abeam. Then you can turn and head directly for it, clearing the shoal completely.

After you clear the red "18" daymark in the narrows proper, the only remaining obstruction is the old drawbridge. The new Route 50 bridge has a vertical clearance of 65 feet at MHW and presents no problem. The old drawbridge is still operational for local traffic; when closed it has a vertical clearance of only 18 feet. Unfortunately, it still does not open on demand for boat traffic but opens every half-hour, on the hour, for any boats waiting to pass through. It is hoped that an open-on-demand policy will be adopted in the near future. (*Warning: on some charts the old drawbridge is incorrectly shown as a fixed bridge.*)

According to the Rules of the Road, vessels with the current behind them are supposed to

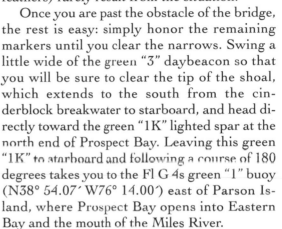

have the right-of-way in proceeding through a restricted passage such as this bridge. In actual fact, vessels holding into the current often display ignorance and manage to pass through first since they do not have to turn around before heading for the opening. The General Prudential Rule takes precedence here, so that significant problems (short of assorted ruffled feathers) rarely result from the situation.

Once you are past the obstacle of the bridge, the rest is easy: simply honor the remaining markers until you clear the narrows. Swing a little wide of the green "3" daybeacon so that you will be sure to clear the tip of the shoal, which extends to the south from the cinderblock breakwater to starboard, and head directly toward the green "1K" lighted spar at the north end of Prospect Bay. Leaving this green "1K" to starboard and following a course of 180 degrees takes you to the Fl G 4s green "1" buoy (N38° 54.07′ W76° 14.00′) east of Parson Island, where Prospect Bay opens into Eastern Bay and the mouth of the Miles River.

Marinas & Restaurants. Although many people use Kent Narrows as a convenient shortcut, possibly making a fuel stop there, it offers a considerable number of attractions. In addition to about half a dozen marinas, with the usual assortment of fuel, supplies, hardware, and repair facilities, there are also several restaurants, all but two on the south side of the bridge. With a little planning, the interval between bridge openings can be put to good use.

Fuel is available only at Piney Narrows Yacht Haven and Mears Pointe Marina. Located on the north side of the Route 50 bridge, on opposite sides of the narrows, both have a marine store and limited groceries, in addition to full marina services. The Harris Crab House and Annie's Restaurant are adjacent to Mears Pointe Marina. At the Red Eye's Dock Bar, also located at Mears Pointe Marina, things sometimes get a bit frantic, especially on holiday weekends in prime boating season. Incidentally, on the pier near the Red Eye's Dock Bar is a collection of rather large palm trees! How they survive the winter there is a mystery to me.

On the south side of the bridge are several restaurants right on the water, many with docking facilities for use while you are dining. Right at the bridge is the casual, classic Eastern Shore

–style Angler's Restaurant and Marina. A little farther south is Fisherman's Village, with the Fisherman's Inn, the Fisherman's Seafood Market, and the Crab Deck. Fisherman's Village has space for docking while you dine. Just inside Wells Cove is the Jetty Restaurant, but you'll have a little trouble trying to lay alongside there. You'll do better to go just past it and take a transient slip at Scott Marine Services to go in for a meal.

Anchorages. Often overlooked in the hurry to pass through the narrows is an excellent anchorage hidden behind Hog Island near the southern end of the Kent Narrows Channel. Kirwan Creek provides a sheltered anchorage with good holding ground in 8 to 9 feet of water about a mile away from the marinas and restaurants in Kent Narrows proper.

To enter this anchorage from the narrows, you first must clear the Fl G 2.5s green "3" marker and proceed approximately two-thirds of the way to the green "1" lighted spar before turning to a course of 330 degrees and entering the approach to Kirwan Creek. This course keeps you roughly midway between Hog Island to port and the cinderblock breakwater to starboard, neatly avoiding both sets of shoals. Once you have reached a line between the northern tip of Hog Island and the center of the breakwater, start swinging to port and remain in the center of the creek until you have reached your selected anchorage anywhere to the west or southwest of Hog Island or farther upstream. There is adequate depth here to anchor within less than 100 yards of either shore. Goodhands Creek, opening due west of Hog Island, offers a good alternate anchorage.

The area is pleasant and quiet with a few small, sandy beaches where you can land to beachcomb, wade, or swim (unless the sea nettles take over the water). It is completely protected from wave action and provides a reasonable amount of shelter from the wind without eliminating the cooling breezes needed in hot weather. In warmer weather, be sure to come equipped with a good set of screens and insect repellent for the evening hours, which is when the sizable mosquito population becomes active. Be careful around the poison ivy at the edge of the beaches.

Queenstown Creek

Charts: 12263, 12270, **12272**, 12273

History. About 2½ miles past the entrance to Kent Narrows Channel is the approach to Queenstown Creek. Although never more than a small village, Queenstown was a small colonial port that was used as an outlet for cargoes of grain, hemp, and tobacco and as a receiving point for manufactured goods from Europe. During the War of 1812 the British considered Queenstown important enough to warrant a joint attack by their land and sea forces.

Today Queenstown Creek is shoaled in, so that only a narrow channel remains, making for a precarious entrance to the pretty, well-protected harbor inside. The entrance channel was dredged to a depth of at least 10 feet in 1985, making entrance much easier, but like most of the Bay, it has a tendency to shoal with the winter storms. If you have a draft approaching 6 feet, pay particular attention to the entering instructions and do not enter on a falling tide.

Approaches. All approaches to the creek entrance should be made by leaving nun "2" close to starboard and heading directly toward the lighted green "3" spar, the first of the actual channel markers. Leave green "3" 50 feet to port to avoid the encroaching shoal and head directly toward the red "2" light well inside the entrance, leaving green "5" about 10 to 20 feet to port. The simplest way to ensure remaining in the channel is to maintain your heading so that the red "2" lines up with the left edge of the white house on the shore behind it. If you line up with the right edge of the house, you may bump. If you keep your speed down on negotiating the entrance, you should pass without difficulty. Running aground here is pretty much a "so-what" situation since the bottom is soft and forgiving; however, it is sticky, so getting free isn't entirely carefree.

Anchorages. Hold this course until you are 30 to 50 yards from red "2" before swinging to port to head for the anchorage area. Assume a course that will take you to a point approximately 30 to 50 yards off the pier to starboard. A duck blind or its remains are adjacent to the

Middle Part of Chester River

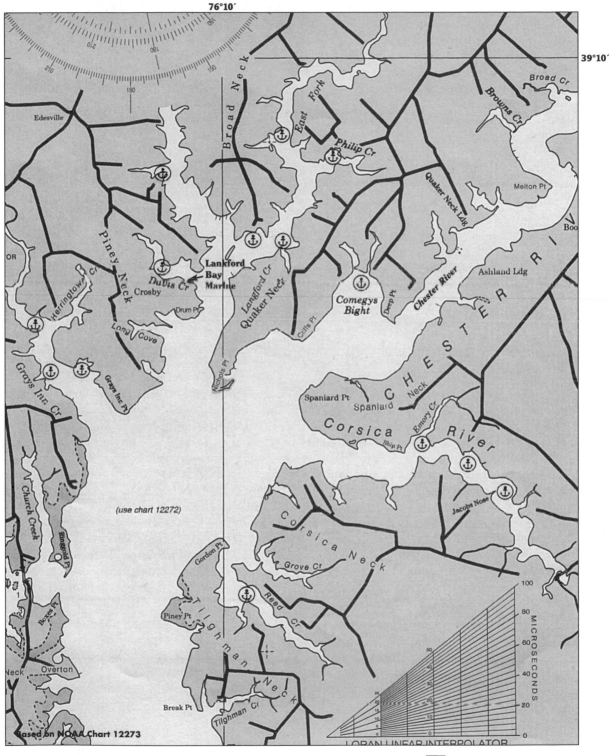

SCALE **0.98"** = **1** NAUT. MILE   ⚓ **Good anchoring**   ⛵ **Marina**   🚤 **Launching site**

Twelve miles above Love Point the Chester sprays into a number of creeks with excellent anchorages.

129

pier on the side closer to the creek entrance. As soon as you come even with the pier, change course to port again to head for the center of the creek in order to avoid the shoal to starboard just past the pier. From here on, you can anchor just about anywhere. There is a minimum depth of 7 feet nearly from shore to shore. Boats with deeper drafts should not proceed very far into Salthouse Cove (to starboard) because the water does start to get thin there.

The upper part of Queenstown Creek, beyond Salthouse Cove, carries at least 6 feet of water until a short distance past Ditchers Cove, where the creek makes a 45-degree bend to the north. There is an overhead power cable in this part of the creek with an authorized vertical clearance of 66 feet. This clearance appears to be a lot less when you are watching your mast approach it! You are better off anchoring short of the cable, although you can find seclusion just around the bend if you have the nerve to go that far.

If you choose to enter Queenstown Harbor, continue around red "2" to starboard as you clear the entrance channel. Once in the harbor, you will see a number of workboats tied to stakes in the water. You can lay alongside the town dock for a maximum of two hours, but finding space is a bit iffy during summer weekends. Alternatively, you can anchor just short of the workboat mooring stakes and take a dinghy ashore if you can find room.

Provisions. From the town dock it is a short walk into town, where you will find a post office and a small convenience store. If you need some groceries or supplies, take Del Rhode Avenue (to the right of the post office) about ⅓ mile to Bob's Mini Mart, at Route 301. Bob's has a nice selection of groceries and an excellent deli.

Grays Inn Creek

Charts: **12272**, 12273, 12278

Approaches. The entrance to Grays Inn Creek, on the northwest side of the river, is about 12 miles up the Chester River from Love Point Light, or about 2 miles past nun "14."

Don't let the unmarked shoals at the creek entrance disturb you; they are no problem if you follow the entrance instructions.

Head due north from can "11" near Hail Point until you pick up Langford Creek can "11," just south of Grays Inn Point. Start your approach from can "1." Set a course of 320 degrees to head directly toward or slightly to the north of the end of the pier on the southwest shore, just inside the creek mouth.

Anchorages. Once you have entered the mouth of the creek, past a line between Grays Inn Point and Little Gum Point, you are in the clear. Simply stay more or less in the middle of the creek until you reach your chosen anchorage.

Not too many cruising boats enter Grays Inn Creek, possibly because cruisers fear the entrance shoals. Those that do enter usually anchor in the mouth of one of the convenient little bights or coves between Browns Point and the entrance to the creek. The character of the creek changes at Browns Point. Before, the land is low-lying and covered in marsh grass with muddy shores. At Browns Point there is a screen of trees above a nice, sandy beach with deep water very close to shore. Then the creek narrows rapidly, and several houses appear.

Holding ground anywhere in the creek is good, and the traffic is usually extremely light. The swimming is excellent through most of the summer, and sea nettles are rare.

Provisions. Ice is available at Steamboat Landing, on the north shore of Herringtown Creek, which branches off to the northeast opposite Browns Point. Gas is available both at Steamboat Landing and at Hills Marine Railway, next to the landing. No other supplies are available. (No, I don't know where Grays Inn was or even if it still exists.)

Chester River, Langford Creek

Charts: **12272**, 12273, 12278

The mouth of Langford Creek is located about 12 miles up the Chester River from Love Point Light, just east of the mouth of Grays Inn Creek. At Cacaway Island, 2 miles upstream from its mouth, Langford Creek splits into the East Fork, the West Fork, and Davis Creek. For cruising, the East Fork, with its rolling farmlands and relatively sparse settlement, is far more attractive than the West Fork. The land in the area is predominantly farmland with a scattering of residences, which are sizable estates, on the western fork.

Anchorages. Langford Creek abounds with excellent anchorages. All are well protected, and most have at least some kind of sandy beach for beachcombing or swimming. While most of the land is low, heavy growths of trees all along the creek provide good shelter from the wind. Throughout the creek, swimming is good whenever the weather and water are warm enough to be comfortable. Sea nettles are rarely a problem even in late August unless it is a particularly bad year for nettles. (In 1987, for example, the nettles were present in quantity all the way to the headwaters.)

History. Like many other areas around the Bay, this region has reminders of times and events that helped shape this country. One of the numerous skirmishes of the War of 1812 was fought at the head of Langford Creek. Men from the British ship HMS *Menelaus* engaged in the harassment of the Eastern Shore were met and repulsed by men of the area in a place called Caulk's Field (inland and between the two forks), near the old St. Paul's Church. A landmark in its own right, the 277-year-old church was constructed in 1713 on the site of the original wooden channel, which dated from 1699.

Approaches. To enter Langford Creek, head due north from can "11" off Hail Point until you pick up either can "1" off Grays Inn Point or the green-red "LC" buoy off Nichols Point. From either of these you can see both can "3" and can "5," which mark the left side of the entrance to Langford Creek. Head directly for can "5," but be sure not to stray to the west of an imaginary line drawn between can "3" and can "5" or you may run afoul of the 1-foot shoal off Deep Cove to port. Incidently, *Deep Cove* is a real misnomer, for it has a maximum depth of only 3 feet and a depth of only 1 foot at the entrance.

If you are navigating upstream, Orchard Point provides a necessary reference. From Langford Creek can "5," set a course that takes you slightly to the left of the watchtower located on Orchard Point (labeled "Lookout Tower" on the chart), but beware of the fishing

stakes often placed to the right of your course. This course takes you to can "7", which is almost impossible to see until you are within ½ mile of it. Do not try to pass west of this can; it appears to be closer to the eastern side of the creek than you would expect, but it is there because of a long shoal that makes out from Drum Point. After rounding can "7," swing to port and remain at least 200 yards off the eastern shore of the creek until you cross an imaginary line between nun "2" at the mouth of Davis Creek to port and the watchtower to starboard. At this point Langford Creek divides into Davis Creek, the West Fork, and the East Fork.

Langford Creek, Long Cove

Charts: **12272**, 12273, 12278

As you proceed upstream from can "5," the marinas in Long Cove offer the first facilities. Long Cove buoys can "1" and can "3" mark the 8-foot-deep channel into the cove. Since the water close to the marinas is a bit on the thin side (the approach depth is 6 feet, but you can't depend on more than 3 feet MLW), other than shoal-draft boats should try elsewhere.

There is no good anchorage here.

Langford Creek, Lawyers Cove

  No facilities

Charts: **12272**, 12273, 12278

The Rock Hall Yacht Club is located in Lawyers Cove, just above Long Cove, but there is even less water than at Long Cove, and I can't recommend trying it without some up-to-the-minute local knowledge.

Langford Creek, Davis Creek

Charts: **12272**, 12273, 12278

Davis Creek, to port, offers a good, easily accessible anchorage. Although somewhat more built up than other areas on Langford Creek, it is pleasant and peaceful enough a little past the marina at its mouth.

Anchorages. The best anchorage is in the first bend of the creek, where it turns to the right. This is a quiet, pretty little area where you can anchor in complete security and good holding in about 7 feet of water.

Marinas & Provisions. If you are looking for marina facilities or a resupply of essentials, the best facilities within 10 miles are at Lankford Bay Marina. It has gas, diesel, ice (block and cube), water, and a small store with a limited amount of marine supplies and even some food. There is no restaurant in the area. The fuel dock is hidden past the last of the boat slips as you proceed toward shore. Just turn sharply to port after passing the last slip and you'll enter a short channel running parallel to the shore, leading to the fuel dock. Hold to within about 50 yards of the marina docks as you approach the fuel dock. It is somewhat chancy for deeper-draft boats, although the water is 8 feet deep alongside the dock.

The Davis Creek Yacht Club, which holds a series of fall races through the first week of November, also operates out of this marina.

While Davis Creek is a pleasant enough anchorage, more attractive anchorages are close at hand in the two forks of Langford Creek.

Langford Creek, West Fork

 3 *No facilities*

Charts: **12272**, 12273, 12278

Approaches. If you proceed up the West Fork of Langford Creek, favor the west side, but watch out for the unmarked, 0-foot shoal that extends a good 100 yards or more off Island Point and the 2-foot shoal off Eagle Point, both to port as you head upstream. (We have personally "surveyed" the shoal off Island Point under full sail and can attest to its presence!)

Anchorages. There are numerous little coves on the western shore of this branch into which you can nestle for the night. Unfortunately, none seems to offer a place to land, and the beaches, if any, leave a bit to be desired. Perhaps the best anchorage is in Bungay Creek, with a close second just inside the entrance to

Shipyard Creek, well upstream. These are small, tight, secure little anchorages, but any location on the West Fork is well protected from both wind and wave.

The entire West Fork is significantly more populated than the East Fork, which is why I feel that the East Fork is a far better choice.

Langford Creek, East Fork

  No facilities

Charts: **12212**, 12273, 12278

Anchorages. As you enter the East Fork of Langford Creek, Cacaway Island, perhaps the best anchorage on Langford Creek, lies to port. Unfortunately, in 1989 "No Trespassing" signs went up on the island. No one seems to know what precipitated this. Even so, if you are wading or on the beach, it is doubtful that anyone will come to chase you off as long as you aren't harming anything. (Note: the island divides the East and West Forks of Langford Creek.) A dense stand of tall trees on the island provides excellent shelter from the critical northwest. The height of the mainland and the trees on it provide good protection from all other directions while still leaving the anchorage open to cooling breezes. At the extreme northern end of the island a sandspit reaches out into the creek, offering a pleasant, sandy beach where you may go ashore to bask in the sun, swim, or build sandcastles. To the west of this spit, along the entire eastern shore of the island, there is deep water almost up to shore. In fact, near the end of the spit, the depth drops to 8 feet at less than that distance from shore! On the other side of the spit, however, the water is no more than thigh-deep all the way across to the mainland.

In the evenings you may see raccoons or opossums (which means "white animal" in some Algonquin language of Virginia) come down to the water to drink or search for clams. Except for the animals, the privately owned island is uninhabited and not very exciting to explore.

A short distance upstream from Cacaway Island is a nice anchorage in the mouth of Wann Cove. Stay at least 100 yards offshore to avoid grounding. There is a small beach around the perimeter of the cove, and due south of where you should be anchored, the sandy hook of Hawbush Point offers a beach where the point partially curves around the mouth of Kings Creek. Stay out of Kings Creek in anything larger than a dinghy or small runabout as there isn't much water.

To the northwest of Wann Cove is an unnamed cove with 9 feet of water nearly up to the southern shore of the entrance, where a small bank rises sharply. If you draw 4 feet or less, you can anchor inside the cove, but it is probably smarter to anchor right in the mouth.

About 1½ miles above Cacaway Island is Phillip Creek, which provides a reasonable alternative anchorage when Cacaway is crowded—as it often is on holiday weekends during the main boating season. Although the entrance is a little tricky, you should have no trouble if you favor the northern shore and do not proceed much beyond 300 yards east of the large house on the north shore. The holding ground is good, and the sandbar at the entrance provides a sandy beach, at least at low tide. There is another bar farther in, closer to where you probably will anchor, but it is all mud.

Across from and a little to the north of Phillip Creek is the Lovely Cove anchorage, which we did not find as inviting as several of the others, although some people like it. It is too "public" for our tastes and has no place to land. Other than that, Lovely Cove is a pretty little place to drop the hook. You can anchor to the inside of the narrow point on the south side of the cove entrance, but watch the depth, as it shoals rapidly.

Just beyond Lovely Cove, in a bend of the river protected by a small bar, is a better anchorage, close to a nice sandy beach. From this point on, you can anchor almost anywhere out of the mainstream of traffic and feel protected from the weather, if not from the occasional power cruiser leaving a large wake.

Don't try to enter either of the two little creeks between Lovely Cove and Island Point; they don't have much water past their mouths.

The East Fork of Langford Creek is navigable as far upstream as Flat Point. Past Flat Point, the water depth drops to 4 feet or less and there are submerged piles off the next upstream point. If you so desire, you can explore the creek for about another mile by dinghy before completely running out of water in the marshy headwaters.

Chester River, Reed Creek

 3 *No facilities*

Charts: **12272**, 12273, 12278

Almost due south of Nichols Point, which marks the eastern side of the mouth of Langford Creek, is the entrance to Reed Creek, an anchorage often avoided by many because of the reputedly "tricky" entrance. However, with a little care this creek can be entered easily.

Approaches. As you round Piney Point on Tilghman Neck while heading upstream in the Chester River, hold to within ¼ mile of the shore of Tilghman Neck. This will guide you directly to can "1" marking the entrance to Reed Creek. The "tricky" part is that you cannot head directly from green can "1" to red nun "2," which is clearly visible in the entrance, because of the unmarked shoal that bows out into the channel from the small point on the eastern side of the entrance. Therefore, from can "1" set a course that would take you about 50 yards to the right of nun "2." Hold this course until you have passed the point on the east shore, then swing to port onto a new course that leaves nun "2" close to starboard (but no closer than 10 yards). Once past nun "2," you are in. Simply remain near the middle of the creek, favoring the west shore until you reach your selected anchorage. The water depths at the entrance are between 7 and 10 feet, and a 7-foot depth is carried for over a mile upstream, with a few deeper areas.

Do not attempt to enter Grove Creek, to port as you pass nun "2," unless you have a draft of less than 3 feet. While there is deep water inside, a bar at the mouth restricts access to very shoal-draft vessels—a shame as it is a pretty little creek. (Gunkholers take note: Here is a challenge.)

Anchorages. As you pass nun "2," swing to starboard and head due west. To starboard is the long sandbar that protects the creek. A sandy beach stretches all along the bar, and you can land here to stretch your legs. In the middle of the bar is a classic mudhole, a playground for those of that particular bent. The first of three excellent anchorages is right here, just before the creek bends sharply to the south.

A small bay halfway up the creek provides another popular anchorage. However, the shore is lined with homes and offers no landing place.

133

Just past this bay, where the creek narrows again, is the third popular anchorage. For about ¼ mile farther up from this point the creek is lined with farm fields and trees. The banks are muddy, but below them are a few small, isolated beaches at low tide where a dog can be "watered." There is no good place to land where you can stretch your legs.

Anywhere you drop the hook in this creek is a good choice. All locations are quiet, serene, and well protected from all directions. There are no marine facilities of any kind on this creek. The closest fuel and supplies are on Langford Creek, 3 to 4 miles away.

Corsica River

  No facilities

Charts: **12272**, 12273

Approaches. A little more than 12 miles up the Chester River from Love Point Light is the Corsica River entrance. A course of 113 degrees (magnetic) from red nun "16," off Nichols Point in the Chester River, takes you directly to nun "2" in the narrowest part of the approach to the Corsica. An alternative approach is to take your departure from the red-green "N" buoy marking the center of the approach to the Corsica and head directly toward nun "2." Favor the north shore as you pass nun "2" to avoid the 2-foot shoal to starboard. This shoal extends to, but not yet past, nun "2." After you clear nun "2," the rest of the river is nearly 10 feet deep from a short distance off each shore, save for a 4-foot shoal extending a good 300 yards to the north about midway between Middle Quarter and Tilghman Coves.

In the mouth of the river, between Town Point and Holten Point, Pioneer Point Manor has been leased by the Russian Embassy for use as an R&R resort. I do not recommend landing on this point to explore.

We were sailing past Town Point a few years ago when we noticed a pompous man strutting down the beach accompanied by another man, quite evidently a bodyguard. Much to our surprise, they suddenly stopped, and the first man peeled off all of his clothes, turned, and strutted into the water. In a few moments it became obvious that he was ordering his companion to join him, which, with

some obvious reluctance, he did. (Note that this took place in mid-July, prime sea-nettle season.) We soon sailed out of sight and never saw the conclusion of the episode, although we could certainly imagine it. Even now, we never pass the mouth of the Corsica without training glasses on Town Point to see whether any more Russians are engaging in that particular form of R&R.

Anchorages. Once within the entrance, you can anchor almost anywhere. However, the three best locations are probably in the bight between Town Point and Middle Quarter Cove, in the bight between Wash Point and Rocky Point, and in the mouth of Emory Creek. All of these have good holding ground and are reasonably well protected from storms from the usual directions. None is likely to be bothered by traffic or water-skiers, and each has some kind of beach on which you can land without bothering the locals. These three areas offer plenty of room for both solitary cruisers and many assorted boats. The shores abound with wildlife, and there are usually clams for the picking.

Above Emory Creek, numerous bends or bights in the river offer excellent anchorages. Simply pick a spot that minimizes the fetch along the river, and you will find a good anchorage.

The last usable anchorage on the Corsica is in the vicinity of Jacobs Nose, a mile upstream from Emory Creek. Just pull to one side to get out of the main traffic pattern and anchor upstream of nun "6."

Although the river is navigable all the way to Centreville Landing, at the headwaters, it is probably not worth going much farther upstream than Jacobs Nose because the river narrows and soon begins to shoal, except for a narrow channel.

There are no facilities readily accessible from the river except for the possible trip upstream to Centreville Landing and a 1-mile walk into Centreville. Centreville is home to the oldest surviving courthouse in Maryland (1792) and a museum. There is also a supermarket.

Comegys Bight

  No facilities

Charts: **12272**, 12273

Anchorages. About 2 miles upstream in the Chester River from the Corsica River entrance is Comegys Bight. This baylike appendage to the river provides a fairly well protected anchorage except from the south to southwest, where it is open to the Chester for several miles. For this reason, and because of the lack of any particular attraction, we have never remained there. There are far better anchorages nearby, such as in the Corsica River.

Island Creek

Charts: **12272**, 12273

The first place on this stretch of the river where a cruiser might practically consider stopping is Kennersley Pointe Marina (410-758-2394), on Island Creek, off Southeast Creek, about 7 miles above the mouth of the Corsica River. Until recently Island Creek was inaccessible to most boats, and there was no reason to try it anyway. Now there is a pleasant little marina, and a channel has been dredged to a depth of 8 feet for a width of 50 feet.

Approaches. Five private markers make the approach relatively easy, provided you pay attention. As you approach Southeast Creek, continue past most of its mouth to round nun "2," which is close inshore to Deep Point, on the far side of the creek mouth. Give nun "2" a wide berth and favor the shore side until you clear the marker. Then hold close to the five private markers, leaving them to starboard and the small island to port. The marina will be directly ahead of you. There is not much room to anchor. Don't plan on it.

Marina. This is one of the increasingly rare family-run marinas on the Bay, and it is quickly recognized as such by the relationship of the Navis family with the boaters there. Usually, 9 of the 50 slips are kept open for transients and can accommodate rather large boats. Reservations are recommended. In addition to marine services, with the exception of diesel fuel, the Navis family provides free transportation to church or Chestertown (11 miles away by road) in a 15-passenger van. This marina has a pool, a welcome item if the nettles

are in (and they do sometimes come this far up the Chester). Both block and crushed ice are available.

Rolph's Wharf

Charts: **12272**, 12273

Approaches. The next potential stopping place is Rolph's Wharf Inn and Marina (410-778-6389), about 1 mile beyond the mouth of Southeast Creek. Start looking for the marina to starboard about ½ mile after passing Southeast Creek.

Provisions. Both gasoline and diesel are now available here, as is pumpout, but ice is a little scarce. During the summer there is a pleasant little restaurant. The marina also offers some groceries and a small marine store.

Dockage. Transients are welcome, but unless you prefer to rent a slip or a mooring, it is not a good place to remain overnight. Aside from the fetch along the river, the slips are totally exposed to wakes from powerboat traffic on the river.

Chestertown

  All facilities

Charts: **12272**, 12273

Once past Rolph's Wharf, the next stop is Chestertown, on the west side of the river just before the Route 213 bridge. At Chestertown you will find a full set of marine facilities, although repairs are limited. Between Chestertown Marina (410-778-3616) and Scotts Point Marina (410-778-2959), you should be able to find a slip, fuel, marine supplies, and more. If you can't find everything you need here, you aren't asking the right people!

Marinas, Restaurants, & Provisions. The Old Wharf Restaurant is right on the riverfront, next to Chestertown Marina. In town are Andy's and the Blue Plate on High Street and Play It Again Sam's snack bar and music store on Cross Street. P.J.'s Market, on High Street, has groceries, and a longer walk, to Route 213 at the north end of town, will take you to a shopping center with a supermarket, bakery, drugstore, department store, and more.

Anchorages. Anchoring in the river near the Route 213 bridge can get "interesting" due to the 180-degree change in the current flow with the change of tide. A plow is the best anchor to use; a Danforth tends to break out as the current reverses. We were anchored here one Fourth of July to watch the fireworks. Even though we had three other boats rafted to us, thanks to our 35-pound plow and all-chain rode we were one of the relatively few boats, in a rather large crowd, that did not drag when the current changed.

The Route 213 drawbridge has a vertical clearance of 12 feet at mean high tide. The bridge opens on demand between 6:00 A.M. and 6:00 P.M. from 1 April to 30 September. At all other times you must give six hours' notice. Instructions are posted on the bridge near the drawspan.

Although the river has at least 7 feet of water all the way to Crumpton, about 7 miles past Chestertown, and about 5 feet for a mile past Crumpton, the trip is probably not worth the effort. It is a pretty river with no special points of interest and no appealing anchorages.

History. Chestertown was established as the county seat in 1698 and was an important and busy port in colonial times. Washington College, founded in 1782, is located here. While Annapolis has more surviving beautiful 18th-century homes, Chestertown has a whole street

of them, all together. Several homes on Water Street were built by shipping merchants during the 18th and 19th centuries.

Chestertown has a favorite historical tale, which any of the residents will be happy to recount in detail. It seems that the citizens of Chestertown held their own "tea party" on 23 May 1774, when they boarded a ship just arrived from England, the brigantine *Geddes*, and dumped her cargo of tea into the water to protest the 1774 tea tax imposed by England on the colonies.

Each year the town celebrates the anniversary of its "tea party" with parades and other activities on Memorial Day weekend. Festivities start on Friday evening with a cocktail party at the Wilmer Park Pavilion overlooking the Chester River. On Saturday a parade begins at 10:30 A.M., with horse-drawn carriages, a fife and drum corps, and more. Around the area, craftsmen — blacksmiths, potters, broom makers, weavers, woodworkers, and others — work at colonial crafts and display their wares. There is also music in the air and food a-plenty, including local and Eastern Shore delicacies. At 2:00 P.M. a crowd of shouting citizens dressed in colonial garb race to the waterfront, row out to the "British ship" in the harbor, and, with some brawling, throw crates of "tea" overboard. Not infrequently, ship crewmembers are added to the "tea" in the harbor. The official closing of the event is 6:00 P.M.

WESTERN SHORE

GUNPOWDER RIVER

Charts: 12272, 12273, **12274** (see also p. 112)

The entire region of the Gunpowder River, from Oliver Point to the Bay, lies within the restricted area belonging to the Aberdeen Proving Grounds (APG). The entire area is normally closed from Monday through Friday, 7:30 A.M. to 5:00 P.M., except on national holidays. The area is also closed at other times, which are an-

nounced over VHF-FM radio; patrol boats direct personnel out of the danger area during periods of active artillery-range firing.

When the area is open, boats may navigate through it, fishing or crabbing is allowed, and water-skiing more than 200 meters offshore is permitted. At no time is swimming allowed, nor may any person or boat touch the bottom, the shore, or a pier within the restricted area. (This regulation is undoubtably due to the probable presence of dud shells and explosives lying on the bottom.)

Saltpeter & Dundee Creeks

 No facilities

Charts: 12272, 12273, **12274**

A short distance inside the mouth of the Gunpowder River, Saltpeter and Dundee Creeks share a common entrance, which is completely within the Aberdeen restricted area. Even without that problem, both creeks are fairly shallow, limiting access to boats of less than a 4-foot draft. Even shallow-draft vessels risk grounding on the unmarked shoals. This is normally runabout country only, and that by virtue of a launching ramp on the east side of Dundee Creek.

There are better anchorages nearby; skip this one.

Upper Gunpowder River

Charts: 12272, 12273, **12274**

While there are launching ramps and small-boat facilities above the fixed bridge (vertical clearance 12 feet), much more accessible launching and other facilities may be found elsewhere. There are no anchorages worthy of the name on this river.

For the above reasons, any detailed description of this area is omitted here. We recommend that all transient cruising boats avoid it. This is runabout country.

SENECA CREEK, MIDDLE RIVER, & BACK RIVER

Charts: 12273, **12278**

This is a busy, built-up area of the Bay. You'll find plenty of provisions and places to eat but little peace and quiet. These three bodies of water share the same entrance to the Chesapeake.

Seneca Creek

Charts: 12273, **12278**

Approaches. Seneca Creek is located just above the mouth of Middle River, and the entire eastern shore of this creek is within the restricted area of the APG.

Anchorages. A possible anchorage in 5 to 8 feet of water is just past the point where the creek turns to the west. Although there are three marinas on this creek, the creek is shallow, except for a narrow channel, and heavily built up, offering little to interest the transient cruiser. This is predominantly powerboat country, and even the powerboats belong to residents.

Hawthorn Cove, right at the mouth of Seneca Creek, looks much more appealing but lies entirely within the restricted area, and it is totally open to the south.

More interesting creeks and far better anchorages exist nearby. Skip this one too.

Middle River

  All facilities

Charts: 12273, **12278**

Approaches. This river is probably the most civilized tributary on the Bay. A cursory exploration reveals every inch of shoreline to be privately owned and built up. Although a number of navigable creeks splinter off Middle River as you proceed upstream and there are numerous marinas all over the area, if you are looking for quiet and solitude in unspoiled surroundings, look elsewhere. There are marina facilities and restaurants on virtually all the little creeks off the main part of the river. Pay attention to your chart because there are a number of shoals, not all of which are well marked. In particular, stay well off Booby Point, on the south side of the mouth of the river; an unmarked shoal there extends east for a good 1/3 mile. (Is it possible that the frequency of inattentive mariners "surveying" this shoal is the source of the name of the point?)

SENECA CREEK, MIDDLE RIVER, & BACK RIVER

Baltimore
See Detail Map

Bayside Bridge

Fort
McHenry

Dundalk
Marine
Terminal

Buoy site of
Star Spangled Banner
Francis Scott Key N BnRW

Sollers
Point

North Poi
Creek

Curtis Bay

Hawkins Point

Old
Road
Bay

Curtis Creek

North Point

Coast Guard

Patapsco
River

White Rocks

Rock Creek

Fort Smallwood

Nabbs Creek

Stony Creek

Hog Neck

Main Creek

Based on NOAA chart 12278

SCALE **1″ = 1.72** NAUT. MILES ⚓ **Good anchoring** ⛵ **Marina** 🛥 **Launching site**

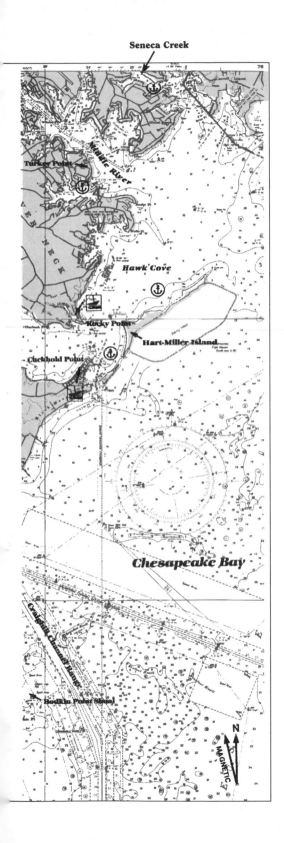

Seneca Creek

Turkey Point

Middle River

Hawk Cove

Rocky Point

Hart-Miller Island

Cuckhold Point

Chesapeake Bay

Craighill Channel Range

Bodkin Point Shoal

N

MAGNETIC

Warning: If you are in a sailboat with a mast higher than 37 feet, be very careful when entering Frog Mortar Creek. Aircraft using the runway at Martin State Airport, on the northwest side of the creek entrance, may find you to be an obstruction. Contact the Martin State Airport control tower on VHF-FM channel 16 to warn them of your presence before transiting this area.

If you are not looking for marina facilities, this river holds little of interest. Sue Creek, on the southwest shore near the mouth of the river, may be the exception. It is the location of the hospitable Baltimore Yacht Club, which has an attractive clubhouse situated on the top of the hill on Sue Island, at the mouth of the creek.

You have to negotiate two unmarked shoals in order to enter Sue Creek. One extends to the east from Sue Island, and the other to the southeast from Turkey Point on the other side of the creek entrance. The easiest way to find the entrance for the first time is to take your departure from the red "4" buoy just off Bowley Point ("Bowley Bar" on some charts). From red "4," head directly for the green "1" flasher on a 14-foot-high piling at the entrance, and you will neatly avoid both shoals. Hold close to the "1" marker and the docks to port as you enter the creek—a shoal on the starboard side extends roughly to the middle of the entrance.

Marinas & Restaurants. Don't go farther than the yacht club docks if you draw close to 6 feet as the water starts to get thin. Slips are usually available for visiting yachtsmen from other recognized yacht clubs. Other than gas, diesel fuel, and a restaurant, no supplies are available here or elsewhere on Sue Creek.

If you draw less than 5 feet, you can proceed well up the main branch of the creek, as far as the Red Eye Yacht Club, which is on the south side of the creek, nearly to the headwaters, near the last fork in the creek. The Red Eye claims to have transient slips available.

Anchorages. If you choose to anchor, the best location is probably under the lee of the high bank on the south shore, opposite Sue Island. The bottom is soft mud with good holding, and the immediate vicinity is relatively unpopulated.

SENECA CREEK, MIDDLE RIVER, & BACK RIVER

Back River

Charts: 12273, 12278

History. The mouth of Back River is guarded on the Bay side by Hart-Miller Island. Older charts show these islands as separate, but the gap between them no longer exists. In the early 1980s, Hart and Miller Islands were selected as the site where the spoil from the dredging of Baltimore Harbor would be dumped. For some time this decision was quite controversial. As it turned out, the dumping created no problem and may have actually enhanced the islands. On the Bay side, a long bulkhead has been constructed to retain the spoil. This wall extends from the south end of Hart Island and curves around to the northern tip of Miller Island, where it terminates.

What to See & Do. Hawk Cove, on the Back River side of the islands, provides the primary point of interest to the boating population. The bulkheading company has deposited a huge amount of sand, which not only filled in the gap but also created a nice beach area that is open to the boating public. The main parts of the islands are marked by "No Trespassing" signs.

While the beach is a nice attraction during the warm summer months, don't plan to stay aboard your boat for any length of time while anchored in that region. The Back River entertains considerable powerboat traffic, which causes an unpleasant chop during most of the day. In addition, there is a long fetch to the north and northwest; a wind from that direction can make this an uncomfortable anchorage. I don't recommend remaining overnight here unless you are sure that the wind will be out of the south or southeast (the prevailing direction during the summer).

Approaches. The primary approach to Back River is the same as for Middle River. Although there are plenty of navigation markers, all you have to do to enter Back River is to guide on Hart-Miller Island, staying off at least 100 yards. Once you reach the southwest corner of Hawk Cove, simply honor any markers you see. A dredged channel passes between the mainland and the tiny island just south of Hart Island, providing a shortcut to Hawk Cove or to the upper part of Back River from the main

Bay. The entrance is easy to find from the Bay: a 105-foot-high tower, which is the rear Craighill Channel Range light, marks the east side of the channel entrance and can be seen from miles away. However, this channel is narrow, and shoaling to 2 feet has been reported, so it is best left to shoal-draft powerboats.

There are numerous unmarked shoals in the Back River, the shoreline is heavily populated, and there are no interesting creeks or tributaries to explore. Other than a number of marinas, if you are in need of supplies or repair, it has little to recommend it.

PATAPSCO RIVER

Charts: 12273, 12278, 12281

The Patapsco River points like a finger into the heart of Baltimore, one of the world's largest ports. Located about 150 miles from Cape Henry and about 50 miles from the Chesapeake & Delaware Canal, the Port of Baltimore is even busier today than it was in the heyday of the clipper ships.

Just a few years ago, yachts cruising the Bay did not go beyond Rock Creek, near the mouth of the Patapsco, without some specific reason. But things have changed rapidly. The harbor is cleaner, and Baltimore completely renovated the Inner Harbor area in the late 1970s and is still continuing the process toward Fells Point and other parts of the city.

The Patapsco has three distinctly different portions. Two—the outer portion, from the Francis Scott Key Bridge to the Chesapeake Bay, and the Inner Harbor of Baltimore—offer harbors of interest to cruising boats. Between them, the third portion, consisting of the part of the river from the Key Bridge to Fort McHenry (with the possible exception of some of the upper portions of Curtis Creek), is lined with the shipping port facilities and shipyards, which, while of direct interest only to commercial shipping, can be fascinating to observe as you cruise past.

The outer portion of the Patapsco River constitutes the real cruising ground of this river. This area is roughly bounded to the northwest by the Francis Scott Key Bridge, to the northeast by North Point, and to the southwest and south by Rock Point and Bodkin Creek.

Until the spring of 1989, Sevenfoot Knoll Lighthouse served as a convenient aiming point for an approach from the south or east. The squat, 42-foot-high, red screwpile-type structure has been moved to Baltimore's Inner Harbor, where it is part of the permanent maritime displays. Functioning in its stead is a much less obvious platform light. The easiest approach is to plot a course to take you a good mile to the north of Bodkin Point. Bodkin Point Shoal extends more than ¾ mile to the east of the tip of Bodkin Point.

If you are approaching from the north, the front Craighill Channel Range light, a 39-foot-high, cylindrical white concrete lighthouse, serves as your guide. You can leave this light to either side, but be careful of the 4-foot shoal 1 mile to the east-southeast of it.

Beware of the unmarked shoals that extend from North Point, on the north side of the Patapsco River entrance, and from Rock Point, on the south side. Once clear of these shoals, you can choose to enter Old Road Bay and continue on up the Patapsco toward Baltimore or approach either Rock Creek or Stony Creek.

Ahead of you, clearly visible from miles away, is the Francis Scott Key Bridge, spanning the Patapsco River between Hawkins and Sollers Points. With a vertical clearance of 195 feet, this bridge presents no obstacle to boating traffic (although a ship did manage to hit one of the bridge supports a few years ago).

To the north of the shipping channel, just before the Francis Scott Key Bridge, is the abandoned Fort Carroll. Started in 1848 as part of the defense structure for Baltimore, this was supposed to be a four-story, 40-foot-high fortress that would hold as many as 350 cannons. Robert E. Lee, then a lieutenant, was in charge of the construction. After three years of effort and an expenditure of more than $1 million (a much more impressive amount of money in those days), Congress refused to provide more funds, and construction ceased. In 1854, a small lighthouse was erected on the unfinished fort. Today Fort Carroll remains unfinished, unmanned, and inhospitable to visitors. "No Trespassing" signs are posted, but visitors can tour around the structure by boat.

Past the Francis Scott Key Bridge, you can see Fort McHenry in the distance. In the water past the bridge a buoy painted red, white, and blue marks the spot where the ship upon which Francis Scott Key wrote "The Star Spangled Banner" was anchored during the 1814 bombardment of the fort. Seeing Fort McHenry from the water is still a bit of a thrill, especially if you have first toured the fort by land. Unfortunately, docking is neither permitted nor practical at the fort. In calm conditions, you might try anchoring southwest of the fort, near the discontinued spoil area, and land by dinghy. However, watch the depth carefully, and be prepared to haul your dinghy out of the water over the riprap (big rocks) protecting the shoreline. Be very careful not to anchor in the pipeline area extending south across Middle Branch from the southern tip of the point on which the fort is located.

At Fort McHenry the river forks. The north fork leads to Baltimore's fascinating Inner Harbor. The south fork offers only a couple of marinas.

The various creeks branching off the Patapsco River provide a range of cruising grounds, some well worth the visit, others probably not worth it.

Bodkin Creek

Charts: 12273, 12278, **12281**

At the mouth of the Patapsco River, on the southern shore, is Bodkin Creek. Although it is neither as scenic nor as secluded as many of the rivers and creeks on the Eastern Shore, Bodkin Creek holds several attractions for those who enjoy being in and around the water as well as on it.

Marinas & Restaurants. There are no supply facilities within reasonable access of the water, although ice is available at Ventnor Marina, on Ventnor Point (marked as "Graveyard Point" on most charts, but no one calls it that), just a little way up Main Creek. Haulouts and repairs are available at Ventnor Marina, Carback's Pleasure Cove Marina well up Main Creek (which has the only restaurant and the only self-service laundry on the creek), and Bodkin's Boat Yard on Back Creek. Germershausan's and Pinehurst Boat Yards, on Locust Cove, also offer repairs, mainly for powerboats.

Approaches. Although narrow, the entrance to the creek is well marked, and with a little prudence it is not difficult to negotiate. If this is your first time, enter the creek slowly, under power. The entrance should be approached well north of Bodkin Point Shoal, marked by green spars "3" and "5." Not only has the shoal shifted but the buoyage system and spar locations were changed in 1976, and another green daymark was added in 1986, so be sure to use a current chart. Leave the green "7" dolphin near the entrance close to port and head directly between the red "10" and green "9" daymarks. These daymarks are located at both the narrowest (about 50 feet wide) and the shallowest part of the channel. If your draft is much over 5 feet, enter only at high water. A bar across the entrance just inside the "9" and "10" daymarks allows creek access only to vessels with a draft of 6 feet or less. Head from the daymarks to leave the green "11 " dolphin on Cedar Point (opposite Old Landon Point) close to port. Beyond this marker the creek maintains a fairly constant 8- to 10-foot depth all the way to the headwaters. Don't try to cut inside the red "12" daymark off Spit Point (between Main Creek and Back Creek); you won't make it.

Anchorages. There are two excellent anchorages off sandy beaches on the main creek. The first, and the more heavily used, is just inside Cedar Point off Bodkin Neck, where you can anchor in 8 to 10 feet of water to within 50 yards or less from the shore. Unfortunately, the pleasant, sandy beach inside the creek entrance is no longer accessible. Condominiums and a condominium marina have been constructed there, closing the beach to all others. Everything else along the shore is private property. This area is also subject to almost constant powerboat wakes as boats roar in and out of the creek.

The second anchorage is about a mile upstream, on the southern side of Main Creek between Jubb Cove and Goose Cove. Although it is smaller than the first anchorage and doesn't have much of a beach, we prefer this spot over the other—water-skiers are much less of a nuisance; it is quieter, less frequented by other

boats; and we rarely ever see a sea nettle. The short beach used to end in a 15-foot cliff. Until the mid-80s the top of the cliff was uninhabited and thickly wooded. Now the whole area has been developed, and the top of the cliff is thick with houses. There is no longer a place to land here.

To the south of Spit Point is a third attractive anchorage, in the little cove to the north of Old Bee Point. While it is well protected from weather, as is the entire creek, there is no place to land, and you are still exposed to powerboat and water-skier wakes.

The other two branches of Bodkin Creek, Back Creek and Wharf and Locust Creeks, are both packed solid with homes; there is little to see and no place to land.

Old Road Bay

Charts: 12273, 12278, **12281**

Approaches. Old Road Bay is located on the north side of the entrance to the Patapsco River, just past North Point. A relatively narrow, well-marked channel leading from the main part of the Patapsco into Old Road Bay is intended for deep-draft ships. Cruising boats can ignore it for all practical purposes. In fact, if you hold a course to leave the red "2" daymark west of North Point well to starboard, you can enter with no problem.

Marinas. The west fork, Jones Creek, has about four marinas but should be left strictly to shoal-draft vessels. The surroundings are heavily industrial.

The east fork, North Point Creek, has several marinas and a narrow channel that carries at least 7 feet up to the headwaters. This branch is not as industrial, but other than to put in for fuel (gas only) or supplies, you should look elsewhere for an overnight stay.

Rock Creek

Charts: 12273, 12278, **12281**

Approaches. Past Rock Point, on the south side of the Patapsco River, approximately 4 miles upriver from Sevenfoot Knoll Light, Rock Creek is an excellent refuge in rough weather and probably the most convenient stopover en route to and from Baltimore's Inner Harbor. Stay well off Rock Point, as a shoal extends more than ½ mile to the north.

The mouth of the creek is easily identified by the White Rocks, a large rock formation located about ½ mile northwest of Rock Point. A friend of ours claims that the seagulls maintain the whiteness of these wonders of the Bay, the only known rocks of this size in the entire Chesapeake. With 12 feet or more of water all the way to most of the marinas, the wide, well-marked channel extends straight into the creek, due southwest of the White Rocks.

Marinas. Of the six marinas on this creek, only the Maryland Yacht Club, just inside the entrance, and the Pasadena Yacht Basin, a mile upstream, offer gasoline and diesel fuel. Most of the six have repair facilities and a marine railway or travelift. Both White Rocks Marina and the Cross Current Inn have a bar and a restaurant. For those with a membership in a recognized yacht club, bar-and-restaurant service is also available at the Maryland Yacht Club, immediately to port as you clear the green "3" light off Fairview Point. Oak Harbor Marina, a mile upstream, is a friendly place offering excellent repairs of all sorts.

Transient slips are usually available at the marinas, and there are well-protected anchorages in the mouth of Tar Cove and Wall Cove. No anchoring is permitted upstream of Water Oak Point due to a state water purification system. Bubbles welling to the surface and a series of warning buoys mark the no-anchoring area. Marinas and residences take up the shore, leaving no place to land.

Stony Creek

Charts: 12273, 12278, **12281**

Approaches. On the south side of the Patapsco River, about a mile to the west of the White Rocks, is the entrance to Stony Creek. Be sure to start your entrance from nun "2," about ½ mile northeast of the reddish brown rocks that guard the entrance to the creek. From nun "2," a heading of 240 degrees takes you to the red "4" lighted marker on a piling. (This flashing 4-second red "4" is nearly onshore and hard to make out on the chart.) Maintain this course until you have passed the reddish-brown rocks to port and are quite close to red "4." (You may have the feeling that you are going to hit the shore.) When the lighted, flashing 4-second green "5" is abeam, swing to port to pass midway between green "5" and red "6." The channel is narrow here, so be sure to stay in the middle. As soon as you pass red "6," swing to starboard toward nun "8." Once past nun "8," you are in, and the creek opens up with deep water from shore to shore. From here on, you have about 15 feet of water.

The next obstacle is the drawbridge (vertical clearance 18 feet MHW), about ½ mile from the entrance. This bridge is manned 24 hours a day and opens on demand except from 7:00 to 9:00 A.M. and from 4:00 to 6:00 P.M., during weekday rush hours. Blow one long and one short blast on your horn to request that the bridge be raised. For emergency passage, you can call the bridge tender on VHF-FM channel 13.

Anchorages. Anchor anywhere past nun "8." Although the area is well settled, the creek is quiet, peaceful, and fully protected from the weather. A 6-mph speed limit, instituted in 1990, makes the entire creek beyond the bridge a no-wake zone. Water-skiers can use the area from the Patapsco River creek entrance to the bridge. Nabbs Creek, well up Stony Creek, and Back Cove, off Nabbs Creek, also offer protected, quiet anchorages. All have depths over 10 feet.

Marinas & Restaurants. Gas (no diesel) used to be available at Stony Creek Bridge Marina, to starboard just past the bridge. However,

I have been told that this is no longer the case. There is a restaurant and pumpout station at Maurgate Marina, on the south side of Nabbs Creek. There are also restaurants at Hand Brothers Marina, at the head of Nabbs Creek, and Thomas's Railway and Marina, in Back Cove.

Bear Creek

Charts: 12273, 12278, **12281**

Approaches. The entrance to Bear Creek is on the north side of the Patapsco River, just before the Francis Scott Key Bridge. In spite of the number of marinas and boatyards on the creek, several of which hope to attract transients as well as residents, there is little here to entice the transient cruiser. The area is simply too commercial and built up. In addition, the water is usually discolored by pollution from the local industries; never swim here.

Anchorages. To get to the only anchorages that might even be considered, you must first negotiate four bridges. The first bridge (actually an extension of the Key Bridge) is a fixed bridge with 53 feet of clearance MHW. The second bridge, once a drawbridge, has been discontinued, and its span has been removed. The third and fourth are a drawbridge and a swing bridge, with normal vertical clearances of 25 and 8 feet MHW, respectively.

Passing a fifth bridge (a drawbridge with a vertical clearance of 12 feet MHW when closed) will take you to the Bear Creek headwaters, which carry 8 to 9 feet of water almost to the end. However, the shore is built up, and we see no good reason to go there, not even to anchor for the night.

There is one relatively secluded area where you can anchor, to starboard just after you negotiate the fourth bridge. The shore is wooded, and a sandy beach stretches about 100 yards. We used to recommend Lynch Cove, to port after the fourth bridge, as an anchorage, but now the shore is completely built up. Anchor Bay East Marina, to port in the mouth of Lynch Cove, and Lynch Cove Marina, near the headwaters, both have fuel.

Curtis Creek

Charts: 12273, 12278, **12281**

Approaches. On the south side of the Patapsco River, about 1½ miles past the Francis Scott Key Bridge, is the entrance to Curtis Bay and Curtis Creek. One of the largest U.S. Coast Guard bases on the East Coast is located just past Stedds Point near the entrance to this creek. This is a shipbuilding and buoy-maintenance facility capable of constructing both steel and fiberglass Coast Guard vessels. The base is normally closed to the public; group tours can be arranged on weekends. The base is open to the public on Armed Forces Day, when there are demonstrations of Coast Guard activities.

Marinas. Hull repairs are available at Smith & Sons Shipyard, on the east side of the creek before you reach the Coast Guard station. Gas (no diesel) is available at the Launching Pad Marina, in Marley Creek, near the headwaters of Curtis Creek.

Anchorages. The first half of Curtis Creek is heavily commercial; the water is dirty, and the area could hardly be called scenic. However, if you pursue your course upstream past the industrial area, the upper reaches of the creek offer a couple of nice anchorages in Marley Creek and Furnace Creek. Swimming is not recommended because the water quality is questionable. The region does offer an alternative to anchoring in Baltimore harbor or traveling several more miles to another creek.

Baltimore

 All facilities

Charts: 12273, 12278, **12281**

Approaches. As you approach Fort McHenry the Patapsco River forks. Although there are a couple of small marinas located in the Middle Branch, to port past the swing bridge, most of the left fork is highly industrialized and of little interest. The right fork leads to the Inner Harbor of Baltimore, a trip worth taking.

On the Fourth of July each year a huge fleet of boats descends on the Inner Harbor area and

PATAPSCO RIVER

its outer reaches to watch the city's elaborate fireworks display. Watching fireworks near Fort McHenry, the birthplace of our national anthem, on Independence Day provides a thrill found in few other places in the country.

Anchoring anywhere in the region between the Francis Scott Key Bridge and Fort McHenry is not normally recommended because of the shipping traffic. Each year, more than 4,000 ships (about 11 per day) enter Baltimore Harbor. Hundreds of business organizations in the area are associated with the shipping industry in one manner or another. Except for companies that provide a direct service to the private boating population, most people are only vaguely aware of the surging and varied activities associated with each ship that enters the harbor. All most of us see are the piers, factories, and ships as we cruise by, especially the huge Dundalk Marine Terminal, to starboard past the bridge. Enough cargo passes through these terminals to make Baltimore the third largest seaport in the United States, just behind New York City and Norfolk.

Leave Fort McHenry to port and proceed up the north (right) fork, labeled "Northwest Harbor" on the chart. Just past the fort, the Canton Marine Terminal lies to starboard. This is

North branch of the Patapsco River: Baltimore Inner Harbor to Fort McHenry.

Fort McHenry: Birthplace of "The Star-Spangled Banner."

the largest privately owned marine terminal on the East Coast and one of the oldest, founded in 1829. The name stems from the estate of John O'Donnel, a captain in the East India merchant service and a colonel in the Maryland Militia, who settled in Baltimore in 1780. He named his waterfront estate after Canton, his favorite Chinese port. Nearly 50 years later his son formed the Canton Company, which eventually became today's terminal.

What to See & Do. As you proceed upstream, a cluster of marinas at Fells Point will be to starboard. Baltimore's original shipbuilding and maritime center, the Fells Point area is alive with the port's commercial activities, and the market there is well worth a visit. Cobblestone streets lead to an assortment of shops, pubs, restaurants, and the Fells Point Fishmarket. More than 350 of the original residences in this area still remain, many of them restored to their former elegance under Baltimore's downtown renewal project. All but one are still private residences. The "one" has been converted into an inn, right on the waterfront at the end of Broadway. Here also is Brown's Wharf, a group of renovated brick warehouses, houses specialty shops.

There is some public dockage at Brown's Wharf, just past the tip of Fells Point itself, and at the end of Broadway, to the west of the large, redbrick Recreation Building on—what else?—the Recreation Pier. If you are lucky, or if you plan far enough ahead, you can tie up for a few hours to visit Fells Point or even remain overnight. Tie up only on the west side; the east side, along the Recreation Pier, is reserved exclusively for tugboats. Call ahead to the Brown's Wharf harbormaster's office (410-563-3900) between 8:30 A.M. and 4:30 P.M., Monday through Friday, especially if you wish to spend the night. If you just show up and take your chances, be sure to check in with the dockmaster promptly. If you decide to put in on the spur of the moment, especially on a weekend, give it a try. However, for the reasons just cited, it is a better idea to plan ahead and contact the office beforehand.

As you pass Fells Point and the huge landmark sign of the Domino Sugar Company (reputed to be the largest neon sign in the world), you are entering Baltimore's Inner Harbor. Space does not permit anything close to a full description of the Inner Harbor. It would take a full book to describe all the activities and things to see and do there. Revitalization of the downtown Baltimore area began in 1959, and the Inner Harbor, in particular, now bears no resemblance to what it replaced. The following list of attractions barely scratches the surface and does not even include everything on the Inner Harbor.

To starboard is the huge, tentlike structure of the Pier 6 Concert Pavilion, a summertime concert hall with programs ranging from jazz to performances of the Baltimore Symphony Orchestra. In the huge building just to the east of Pier 6 is the Baltimore Public Works Museum.

Pier 5 contains the Clarion Hotel, Harrison's Restaurant, and the Lady Maryland Foundation.

Pier 4 is the Baltimore Maritime Museum, with its collection of ships and the old Sevenfoot Knoll Lighthouse, which used to stand off Bodkin Point, in the mouth of the Patapsco River. This is also the location of the "Power Plant." Once it supplied electric power to the city's streetcars, and for a while it held four nightclubs called P. T. Flagg's. Now it contains the Hard Rock Café, Barnes & Noble Bookstore, Gold's Gym, and Disney's ESPN Zone.

Pier 3 holds the fabulous National Aquarium (410-576-3800), which contains more than 5,000 specimens of marine creatures in natural environments, as well as the largest coral-reef exhibit in the continental United States. It even has a large room in which a tropical rainforest is recreated. The submarine USS *Torsk* and the lightship *Chesapeake* are tied to the west side of the aquarium pier. (Note: the ships' locations are subject to change.) There is some space for private boats to tie up along the east side of the pier.

Just past the aquarium, the 30-story, pentagonal tower of the World Trade Center dominates the skyline. The top floor of the building, ostentatiously called the "Top of the World," is open to the public (Monday through Saturday, 10:00 A.M. to 5:00 P.M.; Sunday, 12:00 P.M. to 5:00 P.M.) and sponsors various art exhibits, including oil paintings and marine photography. The five-sided panoramic view of Baltimore and the Patapsco River from the top of this building is spectacular. There is an admission fee.

Next is the sloop of war USS *Constellation* (visiting hours: 15 May–15 October, 10:00 A.M. to 5:45 P.M. daily; 16 October–14 May, Monday through Saturday 10:00 A.M. to 3:45 P.M., Sunday 10:00 A.M. to 4:45 P.M.). Arguably, the oldest American warship continuously afloat and in commission since she was launched. Visitors can examine this ship both above and below decks and ponder on the days of "wooden ships and iron men" (see the Navy's Last Sailing Ship, USS *Constellation* sidebar, page 152).

In the northwest corner of the Inner Harbor is Harborplace, comprising two large buildings. Each of these buildings is not really one place but many. The two-story, glass-and-metal pavilions contain markets for produce, fish, meat, and dairy foods; a trading hall featuring other food items; an indoor park where a variety of international foods are served over the counter; a bazaar for crafts and gift items; and about a dozen traditional and contemporary cafés and restaurants. The building to the west is almost completely food oriented, whereas the one to the east is retail oriented.

In the southwest corner of the Inner Harbor is the Maryland Science Center. The hours are Tuesday through Thursday, 10:00 A.M. to 5:00 P.M.; Friday and Saturday, 10:00 A.M. to 10:00 P.M.; Sunday, 12:00 P.M. to 6:00 P.M.; closed Monday. The unusually shaped building houses a variety of technical exhibits and displays, as well as a planetarium. The center encourages visitors to see, touch, and use many of its exhibits of the Chesapeake Bay, Baltimore, and general science. Be sure to pay it a visit.

When it is in port, the *Pride of Baltimore II*, a replica of a Baltimore clipper, is berthed in front of the science center (on the loss of the *Pride of Baltimore I* and the construction of the *Pride II*, see the *Prides of Baltimore* sidebar, page 151).

Just to the east of Federal Hill, sandwiched between the Inner Harbor Marina and the Harbor View Marina, is the American Visionary Art Museum, the only one of its kind in the United States, dedicated to presenting works of "self-taught visionary" or "outsider" artists.

Immediately to the east of the Harborview Marina is Baltimore's Museum of Industry, which includes a real production line from a turn-of-the-century oyster-canning factory. You can even take a turn on the line!

Probably the best way to get around Baltimore's harbor area is by one of the two water-

Baltimore's Inner Harbor and Fells Point

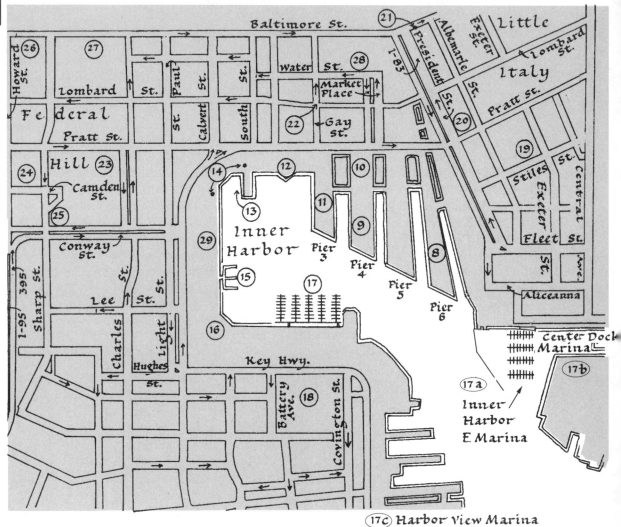

BALTIMORE INNER HARBOR / FEDERAL HILL

- ⑧ Pier 6 Concert Pavilion
- ⑨ Baltimore Maritime Museum
- ⑩ Hard Rock Café & ESPN Zone
- ⑪ National Aquarium
- ⑫ World Trade Center
- ⑬ USS *Constellation*
- ⑭ Harborplace
- ⑮ City Piers
- ⑯ Maryland Science Center
- ⑰ Inner Harbor Marina
- ⑰a Inner Harbor East Marina
- ⑰b Center Dock Marina
- ⑰c Harbor View Marina
- ⑱ Federal Hill Park
- ⑲ Little Italy
- ⑳ Star-Spangled Banner House
- ㉑ Shot Tower
- ㉒ "Corned Beef Row"
- ㉓ Convention Center
- ㉔ Festival Hall
- ㉕ Old Otterbein United Methodist Church
- ㉖ Baltimore Arena
- ㉗ Morris Mechanic Theatre
- ㉘ ㉙ Information

SCALE 1" = **664** FEET

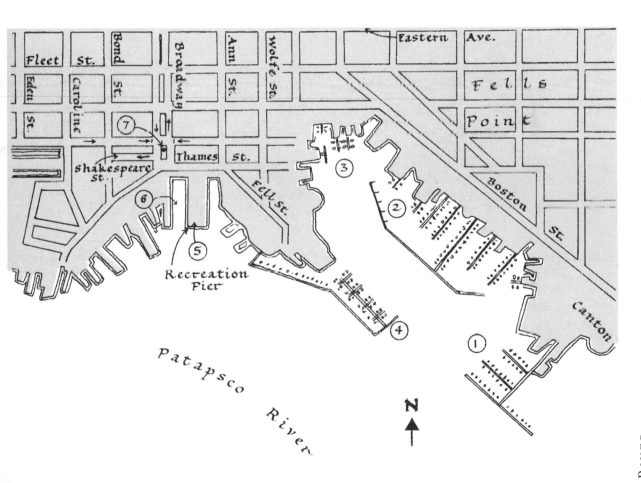

FELLS PT.

① Baltimore Marine Center
② The Anchorage Marina
③ Bay View Marina
④ Henderson's Wharf Inn
   & Marina
⑤ Recreation Pier
⑥ Brown's Wharf
⑦ Fells Pt. Fishmarket

Fleet St.

Bond St.

Broadway

Ann St.

Wolfe St.

Eastern Ave.

Eden St.

Caroline St.

F e l l s

P o i n t

Boston St.

⑦ Thames St.

Shakespeare St.

③

② Canton

⑥

Fell St.

⑤

Recreation Pier

④

①

Patapsco River

N

Note: Arrows indicate flow of traffic on one-way streets.

taxi services, which stop at several points in the Inner Harbor, Fells Point, Captain James Landing, and Canton Waterfront Park. For a nominal fee you can ride around the harbor all day, whenever you feel like going from one area to another. Ed Kane's Water Taxi (410-563-3901) and the Harbor Shuttle (410-675-2900) both offer a great way to see the harbor as well as to get around.

Marinas & Provisions. If you can find space, you can tie up along the seawall in the Inner Harbor, right off the west pavilion of Harborplace. To the south of Harborplace are the public piers, where you can get a slip, if you are lucky. It's first come, first served, no reservations taken. See the harbormaster as soon as you get in; the office is just south of the Harborplace food pavilion. There is a fee both for berthing in slips and for tying to the seawall. This fee has increased each year. Both choices are very public; people will be wandering by above you at all hours of the day or night. You can anchor out in the harbor (depth greater than 30 feet), but that too has a fee, and a paddleboat flotilla runs around the harbor constantly, reducing that option's appeal.

On the south shore of the Inner Harbor, directly opposite the National Aquarium, is the Inner Harbor Marina of Baltimore (410-837-5339), probably the best place for a cruiser to tie up while visiting Baltimore. There are more than 150 slips arranged along floating piers, with water and electricity at each. Showers and restrooms are close ashore; gas and diesel fuel are available, as is a fair-size marine store. There is even a small convenience store nearby. Transients are welcome, but prior arrangement for a slip is a must. This marina is so popular that slips are booked well in advance. Here you can leave your boat in perfect security. The docks are closed off by a fence, and the area is patrolled constantly. Only those with boats there, and their guests, are allowed on the dock. The marina has an agent for both dinner and theater reservations and can provide information on Baltimore events and activities.

The Inner Harbor East Marina (410-625-1700) is on the north side of the entrance to the Inner Harbor, behind an artificial breakwater. It is very near Little Italy, a small section of Baltimore full of excellent Italian restaurants.

Directly across the harbor from Little Italy, on the south side, is the easily identified Harbor View Marina (410-752-1122), with all the facilities you may need, including a marine store with grocery.

Between the Inner Harbor and Canton are at least a baker's dozen of marinas, all of which offer transient slips and most marine facilities. Just find one with space and use the water taxis to get around.

What to See & Do. Behind the marina is a field where the city holds ethnic festivals representing one or more of the Baltimore's neighborhoods nearly every summer weekend. Numerous public holiday activities are held here too.

Dominating this field is the rectangular knoll of Federal Hill. Once used as a lookout point for ships approaching the harbor, it is now a public park and still provides a magnificent view of the harbor and its approaches.

You can easily discover more of Baltimore by walking a few blocks in nearly any direction from the Inner Harbor.

To the east, just beyond Pier 6, is the well-known neighborhood of Little Italy.

Just north of Little Italy is the Star-Spangled Banner House, or Flag House, once the home of Mary Pickersgill, the woman who made the huge flag that flew over Fort McHenry during the British bombardment and inspired Francis Scott Key to pen his poem "The Star-Spangled Banner." The house is now a museum; in its garden is a map of the United States in which each state is constructed from its native stone. Visiting hours are Monday through Saturday, 10:00 A.M. to 3:30 P.M.

Almost next door to the Flag House is Port Discovery (410-727-8120), an interactive, kid-powered museum designed in collaboration with Walt Disney Imagineering. It is open Tuesday through Sunday, 10 A.M. to 5:30 P.M.

Also quite close to the Flag House is Carroll Mansion, home of the longest-lived signer of the Declaration of Independence, Charles Carroll.

Another block to the north, easily visible from quite a distance, is the 234-foot-high, redbrick Shot Tower. Built in 1828, the tower was used to produce shot of various sizes for guns from shotguns to cannon. Molten lead was poured through a sieve with holes of appropriate size at

THE PRIDES OF BALTIMORE

In the latter part of the 18th century, American shipbuilders recognized and responded to the need for fast and maneuverable ships as a means of countering the British command of the high seas, especially during the Revolutionary War. Chesapeake Bay shipbuilders were the first to respond to this need, creating the Baltimore clipper. These small, swift, sleek vessels were among the fastest ships of their day.

Even after commercial needs outgrew the capacity of these relatively small ships, they remained a model for later ship designs, ultimately leading to the design and construction of the giant Yankee clippers, which helped to make America a world maritime power. The yacht *America*, which won the prize (later to be called the America's Cup) in a regatta held at the British World's Fair of 1851, was also based on the design of the Baltimore clippers.

"Pride of Baltimore" was the affectionate title given to another Baltimore clipper, the *Chasseur*, which operated out of Baltimore during the War of 1812. The *Chasseur* and her captain, Thomas Boyle, became world renowned for harassing ships along the English seacoast and single-handedly blockading the coast of England.

In 1977 a replica of one of the Baltimore clippers, the *Pride of Baltimore*, was launched and set sail from the Inner Harbor of Baltimore to serve as a goodwill ambassador for the state of Maryland and, of course, the United States. For nine years it sailed the world, visiting more than 125 ports and accepting visits aboard from more than a million people from all walks of life. Then in May 1986, the *Pride*, along with her captain and three of her crew, disappeared in a violent Atlantic storm.

The loss of the original *Pride* was a catalyst to begin the construction of a new clipper ship, the *Pride of Baltimore II*. The tradition would continue.

Launched in April 1988, the *Pride of Baltimore II* is owned by the state of Maryland as represented by the Department of Transportation acting by and through the Maryland Port Administration. (Donations are still needed to support and maintain the *Pride II*. Tax-deductible contributions can be sent to: Pride of Baltimore, Inc., 100 Light St., Baltimore, MD 21202.)

The maiden voyage of the Pride of Baltimore II.

the top of the tower. As they fell, the droplets formed round balls, which were quenched into that shape in vats of cold water at the bottom of the tower. While the tower is no longer in actual use, a sound-and-light show recreates the process for visitors. It is open Tuesday through Saturday, 10:00 A.M. to 4:00 P.M., and Sunday, 12:00 P.M. to 4:00 P.M. There is no admission fee.

A little to the west of the tower are two blocks of East Lombard Street known as "Corned Beef Row," home of the best kosher delicatessens in the city.

Just north of the Inner Harbor, within a couple of blocks, are the Convention Center and the Civic Center, where circuses, sporting events, exhibits, and assorted other activities are held.

About six blocks north, near the junction of Eutaw and Lexington Streets, is the Lexington Market, two square blocks of assorted foods, both raw and prepared. Just short of the market is the Old Europe, a German deli with some of the best sausage you'll find anywhere, as well as enough other German items to make you feel as if you have walked into old Germany!

THE NAVY'S LAST SAILING SHIP, USS CONSTELLATION

On 26 August 1854 the Navy's last all-sail vessel, a sloop of war named the USS *Constellation*, was launched in the Gosport Navy Yard in Portsmouth, Virginia. Historians believe that some of the timbers from its famous namesake, the frigate *Constellation*, may have been used in her construction for sentimental reasons.

After her commissioning in 1855, the *Constellation* spent time along the Atlantic coast of the United States, and in 1859 it was assigned to a deployment in the Mediterranean to interdict slave trade along the coast of Africa. After the Civil War, it was used to ferry supplies to Ireland to assist in the famine relief and to carry precious works of art to the 1878 Paris Exposition, and it served as a training ship for the midshipmen at the U.S. Naval Academy in Annapolis. The *Constellation* even saw duty in World War II as a relief flagship of the Atlantic Fleet and was the flagship of Battleship Group 5.

After World War II, however, maintenance of the *Constellation* was discontinued, and in 1955 its broken, dilapidated hull was delivered to Baltimore. When a renovation effort was finally begun in the 1960s, the ship, for whatever reason, was configured to look like the 1797 frigate *Constellation*, built at Baltimore's Fells Point. In 1994 the *Constellation* was closed to the public due to internal decay.

After a second restoration, the *Constellation* again rests in its familiar location at Pier 1 in Baltimore's Inner Harbor. While all wooden vessels need extensive maintenance, this current effort is estimated to be good for 50 years. More than half of the timbers in the *Constellation* are from the original 1854 construction, including some of the hand-carved dead-eyes, and the ship is well worth a stop if you're visiting the Inner Harbor either by boat or by land.

A few more blocks to the west, at 203 Amity Street, is the home of Edgar Allen Poe. In fact, Poe is buried in Westminster Churchyard nearby, on Fayette and Green Streets.

Of course, for baseball fans, Camden Yards, home of the Orioles, is only a short walk due west from the Inner Harbor.

Beyond easy walking distance of the harbor are many more points of interest, all accessible by bus, subway, or taxi. There are museums, the Baltimore Zoo, seven theater and concert halls (not counting university and assorted amateur performance centers), soccer (the Blast), ice hockey (Skipjacks), and Pimlico Race Track, where the Preakness (the middle leg in the Triple Crown) is run on the third Saturday in May.

There are probably more than 25 restaurants in easy walking distance from the Inner Harbor, as well as theaters, stores, and many other points of interest. More projects for the area are on the drawing board now, and even more are promised in the future. Baltimore has revitalized itself, and its character has changed for the better.

For more information than you can ever hope to use, contact the Baltimore Convention and Visitor's Center, 110 West Baltimore St., Baltimore, MD 21202; 410-837-4636.

MAGOTHY RIVER

Charts: 12273, **12278**

The mouth of the Magothy River is located at the southern tip of Gibson Island. If you are in doubt, look for the 52-foot-high white column of Baltimore Light positioned a little more than 1½ miles to the east of the entrance. Although traffic tends to be heavy through this relatively

Baltimore Light, a caisson-style lighthouse, is about 1½ miles to the east of the entrance to the Magothy River.

Magothy River, Bodkin Creek, Rock Creek, and Stony Creek

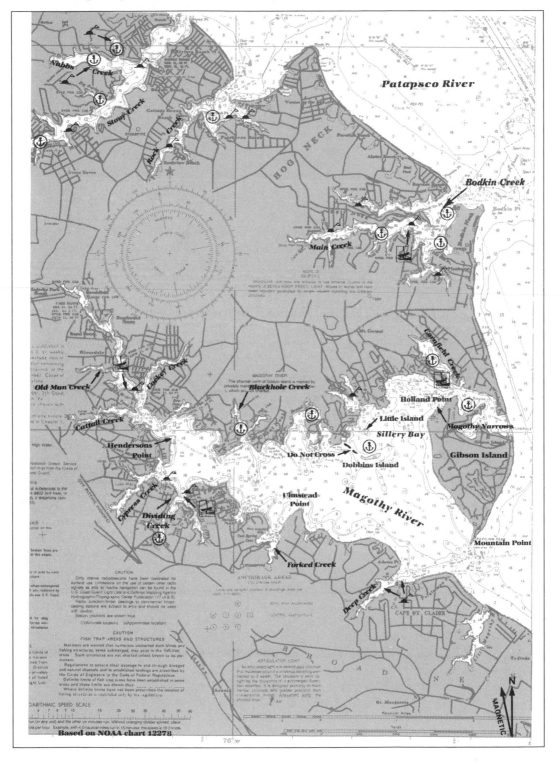

Patapsco River

Bodkin Creek

Nabbs Creek

Stony Creek

Rock Creek

HOG NECK

Main Creek

Carr's Creek

Gooster Creek

Old Man Creek

Blackhole Creek

MAGOTHY RIVER

Holland Point

Catfall Creek

Little Island

Magothy Narrows

Hendersons Point

Sillery Bay

Gibson Island

Do Not Cross

Dobbins Island

Cypress Creek

Dividing Creek

Ulmstead Point

Magothy River

Mountain Point

Forked Creek

Deep Creek

CAPE ST. CLAIR

B R O A D N E C K

Based on NOAA chart 12278

76° 30'

N

MAGNETIC

SCALE **1" = 1.24** NAUT. MILES   ⚓ **Good anchoring**   ⚓ **Marina**   **Launching site**

narrow entrance, it is well marked, and nearly everyone seems to have sense enough to keep to their right as they pass through it. The bar extending to the south from Gibson Island does not extend all the way to the markers, and it drops off sharply from the point where it is no longer clearly visible under the water.

Once you are clear of the entrance, the river opens out, providing a broad sweep where sailboat races with fairly large boats are frequently held. From here you can choose from among a considerable number of creeks or coves in which to anchor and explore.

Deep Creek

Charts: 12273, **12278**

Approaches. On the south shore of the Magothy River, Deep Creek is the first creek to port as you enter the river. There is no good, attractive anchorage here, and we do not recommend spending the night except in a slip.

Marinas & Restaurants. The two marinas located here are the only source for gasoline and diesel for some distance. Fairwinds Marina is on the south shore, just before the lighted "3" marker, and Deep Creek Marina (formerly Capt. Clydes Marina) is on the opposite shore a little farther into the creek. Deep Creek Marina also has a small package store and a restaurant and bar, but space to tie up alongside is rather limited, and boats with drafts of 5 feet or more should not try it. The restaurant features seafood, and the service is friendly and efficient. Both the bar and the restaurant are well patronized by locals, always a good sign. Incidentally, there is good lighting at the fuel dock, so that approaching after dark is easy.

Deep Creek occasionally serves as a temporary port for some of the skipjacks during their winter dredging for oysters. There is some debate about whether this is because the marina and restaurant stay open throughout the winter, or vice versa.

Gibson Island

Charts: 12273, **12278**

Gibson Island is the large island to starboard as you enter the Magothy. This island is unique to the Bay in that it is a totally private island, connected to the mainland by a narrow causeway blocked by a guardhouse on the mainland side. Only members of the Gibson Island Club and their guests are permitted on the island.

Moorings. Members of recognized yacht clubs who arrive by boat at the Gibson Island Yacht Yard, on the north side of the island, adjacent to the causeway, will be welcomed. However, the club has only a few guest moorings, and arrangements for their use should be made in advance with the commodore or a member of the squadron. During the main boating season a club launch provides water-taxi service to the club boathouse. The clubhouse is on the Bay side of the island, about a half-mile walk from the boathouse.

Approaches. As you clear the end of the sandspit off the southern tip of the island, swing to starboard and head for the gap between Dobbins Island and Gibson Island. Stay at least 300 yards off Gibson Island to avoid all shoals. Continue paralleling the shore into Magothy Narrows (west of Holland Point). Be sure to leave the lighted green "3" to port and the lighted red "4" to starboard. There is 10 feet of water all the way into the yacht basin.

Anchorages. Directly opposite Holland Point is Cornfield Creek, on the mainland. Fuel (gas and diesel) is available at Weder's Marina. There are no other supplies in the immediate area. You can anchor here in full security, but the next anchorage is a bit more attractive.

As you pass Holland Point, Eagle Cove opens to starboard. You won't find the name on any chart that we know of, but that is what locals call this cove. Favor the Purdy Point side as you enter and anchor closer to Purdy Point than Holland Point to avoid the shoal in the west side of the cove. This is a well-protected anchorage that appears to be uninhabited. A small, sandy beach is backed by a marsh and woods. None of the houses on Gibson Island are visible from here.

If you proceed past Eagle Cove, as soon as you pass Purdy Point the Gibson Island Yacht Yard Basin opens up to starboard. Here is a completely landlocked harbor where you can watch ships and small boats pass on the Bay while being completely protected by the causeway to the island. Space is limited here.

Dobbins Island

 ⭐ 3 *No facilities*

Charts: 12273, **12278**

Approaches. To the west of the center of Gibson Island, approximately 2 miles from the mouth of the Magothy River, lies Dobbins Island, usually called Dutch Ship Island by the locals. The narrow, ¼-mile-long, wooded island has sheer cliffs rising in excess of 20 feet above the water; it is clearly visible as you finish negotiating the entrance channel to the Magothy River from Chesapeake Bay.

Be sure to honor the green "1" lighted marker at the edge of the shoal extending from the eastern end of Dobbins Island. After rounding this marker, give the shoal a reasonably wide berth and head for the sandy beach extending from the western tip of the island.

Anchorages. This will take you directly to the prime anchorage north of the island. The preferred area to drop the hook is close off the northwest corner of the island, where a sandy spit extends into a narrow finger of a shoal stretching to the mainland. At low tide, more than a third of this shoal is above water and it is possible to wade from the island to the mainland without getting into water deeper than your hips. Do not attempt to enter the anchorage from the west.

The island is virtually unapproachable from the south because of a skirt of very shallow (1 foot or less) shoals leading to sheer cliffs of red clay rising from a minuscule beach. The northern side of the island has deep water (8 to 12 feet) ranging from 20 yards offshore in the central northern portion to as close as 10 feet offshore in the extreme northwestern portion of the island. The anchorage itself is protected from weather on all sides except the northeast, where it is open to Sillery Bay for a maximum reach of about 1½ miles. Although the chart indicates a soft bottom, oyster shells and leaves littering the sticky clay bottom in the western part of the anchorage make it difficult to properly set a lightweight anchor, such as a Danforth. Once the anchor is set, holding appears to be good, and there is plenty of room for several dozen boats to swing.

A half-mile due north of Dobbins Island is Little Island, on which there is a solitary house nestled deep in the trees. Under no circumstances should you anchor to the west of Little Island because the utility cables for the island run across the bottom to the mainland here. Circumnavigation of Little Island is quite easy, but please note that the island is very firmly private.

What to See & Do. Dobbins Island, although privately owned, is uninhabited, and the owners apparently do not object to people from boats landing on the island. Every day during the summer, especially on weekends, numerous people take advantage of this generosity. However, there are signs requesting that you take all trash with you, and if this warning is ignored, the island might be closed to the public.

In the northwest corner of the island is a very nice, sandy beach that stretches from the narrow finger of a shoal, mentioned earlier, to a steep slope leading to the pleasantly wooded upper crest of the island. The view from the crest is a panorama of the lower Magothy River with a vista extending to the Chesapeake Bay Bridges, 7 miles away. Tall trees cover the entire island, while the undergrowth, ranging from light to dense, is crisscrossed with trails providing shaded avenues for exploring.

During the peak boating season this anchorage usually contains a considerable number of boats, and particularly on weekends it is very popular with water-skiers. By all means avoid this anchorage over the Fourth of July weekend, which is a mob scene. Prior to Memorial Day and after Labor Day the island and the anchorage are relatively deserted.

The closest facility for gas, ice, and soft drinks in the vicinity of Dobbins Island is Grays Creek Marine Railway, just inside the right fork of Grays Creek.

Grays Creek

Charts: 12273, **12278**

Approaches. The entrance to Grays Creek is a rare exception, much deeper and easier to negotiate than you would expect from all the indications on nautical charts. Although it is quite narrow, the entrance channel is well marked and used regularly by boats with drafts of 5 feet. The entrance itself is hard to see until you are almost on top of it. To find it, simply head for the eastern side of Little Island. Before you get very close to the island, you will be able to see the red "2" daymark, followed by the rest of the entrance channel daymarks. None of the markers are lighted, so do not try this at night, at least not on the first try.

Once you are past the entrance, the creek opens up into two forks. Do not continue up the right fork past the marina as it shoals fairly quickly.

Anchorages. The best anchorages are in the left fork, which has 9 feet of water and protection from the weather in all directions. The second cove to port is probably the best place to anchor, in 7 feet of water. Don't expect to find a convenient place to land except at the small marina on the right fork. The shoreline is completely built up, and all the property is privately owned.

Broad Creek

 No facilities

Charts: 12273, **12278**

Approaches. Located on the north shore of the Magothy River, Broad Creek is easily accessible and offers a couple of well-protected anchorages. A course of 310 degrees from the entrance to the Magothy River from the Chesapeake takes you directly to the pair of red and green daymarks at the entrance to Broad Creek. Favor the starboard side until you are at least 200 yards past the green "3" daymark to avoid the edge of the shoal that stretches from Rook Point to well south-southeast of the marker. Although there is 13 to 14 feet of water nearly shore to shore, continue to favor the east

shore in order to avoid the 2-foot shoal that reaches halfway across the creek from the west shore midway between Broad Point and the head of the creek. Don't get too close to the east shore until you are well past the little cove to starboard as there are 3-foot shoals projecting out into the creek on either side of the entrance to the cove. (The cove is shallow, so don't try it in anything but a dinghy or a runabout.)

Broad Creek makes an abrupt, right-angle turn to the east just past the 2-foot shoal to port. As you reach this turn, you'll see a tiny island ahead of you. A shoal extends to the southwest and around to the mainland from the island, so leave it well to port. You can hug the starboard shore closely with no problems.

Anchorages. The best anchorage is in 9 to 10 feet of water in the fully protected hook of the creek past the small island. The shoreline is unsettled except for the small North Shore Marina, on the north side of this hook of the creek. Tall trees grow almost to the edge of the high bank on the south shore, making a snug little anchorage, and the island has an attractive beach where you can land. Wading can be a little sticky; the bottom is soft mud just a short distance off the sandy beach.

Going aground here is easy, but the bottom is so soft that it is only a minor inconvenience, and with a little care it can be avoided. This is probably the most secluded and best-protected private anchorage on the Magothy River.

Forked Creek & Cool Spring Cove

  No facilities

Charts: 12273, **12278**

On the south shore of the Magothy River, just past Ulmstead Point, Forked Creek offers a pleasant, well-protected anchorage.

Approaches. A long sandbar nearly closes off the entrance to Forked Creek, but you can easily squeeze past it by holding close to the red "4" daymark opposite the end of the bar. The water is at least 5 feet deep in the channel until you pass the end of the bar. Then the depth is 10 to 13 feet nearly to the head of the creek. The surrounding land is high and wooded except where the large houses of Ulmstead Estates stand. The docks belonging to Belvedere Yacht

Club, part of the Ulmstead development, are on the east side of the creek, just inside the entrance bar. No facilities or supplies are available here.

Do not attempt to enter Cool Spring Cove. A 1-foot bar at the entrance keeps you from the depths of 10 to 13 feet indicated inside the cove.

Blackhole Creek

 No facilities

Charts: 12273, **12278**

Approaches. On the north shore, about 3½ miles from the entrance to the Magothy from the Bay, is Blackhole Creek. This secluded, well-protected little harbor is the home of the Potapskut Sailing Association.

Many experienced cruisers manage to run aground coming in, but if you honor the red "10" light in the middle of the Magothy River before turning to the north, you will easily avoid the first hazard, which is the long, thin shoal extending south from Chest Neck Point, on the east side of the entrance to Blackhole Creek. From red "10," head directly toward the red and green entrance markers to the creek, and you will enter nicely.

Anchorages. The first anchorage is in the bight to port immediately after you pass the green "1" light at the entrance to the creek. Directly ahead after you enter is the green "3" marker, on an island owned by Mr. Robert Pascal, a former Anne Arundel County executive. Past the island is a forest of masts belonging to the Potapskut Sailing Association. Visitors are welcome, but you probably should anchor well off and land by dinghy. You can anchor in 8 to 10 feet of water with complete security anywhere here, but do not proceed upstream through the next narrows in anything but a dinghy because it gets shallow quickly.

The swimming is excellent. There is little traffic, and that is limited to a 6-knot speed. Blackhole Creek is a wildlife sanctuary. You may find pike and perch here—and perhaps some soft crabs in the shallows.

No facilities or supplies are available here.

Mill Creek

Charts: 12273, **12278**

Located on the south shore of the Magothy River, this creek provides an excellent sheltered anchorage. Dividing Creek and Mill Creek share the same entrance approach, with Dividing Creek forking to the west and Mill Creek to the east. If you are short on groceries, there is a small beach on the west side of the approach (Crystal Beach side) where you can land and walk a short way to a good store. Don't plan on staying here: it is too exposed both to weather and to the wakes from boats passing by in the Magothy.

Approaches. While no navigation aids are shown on a chart, there are private markers to assist you in entering Mill Creek. There is a red barrel where the two creeks separate, which should be left to starboard. From there, swing to port and thread your way between the shoals off the southern shore and the sandspit off Stony Point. Head for a second red barrel just past the sandspit. Pass between the barrel and a stake (if it is still there), and you are in. From here on there is 7 to 12 feet of water nearly shore to shore up to the head of the creek. *Warning: About halfway up the navigable part of the creek is an overhead cable with a clearance of 48 feet.*

Anchorages. Anchor anywhere here; the high, wooded bank protects you from weather and wakes. All of the homes in this residential area are well back from the water, giving the illusion of seclusion.

To port just inside the sandspit at the entrance is Ferry Point Yacht Basin, which offers gas (no diesel), ice, limited hardware, and a snack bar. There is also retail seafood. There is 10 feet of water alongside the gas dock; one or two transient slips may be available.

The best anchorage is past the next bend in the creek, where it opens out a bit. Anchor either the small cove to starboard or immediately past this cove near the head of the creek. The high banks provide plenty of shelter, but they tend to minimize the cooling breeze that is so essential in midsummer.

Dividing Creek

  No facilities

Charts: 12273, **12278**

Most of what has been said about the surroundings in Mill Creek applies to Dividing Creek. There are more houses along the latter, and they are more visible. Still, this is a pretty anchorage with complete protection from weather and wakes.

Approaches. After you pass the first red barrel (left to starboard), just before the junction of Mill and Dividing Creeks, swing to starboard to enter the creek. Favor the starboard shore until you have passed the first point to port at the entrance to the creek.

Anchorages. The best anchorage is to port just after you clear this point. The high banks and tree-lined shore make for an attractive spot.

If you proceed upstream, favor the west shore as you pass the next point to port. A shoal off this point is not clearly indicated on the chart. Past this point the creek forks. Stay out of the starboard (west) fork, as it shoals quickly. You can continue about half the remaining distance up the south fork in 7 to 8 feet of water before it too begins to shoal. There is a small boatyard where the creek forks but no supplies or facilities for the cruiser.

Cypress Creek

Charts: 12273, **12278**

Approaches & Anchorages. Still on the south side of the Magothy River, Cypress Creek offers sheltered anchorages in both forks of the creek. Simply honor the two green daymarks, "1" and "3," and you can enter the creek with ease. Stay in the middle, where you will find 8 to 9 feet of water to at least halfway up either fork.

Marinas. Just before you enter the creek, Magothy Marina, to port, offers gas and diesel fuel, as well as premix for outboards. You can get ice but little else in the way of supplies. To port inside the creek, just before the fork, is Cypress Marine, Inc., which stocks some hardware and has a laundromat (no fuel, though).

Struble's Marina, on the west fork of the creek, does not offer much for the transient cruiser.

Cypress Creek is protected from weather, and the holding is good. The area has a high population density, and the shore is lined with private homes. Many outboard enthusiasts come here, perhaps because no speed limit is posted.

Cattail Creek

  No facilities

Charts: 12273, **12278**

Approaches. Before you reach the entrance to this creek the Magothy River begins to narrow, and there is at least one shoal waiting to trap the unwary. As you pass Hendersons Point, with its green "13" light, look carefully for the red "14" light and be sure to honor it. Red "14" is located at the end of a 0- to 2-foot shoal, which extends nearly two-thirds of the way across the river from the north shore. It is even harder to find when you are returning from upriver, so make note of the landmarks after passing it so that you will be sure to honor it on the way back.

Cattail Creek opens to port about ¼ mile past red "14." There is a green "15" daymark at the end of the shoal off Focal Point ("Falcon Point" on older charts), on the north side of the entrance. Favor the south side of the entrance, staying off green "15" since the shoal extends well to the southwest of the marker. There are two privately maintained, lighted markers at the end of two piers to port on the south side of the entrance.

Anchorages. As you pass these markers, hold to the middle of the creek to avoid the ½-foot shoal extending from the west side of the little cove to port. From here on, just stay in the middle and pick your anchorage.

While this is another populous area, the shores are high and wooded and the houses blend into the scenery. The high banks provide protection from weather, and traffic is light. There are no facilities here and no place to land, but this is a pretty anchorage, well worth the visit.

Cockey Creek

  No facilities

Charts: 12273, **12278**

Approaches. About ¼ mile past the green "15" daymark at the mouth of Cattail Creek, Cockey Creek forks to the right off the Magothy River. Entrance to the creek is easy. There are no projecting shoals, and 7 to 12 feet of water is carried at least three-quarters of the way up the creek. The largest boats need to beware of the overhead power cable at the mouth of the creek, although the clearance of 63 feet MHW is more than adequate for most.

Anchorages. This is a creek of strange contrasts. The eastern bank is high and wooded, with unobtrusive houses nestled in the trees. The western bank is overbuilt, with houses looming over the edge of the high bank. This means that there is no privacy for anyone anchored below. If that bothers you, as it does us, go elsewhere. Otherwise this anchorage is quite attractive and well protected.

Upper Magothy River

Charts: 12273, **12278**

Past Cockey Creek the Magothy River becomes more a small creek than the wide river it is downstream. There are no projecting shoals to cause you problems until you reach the head of navigation ¼ mile short of the bridge over the river. The built-up shores leave no place to land except at the two marinas and the Riverdale Inn Restaurant.

Marinas & Restaurants. Cyr's Marina, on the west shore of the Magothy just past Cockey Creek, offers gas, ice, and complete engine and hull repairs.

Old Man Creek, which forks to the left just past the wide spot on the Magothy, is more attractive than the main river in this area. However, the shoreline is completely built up, and it is all private property. The Beall Boat Shop offers nothing for the transient cruiser.

Cruisers may wish to investigate the Riverdale Inn Restaurant, on the west shore of the Magothy, a few hundred yards past the entrance to Old Man Creek. The Riverdale has some of the best food on the Bay at reasonable prices, as well as at least a dozen slips where diners can tie up rather large boats. The service is good and the people are friendly.

Sandy Point

Charts: 12270, 12273, **12278**

Sandy Point State Park is located on Sandy Point, just to the north of the western end of the Chesapeake Bay Bridges. It features a fine, sandy beach and a dredged channel and basin, where you can enter and anchor in complete security if you want to make use of the beach or park facilities.

While not really intended for use by larger, deep-draft boats, the basin provides launch ramp facilities and a refuge for small craft. To find the entrance, head for the northwest corner, where the Bay Bridges meet the mainland. Parallel the bridges, and the marked entrance with its long breakwater will open ahead of you. Simply follow the markers into the basin in Mezick Ponds. Anchoring overnight is not permitted. (I have little doubt that in the case of a blow this restriction would be waived.)

The controlling depth in the entrance and the basin is in excess of 7 feet, so most cruising boats

Sandy Point Lighthouse and the Bay Bridges.

The entrance to the Sandy Point State Park launch basin from the Bay.

can use it, but the only good reason to use it would be as refuge from a storm. This facility with its dozen or so launching ramps is intended to be used solely as a small-boat launching facility. This and the availability of gasoline are the attractions for cruisers.

Sandy Point State Park is the site of the annual Chesapeake Appreciation Days celebration, usually held the first weekend in November (subject to a week's variation in either direction). This event, which runs from 9:00 A.M. to 5:00 P.M., Saturday and Sunday, features Maryland seafood, exhibits on Bay life, air shows, and live entertainment—in short,

something for everyone. There is an admission fee.

The annual skipjack races are usually held the same weekend, in the main Bay, some distance off the point. This is a competition to determine the fastest boat in the nation's only remaining sailing oyster fleet. Weather permitting, there is often a large fleet of spectator boats anchored between Sandy Point and Sandy Point Lighthouse, ½ mile offshore, to get a better view of the races. If you want to watch the races from shore, bring a good pair of binoculars or a strong telescope.

MAGOTHY RIVER

Maryland Tourism

Skipjack races off Sandy Point.

Region 3

BAY BRIDGES TO LITTLE CHOPTANK RIVER

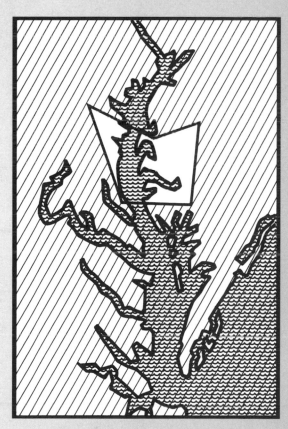

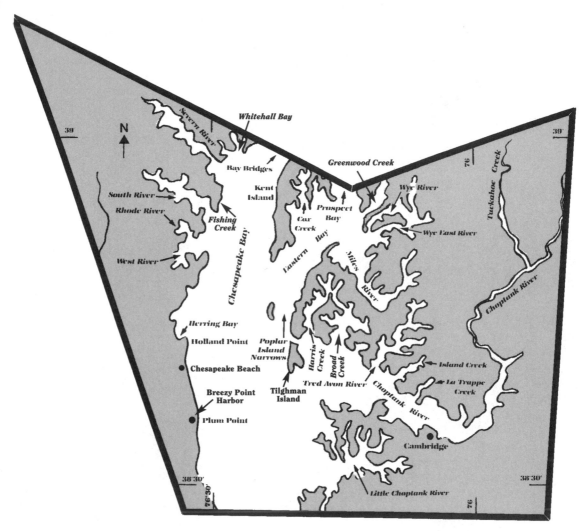

Region 3

SCALE **1″** = **9.8** NAUT. MILES

A S YOU PASS UNDER the Bay Bridges, avoid the center span, which is used by large ships transiting the Bay. There is no need to use the center span; all of the other spans have plenty of clearance (see table at right).

Fluky wind shifts often trouble those sailing under the bridges, so give yourself plenty of room to maneuver in case you are suddenly headed by the wind and have to bear off.

A fleet of ships usually is anchored south of the bridges, off the mouth of the Severn River. With few exceptions, these ships are bulk carriers waiting to enter Baltimore Harbor to take on or off-load cargo. Most carry grain or coal and are waiting their turn at Baltimore's port facility. The grain carriers must be inspected by the U.S. Department of Agriculture. Those that are not clean or are infested with insects or rats must be fumigated, which causes additional time at anchor.

Past the Bay Bridges the Bay water suddenly increases in salinity. As a result, you see different marine life, more ocean-dwelling creatures appearing as you move farther south. Horseshoe crabs and cow-nosed rays are the most obvious. You will find the shells of the crabs on shore and during the summer months you will see plenty of rays cruising just under the surface or making short rushes along the surface with a lot of noise and spray. The rays also have a habit of swimming slowly just under the surface with one or both tips of their "wings" just above the water, looking for all the world like the fins of a couple of sharks. (Sharks are so rare that I doubt you will see one, and if you do, don't worry; there is no record of a shark attack in the Chesapeake Bay.)

One of the most striking features of this part of the Bay is the cluster of islands that enclose a small, shallow bay known as Poplar Harbor. These low islands, visible from more than 5 miles away, are all that is left of what was a 1,000-acre island in colonial times. Now they serve as a convenient reference for those trying to find the entrance to Knapps Narrows from the Chesapeake Bay.

Bay Bridge Clearance Heights

Region 3

Pylons are numbered from Sandy Point, on the Western Shore, to Kent Island, on the Eastern Shore. Clearances are listed in feet between MHW and the lowest point of the structure in the center of the span. Some of the spans have a lower portion, called a knee, not listed here.

SOUTH BRIDGE		NORTH BRIDGE	
PIER NO.	CLEARANCE, FT.	PIER NO.	CLEARANCE, FT.
Western Shore			
6–7	31		
7–8	33		
8–9	23		
9–10	28		
10–11	34		
11–12	19		
12–13	27		
13–14	34		
14–15	42	21–22	42
15–16	43	22–23	43
16–17	52	23–24	52
17–18	61	24–25	61
18–19	70	25–26	70
19–20	79	26–27	79
20–21	88	27–28	88
21–22	98	28–29	98
22–23	115	29–30	115
23–24	**	30–31	125
24–25	168	31–32	168
*25–26	186	*32–33	186
26–27	168	33–34	168
27–28	**	34–35	127
28–29	119	35–36	119
29–30	98	36–37	108
30–31	88	37–38	99
31–32	**	38–39	88
32–33	78	39–40	78
33–34	67	40–41	67
34–35	58	41–42	58
35–36	47	42–43	47
36–37	77	43–44	53–60
37–38	63	44–45	63
38–39	52	45–46	37
39–40	38	46–47	38
40–41	34	47–48	34
41–42	40	48–49	30
Eastern Shore			

*Main Span—Shipping Channel
**Information not available, presumed same as north bridge.

Source: Chesapeake Bay Yacht Racing Association's *The Traveler* (newsletter)

EASTERN SHORE

KENT ISLAND (BAY SIDE)

Charts: 12263, **12270**, 12273, 12282

As you proceed south from the Bay Bridges, the only harbors on the 9-mile stretch of Kent Island to Bloody Point, at the southern tip of Kent Island, are four marinas in artificial harbors. Some of these can accommodate vessels with a relatively deep draft; others are better left to those with shoal drafts.

Bay Bridge Marina

Charts: 12263, **12270**, 12273

Approach. The first of these harbors is the Bay Bridge Marina (410-643-3162), just south of the Bay Bridges. The entrance channel is 6 to 8 feet deep and nearly ½ mile long, dredged through the shoal off Kent Island. It is well marked with ranges and leads into a protected inner basin capable of handling very large boats. The marina maintains both a restaurant and a motel and claims to have 8 feet of water beside the long fuel dock.

Marinas & Restaurants. A boat drawing at least 4 feet can negotiate the entrance chan-

nel. This is primarily powerboat country. There is no anchorage, although boats can tie up along the fuel dock, away from the pumps, long enough to visit the excellent restaurant, Hemmingway's. For an overnight stay you need a slip at the marina, assuming one is available.

Matapeake Harbor of Refuge

 No facilities

Charts: 12263, **12270**

Approach. Matapeake Harbor of Refuge is located about 2 miles below the bridges. Established on the site of the old ferry landing, the harbor has made effective use of the bulkheads and breakwaters left from the ferry. Be careful when you enter Matapeake: the entrance channel has shoaled in recent years, and vessels with more than a 5-foot draft shouldn't try it.

This harbor is intended for use in emergencies only; visiting boats are not encouraged to remain overnight except in a genuine emergency, such as a severe storm. There is a picnic area and a public launching ramp for small boats, used mostly by fishermen, inside the bulkheaded area. A few slips next to the Maryland Marine fisheries Repair Base dock may be used on occasion. There is also some room to anchor, but not much.

Kent Island and Eastern Bay (with Rich Neck)

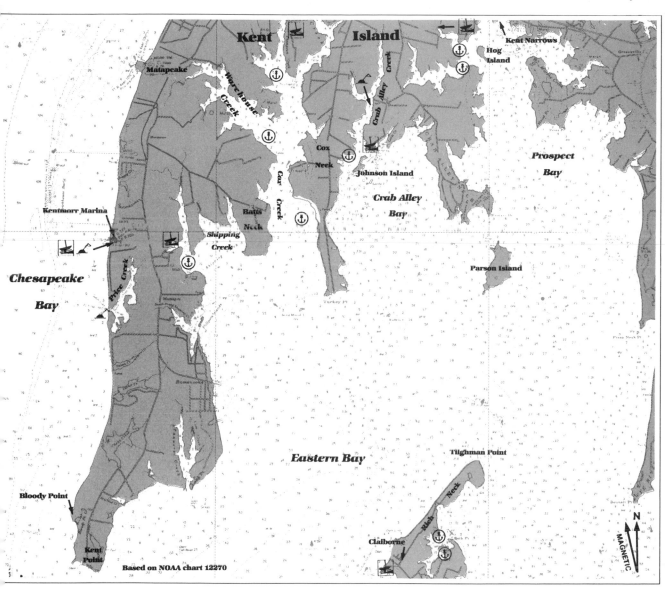

Kent Island

Kent Narrows

Hog Island

Matapeake

Warehouse Creek

Crab Alley Creek

Cox Neck

Prospect Bay

Johnson Island

Crab Alley Bay

Car Creek

Batts Neck

Kentmorr Marina

Shipping Creek

Parson Island

Chesapeake Bay

Price Creek

Eastern Bay

Tilghman Point

Bloody Point

Rich Neck

Claiborne

Kent Point

Based on NOAA chart 12270

N

MAGNETIC

SCALE **1"** = **1.37** NAUT. MILES   ⚓ **Good anchoring**   ⚓ **Marina**   🛥 **Launching site**

165

Kentmorr Marina

Charts: 12263, **12270**

Approach. Kentmorr Marina is located roughly midway between the Bay Bridges and Bloody Point. The easiest way to locate the entrance from the Bay is to take your departure from the south white-orange "S" measured mile marker positioned just under a mile offshore. A course of 120 degrees from this marker takes you directly to the harbor entrance.

This harbor is totally man-made, and the entrance is subject to frequent shoaling. As a result, we cannot recommend it for any boats with more than a 4-foot draft; powerboats or other shoal draft boats should have no trouble. In fact, a fleet of more than 20 charter fishing boats is based here, which indicates the focus of activities.

Marina & Restaurant. The marina is quite large, with all the facilities you may want or need except a self-service laundry. If you ask nicely, the management can probably help you out there also. There is a restaurant, a cocktail lounge, and a snack bar to assuage hunger or thirst. There is also a swimming pool.

Dockages. There is no anchorage here. If you plan to stay overnight, you must reserve a slip, preferably in advance.

Queen Anne Marina

Charts: 12263, **12270**

Approaches. This marina is a little more than 1 mile below Kentmorr Marina (410-643-0029), near the entrance to Price Creek. Price Creek is actually a shallow salt pond that has been dredged near the marina, originally to a depth of 5 feet MLW. The dredged channel has a tendency to shoal, so vessels with a draft of 4 feet or more should not try to enter without recent local knowledge, especially if the sea is running. The marina monitors CB channel 2, a good clue that it caters primarily to power-

boats. It also monitors VHF-FM channels 9 and 73.

Marina & Restaurant. Shoreside facilities are available at the marina, and it is a center for fishing-boat charters. Transient slips are offered, but they are reputed to be in short supply. Don't plan on anchoring out. There isn't any room with adequate depth in the pond for anchoring.

The Pelican Bay Restaurant (410-643-0230), adjacent to the marina, has some dock space for patrons to lay alongside. The restaurant requests a call if you are on your way in to tie up there.

EASTERN BAY

Charts: 12263, **12270**

As you reach the southern tip of Kent Island, the slightly tilted Bloody Point Bar Light, a 54-foot-high redbrick cylinder, is the primary reference for entry into Eastern Bay when approaching from the north. You can pass to

Bloody Point Bar Light is the primary reference for entry into the Eastern Bay from the north.

either side of this lighthouse (but it's best to stay west of it) and head straight for the green "1" bell buoy directly south of Kent Point. While you can cut inside of the "1" bell buoy, it is better to honor it, as you will need this as a reference to be sure of clearing the shoal that extends to the southeast from Kent Point. From green bell buoy "1," set a course of 72 degrees to the red "2A" buoy off Claiborne, on Tilghman Island; hold this course for at least a mile beyond the green "1" to clear the shoal. Once past the shoal, you can bear off to the north if you are heading for one of the creeks on the southeast side of Kent Island or come left a little to head around Tilghman Point into the Miles River or proceed around Parson Island and on up to Kent Narrows.

If you are approaching Eastern Bay from Poplar Island Narrows to the south, simply hold at least ½ mile offshore until you reach the red "2A" buoy off Claiborne. Take your departure from there to any of your destinations on or beyond Eastern Bay.

Shipping Creek

 3 *No facilities*

Charts: 12263, **12270**

Approaches. A course of 5 degrees from the red "2A" off Claiborne takes you to the flashing red "2" marker at the mouth of Cox Creek. The green "1" daymark, which indicates the southern side of the entrance to Shipping Creek, will be clearly visible to the west. Give green "1" about 100 yards clearance as you round it because the shoal extends about that far northwest of the marker. If you bump, alter your course a little farther north and you should quickly find 12 feet of water. Another shoal (off Batts Neck) on the right side of the channel prevents you from heading directly into the mouth of Shipping Creek. Try heading midway between the largest of the houses onshore and the south side of the creek entrance until you are about halfway between the shore and the green "1" daymark. Then head north-northwest until you can see the opening of the entrance into Shipping Creek to port. Don't make the mistake of heading toward the right fork; there

isn't much water there. Once into Shipping Creek proper, simply keep to the middle.

Anchorages. You can anchor anywhere up to the first cove to port in at least 6 feet of water. The anchorage is well protected, with farmland on the western shore and a scattering of attractive homes to the east and farther up the creek.

Don't proceed past this cove as the creek quickly shoals. (Although you may see several workboats and perhaps a sailboat or two upstream, don't try it without current local knowledge.)

If there is a strong easterly wind, pass up this creek—the anchorage will be lumpy.

Cox & Warehouse Creeks

  No facilities

Charts: 12263, **12270**

These two creeks share a common entrance and really should be considered as two forks of the same creek. Both are attractive, but we prefer to anchor in Warehouse Creek.

Approaches. As you pass the flashing red "2" at the entrance to Cox Creek, continue on course for about 100 yards before swinging slightly to starboard to head for the next marker. This will ensure that you clear the shoal off Turkey Point. (If you are in doubt, hold a course about midway between Cox Neck and Batts Neck shores, favoring the west side.) You may choose to anchor here or proceed upstream past the red "4" to where Warehouse Creek splits to the northwest from Cox Creek. Be sure to stay in the middle of the creek and proceed slowly, preferably with a depth-sounder running, as the edges of the creek shoal a bit abruptly.

Anchorages. This is a pleasant location with a few large homes on the south shore of Warehouse Creek and a wooded marsh on the north shore. You can anchor anywhere here, completely protected from weather and waves. Plan to use a relatively short anchor rode because of the shoals and shallows on both sides. To the north-northwest you can clearly see the Bay Bridges, but you will be in nearly complete solitude. Good screening is essential in the warmer weather since the nearby marshes provide excellent mosquito habitat.

EASTERN BAY

Region 3

Crab Alley Creek

Charts: 12263, **12270**

Approach. The entrance to Crab Alley Creek is on the west side of Crab Alley Bay, but you cannot head directly for it from anywhere outside of this little bay as there are several unmarked shoals.

When approaching from the south through Eastern Bay, take your departure from red "2A" off Claiborne. From "2A" a course of 35 degrees, on a line midway between Bodkin Island and Parson Island, takes you past the shoals off each island. Bodkin Island used to be easily recognized from a long way off by the single pine tree that grew on it, resembling the classic palm tree usually depicted on cartoons of a desert island. In the late 1990s, it fell, and the island no longer has any unique distinguishing marks. Once Bodkin Island is abeam to port, head due north (010 degrees magnetic) to leave the green can "1" ahead of you to port.

When approaching from the Miles River, a course of 341 degrees from red "4," north of Tilghman Point, takes you directly to the Crab Alley Bay can "1." From Kent Narrows, simply stay at least ¾ mile off Parson Island (hold the distance you have off the island as you round green "1") at all times until you can assume a course of about 340 degrees to can "1."

From Crab Alley Bay can "1," swing a little to port and pass between the red "4" daymark and the green "3" buoy to enter Crab Alley Creek. Once past red "4," swing to starboard to leave the red-green daymark close to starboard and pass up the left fork of the channel. The right fork leads up a narrow channel that is reportedly shoaled past its red "2" daymark.

Marinas. There are a few tiny marinas and boatyards at the end of the right fork, but they have little in the way of supplies and there is no fuel available. The Bay Boat Shop, located well up the main creek, is another tiny marina that offers repairs and marine supplies, mostly oriented to powerboats. The Wher's Crab House is located in Little Creek, north of Johnson Island, adjacent to the cluster of small marinas there.

Anchorages. Hold close to Johnson Island, forming the east side of the creek, as you

pass its southern tip to avoid the shoal to port. You will find the best anchorage in the mouth of the small cove to port, opposite the middle of this island. If you proceed farther upstream, simply remain in the middle and you can continue to at least the point where the creek forks before it begins to shoal. If you anchor up here, keep a relatively short rode because of the shoals to either side of the narrow creek.

The entire creek is well protected from weather and waves but not from the wake from the occasional workboat. As you would for most of the creeks on Kent Island, come prepared with good screens and mosquito repellent in warm weather.

Claiborne

  No facilities

Charts: 12263, **12270**

Prior to the completion of the first of the Bay Bridges, in the early 1950s, there was a ferry dock at Claiborne Landing, used by the ferries from Romancoke on Kent Island and by Bay steamers. When this service was discontinued, the landing became a public dock and launching ramp, used mostly by local small craft.

What to See & Do. This is not a good harbor for cruising boats. Until 1992 there was an interesting country store and post office in Claiborne, a short walk from the public dock. The owners of the store and the post office have won a battle against the U.S. Postal Service to keep the post office open, but the country store has closed, replaced by a public telephone and soda machine. Martha Hamylin still runs the post office and would love cruisers to stop and chat.

Tilghman Creek

  No facilities

Charts: 12263, **12270**

A well-protected, attractive anchorage, Tilghman Creek is reached easily from anywhere in this part of the Bay. It makes a convenient stopping place for those bound across the main Bay from the Eastern Shore or to the Miles River–Kent Narrows area from the Bay.

Approaches. Except for the final stages of the approach to the entrance, navigation is easy. Swing wide around Tilghman Point and

EASTERN BAY

168

continue south or south-southwest until you are due east of the green "1" light at the mouth of Tilghman Creek and you will have no trouble with the pair of finger shoals extending south and south-southwest from Rich Neck below Tilghman Point. A compass course of 270 degrees brings you safely to the green "1" light on a spar at the mouth of the creek. Leave the "1" marker at least 50 yards to the south of your course until it is abeam to port, then swing to a course that brings the green "3" daymark close to port (to within 30 feet) to avoid the entrance shoal to starboard. Once you pass the red "4" daymark (don't cut red "4" too close), you are in. The creek opens out, and the water is deep enough to allow you to maneuver easily. (We don't recommend entering under sail.)

Anchorages. Leave the first cove to port alone, it is shallow except for a narrow segment along the north shore. The best anchorage is in the first cove to starboard in 11 feet of water off a long sandy beach. There is plenty of room for several boats.

In the event that this cove is full, the mouth of the second cove to port makes a nice alternative. Don't go much past the two piers as the water in the cove gets a bit thin farther in.

Farther up, where the creek forks, is another nice place to anchor, although it is not a good place to land. You can take a dinghy over to what is left of the tiny boatyard, Locust Hill Boatworks, at the end of the left fork, to land and walk into Claiborne. From the boatyard, walk to the end of the road and turn right. About ¼ mile down this road is Claiborne's post office.

No marine facilities are available to cruisers on this creek; come prepared.

Unnamed Cove

 NO RATING | 3 | *No facilities*

Charts: 12263, **12270**

Just over ½ mile southeast of the entrance to Tilghman Creek is a cove, unnamed on any chart I have checked, that presents a little bit of a puzzle. According to the latest and largest-scale chart I have been able to find, the entrance is barred with an extensive 2-foot shoal. From the outside of this cove, I see no obvious evidence that it has been dredged recently. We have seen one good-sized sailboat in there, so

there must be a way in. Unfortunately, we have never looked more closely.

It appears to be a nice anchorage in 9 to 10 feet of water. I leave entering this one as a challenge for other incurable gunkholers.

Porter Creek

 | 3 | *No facilities*

Charts: 12263, **12270**

Approaches. About 1½ miles below Tilghman Creek, just short of Hambleton Point, is the entrance to Porter Creek. For this creek too the chart indicates no navigation aids nor a deep entrance channel. However, a privately marked, dredged entrance channel leads to a pleasant little anchorage in 7 feet of water, surrounded by a few fancy houses on expansive plots of land. (I don't know the entrance depth, but I have seen some fair-sized sailboats inside and thus assume that it must be 4 feet or more.)

Anchorages. There is no place to land, but if that isn't a requirement, this is a nice spot. To enter, simply follow the markers in. Then swing to port and continue upstream until the water just starts to shoal.

Porter Creek is relatively open to the north and northwest, which means that it could get uncomfortable in a strong northerly. There are far better anchorages nearby. Except to say that you have been there, pass it by.

Greenwood Creek

NO RATING

Charts: 12263, **12270**

Greenwood Creek is located on the eastern shore of Eastern Bay, just east of Piney Neck Point. We have seen several good-sized sailboats negotiating the entrance to this creek, but it is totally unmarked, so you would have to feel your way in. We have been told that there is an elusive 5-foot channel. By now, it is probably no more than 4 feet. In any event, we haven't tried it.

If you draw less than 4 feet, you should be able to make it past the entrance bar and find a scenic, well-protected creek 8 feet deep all the way to the headwaters. This creek has no facilities of any kind.

Eastern Bay, Wye East River

Charts: 12263, **12270**

Most of the rivers and creeks on the Eastern Shore are appealing, but the Wye River is special. The river splits into two main forks, the Wye East and the Wye Rivers, which enfold Wye Island. Wye Narrows connects the East Wye and Wye Rivers north of Wye Island, completing the ring of water to make it an island. The small, fixed bridge (vertical clearance 10 feet) that connects Wye Island to the mainland prevents circumnavigation of the island, which otherwise would be easy since there is deep water all the way around.

Wye Island itself is sparsely settled. It was once a wildlife refuge, and most of the island is still a Natural Resources Management Area; there are only one or two houses on the main body of the island now. We have been told that there are future plans to develop at least part of Wye Island. In fact, there are now several large homes along Wye Narrows, south of the connecting bridge. There will probably be more soon.

On other shores of the Wye you will find manor houses, estates, and many lesser but large homes. The water is sometimes discolored from sediment but unpolluted and clean. There is rarely any sign of the refuse or trash you often will find washed ashore in other rivers on the Bay. No matter which part of the Wye you cruise, snug anchorages abound in the numerous creeks or coves on the river.

Approach. If you are approaching the mouth of the Wye from the north through Eastern Bay, plot a course to take you between the green can "3" buoy at the end of the shoal off Bennett Point and the red nun "2" buoy at the north end of a shoal off the mouth of the Wye— all that is left of an island. You can pass into the mouth of the Wye on either side of can "3," but if you pass inside of it, hold to within less than 50 yards of the can or you may run aground on the long shoal off Bennett Point. An intriguing, private lighthouse on the tip of Bennett Point makes identification of this point easy from a substantial distance.

If you approach from the south, out of the Miles River, simply guide on the eastern shore, holding about ½ mile off it. This equates to a course of 18 degrees from nun "12" at the mouth of the Miles River to red "4" in the mouth of the Wye River and neatly avoids the shoals to port and starboard.

Once past can "3," head into the Wye favoring the eastern side of the river until you are well past the lighted red "4" marker on a piling just inside the mouth of the river. As you approach Bruffs Island, you must decide whether to cruise the Wye East River or the Wye River. Regardless of which you choose, good anchorages abound; we list here only a few of those we consider the best.

As you round Bruffs Island to enter the Wye East River, hold at least 50 yards off the shore of the island to avoid its shoal, but watch out for the shoal extending south from Bordley Point on the other side, which juts out farther than indicated on the chart. You must beware of a few other unmarked shoals on this branch of the Wye. Except for these, you will have no problems if you stay near the middle of the river. (Note: All marks in the Wye are maintained by the state of Maryland and might not appear on NOAA charts.)

Leave the red "2" daymark past Shaw Bay fairly close to starboard and assume a course to leave the green "3" daymark ahead at least 25 yards to port. (Green "3" blends into the shore behind it, so it may be a little hard to see until you pass red "2.") When you pass green "3," continue on the same course until you reach the middle of the Wye East segment that runs from north to south. The shoal off the point to port extends well to the east of green "3."

The next shoal to guard against may not be apparent on the chart. This one extends well to the south from the east side of the entrance to Dividing Creek. However, if you stay at least 100 yards off that point until it is past your beam and you are 50 to 75 yards from the south bank of the Wye East before you turn to port to head upstream, you will clear the shoal easily.

The last unmarked shoal is opposite the Wye Heights Boathouse, just before the entrance to Skipton Creek. Give the point to port a wide berth: this shoal is hard and harbors a submerged piling.

Wye River Region

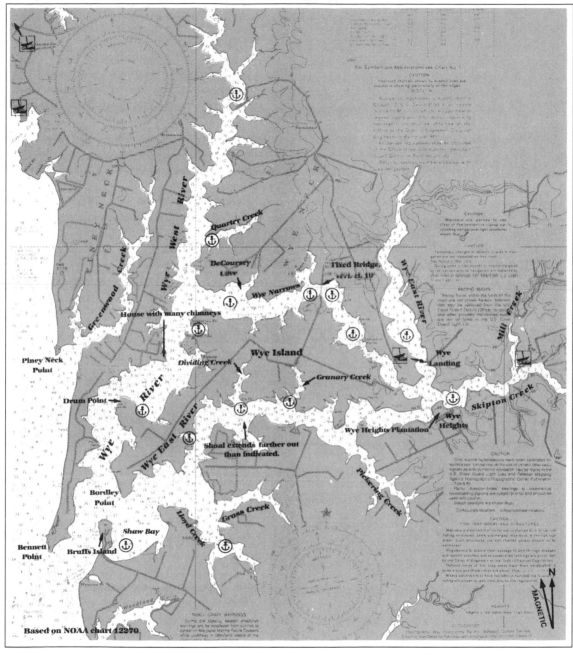

SCALE **1" = 1.21** NAUT. MILES   **Good anchoring**   **Marina**   **Launching site**

Wye East River, Shaw Bay

 ⬡ ★   3   *No facilities*

Charts: 12263, **12270**

Anchorages. Shaw Bay is the first good anchorage on the way up the river. Here you can anchor anywhere in good holding, but most choose to anchor well into the southwest corner of the bay. Do not attempt to land anywhere on Bruffs Island; it is private property and closed to the public. The shore opposite Bruffs Island is sandy and extends almost the entire length

171

Aerial view of the Wye River area.

National Geodetic Survey

of the east side of Shaw Bay. You can land here to walk and beachcomb to your heart's content. We usually find horseshoe crab shells, as well as indications of some marine life more common to the ocean.

Shaw Bay is a beautiful anchorage. On summer weekends it is usually crowded, but it can hold many boats comfortably. For more seclusion, continue upstream.

Wye East River, Lloyd Creek

  No facilities

Charts: 12263, **12270**

Although this creek is not quite as snug as others farther upriver, it is comfortable and well protected except from the northwest. If you happen to like Canada geese, it is a fantastic anchorage in the fall, when literally thousands of geese land to feed in the fields on all sides of this creek. They are noisy, which may keep light sleepers awake at night.

Approaches. A select group of cruisers manage to keep running aground here; we have never been able to understand why. Stay near the middle of the creek, favoring the west side of the center line, as you enter, and you should avoid the 2-foot shoal that extends to the west from the eastern shore of Lloyd Creek, south of Gross Creek, nearly to the center of the creek.

Anchorages. The best anchorage is well into the creek, in the area where the creek hooks sharply to the southwest. Most charts indicate a tiny island at this bend in the creek, but it is just a duck blind. Don't expect to land; there is no good place for it.

Wye East River, Gross Creek

  No facilities

Charts: 12263, **12270**

Approaches. Gross Creek extends to the east just past the entrance to Lloyd Creek, but a bar at its entrance restricts access to vessels with less than a 4-foot draft. (That was the depth when we last visited; it may be less now.)

Anchorages. If you can get past the bar, you will find a 6- to 8-foot depth inside all the way up to the fork in the creek, so you can anchor where you will. Don't enter either fork since the water is less than 3 feet deep despite what the chart says.

Wye East River, Wye Island Cove

  No facilities

Charts: 12263, **12270**

Approaches. This cove is unnamed on the chart, so we dubbed it "Wye Island Cove" for want of something better. The entrance is easy: simply continue up the Wye East River until the entrance to this cove is abeam, then turn and head straight in. Don't proceed more than three quarters of the way to the head of the cove unless you draw less than 4 feet. Up to there the water is 7 to 10 feet over a mud bottom. A small beach here, near the entrance, is a mixture of sand and mud. While minimal, it does allow you to land and stretch your legs a little.

This is a superb anchorage in the late fall, when the winds howl and the geese fly.

Anchorages. Located on the western shore about midway up the north-south part of the Wye East River, about ½ mile past the green "3" daymark, this snug anchorage can accommodate about a half-dozen boats. The cove is lined with trees, which break the wind nicely but not the cooling breezes in the hot summer months. Behind the trees are the fields of Wye Island, providing a very secluded anchorage.

Wye East River, Dividing Creek

  No facilities

Charts: 12263, **12270**

This creek is narrow and relatively deep, with high banks (for the Chesapeake) covered with tall trees forming a screen of woods between the water and the fields of Wye Island. Here a great blue heron stalks the shallows, and osprey and numerous other birds circle overhead. Raccoon and muskrat can often be seen along the shores, especially in the early morning or late afternoon. You are in the minority if you miss sighting a variety of wildlife here.

Approaches. The entrance is easy if you pay proper respect to the shoals extending out into the Wye from either side of the entrance. Keep to the middle of the river until the entrance to Dividing Creek is abeam, then turn and head directly into the middle of the entrance. Favor the port side of the creek until you clear the point to starboard.

Anchorages. From here on, you can anchor anywhere in complete security. Dividing Creek is well sheltered from both weather and the wakes of passing boats.

The depth is 7 to 9 feet almost to the head of the creek. It begins to shoal within about 100 yards of the end of the creek, so be careful if you venture that far. This creek is such an attractive anchorage that on weekends it draws many boats. One early October, we counted 99 boats at anchor, probably because the wind was blowing pretty hard and this creek provides the best protection in the area. During the week you often can have this spot to yourself.

OSPREY

The osprey, or fish hawk (*Pandion halidetus*), is a large, impressive bird with a wingspan reaching 5 to 6 feet. White underneath, it has a striking brown, black, and white pattern under its wings and tail and on its upper side. A black streak extends back from each eye, and it has the classic fiercely curved beak of a raptor.

The ospreys inhabit the Bay from early April until the fall, nesting from late April through July and sometimes even later. Then they go south for the winter, returning each spring.

As recently as the 1960s ospreys were relatively rare in the Bay area. Pesticides washing into the Bay were absorbed into the food chain, concentrating more and more heavily in creatures higher up in the chain. DDT, especially, reached a high concentration in fish, the sole diet of the osprey. The result was a thinning of the shell of the bird's eggs, so that the weight of the brooding parents crushed the fragile eggs. The young that did hatch often were deformed. The osprey became an endangered species.

With the banning of DDT and other pesticides, the osprey is once again a common sight on the Bay. It seems as if every daymark and lighted spar in the Bay sports an osprey's untidy nest.

Wye East River, Quarter Cove

  No facilities

Charts: 12263, **12270**

Approaches. Almost directly opposite the entrance to Dividing Creek, this "cove" looks as much like a creek as many that are so named, at least in this area. The approach to the entrance is wide open, and 7 to 9 feet of water is carried all the way to the head of the cove. From the point where the cove narrows, simply stay in the middle and you will remain in deep water.

Anchorages. This anchorage is pleasant enough but not secluded; there are several homes on the shore. You can land on the sandy

beach on the east side of the mouth of the cove to walk, swim, or beachcomb. However, there are better anchorages nearby.

Wye East River, Granary Creek

  No facilities

Charts: 12263, **12270**

This creek is very similar to Dividing Creek. In fact, everything said about Dividing Creek applies to Granary Creek. However, one house on the west bank about halfway down the creek and another on the opposite shore where the creek bends to the west break the bucolic splendor.

Approaches. The entrance is simplicity itself. Just pay attention to your chart and head directly into the mouth of the creek. Favor the west side of the entrance to avoid the short shoal that projects a little off the east side of the entrance. There are no other shoals to worry about. Seven to 8 feet of water is carried all the way to the headwaters.

Anchorages. You couldn't ask for more protection in an anchorage. This creek doesn't seem to attract quite as many boats as Dividing Creek, perhaps because it is a little farther up the Wye East River. Anchor anywhere once you are in.

Wye East River, Pickering Creek

  No facilities

Charts: 12263, **12270**

Approaches. Pickering is a relatively long and narrow creek with a number of unmarked shoals waiting to snag the unwary. Although the water depth ranges between 8 and 10 feet to the head of the creek, the shores are well built up with homes, making this creek less attractive to us than several others in the region.

Anchorages. The banks are high and lined with trees, providing good protection from weather. If you sound your way in carefully, you will find a secure anchorage, but you may not find anywhere to land. The shore is all private property.

OF TURTLES AND TERRAPINS

One of the largest and most frequently seen of the tidewater creatures, the **common snapping turtle** (*Chelydra serpentina*) inhabits nearly all of the creeks and rivers in the Bay, from brackish to fresh waters. These creatures can grow to as large as 18 inches across and can weigh up to 90 pounds. Most weigh in at around 30 pounds, which is still a lot of turtle! Mortality due to predation is high among the juveniles, but the adult snapper fears only humans; if not caught and killed, they may live to an age of 50 years.

The snapping turtle is caught commercially with traps, handlines, and dip nets and sold as food, especially as the main ingredient in turtle soup. (The state of Maryland prohibits catching snappers from state waters by the use of a hook and line, trotline, bow and arrow, spear, gig or gig iron, or any other device capable of piercing any part of the turtle.) Frequently, hibernating snappers are harvested in the winter from the muddy creek bottoms by probing for them with a pointed stick. The captured turtles are sent to Baltimore, Philadelphia, New York, and other markets.

A less pervasive but better-known Bay turtle is the **diamondback terrapin** (*Malaclemys terrapin terrapin*). This turtle was once plentiful, but by the late 18th century, it was considered such a delicacy that it was hunted almost to extinction. Today legal restrictions and a greatly reduced market are helping this turtle make a comeback.

Diamondbacks are found in brackish creeks and marshes, although they can survive in freshwater. They feed underwater on mollusks and crustaceans but aren't so picky that they won't eat all sorts of other fare, including insects and an occasional fish.

Although there are no regulations regarding snapper eggs, Maryland prohibits the possession, destruction, or disturbance of diamondback terrapin eggs. The young turtles are the favored prey of crows and herons until they are big enough that their size protects them. Even so, the real limits to the diamondback population are shrinking habitat and human predation.

Diamondback terrapin.

Nell Baldacchino/U.S. Fish & Wildlife Service

Wye East River, Skipton Creek

  No facilities

Charts: 12263, **12270**

We feel that this creek is special, if only because the anchorage is within sight of the gardens belonging to Wye Heights Plantation, a replica of an old colonial estate. The house itself can be seen as you approach the mouth of the creek. The imposing brick structure, with its four large, white columns, overlooks the junction of Wye Narrows, Skipton Creek, and the Wye East River. A herd of coal-black sheep wanders the grounds between the house and the river, presumably keeping the grass trimmed. Farther back from the water is a compound with a herd of reindeer! Twice while anchored here we have been invited by the owner to land and stroll through his classic English gardens.

Approaches. The Skipton Creek entrance is easy, provided that you avoid the shoal off the point opposite the Wye Heights boathouse in the Wye East River and give the point on the right side of the mouth of the creek a wide berth.

Anchorages. The best anchorage is located just past the entrance to the creek, in 7 feet of water. Boats with drafts of 4 feet or more shouldn't try to proceed any farther than a little beyond the next point because the creek shoals from there on. Cube ice is available at Wye Landing, on the upper Wye East River, just past the entrance to Skipton Creek.

This creek is one of the prettier anchorages on the Wye, and the sea nettles don't usually show up here. There is a healthy population of snapping turtles; we always have been inspected carefully by one or more of these critters shortly after anchoring.

Wye East River, Eastern Wye Narrows

  No facilities

Charts: 12263, **12270**

The eastern half of Wye Narrows branches off the Wye East River directly opposite the mouth of Skipton Creek. Although Wye Narrows runs between the Wye East and Wye West Rivers, the bridge that connects the north end of Wye Island with the mainland divides Wye Narrows into halves both geographically and in terms of the character of the surroundings.

Approaches & Anchorages. Pay careful attention to your chart and stay in the middle of the waterway until you reach the first of two wide spots southeast of the bridge. This is the best anchorage in this half of the narrows. The water is 7 feet deep nearly up to the shore, except for a shoal that projects to the east from a point in the northwest corner of this miniature bay. The holding is good, but the land is low and the banks are muddy, rising directly from the water—there is no beach.

If you continue toward the bridge, favor the east shore to avoid the shoal that projects into the middle of the channel. The next anchorage is just short of the bridge in 8 to 12 feet of water. Anchor near the bridge on the north side of the waterway, but to avoid the shoals there don't get too close to the northeast corner of this "wide spot." There is almost no traffic over the bridge, so you need not worry about noise from that source.

As noted, the bridge is fixed, with only about a 10-foot vertical clearance. For all practical purposes and most cruising vessels, this is the head of navigation on the eastern half of Wye Narrows.

Upper Wye East River

Charts: 12263, **12270**

Approach & Provisions. Just above the junction of the Wye East River and Wye Narrows is Wye Landing, on the east side of the river. This is a public launching ramp for trailered boats, so it tends to be rather busy on summer weekends. Wye Landing is also the sole place on the Wye where you can replenish your ice supply. Both blocks and cubes are available, as is bait for fishing and crabbing. No other supplies are available. While it may be possible to tie up briefly alongside the pier upstream of the launching ramp, deeper-draft boats should anchor and land by dinghy. This spot is popular with runabouts, making it too active an anchorage for us.

Although the Wye East River is navigable by shoal-draft vessels for up to 2 more miles, most cruising boats have to call it quits less than a mile past Wye Landing. The first point on the starboard side is about as far as the river carries 5 feet of water. From there on, the river shoals, and depths of 2 and 3 feet occur with regularity.

History. The nearby village of Wye Mills is home to the Wye Oak, the oldest white oak in Maryland, reputed to be more than 400 years old. More than 95 feet high with a horizontal spread of about 165 feet, it is the largest of its kind in Maryland and one of the largest in the United States.

Eastern Bay, Wye River

Charts: 12263, **12270**

The Wye River doesn't have as many attractive anchorages as the eastern branch, but it has enough well-protected coves, creeks, and bights to keep this branch high on the cruiser's "must-visit" list.

Navigation here is straightforward. The few projecting shoals are well marked for the most part. Those that do not have markers are obvious on the chart and easily avoided.

Wye River, Drum Point

 2 *No facilities*

Charts: 12263, **12270**

Anchorages. The first good anchorage on the Wye River is just off the south shore, in a bight due east of Drum Point. This bight is about ½ mile wide and has room for a lot of boats. The shore is sandy, and especially on Drum Point itself it provides an excellent beach for swimming, wading, or simply sunbathing. Unfortunately, nearly all of it is now private property, and there is little or no room for the cruiser to land.

The area is fairly open to winds from the north and northeast, and a blow from that direction can make this a lumpy anchorage. The bottom is soft, and the holding is not very good even with a plow anchor. We were once in the middle of a small raft that was caught by a blow with winds of 20 to 30 knots. The anchor boat had a 35-pound CQR plow anchor down with a 9:1 scope out; it plowed a furrow in the bottom for about 100 yards before we managed to break up the raft.

Probably the most popular anchorage on the Wye River, Drum Point is a crowded anchorage for the whole boating season. For more seclusion, continue on.

Wye River, Bigwood Cove

 3 *No facilities*

Charts: 12263, **12270**

The first cove to starboard, about a mile past Drum Point, is Bigwood Cove. There is a large house with a surprising number of chimneys on the point opposite this cove. Once we were so engrossed in trying to count them that we managed to run aground off the point. That took a certain amount of talent since the shoal doesn't project all that far.

Approach & Anchorage. Entering the cove is relatively easy. Simply continue up the Wye River until the entrance to the cove is abeam, then turn and head directly for the center of the entrance. Within less than 100 yards the cove forms a crude T. Stay out of the south fork; it is too shallow. The best anchorage is just inside the north fork.

Bigwood Cove provides a nice, secluded anchorage in 6 to 8 feet of water for one or two single boats. The shore is uninhabited, and privacy is virtually assured. However, the shoreline is marshy, and the cove is open for a reach of about a mile to the southeast. The cove is worth poking into, but an extended stay may not be a good idea.

Region 3

Wye River, Grapevine Cove

 4 *No facilities*

Charts: 12263, **12270**

Anchorages. Grapevine Cove opens to starboard just a few hundred yards past the big house on the point opposite Bigwood Cove. If you like privacy, try this cove, a secluded, well-protected little anchorage in 6 to 7 feet of water for up to half a dozen boats to anchor. There are rarely any boats in the cove, and once you are well in, you cannot be seen from most of the main river. The shoreline is undeveloped, and the banks rise rather steeply from the water. The only beach is revealed at low tide and is muddy. Holding is good, but the cove is so well protected that you probably could use a brick for an anchor and never know the difference. Conversely, it is a little too snug to be comfortable in the sticky, hot summer weather.

Approaches. Although there is 6 to 8 feet of water in the entrance channel, you have to feel your way in because of the shoals on either side and because the channel, like many areas of the Bay, is becoming both narrower and shallower every year. Be careful. Approach the entrance on a southeast course to avoid the shoal on the south side of the entrance.

Wye River, Unnamed Cove West Shore

 3 *No facilities*

Anchorages. On the west side of the Wye River, directly opposite Grapevine Cove, is an unnamed cove with two "horns." Either of these horns provides a secure albeit unsecluded anchorage and is easier to enter than Grapevine Cove. However, the shoreline is all private property, and you cannot land without the owners' permission.

Wye River, Western Wye Narrows

 No facilities

Charts: 12263, **12270**

Just past Grapevine Cove the western part of Wye Narrows opens up to starboard. The entrance is broad and deep (10 to 14 feet), and its navigation is straightforward. You can anchor anywhere fairly close to the south shore, where a series of sandy beaches stretch all the way from the entrance to the bridge.

Approaches & Anchorages. DeCoursey Cove is the first cove to port, about ½ mile from the entrance to the narrows. This cove provides a secure anchorage in 6 to 7 feet of water, but feel your way in because the shoals on either side of the entrance extend a long way across. Head directly north from the middle of the narrows toward the lone house onshore and you will clear the shoals easily. Don't look for the tiny island shown in the mouth of the cove on some charts; it no longer breaks the surface of the water. In midsummer you may want to anchor well out from shore to avoid the clouds of no-see-ums that inhabit the shore.

As you pass DeCoursey Cove, beware of the shoal projecting into the narrows from the east side of the cove entrance and the one projecting to the north directly opposite the point on the east side of DeCoursey Cove entrance.

The next cove to port is Covington Cove, a sheltered anchorage with 5 to 6 feet of water. The entrance is easy. There is 7 feet of water almost from shore to shore in the mouth of this cove. Don't travel up either horn of this cove, as the water gets a bit thin for deeper-draft boats. In hot, sticky summer weather you should avoid this cove. It is too protected to permit any breeze, which means no relief from heat or no-see-ums.

At this point you will have reached the fixed bridge (10 feet MHW vertical clearance) mentioned in the Eastern Wye Narrows section and must stop.

Wye River, Quarter Creek

 No facilities

Charts: 12263, **12270**

Approaches. Continuing up the Wye River, to starboard, just past the mouth of the Wye

Narrows, is Quarter Creek. The entrance is straightforward, and the creek carries 6 to 8 feet of water to its headwaters.

Anchorages. You can anchor anywhere here in good holding. The relatively high banks and the surrounding tall trees provide full protection from the weather, and the curved entrance cuts off wakes from the Wye River.

Few houses are visible from the creek, so this anchorage is quiet and secluded. The first point to starboard after you enter has a small, sandy beach where you can land to swim or wade at other than extreme high tide. Most boats do not venture this far up the Wye River, making this anchorage more private than you might expect, considering its attractiveness.

Upper Wye River

 No facilities

Charts: 12263, **12270**

Past Quarter Creek the Wye River narrows. Here numerous coves and creeks provide tight, secure anchorages. Be sure to check your chart before entering any of them and carefully feel your way in. Most shoal quickly past the entrance.

Anchorages. You can probably anchor anywhere on this part of the Wye River. Just pick a nice-looking spot and drop the hook. The whole river, from Quarter Creek north, is a gunkholer's delight.

Eastern Bay, Miles River

Charts: 12263, **12270**

If you are approaching from Eastern Bay, a course of 161 degrees from the red "4" buoy off Tilghman Point takes you directly to the nun "12" buoy off Deep Water Point, where the Miles River begins to constrict. This course also neatly skirts a shoal, all that is left of an island, off the mouth of the Wye River.

If you are approaching from Kent Narrows, you may pass to either side of this shoal without lengthening your course. From the green "1" can off Parson Island a course of 182 degrees takes you west of the shoal to the red "10" buoy. Then a course change to 160 degrees takes you to the nun "12" buoy off Deep Water Point. Alterna-

St. Michaels Area

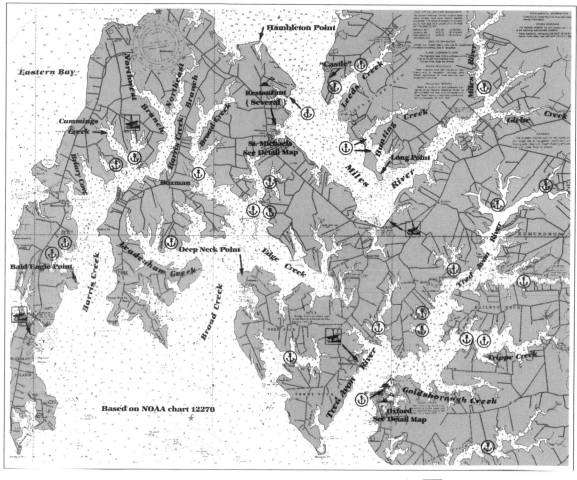

SCALE **1" = 2.12** NAUT. MILES   Ⓐ **Good anchoring**   ⚓ **Marina**   ⛵ **Launching site**

tively, a course of 174 degrees from the Parson Island green "1" takes you to can "11," which marks the eastern edge of the "late island" shoal. Beware of altering course too far to the east because a shoal extends well to the southwest from Bennett Point, at the mouth of the Wye River. From can "1" a course of 186 degrees takes you to the Deep Water Point nun "12." The compass courses are helpful because the buoys are almost impossible to see from more than a mile away.

Nun "12" serves as a reference for all of these approaches, but this red nun is difficult to see until you are within about ½ mile of it. From nun "12" you can navigate virtually unaided the rest of the way up the river.

At Deep Water Point the system for numbering buoys changes from the Eastern Bay system to the Miles River system. A half-mile south of nun "12" is the green "1" lighted (Fl G 4 sec.) spar, southeast of Deep Water Point; this marks the tip of the shoal extending west from Fairview Point. You must honor this marker and nun "2" beyond it. You can ignore nun "4" for all practical purposes if you remain at least 300 yards off the western shore when heading into St. Michaels. The region between nuns "2" and "4" in the mouth of Long Haul Creek is often the scene of round-the-buoy regattas on summer weekends. Steer clear of here if a race is in progress.

At nun "4" St. Michaels is to starboard and the mouth of Leeds Creek is to port. Directly ahead, the Miles River continues for several more miles.

About 2½ miles past nun "4" the river makes a right-angle turn to the northeast, around the end of Long Point. As soon as you clear Long Point, the mouth of Hunting Creek opens up to port. The river continues to be navigable for another 5 miles, with more anchorages beyond the drawbridge, 3 miles ahead.

Miles River, Long Haul Creek

Charts: 12263, **12270**

Approaches. Long Haul Creek, to starboard as you pass the red "2" daymark, is the home of the Miles River Yacht Club. The entrance to this creek is not difficult, even without the club buoys put out during the yachting season. After rounding the red "2" daymark, simply line up the range lights on the club dock, on the southwest shore of the creek, and follow the range all the way to the dock.

Marinas & Anchorages. If you choose to stop in this creek, you can often obtain a slip at the club. Failing that, you can anchor out in either the south or the north fork of the creek. Should you choose the former, stay near the south shore to avoid the shoal waters along the opposite side. For the north fork, simply stay near the middle until you pass the little point to port. You can anchor just past this point in about 8 feet of water, fully protected from weather and wakes.

Water and electricity are available at the yacht club dock. For fuel or supplies, head for St. Michaels, about a mile away.

Miles River, St. Michaels

Charts: 12263, **12270**

For most of its 300-year history St. Michaels has been a workingman's community. Like many of the towns on the Chesapeake Bay, it has now become a tourist attraction.

The town is small for its reputation. St. Michaels is famous for its yacht harbor, its maritime museum, its crab and seafood restaurants, and its old houses, dating back 200 or more

years. In St. Michaels harbor expensive yachts can be found docked hull to hull with the workboats of clammers, oyster tongers, and trotline crabbers. Boutiques, gift shops, and even an art gallery are interspersed with hardware stores, self-service laundries, and a foundry.

History. According to the Chesapeake Bay Maritime Museum, the earliest recorded reference to St. Michaels was made in 1631 by a Captain Claiborne, of Kent Island, who traded at a town on "Shipping Creek." The town, unnamed at first, grew up around a log church built in 1670 by Edward Elliot. The church was rebuilt on the same site three times, resulting in the present handsome, 100-year-old building made from massive stones quarried near Havre de Grace.

In 1680 the town was named St. Michaels, after the archangel. Later it became a shipbuilding center. By the time of the American Revolution there were about 25 boatyards building everything from punts to schooners. During the War of 1812, St. Michaels shipyards produced privateers and gunboats that harassed British shipping.

The British finally became so incensed that several men-of-war were ordered up the Chesapeake to shell St. Michaels and destroy her shipyards. On the evening of 10 August 1813 the fleet arrived off St. Michaels and commenced shelling the village. Anticipating the attack, the townsmen, under the leadership of Brigadier General Perry Benson, hung lanterns high in the trees around the town and darkened all the houses and outbuildings. The British gunners, thinking that the town was on a hill, overshot it with every round except one. That one cannonball crashed through the roof of a house owned by William Marchant, a shipwright, and bounced downstairs past Mrs. Marchant, who was carrying her daughter down those same stairs at that very moment. The house has since been known as "the cannonball house."

Most of the shipyards are gone, and the main industry is now seafood—both the catching and the serving of it. The 1,500 residents of St. Michaels still carry on their daily business much as they always have, and their lovely, placid town holds a strong attraction for cruising people.

St. Michaels

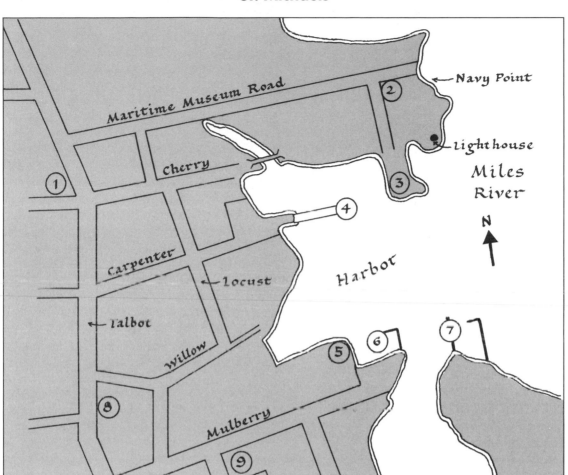

Maritime Museum Road

Cherry

Carpenter

← locust

← Talbot

Willow

Mulberry

St. Mary's Square

chestnut

chestnut

Harbor

← Navy Point

• Lighthouse

Miles River

N ↑

Region 3

KEY

1. Grocery Store
2. Maritime Museum
3. Crab Claw Restaurant
4. Higgins Marine Service
5. Longfellow's Restaurant
6. Miles River Marina
7. St. Michaels Marina
8. Cannonball House
9. Cannonball Church

Approaches. As you pass nun "2" in the Miles River, stay at least 300 yards off the western shore and head for flashing red "2" and green can "3" at the entrance to St. Michaels harbor. (You can pretty much ignore the nun "4" buoy in the Miles River.) As you pass between red "2" and can "3," you will be heading directly toward the Chesapeake Bay Maritime Museum, on Navy Point. There is no mistaking Navy Point. Perched on the end of the point is the six-sided, cottage-type lighthouse, which was moved to the museum from Hooper's Straight in 1966 to save it from demolition. First lighted in 1879, it is one of only three lighthouses of this type left in the Bay region. Not many people notice that the lighthouse is working and that the sequence it flashes is Morse code: C-B-M-M, for Chesapeake Bay Maritime Museum. To starboard is a little creek where you can anchor in relative peace and quiet, or you can head for the marinas and restaurants in the main harbor to port.

Restaurants. During the main boating season, several of the restaurants maintain free water taxis to transport diners to and from boats or the Maritime Museum.

As you enter the main harbor, you can't miss The Crab Claw Restaurant. One of the four restaurants directly accessible from the water, it has several slips on its west side where you can tie up a boat as long as 40 feet while dining there. From the dining room on the second floor there is an excellent view of the harbor, and you can often watch oyster boats unloading their catch at the main dock directly below. As the name suggests, the emphasis at The Crab Claw is on crab and crab dishes, although other fare is offered. We have yet to be served a meal that has been less than excellent, and the prices are reasonable.

In the southwest corner of the harbor, diagonally across from the lighthouse, is Longfellow's Restaurant, certainly the fanciest of the four restaurants on the main harbor. If you go by water, you need a dinghy, because the landing dock is inadequate for anything larger. Longfellow's has a wide selection of delicious meals offered in an elegant, air-conditioned room overlooking the harbor. The service is excellent; the prices are fairly high, but Longfellow's accepts major credit cards.

If you are on a tight budget, try the Quarterdeck Restaurant, next to Longfellow's. It is associated with the St. Michaels Town Dock Marina, where you can either tie up during dinner or rent a slip for the night. The Quarterdeck

Old Hoopers Straight Lighthouse was moved from the Strait to the St. Michaels Maritime Museum, at Navy Point, in 1966.

is more representative of Eastern Shore water-front restaurants.

In the cove on the other side of Navy Point is The Inn at Perry Cabin. Previously a nightclub, it is now a sophisticated bed-and-breakfast and restaurant (coat and tie required).

What to See & Do. With the exception of The Crab Claw, Navy Point is occupied entirely by the Chesapeake Bay Maritime Museum. Some of the buildings are new, but others date back to the mid-1800s. All visitors to the Museum are invited to dock free of charge for the day on a first-come basis. Call the dockmaster on VHF-FM channel 16 or 410-745-2916. Simply tell the dockmaster or the Navy Point staff how many family members and guests you have on board. An admission fee or guest pass is required for all nonmembers on board. Day dockers must leave by no later than 4:00 P.M. No electricity is available at the docks, but water and facilities for trash disposal are. Showers, restrooms, and a pumpout station ($5 fee) are available as well. Overnight dockage is restricted to CBMM members at the level of "contributor" or above.

The main part of the museum is located on the outer half of Navy Point. The buildings house a waterfowling exhibit, a waterman's exhibit, and a display of small boats indigenous to the Chesapeake. Outside are more exhibits, such as the fog bell tower and the original 1,000-pound bell from Point Lookout, a boat workshop, the Hooper's Straight Lighthouse, and the floating exhibits. Newly recovered boats are restored and the existing fleet maintained with the museum's own marine railway and boat shop. Relics of the sailing past discovered on the salt marshes of the Bay are often brought to the museum for restoration. As a result, the fleet is growing every year. In 1998 the drawbridge from Knapps Narrows was transported to St. Michaels and installed at the entrance to the Museum. Cars now pass under the partly raised drawbridge to enter the museum grounds, providing nonboaters with the sensation of negotiating a drawbridge by water. Whether or not you decide to tour the museum, don't miss a visit to the museum store, near the Crab Claw Restaurant.

Higgins Yacht Yard (410-745-9303), St. Michaels Town Dock Marina (410-745-2400), and St. Michaels Harbour Inn & Marina (410-745-9001) offer transient slips and pumpout.

The latter two also have self-service laundries. Fuel is only available at the St. Michaels Town Dock Marina.

Anchorages. Transient slips are usually available at the harbor marinas, but if a slip is not available or if you choose to anchor out, you will find the anchorage in the harbor to be quite small, and it is crowded on holidays and weekends during the cruising season. The holding here is also far from the best. Alternative anchorages are available across the Miles River in Leeds Creek or in either branch of Long Haul Creek beyond the Miles River Yacht Club.

Miles River, Leeds Creek

  No facilities

Charts: 12263, **12270**

Leeds Creek is located directly across the Miles River from St. Michaels. For decades this creek has provided a convenient, easily entered alternative to remaining overnight in the St. Michaels harbor. Recently the shoals at the mouth of the creek have been encroaching on the entrance channel, making the proper channel more difficult both to find and to follow.

Approaches. If you are approaching from the north, give the green can "1" buoy off Fairview Point a wide berth until it is abeam. The shoal extends well to the north and west of the buoy. Once the buoy is abeam, turn to port and, leaving can "1" about 50 yards to port, assume a course toward the end of the first point on the south side of the creek until you are a little more than 200 yards past can "1." Then swing to port to assume a course that will take you about three-quarters of the way to the north side of the creek mouth. Proceed slowly and sound your way in because the shoal has been growing each year. Once the tip of Fairview Point is abeam, you are in. Favor the north side of the creek as you proceed upstream in order to avoid the two shoals protruding from the south side of the creek.

Anchorages. The first anchorage is in the cove to port after you enter. A fascinating "castle" stands at the head of the cove. The story is that it was built by a member of the Winchester family who was afraid of being assassinated, so he constructed his home like a fortification, complete with secret rooms and "hidey holes."

We can't vouch for the truth of this story, but the building is an impressive sight, and the cove is a nice anchorage in its own right.

The next good anchorage is in either of the twin coves to port just under a mile from the creek mouth. The first cove is more secluded, with no buildings or tall trees lining the banks. Favor the west side of the cove to avoid the shoal to the northeast. The second cove has deep water shore to shore, but a couple of houses there reduce the privacy. For some reason, the first little cove is a favorite haunt of horseshoe crabs. We find several complete shells from these interesting creatures, ranging in size from a couple of inches to more than a foot across, every time we come here.

From here on, the creek is protected by a small dogleg, allowing you to anchor anywhere in full protection from the weather. Both sides of the creek in this area are lined with homes. All but shallow-draft powerboats should stay out of the inviting cove to starboard past the dogleg. There is a bar at the mouth, and the water inside is only about 4 feet deep.

You can proceed upstream almost to the fixed bridge, just short of the towns of Copperville and Tunis Mills. The bridge's 6-foot vertical clearance bars passage to all but small runabouts or dinghies; besides, the water starts to shoal here. Beware of submerged pilings off the point to starboard a couple of hundred yards short of the bridge.

Miles River, Hunting Creek

 No facilities

Charts: 12263, **12270**

Approaches. About 2½ miles past St. Michaels, after the Miles River makes a sudden hook to the northeast, the entrance to Hunting Creek will be to port. Even though there is about 10 feet of water very close to the southern tip of Long Point, stay well off since there are some submerged pilings.

To enter the creek, just stay in the middle, avoid the points, and honor the red and green daymarks. The creek is navigable for a good 2 miles from its mouth.

Anchorages. Anywhere you anchor here is fully protected from wind and wave; passing traffic is limited to an occasional workboat.

There are no facilities on this creek; most of the banks appear unspoiled, and houses are sparse, although this is unlikely to be true for much longer. For now, it is a beautiful, serene creek.

This creek holds at least one very vivid memory for us. One October we anchored here in temperatures over 80°F. The following morning we awoke to a blizzard with 2 inches of snow already on the deck! Looking ashore to the island, we saw a small herd of deer peering back at us through the blowing snow. I still wonder which of us was the more perplexed. Needless to say, we stayed put until it cleared.

Upper Miles River

  No facilities

Charts: 12263, 12266, **12270**

From Hunting Creek the Miles River is navigable for another 5 miles. The banks are lined with beautiful homes, and the river is peaceful. The drawbridge 3 miles above Hunting Creek opens on demand from sunrise to sunset. Otherwise, 6 hours' notice is required.

Anchorages. It is feasible to anchor anywhere along the sides of the river in full security, having only to contend with the wakes from local powerboats.

Past the bridge the river splits into three forks. The first fork, Glebe Creek, shoals fairly rapidly about ½ mile past its mouth; however, the entrance offers a nice anchorage. The next fork, Goldsborough Creek, is navigable for about a mile and also offers well-protected anchorages. The third fork, the main Miles River, continues for about 2 miles, although here it is narrow and looks more like a small creek than the wide river you have been negotiating up to this point. It too provides secure anchorages anywhere along its length.

POPLAR ISLAND NARROWS & POPLAR HARBOR

Charts: 12263, 12266, **12270**

At the northern entrance to Poplar Narrows, which runs between the islands and the mainland, is red nun "8," a reminder that the buoyage system in the narrows is still referenced to

Eastern Bay. When entering Poplar Narrows from the north you must treat the navigation markers as if you were leaving Eastern Bay. The red markers are left to port and the green markers to starboard until you reach the lighted green "1" marker south of Poplar Island. Navigation here means threading your way through numerous crab pots. Even though regulations state that from Memorial Day to Labor Day no crab pots are to be placed in a 50-foot channel through Poplar Island Narrows, you usually have to avoid many pots.

A shoal extends nearly a mile to the northeast of Valliant Point on Jefferson Island, one of the islands in the Poplar Island group. Allow plenty of room to clear it as you enter Poplar Island Narrows. If you are not a good judge of distance, hold close to nun "8" and then come to a course of 192 degrees until you pick up can "5" east of Coaches Island, the southernmost island in the cluster. From there, follow the markers until you reach the lighted green "1" marker at the southernmost part of Poplar Island Narrows. Give the last two markers a wide berth because of the shoal southeast of Coaches Island. Boats drawing 6 feet or more probably should not attempt the passage through the narrows because of shoaling in this area. (We once led a good friend whose boat has a 6-foot draft through the narrows, warning him that he might bump a couple of times, and he did—exactly twice.)

Poplar Harbor was once a viable harbor, if rather shallow and difficult to enter. By the late 1990s it had shoaled in to the point that it was accessible only by boats drawing less than 3 feet. In addition, the northern and western islands had eroded to the point where they were almost completely awash. In 1999 a proposal was made to turn the cluster of islands into a dredging spoil area and build it back up into a single island, much as it had been a century ago. The approach would be similar to the process that has been reclaiming Hart-Miller Island, north of the mouth of the Patapsco River. This proposal has been accepted and implementation has started. But it really doesn't matter much to the cruiser: Poplar Harbor is no longer a viable anchorage.

CHOPTANK RIVER

Charts: 12263, 12266, **12268**, 12270

The Choptank River is the largest river on the Eastern Shore. Although it is navigable for most boats as far as Denton, 45 miles upriver from the mouth, and for shoal-draft boats as far as Greensboro, there is little reason for any but the confirmed gunkholer to proceed much beyond the town of Choptank, 8 miles above the bridge at Cambridge (vertical clearance 50 feet). The river is deep, well marked, and protected enough for you to anchor nearly anywhere along the banks, but it winds among low-lying, buggy marshes beyond Choptank, and the best cruising grounds are below this point.

At one time a substantial island was located in the mouth of the Choptank River, south of Tilghman Island. In 1675 the island measured nearly 900 acres and belonged to a doctor, Peter Sharp, for whom it was named. By 1847 the wind, waves, and storms of the Chesapeake had eroded to island to half its size, about 473 acres. After that the erosion accelerated, reducing the island to a mere 94 acres in 1900 and finally to nothing but a shoal in 1963. A series of lighthouses were built on the island, all but the last undermined by the waters or ice and destroyed. The present lighthouse was originally built in 1882 on a 5-acre circular plot of land that disappeared along with the rest of the island. The lighthouse now stands in 10 feet of water. The circular lighthouse, painted brown, was tilted by ice in 1973 and tilted even further by more ice in 1976. Marking the north end of the shoal that was once Sharps Island, it has assumed a rakish angle, making it easily identifiable from a distance. Periodically, the Coast Guard proposes to remove the lighthouse. So far it has survived both the weather and the Coast Guard proposals.

Knapps Narrows

Charts: 12263, **12266**, 12268, 12270

At the mouth of the Choptank River is a peninsula pointing south toward the now submerged Sharps Island. The southern half of this peninsula is actually an island by virtue of a narrow channel from the Bay to the Choptank River, which separates Tilghman Island from the mainland. This channel, Knapps Narrows, saves 5 miles in the passage from the northern Bay into the Choptank River. The channel is heavily used by both local watermen and pleasure boaters who cruise the Choptank River and its tributaries.

Knapps Narrows is not merely a convenient passage for casual yachtsmen. For more than 400 years it has been the home of a sizable fleet of the traditional workboats of the Bay watermen. From late spring through early fall, pleasure craft mingle with the workboats. The yachts disappear before winter, leaving the water to the workboats.

Approaches. As you pass the southern end of Poplar Island, you can see the lighted green "1" marker at the entrance to Knapps Narrows. If you have trouble picking it out from the shoreline, a course of 155 degrees from Poplar Island "1" will take you directly to it.

There is usually shoaling on the Bay side of Knapps Narrows, particularly if winter gales have been severe. After it was dredged in 1980, another red marker was added. (The narrows is redredged periodically, most recently in 1999.) The new marker has eased the approach. The controlling depth is typically 6 to 7 feet in the center of the channel. Even so, check with someone who has been through recently if you are making your first passage for the season. It has a bad habit of shoaling in the vicinity of the red "4" light on the Bay side.

Be sure to hold close to the red "4" light as you approach it, then swing sharply to starboard and head directly for the middle of the entrance to the narrows. In this way you can easily avoid the encroaching shoal northeast of red "4" and allow yourself to enter the narrows proper. From here, favor the south side of the channel until you reach the bridge. You can hold to within 10 feet of the south shore in this section, but don't try it on the north side unless you like plowing through mud.

At the bridge the buoyage system reverses. In other words, when you enter from the Bay side, all green markers are left to port, but immediately after you pass the bridge, you must leave all green markers to starboard.

Although I don't recommend passing through the narrows at night, the bridge opens on demand 24 hours a day, and the passage is fairly safe if there is some moonlight to show you the way on the approach and exit to the narrows. Each time we have made the passage, the bridge operator has been alert and very responsive. Everyone we have met there on both commercial and private craft has been courteous, and the narrow section by the bridge is devoid of the "me first" attitude often encountered in Kent Narrows. Sometimes the current through the narrows is fairly strong, but it has never caused us any problems. The drawbridge was replaced in 1998 with a new drawbridge that looks very much like the old one. The old drawbridge was moved to the St. Michaels Maritime Museum, where it was installed by the museum's new entrance drive. There it remains partially opened to give incoming visitors an idea of what it is like to pass under the bridge by boat.

Once you clear the bridge, you are in deep water throughout the passage until you reach the flashing red "6" marker at the start of the channel into the Choptank River from the narrows proper.

Leave red "6" close to port and hold a course parallel to a line drawn between the green markers to starboard but no closer than 50 feet to them. The markers are not directly on the edge of the channel, but offset about that distance to the south of it. Don't get too far to the north either, as the channel is not more than 100 feet wide. Hold this course until you have passed the lighted green "3," the last channel marker. If you are proceeding north into Harris Creek, hold this course for at least another 400 yards before heading toward the mouth of the creek so that you will clear the shoal to the north. For any other destination on the Choptank, you can come to your new course as soon as you reach green "3."

Marinas & Restaurants. Although definitely a waterman's harbor, Knapps Narrows is also frequented by pleasure craft and has facilities designed for them. Three large marinas cater to yachts and smaller pleasure boats, and four other boatyards cater primarily to the local watermen and their craft.

The Tilghman Island Inn is on the south side of the narrows just inside the entrance from the Bay side. The Inn has slips where you may tie up while dining, but you may have some fun getting into one of them if the current is flowing strongly. Enter bow-first as the slips are fairly shallow and even the bow may bump the bottom. There are at least two restaurants right on the waterfront near the bridge. One of these, the Bay Hundred, is located at Knapps Narrows Marina, adjacent to and northwest of the drawbridge. Temporary dockage is available for diners at Bay Hundred; however, the depth at the fuel dock can be iffy. Directly across the channel is the Bridge Restaurant. The "Bridge" changed hands recently, and we are unaware of any changes the new management may have made (the name may have changed, so don't use that as a reference point) One thing hasn't changed: you can still see watermen off-loading their catch at the pier. *Warning: Do not fill your freshwater tanks from the hoses so conveniently placed outside the Bridge Restaurant. Those hoses pump seawater from the narrows to wash down the area of the pier where oysters and clams are unloaded.*

Although it's not obvious to the casual observer, the Tilghman County Dock is in the artificial cove adjacent to the Bridge Restaurant. There is some confusion about exactly where the part of the pier belonging to the restaurant (which charges a fee to tie up overnight) ends and where the County Dock (which doesn't charge a fee) begins. The rule of thumb that we use is that the County Dock starts immediately south of the corner of the restaurant building and continues clockwise all the way around the cove. However, finding space among the boats belonging to watermen is problematic.

The narrows is an excellent place to refuel, to restock supplies, or to sit down to a meal at a good restaurant, but it is not a good place to spend a quiet night. The waterway is always busy, and even if you can find a place to tie up for the night, you are sure to be awakened in the wee hours of the morning as the watermen get underway.

On the Choptank River side of Tilghman Island, about a stone's throw south of Knapps Narrows, is a small basin populated by workboats and a few skipjacks. Harrison's Chesapeake House (hotel and restaurant) is located here. If you have a draft that permits entrance (the channel was just under 6 feet MLW in 1988) and are looking for a super meal, try it! You can tie up off the end of any of the three piers just inside the entrance channel long enough for a meal (which, incidentally, we guarantee will be outstanding). I don't recommend anchoring overnight even though the channel and basin are dredged to a mean depth of 6 feet. A strong east wind makes mooring at Harrison's piers uncomfortable at best.

Choptank River, Harris Creek
Charts: 12263, **12266**, 12270

Once you have cleared Knapps Narrows, the approach to Harris Creek is easy. Simply honor the markers as you proceed up the creek. You have to contend with only one unmarked shoal, which extends to the southwest from Indian Point on the east side of the creek, just past Dun Cove. If you hold to within a couple of hundred yards of green "7" off Seaths Point, you will avoid it easily.

This creek has many anchorages. The most popular one, in Dun Cove, provides excellent protection from weather and is the closest harbor for convenient passage to or from Knapps Narrows. If you are looking for more seclusion, pick one of the creeks or coves farther up Harris Creek.

Darrell Luskin

The new Knapps Narrows Bridge. The old bridge was moved to the St. Michaels Maritime Museum in 1999.

Harris Creek, Dun Cove

  No facilities

Charts: 12263, **12266**, 12270

Two miles to the north of the eastern end of Knapps Narrows, Dun Cove is an appealing spot to spend the night. Both arms of this cove are excellent anchorages.

Approaches. After passing the green "5" marker in Harris Creek, due east of Bald Eagle Point, head directly for the red "6" marker east of Dun Cove before turning to head directly into the middle of the entrance to the cove. Shoals project from both the north and south sides of the entrance, so keep to the middle at all times.

Anchorages. Anchoring in the south arm of the cove is perfectly satisfactory, but the north arm of the cove is more popular because it is better sheltered. In either case, the bottom is mud and clay, which serve as good holding ground, and the surrounding trees break the wind. It is surprising how suddenly a howling wind and foul weather moderate as soon as you turn into the protection of either arm of Dun Cove.

Except for the farmhouse at the extreme end of the north arm of the cove, the surroundings are woods on one side and fields on the other; however, additional houses seem to be appearing rapidly now. There are sandy beaches where you can land to stretch your legs, although the land off the beach is posted with "No Trespassing" signs. It is not surprising that this anchorage is a favorite spot for cruisers. As a corollary, the cove is often crowded on weekends during the boating season.

Harris Creek, Waterhole Cove

   No facilities

Charts: 12263, **12266**, 12270

The next anchorage above Dun Cove is Waterhole Cove. There are several homes on the shore, but the impression is of a relatively unspoiled shoreline. The holding is generally good, and there are some small, sandy beaches to the west and one off Smith Point to the north.

While you can tuck well into the west side of the mouth of the cove to gain the protection of Smith Point from the north to northeast, in warm weather most cruisers elect to anchor farther out to catch the cooling breezes. This anchorage's main disadvantage is being wide open to the east and southeast. Normally, this is no problem, but one night we did have to break up a raft at 2:00 A.M. when the wind shifted and started to blow hard from that direction.

Harris Creek, Briary Cove

  No facilities

Charts: 12263, **12270**

Briary Cove is almost a clone of Waterhole Cove. The same description fits it except that there is less room to anchor because of the shoaling along each shore, and an unmarked 4-foot shoal extends two-thirds of the way across the entrance from the point on the northeast side of the mouth. Since there are better anchorages nearby, we recommend passing this one up.

Harris Creek, Unnamed Cove

  No facilities

Charts: 12263, **12270**

Between Briary Cove and Cummings Creek is an attractive little cove that is not named on any of our charts. It is a pretty spot but relatively open to the southeast unless you draw less than 5 feet and can get around the point into the left fork. The bottom is soft mud. You may drag a bit if the wind pipes up, but you probably won't drag very far as your anchor will soon bury itself deep into firmer mud.

Our general impression of this cove is one of pristine surroundings. Try it. You probably will find yourself in your own private anchorage!

Harris Creek, Cummings Creek

Charts: 12263, **12270**

If you feel your way through the narrow entrance channel into Cummings Creek, you are likely to have a private little anchorage all to yourself. Leave the quick-flashing marker close to starboard and stay in the middle to enter.

The depth of Cummings Creek is 6 to 7 feet inside the left (west) fork, but you can anchor in 7 to 8 feet of water in the left fork or right in the mouth of the right fork, well protected from weather in all directions except the southeast. Don't proceed past the mouth of the right fork; it shoals quickly. The couple of small boatyards here offer nothing for the transient. The concrete launching ramp indicates some runabout traffic, which may make you decide to anchor elsewhere. Even so, it is worth a look around.

Upper Harris Creek

 No facilities

Charts: 12263, **12270**

The creek is navigable for more than a mile above Cummings Creek, and you can anchor in numerous places along the way, all the way up into the Northeast Branch. Don't try to enter the Northwest Branch; there is a 2-foot bar across its mouth.

Choptank River, Broad Creek

Charts: 12263, 12266, **12270**

Perhaps one of the most underrated cruising grounds in the vicinity of the Choptank River is the Broad Creek area. In discussions of cruising the Choptank River you seldom hear Broad Creek or its several tributaries mentioned. The reason is not clear, but it may have to do with the lack of fuel and supplies on Broad Creek or its tributaries. The nearest point for fuel and supplies is in Oxford, on the Tred Avon River, about 7 miles from the green "1" light at the mouth of Broad Creek. I find the lack of facilities odd since the region abounds in attractive scenery and excellent anchorages in both the main creek and its offshoots.

Broad Creek winds its way north for about 6 miles from its mouth on the Choptank River to its headwaters. From the flashing green "1" light at the mouth of Broad Creek, a course of 10 degrees takes you directly to the lighted red "4" marker off Deep Neck Point. Do not stray very far to the east of this course or you may run afoul of the wide shoal off Deep Neck near the course midpoint.

As you approach the red "4" do not let the group of red and green daymarks visible beyond it confuse you. Simply ignore all the daymarks until you clear red "4," then change course to head either into Leadenham Creek to the west or to a northeast course to head farther up Broad Creek proper. Be sure to leave the red "6" daymark to starboard. At red "6" you can either swing to port to head up Broad Creek or swing right toward red "8" to enter Edge Creek or San Domingo Creek. In either direction attractive anchorages beckon, and worrisome shoals are well marked.

Broad Creek, Balls Creek

 No facilities

Charts: 12263, **12266**, 12270

The first creek to port as you proceed up Broad Creek, Balls Creek is home to a fleet of watermen. Although well marked, the entrance, with its three doglegs, is nerve-racking the first time through, and the creek itself offers little. The low banks are muddy, and the bottom is stony toward the sides of the creek, making anchoring a little uncertain. We recommend passing it up.

Broad Creek, Leadenham Creek

No facilities

Charts: 12263, **12266**, 12270

Approaches. As you approach the red "4" light off Deep Neck Point you can begin to swing to port as soon as you can see the pair of red and green daymarks marking the entrance to Leadenham Creek. There are no more markers after these two, but that presents no problem. Just stay near the middle of the creek. If you plan to continue up Leadenham Creek, swing to port immediately after passing the green "1" daymark; otherwise you may find yourself heading up Grace Creek.

Anchorages. The best anchorage on the Leadenham is in the unnamed cove that opens to starboard about ½ mile past green "1." This pretty cove, with 10 feet of water and good holding, is well protected from all directions except the south. Even from the south the maximum fetch is little more than ½ mile. We once weathered a pretty good blow here in complete comfort. There are only a couple of houses in the northwest corner of the cove, and although all of the land is private property, there are lots of sandy beaches along the eastern side, backed by a screen of trees in front of a farm field, where you can land to stretch your legs a little.

The next opening to starboard is Caulk Cove, where you can anchor securely in 8 feet of water. This is an attractive anchorage, but the muddy banks offer nowhere to land. The same can be said about the remaining portion of Leadenham Creek. Don't travel much beyond the point where the creek bends sharply to the northwest; there it begins to shoal.

Broad Creek, Grace Creek

Charts: 12263, **12266**, 12270

Approaches. As you pass the red "2" daymark at the entrance to Leadenham Creek, swing to starboard and you will easily enter Grace Creek. There is no tricky channel, and the creek is well marked where needed.

Anchorages. The first and best anchorage is in the little cove to port less than 400 yards past red "2." This is out of the way of any traffic, and the holding is good, in soft mud. To the west there is a beach, which appears to be sandy, backed by a screen of trees in front of a field.

As you continue up Grace Creek toward Bozman, you'll find a series of watermen's docks and the P. T. Hambleton Marine Railway. On a good day you may be able to purchase some seafood. No fuel is available.

Upper Broad Creek

 No facilities

Charts: 12263, 12266, **12270**

Approaches. If you swing to port on reaching red "6" at the junction of Broad and Edge Creeks, you can continue into the upper reaches of Broad Creek for 3 miles. Simply stay to the middle of the creek. The few projecting shoals are well marked, and the many bights offer a number of spots where you can pull in and anchor.

Anchorages. With the exception of Hambleton Island, to starboard, most of the shoreline is lined with private homes until you get well up into the headwaters.

From the part of the creek that runs north-south up to the head of navigation, you have a number of attractive spots in which to anchor in relative seclusion. All are well protected and have the mud bottom that offers good holding. Once while exploring this part of the creek, we were overtaken by a line squall. We simply dropped the hook right where we were and rode it out in comfort and security.

Broad Creek, Edge Creek

 No facilities

Charts: 12263, 12266, **12270**

As you reach red "8" to the north of Cedar Point, you will enter the mouth of Edge Creek. Unless you have a definite reason for doing so and some local knowledge, do not try any of the tributaries off Edge Creek except San Domingo Creek. They are full of shoals, and in most the water is uncomfortably thin. We recommend proceeding no farther than Drum Point, just past the mouth of San Domingo Creek, if you are in a sailboat.

There is an overhead power cable across Edge Creek with a vertical clearance of only 26 feet. This is normally not a problem since it is nearly at the headwaters and the water is too shoal for any sailboats, but powerboats with tall antennas should be careful.

Broad Creek, San Domingo Creek

 No facilities

Charts: 12263, 12266, **12270**

Approaches. As you clear red "8" in Edge Creek, come to a southeast course to the green "9" marker. Give this marker a wide berth as you turn to enter San Domingo Creek. The shoal from the south end of Hambleton Island is gradually extending to the southeast; at the time of our last trip it had progressed well past the marker. Keep a good 50 yards or more off the marker and you will enter San Domingo Creek with no trouble.

Once into the creek, stay in the middle. There are only two projecting shoals, both well marked by daymarks green "11" and red "12." If you have a draft of 4 feet or less, you can proceed to within ½ mile of St. Michaels in the headwaters of the creek. There is a public dock where watermen tie up at the extreme end of the east fork of the very northern end of the creek. If you have a draft of more than 2 feet, you must approach in a dinghy. From here it is about a ½-mile walk into the town of St. Michaels, entering by the "back door."

Anchorages. There are several excellent anchorages on San Domingo Creek. If you have no need to go ashore to stretch your legs or explore, proceed past Hopkins Point, where you can anchor almost anywhere with full protection from wind and wave. Some of the better anchorages are in the fork of the creek to starboard, immediately past the red "14" daymark.

Alternatively, you might choose the mouth of the branch to port, about 600 yards past red "14." Beyond that, you are into the headwaters of the creek, where the water starts to shoal.

In all cases the bottom is mud over a clay base, which makes for very good holding ground.

If you are looking for relative solitude and a place to land and explore, Hambleton Island offers at least two secure anchorages and several small, sandy beaches. The charted depths are deceptive. There is actually more water, and the deep water is closer to shore, than indicated by the NOAA charts. At least this was true in places we tried.

Hambleton Island is actually two islands. From the evidence of the shoal between them it is obvious that these two islands were connected in the not-too-distant past. We have explored this connecting shoal by dinghy and found what looked to be about 1 foot of water between the two parts of the island, so we were floored to observe a medium-size workboat blithely cross over it and proceed on into Broad Creek. The attitude of the local watermen toward shoals and their ability to avoid or ignore them never ceases to amaze us!

There are two good potential anchorages off Hambleton Island, both attractive to cruising boats of any size. The first is off the southern portion of the island, in a little bight immediately to the southwest of the green "11" daymark (middle of the lower island). Do not try to anchor immediately to the northwest of green

"11" or even get close to it; there are submerged pilings and a shoal there. The island has a nice beach right near this anchorage and a somewhat larger one on the north side just around the point.

The second anchorage is anywhere to the east of the northern portion of the island; you can anchor to within 50 yards of the beach in 9 to 11 feet of water over a soft bottom of mud and clay. Don't go into the inviting cove to the north of the island; there is only 1 foot of water between the island and the mainland.

Once you have passed the initial barrier of high banks and brush above the beach, you can try exploring the islands. It is easier to land at high tide either by beaching a dinghy or tying to one of the fallen trees and using the tree as a bridge onto the island proper. At low tide, a dinghy grounds 20 to 50 yards from the beach, and you have to wade through the mud and sea nettles in order to land. It is also harder to reach any of the fallen trees. At high tide, most of these problems do not exist.

Once you are on the island, walking is fairly easy and the poison ivy, although present, is not profuse enough to deter exploration.

The southern portion of the island is about ⁶⁄₁₀ mile long; the shoal between the two parts is about ²⁄₁₀ mile, and the northern portion of the island is also about ²⁄₁₀ mile, for a distance of just over a mile from the southern tip of the southern portion to the northern tip of the northern portion of Hambleton Island. Either portion has ample room for you to exercise your legs.

Wherever you choose to anchor on San Domingo Creek, you should have peace and quiet. In spite of the numerous piers and sizable boats in this area, everyone is extremely courteous and considerate of anchored visiting boats, and the water traffic is very light.

Choptank River, Irish Creek

 No facilities

Charts: 12263, **12266**

Approaches. Despite its straightforward appearance on the chart, the entrance to this creek is tricky. Although sailboats as large as 35 feet regularly negotiate Irish Creek, the channel is a true test of piloting skills and a challenge to every dyed-in-the-wool gunkholer.

The first part of the entrance is straightforward. Pick up the green "1" can and head to leave the red "2" nun close to starboard. After rounding red "2," head to leave the green "3" daymark less than 50 yards to port. Now comes the test. You cannot take a straight course from green "3" to red "4." A shoal protrudes from the southwest shore at Lucy Point, so you must take a gentle arc to port until halfway between the markers and then follow the same curve back to red "4." Proceed slowly and use a lead line or pole on either side of the boat to warn you when you are getting too far to one side or the other of the channel. If the duck blind off Holland Point is still there, you can use it as if it were another green marker to guide you.

Anchorages. Once you pass red "41," you are in. Be sure to honor the red "6" daymark off Edwards Point before swinging to starboard. Anchor anywhere in this quiet, well-protected harbor, where there are few other boats besides those belonging to people who live there. Perhaps the most attractive anchorage is in 9 feet of water right in the mouth of Haskins Cove.

The creek carries 6 to 10 feet of water except in the extreme eastern portion, where it bends sharply to the north. Don't enter very far into the attractive little cove between Lucy and Edwards Points as it shoals quickly.

Choptank River, Tred Avon River

Charts: 12263, **12266**

About 7½ miles from the mouth of the Choptank River is a large, 35-foot-high, lighted spider (Choptank River Light) marking the mouth of the Tred Avon River. From this point the river wanders to the north and east, with a variety of creeks and coves offering anchorages ranging from secluded to commercial. Many of the shoals upriver used to be unmarked, presenting a minor navigational hazard. Now there are enough strategically placed markers to keep you off the mud if you are prudent.

Although the Choptank River Light serves as an excellent reference, visible for several miles, it need not be honored when approaching the Tred Avon. Definitely leave the lighted green "1" marker off Benoni Point to port. From Benoni Point a course of 18 degrees takes you to the lighted red "2" spar west of Oxford, a distance of just over 2 miles. From there, with a few exceptions in the tributaries, piloting upriver as far as the head of navigation at Easton Point is a matter of honoring the markers.

Anchorages abound along the 6 miles of river between Oxford and Easton Point. You can drop the hook in varying degrees of sylvan surroundings and still be no farther than a few miles from resupply points for ice and other amenities. If you are looking for restaurants or need supplies or repairs, Oxford is the place to go. If you seek seclusion, head upriver.

Tred Avon River, Oxford

Charts: 12263, **12266**

Marinas & Restaurants. As you clear Bachelor Point, civilization appears to starboard in the form of the Pier Street Marina and Restaurant in Oxford. There is deep water and dock space available for those visiting the restaurant. Use caution when laying alongside the dock in the face of a strong breeze from the southwest quadrant as the area is unprotected from that direction. If you want to spend the night, transient slips are available. The restaurant has reasonable prices and high value for your money, but fancy it isn't.

Almost immediately after rounding the red "2" marker off the Tred Avon Yacht Club, you come to a wharf commonly called the Oxford "town dock," although its name is the Oxford-Bellevue Ferry Dock. This is one of the terminals for the Tred Avon Ferry, the oldest free-running ferry route in the United States, established in 1760. One story holds that the first ferry route here was established in 1683. Whatever the actual date, this is the best-known car ferry on the Eastern Shore. Except for the period from Christmas to the first of March, the ferry operates seven days a week. Although the hours vary for summer and winter, basically it operates from a little after sunup to sundown. In 1988 the tolls were $3.75 per car and driver plus $.25 for each additional passenger; $1.50 for bicycles and trailers; and $2.00 for motorcycles.

The 300 feet of dockage space along the wharf is available to transients at no charge (2-hour limit, no overnight), but it is too exposed to wakes and weather for a lengthy tie-up. You would do better to anchor off the long, sandy town beach (The Strand) and take a dinghy in to shore. There are signs prohibiting dinghies, but they do not apply to transients, who are welcome there for short-term beaching of dinghies. The Strand extends from the ferry dock eastward about halfway to the Town Creek entrance. In warmer weather, be aware of children swimming and diving near the town dock as you pull in.

Within about 100 yards straight inland from the dock is the Robert Morris Inn, an excellent restaurant but a bit on the expensive side. Most major credit cards are accepted. On Friday and Saturday nights dinner is served on a first-come basis, and there are no reservations. The structure of the inn incorporates the original home, built in 1710, of Robert Morris Sr., one of the financiers of the American Revolution.

Much more appealing for either a temporary stop or an overnight stay in Oxford is Town Creek, whose mouth is less than ½ mile beyond the Oxford town dock. The first marker is a lighted red "2" spar, not to be confused with the lighted red "2" to the west of Oxford, mentioned earlier. The Town Creek channel is well marked with pairs of red and green daymarks all the way to the end of the creek. The first facility to come into view is Mears Yacht Haven, to

Tred Avon River Region (Irish Creek to Island Creek)

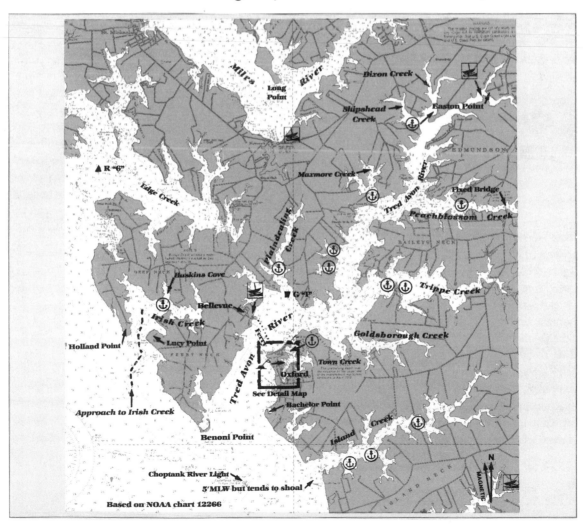

SCALE 1" – **1.65** NAUT. MILES   ⚓ **Good anchoring**   ⚓ **Marina**   **Launching site**

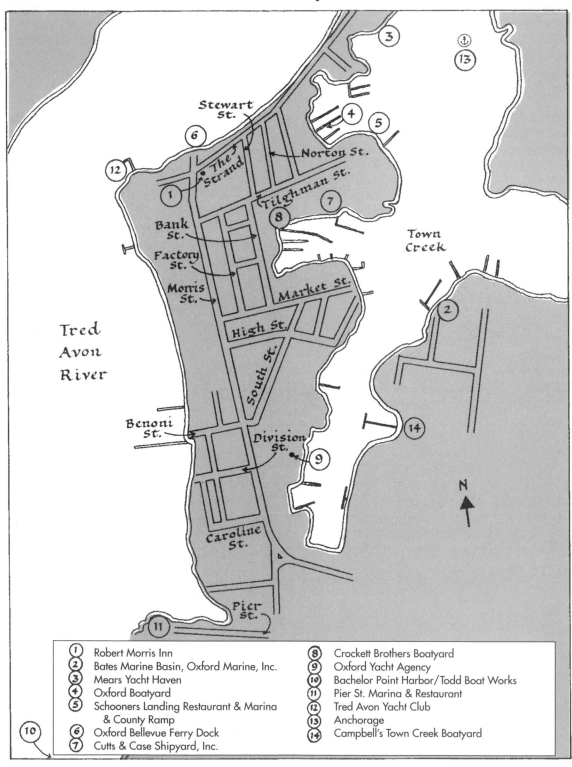

Oxford, Maryland

Stewart St.

The Strand

Norton St.

Tilghman St.

Bank St.

Factory St.

Morris St.

Market St.

Tred Avon River

Town Creek

High St.

South St.

Benoni St.

Division St.

Caroline St.

Pier St.

N

①	Robert Morris Inn	⑧	Crockett Brothers Boatyard
②	Bates Marine Basin, Oxford Marine, Inc.	⑨	Oxford Yacht Agency
③	Mears Yacht Haven	⑩	Bachelor Point Harbor/Todd Boat Works
④	Oxford Boatyard	⑪	Pier St. Marina & Restaurant
⑤	Schooners Landing Restaurant & Marina & County Ramp	⑫	Tred Avon Yacht Club
		⑬	Anchorage
⑥	Oxford Bellevue Ferry Dock	⑭	Campbell's Town Creek Boatyard
⑦	Cutts & Case Shipyard, Inc.		

SCALE 1" = 730 FEET

starboard, perhaps the most convenient place for resupplying ice and fuel. It is very busy during in-season weekends, and you may have to hold off and wait your turn to approach the fuel dock.

Just beyond Oxford Boatyard, following Mears, is the Schooners Landing Waterfront Restaurant & Deck, with almost 200 feet of free dockage for customers. (It replaced the old Town Creek Restaurant and the Oxford Carry-out.) The reasonably priced meals are excellent, and except for holiday weekends, you might get permission to leave your boat tied up at the pier long enough for a tour of the town. Everything in town is within easy walking distance of wherever you may land.

Farther up Town Creek are four more marinas or boatyards, each with varying degrees of capability and facilities. Just across the street from Oxford Yacht Agency is Pope's Tavern, one of Oxford's more "interesting" restaurants. Here you may take yourself back to the turn of the century, complete with ceiling fans, wooden floors, and a selection of penny candy. The room is not large, but the sandwiches and crab-cakes are good, as is a glass of cold beer on a hot summer's day.

Anchorages. If you so desire, you can anchor out in Town Creek away from wave action, if not always protected from the wind. However, the grassy clay bottom makes it difficult to set a lightweight anchor, such as a Danforth, and the surrounding land features cause the wind to come in puffs from fluky directions. Town Creek has a fair amount of boat traffic at times. For these reasons, one of the other anchorages off the Tred Avon may be a better choice for anchoring overnight. Of these, Plaindealing Creek and the unnamed creek southwest of it, directly across the Tred Avon from Oxford, are prime candidates.

Tred Avon River, Plaindealing Creek

 2 *No facilities*

Charts: 12263, **12266**

Approach. Due north of the mouth of Town Creek is Plaindealing Creek, its entrance shoal clearly marked by a green "1" daymark. Legend holds that the creek was named after the Quakers, who did some trading along its banks.

Anchorages. Less than ½ mile past the daymark you can drop your anchor in a little cove to port in good holding ground, sheltered from both wind and wave, except from the southeast.

There is deep water for about another ½ mile, but this cove is the best anchorage. It is possible to land on a narrow strip of sandy beach on the point of land to the north of the cove. The surroundings are quiet and pleasant with a few houses and plenty of trees. We prefer other places on Tred Avon for longer stays.

Tred Avon River, Unnamed Creek Southwest of Plaindealing Creek

 2 *No facilities*

Charts: 12263, **12266**

This unnamed creek is not a bad anchorage unless it breezes up from the southeast. A depth of 6 feet is carried up to the point where the creek bends to the west. Then it shoals rapidly to 3 feet or less as you proceed upstream. The soft bottom provides good holding under most conditions.

There is no place to land as the shoreline is all privately owned, with the possible exception of the marshy point on the west side of its mouth. There is at least 5 feet of water in the little fork to the west inside this marshy point, where you can find full protection from wave, if not wind, in the event of a southeastern blow.

This creek provides a quieter alternative to Town Creek that is still within about a mile of the town of Oxford. You can take a dinghy around the point and southwest to the western (Bellevue side) termination of the Oxford-Bellevue ferry. Leave your dink inside (north) of the quay leading to the ferry dock and ride the ferry (toll) to Oxford to avoid taking a small dinghy across the busy Tred Avon. It saves about a mile of rowing distance, and the ferry is fun to ride.

Tred Avon River, Goldsborough Creek

  3 *No facilities*

Charts: 12263, **12266**

Heading east from Oxford on the Tred Avon, you pass Goldsborough Creek to starboard. Although I am sure that it has its good points, it is too civilized for our tastes.

There is a good anchorage in 8 feet of water just past the small point on the north shore, but you won't find a place to land.

Tred Avon River, Trippe Creek

  No facilities

Charts: 12263, **12266**

Approach. The entrance to Trippe Creek is straightforward, but a couple of shoals lie in wait for the unwary. The first, which extends off the eastern shore, can be avoided easily by holding close to the green "1" daymark at the mouth of Trippe Creek. After clearing this daymark, steer north-northeast until you are approximately due east of the point north of green "1" at the creek entrance. From there, simply stay in the middle of the creek until you clear Deepwater Point. This brings you clear of the shoal west of the point. Unfortunately, each year that shoal has been growing and the channel becoming more shallow. If your boat drafts more than 4 feet, don't try it unless you're willing to chance a grounding.

Anchorages. Although you can anchor almost anywhere once you are fully within Trippe Creek, there are three ideal locations. Our favorite is in the mouth of the unnamed cove to the southeast of Deepwater Point, close to a tiny strip of sandy beach on the outside of the point of land by the cove. If the wind is from the northern quarter, many people seem to like Snug Harbor, on the north bank. We prefer the second unnamed cove to the eastern end of the north bank because Snug Harbor's banks are lined with private homes. Wherever you anchor, holding is good, and the water is clean, with a depth of 7 to 15 feet.

Tred Avon River, Unnamed Coves

  No facilities

Charts: 12263, **12266**

A little above the mouth of Trippe Creek, to the west of the red "10" lighted spar, two unnamed coves provide secure, secluded anchorages in 7 feet of water with tree-lined banks that screen farm fields. The lower cove was promptly

dubbed "Turtle Cove" by the younger members of our crew after we watched about two dozen turtles swimming into the entrance one morning. Both coves have sandy beaches, excellent for swimming, wading, or beachcombing. This land is private, so stay below the high-water mark. In 1990 this area was marked for housing development, and it is now rather built up. There goes another secluded cove!

These coves also share a problem common to many of the low-lying areas along the Eastern Shore—biting gnats, or no-see-ums; unfortunately, the coves are not large enough to permit anchoring far enough offshore to be out of their range. These anchorages are untenable during the late spring and summer months unless you come prepared with adequate screening and appropriate repellents and insecticides.

Tred Avon River, Maxmore Creek

  No facilities

Charts: 12263, **12266**

The mouth of Maxmore Creek, just north of Long Point, provides the next anchorage along the Tred Avon. There is 8 feet of water almost up to shore on Long Point. Most of the rest of the creek is navigable if you have a 5-foot draft or less.

Inside Long Point is the best place to anchor. The voracious no-see-ums frequent this cove, too, so come prepared for them.

Tred Avon River, Peachblossom Creek

  No facilities

Charts: 12263, **12266**

Peachblossom Creek, to starboard, is well worth a visit even if you never get your anchor wet. The steep banks are lined with large houses, perhaps estates, nestled in the trees. All of the land appears to be privately owned and developed. The creek is wide and carries at least 6 feet of water (with no protruding shoals) to within ½ mile of the Route 333 bridge.

You can anchor almost anywhere in the creek proper, but stay out of Le Gates Cove; past the entrance it gets rather shallow.

Tred Avon River, Shipshead & Dixon Creeks

  No facilities

Charts: 12263, **12266**

The last proper anchorage off Tred Avon River is in Dixon Creek, to port. Shipshead and Dixon Creeks share an entrance, and both are navigable, but Dixon Creek is a better choice. Stay well off the point of land to starboard as you enter the creek since the shoal projects somewhat farther out than is apparent from the chart.

You can travel almost to Bloomfield if you have less than a 5-foot draft, but the best anchorage is along the western bank of Dixon Creek, just before the point where the creek splits.

There are low-lying fields on either side of the creek but no beaches, except for one or two small, muddy ones at low water. It is possible to land briefly, if necessary, but this is all privately owned farmland. Although there are gnats here, they are not as bad as in the other anchorages on the western side of the river. Be prepared for them if you do anchor.

Tred Avon River, Easton Point

Charts: 12263, **12266**

Marinas. Just over a mile above the mouth of Dixon Creek is Easton Point. Here you can get marine supplies and gas (no diesel) at Easton Point Marine, which has a head and showers that are yours to use for the asking—something to remember if the weather is sticky or you have been out for several days. The people running the store are courteous and pleasant, characteristics common to most people we have met on the Eastern Shore.

Restaurants & What to See & Do. The city of Easton, the Talbot County seat, is 1½ miles away from Easton Point. With a population of more than 8,000, Easton offers a wide range of stores, movie theaters, and restaurants. The Tidewater Inn, a 120-room colonial hostelry, has a good reputation, especially for local seafood dishes. Each November it is the

site of the annual Waterfowl Festival, which attracts literally thousands of people. Easton is close enough to walk to, or you can call a taxi from Easton Point Marine.

Upper Choptank River

Charts: 12263, **12266**

This section covers both shores of the Choptank River from Island Creek and Castle Haven Point upriver to Cambridge.

Upper Choptank River, Island Creek

  No facilities

Charts: 12263, **12266**

Approaches. The entrance to Island Creek, due east of the Choptank River Light, has been progressively shoaling in. Although the chart indicates 5 feet in the channel, if you have a draft approaching that, you should verify the actual controlling depth in the channel before trying it.

Once you are in, you will find plenty of water depth (9–20 feet) throughout the creek. There are, however, two places where you need to watch your depth carefully. Both are near the creek's headwaters, off the last two points on the northern shore where it forks. The second of these shoals projects more than halfway across the mouth of the northern fork at the end of the creek.

Anchorages. Any anchorage out of the mainstream of traffic is in good holding and fully protected from weather. This Eastern Shore creek is one of the few with a completely developed shoreline, which means there is no place to land. If landing is not a criterion and you have a draft that allows you to get into Island Creek, it is an attractive anchorage. The closest facilities are in Oxford.

Upper Choptank River, Castle Haven

  No facilities

Charts: 12263, **12266**

Approaches. About 2 miles southeast of the Choptank River Light, on your way up the Choptank River, you can see a sizable cove to starboard. Under no circumstances should you head directly for it. A long finger of a shoal, barely submerged, extends from the tip of Castle Haven Point to the red nun "2" buoy past the mouth of this cove. Swing wide round this buoy and head for the south side of the cove entrance until you are a good 300 yards past nun "2." Then swing a little to starboard, to head for the end of the point on the northern side of the entrance, until you are just past the center of the entrance.

Now you can head directly into the cove, keeping in the middle until the first constriction, where two small points on opposite sides stretch toward each other. Proceed beyond here with caution; it starts to shoal rather quickly.

Anchorages. The land is low lying and marshy except for the site of a lone house on the northern shore. Castle Haven offers good protection from all but the east, where it is wide open to a fetch of more than 2 miles. This gunkhole is interesting to poke into—once.

Upper Choptank River, Lecompte Bay & Creek

  No facilities

Charts: 12263, **12266**

Just below Castle Haven is the wide mouth of Lecompte Bay. This bay has 7 to 10 feet of water throughout but is wide open to the entire northeast quadrant. A nice place to visit but not a snug harbor.

The chart indicates a well-marked channel into Lecompte Creek. This channel has had a lot of shoaling, so don't expect to get through it with anything over a 3-foot draft.

A nice little anchorage sits just inside the entrance, but the shores are marshy and the area is a bit on the "buggy" side. Look elsewhere!

Upper Choptank River, La Trappe Creek

Charts: 12263, **12266**

Approach. La Trappe Creek is located on the northeast shore of the Choptank River, directly opposite Lecompte Bay. The entrance is marked by a large, black beacon (perhaps replaced with a green one by now) that resembles a miniature lighthouse. Swing wide around the point on the west side of the creek mouth before approaching the beacon. Stay 20 to 40 yards off the beacon and head so that the red "2" (also a miniature lighthouse) beyond it is a little to starboard; the water is 10 feet deep all the way into the creek.

Anchorages. To port just inside the creek is one of the finest anchorages in this part of the Bay. Give a wide berth to the end of the sand spit as you swing around it, and you can anchor behind Martin Point in 7 to 8 feet of water. There is deep water to within a few feet of the sand spit, but don't get too far to the west side of the cove because it starts to get shallow. Martin Point is posted with "No Trespassing" signs, but you may land at the end of the sand spit to swim, wade, or beachcomb. The rest of the point, with a nice, sandy beach, is closed to the public as a result of the thoughtless boaters who left piles of litter here in the past.

The next attractive anchorage, with 10 feet of water and good holding, is in the bight just past the first point to starboard on your way upstream. The high, wooded shores provide plenty of protection from wave and weather. The shoreline is uninhabited, and you can land on a small, sandy beach.

There is a pretty little anchorage with 6 feet of water in the mouth of Sawmill Cove, about a mile upstream from the mouth of the creek. There are a couple of houses here, but they don't detract from the scenery.

The creek is navigable (6 to 7 feet of water) to Trappe Landing, the home of Dickerson Boat Builders.

The La Trappe is one of the most beautiful creeks on the Chesapeake Bay. On the way upstream it narrows, and the trees lean over the water, giving it an otherworldly feel. The water is a deep shade of chocolate, which makes you feel more like you are driving down a road than cruising a waterway. Don't let this otherworldliness keep you from taking a look at the many large mansions and estates along the way. Don't attempt to travel beyond Trappe Landing, or you will promptly run out of water.

Upper Choptank River, Cambridge

  All facilities

Charts: 12263, **12266**

Approach. Cambridge is located about 7 miles southeast of the Choptank River Light, just short of the Route 50 bridge over the river. As you pass Hambrooks Bar and Gray Marsh Point, just northwest of Cambridge, be sure to honor all the red markers to avoid the 2-foot shoal that extends way out into the river. From can "23" off Hambrooks Bar, head for a point on the bridge about a third of the way across from the Cambridge side, a course of 148 degrees. This takes you directly to the pair of green and red markers where the deep, dredged channel into Cambridge Creek harbor begins. You can either follow the markers into Cambridge harbor or use the outer markers as a takeoff point to enter the Municipal Yacht Basin, also the site of the Cambridge Yacht Club.

If you choose the yacht basin, look for the wooden bulkhead just to the right (about 350 yards) of the entrance to Cambridge Creek. A pair of red and green lighted markers on this bulkhead indicates the entrance into the basin. Head directly to these markers from the outer green "1" at the beginning of the Cambridge channel. This course takes you through the channel to the basin entrance with ease. Don't enter the basin if you draw more than 5 feet.

Marinas & Restaurants. The clubhouse of the Cambridge Yacht Club (410-228-2141), a gift from Francis Du Pont in 1938, is immediately to the right as you enter the basin. The club honors membership cards from other yacht clubs and maintains a few guest slips. The water depth is a little uncertain, more amenable to powerboats than to sailboats. Fuel, water, and showers are available here.

Cambridge, Maryland, Area of the Choptank River

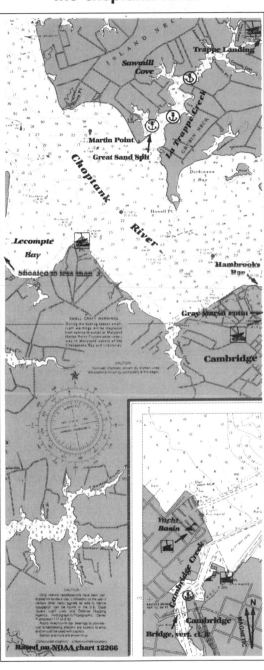

Based on NOAA chart 12266

SCALE **1"** = **1.45** NAUT. MILES

⚓ **Good anchoring**

⚓ **Marina**

 **Launching site**

The Municipal Yacht Basin (410-228-4031) is to port upon entering the bulkhead area. The basin has a few slips for transients up to 60 feet, but the same caveat on water depth as for the yacht club applies here. A restroom, shower, and self-service laundry are located in the building that houses the dockmaster, to the far right of the basin on the shore side. The dockmaster is on duty most of the year, with extended hours in the summer months.

To enter Cambridge Creek, simply follow the markers into the turning basin at the mouth of the creek, 10 feet of water all the way. Once in the turning basin, swing to starboard into the narrow channel leading to Cambridge Creek proper. The Yacht Maintenance Company comes up quickly on your left. Primarily a repair facility, it also has numerous slips, some of which may be available to transients.

Ahead to starboard is the 600-foot-long service dock of the previous Phillips Oil Company Marina, now called Wise Mart, an automobile service station and convenience store, with pumps near the water to serve boats. Tie up alongside and walk into town. East of the Wise Mart is Snapper's Waterfront Café (410-228-0122), with plenty of free dockage in 6 feet of water.

Anchorages. Anchor out in the basin, but stay out of the middle to avoid the boat traffic, mostly watermen but occasionally some rather large vessels.

Past the bridge, there is some room to anchor, but it is a little narrow and in the company of numerous condominium slips. Except during the noon hour the bridge opens on demand to the standard call of one long and one short blast on a horn, or you may call on VHF-FM channel 13. We prefer to anchor in the turning basin before the bridge but recommend going elsewhere for the night.

What to See & Do. The town has several restaurants, self-service laundries, convenience stores, and grocery stores—in short all the shopping you could wish for in a small city. Although founded about 300 years ago, Cambridge has few of the original, colonial buildings due to a series of fires over the years. On the bright side, the cutesy tourist shops and fast-food places common to several other waterfront towns are also missing here. If you hunger for fast food,

take the 1- to 2-mile walk to Route 50, "fast-food paradise." The Rouse Company has put together a redevelopment plan for Cambridge Creek that will soon cause some significant changes to the area. Already a mini-mall has opened and a couple of townhouse complexes have sprung up. A large hotel and a marina complex were still on the boards as of 2000.

Cambridge offers plenty to see and do, but we don't recommend spending the night there, except perhaps in a slip at the municipal basin. We like to leave in time to get back into La Trappe Creek, 4 miles away, to anchor for the night.

Upper Choptank River to Headwaters

Chart: **12268**

The Route 50 drawbridge has been replaced with a fixed bridge that has a maximum vertical clearance in the main channel of 50 feet. The center portion of the old drawbridge has been removed, and the remaining portions jutting out from either shore have been converted into fishing piers.

Approaches. Do not run upriver for the first time after dark: the river is well marked, but an unmarked shoal extends to the north from Whitehall Creek to starboard just past where the river bends to the northeast, and there is a narrow section just west of Goose Creek, marked by buoy cans "33" and "35" and the lighted red "34" marker. Until you reach the Warwick River, none of the little creeks are navigable.

Marinas, Restaurants, & Anchorages. The Warwick River has a narrow, dredged channel up to the Dorchester Oil Company, at Secretary, where you could probably get permission to dock, but why bother? Anchor in the Choptank for the night or land by dinghy. Secretary was named in honor of Lord Dewall, who owned the land while serving as secretary of the province of Maryland in the mid-1600s. The oldest church in the United States in continuous use, Old Trinity Church, built in 1675, is located here.

The next creek up offers a small marina and restaurant by "Suicide Bridge." (If you know how the bridge got its name, I would like to hear the story.) The creek shoals to 3 feet, accessible only to shoal-draft vessels.

The next reasonable place to anchor is near the town of Choptank. Do not enter the old steamboat basin, which has less than 2 feet of water. Anchor out on the edge of the channel. You could also try the Choptank-Towne Yacht Basin, which offers gasoline and some transient slips.

Although there is deep water all the way, unless you are a real diehard, don't bother proceeding beyond Choptank. There are no other creeks or coves to pull into until Tuckahoe Creek, which is more than 40 miles up the Choptank River past winding, marshy banks. If you make it as far as Tuckahoe Creek and brave its winding marshy channel, you qualify as an expert gunkholer.

LITTLE CHOPTANK RIVER

Charts: 12263, 12264, **12266**

On the Eastern Shore, just south of the mouth of the Choptank River, lies the Little Choptank River, with several first-class harbors beckoning the cruiser. It is a trip of 5 to 6 miles from the green "1" lighted spar, positioned nearly a mile to the southwest of Hills Point in the mouth of the river, to the nearest good shelter. The land in this region is low lying—nothing is more than 20 feet above sea level—but the trees on the shore provide an adequate windbreak and the nooks and crannies provide good shelter from the waves. Because easily identified landmarks are lacking, you need to pay careful attention to your position because there are a number of unmarked shoals. As in most of the Bay, the bottom here is forgiving; the only damage likely to result from grounding is to your dignity.

Whether you approach the Little Choptank from the north or from the south, James Island serves as a convenient reference. It is characteristically low, but the trees on it are visible from a good distance away. From the west to the northeast, approach no closer than ¾ mile in order to avoid the shoal around it. Since the green "1" marker between James Island and Hills Point is

difficult to see from a distance, simply guide around James Island and head directly for the lighted green "3" beacon to the southwest of Ragged Island as soon as you can see the beacon. From green "3" you should be able to see the lighted green "5" beacon to the southeast. Leave both markers well to port and you will travel in 20 to 50 feet of water until you are about 200 yards past beacon "5." From there on, typical depths are between 9 and 20 feet, with some deeper spots. Green "5" is your departure point for approaching the assortment of creeks off the Little Choptank that offer the best anchorages.

Slaughter Creek

Charts: 12263, **12264**, 12266

Approach. A course of 190 degrees from green "5" in the Little Choptank takes you to the first channel marker into Slaughter Creek, although you should be able to see the marker from green "5." Subject to continual shoaling, the channel has been dredged recently, so there should be 6 to 10 feet of water throughout. Make sure that you stay in the channel through the bar. A storm may have caused additional shoaling, so go slowly. Leave the lighted red "2" beacon about 20 feet to starboard on the way in, then bow a little to port and swing in a smooth arc back to the red "4" beacon because the shoal tends to encroach from the west. Then swing right to head between the red "6" and green "7" markers.

Once into the creek proper, stay in the middle, where you will have a minimum of 7 feet of water all the way to the Coast Guard station and Taylor Island Marina, just before the fixed bridge. The only reasonable way to explore past the bridge is by dinghy. Bring plenty of repellent as the marshy shores are well populated by mosquitoes. There is no place to land except at the marina; the banks are muddy, and there are no beaches.

Marinas & Provisions. Taylor Island Marina is a small place, but it offers transient slips, gas, diesel, ice, and a few other supplies. It

Little Choptank River

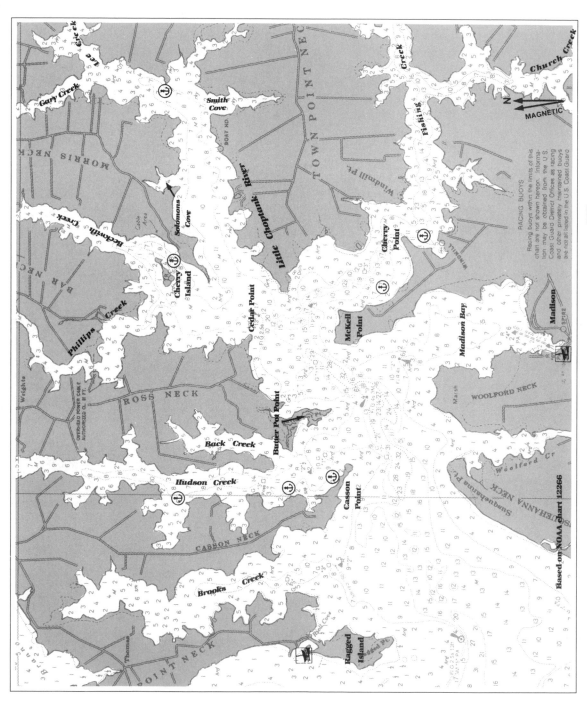

Little Choptank River

RACING BUOYS

Racing buoys within the limits of this chart are not shown hereon. Information may be obtained from the U.S. Coast Guard District Offices as racing and other privately maintained buoys are not assisted in the U.S. Coast Guard

Based on NOAA chart 12266

SCALE 1" = **0.80** NAUT. MILES

⚓ Good anchoring   **⚓ Marina**   **⚓ Launching site**

also has a pumpout station and that boon to cruisers, a self-service laundry. There is also a small snack bar. Believe it or not, the Coast Guard station here is a houseboat at the marina! At the other side of the bridge, about ½ mile by road, is a general store. It also can be reached by dinghy or by boats with less than a 3-foot draft.

In earlier editions we recommended passing this creek by, but the channel dredging, the better marking, and the current facilities offered amid bucolic surroundings have led us to change our minds. The very remoteness of this area definitely adds to its attraction. Give it a try.

Brooks Creek

  No facilities

Charts: 12263, 12264, **12266**

Approaches. The entrance to Brooks Creek is to the north of the green "5" beacon in the Little Choptank River. Swing wide around green "5" and head directly for the pair of daymarks designating the narrow entrance to the creek. With careful piloting you can get about another mile into the creek through the relatively narrow channel. The creek has shoaled badly since the charts were updated—this is now shoal-draft country. If you are in a sailboat of any size, don't try it; you will have to turn around and go back out. Our last time in we surveyed the channel the hard way.

Even so, many fairly large sailboats often anchor in the center of Brooks Creek as far as several hundred yards past the two points at its mouth. This is exposed to the entire south quadrant, and although we don't find it particularly appealing, some do.

Anchorages. The first cove to port is a snug, attractive, tree-lined anchorage for those with a draft of less than 3 feet. The rest of the creeks off the Little Choptank offer better anchorages, so we skip Brooks Creek.

Hudson Creek

  No facilities

Charts: 12263, 12264, **12266**

Approaches. To enter Hudson Creek, assume a course of 76 degrees from the Choptank River

green "5" beacon and start looking for the green "7" daymark, about 1½ miles ahead. From here on, pay careful attention to your navigation; it is easy to become confused if your attention lapses. Daymark "7" is the turning mark for the entrance to Hudson Creek. As you pass the marker, maintain your course for at least another 100 yards before swinging slowly to port to a course of about 15 degrees. Do not head directly for the green "1" daymark in Hudson Creek from green "7" since a shoal bows to the east of a line between these two marks. (And do not proceed east of a line between Hudson Creek green "1" and Little Choptank green "9," off Butter Pot Point, because there's another shoal there.) Hold close to green "1" as you pass it and head directly toward the red "2" daymark.

Leave red "2" close to starboard as you swing around it. Less than ⅓ mile past red "2" you'll pass the green "3" daymark, which should be left close to port. From here you are on your own; there are no more markers, but neither are there more projecting shoals. Stay in the middle and proceed slowly (as you should in any case) and you will have no problems.

As you move upstream, to starboard there are widely scattered homes with well-kept lawns on large plots of land. To port the land is undeveloped and marshy. All of the land is close to the same level as the water, which must make the residents rather nervous during the spring tides.

Toward the headwaters the feel is noticeably yet indefinably different. Perhaps *peaceful* best describes it. In any event, it is worth traveling up the creek at least once, if only to see the sights and return immediately. Several inviting coves beckon from the western shore, but if you draw more than 4 feet you are better off viewing them from a distance.

Anchorages. The creek is navigable for 3 miles from its mouth, up to the point where it forks near the head of navigation, less than ½ mile from the town of Hudson. However, the best anchorage is near the mouth, just inside Casson Point. Here you can pull well out of the channel and anchor in 7 feet of water within 100 yards of an inviting, sandy beach. This anchorage is well protected from any wave action, and thanks to the trees, it is reasonably sheltered from the wind save from a north or south direction. The traffic on this creek is light, and there are few houses in sight. Holding is good, and most cruising boats that visit Hudson Creek anchor here or in the mouth of the next cove to port upstream.

Now for the fly in the ointment: the inviting beach just mentioned is posted "Private No Trespassing." A little investigation, however, reveals a similar beach on the inside of the tip of Casson Point, past the clump of trees, that is devoid of legal deterrent. No one seemed to object to our landing there.

Back Creek, to the northeast of red "2," offers an anchorage in about 6 feet of water, provided you can get past the 3-foot bar at the entrance to the creek.

Immediately to port past the green "3" daymark a beguiling cove presents itself. Proceed on a course up Hudson Creek until you are well past the center of the mouth to the cove before attempting to enter. Favor the north shore as you approach and anchor just within the point on the southern shore in 5 to 6 feet of water. It looks as though you could pull very close to the southern shore just inside this point and still be in 5 feet of water.

Farther upstream there is a larger cove about ¾ mile beyond green "3." Except right at the entrance it is no deeper than the first cove, and it is less snug. The chart shows 5 feet of water in the middle of the cove, but 2-foot shoals line the perimeter.

A half-mile beyond the second cove are two small coves open for exploration if you draw less than 5 feet. In both coves you can pull in close to shore and anchor in about 5 feet of water. These coves abut a marsh, which offers some solitude and the songs of the wild at night. At least this used to describe the area, which has been subdivided for development.

On the eastern side of the creek, about midway between the second cove and the pair of coves just mentioned, is an inviting cove. Decline its invitation; there is a 1-foot bar at the entrance.

From here to the head of navigation there are no more suitable anchorages. Shallow-draft boats can travel up the left fork of the creek almost as far as the town of Hudson, but for most cruising boats the fork in the creek should be considered the head of navigation.

Madison Bay

Charts: 12263, 12264, **12266**

Approaches. A lighted red beacon southeast of Hudson Creek marks the entrance to Madison Bay. Hold close to this marker on a course from the Little Choptank green "9" until you are 100 yards past it. Inside, the channel opens up into a wide bay with 7 feet of water in the middle third.

Anchorages. While it is quite feasible to anchor in most of Madison Bay, it is exposed to the northwest, and the screen of shoaling around the perimeter doesn't permit approaching much closer than 400 yards offshore. It is quiet, and there is little boat traffic through the area, but we much prefer other anchorages on the Little Choptank.

Marinas, Restaurants, & Provisions. Madison Landing is tucked away in the southernmost corner of Madison Bay. A few years ago Madison Bay was a real chore to navigate. Today it has a well-marked, dredged channel. At Madison Landing you can get gasoline and diesel fuel, soft drinks, beer, some groceries, and even a pretty good meal (or so we have been told). The approach to Madison Landing is well marked, and you can carry 6 feet all the way to the fuel dock.

Most of the slips at the marina are for workboats, which means a noisy, early morning departure, so we don't spend the night here.

Fishing Creek

  No facilities

Charts: 12263, 12264, **12266**

Approaches. The entrance to Fishing Creek is past McKeil Point, which separates Fishing Creek and Madison Bay. You must hold a course fairly close to the Little Choptank green "9" and "11" markers in order to avoid the unmarked shoal that extends well to the west of the tip of McKeil Point. From green "11" swing to starboard and head directly toward the red "2" daymark in the entrance to Fishing Creek. Leave this mark close to starboard as you swing around it to head for the green "3" daymark in the creek.

Anchorages. Once past green "3," you can anchor anywhere along Cherry Point, off a very nice, sandy beach. Since this spot is exposed to the northwest, anchor here only if the weather promises to remain fair.

Squeezing past the end of Cherry Point to obtain access to the rest of the creek can be a little tricky. A draft of more than 5 feet may deny you the better anchorages on Fishing. From green "3" head directly toward red "4" until you are within 50 yards of it. Then swing to port to pass within 50 feet of it. As red "4" comes abeam, start to swing gently to starboard to keep it abeam until you are pointing straight into the middle of the rest of the creek. Hold this course until you are past the tip of Cherry Point. From here on, the creek opens out, and you only need to remain somewhere near the middle to go nearly to the headwaters. (No, the chart doesn't lie; there are shoals in Fishing Creek, but passage is nowhere near as scary as it may appear.) The best anchorage on the creek is in the bight to the south immediately after clearing Cherry Point. You can anchor in 9 feet of water off a sandy beach, well protected from weather.

If you like crabs, pull into the mouth of the little cove near the house on the shore, but feel your way carefully. This is one of the best places to crab. We once pulled up 25 crabs in 30 minutes using 6 baited lines along the sides of the boat! We would have done even better, but "Dad" had some trouble extracting crabs from the twine dip net we used.

The area upstream is more populated, although the mouths of the unnamed creeks branching off the main creek offer several places to anchor. There are a couple of snug little anchorages in Church Creek, about a mile beyond Cherry Point. These are in the first two coves to port after you enter Church Creek. Past the second cove the creek shoals to about 4 feet or less, effectively limiting further exploration to shoal-draft boats or dinghies.

By all means, put Fishing Creek on your "must-try" list.

Phillips Creek

  No facilities

Charts: 12263, 12264, **12266**

Approaches. Phillips Creek splits off the Little Choptank to the north just past the last navigation marker, the flashing green "13" off Cedar Point. Watch out for the long bar off the tip of Morris Neck on the east side of the creek entrance. If you head from green "13" to the end of the point directly to the north, where Phillips Creek swings to the northwest away from Beckwith Creek, you can clear all the shoals.

Anchorages. You can anchor anywhere in the little bay west of Cherry Island with 6 to 7 feet of water. There is only one house in the vicinity, making this one of the area's more private anchorages. Usually few, if any, boats are anchored here.

If you sound your way carefully, you can follow the unmarked channel around the point of land west of Cherry Island for nearly ½ mile up Phillips Creek. Proceeding beyond Cherry Island into the main part of Phillips Creek is a good test of a gunkholer.

Beckwith Creek

  No facilities

Charts: 12263, 12264, **12266**

On the east side of the little bay on Phillips Creek is Cherry Island with its large square tower. You can enter the mouth of Beckwith Creek by heading north through Phillips Creek until the tower is nearly abeam and then heading east until it is again abeam on the port side.

Once past the tower, you can anchor to the southeast of Cherry Island in 8 feet of water.

It is possible to feel your way about ½ mile upstream, but only confirmed gunkholers should try it. Be ready to survey a few shoals on the way.

Little Choptank River Headwaters

  No facilities

Charts: 12263, 12264, **12266**

The Little Choptank is navigable for about

2 miles past the mouth of Phillips Creek. There are alluring anchorages in the mouths of Solomons Cove (4 feet of water), Smith Cove (5 feet), and the unnamed cove beyond Smith Cove (5 feet near the north side of the mouth).

In this part of the Little Choptank you can anchor anywhere that appeals to you. The river has 5 feet of water all the way up to the last fork, where it splits into Gary and Lee Creeks, which shoal rapidly beyond both entrances.

WESTERN SHORE

The western side of the Bay is much more populated than the eastern side. There is little of the shoreline that has not been developed into residences or businesses. However, you still can find excellent anchorages that give the illusion of seclusion even if they don't actually provide it. Many are attractive even though the shore is lined with homes.

WHITEHALL BAY

Charts: 12263, 12270, **12282**, 12283

Whitehall Bay is a popular good-weather anchorage, and the three creeks branching off it offer secure, attractive anchorages plus assorted marine facilities. It is only a short run to Annapolis from here, making the area a popular anchorage for those who want to visit Annapolis but don't want to contend with its crowded, busy harbor for the night.

Whitehall Bay Anchorage

 No facilities

Charts: 12263, **12282**, 12283

Approaches. Because North Shoal extends a surprising distance to the west and south of Hackett Point, it is easier to approach the 4-second flashing red "2" spar marking the entrance to Whitehall Bay from the south than from the north. A course midway between Hackett Point and Greenbury Point brings you directly to the red "2" marker with no problems. You can't miss Greenbury Point; it's the one sprouting the three large antennae. There used to be a lot more antennas until the Navy took them down in 1999.

When approaching from the north, stay at least ½ mile offshore from Hackett Point. Underestimate that distance and you may be grounded.

Leave the red "2" marker close to starboard on entering Whitehall Bay. Hold your course, which should be due north, until you are about 300 yards past the marker, then head for your chosen anchorage.

Anchorages. The best anchorage in Whitehall Bay itself is in the northeast corner, off the long, sandy beach. This beach is private, which means that you are not likely to get permission to land there. The anchorage is protected from all but the south. Normally, this presents little of a problem as most southerlies are mild. However, in a strong blow from the south or southwest the long fetch quickly makes this anchorage uncomfortable. Should this happen, the prudent course of action is to move into one of the nearby creeks off Whitehall Bay Mill Creek, Whitehall Creek, or Meredith Creek. All three offer full protection from all directions, and only Meredith Creek is difficult to enter.

Mill Creek

Charts: 12263, **12282**, 12283

Mill Creek lies tucked away in the western corner of Whitehall Bay. Its narrow entrance and high banks are well camouflaged by the scenic shoreline. It offers complete protection from wind and weather in any of the several possible anchorages, as well as a couple of "hurricane holes." On the down side there is no convenient landing place on the creek other than at the Riverside Inn. Private property or terrain makes landing elsewhere impossible.

Approaches. After entering Whitehall Bay and proceeding about 200 yards past the red "2" spar, swing northwest on a course of 310 degrees to head directly toward the first of the daybeacons marking the entrance to Mill Creek. As you pass between the first red and green markers, stay in the center of the umbrella-handle-shaped entrance channel; the edges rise very quickly. While there is some shoaling between nuns "2" and "4," the charts claim a 6-foot controlling depth for the channel. The charts are correct, but you may want recent local testimony to confirm them.

Anchorages. The first anchorage on the creek, and perhaps the best, lies just inside Possum Point as you clear the entrance channel. The high banks of the creek provide a windbreak from all directions except the southeast. To the southeast, Possum Point, which is a large sandbar, provides complete shelter from wave action while permitting a cooling breeze to sweep the anchorage. The sandy beach of Possum Point provides a very attractive place to stretch your legs, but don't land there. The impressive antennas on the shore used to belong to a Navy communications facility. In the past a few trespassers shot at insulators on the towers, and as a result the Navy used to keep a close watch on anyone approaching the area. Now things may be a bit more relaxed. I have been told that the Naval Academy has assumed responsibility for the towers.

Immediately to starboard at the entrance to Mill Creek is Burley Creek. The surrounding high banks and trees make it a very snug hurricane hole. It also provides a very comfortable anchorage on chilly spring or fall evenings. Conversely, Burley Creek is not the place to spend a hot, muggy night. There are a number of large, attractive homes on this creek, but there is no place to land, and there is room for only a couple of boats to anchor.

Martins Cove lies to port about ½ mile past Possum Point. More a small creek than a cove, it is very similar to Burley Creek. The homes lining the banks, although far less ostentatious than those on Burley Creek, appear to be well

kept. Martins Cove offers a nice, snug anchorage for two or three boats that need to ride out some very unpleasant weather, but avoid it in hot weather because breezes are rare.

Restaurants. For an excellent, inexpensive meal, continue upstream on Mill Creek to the Riverside Inn. This bar-restaurant sits on top of a 30-foot-high bank to port just beyond Martins Cove. It is easily identified by its sign and its large pier with a pair of fuel pumps and tray-like tanks of water holding scores of crabs. An open-air patio with tables overlooks the creek. Most diners use the main building only in bad weather. Don't expect a lot of frills—just good food and drink.

Additional Anchorage. You can continue up the creek almost to the headwaters, passing large, expensive homes to starboard and much smaller, perhaps more interesting ones to port. Be sure to leave the point above the Riverside Inn well to port to avoid the unmarked shoal that extends more than halfway across the creek. A distance of about two-thirds of the way across the creek from the point to port will keep you out of trouble. The end of the shoal is now marked with a small green buoy, but it is easy to miss and looks like it is too far to that side of the creek to be correct. Believe it!

Once clear of the point, you can anchor in the north corner of this loop of the creek. If you do, try to stay well out of the channel; a number of watermen leave at sunrise or earlier and will have to pass you.

Just past what we call "Sneaky Point" are a couple of small marinas to port on the southeastern shore, but neither has fuel or facilities for transient yachts.

Past the marinas the house lots become more spacious, and the creek rapidly narrows, begins to shoal, and is quiet (except when there is a shoot at the nearby gun club). If you can see the bridge over the headwaters of the creek, turn around and get out.

Whitehall Creek

Charts: 12263, **12282**, 12283

Whitehall Creek has a number of features to

attract the cruiser—an easy entrance, a number of well-protected, attractive anchorages, and marine facilities for transients. It also offers a few places to land and stretch your legs.

Approaches. After passing Whitehall Bay red "2," continue another 200 yards before swinging to a northeast course to pick up the red "4" daymark at the entrance to Whitehall Creek. From red "4" simply honor the next two markers and you will enter the creek, easily clearing the sheltering bar at its mouth. As soon as you round red "6," you are in well-sheltered waters and can anchor in full security nearly anywhere that strikes your fancy.

The first cove to port, just before the green "7" daymark, contains Scott's Marine Services. This tiny marina with limited facilities specializes in fiberglass repairs. One or two boats could anchor here for shelter from storms, but there are much better anchorages farther up the creek.

As you proceed up Whitehall Creek, be sure to find and honor the green "7" daymark. This marker warns of the last extensive shoal of any significance, which lies in wait for the unwary.

Anchorages. The next branch of the creek to port is called Ridout Creek. This creek is perhaps the finest anchorage on Whitehall Creek. It is navigable for nearly a mile from its entrance, progressively narrowing to allow you to select your desired degree of "snugness." There are still a few places to land, mostly on the south side of the creek, but you have to look for them. It is usually not crowded except for the occasional rendezvous weekend at one of the larger yacht clubs there.

Just past the mouth of Ridout Creek a small cove opens to starboard, offering a secluded anchorage with 8 feet of water for more than half its length. It is worth looking into.

Marinas. Minnow Creek, the first creek to port, contains Scott Marine Services, which offers complete engine and hull repairs but little for the transient cruiser. Farther up the main branch of the creek the Whitehall Yacht Yard may be found to starboard. Here you can anchor anywhere in 8 to 10 feet of water unless you want to wait for the snuggest anchorages, which lie around the next bend in the creek past the marina.

Meredith Creek

 ⭐ ③ *No facilities*

Charts: 12263, **12282**, 12283

Approaches. On a chart Meredith Creek appears to be impossible to enter because of a 1-foot shoal barring the entrance. This is not quite true. You can get into the creek, but don't try it without recent local knowledge, or have someone precede you in a dinghy, sounding for the channel every foot of the way. Do not attempt this in windy conditions. However, if you do manage to negotiate the entrance, you will find a lovely spot, secluded and serene, in which to drop the hook.

Any cruiser who succeeds in entering this creek automatically becomes a member of the unofficial "Meredith Creek Gunkholers Association" and must swear to keep secret the information on how to negotiate the entrance. Am I kidding? See for yourself, but be prepared to pull yourself off a shoal!

SEVERN RIVER

Charts: 12263, 12273, **12282**, 12283

The Severn River offers a plethora of harbors, anchorages, and sights to see, ranging from the cosmopolitan to the provincial and wild. A beautiful river in its own right, its alluring creeks and coves beckon the boater. The major attractions are close to its mouth—harbors for easy stopover on the way up or down the Bay; all the marine facilities, supplies, and attractions that you can imagine; and Annapolis, the state capital, home of the U.S. Naval Academy, and much, much more. Farther up the Severn are an assortment of quieter anchorages, many of which are worth a visit.

Approaches. If you remain on the Severn River itself, you must continue upstream beyond at least the first of the two bridges over the river; anchoring below that bridge is prohibited. The first, a drawbridge, has now been replaced by a fixed bridge with a vertical clearance of 60 feet at MHW. Part of the old bridge remains for use as a fishing pier.

There used to be a second bridge, an old, unused, permanently open swing bridge that once served a railroad line. The entire bridge has been removed, so there is no obstacle to water traffic.

The last bridge (Route 50) presents no difficulty in terms of its vertical clearance (80 feet). And the orange rectangles painted on two of the supporting columns for one span no longer have any meaning.

After clearing the Route 50 bridge you can enjoy the peace of many quiet anchorages, as well as the excitement and bustle of Annapolis, just minutes away.

Anchorages. You can anchor in 15 feet of water on the north shore in a bight about midway between the two bridges, but there are old pilings there, some of which may be just below the surface. I recommend forgoing that spot in favor of the mouth of Weems Creek, to the southwest, just short of the last bridge. If that fails to suit your fancy, you can choose from the many excellent anchorages farther up the river, all of which are obvious from a glance at the chart and easy to find.

Lake Ogleton

 No facilities

Charts: 12263, **12282**, 12283

Approaches. On the southern side of the mouth of the Severn River, about a mile in from Tolly Point, is the entrance to Lake Ogleton. The outside marker for the 8- to 10-foot-deep dredged entrance channel is difficult to discern until you are within a mile of it. Some charts appear to show the green 4-second flashing "1" marker on the wrong side of the channel. Don't worry about it; just leave green "1" to port on entering as you normally would. Line up the first two green markers as you approach the channel to avoid the shoals on either side of the entrance, which extend well to seaward from the first marker. Once past the first marker, simply honor the red and green markers until you pass the last green marker.

Anchorages. Beyond the last mark, on the southern shore you face Oak Point, which divides Lake Ogleton roughly into two parts. You can anchor in comfort on either side if you don't push too far to the extreme east or west, where it starts to shoal.

Don't expect to be able to land. The entire waterfront is private property, with the possible exception of a community marina at the far southeast end of the basin. The anchorage is

fully protected from weather in all directions, and the holding, although mud, is normally adequate. This is an excellent anchorage for those who wish to be close to Annapolis without spending the night in Annapolis Harbor or those who want to get a jump on a trip farther up or down the Bay the next day. We have entered this anchorage late at night many a time for just that reason.

Back Creek

 All facilities

Charts: 12263, **12282**, 12283

Back Creek may be the first option that comes to mind as an alternative to anchoring in Annapolis Harbor. Unfortunately, it too suffers from congestion and heavy traffic. The entrance is fairly wide but tricky when visibility is poor or restricted, and anchorage room is limited to nonexistent. Unless you plan to tie up at one of the many marinas here, we advise you to move upstream on the Severn River or back around Greenbury Point to one of the anchorages off Whitehall Bay.

Spa Creek (Annapolis)

 All facilities

Charts: 12263, **12282**, 12283

Here is where you will find Annapolis. The sound of its name conjures visions of fleets of pleasure craft gliding through the harbor and beyond in a kaleidoscope of motion, which is actually pretty close to the truth.

Approaches. Entering the harbor is easy. On the way into the Severn simply honor the 40-foot-high "spider" light (red) and the nun "10" beyond it. From nun "10" head to leave the green, flashing 6-second light off Horn Point well to port. Once clear of Horn Point shoal, you can turn and head directly into the harbor, where there are no shoals.

Marinas. For all practical purposes, Spa Creek is synonymous with Annapolis. The mouth of Spa Creek is Annapolis Harbor. Both sides of the creek are lined with hundreds of boats in marinas, boatyards, and private piers. If you arrive reasonably early in the day, you should be able to find a transient slip at one of the marinas in the area. However, if your heart

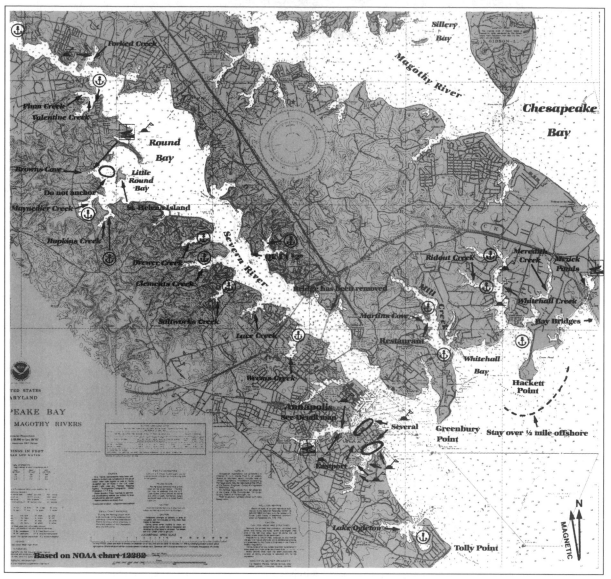

SCALE **1″ = 1.55** NAUT. MILES   ⚓ **Good anchoring**   ⛵ **Marina**   🚤 **Launching site**

is set on tying up in Annapolis, make advance reservations.

Between Back Creek and Spa Creek, which bracket the Eastport section of Annapolis, there are close to 30 marinas, not counting yacht clubs, sailing associations, and temporary tie-ups. This count includes only the ones in the immediate Annapolis Harbor area. There are even more marinas farther up the Severn River, across the mouth of the Severn in Mill and

Whitehall Creeks, and in the South River, just a short run around Tolly and Thomas Points. Most of these marinas welcome transients. Supplies and fuel are readily available throughout the area.

The Spa Creek Bridge does not necessarily open on demand, especially during landlubbers' rush hour (7:30 to 9:00 A.M. and 4:30 to 6:00 P.M.). This makes anchoring upstream impractical; passing under the bridge two times is a nui-

National Geodetic Survey

Aerial view of the Severn River region. Annapolis is to the left, and Whitehall Bay, with Mill, Whitehall, and Meredith Creeks, is to the upper right.

sance. Upstream there is little room to anchor, and transient dockage is limited. Better choices are to spend the night at Lake Ogleton, sail across the mouth of the Severn to Whitehall Bay, or move farther upstream on the Severn.

Slips and bulkhead space are available on the Annapolis city dock on a first-come basis. The normal procedure is to pull into a vacant space not roped off or to tie to a bulkhead before paying the dockage. The city has also placed 40

moorings in the harbor area, leaving no room to anchor. The mooring fee is $15 per day from Memorial Day through Labor Day. In April and May and again in September and October, a one-month mooring is available at half-price. However, you can anchor farther up Spa Creek for free. Anchoring is prohibited between the green-red buoy GR "SC," south of the Naval Anchorage, to the G"3" daymark in Spa Creek.

On weekends during the boating season, especially holiday weekends, casual transients should stay clear of the congested harbor and perhaps even the mouth of the Severn River. If you plan to visit the harbor area, try to do so during the week, or wait until the off-season. Even then you will have plenty of boats to keep you company, but you will also have more room to maneuver.

Annapolis is expensive. Supplies usually fetch full price, the restaurants are not cheap, and dockage fees and repair costs can be significantly higher than in outlying areas.

In 1988 and again in 1989 the mayor of Annapolis, Dennis Callahan, opened the city dock to free use by workboats from late fall through 1 April. He also initiated an effort to reopen the old McNasby's Oyster House in Eastport with the idea of joining with the Maryland Waterman's Association to turn the building into a seafood-buying-and-packing coop. These were the first of several steps taken to reverse the tide of watermen leaving Annapolis as a result of the conversion of waterfront buildings and warehouses into offices and condominiums, as well as the raising of docking fees.

What to See & Do. Every visitor must tour Annapolis itself. There is a lot to see: more than 100 18th-century houses, the oldest statehouse in the country, the home of William Paca (a signer of the Declaration of Independence), St. John's College (founded in 1696), the U.S. Naval Academy, restaurants, shops, and more. There are marinas, marine-supply stores, yacht sales agencies, sailmakers, repair facilities, and dockage; anything that has to do with boats probably can be found in Annapolis.

Each year, during a two-week period in October, in-the-water boat shows are held at the city dock, one week for sailboats and one week for powerboats. These shows get bigger and better every year. The shows are so popular that visitors have to park at the Naval Academy football stadium and take special buses from there to the show site. Incidentally, don't try to visit the show by water, at least not in Spa Creek. This area is also known as "Ego Alley" because boats sometimes parade through the dock area up to Market Square and back out, apparently only to show themselves off.

Sightseeing here is best done on foot, especially in the summer, when the streets are

Each October, Annapolis is the site of a two-week boat show—one week for sailboats (shown) *and one for powerboats.*

Annapolis Chamber of Commerce

clogged with traffic and parking space is almost nonexistent.

Regardless of where you land, the starting point for any cruiser's tour of Annapolis has to be at the city dock. The harbormaster's office and the visitor-information center here can provide you with far more information than this book can include. Surrounding the city dock are a variety of restaurants, several watering holes, the seafood market, assorted stores of all types, and Fawcett Marine Boat Supplies (410-267-8681), right on the waters of the dock area.

A short walk north along Randall Street takes you to the Naval Academy. You can enter there at gate 1 or turn left on King George Street and enter at gate 3, a couple of hundred yards up the street. Gate 1 takes you to Ricketts Hall, the Visitor Center, where you can arrange for a guided tour of the academy seven days a week throughout the year. Gate 3 takes you directly to Preble Hall, where the museum is located, and a quick right turn takes you to the Navy Chapel, where the body of John Paul Jones, the "Father of the U.S. Navy," lies preserved in an alcohol-filled crypt. Wander the grounds and try to catch the Brigade Noon Formation.

The historic areas of the city are centered on Maryland Avenue and State Circle, where the original town was laid out by Governor Francis Nicholson in 1696. As you leave gate 3 of the Naval Academy and proceed south along Maryland Avenue, you come upon the fabulous Georgian Chase-Lloyd House and Hammond-Harwood House, which face each other just south of King George Street. Both were built in the 1760s, and both are open to visitors.

A short jaunt down Prince George Street takes you to the not-to-be-missed William Paca House & Garden. Built by Paca, another signer of the Declaration of Independence, before he became governor of Maryland in 1782, the building was scheduled to be demolished in 1965. Historic Annapolis, Inc., not only prevented its demolition but went on to restore the house and its once magnificent garden. Archaeologists helped unearth most of the garden from beneath a parking lot and the deteriorated Carvel Hall Hotel building.

The focal point of Annapolis is the State House, located on the highest point of land in the area and ringed by State Circle. Built between 1772 and 1779, this is the oldest state capitol still in continuous legislative use, and a National Historic Landmark. It is also the only statehouse to have served as the nation's capitol, which it did from November 1783 to August 1784. Tours of the State House are available year-round at no charge at 11:00 A.M., 2:00 P.M., and 4:00 P.M. daily except Thanksgiving, Christmas, and New Year's Day. The tour includes a slide show.

Nearby are the Governor Calvert House, now an inn for dignitaries, and Government House, the residence of the governor of Maryland.

A little farther on is Church Circle, dominated by St. Anne's Church and the Anne Arundel County Courthouse. A hundred yards down Franklin Street is the Banneker-Douglass Museum, featuring the history of Afro-American life and culture in Maryland.

A walk down Duke of Gloucester Street toward the Spa Creek bridge takes you past St. Mary's Church and the Charles Carroll Mansion, the home of yet another signer of the Declaration of Independence (not open to the public).

Cross over the bridge and you are in the Eastport section of the city, with more marine-supply stores, marinas, restaurants, and water-

ing holes than can be described here. Call the Annapolis Information Center at 410-268-TOUR (410-268-8687) or the dockmaster at 410-263-7973 for more information. Discover the rest for yourself.

Weems Creek

  No facilities

Charts: 12263, **12282**, 12283

Although Weems Creek is navigable for more than a mile from its mouth, the bridges over it limit normal cruising boats to the area just inside the mouth. The shore is all private property, leaving no place to land without express invitation.

Approaches. When approaching the mouth of the creek, be sure to steer clear of the shoal on the north side of the entrance, marked by the red-green buoy. Leave the buoy well to starboard on entering and head for the center of the creek mouth.

Anchorages. You can anchor anywhere inside the creek mouth up to the first bridge. The entire area is well protected with good holding in about 10 feet of water. Don't bother to try to pass the pair of bridges over the creek. The first bridge is a swing bridge with a 5-foot vertical clearance when closed. Trying to get it to open is more of a problem than it is worth. Past the swing bridge is a fixed bridge with a 28-foot vertical clearance, so only powerboats have access to the upper part of the creek. There is a dinghy dock at the Tucker Street Landing on the southeast side of the creek, a little short of the first bridge. Unfortunately, this does not land you within easy walking distance of anything useful.

Cool Spring Creek

  No facilities

Charts: 12263, **12282**

To starboard just past the Route 50 bridge, Cool Spring Creek lies almost hidden amid the high banks of the northeast shore of the Severn River. Provided that it hasn't shoaled in, the entrance is easy to negotiate but hard to see unless you know where to look. Beware of the shoal protruding to the south from the north side of

Region 3

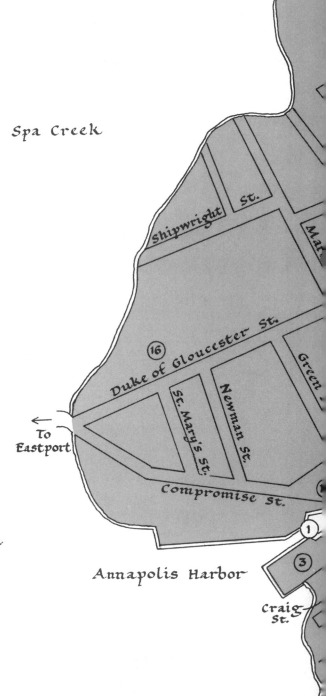

Spa Creek

KEY

1. City Dock
2. Maryland State House
3. Visitor Information Center-
   City Dock, Harbormaster
4. Visitor Center, U.S.
   Naval Academy
5. U.S. Naval Academy
6. Navy Chapel & Crypt
   of John Paul Jones
7. Naval Academy Museum
8. William Paca House
   & Garden
9. Hammond - Harwood House
10. Chase-Lloyd House
11. Governor Calvert House Inn
12. Government House
13. St. Anne's Church
14. Banneker - Douglass Museum
15. Anne Arundel Co. Courthouse
16. St. Mary's Church
17. Market House

Annapolis Harbor

SEVERN RIVER

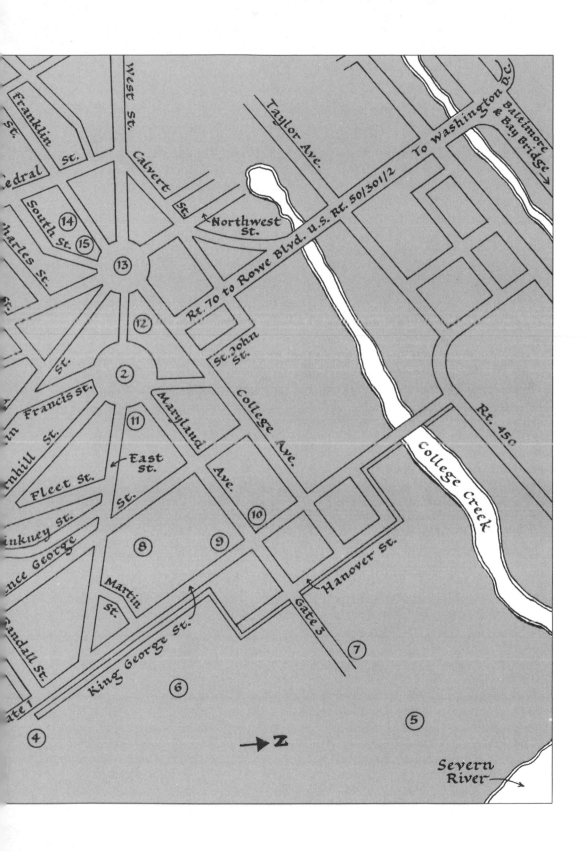

SEVERN RIVER

the entrance. Sound your way in carefully.

Once in, you are in a snug, well-protected anchorage for just a few boats. In warm weather it is so snug that there are no cooling breezes. Here too the shore is all private property and there is no place to land. Unless you want to try it just to see if you can negotiate the entrance, try elsewhere.

Luce Creek

 No facilities

Charts: 12263, **12282**

At first glance Luce Creek seems to be an attractive anchorage. A second look at the chart shows a 4-foot bar at the entrance with the expectation that it will shoal in over time. Although it is well protected, we suggest that only shoal-draft vessels or cruisers with recent local knowledge attempt the entrance.

The community marina here has no transient facilities. The shoreline is private property, so there is no place to land. Head for the more attractive anchorages farther upstream.

Saltworks Creek

 No facilities

Charts: 12263, **12282**

An intriguing, well-protected, easily entered creek, Saltworks Creek bears your investigation. Steep banks provide more than adequate shelter from weather.

Once you are clear of the shoal extending eastward from the north side of the creek entrance, you have 8 to 10 feet of water all the way to the overhead power cable (vertical clearance 46 feet) at the headwaters. This is an attractive anchorage, but as at most anchorages in this region, the private shoreline offers no place to land.

Chase Creek

 No facilities

Charts: 12263, **12282**

Almost directly across the Severn River from Saltworks Creek, Chase Creek has a quick-flashing red "2" buoy marking the shoal on the

upstream side of the entrance. This not only provides warning of the shoal but also makes the entrance easy to find in almost all conditions. As you pass the small spits that guard both sides of the entrance, the creek opens out into a Y. Other than the one by the red "2" buoy at the entrance, there are no shoals.

Moored or anchored boats, predominantly sail, fill the left branch. The right branch has fewer boats and is slightly less developed. The high banks provide plenty of protection, and even though the shore is all private property, you have the illusion of partial seclusion. A sandy spit of land here is a possible landing, at least at low tide.

Clements Creek

 No facilities

Charts: 12263, **12282**

Although a little wider, Clements Creek is nearly a clone of Saltworks Creek. It has the same high banks, good protection, and private shoreline. There is no place to land.

This is an attractive anchorage, so you will find plenty of boats anchored or moored here. No supplies or marine facilities are available.

Brewer Creek

 No facilities

Charts: 12263, **12282**

Just upstream from Clements Creek, Brewer Creek provides a snug, secure anchorage. Simply stay in the middle on entering and you will find 10 to 15 feet of water almost to the end of the creek.

The best anchorages are from halfway to three-quarters of the way up. Not too long ago this anchorage was surrounded by high, wooded banks; now it is solidly residential, and the shoreline is all private property.

There are no facilities or supplies, and there is nowhere to land.

Asquith Creek

 No facilities

Charts: 12263, **12282**

Approaches. About ½ mile past the mouth of Brewer Creek on the north side of the Severn River, is a neat little anchorage that goes largely unnoticed by most casual cruisers. Admittedly, there are more attractive anchorages nearby, but this one does deserve a look. However, it takes a bit of effort to enter successfully on the first try.

Do not head directly toward the Fl 4s G"5" marker as you head up the Severn. Be sure to swing wide of Brewer Point to avoid the rather abruptly rising shoal northeast of the point. As you come even with the tip of Brewer Point, head due north toward the west (left) end of the 100-yard-long bulkhead at the entrance to Asquith Creek. A large, 6 mph speed-limit sign attached to the west end of the bulkhead makes a good aiming point. About 200 yards from the speed limit sign, turn to port to maintain a course parallel to the shoreline to starboard. Dead ahead you should see a set of small, private markers that define a 200-yard-long, narrow dredged channel 6 feet deep leading into the basin inside.

Be sure to give the point to starboard (east) a wide berth as a shoal extends farther out into the river than you might expect. For that reason, do not head directly toward the first green private marker (N39° 02.0′ W76° 31.6′). Run parallel to the shore until you can turn to head straight into the channel. Proceed slowly with your depth-sounder running and remain on a course to keep the set of red markers about 5 feet to starboard. *The channel is narrow,* only about 15 feet wide. One's first entrance is definitely a time for white knuckles.

Anchorage. There is plenty of deep water (7 to 13 feet) inside the basin, extending practically from shore to shore. Pick your spot and drop the hook. Here you are fully protected from weather, waves, and wakes from all directions. Even so, it is sufficiently open from the south to the southwest to permit a cooling breeze in hot weather. There are no marine facilities here, and with the possible exception of the little island at the entrance, there is no place to land. It is all private property.

Round Bay

Charts: 12273, **12282**

Round Bay provides no secure anchorages but deserves mention because of its unique character. Located about 5 miles up the Severn River, Round Bay opens out to provide an excellent, protected area for sailing small boats. If it weren't for the brackish water, you might think that you were in a large landlocked lake.

On the west side of Round Bay is St. Helena Island, a private island located right in the middle of Little Round Bay. In mild weather you can anchor inside Long Point, to the north of the island. Be sure to stay clear of the cable area to the west of St. Helena Island. You can anchor anywhere else in Little Round Bay in reasonable protection, but all of the shore is private, and there is no place to land except at Smith's Marina, just inside the mouth of Browns Cove. Gas, but not diesel, is available at the marina. The approach is risky for boats with drafts of more than 4 feet.

Maynedier Creek

 No facilities

Charts: 12273, **12282**

Approaches. Maynedier Creek and Hopkins Creek share a common entrance to the southwest of St. Helena Island. Although both of these creeks are unmarked, there is only one shoal to watch out for on your approach. This shoal extends to the northwest from the little point on the mainland due south of St. Helena Island. If you hold close to the red "2" marker off St. Helena Island, even this shoal presents no problem. You don't even need instructions to enter: just stay near the middle of the passage and you will have no problem entering.

Anchorages. Once you've entered the creek proper, it opens out into a bowl shape. The steep banks provide good protection from weather all around except to the southwest, where you can look right up a small valley. Anchor anywhere on the eastern half of this circular "bay," which has 8 to 10 feet of water; the western half is shoal. Unfortunately, a water-skiing course is set up in part of the circular bay, which means that the anchorage will probably be uncomfortable during the day, at least in warmer weather, due to ski-boat wakes.

Hopkins Creek

 No facilities

Charts: 12273, **12282**

As you enter the mouth of Hopkins Creek, hold close to the sand spit to port to avoid the shoal offshore to starboard. This is one of those sand spits from which you can dive into about 10 feet of water.

Once past the sand spit, you can anchor anywhere in the creek in 8 to 11 feet of water. The steep banks all around make Hopkins Creek one of the snuggest "hurricane holes" you are likely to find anywhere on the Bay. The same snugness cuts off breezes, so Hopkins is not a comfortable hot-weather anchorage.

Upper Severn River

Charts: 12273, **12282**

Past Round Bay the river narrows. You can find numerous anchorages in Valentine, Plum, or Forked Creeks or in a bight of the Severn River itself. It may be possible to squeeze into Yantz Creek, but I don't recommend trying it unless you are in a small boat with a shallow draft that you can get out of and push.

The river remains deep as far as Indian Landing, where the Anne Arundel County Department of Education has a dock and recreational facilities that may be used by cruising people if prior arrangements are made. Beyond Indian Landing the river shoals rapidly, so don't go past this point.

FISHING CREEK

Charts: 12263, **12270**

This little-known creek lies between the Severn and South Rivers, tucked away just north of the tip of Thomas Point. The entrance must be

approached from the northeast because of the shoal extending to the east from the tip of Thomas Point. Stay to the northeast of a line between Thomas Point Lighthouse and the point on the north side of the creek mouth until you can leave the flashing red "2" marker close to starboard. From there on, simply honor the markers until you reach the basin near the Coast Guard station.

 No facilities

Anchorages. There is 56 feet of water at MLW through most of the basin. However, be sure to anchor away from the Coast Guard station and well out of the path to the exit markers. The "Coasties" may be called to depart at all hours of the day and night, and they tend to do so at top speed. Their wakes can be impressive.

There is nothing in particular here to attract the cruiser except that it makes a convenient stopover point for the night on a passage up or down the Bay to save some distance. There are better anchorages nearby. I'd recommend passing this one by.

SOUTH RIVER

Charts: 12263, **12270**

Prior to the American Revolution, the South River was used in the shipping trade. In fact, Londontowne, about 2 miles upstream from the river's mouth, rivaled Annapolis. It was one of three Anne Arundel County sites addressed in a 1683 General Assembly act designed to promote trade. The water was not deep enough at Londontowne to serve the traffic a state capital would generate, and Annapolis quickly eclipsed it. The London Towne Publik House is now the only surviving structure from the original town.

Scattered throughout the South River region are numerous marinas and boatyards, as well as many restaurants accessible from the water. Although commercial traffic is light, the South River carries a substantial amount of traffic, much of it from Selby Bay. Even so, it is not nearly as busy as the Severn or Middle River in spite of comparable population densities.

Navigation here is easy. Although you have to contend with several shoals during your approach, they are well marked, so you have only to use a bit of prudence to stay out of trouble. The approach to the mouth of the South River is simplicity itself. The Thomas Point Lighthouse is as a highly visible, picturesque reference point that aids in the recognition of and approach to the entrance to the South River. The red nun "2" can be ignored with impunity—it is located in 13 feet of water—but honor all the other markers on the river.

Two bridges cross the river. The first is the Route 2 bridge at Edgewater. This bridge was rebuilt recently with a center arch 53 feet high, high enough for all but the very tallest sailboats to clear. The second bridge, at Riva, is a fixed bridge with a 50-foot vertical clearance; it will stop some sailboats. In 1987 this bridge replaced an unreliable and almost always broken drawbridge.

Selby Bay

Charts: 12263, **12270**

Tucked away just inside the mouth of the South River lies a small body of water that gives cruisers a choice. In Selby Bay the visiting yacht can enter the busy, bustling world of heavily populated marinas, with all their attendant facilities, or anchor out in relative seclusion. The latter option offers the best of both worlds: you can anchor close to an undeveloped shoreline full of small wildlife, yet never be more than minutes away from facilities you might need.

Approaches. As you enter the mouth of the South River a course of 321 degrees takes you to the green "5" daymark off Turkey Point. Hold your course for at least 200 yards past the green "5" daymark before swinging to port to head directly for the red "2" lighted mark at the entrance to Selby Bay. This will ensure that you clear the shoal off Turkey Point, as well as the submerged pilings reported there.

Anchorages. As you approach the red "2" marker you must quickly decide which Selby Bay you wish to enjoy. For marina facilities, continue on; to anchor out, let red "2" slide past, then turn to starboard to a northwest course, which leaves the red "4" marker well to port.

Two fingerlike shoals parallel to this new course extend from the shore to these two red markers; you now pass between them.

Once inside the shelter of Long Point you can anchor just about anywhere. The relatively low surrounding land allows a cooling breeze, but you are well protected from wave action, and the holding ground is good. Stay out of the inviting little cove to starboard on Long Point: it has only 2 feet of water.

Long Point is an uninhabited, marshy peninsula with some sandy beaches where you can land to beachcomb or, if the jellyfish have not yet come in, swim. The remains of a wrecked boat still should be visible on the shore. In the evening the crickets and tree frogs sing you to sleep, while on the opposite shore the lights of the houses and marinas announce considerable human activity. Very little human noise carries the distance to this anchorage, and what little sound does carry is drowned out by nature's serenade.

The amount of boating activity in this area makes it necessary to display a good anchor light. In addition, I highly recommend the use of good screens in the summer—mosquitoes like this marshy shoreline.

Marinas. If you opt for the world of marina facilities, you have a choice of two courses from the red "2" marker at the bay entrance. One larger marina, Selby Bay Yacht Basin (410-798-0232), is located in the northwest corner, but most of the facilities are clustered in the southern part of Selby Bay.

To reach the marina cluster, head south-southwest from red "2" off Long Point. Keep the green "1" daymark to port and the lighted red "4" to starboard and you will have no problem reaching your destination. A casual glance at the chart will disturb you: the southern part of the bay shows 1, 2, and 3 feet of water. But don't be alarmed. A careful examination reveals a reasonably deep channel that runs near the southern shore most of the way around the bight where the marinas are located.

As you approach Holiday Point Marina (410-956-2208), watch out for runabouts and small power cruisers exiting Ramsay Lake through the fixed bridge to port.

Do not attempt to anchor anywhere in the bight where these marinas are located. You will either run aground or block traffic.

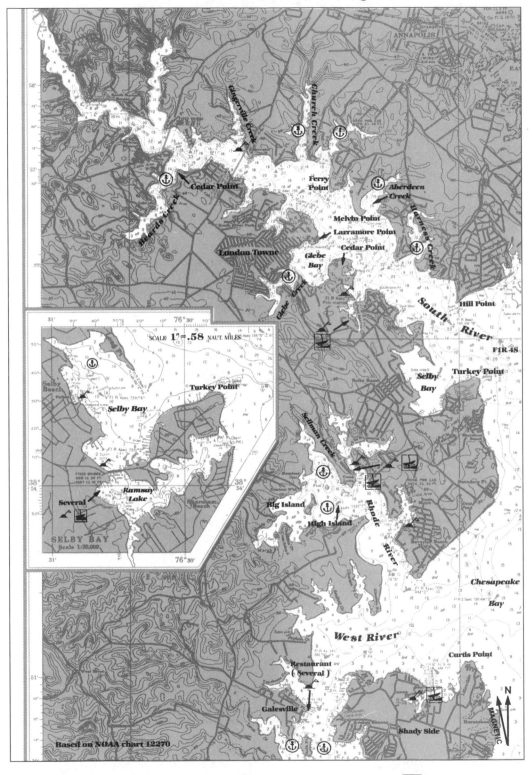

SCALE 1" = .58 NAUT. MILES

Based on NOAA chart 12270

SCALE 1" = **1.16** NAUT. MILES   ⚓ **Good anchoring**   ⚓ **Marina**   **Launching site**

The Thomas Point Lighthouse was the last manned lighthouse on the Chesapeake. It is still one of the most famous Bay landmarks.

Somewhat more accessible and less congested is Selby Bay Yacht Basin, located due west of the red "2" marker off Long Point. Head west from red "2" so that you leave the red "4" marker close to starboard. When you clear red "4," head directly toward the green "5" marker on the corner of the large building ahead of you. That building is the part of the marina containing the fuel dock and a platform from which you can view all of Selby Bay. Children, especially, seem to enjoy climbing to the top of this observation platform and looking around.

Associated with Selby Bay is Ramsay Lake, a nearby landlocked tidal pond. The only real access to the lake is through the stone abutments of the bridge connecting Turkey Point to the mainland. During changes of the tide there is a substantial current through these abutments. Despite the current, the water is quite shallow, marked as 2 feet on the chart. The bridge itself has a vertical clearance of only 10 feet, which, together with the shallow water, restricts access to the lake to relatively small powerboats. Even so, traffic is substantial, especially on weekends.

Duvall Creek

  No facilities

Charts: 12263, **12270**

The markers in the mouth of Duvall Creek are privately maintained, and the channel is narrow. Though charts show a 2-foot shoal across the mouth, the channel depth holds at a minimum of 5½ feet MLW, making it accessible to most sailboats unless there is a strong northerly, which can blow the water out.

Approach the first two markers, "1" and "3," on a line roughly midway between the two midriver markers "6" (off Turkey Point, to the south) and "8" (off Hill Point, to the north). Head directly for the green "1" daymark, turning to starboard at a distance of 15 to 20 feet to leave it, a small green buoy, and the green "3" daymark all fairly close to port. Maintain this course until you are past the end of the sand spit to port. Anchor anywhere.

Harness Creek

  No facilities

Charts: 12263, **12270**

Approaches. Harness Creek is the first good foul-weather anchorage on the South River.

The entrance is unmarked but not difficult. After you pass the red "8" marker off Hill Point, maintain your course until the opening into Harness Creek is at about a 45-degree angle off your starboard bow. Then turn and head directly for the entrance. As you enter, favor the east side, where you'll have a minimum of 11 feet of water all the way in.

Anchorages. Once in the creek you can anchor anywhere, secure from foul weather from any direction. The sandy point to starboard on entering offers a nice beach where you can stretch your legs or "water" a dog. If you follow the eastern shore carefully, you'll come to the gap in the marsh that allows entrance to the famous Harness Creek "hurricane hole." You can negotiate this gap with a good bit of water *under* you but not much *around* you until you are through it. In this hurricane hole a couple of boats can weather any blow, completely protected by the high banks and dense woods. This very protection makes it the last place to anchor in hot, sticky weather.

Although we never have had a problem here, we have heard several reports of boats having trouble getting their anchors to set properly and hold in the upper part of the creek. Since this is quite a popular anchorage during the main boating season, we recommend that you get in early, set your anchor carefully, and check it even more carefully before turning in.

If this anchorage is too crowded for your taste, simply head for one of the other creeks up the river.

Brewer Creek

Charts: 12263, **12270**

Just across the South River from Harness Creek, Brewer Creek offers anchorage in pretty, wooded, high-banked surroundings. The creek is open to the north for some distance unless you have a shoal draft, which enables you to pass the 2-foot bar into the inner cove.

If the weather is expected to remain fair, give Brewer Creek a try; otherwise head for another anchorage.

Aberdeen Creek

  No facilities

Charts: 12263, **12270**

The next creek on the way upriver is Aberdeen Creek. For some reason, many cruisers fail to pay attention to the shoal that extends to the east from Melvin Point, to port, when entering this creek. Even though the creek is unmarked, there is no good reason to run aground. If you keep in the eastern third of the creek's entrance, you have 15 to 17 feet of water all the way in. Once you have passed the mouth, the creek opens out and all you need to do is keep a prudent distance offshore.

To starboard on entering is a group of buildings belonging to a children's camp. Melvin Point is wooded, curling down and to the east, where it ends in a marsh. The shoal mentioned above extends from this point.

The shoreline around the creek is wooded but relatively low, permitting a welcome breeze on hot summer nights. The creek is open to the south-southeast unless you proceed nearly to the headwaters. This is not the usual direction for a significant blow, however, so the openness is not a problem.

An attractive anchorage and a favorite rendezvous spot for boating clubs, this spot is rarely crowded.

Glebe Creek

Charts: 12263, **12270**

Approaches. Directly across the South River from Aberdeen Creek a green "11" flashing marker indicates the tip of the shoal off Cedar Point, on the east side of the entrance. Do not cut inside this marker! In addition to the shoal, there is a collection of old pilings (indicated on the charts), some of which are still visible above the water. Favor the south side of the entrance to avoid the shoal that extends to the east from Larramore Point and has its own collection of pilings. Stay with the south shore as you continue through Glebe Bay; there is a 2-foot shoal right in the middle of the bay. There is a piling in the water about where you would expect to find this shoal; although it really doesn't mark the shoal, give it a wide berth and you will avoid the shoal and pass through Glebe Bay with no problems.

Glebe Bay is attractive, but it is too exposed to provide a comfortable anchorage, and the shoals extend farther from shore than the charts indicate. Continue on and pass into Glebe Creek. By skirting the southeast shore of Glebe Bay about 150 to 200 yards offshore, you will easily reach the low-lying point of land that protects the entrance to Glebe Creek.

Anchorages. From here on, there is deep water (11 feet) from a short distance offshore all the way across the creek. You can anchor anywhere here well protected from wave and weather. Be careful how you set your hook! The bottom is covered with leaves, which make it difficult for a Danforth to dig in, so test your anchor accordingly.

This anchorage is lined with modest homes. It is attractive but can be a bit noisy, at least during daylight hours.

Almshouse Creek

 3 *No facilities*

Charts: 12263, **12270**

History. The next creek upstream to port is Almshouse Creek, named for the almshouse in Londontowne, which was once the Cortelyou Mansion and is now known as the London Towne Publik House. As mentioned earlier, Londontowne was a leading port before Annapolis became Maryland's capital.

From 1694 until the 1790s a public ferry connected Londontowne with Annapolis. As one of the provisions of the ferry's license, the ferry operator had to maintain specific service standards, which included providing meals and lodging to those waiting to cross on the ferry. The license holder, William Brown, therefore constructed the London Towne Publik House in the mid-1760s. For a while the building served as the governor's residence. In 1828 it was purchased by the county for use as a poorhouse, a role it served until 1965.

What to See & Do. In 1970 the London Towne Publik House & Gardens was desig-

nated a National Historic Landmark, restored to its colonial appearance, and now operates as a historic site museum. It is open to the public 10:00 A.M. to 4:00 P.M., Tuesday through Saturday, and 12:00 to 4:00 P.M. on Sunday. It is closed Mondays, Easter Sunday, Thanksgiving, Christmas, and the months of January and February. Boats may tie up at the public pier here at no charge during the regular hours of the Publik House.

Approaches. Entering Almshouse Creek is easy: Keep clear of the green "15" marker at the west side of the entrance and you'll have 11 to 14 feet of water all the way in. The area is built up and has become entirely too "public" for our tastes. Since no fuel or facilities are available, we recommend visiting the Publik House but anchoring elsewhere for the night.

Crab Creek

 3 *No facilities*

Charts: 12263, **12270**

Approaches. Although completely unmarked, the approach to Crab Creek is relatively easy. After you pass red "14" off Ferry Point, maintain about the same distance offshore and swing around Ferry Point to the entrance to Crab Creek. Favor the starboard side of the entrance, leaving a piling there well to port.

A small cove to port right after you enter makes anchoring possible for one or two boats. However, there are better anchorages farther up, past the sandy hook on the east side of the creek. A glance at the chart may cause you to pause, but the narrow channel carries plenty of water (12 feet). Hug the sandy spit at a distance of 75 to 100 feet off the beach and you can pass into the upper part of the creek with relative ease.

Anchorages. Although you can anchor anywhere here, the better anchorages are past the second point to starboard, in 10 to 12 feet of water. Most boats can proceed almost all the way to the headwaters, although the creek shoals to 5 feet in the last ¼ mile.

The high banks inside provide plenty of shelter from the weather, and the only waves you get are from other boats. There are no marina facilities, and the houses, well screened by trees

SOUTH RIVER

223

and shrubbery, are relatively secluded. By all means try this anchorage.

Church Creek

  No facilities

Charts: 12263, **12270**

Church Creek shares share more than a common approach with Crab Creek; it shares all the latter's positive aspects as well, making Church Creek another recommended anchorage.

Approaches. Approach as if you were going to enter Crab Creek, but just before you would enter it, swing to port to head directly for the entrance to Church Creek, which then is clearly visible. This course neatly avoids the 2-foot shoal to port.

Anchorages. Pass the first point to starboard before anchoring to provide yourself with full protection from wave and weather. Although you can anchor anywhere here, the best anchorage is in the north fork of the little cove to port after you enter. The description of Crab Creek's surroundings applies here as well.

Warehouse Creek

Charts: 12263, **12270**

On the southern shore, just before the Route 2 bridge at Edgewater, is Warehouse Creek. As with most of the creeks on the southern side of the South River, the shores are developed and therefore less attractive as anchorages go.

The Warehouse Creek Boatyard is located here, but it has neither fuel nor other facilities for transient boats other than inboard engine repairs.

Upper South River

Charts: 12263, **12270**

Past the Route 2 bridge are several other creeks or anchorages worth exploring. Gingerville Creek, to starboard immediately past the

bridge, provides a couple of coves and bights below high banks where you can anchor in security. Just past Gingerville Creek is a small, interesting cove to starboard. Beards Creek, to port just before the Riva Road bridge (the second bridge on this creek), offers some anchorages near its mouth. Past the South River Boat & Engine Works is a cable area that covers most of the navigable portion of the creek, which precludes anchoring there.

The vertical clearance of 53 feet for the fixed Route 2 bridge allows most boats to proceed another mile upstream to the fixed Riva Road Bridge (vertical clearance 25 feet), which will stop virtually all sailboats. Powerboats can continue past the bridge into Broad Creek and the headwaters of the South River itself.

RHODE RIVER & WEST RIVER

Charts: 12263, **12270**

Approximately 4 miles southwest of the Thomas Point Lighthouse lies the Rhode River with its three distinctive little islands. The area is much more reminiscent of many of the Eastern Shore anchorages than it is of those on the more congested and more built up Western Shore of Maryland. Once you are well into the river, you'll find the shoreline relatively sparsely settled with high, wooded banks.

Rhode River

Charts: 12263, **12270**

Approaches. The approach to the mouth of the West River, from which the Rhode River branches off, is easiest from the north. A compass course of 240 degrees from Thomas Point Lighthouse brings you past the green "1" buoy to the red "2" light in the mouth of the West River, just about a mile north of Curtis Point.

The approach from the south is a little more complex due to a long, wide 3- to 4-foot shoal that extends for about 1½ miles northeast of Curtis Point. Although shoal-draft boats can pass over the outer third of this shoal, it is more prudent to hold close to the green "73" bell buoy of the Chesapeake Bay main shipping channel. (Note: The Coast Guard is in the process of changing these buoy numbers. This buoy is the one about 2½ miles east-northeast of the tip of Curtis Point.) Next follow a course of 292 degrees to the green "1" buoy at the approach to the West River. Then a course of 240 degrees takes you to the West River red "2" marker.

A course of 284 degrees from red "2" takes you directly to the red "2" lighted beacon at the entrance to the Rhode River, which is difficult to see until you get fairly close. Be sure to honor the Rhode River red "2" unless you enjoy kedging off shoals.

Marinas & Restaurants. There are several small tributaries on the Rhode River, where you can restock supplies and fuel or perhaps explore, but we do not recommend anchoring in any of them for an extended period because the anchorage near the three islands is far superior in every respect. Bear Neck and Cadle Creeks are the closest places for resupplying fuel and provisions. One caution: While the chart shows 5 to 7 feet of water in Cadle Creek, a 4-foot (or less) bar at its mouth restricts entrance to shoal-draft vessels. For groceries or a restaurant, head for Galesville, just over 3 miles away on the West River.

Anchorages. The first reasonably good anchorage on the river is in the large bend, Canning House Bay, to the west of the mouth of Cadle Creek, where you can anchor fairly close to shore near some attractive, sandy beaches. The holding is good, and the area is well sheltered from wave action and somewhat sheltered from the wind, but it is exposed to wakes from the plentiful passing traffic. For that reason, most people continue upstream to anchor near the three islands.

After clearing the red "6" daymark, give the green "7" light, where the Rhode River bends sharply to the west, a wide berth as you approach it. This course avoids the shoal between the green "7" light and the mainland to the south of the light. As you clear the marker you will have a clear view to port of the anchorage among the islands. We recommend passing to the south of High Island so that you avoid the shoals extending north from that island and south from Flat Island. These shoals don't pre-

sent any real problem, but we see no reason to flirt with even possible trouble.

Holding in the area is excellent; the heavy mud bottom provides good security with any type of anchor. The best place to drop the hook is to the east of Big Island unless there is a strong easterly wind. In that event, simply run around the north side of Big Island and anchor in its lee. There is about 7 feet of water to within roughly 50 yards from the shore. Do not try to pass to the south of Big Island as the water shoals to 2 feet or less between the island and the mainland. The only real problem is caused by the wakes of powerboats, both cruisers and the runabouts from the water-ski school located there, a good reason to anchor here during the off-season rather than during the prime warm-weather boating season.

Muddy Creek, to the southwest of Big Island, is just that—muddy and shallow. Sellman Creek, to the north of Flat Island, is a nice anchorage to use if the Big Island anchorage is too crowded. As the names might lead you to expect, High Island is relatively high in relation to its size, whereas Flat Island is so low that it appears in danger of submerging at any time. Flat Island is all that remains of a small peninsula that used to extend from the mainland. High Island is also disappearing, its high banks crumbling into the water. You can land on both these islands and explore, but be careful of the poison ivy that flourishes on High Island. Big Island, the last of the trio, is big only in comparison with the other two. It is approximately 500 yards long and 100 yards wide, its high banks covered with heavy underbrush and pine trees. It is posted with "Private, No Trespassing" signs. Evidently this prohibition is enforced, for no one tries to land there even though it is uninhabited.

To the north of High Island, on the mainland, is Camp Letts, which is a well-maintained, pleasant place to stretch your legs if you land well to the west of the main camp, inside Sellman Creek.

The Rhode River is a popular anchorage, especially with power cruisers, and the area between Big and High Islands is usually peppered with anchor lights after sundown during the height of the boating season (Memorial Day to Labor Day).

West River

Charts: 12263, **12270**

Approaches. The approach to the mouth of the West River is the same as the approach to the Rhode River up to the West River red "2" north of Curtis Point. Although there are several marinas in Parrish Creek, just inside Curtis Point, normally only boaters who have slips there traverse the narrow, dredged channel.

From red "2" a course of 260 degrees takes you to the flashing 4-second red "4" spar, leaving the green "3" can to port. The creeks along the north shore of the river are too shallow to be of interest. Once you reach red "4," you need to pay careful attention to your navigation as the channel narrows and bends, with shoals extending from both shores.

A course of 200 degrees from red "4" takes you to the green "5" daymark opposite the mouth of Cox Creek. If you draw less than 5 feet, you can enter Cox Creek, which provides a pleasant, well-protected anchorage. Favor the south side of the creek on the way in. The best anchorage is just opposite the mouth of Tenthouse Creek in about 5 feet of water.

As you clear green "5," find and leave the flashing 4-second red "6" marker off Councilors Point, on the south side of the mouth of Cox Creek, well to starboard. For some reason this marker is easy to miss, and if you fail to honor it, you will find yourself trying to plow another channel.

Marinas, Restaurants, & Provisions. After you clear red "6," the channel opens out again and you can head directly for your destination. All the marina facilities you may need, as well as a couple of restaurants and a small grocery store, are in Galesville. Clustered on Councilor's Point are: West River Yacht Harbor (410-721-2373), Pirates Cove Marina & Restaurant (410-867-2300), Steamboat Landing Restaurant (410-867-4600), and the Hartge Yacht Yard (410-867-2188).

Lawrence Hartge, of the Hartge Yacht Yard, recently took advantage of the yard's long-held relics from the past and established the Hartge Nautical Museum in a portion of the house built in 1879. The exhibit wraps around the room, displaying a chronological sequence of the Hartges' history, starting in 1832 and ending with recent aerial photos of the yard.

Anchorages. Anchor in the basin where Smith Creek bends to the west or pass to the east of Chalk Point and anchor in South Creek. Unless you draw well under 5 feet, don't proceed up South Creek much past the Chesapeake Yacht Club, to port in Shady Side.

All the shore is privately owned. If you decide to go ashore, you have to land at one of the marinas. The West River offers marina facilities and well-protected anchorage but no seclusion.

HERRING BAY TO PLUM POINT

Charts: 12263, **12270**

South of West River, Rockhold Creek is the last harbor for a distance of more than 30 miles along the Western Shore, not counting a handful of man-made basins. Even so, it is only for those who draw less than 4 feet. There is little room to anchor, so if you stay, you will probably have to tie up at a marina.

Long Bar extends southward from Parker Creek to beyond Fairhaven. Boats with drafts of less than 4 feet can cut across the southern half of the bar, but proceed carefully—the bottom is hard oyster shell.

Rockhold Creek

  All facilities

Charts: 12263, **12270**

Approaches. Pay close attention as you travel up the dredged entrance channel. Although it is well marked, you can easily drift out of the channel between the marks and find yourself on the flats. At one time only boats with a very shallow draft could approach the two marinas in the mouth of Tracy Creek, preferably inboard/outboard or outboard boats. The considerable number of large sailboats there now indicates an improved channel depth. No boats can proceed past the fixed bridge over Tracy Creek, for the bridge is low and the creek promptly shoals to almost nothing.

Marinas & Restaurants. Most of the marinas are clustered along the shores of Rockhold Creek below the fixed bridge (vertical clearance 14 feet); there are a few on the eastern shore above the bridge, where the water depth drops to 3 feet MLW. On the west side of Rockhold Creek, just before the bridge, is the Happy Harbor Restaurant. It is a "just plain folks" place that hasn't changed much in several decades. You can still get a great meal there at a reasonable price. There is room for one or two shoal-draft boats to tie up at the dock for dinner. (Remember, this is powerboat country.)

Provisions. Supplies and fittings are available in a number of places, and the town of Deale, about a mile above the fixed bridge, has an excellent hardware store that caters to the marine trade.

This is not an anchorage. To spend the night, you must take a slip at one of the marinas or go elsewhere.

Herrington Harbor

 3 *All facilities*

Charts: 12263, **12266**, 12270

Once called Rose Haven, Herrington Harbor has had a somewhat spotty history. The Rose Haven Yacht Club, founded in 1947, was intended to be the focus of the Rose Haven community. The club fell into disrepair, and both the entrance and a large part of the basin silted in. In 1978 the club was sold, and the new owners dredged and enlarged the entrance and basin and refurbished the shoreside facilities. They also opened the facilities to the public, with the intent to cater to cruising groups.

Approach. The entrance to Herrington Harbor is in the southern part of Herring Bay, just to the west of Holland Point. If you approach from the north, remain a good 1½ miles offshore until you can pick up the quick-flashing green "1" marker at the entrance to Herrington Harbor channel. Leave the green "1" marker to port and follow the daymarks into the basin. The channel has a controlling depth

of 5 feet for a width of 60 feet. Boats with close to a 5-foot draft should proceed cautiously as the entrance is always in danger of shoaling. Most of the resident boats are large powerboats, but as many as one-quarter of the boats are good-sized sailboats, indicating some serious effort to keep the entrance channel open to a reasonable depth, so perhaps it is now deeper than the previous 5 feet.

Marinas & Restaurant. The fuel dock is the third pier to port on entering. Tie up here for directions to where you can stay if you decide to visit the restaurant (clearly defined by the "lighthouse"). If you are looking for a slip for the night, make advance reservations during the boating season (401-741-5100). Don't plan to anchor out; there is no room.

Although it is open to the public, Herrington Harbor has all the trappings of a yacht club, complete with pool, tennis courts, a restaurant and lounge, and a motel. It also has a laundry. The facilities are open to slip holders and guests, but the harbor does advertise slips for transients.

Herrington Harbor offers high-class shoreside accommodations and lots to do. Try it, unless you "want to be alone."

Chesapeake Beach (Fishing Creek)

 3 *All facilities*

Charts: 12263, **12266**

About 2 miles south of Holland Point is the entrance to Fishing Creek, better known as Chesapeake Beach. Unless it has been dredged recently, we recommend that boats with drafts of more than 3 feet stay out. As with many such places on the Bay, the problem is not the water depth in the basin but the shoaling in of the entrance channel. The controlling depth of the entrance was 6 feet in 1983; I don't know what it is now.

Approaches. Stay at least a mile offshore until you are able to pick out the green "1" entrance marker outside the breakwaters with a pair of red and green markers at the end of each jetty. Your approach should be roughly perpendicular to the shoreline. Favor the north side of the approach to avoid the ruins of an old pier on the south side.

Anchorages & Dockages. Once you are inside, there is some room (not much) to anchor in about 7 feet of water, or you can get a slip at Kellam's Marina. You may tie up alongside the Rod & Reel Dock at no charge if you plan to eat at the restaurant; some dockage for transients is available. The Rod & Reel and Kellam's both sell fuel, and groceries are available nearby.

A sizable fleet of charter fishing boats is located here. The harbor is not pretty, but it does offer good shelter from wind and wave—if you get in the channel entrance before the storm hits. Don't try the entrance in a storm!

Two hundred yards inside the entrance is a low, fixed bridge (10-foot clearance), so only small powerboats can continue farther. The covered and open slips past the bridge belong to the marina and two restaurants.

Breezy Point Harbor

Charts: 12263, **12266**

Just north of Plum Point is Breezy Point Harbor, an artificial basin dredged into a marsh. There is plenty of water in the basin, but the entrance frequently shoals, presenting transients with an iffy situation. This is a shame because inside is a rather nice marina with a restaurant, a snack bar, and some limited marine supplies. Our advice is to stay out if you are not in a powerboat without a fixed propeller and rudder, that is, unless you know that the entrance has recently been dredged. You can contact the marina (410-257-2561) to check on the controlling depth.

Region 4

LITTLE CHOPTANK RIVER TO POTOMAC RIVER

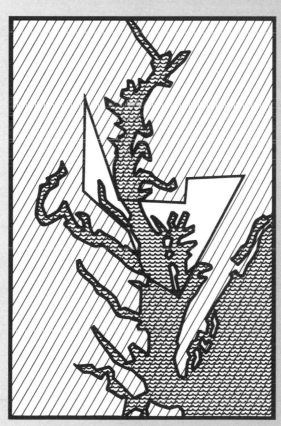

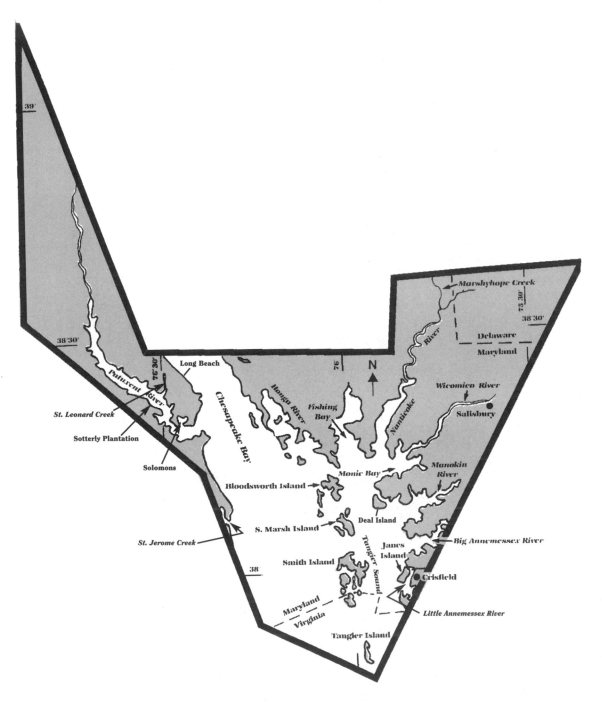

LITTLE CHOPTANK RIVER TO POTOMAC RIVER

SCALE **1"** = **14.2** MILES

Between the Little Choptank and the Potomac River the character of the Bay changes again. On the Eastern Shore the harbors disappear, and there is a long stretch of low-lying marshy islands with no receptive harbors until you reach Hooper Strait. Even then, attractive harbors on the Eastern Shore are rare until you reach Smith Island.

The Western Shore, similarly short of harbors until you reach the Patuxent River, has a totally different character. There you find the high, fossil-laden Calvert Cliffs, which stretch from just south of Herring Bay to Cove Point. After a short interruption they resume to sweep on into the mouth of the Patuxent River. High on these cliffs, about 4 miles north of Cove Point, is the Calvert Nuclear Power Plant. In fair weather you can go ashore (by dinghy) and tour the plant, which has an interesting display of fossils from the Calvert Cliffs.

Just north of Cove Point is the Cove Point Natural Gas facility; a huge, imposing structure with a pier that looks like it was designed for giants. Most charts warn you to stay a minimum of 200 yards away from this facility, but we prefer a minimum distance of at least ½ mile. Don't miss the Cove Point Lighthouse. It is a classic lighthouse, complete with a lightkeeper's house.

South of the Patuxent River you pass some peculiar-looking structures about 2 miles offshore, midway between Cedar Point and Point No Point. Stay well away from them; they are targets for a U.S. Navy bombing range.

If you are headed for the Potomac River, you can cut well inside Point No Point Lighthouse to save some distance. The light is really intended for large-ship traffic.

EASTERN SHORE

HONGA RIVER

Charts: **12230**, 12261, 12263, 12264

The Honga River opens to the north off Hooper Strait, at the south end of Hooper Island. The river has a deep, wide channel for most of its length but no anchorages. The Honga is worth the trip if you are interested in the three relatively unspoiled fishing villages along its shores. These workboat harbors have narrow, dredged channels and small basins where gasoline and some supplies are available.

A passage called Fishing Creek offers a shortcut into the Honga River at the northern end of Hooper Island. Unless it has been dredged recently, it is only suitable for the shallow-draft workboats skippered by local watermen. It was dredged to a depth of 8 feet in autumn 2000. However, it keeps shoaling. Don't try it in anything but a light-displacement, shallow-draft boat unless you have recent knowledge of the controlling depth.

Fox Creek

Charts: **12230**, 12261, 12263

Approach. Hearns Cove is off the eastern side of Fox Creek, around Crab Point and up a narrow, dredged channel with a reported controlling depth of 5 feet. Swing wide around the red "2" marker off Crab Point and head straight to the first of the channel markers into Hearns Cove. Supplies are available within a short walk of the basin in the small village of Wingate. The quarters here are tight, and there is no place to anchor. You may have trouble even finding a place to tie up among the workboats.

Anchorages. Just past the green daymark off Pauls Point, Fox Creek makes a right-angle bend to the northwest. Six feet of water is carried in a nearly straight line to within 400 yards

231

of the shore of Asquith Island, forming the west side of the creek. This region presents a possible anchorage in a nearly unpopulated region. It is open for more than 2 miles to the southeast, and the low land provides limited protection from the wind. This may well be the closest thing to a good anchorage (with more than 2 feet of water) that you'll find on the Honga River.

Muddy Hook Cove

Charts: **12230**, 12261, 12263

Almost due west of the entrance to Fox Creek, on the western side of the Honga, is Muddy Hook Cove, a small basin up a narrow channel with a reported controlling depth of 6 feet. There is a 200-foot-long dock at Rippons Harbor, where you can tie up. Fuel is available. Close by, in Hooperville, is a crab house where you can get fresh seafood in season. The harbor is exposed to the east, and space at the dock is scarce. There is no anchorage, and unless you can manage to rent a slip, remaining overnight here is not a good idea (unless there is a hard blow).

Back Creek

Charts: **12230**, 12261, 12263, 12264

Six miles up the Honga River from Muddy Hook Cove, also on the western shore, is Back Creek. This is the snuggest of the three potential harbors on the Honga River, thanks to a dogleg in the narrow, dredged channel. The controlling depth in the channel is somewhat uncertain, so unless you are in a shallow-draft boat, check the depth with one of the locals before trying it. Even then, proceed slowly and with caution.

Fuel is available at Rippons & Tolley, right by the dogleg, and you can get some supplies in the nearby town of Fishing Creek.

FISHING BAY

Charts: **12230**, 12231, 12261, 12263

At the eastern end of Hooper Strait the broad expanse of Fishing Bay opens to the north. This is a wide, shallow bay surrounded by low, marshy shores. Why this body of water is called a bay and not a river or creek is beyond me; it looks more like a river than the nearby Honga. There are no good anchorages or cruiser-oriented harbors.

A number of small streams wind their way through the marshes into Fishing Bay, but only four are identifiable by channel markers leading into them. The first one, on the western side, is Tedious Creek. About 2 miles north of that creek, still on the western shore, is Goose Creek. Just over a mile above Goose Creek, on the eastern shore, is McReady's Creek, and 2 miles past that, on the western shore, is the last available harbor on Fishing Bay, Farm Creek. These are all workboat harbors, and, except for Goose Creek, you can't get into them unless you have a draft of 3 feet or less. Goose Creek is reputed to have a controlling depth of 5½ feet. All have some gasoline available, and except at Goose Creek, supplies are available relatively nearby, but you'll have to ask for directions.

After you pass the entrance marker to McReady's Creek, there are unmarked shoals on both sides of Fishing Bay. Proceed with caution to the entrance to Farm Creek. Above Farm Creek the bay rapidly shoals to depths of 2 to 5 feet. Cruisers with a draft of 3 feet or less can continue on to explore the rest of Fishing Bay, but the water depth is iffy all the way. This is an area reserved for small, shallow-draft boats.

NANTICOKE RIVER

Charts: 12230, **12261**, 12263

Most cruising boats can navigate the Nanticoke River all the way to Seaford, Delaware, a distance of more than 35 miles from its mouth. The channel is well marked; the shoreline is low and marshy. You can anchor anywhere out of the main part of the river once you pass upstream of Chapter Point. The bends in the river provide adequate protection from weather, but you need good screens for protection from the flying, bloodthirsty insects. Below Chapter Point there are three possible harbors for boats with a relatively shallow draft.

Nanticoke

  No facilities

Charts: 12230, **12261**

The town of Nanticoke offers a dredged cove on the eastern side of the river just past Roaring Point. A pair of jetties provide protection to the small harbor. The controlling depth is reputed to be 5½ feet, with deeper water in the turning basin. This is a county boat landing, intended for small boats; it is not made to cater to larger cruising boats.

Provisions. Although supplies should be available in Nanticoke, you may have trouble finding room to tie up at the dock. The county boat landing has some slips, but their availability is problematic.

Bivalve

Charts: 12230, **12261**

The town of Bivalve offers a short entrance channel and a well-protected basin, but the controlling depth is about 4 feet. To get there you have to negotiate the somewhat tricky eastern channel on the Nanticoke River between Ragged Point and Wetipquin Creek.

Fuel and ice are available on weekends during the boating season at the Cedar Hill Boat Ramp & Park. Cedar Hill has 150 slips and welcomes transients. To stay overnight, you must take one of the slips; this is no anchorage.

Wetipquin Creek

  No facilities

Charts: 12230, **12261**

The entrance to Wetipquin Creek is unmarked and difficult to follow, and the controlling depth is reputed to be 4 feet. If you line up with a clump of trees on the western shore and head toward the right side of the wharf ahead, you

should be able to follow the channel into the creek. Proceed carefully, preferably using a lead line or pole to feel out the channel. You should find 4 feet if you manage to stay in the channel. Unless you can squeeze well into the creek, this area is exposed to the northwest. Most shoal-draft boats should be able to get far enough in to find good shelter.

Try anchoring farther up the Nanticoke, past Chapter Point, where you will feel much more secure. The Wetipquin is a little too tight for comfort.

Rewastico Creek

  No facilities

Chart: **12261**

This creek is an anchorage for shoal-draft boats that can manage to get over the 3-foot bar at its mouth. If you can get in, you can explore this little creek for more than a mile. If you have a shoal draft and nerve, proceed for 3 miles upstream as far as Jenkins Landing. After you pass the mouth of Manumsco Creek, you can get out and walk!

Just past the second bend in the creek is a possible anchorage. I can almost guarantee that you will find yourself all alone in this pleasant little creek, which meanders through a tidal marsh. Don't expect to land—it's all mud.

The Inlet

  No facilities

Chart: **12261**

About ½ mile past the mouth of Rewastico Creek is a barely visible entrance labeled "The Inlet" on the chart. The Inlet offers gunkholers a unique experience: the opportunity to explore a tidal marsh uncorrupted by civilization. Any cruising boat worthy of the name can travel this narrow but deep body of water, which winds its way through a couple of miles of marsh. Here you can observe wildlife and plants in their wetland habitat, something usually possible only for small boats whose drafts are measured in inches rather than feet.

Approaches. About a mile into the passage there is a fork to the left, which you can follow for nearly ½ mile before it shoals at another split. The right fork leads on for another mile, where it connects with two other waterways through the marsh. The left branch is Rags Thorofare, which, if you could get past the 1-foot shoal about ⅓ mile into it, would lead you back to the Nanticoke River just above Marshall Point. The right branch is Bridge Thorofare, which leads into Rewastico Creek at its second bend if you can clear the 2-foot shoal that is ⅔ mile past the junction of the three "thorofares." These little passageways have 6 to 21 feet of water depth until you reach the two shoaling spots mentioned.

Although I don't recommend trying to anchor here, if you are looking for a good introduction to the "art" of gunkholing, I can't think of a better place.

Vienna

Chart: **12261**

History. Vienna is one of the oldest settlements in Maryland, dating back to the late 1600s. It has had two ferry services alternating with two bridges. The first ferry was established in the 1670s and remained in service until 1828, when the first bridge was built. In 1860 the bridge was declared unsafe and dismantled, and the ferry service was reestablished, continuing in operation until 1931, when the present Route 50 bridge over the Nanticoke was built.

During the American Revolution, Vienna was such an important source of supplies for the Continental Army that the British raided it at least five times. They also raided it during the War of 1812 but were repelled from a breastwork constructed from ship ballast set up along the river. The remains of this breastwork can still be seen on the south side of the town, near the Nanticoke Manor House.

What to See & Do. Much of Vienna's past survives today in its architecture. The town has made a determined effort to restore many of its fine old homes, and it has produced a brochure to guide visitors around the two-block historic area, right on the waterfront. There are 22 points of interest on the tour, including the Nanticoke Manor House, built in 1861; the Governor Hicks House, built between 1780 and 1800; the Federal period Houston House; the colonial Tavern House; the one-room ferry house; and St. Paul's Episcopal Church, one of the earliest churches in Dorchester County. The Customs House, located at the foot of Church and Water Streets, dates back to 1768. In that year, Vienna was proclaimed to be the customs district of the area by the Maryland Assembly. The Assembly also authorized it to

be the location of the town of Baltimore—this obviously never came to pass, and it was named Vienna, instead. The Customs House was closed in 1865, when the true Baltimore became Maryland's center of commerce.

Anchorages. The bend in the river here provides enough shelter to permit anchoring. The Route 50 bridge opens on demand 24 hours a day. During periods of heavy road traffic you may have to wait a while for a response. The Vienna public launching ramp, just south of the Route 50 bridge, makes a good place to land and leave a dinghy if you decide to tour the town or buy some groceries. I wouldn't recommend trying to bring in a large boat.

Marshyhope Creek

  No facilities

Chart: **12261**

About 4 miles above the town of Vienna, Marshyhope Creek splits off to the west from the Nanticoke River. There are no navigation markers on this creek, but you can follow it all the way to the town of Federalsburg, a distance of more than 12 miles, in water never shallower than 5 feet. Except for the shoals at the entrance, there is plenty of water nearly from shore to shore.

Approaches. To enter the creek, take your departure from the red "38" marker in the Nanticoke River and head straight for the tip of the point on the right (north) side of the first bend of Marshyhope Creek. About midway between this point and the one just before it on the Nanticoke River side, swing to port slightly to head for the center of the creek. You should find a minimum of 7 to 8 feet of water if you are in the right place. If the creek starts to shoal, stop and use a sounding pole or lead to determine which way to turn for deeper water. Once you are past the aforementioned point, you are in, and should have no more problem with water depth, although a 5-foot spot at the end of the first U-bend in the creek could catch you by surprise.

Anchorages. Here you can anchor nearly anywhere in security; other traffic is usually a rarity.

Sharptown

   No facilities

Chart: **12261**

The swing bridge over the Nanticoke River here has a vertical clearance of 8 feet but will open on demand on a 24-hour-a-day basis. Call the bridgetender on VHF channel 13 or blow horn (one long and one short blast). I have not investigated this area because it hosts too much come-and-go traffic from small craft, the result of the launching ramp there.

Broad Creek

  No facilities

Chart: **12261**

Three miles beyond the bridge at Sharptown, the entrance to Broad Creek opens to starboard. The entrance is easy; simply stay in the middle. There are enough bends to protect you from waves, but the land is too low to offer a windbreak. This is a pretty little creek. If you are looking for an anchorage, give it a try.

This winding, well-marked creek is navigable as far as the town of Laurel, 6 miles upstream. The controlling depth is reputed to be 5 feet, but there is deeper water as far as the town of Bethel, halfway to Laurel. Here a fixed bridge with a vertical clearance of 30 feet effectively stops any cruising sailboat. Just past Laurel a fixed bridge with a vertical clearance of 2 feet puts a halt to virtually all boat traffic.

Seaford

Chart: **12261**

Approaches. The town of Seaford, Delaware, represents the head of navigation for the Nanticoke River, although there is water for some distance beyond it. There is a swing railroad bridge (no vertical clearance when closed), followed by a drawbridge (3 feet vertical clearance). Nothing beyond these bridges has beckoned enough to motivate me to go to the trouble of getting either one to open.

Marinas & Provisions. Walkers Marine, near Lewes Creek, 2 miles downstream from Seaford, offers fuel, repairs, and some marine supplies. Select groceries are available in the town of Seaford, a short walk from the public launching ramp just below the railroad bridge.

WICOMICO RIVER
Charts: 12230, **12261**

With the possible exception of Webster Cove and Wicomico Creek, there are no good harbors on this river until you reach Salisbury, about 20 miles upriver from its mouth. On the way upstream the banks are low and marshy, and the water sometimes changes to "interesting" colors. The channel is wide and well marked all the way, and the controlling depth is at least 10 feet. Keep a lookout for fairly large commercial traffic and give it plenty of room. Although the many bends in the river seem to offer protection from the weather, the commercial traffic makes this an unsuitable anchorage unless you can really get well off to the side.

Monie Bay
 No facilities

Charts: 12228, 12230, 12231, **12261**

Monie Bay is wide and shallow and offers shelter in only two of its tributaries, Dame Quarter Creek and Monie Creek. Even those can be used by shallow-draft boats only.

Anchorages. A marked channel leads into Dame Quarter Creek from the south side of the entrance to Monie Bay. The controlling depth in the bay is reputed to be 4 feet, but it seems to be less than that. If you can get in at all, there is a reasonably protected anchorage just inside its mouth, well short of the launching ramp there. I do not recommend spending time here in anything larger than an inboard/outboard.

Monie Creek is located at the extreme northeast corner of Monie Bay, and there are no channel markers. The controlling depth is 3 feet, and if you can handle that, there are a couple of possible anchorages. Favor the eastern side of Monie Creek until you reach Nail Point. Then favor the left side of the creek until you

round the next bend in the creek. A possible anchorage in 7 feet of water lies just inside Nail Point, in the western corner of the creek's first bend. There is a 3-foot spot just past the bend; then the water deepens and you can proceed for at least another mile, anchoring at whim. Your effort to get in will undoubtedly be rewarded by seclusion.

Ellis Bay
NO RATING

Charts: 12230, 12261

The wide expanse of Ellis Bay opens up to the west just past Mollies Point. It is too shallow and too exposed for anything but wading.

Webster Cove

Charts: 12230, **12261**

Webster Cove is an artificial harbor located a good ½ mile up a narrow, dredged channel. At one time the controlling depth was 6 feet, but I don't know what it is today. In any event, don't even think of entering it with a draft much over 3 feet unless you have first checked locally.

The main attraction here is the Harbor Club, operated by Harvey Hastings. It has 120 feet of dock space, including the gas (no diesel) dock, for those who want to try the restaurant. There are also some slips of uncertain depth at the nearby Somerset County dock and ramp.

Whitehaven
NO RATING

Charts: 12230, **12261**

History. Whitehaven is a quiet Eastern Shore town with a collection of old, stately homes. It dates back to 1685, when its charter was granted by Lord Baltimore. Today its main point of interest is the cable ferry, one of two on the Wicomico River. There has been a ferry of one kind or another in operation here since the first one was established in 1692. Now the ferry is a free, cable ferry much like the one at Woodland, on the Nanticoke River.

Since rarely as many as 300 cars a day cross on the ferry in the summer, the peak season, this ferry is likely to continue in operation for the foreseeable future. The reason is simple: it's cheaper to operate and maintain the ferry than it would be to construct a bridge.

Navigation Alert. The Whitehaven ferry can carry three or four vehicles, depending on their size, on each trip across the 1,000-foot width of the river. Be sure to stay well clear of the ferry if you approach while it is in transit to avoid the steel cable, which is brought near the surface in the vicinity of the ferry.

Wicomico Creek

Charts: 12230, **12261**

Approaches. Two miles above Whitehaven, Wicomico Creek opens to starboard. The channel into this creek is well marked, but pay close attention to the markers. Look for the red "2" daymark in what looks like the middle of the main Wicomico River. You must round this before swinging to starboard and heading for the green "3" daymark in the creek itself. From green "3" stay in the middle until you clear the next marker to port. From there on, it is deep water all the way to Walkers Marine, past the big horseshoe bend in the creek.

Anchorages. Once into the horseshoe, you can anchor just about anywhere in good security. Just get over to one side so that you don't block traffic from the marina.

I am not sure just how far the creek is navigable, but it looks like it may be worth exploring.

Upper Ferry

NO RATING

Charts: 12230, **12261**

Upper Ferry is just that—the upper of two cable ferries across the Wicomico River. Like the one at Whitehaven, this ferry is free, operated by Wicomico County since the early 1950s. Prior to that time the ferry was privately operated, and a toll was levied for the 3-minute crossing. Apparently some of the road maps haven't caught up with the times, as several still indicate a toll.

Navigation Alert. This ferry is smaller than the one at Whitehaven and carries no more than two vehicles. It is powered by an outboard motor mounted alongside the pilot house. To change directions, the whole motor is turned around, a simple yet elegant solution. Differences aside, the same caveat regarding the steel cable applies: give the ferry plenty of clearance if you approach when it is in transit.

WOODLAND FERRY

Woodland Ferry is neither a harbor nor an anchorage. It is the site of one of the four remaining ferries on the Delmarva Peninsula and the only one operated in Delaware. The other three are in Maryland.

The first ferry in this location was established in the 1790s and continued to be operated by the Cannon family until 1843, when the operation was taken over by Sussex County. Nearly a hundred years later, in 1935, it became a state-run free ferry, and so it continues to be today.

The ferry operates year-round, from sunrise to sunset seven days a week, averaging 70 crossings a day. Each crossing takes 2 to 3 minutes, and the ferry can carry only three or four vehicles each trip, depending on their size. It has one motor, but a transmission directs the power to the proper propeller. With a propeller at each end, the ferry is always going "forward" regardless of the direction in which it is crossing the river.

If you are boating in this area and see the ferry start to transit, you must give way to it. This is a cable-guided ferry. That is, it is hitched to a steel cable stretched from shore to shore, which guides the ferry across the river. Normally, the cable lies on the bottom and is no impediment to other boating traffic. However, passing ahead of or behind the ferry while it is in transit is not a good idea since the cable is raised by the ferry as it passes and rests near the surface for some distance from the ferry. There are cable ferries at Whitehaven and Upper Ferry, on the Wicomico River, as well.

Marinas. In the bend of the river just below the cable ferry is White Marine, which offers complete hull and engine repairs. However, there are no transient facilities.

Salisbury

Charts: 12230, **12261**

Those who travel all the way up the Wicomico River to the town of Salisbury will find 20 slips reserved for transients at the Port of Salisbury Marina. The marina offers most basic marina services, including a dockside sewage pumpout facility, and there are plans to make it a full-service marina. A short walk into the town of Salisbury enables you to restock groceries and other supplies, as well as shop, eat at a restaurant, or both.

What to See & Do. Salisbury, the county seat of Wicomico County, is both an industrial and a shipping center. If you have just made the long trek up the river, you may be surprised that it is a shipping center, but shipping goes hand in hand with industry here. Because of a pair of fires in 1860 and 1886, virtually everything in the town belongs to the 20th century, with the single exception of the Poplar Hill Mansion, built in 1795. The mansion, known for its architectural work (especially the cornices), is a short distance from the river on Elizabeth Street. It is open to the public on Sundays from 1:00 to 4:00 P.M.; a donation is requested.

The Wildfowl Carving and Art Museum is located in Holloway Hall at Salisbury State College, a moderate walk down Camden Avenue from the river. The museum has a collection of exquisite bird carvings and antique duck decoys, as well as some fairly elaborate displays of prairie falcons and doves. The museum is open daily from 10:00 A.M. to 5:00 P.M. There is a small admission fee.

DEAL ISLAND

Charts: 12230, **12231**

238 Between the east side of Tangier Sound and the north entrance to the Manokin River is Deal Is-

land with its two harbors, Chance, at the north end of the island, and Wenona, at the south end. In spite of a scattering of summer cottages along the waterfront, mostly near Chance, this is very much a waterman's island, with a way of life reminiscent of several decades ago.

A good half of the island is marsh, and even the "high ground" is very close to water level. Just wander by a churchyard and notice the large, heavy slabs of stone atop most of the graves. The water table is really close to the surface here.

The people are friendly and helpful, but there is little reason to wander far from either of the harbors other than to see a slice of life on the Chesapeake. The low, marshy island is a good breeding ground for mosquitoes; be prepared for them if you plan to spend the night.

Chance (Upper Thorofare)

Charts: 12230, **12231**

The harbor at Chance, Maryland, is on Upper Thorofare, the narrow body of water that separates Deal Island from the mainland. To be strictly correct, the town of Chance is on the mainland, north of Upper Thorofare, not on Deal Island itself. However, since nearly everyone refers to the harbor simply as "Chance," we'll do the same.

Approaches. The entrance channel to Chance was dredged to a depth of 10 feet in 1987, and as of 1989 there was still at least 9 feet of water at mean low tide. Entrance is easy: honor the buoys on the way in. For those approaching at night, there is now a lighted range, which you may use to keep in the entrance channel until you can rely on the harbor lights to see where you are going.

Anchorages, Marinas, & Provisions. When you enter the turning basin of the harbor, you will see that this is very much a working waterman's harbor. Even so, it is attractive enough to draw rendezvous from several of the cruising clubs on the Bay during the summer. During the fall it is likely to be crowded with workboats, so you may have some trouble finding a space to anchor, let alone tie up. There are three marinas, a hardware store, and a seafood store—restaurant right on the water in the harbor.

Two of the marinas, Last Chance Marina and Scott's Cove Marina, are on the north side of the turning basin. Both have fuel, ice, water, engine and hull repairs, and some transient slips. Scott's Cove Marina has a bulkheaded basin at the end of a dredged channel. Last Chance is slightly farther into the harbor. The third Marina, Windsor's Marina, is located past the fixed bridge (vertical clearance 10 feet) and offers only slips and a shell launching ramp for small powerboats.

On the south side of the turning basin is Island Seafood, Inc., which has 200 feet of dockage for those who want to buy seafood or to take a meal at the small restaurant. The wharf next to Island Seafood is Deal Island Hardware, which offers fuel, ice, marine supplies, and some groceries. Be careful when approaching the wharf. I am not certain about the depth alongside, although I have been told that it is "adequate."

Additional groceries and some other supplies are available south of the bridge, on the road through Deal Island to Wenona. The short walk down this road takes you to the grave of Joshua Thomas, the "Parson of the Islands." There is a chapel dedicated to him nearby.

Wenona (Lower Thorofare)

Charts: 12230, **12231**

At the south end of Deal Island is a long, narrow, dredged passage—Lower Thorofare—between Deal and Little Deal Islands. It leads to the harbor at the little town of Wenona, another working waterman's harbor.

Approaches. The channel was dredged to a 10-foot depth in 1987, and a small fleet of skipjacks uses it regularly. The depth in the channel is still reasonably close to 10 feet; however, the channel itself is narrow and poorly marked.

Anchorages & Dockage. Most of the harbor is shoal, so if you do make it in, you won't be able to anchor unless your draft is 1 foot or less. The piers to port have about 8 feet

of water alongside and up to about 80 feet out from them. This is the only place for deeper-draft boats to maneuver or stay. You will probably find a couple of skipjacks and some crab skiffs tied up alongside the piers. The locals are friendly; hail someone and ask where you can either tie up or anchor.

Provisions. Some groceries and ice are available nearby. One of the piers has a peeler pound for crabs. However, the greatest appeal of the Lower Thorofare is to the gunkholers among us. Those who suffer from grounding angst had better pass it by.

MANOKIN RIVER
Charts: 12230, **12231**

This wide river is rather disappointing in that it has no good anchorages and is full of outlying shoals. The only place to put in is at Goose Creek Marina, in the mouth of Goose Creek, on the south side of the entrance to the Manokin River. Deep-draft boats will find this difficult to reach.

A well-marked channel goes past Carmel Point, where some shelter can be found. Even so, I consider it too exposed to be a secure anchorage. Those who travel up the Manokin do so simply to see what the river looks like. It looks as if you could take a 4- or 5-foot draft up to St. Peters Creek.

BIG ANNEMESSEX RIVER
Charts: 12230, **12231**

Daugherty Creek, on the south side of the Big Annemessex, leads to the Daugherty Creek Canal, the back door to Crisfield. Proceed slowly into Daugherty Creek past the markers until you enter the canal. In the canal the water is 6½ feet deep for a width of 60 feet all the way to the Little Annemessex River. At the south end of the canal the buoyage system changes. Leave the red markers to port from here on; they are now referenced to the Little Annemessex River.

Boats drawing less than 5 feet can make their way upriver as far as Persimmon Point. Thanks to the bend in the river, some shelter can be found here.

239

Region 4

Anchorage. The only anchorage on the Big Annemessex River is Colbourn Creek, which offers a well-protected spot with 5 feet of water if you stay in the middle and don't go beyond the first bend in the creek. Feel your way in carefully. Although there is 5 to 7 feet of water in the entrance channel, it is unmarked and curves close to Long Point.

LITTLE ANNEMESSEX RIVER
Charts: **12228**, 12230, 12231

When approaching the mouth of the Little Annemessex River from any direction, head for the 37-foot-high, black Janes Island Lighthouse, southwest of Island Point on Janes Island. If you are coming from the north, be sure to pass at least ½ mile to the west of the lighthouse, honoring the red "8" buoy. As soon as

Manokin and Big Annemessex Rivers

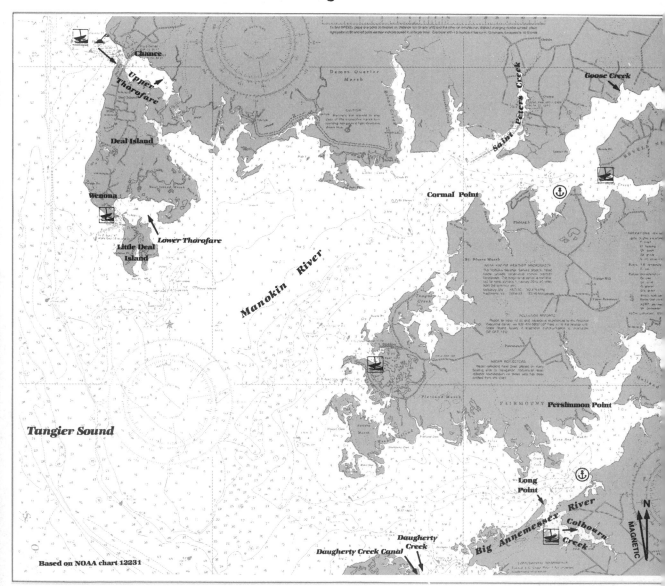

Based on NOAA chart 12231

SCALE **1" = 1.53** NAUT. MILES   **Good anchoring**   **Marina**    **Launching site**

you can see the small green "1" can southeast of the lighthouse, turn to head directly toward it. You can leave it to either side because there is at least 7 feet of water for about 200 yards north of it. From can "1" on, the channel is well marked and easy to follow.

The river makes a right-angle bend to the north around the southern end of Janes Island and continues past the town of Crisfield until it turns into Daugherty Creek Canal, a shortcut inside Janes Island to the mouth of the Big Annemessex River. Janes Island is all tidal marsh except for the area at the southern end of Daugherty Creek Canal, where Janes Island State Park offers campsites and slips for campers.

Harbors on the Little Annemessex River are remarkably few. In fact, it is possible to get into a total of three creeks plus the canal. The real place of interest on the river is the town of Crisfield.

Old House Cove

 3 *No facilities*

Charts: **12228**, 12230, 12231

The first cove to port as you enter the Little Annemessex River is Old House Cove, a fair-sized basin at the southern end of Janes Island. The entrance was dredged to a depth of 5 feet in 1979; what it is now is anyone's guess. Inside, the water depth ranges between 3 and 4 feet, at least in the middle. If you are in a shoal-draft boat, such as an outboard or inboard/outboard, give it a try.

Broad Creek

   No facilities

Charts: **12228**, 12230, 12231

This is not an anchorage; in fact, it is called a creek only out of courtesy. It is really a short-cut through the marshes between the Little Annemessex River and about the middle region of Pocomoke Sound. Unfortunately, the controlling depth is only a little more than 3 feet, limiting its use to boats with a very shallow draft. It is probably used only by local watermen and an occasional inquisitive gunkholer.

Crisfield Chamber of Commerce

Crisfield Harbor on the Little Annemessex River (view facing due west).

Jenkins Creek

Charts: **12228**, 12230, 12231

Jenkins Creek is little more than a narrow channel leading to the Crisfield County wharf and launching ramp. While some small, shallow-draft boats might find a few places to anchor, this creek is used as water access for fishermen. The restaurant near the ramp area is there almost by coincidence as it is not cruiser oriented.

Crisfield

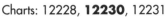

Charts: 12228, **12230**, 12231

Approaches. The only real harbor on the Little Annemessex River is Somers Cove, a good-sized basin serving the town of Crisfield. The entrance to Somers Cove is almost impossible to see until you are on top of it. As you approach the green "11" beacon, you will see a large brick building among a cluster of others on the east side of the river. Head for this building and look for the small sign that points the way into the deep, narrow channel between the packing plants and into Somers Cove.

Marinas. The channel soon opens up into the basin, and the piers and building of Somers Cove Marina appear just off your port bow. While you can anchor out in the basin, this marina is of such high quality that, contrary to our usual counsel, we recommend that you take a slip for your stay here. The marina has become so popular that reservations are a good idea during the peak boating season. We have been told that reservations usually are not accepted during the period of the Crab Festival, from 15 August to Labor Day; during that time slips are available on a first-come basis.

At the Somers Cove Marina you are greeted promptly and pleasantly, and a marina employee not only directs you to your slip but also helps you tie up. The main building houses the marina office. In an adjoining building are very clean

The Somers Cove Marina with the U.S. Coast Guard Station in the background.

heads and showers, as well as a coin-operated laundry. The combination to the locks on the doors is provided to each visitor on request.

The marina's landscaped grounds are large and parklike with a wide walkway bordering the basin. The piers are painted white, and the 14-inch pilings border on overkill for this landlocked harbor. The complex includes a swimming pool, which is very popular in hot weather.

History. The town of Crisfield was established in the mid-1600s as Annemessex, the Algonquin Indian name meaning "bountiful waters." Agriculture was the primary industry until the early 1800s, when fishing became the focus and the town's name became Somers Cove. In 1860, oystering brought the oyster fleet, along with steamships and a railroad line, to Somers Cove. The railroad line was brought largely due to the efforts of a Princess Anne area lawyer named Crisfield, in whose honor the town was renamed again. Legend has it that the real reason for naming the town after Mr. Crisfield was to soothe him after he fell through a rotted pier into the harbor. In any event, the fishing industry really took off, and Crisfield promptly dubbed itself "The Seafood Capital of the World." In fact, much of the town is literally built on oyster shells. The oystering industry has dwindled since its heyday, but crabbing still holds full sway. At the city dock are a crab-barrel factory, shops for repairing oyster dredges, and packing plants.

During half of the year Crisfield is a quiet community, mostly of watermen. From May through October, however, it is one of Maryland's major crabbing centers, fully justifying the new version of its self-adopted title, "The Crab Capital of the World."

What to See & Do. By all means, walk into the town and explore. The shops have a turn-of-the-century atmosphere, and the people are unfailingly pleasant. Buyer beware: this book may be the only place where you receive fair warning about the 5 percent nuisance tax levied on customers who use a credit card!

The J. Millard Tawes Historical Museum provides an interesting and full look at Maryland history from pre-European times to the present, with special emphasis on Governor Tawes and other prominent Crisfield individuals and businesses. Museum hours are 10:00 A.M. to 5:00 P.M. daily from Memorial Day through September and 10:00 A.M. to 4:00 P.M. daily from March through May and in October. The museum closes its doors to the public during the months of November, December, January, and February. The admission fees are $1.00 for adults and 50¢ for children. Adjacent to the museum is an information center, which is worth a look before you continue your exploration of town.

On the waterfront are several ferries that go to Smith Island or Tangier Island. This is a good way for you to visit these islands if you don't wish to negotiate the narrow channel into the harbor and deal with the problem of finding a place to tie up or anchor. The cost is $12 to $20 per person, depending on the cruise line you choose and its options.

Over the Labor Day weekend each year Crisfield holds the Hard Crab Derby, in which specially groomed crabs are raced on a wet, inclined platform. Related activities, including a fishing tournament, a beauty pageant, land and water parades, and many others, make this a real festival that attracts large crowds. It takes an intrepid crew to bring a visiting boat into this maelstrom.

SMITH ISLAND
Charts: **12228**, 12230, 12231, 12261

At the beginning of the 20th century there were several islands with significant populations. Now all but two—Smith and Tangier—have succumbed to the erosion of wind and wave.

Captain John Smith visited Smith Island

The entrance to Somers Cove is a little hard to see. As you approach the green "11" beacon you will see a large brick building among a cluster of others on the east side of the river. Head for this building and look for the sign that points the way into the deep but narrow channel between the packing plants.

Crisfield

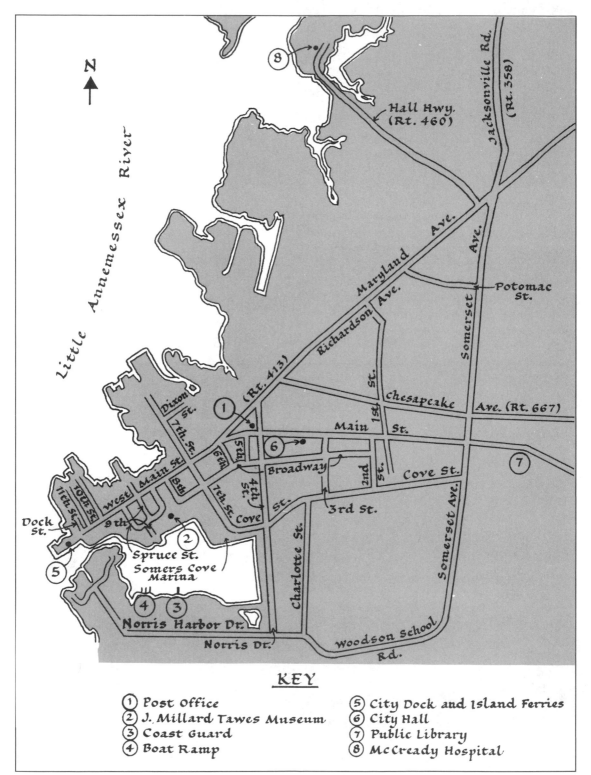

Little Annemessex River

N

⑧ Hall Hwy. (Rt. 460)

Jacksonville Rd. (Rt. 358)

Maryland Ave.

Richardson Ave.

Somerset Ave.

Potomac St.

(Rt. 413)

① Chesapeake Ave. (Rt. 667)

Dixon St.

7th St.

6th St.

5th St.

4th St.

Main St.

1st St.

St.

⑥

Broadway St.

2nd St.

Cove St.

⑦

7th St. Cove St.

3rd St.

West Main St.

8th

9th

10th St.

11th St.

Dock St.

⑤

② Spruce St.
Somers Cove Marina

③ ④

Norris Harbor Dr.

Norris Dr.

Charlotte St.

Somerset Ave.

Woodson School Rd.

KEY

① Post Office
② J. Millard Tawes Museum
③ Coast Guard
④ Boat Ramp
⑤ City Dock and Island Ferries
⑥ City Hall
⑦ Public Library
⑧ McCready Hospital

SMITH ISLAND

SCALE **1″** = **0.25** MILES

during his exploration of the Chesapeake in 1608, giving it his name. By the late 1600s the island had been settled, and much later it took an active part in the War of 1812. All of the settlers were of British origin or ancestry, and even today the population of about 900 is nearly pure Anglo-Saxon, with names such as Evans (a name shared by about half the population), Crockett, Parks, and Tyler. Their speech is laced with a faint touch of Elizabethan English, although it is rapidly being diluted by TV and radio. The island is populated almost entirely by watermen, who work crabbing in the summer and oystering in the winter.

Most of the island is low-lying marshland with a few scattered trees. Marshland means mosquitoes, so come prepared with good screens and repellent if you plan to spend the night. For the same reason, try to visit the island in the spring or fall rather than the summer, but by all means visit.

There are three villages on the island. The largest, Ewell, can be reached from the main Chesapeake Bay or from Tangier Sound through the channel called Big Thorofare. The other two, Tylerton and Rhodes Point, are accessible from Tangier Sound up a long narrow channel (Tyler Creek), provided you can find your way over the bar that stretches from Horse Hammock Point, on Smith Island, all the way south to Tangier Island. There is also a channel in from the main Bay on the west side of the island, but shoaling is a frequent problem there.

Big Thorofare

Charts: **12228**, 12230, 12231

Approaches. There are two entrances to the main Smith Island harbor at Ewell. The shortest approach is from the Bay side, where the entrance is marked by a pair of lighted beacons. The controlling depth in the first part of the channel is 7 feet, presenting no problem to most cruising boats. Immediately after passing the red "10" daymark you must make a 90-degree turn to the south to enter the channel to Ewell. The controlling depth of this channel is indi-

cated as 4½ feet; however, the range of tide here is about 2 feet, and most cruising boats can make it through the passage by taking advantage of the tide. The church steeple in Ewell serves as a good reference point once you have turned into the southbound channel.

The other approach is up a 4-mile-long channel from Tangier Sound. A course of 295 degrees from Janes Island Light takes you to the lighted green "1" beacon at the channel entrance. The controlling depth is 7 feet, so most cruising boats should have no trouble. Watch out for the ferries from Crisfield; squeezing by them can be a little tight in the narrow channel.

If you are passing through Smith Island between the Bay and Tangier Sound, take note that the buoyage system reverses at Ewell.

Anchorages & Dockage. Once you reach Ewell, you can tie up along the right-hand dock on the town side. If you anchor out, the short section of channel running southeast from Ewell is a possibility. A better anchorage, though less convenient to Ewell, is the part of the channel (entrance from the Bay side of the island) that extends to the east of the 90-degree bend at marker "10." Here the channel is unmarked but has 7 feet of water, providing a snug anchorage except when there is a strong west wind.

Restaurants & Provisions. In Ewell, fuel and water are available at the docks; other supplies and a couple of excellent restaurants are in town. Ruke's has great soft-shell crabs and crab cakes. The Bayside Inn has a buffet with a lot of southern-style food, but it's only open until 4:00 P.M. The Driftwood General Store carries a wide assortment of useful items, including coffee and packaged snacks. Don't plan on eating out for breakfast—nothing is open.

Tyler Creek

Charts: **12228**, 12230, 12231, 12261

Approaches. In order to try Tyler Channel to reach the towns of Tylerton or Rhodes Point, you need a draft of 5 feet or less so that you can cross the bar extending to the south from Horse Hammock Point. To cross the bar, depart from

Tangier Sound

the lighted red "6" bell buoy in the middle of Tangier Sound, right on the Maryland–Virginia line. From red "6" a course of 270 degrees (due magnetic west) heading directly toward tiny Herring Island takes you across the bar. You won't be able to make out Herring Island until you are actually crossing the bar. Continue on this course for a good 300 yards after the water starts to get deeper again, then swing to star-

board to a course of 350 degrees to the first of the Tyler Creek channel daymarks, red "2." Past the red "2" daymark head toward red "4," more than a mile away, by feeling your way carefully with a lead line or depth-sounder. Any time the depth drops below 8 feet you are getting out of the channel. Be sure that you make corrections in the right direction as the water gets thin fast.

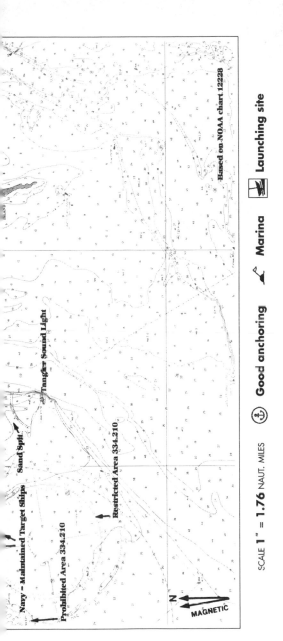

Based on NOAA chart 12228

Navy – Maintained Target Ships

Sand Spit.

Tangier Sound Light

Prohibited Area 334.210

Restricted Area 334.210

N
MAGNETIC

SCALE 1" = 1.76 NAUT. MILES

⚓ Good anchoring   ⚓ Marina   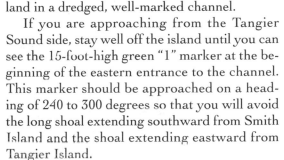 Launching site

TANGIER ISLAND

Charts: 12225, **12228**, 12230

Approaches. About 8 miles south of the entrance from Tangier Sound to Big Thorofare, on Smith Island, is the entrance to Tangier Island. Until the mid-1960s this was the only entrance to the tight little harbor on Tangier Island. Now it is possible to pass completely through the island in a dredged, well-marked channel.

If you are approaching from the Tangier Sound side, stay well off the island until you can see the 15-foot-high green "1" marker at the beginning of the eastern entrance to the channel. This marker should be approached on a heading of 240 to 300 degrees so that you will avoid the long shoal extending southward from Smith Island and the shoal extending eastward from Tangier Island.

Approaching from the Bay side is a little different, especially from the southwest quadrant. Before the island itself is clearly visible, you may be able to see what appears to be a large ship proceeding on an east-west course much farther to the east of the normal shipping channels than you would expect. That ship is a U.S. Navy bombing and gunnery target; stay well clear of it. It is in the center of the 1-mile-diameter prohibited area marked on the chart. It is also the center of a 6-mile-diameter restricted area, which is closed to traffic when the range is in use. There are other wrecks in the vicinity, also part of this Navy bombing range, but they are less clearly visible.

Because of this bombing range, vessels approaching from the south or southwest would be wise to pass east of the Tangier Sound Light at the southern tip of Tangier Island and head for the eastern channel entrance. Otherwise, plot a course to take you well north of the target ship before heading in to the western channel entrance.

As you approach from the Bay side the spire of the church in the middle of the island becomes visible before anything else. Head directly for this spire and you will soon be able to pick out the 15-foot-high green "1" at the channel entrance. Be sure to leave this to port. Although the channel is subject to shoaling, the controlling depth is nominally 7 feet, and prudent cruisers should have no trouble.

Tylerton

there is a line of fish houses in the water just past the green "1" daymark at the beginning of the channel to Rhodes Point. The controlling depth of this channel is reportedly 6 feet, but only for a width of 40 feet; this channel is reserved for the adventurous. At one time boats with drafts under 3 feet could make it all the way out to the Bay via this channel. It may still be possible, but check with the locals before even considering the attempt. Shoaling in Sheep Pen Gut, north of Rhodes Point, is the usual problem.

Peter McClintock/Virginia Marine Resources Bureau

The main harbor at Tangier Island, looking northwest to the entrance from the Bay side.

Be sure to note that the buoyage system changes at the town of Tangier. That is, on entering from either entrance, keep the green markers to port and the red markers to starboard until you reach the town. If you continue through the channel from there, heading either to the Bay or to Tangier Sound, keep the green markers to starboard and the red markers to port. (A simple way to keep this straight is to look at the marker numbers: if the numbers descend, keep the red markers to port.)

Be careful of the ferry from Crisfield if it is heading your way. The channel is narrow, and it can be a bit of a tight squeeze in the region near the center of the island. In fact, the Bay entrance is now considered the main entrance, and if only to avoid the ferry squeeze, it is preferable if you have a choice.

Southwest of Tangier Island the chart indicates a large danger area labeled "*San Marcos* Wreck." This was once the U.S. Navy battleship USS *Texas*, which served during the Spanish-American War. In 1911 it was renamed the *San Marcos* and towed to its current location to serve as a gunnery target. Blasted to a hulk by the

battleship *New Hampshire* in 1911–12, the *San Marcos* again served as a gunnery target during World War II. Afterward, it was said to have been responsible for at least seven shipwrecks, and in the late 1950s it was dynamited to leave a depth of about 20 feet over the highest part of its remains. Although what remains of the *San Marcos* is no longer really a hazard to navigation, the prudent mariner gives its location a wide berth.

Tangier

Charts: 12225, **12228**, 12230

Dockage. There is little room to anchor among the local fishing boats, which are moored to stakes in this harbor. Fuel may be available at the Tangier Oil Company docks, but you are not encouraged to tie up there or at the other docks used by the local fishermen.

In fact, during the boating season (Memorial Day to Labor Day), visiting boats are not always welcome due to crowding of the harbor and its few facilities. Even so, several piers are available for visiting boats, and some signs indicate transient dockage for rent.

The town of Tangier, the only town on the island, is a working fishing village. The people, especially the children, are friendly and somewhat curious about visitors from the "outside." With TV and radio, most of the island mannerisms of speech have all but disappeared. As on Smith Island, a small assortment of surnames serves the islanders. The most common is Crockett, followed by Pruit and Parks.

Restaurants. Go to Hilda Crockett's Chesapeake House for excellent seafood. Be sure to get there no later than 5:00 P.M. Meals are served daily from 15 April through October, and the restaurant claims the food is "good enough to justify the ferry ride."

Bed-and-breakfast lodging is available with reservations. Call ahead at 804-891-2331. The Chesapeake House is closed from 1 November to 1 April. Limited groceries and supplies are available in town, but all shops are closed on Sunday.

Anchorages. If you can't find room in the harbor or if you would like to spend the night in solitude, boats with drafts of less than 6 feet can find their way into the snug little anchorage inside the hook at Sand Spit, at the extreme southern tip of Tangier Island. Stay a good ½ mile off the island until you reach the tip of the hook,

OYSTER WARS

What became known as the "oyster wars" started in 1870. The wars involved two separate conflicts: one between the hand-tongers and the dredgers, and one between the dredge boats from Maryland and those from Virginia (and later, "pirate" dredgers from New England).

When the oyster dredge was first used in the 18th century, it immediately caused conflict with the hand-tongers, who could only work beds in relatively shallow water. Dredgers could take oysters anywhere that they didn't run aground. At first the argument was fairly mild, but by 1871 thousands of dredge boats were invading river waters supposedly reserved for hand tonging, and the argument escalated into a shooting "war" between the tongers and dredgers, a rivalry that continues to a limited extent today. These battles, which peaked on the Chester and Choptank Rivers, led to the formation of Maryland's scandal-ridden "oyster navy," which was later replaced by the Marine Police and eventually the Natural Resources Police we know today.

then hold close to the hook as you ease around it. You will find a well-protected anchorage surrounded by marsh with about 6 feet of water. (Remember, marshes mean mosquitoes, so come prepared with screens and repellent.)

WESTERN SHORE

The Western Shore of the Bay in this region is relatively inhospitable. The long line of the Calvert Cliffs continues all the way into the Patuxent River, broken only by one artificial harbor and the Patuxent River, an excellent cruising ground all by itself.

PLUM POINT TO PATUXENT RIVER
Charts: **12263**, 12264

Long Beach (Flag Harbor)

Charts: **12263**, 12264

Of all of the artificial harbors on the 30-mile stretch of the Western Shore above the Patuxent River, Flag Harbor at Long Beach is probably the most likely to be accessible.

The first guide to look for is the set of domed towers belonging to the Calvert Cliffs Nuclear Power Plant. The entrance to the marina is just over 2 miles north of these towers. If you are in approximately the right area, you should see a line of light-colored houses near the water level, followed by another line of houses higher up on the cliff. Just past this upper line of houses you should see a dark opening in the shoreline:

Calvert Cliffs State Park, Lusby, Maryland.

Maryland Tourism

this is the entrance to the marina.

Head toward this dark opening on a course perpendicular to the shoreline. At the entrance are two lighted markers on dolphins, along with a quick-flashing white range light just inside the

250

harbor to mark a spoiler jetty to starboard as you enter.

Marinas. This is largely a sailboat marina, although there are some sizable powerboats here. There is no room to anchor, but transients are welcome. There are some transient slips for boats up to 38 feet. Individually owned slips are often available for a flat fee. There is no longer any free overnight docking, nor do you have to listen to a condominium sales pitch.

The management is striving to keep the entrance channel open to a depth of 7 to 8 feet and seems to be succeeding. The marina is of modern construction, and its facilities include fuel, water, ice, showers, a swimming pool, and tennis courts.

PATUXENT RIVER

Charts: 12230, 12263, **12264**, 12284

Located about halfway down the Chesapeake Bay's relatively inhospitable Western Shore, between Herring Bay and the Potomac River, the Patuxent River offers some of Maryland's best cruising grounds. While the river is navigable for more than 40 miles from its mouth, all of the good harbors are within about 18 miles of its entrance, and the best ones less than 8 miles above Drum Point.

When approaching the mouth of the Patuxent River from the south, you should be especially careful of two shoal areas. The first of these is off Cedar Point, where the chart shows an abandoned lighthouse in ruins. Until 1999 the lighthouse appeared to be in reasonably good condition when viewed from a distance. Then a storm did it in, and most of the structure collapsed. It is still visible but not nearly as good a landmark as it used to be. Although the bell buoy that replaced the lighthouse is almost a mile farther offshore, you can approach within 200 yards of the lighthouse in at least 10 feet of water on the offshore side. The danger lies in the possibility that the current or wind might push you much closer than you intended because there are rocks there.

The second shoal is off Hog Point, extending due north from the point. If you draw less than 6 feet, this is not a problem, but the ice in winter has a tendency to destroy the lighted "1" spar here, and the temporary buoys used as replacements are hard to see. Should you cross inside of the marker with your depth-sounder running, you will see the bottom come up alarmingly fast. Although there is no real danger, the relatively sudden change from 20–30 feet of water to 6 feet or less can be a real heart-stopper if you are not expecting it.

Flag Harbor Marina has some slips for transients but no room to anchor.

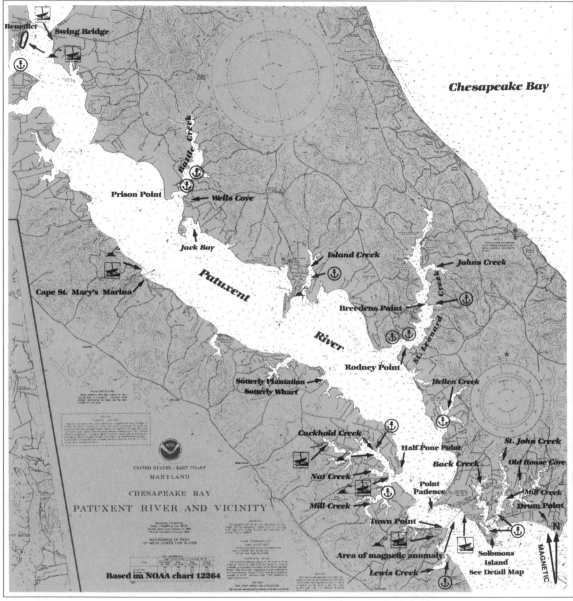

SCALE **1"** = **2.2** NAUT. MILES   ⚓ **Good anchoring**   ⚓ **Marina**   **Launching site**

PATUXENT RIVER

Once clear of the Hog Point shoal, a course of 272 degrees from number "1" takes you directly to the flashing red "6" marker that indicates the southernmost point of the sunken island in the entrance to Solomons Harbor. This course takes you a few hundred yards offshore of Drum Point Light. Mounted on a 30-foot-high tower, Drum Point Light is easily seen

from a considerable distance, even against the shoreline. You can use this tower as a reference, or, within limits, you can ignore it completely since the water is about 40 feet deep to within a short distance of the shore.

A simpler approach to the Patuxent is from the north. After rounding Cove Point, if you stay at least 400 yards offshore, you have to try

Cove Point Light, on the Western Shore, just below the natural gas facility.

really hard to hit anything except crab pot floats, which are abundant, or a few fishing stakes. (Note: If you approach at night, stay more than ½ mile offshore as the fishing stakes are invisible then until it is too late.) Once you can see Drum Point Light, head directly toward it. Actually, you should head a bit to the south of the light, which is on the shore.

Drum Point Light, in the Patuxent River near Solomons, has three red sectors—northeast, south to east-southeast, and west. The first two may be used as guides for entering the Patuxent River at night. From the Bay, locate the Drum Point Light and maintain a course to keep you in the white sector of its beam. If it suddenly turns red, you are off course to either the north or the south. The direction of your needed correction should be obvious. The west red sector is a guide to those exiting the Patuxent River around Solomons to avoid the shoals south and east of Solomons and on past Drum Point. (See the chart if you need clarification.)

About 1 mile to the northeast of Drum Point a series of cliffs appear to starboard. Although they have neither the name nor the fame, these cliffs are essentially the same as the Calvert Cliffs. In actual fact they are an extension of the same formation. It is possible to anchor to within 100 yards of the beach (you can get a lot closer, but we lost our nerve), land, and search the cliffs for sharks' teeth and Miocene fossils (15 to 30 million years old). If you have children aboard, and even if you don't, be sure to visit these cliffs at least once. The main advantage to stopping here rather than at the more publicized

Calvert Cliffs is that in the event of a storm you are not far from shelter in Solomons Harbor.

Once past Drum Point, you have the option of putting in to Solomons for supplies, a meal at a restaurant, or whatever, or continuing on to the more sylvan harbors farther up the Patuxent. Incidentally, the Governor Johnson Bridge, upriver from Solomons, has a 140-foot vertical clearance; you can get under it no matter how high your mast may be. If you use a compass-driven electronic autopilot, be careful in this area; there is a large magnetic anomaly in the vicinity of the bridge.

Solomons

  All facilities

Charts: 12230, **12264**, 12284

Near the mouth of the Patuxent River, Solomons Island beckons to many boaters cruising up or down the Bay. Unless you demand solitude, the area serves as a wonderful stopover during a cruise. It offers anchorages, marinas, restaurants, groceries, hardware, and an interesting marine museum. The harbor is well protected, and the creeks fanning off from it provide anchorages out of the mainstream of traffic. Few other harbors on the Bay offer as much in the way of facilities for the cruiser.

Approaches. As you clear Drum Point on the way in, you have a choice of two channels past the shoal at the harbor entrance. In daylight either channel is acceptable, although the outside channel is preferred by most. Both are well marked. At night the lighted markers "3," "4," and "6" make the outside channel by far the easier approach. None of the inner channel markers are lighted.

As you swing around the bulkhead on the northeastern end of Solomons Island, a triangular man-made island appears off your port bow. This was once the site of a natural island called Mollyleg or Moll's Leg or Molly's Leg, which was wiped out by a hurricane more than 50 years ago. I am not sure why the island was rebuilt unless it was used as a repository for spoil from harbor dredging. In any event, the majority of marinas, restaurants, shops, and other facilities are in the cove to the west and south of this island.

PATUXENT RIVER

253

Solomons Island and Vicinity

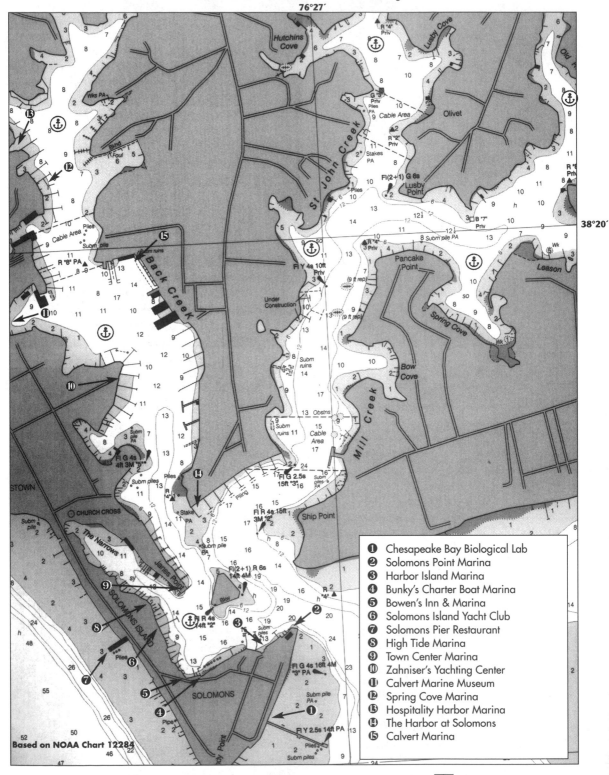

76°27′

Region 4

Based on NOAA Chart 12284

PATUXENT RIVER

❶ Chesapeake Bay Biological Lab
❷ Solomons Point Marina
❸ Harbor Island Marina
❹ Bunky's Charter Boat Marina
❺ Bowen's Inn & Marina
❻ Solomons Island Yacht Club
❼ Solomons Pier Restaurant
❽ High Tide Marina
❾ Town Center Marina
❿ Zahniser's Yachting Center
⓫ Calvert Marine Museum
⓬ Spring Cove Marina
⓭ Hospitality Harbor Marina
⓮ The Harbor at Solomons
⓯ Calvert Marina

SCALE **2.04″ = 0.5** NAUT. MILES   ⚓ **Good anchoring**   ⚓ **Marina**   🚤 **Launching site**

254

Immediately to your left, on the southern side of the harbor entrance, are the docks belonging to the Chesapeake Marine Biology Laboratory. Here you usually can see some of the laboratory's research vessels tied up in the shadow of the huge Exxon tanks.

Marinas, Provisions, & Restaurants. Just past the Exxon tanks are the docks of the excellent Harbor Island Marina (410-326-3441). The pilings and platform of the first dock you come to have a good bit of soft creosote, of which you should be wary when laying alongside. The marina keeps space for visiting boats along its outer piers, and you may wish to take advantage of this courtesy to visit the Harbor Island Inn there.

Adjacent to the Harbor Island Marina is Bunky's Charter Boat Marina, which offers its services to Bay anglers. Just past Bunky's are a package store and a small gift shop, which also carries a good line of boating clothes.

Next is Bowen's Inn & Marina. Transients are welcome to tie up to its pier overnight (space is limited, and there is a charge) or to visit the dining room or bar (no charge to tie up). However, Bowen's Marina is only open from 15 April to 1 October. The restaurant is also closed on Mondays.

In the off-season the Solomons Island Yacht Club (410-326-3718) is an excellent place to spend the night, particularly for members of recognized yacht clubs.

Unfortunately, the Dockside Grocery, which used to be just past the Solomons Island Yacht Club, is no more. In 1999, the building was empty. I do not know if anything has taken its place.

The Town Center Marina (410-326-2401), at the end of a little peninsula northwest of Molly Leg Island, has a long bulkhead where you may tie up to take on fuel or water and to visit the marine store.

Most of the marinas in the area have pump-out stations.

On the Patuxent River side, directly across the thin neck of land from the Solomons Island Yacht Club, is Solomons Pier Restaurant. The restaurant is located on a long finger of a pier extending out into the Patuxent River. There is dock space for a few boats to tie up, but the water depth is uncertain, and there is no protection from waves or wakes from the river. The restaurant changed hands in 1985 and has become a "fancy" place instead of the "just-plain-folks" place it once was. It's also quite a bit more expensive.

Between Solomons Island Neck and Langley Point is a small body of water called the Narrows. On the northeastern shore of the Narrows are the large Langley Point Marina and the Pier 1, a busy little restaurant that has docks where you may tie up while enjoying a meal there. On the western side of the Narrows is a place that offers charter fishing boats. The Narrows is far too busy a place for anchoring at any time.

Often overlooked by newcomers, Back Creek, extending to the north of Molly Leg Island, has several marinas and the intriguing Calvert Marine Museum.

Zahniser's Marina & Boatyard (410-326-2166) is located in the first cove to port, less than ½ mile past the tip of Langley Point. There are a gift shop and a nice marine store in the main building.

Off the starboard bow is the large and hospitable Calvert Marina (410-326-9251). Calvert has a pier set aside for transients adjacent to its carry-out restaurant, which is open in the summer months. It also has a ship's store, a swimming pool, and that site of washday miracles, a laundry.

Near the end of Back Creek is Spring Cove Marina (410-326-2161), a large marina with transient slips, fuel, pumpout, a marine store, and limited groceries. From the marina it is only a short walk through the Comfort Inn & Hospitality Harbor Marina (410-326-1052) parking lot, next door, to a little shopping center on Route 2.

The shopping center has a pizza parlor, post office, liquor store, convenience store, laundry, and the considerably expanded Woodburn's Food Market. The marine store (1st Marine) is one of the few places that can repair and recondition propellers. (The owner tells me that he can handle only small propellers, no larger than 5 feet in diameter.)

What to See & Do. Tucked away back in the cove is the Calvert Marine Museum (410-326-2042). Operated by the Calvert County Historical Society, the museum is open daily year-round. Although reputed to have as much as 200 feet of dock space for visitors at the museum pier, there is really only one space, a floating dock in front of the lighthouse, to lay alongside the pier. Museum boats take up most of the dock space, and the museum would prefer that only dinghies attempt to tie up there. You can either anchor out in the cove and land by dinghy or pull into a transient slip at Spring Cove Marina and walk to the museum from there—or, for that matter, from any part of Solomons. Whatever you have to do to get there, by all means visit the museum.

For admission the society requests a voluntary donation to help support the museum. Inside, there are exhibits on local maritime history, estuarine natural history, and paleontology. In addition, there are a ship-carving and model-making shop and underwater exhibits—by themselves worth the trip. There is also a small gift shop. Outside are a few small exhibits, a small boat shed, and the screw-pile Drum Point Lighthouse. (The lighthouse, which is open to visitors for only certain hours of the day, appears to be typical of the type. In fact, it seems to be a twin of the lighthouse at the St. Michaels Marine Museum.) The museum also offers hour-long cruises on a converted 1899 bugeye, *Wm. B. Tennison*. From September through March visitors can see working oyster boats at Broomes Island, Chesapeake Beach, and Solomons Island. Across the street from the museum is a Visitor Information Center.

Anchorages. Don't try to anchor for the night anywhere in Back Creek. It is crowded with boats and will not make for a restful night. Instead, head up into Mill Creek, to the northeast of Molly Leg Island. Anchorage here is adequate, but most of the shore is private property, so you should not expect to be able to land.

There is a pleasant anchorage at Old House Cove, either just inside the mouth of the cove or in the broad part of Mill Creek just past the cove. The bottom in both places is hard mud, making for good holding. Don't try to anchor in Leason Cove; the holding there is reputed to be as poor as the holding in Old House Cove is good.

If you don't have to go ashore, you can anchor almost anywhere in either Mill Creek or St.

A view of the Calvert Marine Museum's waterfront and Drum Point Lighthouse. The Patuxent Small Craft Guild maintains the museum's small-craft collection, including the skipjack Marie Theresa in the foreground.

Paula Johnson/Calvert Marine Museum

John Creek and spend a peaceful night. You can follow Mill Creek upstream until you start to plow mud or poke into any of the other branches until the water gets uncomfortably thin. In spite of the population density, the water traffic on Mill Creek is surprisingly light. You cannot anchor in the basin on the south side of the Patuxent River, across from Solomons, because it is part of the Patuxent Naval Air Test Center and therefore is not open to the general public.

Lewis Creek

  No facilities

Charts: 12230, **12264**, 12284

Virtually unnoticed by cruisers, Lewis Creek is hidden on the western shore of the Patuxent River just south of Town Point. Nearly everyone who ventures into this area bypasses this creek in favor of Town Creek or to continue up the Patuxent. This is probably because the chart indicates that the entrance is impassable by cruising boats, which is not the case; you just have to know how to get through the entrance.

Approaches. On the south side of the entrance is a sandy hook with a green "1" daymark at its tip. On the opposite side of the entrance is a large patch of marsh grass backed by a small hillside, which gives warning of shoaling on that side. The entrance is best approached on a due-west course, guiding directly at the middle of the sandy beach of the hook. Approach slowly, holding almost close enough to the beach to jump ashore, and follow the beach around the point. Don't get too close to the green "1" as you can expect a little shoaling past it. Once on a course toward the big boathouse to starboard, you are in.

Anchorages. The creek has 6 to 11 feet of water right up to its end. The banks are high and wooded, providing a well-protected, secluded anchorage for boats adventurous enough to negotiate the entrance. There are only a few houses on the shore. This is a truly secluded spot.

Town Creek

Charts: 12230, **12264**, 12284

Town Creek, the second navigable creek on the western shore of the Patuxent River, literally lies in the shadow of the Governor Johnson Bridge, which crosses the river just a little to the northwest of Solomons. The right fork of the creek is accessible only to vessels with a vertical height of less than 30 feet.

Approaches. The entrance to the creek is deep and easily negotiated. Simply honor the lighted red "2" marker at the mouth of the creek, leaving it close to starboard. The rest of the creek has 8 to 10 feet of water except in the second half of the creek's left fork, where it shoals to about 4 feet.

Marinas & Restaurants. There are several marinas here, two of which serve transients. To starboard just before the bridge is Homeport

Marina, indicated by a small sign bearing that name. Near the water is a small, tan masonry building that houses the showers and the self-service laundry. Past the bridge, at the head of the creek's right fork, is the Town Creek Marina, which offers package goods, a restaurant, and a bar with nightly entertainment.

Although the area is not unattractive, the creek shoreline is residential, and there are far better harbors elsewhere on the Patuxent.

Mill Creek

Charts: 12230, **12264**

Approaches. Once you pass the bridge and round Point Patience in the Patuxent River, you will soon see the common approach shared by Mill and Cuckhold Creeks off your port bow. A course of 344 degrees takes you from the red "8" light at the tip of Point Patience to the green "9" Patuxent River lighted marker, which also indicates the south side of the approach into Mill and Cuckhold Creeks. As you pass green "9," swing to port and follow the daymarks past Half Pone Point into the creek mouths. As you clear the last red marker off Half Pone Point, swing to port to enter Mill Creek. There is plenty of water in all the branches of Mill Creek; just be sure to give all points a prudent berth.

Restaurants & Dockage. Directly in front of you as you complete the approach is Clarke's Landing. The restaurant and bar here offer slips to transients using their facilities. It would be wise to ascertain the depth in any of these slips before using it.

At the end of the first cove to starboard in Mill Creek is the Placid Harbor Conference Center. Although it does not really cater to the marine trade, it does offer some slips, showers, heads, and ice. Other conference-center facilities are not open to the general public. Contact the dockmaster to obtain permission before using any of the slips.

The rest of the creek is pretty and wooded, although most of the shoreline in the smaller branches is lined with homes.

PATUXENT RIVER

257

Region 4

Anchorages. You can anchor nearly anywhere here with good protection. We have found the best anchorage to be in the bight to port just after entering the creek, near the cliffs. There are some nice, small, sandy beaches along here where you can land to stretch your legs; if you have a dinghy, just inside the point is a small pond in the marsh, which you can explore.

Cuckhold Creek

Charts: 12230, **12264**

Approaches. The instructions for approaching Mill Creek apply here as well. After clearing Half Pone Point, swing to starboard to enter Cuckhold Creek (sorry, we haven't been able to discover the origin of the name). Immediately to port is Nat Creek, which has plenty of water but was too crowded to interest us.

The creek is navigable almost to the headwaters of the two forks at its end. It is interesting that the farther upstream you go, the browner the water gets.

Marinas. About ½ mile past Nat Creek, where the Cuckhold Creek widens a bit, Blackstone Marina appears to port. The marina has a marine store, showers, and heads, as well as gas and diesel fuel. Just past Blackstone's, Weeks Marina offers ice and limited hardware; however, it does not really cater to transients.

Anchorages. You can anchor anywhere in Cuckhold Creek, but we prefer less developed anchorages. We recommend Mill Creek or one of the other harbors on the Patuxent for overnight anchoring, but we think a quick trip up this creek is worthwhile.

Hellen Creek

 No facilities

Charts: 12230, **12264**

To starboard about a mile past the entrance to Mill and Cuckhold Creeks lies Hellen Creek. This creek looks interesting, but unless you can find the narrow, 7-foot-deep privately marked channel, the bar across its entrance limits access to vessels with a very shallow draft. If you can

258

get in, there are well-protected anchorages in 7 to 11 feet of water. Negotiating the bar is a test of nerve and skill.

St. Leonard Creek

Charts: 12263, **12264**

Approaches. A little more than 3 miles past Point Patience is the entrance to St. Leonard Creek, perhaps the prettiest part of the Patuxent River. A course of 355 degrees from the red "8" at the tip of Point Patience takes you directly to the green "1" daymark in the mouth of St. Leonard Creek. The entrance is difficult to see until you are almost on top of it. About 400 yards to the west of the St. Leonard Creek green "1" daymark is the lighted red "14" Patuxent River marker. Do not go between them; they indicate the same shoal. Leave green "1" to port and enter the mouth of St. Leonard Creek. The creek has no more markers, but none are needed.

Give Rodney Point a wide berth as you proceed up the creek. The rest of the creek is easy to navigate, as a glance at the chart shows. There is 7 to 20 feet of water nearly from shore to shore for the entire 3 miles of St. Leonard Creek. Simply stay near the middle and you won't get into trouble while you enjoy the quiet, pastoral scenery on this beautiful creek. There are few houses, and with one exception, there is no commercial development.

History. It was in St. Leonard Creek that the little flotilla of Commodore Barney was bottled up when it fought to turn back the British during the War of 1812. After a valiant effort, the flotilla pulled off a surprise attack that sent the British fleet reeling back to Point Patience, whereupon Commodore Barney was able to escape with his fleet relatively intact upstream on the Patuxent River to Benedict. Unfortunately, the British fleet was soon reinforced, Barney's flotilla was forced to scuttle its gunboats, and the British went on to burn Washington, D.C. Today there are continuing efforts to find and salvage artifacts from the scuttled gunboats.

Library of Congress

The destruction of the U.S. Chesapeake flotilla in Washington, D.C.

Anchorages. The first anchorage is in Mackall Cove, the little cove to port almost at the mouth of the creek. The high, wooded banks and 12 feet of water make this one of the most snug anchorages in the area. Conversely, there is little of the air circulation needed in hot weather. Mackall Cove is definitely a cool-weather anchorage.

Just past Rodney Point is one of the creek's most popular anchorages. From Rodney Point around to the east is a beautiful, white, sandy beach below a wooded bank. Here you can wade, swim, beachcomb, or build sandcastles to your heart's content. Anchor inside the point in about 14 feet of water with good holding. During the boating season you probably won't be alone, but there is plenty of room for all.

The next good anchorage is just below the cliff at Breedens Point. If you really want seclusion, make your way into Hollins Cove, just to the east, where there is room for just a couple of boats to swing, completely protected from all directions.

Directly west of Breedens Point, on the opposite side of the creek, is an unnamed cove between high, wooded banks. This is a great place to duck into in the event of a line squall. The homes on both sides preclude landing, and it is too close for hot-weather anchoring.

Marinas & Restaurants. A little farther upstream, where Johns Creek branches off St. Leonard Creek, is Vera's White Sands Restaurant & Marina (410-586-1182). If you want a slip for the night or plan to go to the restaurant (which you definitely should visit at least once), pull up to the gas dock for a slip assignment from the dockmaster. Showers and heads, as well as the swimming pool, are located in the restaurant building, on the hill above the docks. It is Vera who makes this facility unique. Once a Hollywood starlet, Vera is a gracious lady with a taste for the exotic who still makes a commanding appearance. There is never any question who she is. Once having met her, you'll never forget her. In 1999 Vera became ill, and we were told that the restaurant might not open the next year. It did open in 2000, but if it closes, it will also signal the end of an era and a loss to all of us.

You can proceed farther upstream, but sailboats are advised not to proceed beyond Planters Wharf Creek due to the overhead power cable (vertical clearance 38 feet).

Sotterly Plantation

  No facilities

Charts: 12230, **12264**

Approaches. Almost directly across the river from the mouth of St. Leonard Creek is Sotterly on the Patuxent. The plantation overlooks a large sweep of the river. This is a working plantation that dates back to the early 18th century.

Easily accessible from the water, Sotterly welcomes visitors. There are two docks where you can tie up to visit, although overnight dockage is neither expected nor desirable given the proximity of St. Leonard Creek. One of the docks at Sotterly is a T-shaped pier that juts out into the Patuxent River, but it is a little rickety and probably no longer in use. The other dock, which is perhaps a better choice, is in the little cove just north of the pier. To enter the cove, favor the south side of the entrance, swinging close to the pier, then pull into the dock on the south side of the cove. Here your boat will be well protected from weather and wave while you visit the plantation.

What to See & Do. The dockhouse has a phone that you can use to call the docent, who can probably send a car to take you and your crew up to the lovely Georgian mansion if you are not up to walking. Actually, it is a pleasant half-mile walk up the dirt road past the bordering raspberry bushes. The house is normally staffed and open to the public during the summer from 10 A.M. to 4 P.M. Tuesday through Sunday. However, since the hours and activities seem to fluctuate a bit, it is a good idea to call before visiting.

The staff at the plantation welcome both small and large groups, and for a nominal fee they will conduct a tour of the manor. If you give them advance notice, they will cater luncheons, teas, or receptions for groups of more than 25. The plantation is operated by the Sotterly Mansion Foundation, which may be

Sotterly on the Patuxent, a working plantation, is open to visitors and easily accessible from the water.

reached by phone at 301-373-2280 or by writing to P.O. Box 67, Hollywood, MD 20636.

Originally, Sotterly was part of a 4,000-acre land grant made in 1650 to Thomas Cornwallis by Lord Baltimore. This tract was subdivided in 1710, when the 890 acres that became Sotterly were purchased by James Bowles, who started construction on the manor house. Bowles died in 1727, before much could be completed. Two years later his widow married George Plater II, a prominent lawyer. It was George Plater II and his son, George Plater III, who were responsible for most of the construction of the present manor.

The manor house stands at the top of a sloping bank, now a sheep pasture, which provides a fantastic panorama down to and across the Patuxent River. Be sure to walk in the English country garden, north of the house.

St. Thomas Creek

  No facilities

Charts: 12230, **12264**

Just to the north of Sotterly on the same side of the Patuxent River is tiny St. Thomas Creek. This creek is a gunkholer's delight because it is almost invisible from the river and because it has a difficult and shallow entrance. If you can manage to get over the 3-foot bar in the entrance, you will find a lovely, pristine little anchorage in 7 feet of water with full protection from any weather. Unfortunately, few cruising sailboats will be able to enter because of the shallow bar.

Island Creek

Charts: 12263, **12264**

Approaches. The entrance to this creek, although marked, is tight and subject to shoaling. You have to feel your way in if you have more than a 3-foot draft because the channel meanders more than the chart and the few markers indicate. Keep the Fl R"2" close to starboard and watch your depth until the creek opens up and the water deepens to 8 feet or more. From there on, it's easy until the water begins to shoal again, near the headwaters.

The shoreline is low and marshy to starboard and at the headwaters; and the port side is built up. There is reasonable protection in 8 to 10 feet of water once you get in.

Marinas, Restaurants, & Provisions. There are three small marinas here where you can get limited supplies. Len's Market and Fishing Center, in the little cove to port just after you pass the narrow mouth of the creek, offers groceries. Be prepared to go in by dinghy; it gets shallow there.

On Broom's Island is Stoney's Seafood House (410-586-1888), one of the best crab houses on the Bay. Stoney's has docking for diners (the depth is a little uncertain, so you should go by dinghy) and both an air-conditioned dining room and a patio dining area complete with a Tiki Bar.

Battle Creek

No facilities

Chart: **12264**

Approaches. The entrance to this creek is marked with two buoys at a dogleg in the channel through the shoals in its mouth. There is also a snag indicated to starboard just prior to a 3-foot shoal opposite Prison Point. Swing well north of the red marker in the Patuxent River to the west of Jack Bay and set a course to head toward the east end of the sand spit inside the mouth of the creek past Wells Cove. As the tip of Prison Point comes abeam, swing slowly to port and feel your way in until the water depth drops to about 15 feet. From then on, remain in the middle and you should fare well. There is 7 to 18 feet of water in the first two-thirds of the creek; then it starts to shoal.

Anchorage & What to See & Do. There is good protection here, but the shore is thickly settled until you get away from the mouth of the creek. You can proceed for a distance of about 1½ miles upstream from the creek mouth before the water starts to drop below 7 feet. You can land at a lovely little beach inside the crook of Prison Point. Along the western shore is a series of snug little anchorages off some pretty farmland. Although the eastern shore is rather built up with residences, there is an anchorage in 5 feet of water just inside the entrance to Long Cove.

At the head of the creek is one of the northernmost stands of bald cypress in America—some of the trees are reputed to be 600 years old. It is possible to make the 1½-mile trip to the Battle Creek Cypress Swamp Sanctuary, but you should only attempt it at high water and in a shallow-draft boat, preferably a canoe or a kayak. At low water you will have to get out and carry your boat. It is open from 10:00 A.M. to 5:00 P.M. Tuesday through Saturday and from 1:00 P.M. to 5:00 P.M. on Sunday. Try the self-guided elevated tour.

Marinas. There are no marine facilities on this creek, but the Cape St. Marys Marina, directly across the Patuxent River from the entrance to Battle Creek, has fuel, water, ice, a dockside sewage pumpout facility, engine repairs, a restaurant, and a novelty shop.

Upper Patuxent River

Chart: **12264**

Approaches. Above Battle Creek no protected anchorages outside the main part of the river are passable by other than boats with a very shallow draft. There is some dockage at Benedict, the principal town on the upper part of the Patuxent, just below the swing bridge. Supplies are available dockside or in stores in the town. You can anchor in the mouth of Indian Creek, just below Benedict, but watch the depth as you feel your way in.

The swing bridge at Benedict has a closed vertical clearance of 16 feet, but it opens on signal from 6:00 A.M. to 6:00 P.M. At any other hour advance notice is required (phone, 410-535-1740).

The river is navigable for more than 10 miles above the swing bridge but narrows as you proceed upstream. How far you can actually go de-

pends on your draft and your nerve; NOAA chart 12264 has a chartlet that extends to Nottingham, a dozen miles beyond the bridge.

Anchorages. There are no protected harbors or tributaries off the main river, but none are necessary. Just pull to the side of the river in a comfortable-looking bend and drop the hook. Here the river is still pretty, and if you have the inclination, it is worth a look. Some parts are fairly well populated, but others are nearly pristine. Few cruising boats take the trouble to travel this far upriver; they are missing something.

ST. JEROME CREEK

Charts: 12230, **12233**

Just south of Point No Point, about midway between the Patuxent River and the Potomac, is St. Jerome Creek, a harbor of refuge to vessels with a relatively shallow draft. If you carry a draft of 4 feet or more, don't try it. Under no circumstances should you attempt to enter at night unless you are very familiar with this creek.

Approaches. The approach is straightforward. The course from Point No Point Light to the first marker at the entrance of St. Jerome Creek flashing 2-second green is 258 degrees for 2.3 miles. Once you are close to shore, simply find and honor the markers in the entrance.

Anchorages. Once past the last daymark, turn sharply to the north and anchor anywhere in the northern fork of the creek. Stay out of the shallow south fork.

Marinas. Trossbach Marina, in the southern corner of St. Jerome Creek, offers gasoline, ice, and showers, but there is ready access only for shallow-draft boats.

Region 5

POTOMAC RIVER

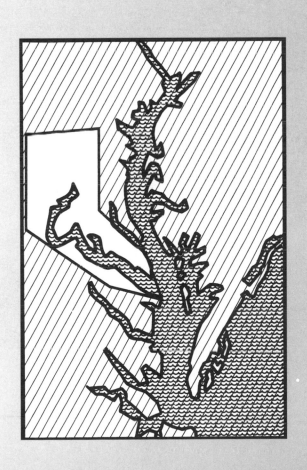

Potomac River Region

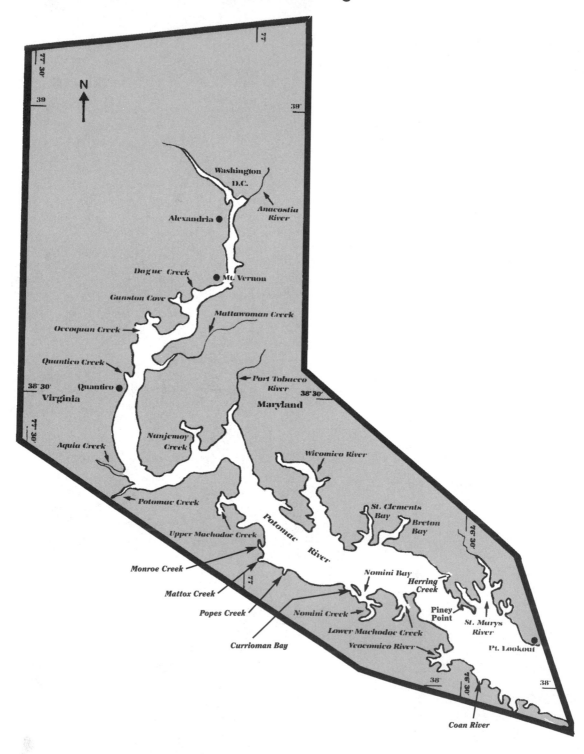

N

77° 30'

39°

39°

77°

Washington
D.C.

Alexandria ●

Anacostia
River

Dogue Creek

Mt. Vernon ●

Gunston Cove

Mattawoman Creek

Occoquan Creek ←

Quantico Creek ←

38° 30'

Port Tobacco
River

38° 30'

Quantico ●

Virginia

Maryland

77° 30'

Nanjemoy
Creek

Aquia Creek ←

Wicomico River

Potomac Creek ←

Potomac River

St. Clements
Bay

Breton
Bay

76° 30'

Upper Machodoc Creek →

Monroe Creek ←

77°

Nomini Bay

Herring
Creek

Mattox Creek ←

Popes Creek ←

Nomini Creek

Piney
Point

St. Marys
River

Currioman Bay

Lower Machodoc Creek

Yeocomico River

Pt. Lookout ●

38°

76° 30'

38°

Coan River

OFTEN OVERLOOKED BY those who cruise the Chesapeake Bay, the lower portion of the Potomac River offers cruising grounds that can rival those of the Bay itself. The mouth of the Potomac is 10 miles wide, comparable to the upper Bay, with low-lying land that creates an illusion of an even greater expanse. Within the 95 miles of river from Point Lookout to Washington there are nearly 30 rivers or creeks—some are inviting, some impassable. The best cruising grounds lie within the first 30 miles of the entrance. Good harbors are scarce in the last 65 miles of the run to Washington, but they do exist.

The mean range of tide varies from about 1½ feet on the lower river to about 3 feet at Washington. As in the rest of the Chesapeake, tide and currents here can be greatly influenced by the wind. Winds from the north or south can make any resemblance between the tide and current tables and the actual conditions purely coincidental. Luckily the waters are forgiving. Like the Chesapeake's, the Potomac's bottom tends to be soft mud; running aground is an inconvenience but no great hazard. The current, however, can be much more of a problem here than in the Bay. You can expect to encounter some currents on the order of 1.5 knots or more. Besides affecting your progress, such currents can throw your navigation well off when visibility is restricted.

Under conditions of opposing wind and current the mouth of the Potomac can become extremely uncomfortable in a surprisingly short time. This area also has a reputation for squalls, so get into port early, particularly in the summer months.

Warnings notwithstanding, the lower Potomac is a vast expanse of placid waters with numerous rivers, creeks, and bays containing plentiful, well-protected harbors, and surroundings varying from secluded without supplies to public with full facilities. The upper portion of the Potomac, although somewhat lacking in harbors, more than makes up for that deficiency with more points of interest.

For sailors, the first 30 miles of the river allow plenty of room for tacking since the river is at least 4 miles wide there. Unless you are a real diehard, we don't recommend cruising the Potomac and its tributaries without power.

The real line of demarcation between the Chesapeake Bay and the Potomac River is Point Lookout, on the Maryland side of the river; Smith Point, on the Virginia side, is not as sharply defined. Under certain conditions a "line"—possibly caused by the effects of wave action on bottom sediment or the mixing of main Bay and Potomac waters—extends southward from Point Lookout for as far as a couple of miles across the mouth of the Potomac. To the east of this line you are in the Chesapeake Bay; to the west and north of it you are cruising the Potomac River.

Point Lookout is now a state park with all sorts of recreational facilities. On the inside of the point, in a bight labeled Cornfield Harbor (it really isn't a harbor), is a channel leading into the public facility for boat launching and rental. However, this "harbor" is strictly for small powerboats; the maximum depth is 4 feet, and it definitely is not an overnight anchorage area.

History. During the Civil War a Union prisoner-of-war camp was located at Point Lookout. Officially called Camp Hoffman, the 26-acre compound was surrounded by a 12-foot-high fence and patrolled by guards on a catwalk on the outside. Inside, there was a ditch marking the deadline, beyond which any prisoner would be shot. For the prisoners Hoffman was hell. In its poor treatment of prisoners it frequently has been compared to the Confederate prison camp at Andersonville in Georgia.

The camp was protected by three earthwork forts, and picket boats patrolled the shores. Today there is little left besides a piece of the prison wall and one wall of one of the forts. Nearby, a monument marks the common grave of the more than 3,000 Confederate soldiers and some civilian sympathizers who died there.

MOUTH OF POTOMAC RIVER TO PORT TOBACCO RIVER

LOWER POTOMAC RIVER

Charts: 12230, **12233**, 12285

Smith Creek

Charts: 12230, **12233**, 12285

The mouth of Smith Creek lies on the Maryland side of the Potomac, about 6 miles from Point Lookout. The entrance, although narrow, is well marked and easy to negotiate. This creek is often used as a harbor of refuge, and the four marinas inside offer all the facilities you are likely to need.

Approach. You may have some trouble locating the first of the entrance markers, a lighted red "2" spar, feeling uncomfortably close to the land before you pick up "2" for certain. This feeling is illusory; your depth-sounder will indicate depths in excess of 20 feet if you are even approximately on course. Hold reasonably close to the green "3" marker right in the middle of the creek as you pass it since there are some shoals to either side, especially to the southwest of the marker. Past green "3" (you have to take a dogleg to the west after passing green "3"), there is deep water from shore to shore all the way to the headwaters of both branches of the creek. There are numerous coves or creeks

here, so there is a good chance of finding one unoccupied if you seek privacy.

Marinas & Restaurants. All of the marine facilities are in the east fork of the creek (Jutland Creek). If you need supplies, fuel, or prefer a slip for the night, head up this branch. Point Lookout Marina, in the mouth of Jutland Creek, is the most transient-friendly. It has transient slips, fuel, a self-service laundry, a pool, pumpout facilities, and a restaurant (Spinnaker's Restaurant), in addition to full repair facilities. The marina also has complimentary bicycles for off-site exploration. There is also Scheibles Crab Pot restaurant at Scheibles Fishing Center, just inside the mouth of Smith Creek. No groceries are available, but you may be able to arrange for transportation to one of the little country markets not too far away.

Anchorages. The west fork offers more solitude. You can anchor anywhere up to a distance of about 1 mile above the point, where the creek forks. Holding is good, and you will be well protected from the weather in all directions. The first cove to starboard is surrounded by tall trees, which makes it private and also gives excellent protection from a blow.

ST. MARYS RIVER

Charts: 12230, **12233**, 12285

For the main part, the St. Marys is a pretty river surrounded by wooded hills and farmland. The few thickly settled areas are quiet and well kept. The St. Marys offers not only sheltered anchorages but also many historic sites to lure the tourist in all of us. Even those with no appreciation for its history will enjoy the 8-mile trip from the river's entrance to the head of navigation.

In 1634 two small ships filled with colonists sailed up the Potomac River, past the mouth of the St. Marys River and landed briefly on St. Clements Island. There they erected an altar and cross, giving thanks for their safe voyage.

Leaving St. Clements Island, the colonists sailed the *Ark* and the *Dove* up the St. Marys River. Led by Leonard Calvert (brother of Lord Baltimore), they established the colony of Maryland and named the first settlement and provincial capital St. Marys City. In 1695 the provincial capital was moved to Annapolis, a blow that caused the settlement at St. Marys to dwindle and almost disappear into history.

Few traces of the original settlement remain, but an 800-acre outdoor museum, including the reconstructed brick State House, the rebuilt Trinity Episcopal Church, and several other colonial buildings, now occupies the original site. (For more information, see the section on St. Marys City, pages 270–71.)

The approach to the St. Marys River is easy. From Point Lookout to the mouth of the river steer a course to keep you at least ½ mile offshore. This will enable you to clear the few shoals that could cause difficulty. Pass well to the south of the red "2" light at the mouth of Smith Creek to avoid the long shoal off Kitts Point, at the mouth of the St. Marys River.

As you enter the St. Marys, continue to keep at least ½ mile offshore, especially as you approach Fort Point, where an unmarked 3-foot shoal to starboard extends about ½ mile into the river. By the time you get to this point, you should have decided whether you want to put into St. George Creek or continue up the St. Marys River.

As you clear Fort Point (which doesn't look like much of a point) you can see the large Naval Test Facility to starboard. There is a Coast Guard facility located nearby, in St. Inigoes Creek. Although you can't see much of the base, you will see some signs of activity, and you cannot miss the Coast Guard aircraft taking off and landing at the airfield.

About here you have to make another decision regarding your destination. You can proceed up the St. Marys River toward St. Marys City, put into Carthagena Creek for fuel or supplies, or enter St. Inigoes Creek, which has some of the best-protected anchorages on the St. Marys River.

Region 5

St. George Creek

Charts: 12230, **12233**, 12285

Marinas & Restaurants. There are a couple of marinas on this creek, and on the Potomac side of the peninsula, about midway between Piney Point and Straits Point, are the Oakwood Lodge & Dinner Theatre, which are within walking distance. However, unless you plan to visit the Harry Lundeberg Maritime Training School or the Oakwood Lodge, I recommend proceeding to more attractive creeks and anchorages up the St. Marys River. The island at the mouth of the St. George Creek is low and marshy with a few clumps of pines.

Anchorages. If you are planning to continue up or down the Potomac the following day, you could anchor in Price Cove. Its proximity to the Potomac makes it a good spot in which to overnight. Price Cove is near the St. George Creek entrance. It is roomy enough that you won't feel crowded if you share the spot with several other boats. Well protected from weather, the cove still gets a cooling breeze, and it is large enough that you can anchor offshore to avoid becoming an insect luau. Tall trees and a nice shore-side beach add to the cove's attraction. On the down side, a few boats have had trouble getting their anchors to hold in the bottom.

ST. MARYS RIVER

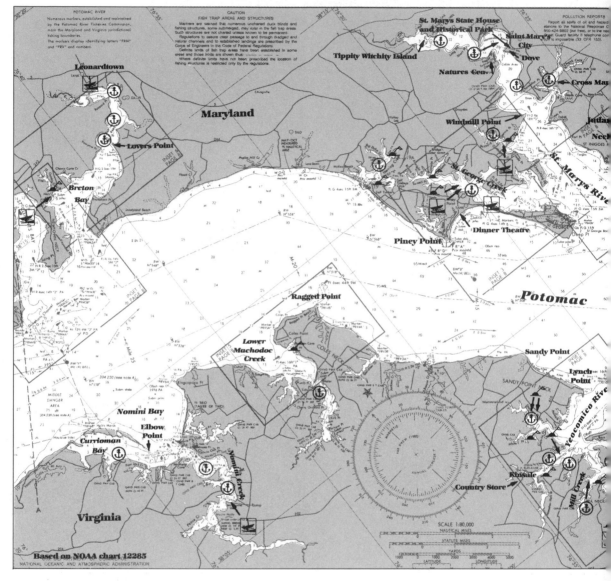

SCALE **1" = 2.65** NAUT. MILES   ⚓ **Good anchoring**   ⚓ **Marina**   🚢 **Launching site**

S T . M A R Y S R I V E R

Carthagena Creek

Charts: 12230, **12233**, 12285

Provisions. The only place on the St. Marys River where supplies are available is Dennis Point Marina, in Carthagena Creek. Just a few

268   years ago, entering this creek was more of an

adventure because it was a little short of markers. Today the entrance is well marked and, if you honor the markers, no trouble to negotiate.

    Approaches. As you approach the flashing green "1" off Edmund Point you can see the first of two green daymarks, "1" and "3," off Graveyard Point. You may have some trouble recognizing them because they tend to blend into the background until you are within ½ mile of them. Leaving the green "3" to port, head directly to-

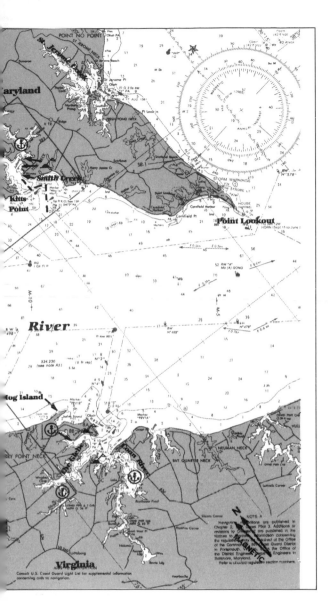

and cooperation of the personnel. This marina has been run by the same family since the early 1970s and reflects that care, interest, and attention.

The shore of Carthagena Creek is wooded, and the entire creek is quiet. You can cruise nearly to the headwaters of the creek, approximately 1 mile past the marina, in 7 feet of water. Except for the marina, there appears to be no convenient place to land, and the banks look pretty muddy.

St. Inigoes Creek

  No facilities

Charts: 12230, **12233**, 12285

Approaches. On the eastern side of the St. Marys River, almost directly opposite the entrance to Carthagena Creek, is St. Inigoes Creek. As you enter St. Inigoes, be sure to stay well off the southern shore. Some shoals protrude well out into the creek there; do not be misled by the sizable dock at the Coast Guard station.

Anchorages. The first anchorage is in the entrance to Molls Cove, which has room for several boats to swing. (There is a shoal on the west side of the shore, but it doesn't bar the entrance.) Holding is good, and the anchorage is sheltered except from the west. Cross Manor, said to be the oldest house in Maryland, is located on the eastern side of Molls Cove. The main house and several of the outbuildings were constructed in 1644, just 10 years after the founding of St. Marys City. This impressive, well-kept structure is not open to the public.

Perhaps the best anchorage in St. Inigoes Creek is beyond the point where Cross Manor stands. Once you clear the point, the creek widens, and you can drop the hook in 10 to 13 feet of water to within 50 yards of shore. On the sandy point nearby is the wreck of what appears to be a steel-hulled boat lying on its side. At low tide less than one-quarter of the boat protrudes above the water. This sandy point is about the only place on St. Inigoes Creek where you can land. The rest of the shore is lined with private homes.

Both Milburn Creek and Church Cove have an anchorage. Be warned that the names of the creeks and coves shown on the chart do not

ward the 15-foot red "4" flasher at the mouth of the creek. Leave the red "4" close to starboard and the green "5" daymark well to port.

Marinas & Restaurants. The fuel dock of Dennis Point Marina lies straight ahead, under the large Gulf sign. In addition to the usual marina facilities (water, fuel, electricity, and slips), Dennis Point Marina has a small snack bar–cocktail lounge and a limited selection of groceries and hardware. On each of our visits we have been impressed by the friendliness

necessarily agree with the local names. For example, what the chart refers to as Molls Cove is locally known as Church Creek. This is one of the rare cases in which local knowledge, normally so valuable, can confuse you or, worse, get you into trouble.

As you leave the mouth of St. Inigoes Creek be sure to honor the lighted "3" marker off Windmill Point. Once you are past Windmill Point, the navigation is straightforward. The entire river contains deep water up to within 50 yards (sometimes less) of the shore.

Chancellor Point

  No facilities

Charts: 12230, **12233**, 12285

Barely 1 mile past the mouth of St. Inigoes Creek, on the east side of the St. Marys River, is a small sandy spit of considerable interest. First, it forms a pocket in the river, providing a surprisingly protected anchorage, even with a 1-mile stretch of the river open to the north. Second, a smooth, sandy beach, open to the public, slopes gently into the water, making for excellent swimming and wading. Third, this is the site of the Chancellors Point Natural History Area & Nature Center. The nature center has an exhibit hall, several nature trails, a picnic area, and a full-time "curator," who is willing to explain the area's indigenous species, both living and fossilized. The natural history area includes a re-creation of a Native American longhouse and an exhibit of the Stone Age tools used to build it.

Those going ashore in midsummer should beware the no-see-ums. While they don't venture far offshore, they will drive you crazy on the beach if you don't use a good repellent. This is the only place on the St. Marys River where we've had problems with these little vampires.

St. Marys City

  – 3 *No facilities*

Charts: 12230, **12233**, 12285

Approach. No visit to the St. Marys River is complete without a visit to Historic St. Marys City. Once you clear Chancellor Point, you can see Church Point, the original site of the city.

Church Point has two landmarks that clearly identify it: Trinity Episcopal Church, on the top of the hill, and the reconstructed redbrick State House, just to the right of the church. Next to the State House some restored houses from the original St. Marys City now house a visitors' center, an exhibit, and a gift shop. Historic St. Marys City includes the *Dove,* a full-size replica of one of the two ships (the other was a supply ship called the *Ark*) that carried the first Maryland colonists. The *Dove,* which is usually tied to a pier directly below the State House, is open to the public for a nominal fee. Built by the well-known Cambridge, Maryland, boatbuilder Jim Richardson, who inspired the boatbuilding section in James Michener's novel *Chesapeake,* the *Dove* is normally staffed by at least one of the crewmembers, if not the master, who will be able to answer any questions about the vessel or its use, often spiced with anecdotes about some of its cruises.

What to See & Do. Historic St. Marys City is an 800-acre living-history museum. Actors play the parts of the villagers and colonists,

The Dove, *a reconstruction by the boatbuilder Jim Richardson of one of the ships that carried the first colonists to Maryland.*

The State House, a reconstruction of the 1676 original. The militia is shown mustering on the river lawn in one of the town's living-history reenactments.

assuming the dress, accents, and attitudes of the period. Their skits never fail to entertain. The museum comprises four exhibit areas: the Brentland Farm Visitor Center, with orientation exhibits, an archaeology exhibit hall, and a gift shop; the Governor's Field, with the *Dove*, the Reconstructed State House of 1676, Farthing's Ordinary (a re-created 17th-century inn and modern outdoor restaurant), and several archaeological sites; the Godiah Spray Tobacco Plantation, a working farm of the 1660s period; and the Chancellor's Point Natural History Area, which is the site of the Chesapeake Indian Lifeways Center. The visitors' center is open daily except on Christmas, Thanksgiving, and New Year's Day. Exhibits are open Wednesday through Sunday from Memorial Day through Labor Day and weekends from the end of March to Memorial Day and from Labor Day to the end of November. The hours are 10:00 A.M. to 5:00 P.M. Wednesday through Sunday. Admission is $7.50 for adults, $6.00 for seniors

and students, and $3.50 for children aged 6 to 12 years.

Anchorages. There is a good anchorage off the dock where the *Dove* is tied up, and a nice beach stretches from the base of the hill to the end of Church Point, where you can land in a dinghy. Alternatively, round Church Point and anchor in the better-protected Horseshoe Bend near the St. Mary's College Boating Center. Sometimes you can tie up at the pier used by the college's sailing fleet long enough to see the local sights. Other than that, there is normally no dockage available at Historic St. Marys City, making anchoring out a necessity if you want to visit the town or the *Dove*.

Headwaters of the St. Marys River

  No facilities

Charts: 12230, **12233**, 12285

Approaches. Past Historic St. Marys City the shores are lined by high, wooded banks and farmland. As you approach the headwaters, you will encounter the improbably named Tippity Witchity Island. Do not pass beyond; the water shoals rapidly, and there is little left of the St. Marys River. As you approach Tippity Witchity Island beware of the ½-foot-depth area to the southeast, where there is supposed to be a wreck.

Anchorages. The best anchorage here is in 7 feet of water to the south-southeast of the island, where you will be sheltered from all but the southeast.

History. Prior to the Civil War this island was called Lynch Island. It seems likely that it was named after the Lynch family, who owned it. There is an interesting story behind its present name. Captain H. W. Howgate, a somewhat disreputable ex-Confederate smuggler, operated several floating bordellos in Washington. In 1879 a flood destroyed most of them, and the survivors were ordered from the city. The good captain purchased the former Lynch Island in the St. Marys River and constructed a gambling house and bar with three bedrooms upstairs dedicated to his "girls." The place was called the Tippling & Witchery House, which quickly corrupted to "Tippity Witchity." Business, dependent on crews from visiting ships, was sporadic, and the doors closed in 1881, just two years later. The house itself persisted into the early 1940s before being destroyed by vandals.

A new house now occupies the site, but it is a private home guarded by a large black dog whose mission is to protect the island from interlopers. Don't try to land.

COAN RIVER

Charts: 12230, **12233**, 12285

Seven miles from Point Lookout, or 13 miles from Smith Point, are the three branches of the Coan River on the Virginia side of the Potomac. Each offers seclusion in well-protected anchorages, and one has marina facilities.

The main entrance to the Coan is marked by the Potomac River 4-second flashing green "5" buoy, about 3 miles offshore. If you are not already familiar with the entrance, use this marker as the starting point for your approach. From here a course of 232 degrees takes you past the nun "2" and nun "4" buoys, which mark the starboard side of the channel into the Coan. From nun "4" take a heading that leaves the lighted 4-second flashing green "5" buoy close to port. The next marker, a red "6" lighted spar, is critical: it marks the end of the long shoal off Travis Point (Lewisetta). Winter ice has taken this spar out more than once. If it is missing, move slowly until you either find a temporary buoy or feel your way around the shoal.

After you clear red "6," swing 90 degrees to starboard and head toward the two red daymarks off Honest Point. A large number of fish stakes and poles mark oyster grounds in this area, so navigate carefully! Usually these stakes are in 8 to 10 feet of water, so grounding should not be a problem. The stakes do tend to confuse you as they seem bereft of pattern and often have no fairways between them. Your best bet is to ignore them and follow the proper navigation markers. As you approach the red "8" daymark, you must choose among the three branches: the main branch, to the south; The Glebe, straight ahead; and Kingscote Creek, to the north. Kingscote Creek is the only branch with marina facilities.

Main Branch

  No facilities

Charts: 12230, **12233**, 12285

Approaches. The entrance to the main branch of the Coan River is a little tight and requires careful attention to the chart, particularly off Walnut Point. Do not assume a straight course between the red "10" and "12" markers; you need to swing to starboard to avoid the shoal.

Anchorages. Many boats choose to anchor just to the south of Walnut Point, but more secluded anchorages lie upstream. There is deep water, 8 to 13 feet, all the way to the headwaters. You have your pick of good places to anchor here. The shores are predominantly wooded with few dwellings. Finding an isolated cove or bight where you can anchor all by yourself should be short work. Low tide reveals a number of sandy beaches where you can land to stretch your legs.

The Glebe

  No facilities

Charts: 12230, **12233**, 12285

Approaches. The entire entrance to The Glebe appears to be blocked by oyster stakes. Don't let them bother you; they are all in deep water. As you enter, stay near the middle of the creek and pick your way through the stakes. Once past this congestion, your passage will be clear, but beware of the unmarked shoals that extend from each point of land.

Anchorages. The first cove to starboard, unnamed on the chart, is called Fishermans Cove locally. You can anchor in its mouth or move around the slight bend to the west. This small anchorage is a perfect, snug place to ride out a storm. Watch out for the unmarked shoal extending to the south from the starboard side of the cove entrance.

The next cove to port has a jumble of oyster stakes at its mouth. A private marker at the edge of the shoal extends to the northwest from the point to port at the mouth of the cove. You can ignore the oyster markers and enter well into this cove if you favor its eastern side. Watch out for the unmarked shoal extending from the south of the cove; it nearly splits the cove in half.

Farther upstream are anchorages galore. You can pull into Wrights Cove or round the bend and anchor in the mouth of Glebe Creek in 7 feet of water. If your draft is less than 5 feet, squeeze through the narrow pass into the headwaters of Glebe Creek, where there is 6 to 8 feet of water. The whole area is well protected from wind and wave in all directions.

Kingscote Creek

Charts: 12230, **12233**, 12285

Provisions. The northern branch of the Coan River, Kingscote Creek, contains a popular harbor at Lewisetta. This is your one stop for fuel, ice, and supplies. An interesting country store is located at the end of a remarkably long dock.

Approaches & Anchorages. Private markers aid your entrance into this creek, but they are not on the chart. If a strong wind from the south to southeast is due, try anchoring farther up the creek, where there is more protection. The wooded banks give the impression of isolation, but the conveniences of Lewisetta are less than a mile away.

YEOCOMICO RIVER

Charts: 12230, 12233, **12285**

The Yeocomico River, 4 miles upstream from the Coan River, offers myriad anchorages and a choice of 10 marinas. The countryside is Chesapeake pretty, and locals are friendly and helpful. The Yeocomico is a very popular stop for yachts. I will mention only a few of the many anchorages. Although all the branches have plenty of water, watch your chart for the shoals that extend from most of the little points of land, not all of them are marked. One other note of caution: Beware of numerous fishing stakes and traps as you approach the mouth of the Yeocomico, especially by Hog Island, in the mouth of Judith Sound to the east. The water is deep, but if you are careless, you could get tangled in the nets while picking your way through.

The flashing red "2" marker about 1 mile to the east of Lynch Point on Sandy Point Neck is the starting point for the entrance to the Yeocomico. The approach is easy because the entrance is broad and deep; however, the fishing and oyster stakes could confuse you. Once you clear the 4-second flashing green "3" marker off Barn Point, you must decide which of the three primary branches of the Yeocomico to enter. The South Yeocomico extends to the south for about 1 mile, then splinters into a spray of creeks and coves. The West Yeocomico extends straight to the west. The Shannon Branch, which extends to the north, offers the least of the three.

South Yeocomico River

Charts: 12230, 12233, **12285**

Approaches. As you clear the green "3" marker, swing to port to head directly for the red "2" daymark at the mouth of the West Yeocomico River. On Mundy Point, just south of the red "2" daymark, are the long, low buildings of the W. J. Courtney fish cannery, now closed. Pass quite close to the docks and you will avoid the long shoal that extends northwest from Tom Jones Point, opposite the cannery.

Anchorages. As you pass the red "4" daymark off Walker Point the river begins to divide. To port is Palmer Cove, an attractive anchorage with 7 to 8 feet of water. The entrance is about 400 yards wide, and inside there is room for a number of boats. The bottom is soft mud, so set your hook accordingly.

To starboard is the entrance to Mill Creek, one of the river's more thickly settled branches. There are no facilities up this creek, just some tidy little homes. However, there is room to anchor if lack of a place to land doesn't bother you.

To port opposite the red "6" daymark is the entrance to Dungan Cove, where you can anchor in relative seclusion with 7 to 9 feet of water. The last time we visited this cove, its shores were still undeveloped.

There are several places to anchor beyond Dungan Cove—just pull over to the side at any place that appeals to you. Our preference, however, would be to head back to Dungan Cove or Palmer Cove for overnight anchorage.

YEOCOMICO RIVER

273

Marinas. If you are in need of fuel, ice, or other services, there are a couple of marinas on this branch of the Yeocomico. On the north shore, opposite Dungan Cove, is Krentz Marine Railway (804-529-6800), which offers fuel, ice, pumpout, and transient slips. On the south shore, just past Dungan Cove, Olverson's Marina (804-529-6868) has fuel, ice, pumpout, and transient slips for powerboats, although it claims 10 feet of water.

West Yeocomico River

Charts: 12230, 12233, **12285**

Approaches. Hold close to the red "2" daymark at the mouth of the West Yeocomico as you swing to starboard to enter the river in order to avoid the shoal that stretches to the north from Mundy Point. Hold to the middle of the river until you are at least 300 yards past the "2" marker or opposite the entrance to Wilkins Creek to port.

Anchorages. Wilkins Creek is readily accessible, so a number of boats choose to anchor there. It is protected and has several sandy beaches at low tide. A small cove immediately past Allen Point also provides ready access to the restaurant at Port Kinsale Marina there. The next cove to starboard, Long Cove, is also a nice anchorage, with a nice sandy beach on the east side of its mouth. Actually, you can anchor just about anywhere in this branch in perfect security. Just pick a spot that strikes your fancy and drop the hook, making sure that you are well away from the center of the creek so that you will not impede traffic.

Marinas & Restaurants. To starboard just inside Horn Point is a little bight that is the home of the Port Kinsale Marina (804-472-2514) and the Moorings (804-472-2971), a little restaurant with excellent food. You can tie up at the marina for fuel, supplies, or a meal. As an alternative you can pass just a little farther upstream, anchor in the next little bight, and then land by dinghy.

Kinsale, the leading town on the Yeocomico, is at the head of this branch. The marina there,

Kinsale Harbour Yacht Club (804-472-2514), reopened as of 1998. We were lucky enough to be there one June when a special country jamboree was being held. We anchored near the town and were serenaded for hours by the sounds of bluegrass.

Shannon Branch

Charts: 12230, 12233, **12285**

Approaches. This branch of the Yeocomico is easy to enter. As you clear the green "3" marker swing to starboard, leaving the green "5" of Shannon Branch close to port. There is deep water fairly close to both shores, and you can hold close to White Point if you wish.

Marinas. The Shannon Branch is the way to White Point Marina (804-472-2977), on White Point Creek. It has fuel, a pool, and a small marine-supply store. We were well treated here.

Sandy Point Marina (804-472-3237) is on the northeast shore, opposite the mouth of White Point Creek. It has a dockside sewage pumpout facility in addition to the conventional marina facilities.

Anchorages. There is a pretty anchorage in 9 feet of water just north of the bar between White Point Creek and Shannon Branch, but to our minds the Shannon Branch cannot stand up to the competition from the South and West Yeocomico Rivers.

HERRING CREEK

Charts: 12230, 12233, **12285**

Almost invisible from the Potomac, Herring Creek is located about 2½ miles above Piney Point on the Maryland side of the river. Once you know that it's there, it's surprisingly easy to approach and enter. Run up the coast, staying a prudent distance offshore, until you can see the pair of flashing 15-foot-high navigation markers and the jetties at the narrow entrance to the creek.

Approach. The entrance channel seems to have stabilized at 6 feet, which permits passage to most cruising boats. Inside the creek the depth ranges from 7 to 8 feet in the middle, with outcropping shoals around the periphery.

Anchorages. Anchor where you will; it is all well protected from wind and wave. There is room for plenty of boats to swing. Be sure to put up a good anchor light since you can expect some traffic well after dark.

Marinas & Restaurants. Tall Timbers Marina (301-994-1508) is to starboard just inside the entrance. Head for it if you need gasoline or supplies. The marina often has a transient slip for the night, but call in advance to be certain. If you are in the vicinity on Friday night, be sure to try the buffet at the Reluctant Navigator.

Cedar Cove Marina (301-994-1155) is straight ahead, near the creek's headwaters. It offers gasoline and engine and hull repairs. Make a careful approach; the depth nearby is 5 feet with only 4 feet alongside.

LOWER MACHODOC CREEK

Charts: 12230, 12233, **12285**

Lower Machodoc Creek, 11 miles above the Yeocomico, is exposed to the northwest, unless you squeeze around the narrow sand spit labeled "Narrow Beach" on the chart.

Approach. Note that the Fl G 4s "1" light at the entrance to Lower Machodoc Creek is very close to the green "1" daymark indicating the start of the channel into Branson Cove. Since they are both green, that they have the same numeral is only a little confusing.

Provisions. You can get supplies at any of the three marinas in Branson Cove, just inside the entrance. A short distance from the marinas is the Driftwood Restaurant (804-472-3892), where you can get a great meal at a

good price. The dining room is small, so you may have to wait. Reservations are a must on Saturday night. Groceries and facilities are also available up the creek at the town of Hague.

Fuel and marine supplies are available at Branson Cove Marina (804-472-3866), immediately to the south after you emerge from the narrow channel into Branson Cove.

Anchorages. If you do squeeze past Narrow Beach Point by markers "4" and "6," you will come upon a well-protected anchorage with 7 to 10 feet of water. You have to feel your way through the narrow channel off the tip of the point. Hold close to the red markers, then favor the side opposite the point in order to clear the shoal extending to the south from the tip of the point. A couple of private stakes in the water mark the two shoals south of the tip of the sand spit.

You can anchor anywhere past the point; we recommend the cove inside the sand spit. There is 7 to 14 feet of water in this part of the creek and at least 6 feet of water as far as Parham Point, which was a sidewheeler steamer dock from 1900 until World War I.

Stay out of Glebe Creek; there's precious little water in it, and there is a 1-foot shoal at the entrance.

NOMINI BAY & CREEK

Charts: 12230, 12233, **12285**

About 3 miles above Lower Machodoc Creek is Nomini Bay. The entrance channel to Nomini Creek is tight—attempt it only in good visibility. The markers, which are sometimes hard to see, must be followed religiously.

Nomini Creek

Charts: 12230, 12233, **12285**

Approaches. Once you pass the entrance, the creek opens up and several attractive anchorages present themselves. Pay careful attention to the chart. You have to contend with several unmarked shoals as well as numerous oyster stakes, not to be mistaken for channel markers.

Once you pick up the lighted green "1" marker at the entrance, the channel is well marked and straight until you reach the lighted green "5" marker, off Icehouse Point. From there it bends to starboard and runs straight to the red "8" daymark, off Hickory Point. Red "8" can be hard to see. If you cannot find it from green "5," point your bow at the white house in the trees on the odd-shaped point about 1 mile ahead, where the creek bends sharply to the east. (On the chart this point resembles a crab's claw.) After you clear red "8," you have to negotiate past the oyster stakes; then you are in the clear. Give the "crab claw" point wide berth to avoid the shoal that extends to the north of it. After you pass the tip of the claw, hold close to the western shore to avoid the 1-foot shoal and (probably submerged) piling on the opposite shore. Then just keep to the middle.

Anchorages & What to See & Do. This is a picturesque anchorage. If you are even an occasional tourist, you should put into Mount Holly and take the short taxi ride to Stratford and Wakefield, the birthplaces of Robert E. Lee and George Washington, respectively. Dock space for boats drawing under 4 feet is available at the Mount Holly Steamboat Inn for those visiting the restaurant. Motorlaunch service is available for boats anchored off the dock.

If you need supplies, try McGuires Wharf, or put in at Nomini just past the swing bridge (vertical clearance 5 feet when closed).

Pierce Creek, beyond Mount Holly, is shallow, accessible only to boats drawing well under 4 feet.

CURRIOMAN BAY

Charts: 12230, 12233, **12285**

At the mouth of Nomini Creek is the entrance to Currioman Bay. It is reputed to be well marked—we haven't tried it—and I've been told that if you manage to pick up the correct red "2" nun (the first one to starboard, not the red "2" for Nomini Creek) and don't get confused by the markers at the Nomini Creek entrance to Currioman Bay isn't

all that difficult. Beware of the long, narrow, submerged tip of Elbow Point to starboard.

The bay is too open to be comfortable if the weather turns bad. If you are looking for supplies or a secure, protected anchorage, Nomini Creek is much to be preferred. On the other hand, the protecting bar on the Potomac side of the bay offers you an isolated beach and a good place to stretch your legs. Try wading out on Elbow Point just to see how far it goes.

BRETON & ST. CLEMENTS BAYS

Charts: 12230, 12233, **12285**

On the Maryland side of the Potomac, 6 miles across the river from Lower Machodoc Creek, Breton Bay and St. Clements Bay share a common approach. They also share a reputation for some of the best cruising waters on the Potomac.

The approach is marked by a red-green nun. While you may pass to either side of this nun, beware of Heron Island Bar, to the west, all that remains of its namesake island. The eastern side of this shoal is indicated solely by a privately maintained marker.

Breton Bay

Charts: 12230, 12233, **12285**

Approaches. From the red-green buoy a course of 027 degrees takes you past the red "2" light marking the mouth of Breton Bay directly to the red "4" daymark inside. Just inside the entrance, Combs Creek and Cherry Cove Creek offer yachtsmen facilities (except diesel fuel). Although the chart indicates that the entrances are unmarked, both creeks have private markers that make the entrance fairly easy. There is about 7 feet of water inside, although the channels are reputed to be no deeper than 5 feet. *Warning: If you do go into Combs Creek, watch out for the overhead power cable (vertical clearance 50 feet) just past Combs Creek Marina.*

Anchorages. The upper portion of Breton Bay offers several good anchorages along the northern shore, just below Leonardtown.

Watch out for the shoal off Lovers Point, marked by the flashing red "8" light, and the obstruction reported to be about 400 yards north of the marker.

Breton Bay is navigable all the way up to and a little beyond Leonardtown Wharf. Beyond this point, there simply isn't any more water, in either a horizontal or a vertical direction.

St. Clements Bay

Charts: 12285, **12286**

History. In 1634 the original Maryland colonists, arriving on the *Ark* and the *Dove*, erected a wooden cross on the southern tip of St. Clements Island, at the mouth of St. Clements Bay, in thanks for their safe crossing of the Atlantic Ocean. Shortly after that

the colonists sailed back to the St. Marys River to found St. Marys City. The original cross is long gone, but a large, new, stone cross was erected in 1934 in memory of that first landing. The new cross provides a landmark that unquestionably identifies the island from a long way off.

Approaches. The large cross on St. Clements not only clearly identifies the island but also serves to warn cruisers headed upriver that they are about to enter the lower limit of what is called the Middle Danger Area. This is a region that has been established to permit firing in this portion of the Potomac by the U.S. Naval Weapons Laboratory at Dahlgren, Virginia. Boats may not enter this area while firing is in progress without the permission of a Navy range boat. These boats can be identified by a square red flag during daylight hours and by a 32-point red light at the masthead at night. If you see one of these boats, you can ask for instructions regarding where you can and

St. Clements Island—Potomac River Museum

Aerial view of St. Clements Island. The island is accessible only by boat.

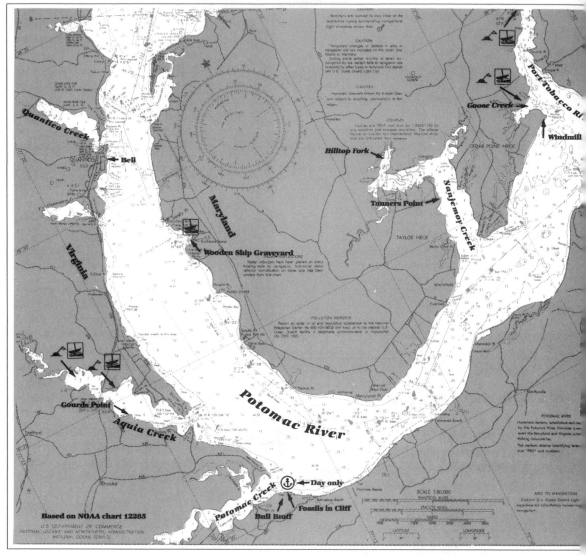

SCALE **1" = 2.78** NAUT. MILES ⚓ **Good anchoring**   ⛵ **Marina**   ⛵ **Launching site**

cannot go. Don't get too worried; this area is rarely used for firing. In fact, I suspect that it is no longer in active use.

The entrance to St. Clements Bay requires careful navigation, mostly due to the Heron Island Bar (see under Approaches for Breton Bay). However, it is well marked, and a little care will keep you out of trouble.

Anchorages. There are several creeks with good anchorages on the western side of St. Clements Bay. All are easily accessible and have at least 6 feet of water.

278

The first is St. Patrick Creek. This is the one to choose if you need marina facilities. The privately marked entrance and channel are fairly narrow. There has been some shoaling, so I am unsure of the present depth. There is no good place to anchor, but you can spend the night at a transient slip, usually available at Kopel's Marina (410-769-3121) or Cather Marine (410-769-3335). Kopel's will supply a courtesy car if you need transportation to a nearby restaurant. If you prefer to swing at your own hook, find another creek.

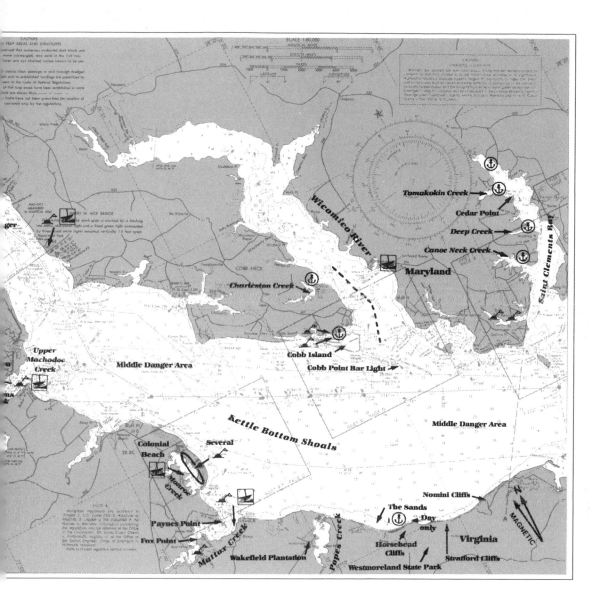

The next creek is Canoe Neck Creek. The entrance is wide and easy, and there are a number of bights with good anchorages. Skip the first two little coves to port; both are chock-full of homes and boat docks, and the second one has a 2-foot bar at its entrance. The rest of Canoe Neck Creek is more inviting. Perhaps the nicest anchorage here is in the first cove to starboard, on the north shore. An extensive shoal projects from the point on the southeast side, so keep well to port as you enter. This anchorage offers relative seclusion, and at low tide you can land on some of the beaches on the

eastern side of the cove. The second cove on the north side is also secluded; there is a single house with a dock at the end of the cove. Actually, you can anchor anywhere in Canoe Neck Creek in complete safety; these are my top choices.

Next is Deep Creek. Although Canoe Neck Creek has more area and bights, Deep Creek has a reputation for more scenery. This single, nearly straight creek doesn't have the usual protecting shoal at its entrance. You could probably enter blindfolded. Regardless, you can anchor anywhere inside.

The last creek, Tomakokin Creek, is the least built up of the three. This little creek is to port as you round the "5" light off Cedar Point. You can proceed about half the creek's length before it shoals. Tomakokin is somewhat exposed to the east, but this far up St. Clements Bay you could probably anchor anywhere in full security.

WICOMICO RIVER

Charts: 12285, **12286**

Slightly more than 4 miles past St. Clements Island is the mouth of one of the four Wicomico Rivers on the Chesapeake. This one has many outlying shoals and no navigable creeks or well-sheltered anchorages, except for Neal Sound, directly north of Cobb Island at the mouth. (Note: The chart shows a reported obstruction to the southwest of Cobb Point Bar Light. Steer clear of that area; ruins and piles lurk just below the surface.)

Neal Sound (Cobb Island)

Charts: 12285, **12286**

Approaches. With the possible exception of Mattox Creek, on the Virginia side of the Potomac, Neal Sound is the last available port for a considerable distance for vessels going up the Potomac. If you are in a boat drawing 4 feet or less, you can enter from the downstream side and leave by the upstream channel, saving quite a distance. (The fixed bridge between the mainland and Cobb Island has a vertical clearance of 18 feet, which effectively prevents sailboats from using this passage.) If you draw more than 4 feet, use only the downstream side. Even then, refer to a current chart and watch out for shoaling near daymark "4." Recent reports indicate that the upper channel is now badly silted in. The entrance to the Wicomico River is well marked and easy to follow if you keep your wits about you. From the red-green nun southeast of the 18-foot-high flashing "1W" on Cobb Point Bar a

course of 357 degrees takes you to the red "2W" daymark. From red "2W" a course of 337 degrees takes you to the flashing green "3W" at the eastern (downstream) entrance to Neal Sound.

From the Fl G "3W" head for the Fl R "2" at the dredged entrance to the Cobb Island Channel. Leave red "2" and the next daymark, red "4," to starboard. Favor the port side of the sound where the water is deepest.

Marinas & Restaurants. Sailboats must berth at marinas located below the fixed bridge between Cobb Island and the mainland, but powerboats can enter the marinas above the bridge. The best anchorage and shore facilities are found in the basin east of (below) the bridge.

Cobb Island Marina (301-259-2879), the last on the left before reaching the bridge, has excellent facilities, including a restaurant, the Portside, and a self-service laundry. Nearby is a grocery store, Cobb Island Market. I recommend a walking tour of the island—it is a pleasant walk, and the islanders are particularly friendly.

Shymansky's Marina (301-259-2221), on the north side at the bridge, offers all the facilities you are likely to need, including a marine store, Shymansky's restaurant, and limited groceries.

Just west of the north end of the bridge is Captain John's Crabhouse & Marina (301-259-2315), where you can get lots of (what else?) crabs. Also available are a small marine store and limited groceries.

Upper Wicomico River

 No facilities

Charts: 12285, **12286**

Approaches. If you choose to explore the rest of the Wicomico, a course of 11 degrees from "2W" at the river's mouth takes you to the flashing green "5W." From there swing to a course of 357 degrees to avoid White Point Bar to starboard and head on up the river.

Anchorages. If you draw less than 5 feet, Charleston Creek, to the west of green "7W," offers the only protected anchorage on the rest of the river. While it is possible to proceed considerably farther up the Wicomico River, the numerous shoals and obstructions and lack of sheltered anchorages make doing so less appealing.

POPES CREEK

Charts: 12285, **12286**

Between Nomini Bay and Popes Creek are the high Nomini, Stratford, and Horsehead Cliffs, where you can search for fossils, much like at the Chesapeake's better-known Calvert Cliffs. Behind the Horsehead Cliffs is the 1,300-acre Westmoreland State Park, well worth climbing the cliffs to visit. (A path leads upward from the beachside picnic grove at the area labeled "The Sands" on the chart.) The park has cabins, camping, hiking trails, and a boat ramp. You can swim at the beach or in the new Olympic-size swimming pool.

At Popes Creek is the Washington's Birthplace National Monument (shown on the chart as northwest of Popes Creek). Wakefield is not only a national monument but also a working 18th-century plantation with a Georgian-style manor house (the original burned long ago), the family burial plot, and a picnic area. You may try to take a dinghy in, but even by dinghy there is no good place to land. (It's a 3-mile walk from The Sands.) Popes Creek itself is inaccessible by water, but Mattox Creek, a couple of miles upstream, offers a quiet anchorage, and you can visit Wakefield from there.

MATTOX & MONROE CREEKS

Charts: 12285, **12286**

Mattox and Monroe Creeks share a common approach, and both offer well-protected anchorages and many marinas. The navigational aids serving these two creeks are somewhat difficult to see against the shoreline as you approach.

Mattox Creek

Charts: 12285, **12286**

Mattox Creek is easily identified by the two large tanks on Paynes Point, on the north side of its entrance. This creek offers a quiet, protected anchorage and all the marine facilities that you are likely to need during a short stay. The entrance is easy, and the channel is well marked. The channel has 6 to 7 feet of water most of the way in; however, boats with a draft of more than 5 feet should not proceed much beyond Fox Point.

Just past Fox Point is the Harbor View Marina & Resort, which is open to the public. Cruisers have a variety of services here, including a self-service laundry and a dockside sewage pumpout facility in addition to the usual amenities. There are also a grocery and a marine-supply store at the marina.

You can either tie up at the fuel dock to arrange for a slip for the night or anchor out just about anywhere in the creek. Swimming is reputed to be good, and the scenery is easy on the eye.

Monroe Creek (Colonial Beach)

  All facilities

Charts: 12285, **12286**

Approaches. If you approach Monroe Creek from the flashing 4-second red "2" east of Gum Bar Point, leave red "4" well to starboard and assume a course of 230 degrees to take you down the middle of the approach to Mattox and Monroe Creeks until you are on a line between Mattox Creek green "1" and Monroe Creek red "4." Then a course of 323 degrees takes you directly to red "4" and the narrow entrance channel into the harbor. Favor the port side of the entrance to avoid the shoals that extend westward from the spit to starboard. This entrance can be subject to strong currents. Plan to pass through when the current is not running strongly. You need a considerable amount of power to buck an adverse tidal current in this area.

Marinas, Restaurants, & What to See & Do. Colonial Beach, on the long peninsula between the creek and the Potomac, has facilities for residents and transients alike, including full-service marinas and restaurants with their own docks. This is the last diesel-fuel source for deep-draft boats (more than 5 feet) until the marinas in Washington. It also serves well as a base from which to branch out and visit nearby historic sites. Monroe Creek is a logical stopping point both for breaking the long run to Washington and for resupplying your boat.

Colonial Beach came into its own as a resort around 1882, and by 1911 it was serviced regularly by the famous side-wheel steamboats. In the 1950s a long pier extended out into the Potomac, capitalizing on the fact that the Maryland border extended along the Virginia side of the Potomac. This was significant because gambling was legal in Maryland but not in Virginia. The pier burned down but was never rebuilt because the laws changed, negating the need for this feature. Colonial Beach is still a popular resort area, drawing people from far and wide, especially for its Potomac River Festival and outdoor art festival.

The first marina to starboard, Colonial Beach Yacht Center (804-224-7230), claims to have about 10 feet of water at the fuel dock and 4 to 10 feet elsewhere. There are at least six more marinas located here, but CBYC offers the most complete services. Facilities farther up the creek offer restaurants, motels, and other amenities for the cruiser. Be careful of the depth; it gets iffier the farther up you go. Do not

anchor out without a great deal of care; there's very little water outside the marked channel. The wiser course is to take a slip for the night or go back to Mattox Creek and anchor there.

The town residents are friendly and helpful, and the tree-lined streets make for pleasant walking. This is the place to get taxis for the drive to Wakefield or Lee's birthplace, Stratford Hall, which has a working gristmill, in addition to more conventional restorations.

UPPER MACHODOC CREEK
Charts: 12285, **12286**, 12287

Seven miles above Mattox Creek is Upper Machodoc Creek, occupied by the U.S. Naval Weapons Laboratory at Dahlgren. Once a prohibited area, it is no longer restricted.

The approach to this creek should start from the flashing 4-second green "29" buoy near the middle of the Potomac River. There is an inshore approach, but I prefer the middle of the river. From green "29" simply follow the markers into the creek.

Boats drawing less than 5 feet can get supplies at Dahlgren Marine Works, near the headwaters, past the Coast Guard station to starboard.

The middle of the creek has 5 feet of water to just beyond the first bend. It shoals toward the sides and in Williams Creek.

PORT TOBACCO RIVER TO WASHINGTON

PORT TOBACCO RIVER

Charts: 12285, **12288**

Continuing upstream from Upper Machodoc Creek, you pass under the Route 301 bridge, which has a vertical clearance of more than 100 feet. Shortly after passing this bridge, you enter the Upper Danger Area, similar to the Middle Danger Area mentioned earlier and with the same caveats. Pay attention to the channel markers in the Potomac; there are several unmarked shoals.

Approach. The Port Tobacco River, which is on the Maryland side where the Potomac makes a sharp bend to the west 5 miles above the bridge, is a pretty place. It is, however, too open to the north and south to be a comfortable anchorage except under optimum conditions. The holding ground is somewhat uncertain. Observe all daymarks in this river, particularly the green "1" off Windmill Point at its mouth.

Marinas & Restaurants. Goose Bay Marina (301-934-3812) in Goose Creek, to port after you clear green "1," is accessible only to vessels with a shoal draft. Port Tobacco Marina (301-870-3133) is at the headwaters. Both are better avoided by anyone with a draft of 4 feet or more in spite of claims by Port Tobacco Marina that the controlling depth in its facility is at least 5 feet. I'm afraid I don't believe it. However, if you can make it that far, the huge Turf Club & Restaurant offers lunch and dinner, an outside Tiki bar, and a great view of the river.

What to See & Do. High on a hill at Chapel Point, overlooking the river, is the St. Ignatius Catholic Church, built in the early 18th century. The view from the hilltop is worth the climb.

The town of Port Tobacco, now a short distance beyond the headwaters of the river, was a busy port in early colonial times. Even though it was a major tobacco shipping port in the 1700s, the origin of the town's name had little to do with tobacco. It is a corruption of the name of a local Native American village, variously reported as Potapaco or Pertafacco.

Anchorage. Once you pass Fourth Point at red "4," you can anchor in reasonable security. However, beware of the 3-foot spot about 400 yards north of the tip of Fourth Point. Head directly from red "4" to red "6" to leave it to port, but watch your depth. There are other shoals in the area, all of which are essentially unmarked.

NANJEMOY CREEK

Charts: 12285, **12288**

The next creek on the Maryland side, Nanjemoy Creek, got its name from a Native American word for "poor fishing." The tendency of the water to get a little thin and a maze of fishing structures, especially at the entrance, greatly reduces the creek's appeal. Blossom Point Proving Grounds is on the point to the east of the creek entrance, as is a 287-acre wildlife sanctuary operated by the Maryland Nature Conservancy. Possibly as a result, this is one of the least populated creeks off the Potomac.

John Wilkes Booth rowed across at Blossom Point during his flight from the capital after shooting Lincoln.

I have been told that depths in the Nanjemoy are greater than indicated by the chart. However, unless you draw well under 5 feet, navigation is going to be touchy. If you try it, hug the eastern shore on your way in until you find the locally maintained buoys near Tanners Point. These will take you the rest of the way up the creek to near Hilltop Fork if your draft is 3 feet or less. Beyond the fork, get out and walk!

Gunkholers may like to poke in here once, but they won't find any good anchorages. The Nanjemoy is an unspoiled creek that would be quite attractive if it only had a bit more water.

POTOMAC CREEK

Charts: 12285, **12288**

Potomac Creek, 9 miles beyond Nanjemoy Creek on the Virginia side, features a tight entrance, big mosquitoes, and thin water. If you draw 4 feet or more, stay out.

For the amateur archaeologist, Bull Bluff, on the south side of the entrance, offers the possibility of finding fossilized sharks' teeth. You can anchor quite close to shore in 6 to 7 feet of water, but the area is exposed, so I don't recommend staying overnight. This is also one of many sites that claim to be where Pocahontas saved Captain John Smith from her father, Chief Powhatan.

Waugh Point

Charts: 12285, **12288**

Waugh Point Marina, on the south shore of the creek near green daymark "5," reportedly has at least 6 feet of water alongside the gas dock (no diesel), but I have not verified this. It does have a dockside sewage pumpout facility.

AQUIA & QUANTICO CREEKS

Charts: 12285, **12288**

Three miles above Potomac Creek, still on the Virginia side of the river, is Aquia Creek. About 8 miles above Aquia Creek is the Quantico Marine Base, just before Quantico Creek. Do not attempt to anchor in the mouth of Quantico Creek—aside from the shoals, there is a noisy railroad line nearby; the main creek is unnavigable.

Aquia Creek

Charts: 12285, **12288**

Aquia is a reasonable anchorage for boats with drafts of less than 5 feet, although it shoals quickly outside the narrow channel. If you draw less than 4 feet, you can proceed upstream as far as the fixed bridge (vertical clearance 26 feet), just over 2 miles from the creek mouth.

There are a couple of marinas near Gourds Point, on the south side—Aquia Creek Marina & Boatyard (by the point, 703-659-2745) and Willow Landing Marina (703-659-2653)—and another, Aquia Harbor Marina, past the fixed bridge. I am not sure of the approach depths, but they are reputed to be between 3 and 4 feet. The Aquia Harbor Marina has a ramp, 50 slips, showers, and a shoreside pool.

THE MISBEGOTTEN WOODEN WARSHIPS

On the Maryland side of the Potomac, about 5 miles above the mouth of Aquia Creek, lies a monument to bureaucratic stupidity, the remains of more than 100 wooden hulls of would-be freighters constructed during World War I. This area is not an anchorage, nor is it a place to take anything other than a dinghy for a closer look. However, if you are on the Potomac, swing by and take a look.

The United States entered World War I in April 1917, nearly three years after its start. The German submarine campaign had destroyed so much shipping that the United States, under the newly formed United States Shipping Board, hastily developed a bold scheme to build and deploy a fleet of quickly and cheaply constructed wooden steamers. The theory was that the ships could be built with semiskilled labor and would not tie up the shipyards engaged in steel ship construction.

The Emergency Fleet Corporation, which was established to execute the task, was unable to live up to the theory's promise. The entire effort was mismanaged and uncoordinated. There were innumerable delays, and costs skyrocketed.

The original plans called for the construction of approximately 1,000 ships in 18 months! However, it took 8 months just to place the contracts for the first 300 vessels. Within a month after that the program was a case study in bureaucratic entropy. The wrong timber had been purchased for keels and hulls, and the proper timbers were only available from West Coast lumber contractors. Railway shipping of the needed timbers from the West Coast was soon at a near standstill because transportation priorities had been improperly planned. As a result, a parallel West Coast program for wooden ships was initiated. Controversy and infighting between the two programs was rampant. The U.S. Navy refused to man the vessels, charging that the ships were not seaworthy. The resulting design changes increased the costs and the length of the delays.

When Germany surrendered in November 1918, only 134 ships had been completed. Only 76 had ever carried any cargo, and these were in the Pacific; not one had been deployed to Europe, the original purpose of the program. The ships leaked and could not carry enough cargo to justify their operating expenses. Even so, by mid-1919, 174 wooden ships were in operation, with more on the way.

After the war most of the ships were mothballed in the James River, kept afloat only by constant effort. Finally, some 200 were sold for scrap. These were towed from the James and up the Potomac to Alexandria, where they were stripped of machinery and equipment and returned downriver for disposal. Tied together with a steel cable, they were burned to the waterline at Widewater, on the Virginia side of the Potomac, then towed across the river to Mallows Bay, where salvage crews removed much of the metal.

The fleet was forgotten until the 1930s, when the ships were searched again to recover any remaining scrap metal. The scrap was sold to metal-hungry Japan, and much of it came back to the United States as shells and other weaponry during World War II. The number of salvagers and, during Prohibition, bootlegging operators in Mallows Bay caused a local population explosion. Well-managed, very coordinated entrepreneurs anchored five houseboats in or near the "Reservoir" part of Mallows Bay. These floating brothels were known as Potomac River arks. At least one of these boats is still visible, aground on the south side of the mouth of the reservoir.

You still can see the hulks of Mallows Bay's misbegotten fleet, as well as some more recently abandoned boats and barges, in the reservoir. Some hulls are difficult to recognize; nature has reclaimed them, turning a war effort into life-supporting islands of bushes and trees.

Region 5

Quantico Marine Basin

Charts: 12285, **12288**

The boat basin, maintained by Quantico Marine Base, is just before Quantico Creek. It is indicated on the chart by the word *bell*. You must get permission from the harbormaster to tie up or use a mooring in Quantico Marine Basin. Beware of strong currents near the approaches to the basin.

UPPER POTOMAC RIVER

Charts: 12285, **12288**

This portion of the river does not offer great cruising but makes up for that lack by offering plenty to do. Despite increased development, there are still plenty of anchorages in addition to the expected yacht clubs and marinas.

Mattawoman Creek

Charts: 12285, **12288**

Mattawoman Creek to Washington, D.C.

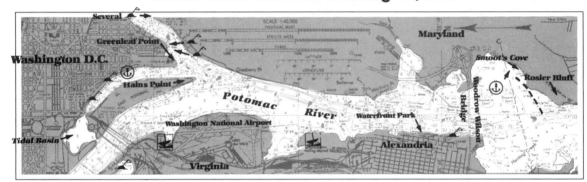

SCALE **1"=1.34** NAUT. MILES

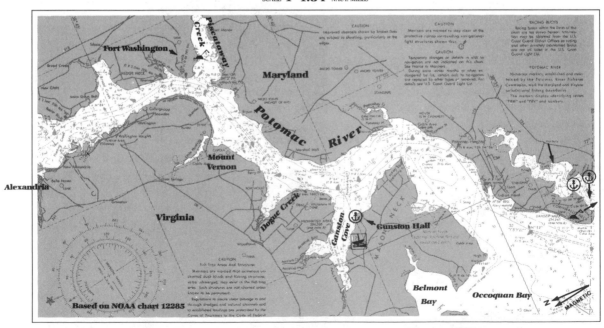

Based on NOAA chart 12285

286   SCALE **1" = 2.64** NAUT. MILES   ⚓ **Good anchoring**   ⚓ **Marina**   🛥 **Launching site**

About 4 miles above Quantico, on the Maryland side of the Potomac, is Mattawoman Creek, with its mouth flanked by the Naval Ordnance Station on the north and the Naval Ordnance Disposal Facility to the south. This is probably the first anchorage where you will encounter weekend cruisers from Washington.

Anchorages. The outer portion of the creek is convenient for anchoring, but it is exposed to the northwest. Better shelter lies farther up the creek. Proceed carefully to avoid grounding, especially on the 3-foot spot between the "5" light and Grinders Wharf. There is a good anchorage just west of Bullitt Neck, but the water shoals rather quickly in this area. Virtually any cruising sailboat will have trouble in this vicinity. You can land at either Marsh Island or Thorofare Island to explore. Throughout the creek the banks are heavily wooded, and the houses are fairly well screened from view by shrubbery, giving a semblance of seclusion.

Marinas & What to See & Do. Just past the first point to starboard on the way in is a small promontory labeled Sweden Point on the chart. This is part of Smallwood State Park (often confused with Fort Smallwood State Park, in the mouth of the Patapsco River), developed by the state of Maryland. In August 1990 the park opened Sweden Point Marina, a 50-slip marina with full facilities (showers, self-service laundry, etc.); the marina eventually will have 200 slips. To ascertain the status of the marina, call the park at 301-743-7613. Each October the marina hosts the Big Kmart Bassmaster top 150 Tournament, perhaps the biggest professional bass tournament on the East Coast. There is a small shop for fishing gear and sandwiches. The highlight of Smallwood State Park is Smallwood's Retreat, the home of General William Smallwood, who was a Revolutionary War hero and Maryland's fourth governor. The original all-brick structure dated from 1762; the present reconstruction, which is completely furnished with period pieces, is open on weekends and holidays from May to September. Guided tours are offered on Sundays from 1:00 to 5:00 P.M. from April through mid-October.

Next to the marina is the Mattawoman Creek Art Center (301-743-5159), which houses not only collections of paintings, sculpture, pottery, graphic arts, textiles, and folk arts but also artists' studios, where you can probably meet and observe local artists at work. It is open Friday through Sunday from 1:00 to 5:00 P.M. year-round.

Technically, you can continue for another mile beyond Grinders Wharf in at least 7 to 8 feet of water, but the narrow, winding channel is unmarked and probably will appeal only to the confirmed gunkholer. It makes for an attractive trip, moving through lily pads and past wooded banks, but a nerve-racking one.

Occoquan River

Charts: **12285**, 12289

On the Virginia side, the Occoquan River offers well-sheltered anchorages, all very far up a narrow channel beyond the first bridge (vertical clearance 65 feet). The channel is reasonably well marked, and a depth of greater than 10 feet is supposedly maintained since the channel is used by commercial barges. In fact, the portion of the channel that passes through Occoquan Bay has doubtful depths. Boats with more than a 4-foot draft are advised to proceed with extreme caution. Be sure to stay in the narrow, marked channel as the water quickly shoals to less than 2 feet outside the channel.

Swimming is good, but holding is poor, and there is a current to contend with.

If you carry less than a 4-foot draft, the southern quarter of Belmont Bay offers a possible alternative anchorage, but you must cross a 3-foot bar to get there.

Although numerous large powerboats and sailboats call the Occoquan home, we do not recommend it for the transient cruiser.

Gunston Cove

 No facilities

Charts: 12285, **12289**

Approaches. Gunston Cove, bordered on the north by Fort Belvoir, offers a fairly well protected anchorage in 6 feet of water once you are well into it. The mouth is marked by red nun "2" near the southwest shore inside Hallowing

Point. The rest of the cove is unmarked; you have to feel your way past the entrance shoals, a relatively easy matter.

Anchorages & Facilities. Once past the Gunston Hall Estate, you can anchor just about anywhere close to the southwest shore. You cannot anchor in the wide pipeline area down the middle of the cove, and the Fort Belvoir restricted area takes up the entire northern quadrant. Pohick Bay Regional Park, well into the cove, has picnic facilities, a launching ramp, and a small dock (for very small, shallow-draft boats only).

What to See & Do. Gunston Hall, the home of George Mason (author of the Virginia Declaration of Rights and Constitution and a contemporary of George Washington), is within walking distance of the boat-launching area. If your draft is more than 2 feet and you want to go ashore, you have to land by dinghy. This colonial mansion, built in 1755, has been beautifully restored and preserved by the state of Virginia in concert with the Colonial Dames of America. There are guided tours of the building, and there is a classic boxwood garden on the side toward the river. It is open daily 9:30 A.M. to 5:00 P.M., except Thanksgiving, Christmas Day, and New Year's Day. Admission is about $5 for adults, $1.50 for children.

Dogue Creek

Charts: 12285, **12289**

A small military marina maintained by Fort Belvoir is located well up this narrow and shallow creek. You may visit the post, but the marina is not open to the public.

The Mount Vernon Yacht Club is on the north shore of the creek. There is a 50-foot-wide channel with 6 to 8 feet of water from the Potomac to the yacht club dock, where gas is available if you are in dire need. The yacht club welcomes transients who have an affiliation with another recognized yacht club.

The rest of Dogue Creek is quite shallow. Do not attempt it if you carry a draft of 3 feet or more; even then, be prepared to feel your way in and proceed slowly. This is not an anchorage.

Mount Vernon

 No facilities

Charts: 12285, **12289**

About 1½ miles past Dogue Creek, on the Virginia side of the Potomac, is Mount Vernon, the home of George Washington. There is a dock where you can tie up temporarily if you want to visit the estate, but you cannot spend the night. The narrow but well-marked channel that you must follow to approach the dock from the main part of the Potomac is supposed to have at least 6 feet of water (9 feet in 1984), but I suggest soliciting recent local knowledge if you are in a deep-draft vessel. The north side of the dock is reserved for visiting private boats. There is an easily recognized cupola at the end of the docks. Visiting yachtsmen are welcomed by a security guard, who collects the admission fee for visiting the grounds, if they have made the necessary arrangements in advance (703-780-2000). Note: Prior arrangement is necessary for docking here.

Mount Vernon is open every day of the year, including Christmas. The hours are 9:00 A.M. to 5:00 P.M. from March through October and 9:00 A.M. to 4:00 P.M. from November through February. In addition to touring the grounds and mansion, you can talk to museum "interpreters," who can give detailed accounts of Washington's life at Mount Vernon and answer any questions. At least two hours are suggested for the tour.

Piscataway Creek

Charts: 12285, **12289**

Approach & Marinas. Almost literally the last stop before Washington is Piscataway Creek, on the Maryland side, less than 3 miles from Mount Vernon. The approach channel is periodically dredged to a controlling depth of 6 feet. However, if your draft approaches that, proceed cautiously as shoals have a way of returning. The approach to Fort Washington Marina, your best bet for an overnight stay, is a bit

Cupola at the end of the Mount Vernon dock.

Darrell Luskin

on the thin side even in the marked channel. In season, make prior arrangements if you intend to stay overnight. This is one of the few marinas on the upper Potomac that carries diesel fuel. It also has a dockside sewage pumpout facility.

What to See & Do. Visit Fort Washington. Walk from the marina or, easier, land on Diggs Point by dinghy and walk up the hill to the fort. It is well preserved, and like the marina, it is operated by the National Park Service.

The original fort was too weak to withstand the British fleet, which sailed up the river to Alexandria in the spring of 1814. In September of that same year, plans were laid to construct a much stronger fort that would be able to repel a naval assault. However, the fort wasn't completed until 1824 and never received a challenge, not even during the Civil War. Abandoned in 1872, the fort later was transferred to the care of the National Park Service.

You enter the fort via a drawbridge over a moat, which leads into a tower with a guardroom on one side and the commandant's quar-

ters on the other. Inside the fort, the officers' and enlisted quarters, all restored, flank the parade ground. The battlements to the right overlook the Potomac River, with a view all the way past the Woodrow Wilson Bridge to Washington, D.C.

The park and fort are open daily from 7:30 A.M. until dark. On Sundays in the summer there is a parade ceremony, which is worth watching (bring your camera).

Swan Creek

Charts: 12285, **12289**

If it weren't for the Tantallon Yacht Club, located up a well-marked 4- to 6-foot-deep channel, Swan Creek could be totally ignored. Transients are accepted for an overnight stay, but yacht club affiliation is expected. Prior arrangements are recommended. To stay here, you must take a slip. There is no anchorage.

Smoot's Cove

  No facilities

Charts: 12285, **12289**

Except for the Tantallon Yacht Club in Swan Creek, there are no safe anchorages or marinas beyond Piscataway Creek until you reach the Woodrow Wilson Memorial Bridge, 5 miles upstream. This drawbridge has a vertical clearance of 50 feet when closed. In 2001, immediately south of the existing Woodrow Wilson Bridge, construction began on a pair of drawbridges to replace it. The closed vertical clearance of the new bridges is designed to be 70 feet, eliminating the need to open it except for passage of occasional commercial or navy vessels. The first bridge is scheduled for completion in 2004 and the second in 2006. After that, I presume that the old bridge will be removed.

Anchorages & Approaches. Smoot's Cove, to starboard just below the bridge, is a possible anchorage. Once you are in, there is plenty of water. The problem is getting over the entrance shoals. Use the red "90" lighted buoy just past Rosier Bluff as your turning mark. Swing to starboard to a course of 85 degrees toward the Maryland shore, feeling your way with your depth-sounder until the water starts to deepen again. Then hold about the same distance offshore and follow the curve of the cove until you find a place to anchor. You must come back out the same way as this is the only route through the shoals.

In early 2000 most of the trees on the shore were bulldozed, and construction started on a hotel and marina complex. It appears that both the hotel and the marina are going to be quite large. Whether there are plans to dredge the entrance and add markers is unknown, but the current signs indicate that this is highly likely. Soon transients may find that they have to tie up to the marina rather than anchor out in order to remain overnight in this cove.

Alexandria

Charts: 12285, **12289**

History. To port immediately above the Woodrow Wilson Bridge is the town of Alexandria, a commercial and cultural hub off and on for more than 250 years. Old Town Alexandria was founded as a seaport in 1749; Scottish merchants were the principal city founders. Known as George Washington's hometown, this is where Washington and his fellow patriots attended the theater, church, and political meetings during the formative years of the Revolution. Old Town Alexandria had been rather seedy, with rotten wharves and grungy warehouses. Today it is a National Landmark by the National Register of Historic Places, and

The Carlyle House is Alexandria's "grandest" house. Begun in 1752 and completed in 1753 by the Scottish merchant John Carlyle, it is the city's only example of a Scottish country manor home. It is at 121 North Fairfax Street, two blocks up Cameron Street from the Torpedo Factory Art Center. Before the waterfront was developed, the Potomac River reached almost to the formal gardens at the rear of the house.

Nina Tisara/Alexandria Tourist Council

Alexandria began as a Potomac River seaport. Today commerce and recreation share its shoreline.

has been transformed into a vibrant center for shopping, dining, and the arts.

Marinas. The Alexandria City Marina (703-838-4265) is probably the best place to tie up to land. It is easily recognized because of the large wooden gazebos on its two piers. As the name would indicate, it is operated by the city. The marina can accommodate about a dozen boats of the 30-foot class and 15 to 17 small powerboats; there is additional space alongside the pier ends, where a vessel of up to 200 feet can be handled. The dockmaster is on duty from 9:00 A.M. to 9:00 P.M. on weekdays and from 10:00 A.M. to 10:00 P.M. on weekends. Transients are expected to arrive during those hours. As of 2000, the fee was $5 for the first four hours. Overnight dockage, if available, is based on the LOA of the vessel at $1.50 per foot, I believe. Reservations are recommended, and don't even think about trying it on the Fourth of July.

What to See & Do. Just above the bridge is Waterfront Park, where the schooner *Alexandria* used to be tied up. Unfortunately, it was sold in 1996, and on the first voyage to its new home it sank off the Virginia capes that same year.

Above the park, immediately inland from the City Marina, is the Torpedo Factory Art Cen-

ter, which is home to 83 studios occupied by more than 165 professional artists, as well as five cooperative membership art galleries, an art school, and an archaeology laboratory and museum. Artists work in the public view, so you can watch the art being created, ask questions about the creative processes, and buy their work. The art center is located in a building constructed at the end of World War I for manufacturing torpedo shell cases. At the end of World War II the building was used by the federal government to store documents and artifacts and by the Smithsonian Institution for an urban archaeology laboratory that focused on 18th- and 19th-century items revealed in excavations in Alexandria. The laboratory and museum, now called Alexandria Archaeology, is open to the public Tuesday through Saturday from 9:00 A.M. to 5:00 P.M.; the laboratory hours are Friday and Saturday from 11:00 A.M. to 5:00 P.M. Alexandria Archaeology is the nation's first municipally supported urban archaeology program. The Torpedo Factory Art Center renovation has been hailed as an imaginative example of adaptive reuse architecture; to me, however, it still looks like a torpedo factory, at least from the outside.

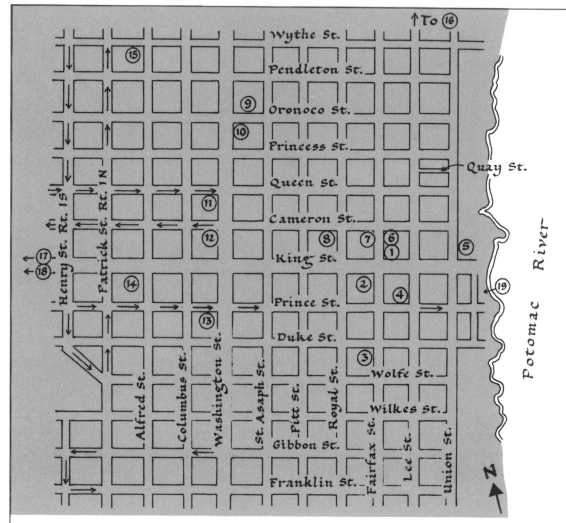

↑To ⑯

Wythe St.

Pendleton St.

⑨ Oronoco St.

⑩ Princess St.

Queen St.

Cameron St.

⑪

⑫

⑧ ⑦ ⑥
⑰ ⑤
⑱ ① King St.

⑭ ② Prince St.
⑲
④

⑬ Duke St.

③ Wolfe St.

Wilkes St.

Gibbon St.

Franklin St.

Quay St.

Potomac River

Henry St. Rt. 1 S · Patrick St. Rt. 1 N · Alfred St. · Columbus St. · Washington St. · St. Asaph St. · Pitt St. · Royal St. · Fairfax St. · Lee St. · Union St.

N

KEY

① Ramsay House Visitors Center
② Stabler-Leadbeater Apothecary Shop
③ Old Presbyterian Meeting House
④ The Athenaeum
⑤ Torpedo Factory Art Center & Alexandria Archaeology
⑥ Carlyle House
⑦ Market Square/City Hall
⑧ Gadsby's Tavern Museum
⑨ Boyhood Home of Robert E. Lee
⑩ Lee-Fendall House

⑪ Lloyd House
⑫ Christ Church
⑬ The Lyceum
⑭ Friendship Veterans Fire Engine Association
⑮ Black History Resource Center
⑯ Alexandria Waterfront Museum
⑰ George Washington Masonic National Monument
⑱ Fort Ward Museum & Historic Site
⑲ Waterfront Park

Note: Arrows indicate flow of traffic on one-way streets.

A little farther upriver is the Alexandria Waterfront Museum, actually the first of four locks built as part of the Alexandria Canal. The tidal lock's excavation and preservation is portrayed in a 10-minute video; additional photographs, maps, and drawings explain how the canal worked.

Just inland on Royal Street, three blocks up Cameron Street from the Torpedo Factory Art Center, is Gatsby's Tavern Museum, known for its Georgian architecture. The tavern was a cen-

BOATING SEASON ACTIVITIES IN ALEXANDRIA

Several special events occur annually between Memorial Day and Labor Day in Alexandria. Busy waters and marinas will be more crowded when these celebrations take place. I have listed the usual time for each event, but you can get details by calling the Alexandria Convention & Visitor's Bureau (703-838-4200).

- *Alexandria Red Cross Waterfront Festival*, second weekend in June. A celebration of Alexandria's historic importance as a seaport and the vitality of the Potomac shoreline today. Historic ships, boat rides, fireworks, children's events, ship tours, arts-and-crafts shows, entertainment, food booths, and water-safety demonstrations. Admission.

- *Civil War Living History Weekend*, date varies in June or July. On Saturday and Sunday authentically equipped Civil War military units demonstrate camp life with drills, music, and a review of the troops at the Fort Ward Museum and Historic Site, four miles from Old Town Alexandria. Torchlight tours of the camp are held on Saturday night. Admission.

- *Virginia Scottish Games*, fourth weekend in July. This two-day annual Celtic festival is one of the largest in the United States. It features Highland dancing, bagpiping, a national professional heptathlon, animal events, and national fiddling competitions, all at the Episcopal High School grounds. Admission.

ter of political, business, and social life in early Alexandria. (Birthright celebrations honoring George Washington were held in the second-floor ballroom.)

There is a plethora of restaurants in Old Town within a short walk of the City Marina. I will mention only a few. Right by the marina are the food pavilion, with a collection of fast-food services and, just past that, the famous Charthouse Restaurant, with a great view of the Potomac from the Woodrow Wilson Bridge and Washington, D.C. Not to slight the other restaurants, I simply have to mention the Fishmarket, a lively placed noted for all kinds of seafood. Next door is Pops, which serves gourmet ice cream made from a 60-year-old Washington, D.C., recipe. Both were established by the late "Mr. Ray," who was the owner of the *America*, a reproduction of the first yacht to win what became the America's Cup. This 100-foot-long yacht was frequently docked in Old Town. I don't know its current fate. As for the other restaurants, simply take a walk around and take your choice.

WASHINGTON, D.C.
Charts: 12285, **12289**

Slightly more than 2 miles above the bridge, on the Virginia side just south of Washington National Airport, is the Washington Sailing Marina, where you will find facilities and supplies and can make arrangements for transportation into Washington. To approach the marina, take your departure from the green "1" can adjacent to the main Potomac Channel and head directly for the pair of red "2" and green "3" daymarks indicating the channel entrance. From there, follow the markers around the point into the marina basin.

About 4 miles above the bridge the Potomac divides into three "channels": the Anacostia River to the east, the Washington Channel in the middle, and the Virginia Channel to the northwest. Haines Point divides the Potomac into the Virginia Channel, which is actually the main Potomac River, and the right fork, or Washington Channel. A few hundred yards farther, Greenleaf Point, on which Fort McNair is located, divides the right fork into the Washington Channel and the Anacostia River.

293

Region 5

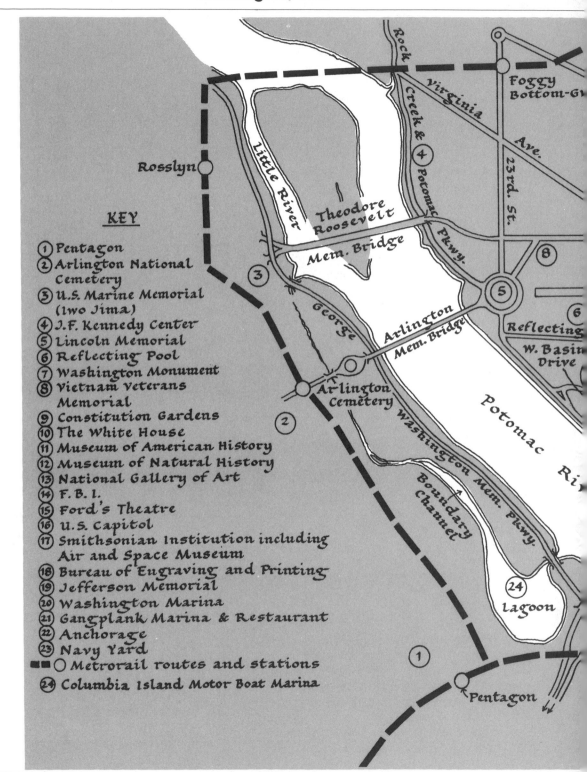

KEY

1. Pentagon
2. Arlington National Cemetery
3. U.S. Marine Memorial (Iwo Jima)
4. J.F. Kennedy Center
5. Lincoln Memorial
6. Reflecting Pool
7. Washington Monument
8. Vietnam Veterans Memorial
9. Constitution Gardens
10. The White House
11. Museum of American History
12. Museum of Natural History
13. National Gallery of Art
14. F.B.I.
15. Ford's Theatre
16. U.S. Capitol
17. Smithsonian Institution including Air and Space Museum
18. Bureau of Engraving and Printing
19. Jefferson Memorial
20. Washington Marina
21. Gangplank Marina & Restaurant
22. Anchorage
23. Navy Yard
◼◼◼○ Metrorail routes and stations
24. Columbia Island Motor Boat Marina

WASHINGTON, D.C.

SCALE 1" = 1,900 FEET

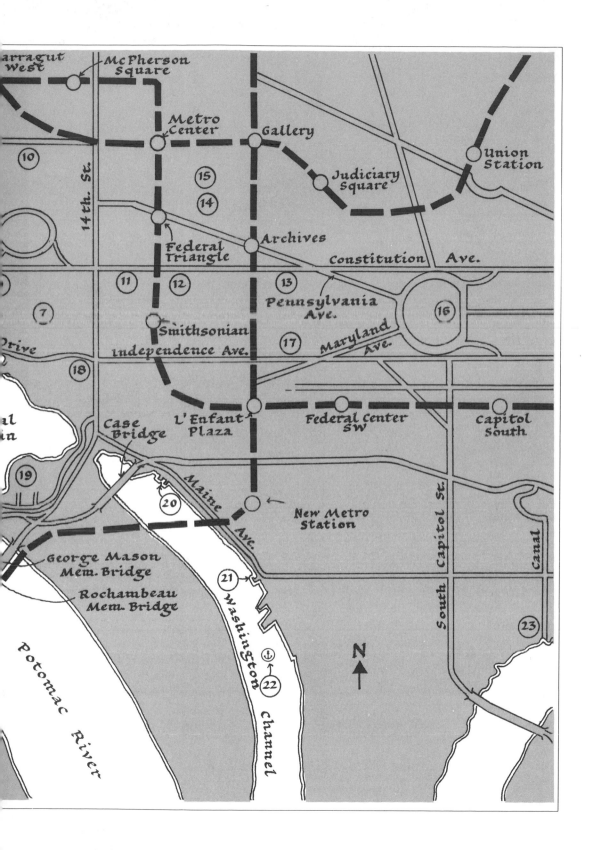

Region 5

Farragut West
McPherson Square
Metro Center
Gallery
Union Station
10
15
14
Judiciary Square
14th St.
Federal Triangle
Archives
Constitution Ave.
7
11
12
13
Pennsylvania Ave.
16
Smithsonian
Independence Ave.
17
Maryland Ave.
Drive
18
L'Enfant Plaza
Federal Center SW
Capitol South
Case Bridge
19
20
Maine Ave.
New Metro Station
George Mason Mem. Bridge
21
Washington Channel
South Capitol St.
Canal
23
Rochambeau Mem. Bridge
Potomac River
22
N

WASHINGTON, D.C.

295

Anacostia River

Charts: 12285, **12289**

Small powerboats can follow the Anacostia River almost to Bladensburg, but the route is uninteresting except perhaps to history buffs interested in following the route taken by the British Marines who set fire to the White House during the War of 1812.

Marinas. The James Creek Marina (202-554-8844) and Buzzard Point Marina (202-488-8400), immediately to the east of Fort McNair, are on Greenleaf Point, in the mouth of the Anacostia River. Both marinas welcome transients. The James Creek Marina is the only one on the Anacostia that offers gasoline and diesel.

What to See & Do. A little above the South Capitol Street Bridge (a swing bridge with a closed vertical clearance of 40 feet) are the Port of Bladensburg & Safford Marine and the Anacostia Marina, both of which offer facilities and a place to tie up while visiting the nearby Navy Museum on the Washington Navy Yard.

The Washington Navy Yard was established in 1799 and has been in continuous operation ever since. It is the oldest naval facility in the country. For many years it was the Naval Gun Factory, the primary facility for design and production of large naval guns and ordnance. The Navy Memorial Museum, housed in one of the old factory buildings, is dedicated to the history of the U.S. Navy in war and peace, from the Revolutionary War to the space age. More than 4,000 items, including the first working submarine built in the United States, and the *Triest*, the deep-sea oceanographic submersible, are on display both within the building and outdoors in the waterfront park. Admission is free, a refreshing change in this day and age. Museum hours are 10:00 A.M. to 5:00 P.M. seven days a week.

The next two bridges are fixed, and their vertical clearance of 28 feet limits passage. Those boats requiring no more than 8 feet vertical clearance can continue upriver almost to Bladensburg, Maryland. The only reason I can

imagine for making the trip is to be able to say that you have done it. I would settle for the Navy Yard or the marinas nearby.

Washington Channel

Charts: 12285, **12289**

The Washington Channel can be considered the headquarters for most of the Washington yachting fleet. Between 1985 and 1990 the area was revamped as a part of the Southwest Washington Redevelopment Program. Initially, long-range plans called for a wide pedestrian mall along the waterfront with several hundred slips for yachts, a commercial dock, excursion steamer docks, and several other attractions designed to upgrade the quality of the waterfront. Although the redevelopment project is still ongoing, it's close to its goals.

Marinas & Restaurants. The main marine facilities, all to starboard as you enter Washington Channel, include the Gangplank Marina, followed by the Capitol Yacht Club and the Washington Marina. All accept transient yachts for a short stay. The yacht club expects you to have some standing with a recognized yacht club, and even then it discourages prolonged stays.

Hogates Restaurant and the Flagship Restaurant are easily accessible on the waterfront side of Maine Avenue. Hall's Seafood Restaurant is located on Buzzards Point, at the foot of 1st Street.

What to See & Do. To the west is the East Potomac Park with its public golf course and visitor center.

For theatergoers there is the Arena Stage, at the intersection of Maine Avenue and 6th Street. Depending on the play and the time of the year, reservations (well in advance) are recommended but not always necessary. The ticket office is close enough to wherever you can tie up in Washington Channel that you can easily stroll over to inquire about available seats.

At the north end of Washington Channel, on the Tidal Basin, is the Jefferson Memorial. This monument is difficult to reach from any of the marine facilities by foot because of the road pattern and the traffic, but it's worth the trouble.

Ranging farther afield, a walk of about ¾ mile takes you to "the Mall," where you will find the Smithsonian Institution, the Washington Monument, the White House, the Lincoln Memorial, and the U.S. Capitol. Often overlooked by tourists, the Botanical Gardens are just before the Capitol. Directly behind the Capitol are the impressive buildings of the U.S. Supreme Court and the Library of Congress.

If you are not up to walking, the Waterfront metro station (on the green line), is located at the junction of 4th and M Streets, just a couple of blocks from Washington Channel. You can get off at L'Enfant Plaza and walk from there or change to the blue line and ride that to the Smithsonian stop. The metro maps are easy to understand, and the system is designed to be user-friendly.

Once you have seen the main attractions of Washington, consider a visit to the Navy Museum, on the Washington Navy Yard, 2 miles east of Arena Stage on M Street. If this is too far to walk, you might consider taking your boat around Greenleaf Point to one of the Navy

docks or to one of the marinas there. Check with the Navy Yard's Visitor Center (202-433-3731) before trying to use any Navy facilities.

Washington has far too many points of interest to list here. In the Washington Channel you are close to the heart of the city and within easy reach of most of its "must see" places—without traffic, parking, and related hassles.

Virginia Channel

Charts: 12285, **12289**

Approaches. For almost all sailboats the first bridge over the Virginia Channel must be considered the head of navigation because of the 18-foot vertical clearance of the fixed bridges. Powerboats may continue upstream some distance above the Key Bridge (which crosses the river by the Lincoln Memorial) to the vicinity of Fletcher's Boathouse and the Kennedy Center, possibly a little farther.

Anchorages & Marinas. Although the river does narrow and you should follow the

Looking west from atop the Washington Monument to the Reflecting Pool and the Lincoln Memorial.

WASHINGTON, D.C.

chart carefully (there are rocks here), the water is 7 to 36 feet deep almost from shore to shore. You can anchor here, but there are no facilities for cruising boats, nor is there any practical place to tie up and land, except for the Columbia Island Marina (202-347-0173), which is in a shallow basin adjacent to the Pentagon. There is a fixed bridge with an 18-foot clearance over the entrance to the marina, restricting it to smaller powerboats. It may be possible to lay alongside Fletcher's Boathouse, on the Washington side, but you must ask permission there at the time and there is precious little room.

Region 6
POTOMAC RIVER TO WOLF TRAP LIGHT

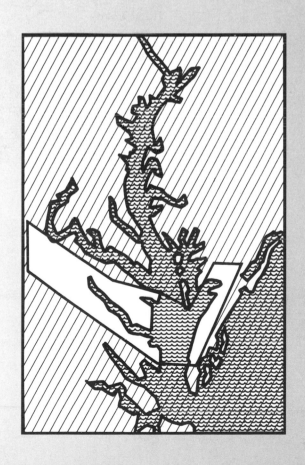

Potomac River to Wolf Trap Light

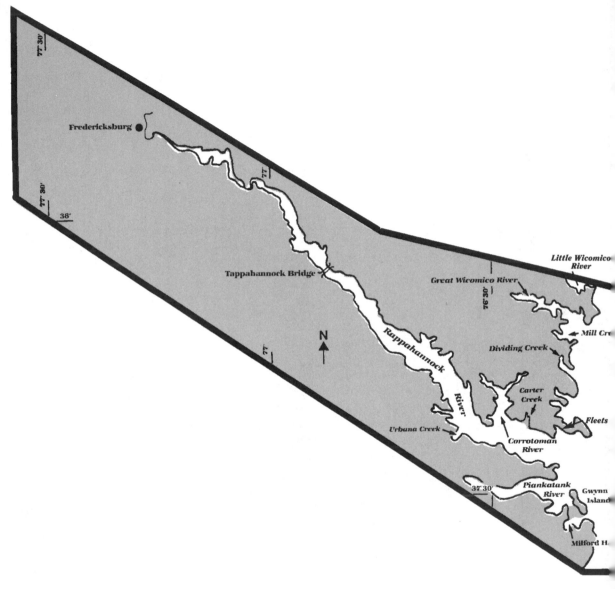

Region 6

Fredericksburg

77°30'

77°30'

38°

77°

Tappahannock Bridge

77°

N

Rappahannock

River

Little Wicomico River

Great Wicomico River

76°30'

Mill Cre

Dividing Creek

Carter Creek

Fleets

Urbana Creek

Corrotoman River

37°30'

Piankatank River

Gwynn Island

Milford H.

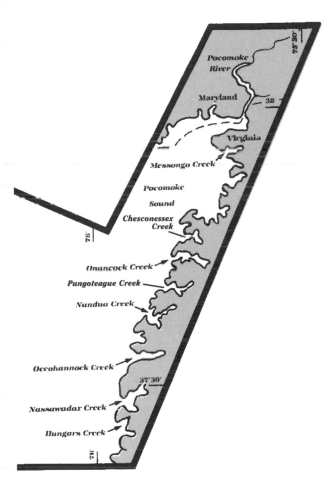

F ROM THE POTOMAC RIVER on south, the Chesapeake Bay widens and the low-lying land on the Eastern Shore makes the Bay look even wider than it is. For some distance below Tangier Island it is more than 20 miles across and you can easily be out of sight of land, an unusual feeling for those used to the upper Bay. The water is almost indistinguishable from that in the ocean, being only slightly less salty and full of comparable marine life. Although the average depth here is still only about 40 feet, the waves tend to be bigger and farther apart than in the more northern regions. Although you are still in what the Coast Guard classifies as "semi-protected waters," you can almost convince yourself that you are sailing "blue water."

You are still in the Chesapeake Bay, how-ever, and never very far from a sheltered harbor. If you are reasonably prudent and alert, you won't be caught out if the weather turns nasty.

Contrary to the character of the Bay farther north, from the Potomac River on south the best harbors are on the Western Shore. With a few notable exceptions, those on the Eastern Shore are small, shallow, and relatively difficult to ne-gotiate. The rivers, creeks, and coves on Vir-ginia's Western Shore are comparable to those on Maryland's Eastern Shore and constitute the best cruising grounds in the southern Bay.

EASTERN SHORE

Although Tangier Island is actually located south of the Potomac River, I included it in re-gion 4, making it part of the Crisfield–Smith Island–Tangier Island triad.

In just about the middle of the Bay, west-southwest of Tangier Island, markings on the chart show a series of shipwrecks within a circle 301 labeled "Prohibited Area." When cruising in this area you will see what appears to be a perfectly normal ship apparently headed in an easterly direction straight toward Tangier Island. This and the other wrecks are all targets for a Navy bombing range, so stay away from them.

Southwest of Tangier Island and due south of the center of the "Prohibited Area" the chart warns of the wreck of the *San Marcos*. (See Tangier Island, page 248, for more on the *San Marcos*.)

POCOMOKE SOUND

Charts: 12225, 12228, **12230**

Of the two approaches to Pocomoke Sound the easiest is from the south, past the southern tip of Watts Island. The other is from the Little Annemessex River, near Crisfield, through the Broad Creek dredged cut, which shortens the run through Pocomoke Sound by about half. However, the controlling depth for this shorter route keeps getting shallower, as it does in all dredged channels on the Chesapeake. If your draft is more than 5 feet, check on the latest controlling depth, especially at the southern end, before trying it. If you have a draft even approaching 5 feet, try this approach on a rising tide to take advantage of the 2-foot average range of tide. Do not attempt this if a strong northerly wind has been blowing for any appreciable period of time.

Pocomoke River

Charts: 12225, 12228, **12230**

The entrance to the Pocomoke River is via a 3½-mile-long, dredged cut across "the Muds," as the shoal in the mouth of the Pocomoke is known, 16 miles up Pocomoke Sound from the southern tip of Watts Island. As a result, most cruisers don't visit this river. It is their loss, I say, because the Pocomoke offers excellent scenery and easy cruising in deep water once you get past the entrance.

Approaches. Once you are into Pocomoke Sound, the navigation is straightforward for most of the way to the cut through The Muds. Be especially careful of the large number of fish stakes, nets, and the thousands of crab-pot floats. Be sure to honor the green and red buoys just west of North End Point so that you will avoid the shoal in the middle of the sound there. Incidentally, the white-orange buoys spaced throughout the sound mark the Maryland–Virginia border. They are not navigational markers.

From the last green marker in Pocomoke Sound (the Fl G 4-second green "12") make a small dogleg to the left and head directly for the lighted green "1" at the entrance to the cut. Proceed slowly and carefully through the cut, sounding all the way. Be especially careful of shoaling in the section of the cut that closely parallels the shore. Once you reach the part of the cut through Fair Island, the controlling depth is fairly reliable at 6 feet minimum. As you clear the last green marker at the end of this cut, you will be in the deep (11 feet or more) water of the Pocomoke River.

From here on, there are no navigational markers, and none are needed as there is deep water from shore to shore and there are no noticeable protruding shoals. For about 8 miles the shore is mostly marsh, with occasional pockets of heavier vegetation.

What to See & Do. About 4 miles above the cut you will see a pair of huge cypress trees at the edge of the water. When you see them, look for a beautiful, 18th-century plantation house known as Thrumcapped (not open to the public).

Eight miles upriver is the town of Rehobeth, which has a post office and a small country store.

Just above Rehobeth the character of the river changes. Here the river passes between high banks lined with tall trees, and the water turns darker, stained almost black by the huge cypress trees lining both sides of the slow-moving, freshwater stream. This is the real cruising ground of the Pocomoke. Dense cypress woods mixed with maple, pine, and dogwood give the impression of virgin territory. The few breaks in the woods, which give glimpses of farms, and the few small boats tied at the water's edge do little to dispel this feeling.

Pocomoke City, about 14 miles upstream from the river's mouth, can provide all kinds of supplies, but other than at the marina, you may have some difficulty finding a good place to land.

Anchorages & Marinas. In Shelltown, to port a mile above the exit from the cut, the small country store has some piles and a bulkhead where a boat can tie up to visit.

Pocomoke City Municipal Park offers 100 feet of service dock, but in boating season space is in demand, so it might be wiser to anchor and land by dinghy there or at the Pocomoke City Municipal Marina, a little farther upstream. The Pocomoke City Municipal Marina offers transient slips, showers, gasoline, a pumpout, and a self-service laundry. However, the maximum LOA that can be accommodated is 33 feet.

A fixed bridge 1 mile above the railroad bridge at Pocomoke City limits further navigation to those boats with a vertical clearance of less than 35 feet, effectively making this the head of navigation for most cruising sailboats. Powerboats can continue for another 14 miles to the town of Snow Hill before shoaling and snags make further exploration unwise, although possible. Ten miles above Pocomoke City is Shad Landing State Park, which has a basin 6 feet deep at the end of a dredged channel. Here you can anchor to enjoy this lovely park and its facilities.

Messongo Creek

  No facilities

Charts: 12210, 12225, **12228**, 12230

On the southeast side of Pocomoke Sound, between the long shoal extending to the southwest from Long Point and Guilford Flats, is Messongo Creek. It looks attractive at first glance, but is too shallow for any save vessels with a very shallow draft, such as runabouts.

Boats drawing less than 4 feet can find a marginal anchorage just inside Drum Point, but it doesn't seem worth the effort since there is nothing else to recommend this creek.

Guilford Creek

  No facilities

Charts: 12210, 12225, **12228**, **12230**

Approaches. Less than 3 miles south of the mouth of Messongo Creek, the approach to Guilford Creek lies between two long shoals. Find the quick-flashing, 18-foot-high light at the western tip of Guilford Flats for proper orientation to start your approach into the harbor. From this light, assume a course of 105 degrees (magnetic), which is aimed slightly south of the tips of Flood and Ebb Points (you probably cannot distinguish them from a distance). As soon as Lower Bernard Island comes abeam, swing in a wide arc to a course of 50 degrees (magnetic) to head directly for the red "2" marker northwest of Ebb Point. Leave red "2" and the red "4" daymark just beyond it close to starboard. From red "4" you need to take a dogleg to the north of a course directly toward the red "6" light east of Sandy Point. A course of 117 degrees from red "4" helps you avoid Bernard Flats to port and the shoal northeast of Sandy Point to starboard. The Muddy Creek green "1" northeast of red "6" can serve as a point to aim for. When red "6" is approximately 45 degrees off your starboard bow, swing to leave it close to starboard.

Anchorages. Once you round Sandy Point, Guilford Creek offers a reasonably protected anchorage in 5 to 6 feet of water in the main part of the creek. Boats drawing 5 feet or less can find a nice anchorage tucked just inside Sandy Point off an isolated beach. If you are looking for seclusion, this spot is hard to beat.

Stay out of Young Creek, to the south, in anything but a dinghy. In spite of the encouraging red "2" daymark at its entrance, the maximum depth inside is 2 feet.

Muddy Creek, to the east, offers a challenge to the gunkholer. If you draw 4 feet or less, you can get in, but feel your way carefully. The markers on Muddy Creek are deceptive. You cannot follow a straight course between them as the channel wanders back and forth. If you do make it in, try the nice little anchorage northwest of Poulson Point.

The upper reaches of Guilford Creek, where it necks down to a tight squeeze at Graven Point, are also accessible to craft with a 4-foot draft. It is unmarked, so you have to feel your way in. Do not proceed beyond the first point to starboard past Graven Point: there isn't any water.

With the exception of Sandy Point, the shores are muddy and marshy. The creek could be used as a jump-off point for a trip to or from the Pocomoke, but it has little attraction on its own.

The Thorofare

Charts: 12210, 12225, **12228**

"Thorofare" seems to be a popular name on the Bay. Usually it refers to a passage from one body of water to another through a section of land. This one goes to a dead end and the town of Hopkins, although it does provide a common entrance to both Hunting and Bagwell Creeks. There are a couple of reasonable anchorages, but no special attractions.

Approaches. The initial approach is the same as for Guilford Creek. First find the beacon at the end of Guilford Flats. From this beacon hold a course of about 120 degrees, toward Simpson Point, until Lower Bernard Island comes abeam. Then swing to starboard to head south-southeast until you can pick up the red and green markers east of Halfmoon Point, at the entrance to The Thorofare. Hold close to the green "3" daymark and swing a little to port after passing it in order to avoid the shoal off Halfmoon Point.

Anchorages. Once inside The Thorofare, you can anchor near the middle in 7 to 8 feet of water. Boats drawing 4 feet or less can find a nice spot tucked in the curve of Halfmoon Island about 300 yards south to about 800 yards south-southwest of the tip of Halfmoon Point. Take your choice, but watch out for shoaling extending southeast from the point to an imaginary line drawn south-southwest from green "3." The land in this area is so low that there is little or no protection from wind, but there is full protection from waves in all directions.

Bagwell Creek offers a well-protected anchorage in near pristine surroundings for boats with drafts of less than 4 feet. Its entrance is easy to negotiate; just swing to port past the green "7" daymark southwest of Weir Point and hold to the middle of the creek. You can proceed for about ½ mile, to where the creek bends sharply to the north, before the creek shoals.

Marinas. Boats with a draft of 5 feet or less can continue to follow the markers into Hunting Creek as far as the little town of Hopkins, where there is a marine railway and a concrete launching ramp. No supplies are available there, and there is little or no room to anchor, so come this way only if you have sustained damage requiring immediate repair.

Deep Creek

 No facilities

Charts: 12210, 12225, **12228**

It is 8 miles up a winding but well-marked channel to the town of Deep Creek. As you approach the green "11" marker just south of Scott Island, the channel narrows drastically to a dredged channel used by watermen from Deep Creek. According to the chart, this channel is for shallow-draft powerboats only; however, the local watermen claim that the water is more than 10 feet deep at high tide. Whatever the real depth, there is little to attract cruising boats up this creek. Although the village of Deep Creek is probably one of the busiest fishing villages on Virginia's Eastern Shore, there is no anchorage here.

Do not attempt to enter Island Bay. Although you can get in if your draft is less than 4 feet, the numerous unmarked shoals make it slow going. Pass this one by.

CHESCONESSEX CREEK TO HUNGARS CREEK

Charts: 12210, 12225, **12226**, **12228**

Chesconessex Creek

Charts: 12210, 12225, **12228**

About 2 miles north of the better-known Onancock Creek on Virginia's Eastern Shore is the channel into Chesconessex Creek.

Approaches. The channel into Chesconessex Creek is wide and well marked—a 5-foot shoal lies between "3" and "4"—until you reach

Chesconessex and Onancock Creeks

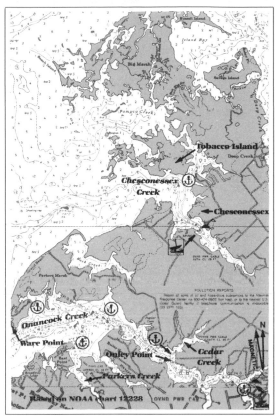

SCALE 1" = **1.45** NAUT. MILES ⚓ **Good anchoring**

⛰ **Marina** 🚤 **Launching site**

up to walk into the village of Chesconessex. From the channel, head directly toward the center of the wharf, then pivot to lay alongside. Be careful when approaching the wharf because there is little water to either side of it, although there is more than 10 feet alongside.

The marine railway has a gas pump (no diesel), but the water depth is debatable. Ask before trying to approach.

At the red "12" daymark the channel turns abruptly to the west, where it ends at the state launching ramp and a small service dock. There is a gas pump on the wharf, but if you draw more than 4 feet you won't be able to lay alongside. Since the channel runs very close to the wharf, you may be able to get close enough to have the hose passed to you, but don't try this on a falling tide. You can obtain supplies at the small country store at the wharf.

If you are the adventurous type, proceed a few hundred yards past the last channel dogleg, but be careful as the creek shoals quickly. Other than this region and a small area to the east of the red "6" daymark near Tobacco Island, there is no good place to anchor out on this creek. The anchorage near Tobacco Island is exposed to the Bay on the west side.

Onancock Creek

Charts: 12225, **12228**

Approaches. This is probably the most easily accessible creek on Virginia's Eastern Shore. The channel is well marked and well maintained with controlling depths of 10 to 11 feet all the way to the town of Onancock at its headwaters, a distance of about 3½ miles. At night the 4-second flashing green "1" beacon at the channel entrance is easily seen from several miles away. If you do enter at night, be sure to have a good spotlight so that you can pick up the daymarks.

Anchorages. If you prefer to anchor out in seclusion, there is an excellent anchorage off a sandy beach to the north of the channel, just inside Ware Point. The area is well protected from wave action, although the low-lying land

the red "6" daymark, where the creek makes a 90-degree turn to the south. Do not head directly toward the next marker; the shoal between markers bows to the west. Keep red "8" on your port bow until you are about two-thirds of the way to it. Then turn to head directly toward it until it is a little more than 50 feet away before swinging to port and heading for the next marker. There is supposed to be a stake opposite red "8" to mark the shoal on the opposite side of the channel, but don't depend on it. The channel carries 6 to 7 feet of water all the way to the last set of markers.

Marinas & Provisions. As you near the red "10" daymark you will see some of the crab buildings ahead of you. On the eastern side of the creek, just past Tom's Railway Service directly across from red "10," is the North Chesconessex County Wharf, where you can tie

does little to stop wind. The marshes here are attractive, but they do mean mosquitoes at night, so be prepared.

There is a secure anchorage in the mouth of Parkers Creek, about 2 miles in from the green "1" marker at the channel entrance. Parkers Creek has more than 6 feet of water all the way to the last marker (which isn't very far), but it is probably best to anchor just inside the tip of East Point.

As you proceed up the creek the channel narrows somewhat, but there is still plenty of room. The marshland at the entrance quickly gives way to farmland. The homes dotting the shore are widely spaced, and many of them date back to the colonial era.

The town wharf is located in North Branch, at the headwaters. It is easily identified by a large sign that proclaims, "Onancock, the Cobia Capital of the World" (cobia is a food and sport fish). Dockage is free for a few hours, not overnight, but you may have trouble finding space on weekends. The harbormaster monitors VHF-FM channel 16, or you can call him at 757-787-7911. The waterfront is busy and noisy well into the evening. A more comfortable anchorage is in the North Branch basin or a little downstream near the mouth of Titlow Creek, also known as the South Branch.

What to See & Do. Founded in 1682, Onancock covers only 1 square mile despite having had 300 years to develop. It is still composed of a considerable number of homes built from the late 18th century through the 19th century. Scotts Hill, built in 1779, looks like the fortress that it was, complete with trapdoors and hiding places.

One of the better-known buildings in Onancock is Kerr Place, built in 1799. It is owned by the Eastern Shore of Virginia Historical Society, which uses it as a museum, complete with period furniture. It is open to visitors Monday through Saturday from 10:00 A.M. to 4:00 P.M. for a small admission fee.

The Hopkins & Brother Store Museum (757-787-3100), on Market Street, contains a general store from about 1842 and a steamboat wharf. It offers cruises to Tangier Island. Recently, it has added a small selection of groceries, a gift shop, and a small restaurant (open April through December) that serves three

meals a day. Gas and diesel fuel are available. Since there are only a few transient slips near the museum, reservations are recommended.

Marinas, Restaurants, & Provisions. Onancock Wharf (757-787-7911), a small marina across from the town dock, offers fuel and pumpout facilities, as well as transient slips.

The town has several shops, at least two drugstores (which serve meals), and a post office. There is a supermarket about 1 mile down the road, and there is an icehouse 2 miles outside of town. You should be able to find all the supplies you need here, although you may have to walk a ways to find them. There are several restaurants in town, and Flounder's (757-787-2233, closed Mondays) has a shuttle service from the town dock for those wishing to dine there.

Actually, it is worth a visit to Onancock simply to walk around the town. As in most places on the Eastern Shore, the people here are friendly and helpful.

Pungoteague Creek
Charts: 12210, 12225, **12226**

About 4 miles south of Onancock, Pungoteague Creek rivals Onancock Creek as an attractive place to visit. The channel is deep and well marked as far as the town of Harborton, about 4 miles from the entrance. There are no good anchorages until you reach this part of the creek. Stay out of Underhill Creek—there's no water. Pungoteague Creek appears broad, but wide shoals on both sides prevent you from pulling far from the center of the creek to anchor.

Approach. A quick-flashing marker lies about a mile into the Bay from the two points of land that indicate the (unnavigable) entrance to Butcher's Creek. The actual entrance to Pungoteague Creek is between the marshy Bluff Point and Finneys Island, about 2 miles northeast of the quick-flashing marker and nearby green "1" daymark, both of which should be left to port on the way in. Just inside the quick-flashing marker is a tilted concrete base, the remains of the old marker. For the rest of the way into the creek just honor the markers; the channel is easy.

Past Harborton the creek is unmarked. Taylor Creek shoals rapidly, so stay out of it. You can proceed, with caution, nearly 2 more miles up the main (north) fork of the creek in 5 to 6 feet of water. Here you can find a number of secluded anchorages. There are few houses here, but there may be a little pulpwood traffic. Past Boggs Wharf, now only a ruin, the water shoals abruptly. Larger boats ought to stop here, although you can still explore by dinghy for a mile or more up both of the remaining forks.

Harborton

Charts: 12210, 12225, **12226**

Probably the best place to anchor for the night is near the red "13" light just short of Harborton. There is room there to swing, and on a hot night you can get a cooling breeze. Pull out of the channel to avoid the workboats, which will probably go out early in the morning.

Harborton has a public wharf where you can tie up to visit the tiny town. At the end of the dock there is at least 6 feet of water, and gas (no diesel) is available here. Be careful as you move toward the end of the wharf where the gas dock is located because the water depth is a little uncertain. An easier stop for gas is at the Eastern Shore Yacht & Country Club, across the creek from Harborton. The post office is in town, and the grocery stores are about a mile down the road.

Nandua Creek

 No facilities

Charts: 12210, 12225, **12226**

Approaches. Just 2 miles south of the entrance to Pungoteague Creek is the winding channel into Nandua Creek. The channel is well marked, but the shoals frequently shift, so proceed cautiously. The controlling depth in the channel was 5 feet a few years ago; it could be less now. Approach the first marker at the entrance to the channel, green "3," on a southeast course to avoid the unmarked shoal on the

south side of the entrance. (The first marker, a green "1" beacon, is more than a mile offshore in 12 feet of water.) The channel is rather narrow until you pass Milbys Point and the channel hooks to the south. From there on it is wider and more forgiving.

Anchorages. Once you are inside the shelter of Milbys Point there are several places to anchor, all the way to the headwaters of the creek. On the north side of the creek are several large homes or estates. On the south side are more modest homes and the village of Nandua. There are no marine facilities, and the public wharf has long since decayed. The anchorages are snug and well protected, and there is little traffic on the water. If you are looking for seclusion, you will find it here; if you need resupply of any kind, you are out of luck.

Occohannock Creek

Charts: 12210, 12225, **12226**

Approaches. This creek is a pleasant, quiet place with some snug anchorages. The channel is easy to find from the Bay and reasonably well marked. Between daymarks green "5" and red "6," southwest of Killmon Cove, the channel is shoaling in. Even so, if you can manage to stay in the channel, the controlling depth is close to 7 feet until you reach red "16," which is just east of Poms Point, well inside the creek. In that region the channel has shoaled to about 5 feet.

Other than that, the channel is wide and reasonably deep as far as Fisher Point, about 2½ miles past the creek entrance at Old Neck. Beyond there the creek is unmarked and the water depth is iffy. Those adventurous souls in shoal-draft boats may be able to pick their way as far as the fixed bridge at Belle Haven.

Marinas. At the place labeled "Morley's Wharf" on the chart are the Wardtown public launching ramp and a small service dock. Morley's Wharf no longer exists save as a ruin.

Across the creek is Davis Wharf, where you can get gas and visit the small store–post office. The depth at the fuel dock is reputed to be 5 feet.

That is the extent of marine facilities on this

creek. It offers quiet, secure anchorages and a good place to visit.

Nassawadox Creek

Charts: 12210, 12225, **12226**

Approaches. This creek is reserved for boats drawing less than 3 feet and skippers with good nerves. The chart indicates that it is a tricky creek to negotiate, and it is. The depth at the entrance to the channel keeps changing. For several years it has held at between 3 and 4 feet, but don't depend on it. I recommend checking with one of the locals before trying the entrance. The channel itself is normally marked with stakes by the local boatowners, in addition to the standard daymarks, and the resulting plethora of stakes can be confusing.

If you can get into this creek, you should be able to go if you give proper consideration to the numerous shoals. You certainly won't be crowded by other boats. Don't try Church Creek; the entrance is closed by a shoal. The rest of the creek is a significant challenge to the true gunkholer.

Marinas. Hull and engine repairs are available at Zimmerman Marine, to port beyond the radio tower. There is another marina to starboard, but it is private.

Hungars Creek

  No facilities

Charts: 12210, 12225, **12226**

Although Hungars and Mattawoman Creeks share a common entrance, only Hungars Creek is navigable. Mattawoman Creek has only 1 foot of water.

Approaches. The channel into Hungars Creek is marked for about 2 miles, which is about as far as you can expect to go. There is 6 to 7 feet of water until a little past the points of land that mark the entrance to the creek proper. Past that the channel shoals to about 4 feet for a little more than ½ mile, after which you would make better progress if you were to step overboard and walk.

Obviously there are no supplies or marine facilities on either creek. Hungars Creek offers some shelter in an emergency, but unless you are an incorrigible gunkholer, you should find more rewarding creeks elsewhere.

WESTERN SHORE

As you pass Smith Point, just below the mouth of the Potomac River, note the wind and current conditions. A significant current can develop in this area, passing over or near shoals, sometimes with an opposing wind. Some rather impressive though localized seas have been encountered just outside Smith Point Light under these conditions. By moving your course ½ mile farther out you can improve the comfort of your passage.

LITTLE WICOMICO RIVER

Charts: 12225, **12233**

One of four Wicomico Rivers on the Chesapeake Bay, the Little Wicomico lies almost hidden beyond the tip of Smith Point at the entrance to the Potomac River. Unfortunately, the entrance shoals are constantly changing, so don't completely trust any charts or entrance instructions, including these, unless you first check with Smith Point Sea Rescue on VHF-FM channel 16 for entrance instructions.

Even then, feel your way in. The bottom here is firm sand, so be careful. The current at the entrance is often strong. I recommend entering on an incoming tide.

Approaches. Make your approach to the jetties from the southeast. Assume a due west or slightly south of west course to keep Smith Point Light dead aft (to the east) until the red "2" marker for the river entrance comes nearly abeam. Then set a course for that marker. Don't pass too close to red "2." Once you can see the red and green markers at the end of the jetties, head to leave the green marker about 200 yards to port before swinging to port to head directly between the jetties. Past the jetties, favor the south (port) side, where you should find at least 6 feet of water. As you enter between the red and green markers, note that the channel doglegs to the north as you pass green "3." The small island ahead of you must be left to port. Once past the daymark "6," you are in, and you can expect to find 6 to 10 feet of water in most of the branches.

Marinas & Provisions. There are three marine railways on the Little Wicomico, but the only marine facilities useful to transient cruisers are in the second branch of the river to the south. Look to port after passing red "4" for the daymarks leading to the two marinas. The channel lies quite close to shore. Don't hold too close to green "5" and "7." As you clear the point into this little branch you can see the Smith Point Marina, which has ice, gas, diesel fuel, and some groceries. Jett's Marina is a little farther in.

Anchorages. There are several anchorages in the other branches of the river with 8 to 10 feet of water where you can drop the hook in relative seclusion. Keep an eye out for bald eagles, which are known to nest here.

Just past green "7" is one of the Chesapeake's few remaining cable ferries. They are interesting to watch in operation, and you can ride this one for free.

GREAT WICOMICO RIVER

Charts: 12225, **12235**

The Great Wicomico River offers numerous anchorages in relative seclusion as well as several points of resupply or refueling. The approach is easy: leave Great Wicomico Light, a steel spider, to starboard, and you will enter Ingram Bay, at the mouth of the river.

Here you have several choices. You can head southwest to enter Mill Creek, which shares a common entrance with the Great Wicomico; north into Cockrell Creek for resupply; or northwest up the Great Wicomico itself, which has many attractive anchorages.

Cockrell Creek

Charts: 12225, **12235**

Cockrell Creek, sometimes referred to by the name of its only town, Reedville, is the home port for much of the menhaden fishing fleet. The fish-processing plant is across the creek in what is actually Fleeton. If the plant is in operation, proceed well north of it to avoid its malodorousness. There are plenty of anchorages.

The area is unique in that it is the center for the entire menhaden fishing and processing industry. Here is where the fleet brings its catch to be turned into fish oil, meal, fertilizer, and scrap, which is used in animal feed, paint, and cosmetics. When the plant is in operation the stacks emit great billows of "smoke," which is actually steam from the process of drying the meal after the oil has been pressed out.

Provisions. Jennings Boat Yard (804-453-7181), in the cove below Tims Point, opposite the large stack marked on the chart, offers gas and diesel fuel, as well as ice (block and cube), limited hardware, and a few slips for transients.

Buzzard's Point Marina (804-453-3543), near the end of the west fork of the creek, offers gas and diesel fuel, repairs, ice, and a few transient slips. Both marinas have pumpout facilities.

You can either anchor in the east branch of the creek and take a dinghy in to the Reedville Marine Railway or tie up to the old wharf at the

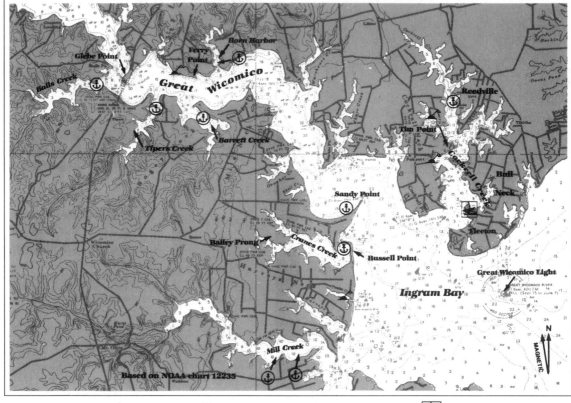

SCALE **1"** = **1.22** NAUT. MILES   ⚓ **Good anchoring**   ⚓ **Marina**   🛥 **Launching site**

southern tip of the peninsula, near the old icehouse, where there also is (or used to be) a good machine shop. The icehouse used to have one of the best block-ice bargains on the Bay. Now, however, it only carries cubes. Ten-pound block ice is available at the gas station about ⅓ mile up the road, a little beyond the church.

Marinas & Restaurants. Elijah's Restaurant (804-453-3621) is now located in the old Reedville Market, near the Reedville Marine Railway. The building has been restored to its early-19th-century condition, and the restaurant is noted for its fresh seafood and homemade soups.

Fairport Marina (804-453-5002), across Cockrell Creek, has a down-home type restaurant with both beef and seafood dishes. Block ice is also available here.

Anchorages. The best anchorages are in the main, north fork of Cockrell Creek. This is far enough away from the processing plant that

it is usually practically unaffected by it, and the surroundings are quiet and pleasant, although heavily residential. You can continue up this branch nearly to the end before it starts to shoal. Anchor wherever you find a place that appeals to you. The entire fork is well protected, and the holding is generally good. Beware of the unmarked shoal protruding into the creek just past the first cove to starboard. Favor the west half of the creek in this region. For the rest of the way, keep to the middle.

What to See & Do. Visiting Reedville, a town on the Virginia Historic Register, is like taking a trip back in time. The only street in town is lined with homes from the turn of the century, the oldest dating to 1875. Partway down the street is a monument to Elijah W. Reed, the town's founder. The Reedville Fisherman's Museum, on Main Street just inland of the Reedville Marine Railway, is open weekdays from 3:00 to 5:00 P.M. and weekends from

1:00 to 5:00 P.M. There is no admission fee, although donations are gratefully accepted.

Cranes Creek

 3 *No facilities*

Charts: 12225, **12235**

A course of 307 degrees from red "6" in the middle of Ingram Bay takes you to the first red "2" daymark at the entrance to this creek. The entrance is tight and a little tricky. If you draw more than 5 feet, you may not be able to get over the bar just west of the tip of Bussel Point.

Approach on a line with the two red daymarks and proceed slowly, holding fairly close to both of them. Hold close to red "4," then swing sharply to port, holding close to the end of the pier just past the marker, and head directly toward the sand spit at the end of Bussel Point. Once you squeeze past the end of the sand spit you will quickly find yourself in a well-protected basin with 8 to 11 feet of water. You can anchor anywhere here in quiet rural surroundings.

Overhead power cables prevent cruising sailboats from proceeding up the forks to either side of Bailey Prong. These cables are supposed to have a vertical clearance of 40 feet, but it may be a little less.

Sandy Point

 2 *No facilities*

Charts: 12225, **12235**

While it is part of the main Great Wicomico River, Sandy Point gets special mention because it is one of the most popular anchorages on the river.

In the bight north of Sandy Point is a well-protected, deep-water (15 feet) anchorage. The deep water holds quite close to the beach, and the area is better sheltered than the chart indicates. There is enough room for many boats to anchor without crowding one another. Unfortunately, the nice sandy beach that used to extend from the tip of Sandy Point is now nothing but a shoal.

Cruisers used to go ashore here to have beach cookouts. Recently, however, some "No Trespassing" signs have cropped up on what is

left of the point, as in many parts of the Bay. The shore is no longer accessible to cruisers.

Horn Harbor

 4

Charts: 12225, **12235**

Other little creeks branch off the Great Wicomico before Horn Harbor, but sandbars block their entrances, making them inaccessible to cruisers.

Anchorages. Horn Harbor, about 3 miles above Sandy Point, is something special. It is one of the snuggest hurricane holes on the Bay. The entrance is a little tricky, but once in, you'll find 7 to 8 feet of water.

Provisions. Just to the west of the entrance is the Horn Harbor Restaurant at the Great Wicomico Marina. Supplies in this area are limited to the fuel and ice available here.

Approaches. The Horn Harbor entrance is unmarked, and the numerous fish stakes around it add to the confusion. Ignore the stakes and approach the beach about 100 feet east of the entrance, then turn to port to parallel the beach until you can turn directly into the entrance. Private floats used to mark the channel, but there is no guarantee that they are still there. Favor the starboard (east) side as you negotiate the entrance. Once in, dogleg to starboard to avoid the little shoal on the west side of Horn Harbor just after you enter. The surrounding fields and woods rise more than 80 feet above the water to provide near total protection, which also means that you don't want to be here on a hot, muggy summer night.

Barrett Creek

 3 *No facilities*

Charts: 12225, **12235**

Approach. Across from and a little upstream of Horn Harbor, Barrett Creek offers a lovely rural anchorage that fascinated us. The mouth of the creek is crowded with confusing oyster stakes. They don't mark shoals, so it is best to ignore them.

Shoals protrude from each side of the entrance. The best approach is to continue up the Great Wicomico to just beyond Ferry Point, then turn and head right for the middle of the entrance to Barrett Creek. Once you pass between the two points of land at the entrance, swing to port and favor the east side of the creek the rest of the way.

Anchorages. Anchor in the region just short of where the creek forks. Here you have good holding in mud with 7 feet of water.

In the southern fork of the creek a small peninsula juts into the water. Several times we watched horses come down in both the morning and evening to play here in the water and with one another, amusing us to no end. Unfortunately, when we were here in 1998, there was no sign of the horses, and many new houses had been constructed along both sides of the creek. Although the peninsula still looks pretty much as it used to, we don't know if the horses are still there.

Directly across from this peninsula is a small marsh pond that is nearly landlocked. When we took our dinghy in to explore, we saw raccoons, deer, and opossums come down to the water in the evening.

There are no facilities here. In spite of the increased number of houses, you still are likely to be all by yourself wherever you anchor, something that is harder and harder to achieve on the Bay.

Tipers Creek

 No facilities

Charts: 12225, **12235**

Tipers Creek, just past Barrett Creek, is another tight little anchorage that few manage to find their way into. A bar here limits access to boats with drafts of less than 5 feet. If you can clear that bar, the entrance is easy.

If you stay in the middle and squeeze over the bar off the tip of the narrow finger of land that nearly closes the mouth of the creek, you will find yourself in a secluded little cove with 10 feet of water. You can proceed about halfway up the creek before the depth drops to less than 6 feet, but the best anchorage is just inside the spit.

Upper Great Wicomico River

Charts: 12225, **12235**

At Glebe Point there is a swing bridge (vertical clearance 9 feet) over the river that presents little obstacle to exploring the headwaters of the river. Until 1984 most cruising sailboats had to consider this the head of navigation because of an overhead power cable on the other side of the bridge that had an authorized clearance of 40 feet. When a violent storm caused one of the power poles to snap, two poles were replaced with 65-foot ones, providing an authorized clearance of at least 54 feet at midchannel, adequate clearance for all but the largest sailboats. Boats can continue to explore the river for about another 3 miles.

There are plenty of attractive and secluded anchorages. Other than to enter Balls Creek, stay in the main part of the Great Wicomico since the remaining offshoots are too shoal. You can anchor just about anywhere in good security.

Balls Creek is also accessible for most of its length, flowing between high, wooded banks. It carries a depth of 7 to 8 feet for about 1 mile before starting to shoal. The creek has no markers, and none are needed provided you stay clear of the small shoal on the north side of the creek entrance. The high, tree-lined banks make this a well-protected harbor in blustery or stormy weather. By the same token, it can be hot on a summer's night. The few houses on this creek are unobtrusive. However, in the mid-1990s a development, Tipers Landing, was planned for a 192-acre site on this creek.

MILL CREEK TO FLEETS BAY

Mill Creek

  No facilities

Charts: 12225, **12235**

Mill Creek, one of the prettiest waterways in the region, shares a common approach with the Great Wicomico. Once you pass the Great Wicomico Light, head directly toward the red

"2" daymark, to the southwest in the mouth of Mill Creek. Be sure to honor the next two markers, giving green "3" a wide berth and holding fairly close to red "4." As you pass red "4," swing sharply to starboard to enter Mill Creek proper. Favor the east side when you enter as a shoal extends from the western point at the entrance.

Approaches. The creek is unmarked from here on, but it has few protruding shoals to snag you. Just be wary of getting too close to any of the points of land. You can proceed nearly to the end of the creek, passing though scenic wooded surroundings that are dotted with homes.

Anchorages. Anchor anywhere that strikes your fancy; the holding is good in soft mud. If you would like to land on a sandy beach, the best anchorage is just inside the mouth of the creek, due south of red "4." You will need to be careful of both the depth and the substantial number of crab-pot floats here, but it's worth the effort.

There are no facilities of any kind on this creek, and you will encounter few other boats. If you are looking for a quiet, secluded anchorage, this is it.

Dividing Creek

 3 *No facilities*

Charts: 12225, **12235**

Although it is exposed to the southeast for most of its length, Dividing Creek offers some secure anchorages in its tributaries. There are no facilities here, so most of the people you encounter will be locals or cruisers looking for an out-of-the-way anchorage.

Approaches. The approach is easy. Simply pick up the first marker, a lighted green "3" (there is no "1" marker), and follow the markers to the northwest into the mouth of the creek. Beware of the unmarked shoals off Kent Point and the point north of Prentice Creek.

Anchorages. There is an excellent anchorage just inside Jarvis Point, although you need to feel your way past the shoal on the way in. Take your course from the green "7A" daymark north of Jarvis Point and head directly toward the red "2" daymark in the entrance to Jarvis

Creek. When you are about 100 yards from red "2," turn to the south and feel your way along the shoal to port until you are 100 yards past the end of the Jarvis Point hook. You can anchor just inside this hook or proceed carefully around the next point to starboard. In either case you will anchor in 7 feet of water, well protected in all directions.

To enter Prentice Creek, depart from a little upstream of the red "8" daymark west of Hughlett Point and head for the center of the opening into Prentice Creek, leaving green "1" close to port. There is good anchorage in 7 to 8 feet of water around the second bend. Some gas and ice may be available in Ditchley, but this is not a sure thing. This area is a little more populated than we anticipated; if you likewise prefer seclusion, try farther up Dividing Creek.

Lawrence Creek, about 1 mile above Prentice Creek, is easy to enter. Simply cruise in and drop the hook anywhere past the first bend. There shouldn't be significant boat traffic.

The last anchorage is in the north fork of Dividing Creek, where it bends to the north. The mouth of Natty Point Cove offers the prettiest anchorage in the area. It is quiet and secluded.

Fleets Bay

Charts: 12225, **12235**

This bay serves as an entryway to four cruising creeks: Indian, Dymer, Tabbs, and Antipoison.

Indian Creek

 2 – 3

Charts: 12225, **12235**

Like Dividing Creek, Indian Creek is easily entered. It is also exposed to the southeast for more than two-thirds of its length, and anchorages are to be found only in tributaries and in the last third of the main creek. Indian Creek has some excellent marine facilities and is much more built up than Dividing Creek. Even so, Indian Creek is pretty cruising ground.

Approaches. The approach and entrance are straightforward. Follow the markers, hold-

313

ing within about 100 yards of a line between the red entrance markers. The channel is wide; the only problem is an unmarked shoal to port off the southern side of the entrance.

Anchorages. The first anchorage is in Henrys Creek, to starboard just before you reach "6." Don't try to enter Barnes Creek, just inside Bluff Point; there is a 1-foot bar at the mouth of that creek. Simply stay in the middle of the entrance to Henrys Creek, favoring the starboard side as soon as you pass between the points of land at the entrance. Usually a stake marks the shoal to port, and more mark the one to starboard a little farther in. Here you can anchor anywhere in 7 to 11 feet of water. *Note: The overhead power cable in the west fork of the creek has a clearance of 30 feet, so sailboats should beware.*

About ½ mile past Henrys Creek, Balls Creek opens to starboard. The entrance is easy if you stay in the middle, avoiding the shoals on either side. Balls Creek offers snug anchorage in 8 to 11 feet of water, depending on how far up you go.

Longs Creek and Arthur Cove, to port and starboard, respectively, offer snug anchorage for the few boats that manage to squeeze in the unmarked entrances.

Pitmans Cove is one of the more attractive anchorages on Indian Creek. Stay in the middle on entering, and anchor anywhere except in the inviting cove to port, which is a little shy of water. The bottom is mud, and the entire creek is well protected from all directions.

Pass up Waverly Cove in favor of either of the two forks at the headwaters of Indian Creek. Both offer snug, well-protected anchorages in pleasant surroundings.

Marinas. The Chesapeake Boat Basin (804-435-3110), located on the point of land labeled Kilmarnock Wharf on the chart, deserves special mention. Kilmarnock Wharf was once a steamboat landing in the days when steamers were a major source of transportation in the Bay. The marina is nicely laid out and has some transient slips, ice, gas, and diesel fuel. The marine store's inventory is a little spotty but they can probably get whatever you need fairly quickly. There is also a gift shop. The town of Kilmarnock lies about 2 miles down Wharf Road from the marina. Transportation to town can usually be arranged at the marina.

Dymer Creek

Charts: 12225, **12235**

Like Dividing and Indian Creeks, Dymer is exposed to the southeast for most of its length. Entering is easy if you honor the markers on the way in. The best anchorages are in the tributaries or coves off the main creek. Virtually all are readily accessible, and except for Lees Cove, Chases Cove, and the unnamed cove just before Chases, all have 6 or more feet of water.

Marinas. There is a marine railway at the entrance to Georges Cove, and the Ocean Boat Shop, with 165 feet of dockage, is farther into the cove. No fuel or ice is available on the water, but transportation can be arranged into Kilmarnock for supplies.

Anchorages. The first cove to starboard on the way in, Rones Bay, makes a nice anchorage. Favor the starboard side when you enter, then stay well offshore. Watch out for the shoal extending out from the northeast corner of the cove.

The third cove to starboard, Hunts Cove, provides the best anchorage on this creek. Stay in the eastern half of the entrance on the way in to avoid the shoal on the other side. Look for a stake, which you should leave to port. Once you are well into the creek, stay in the middle until you select your anchorage.

If you are looking for more seclusion, continue toward the headwaters of Dymer Creek proper, past Chases Cove, where you have a choice of relatively private spots in which to drop the hook.

Tabbs Creek

  No facilities

Charts: 12225, **12235**

This creek is just south of Dymer Creek and shares a common approach. The entrance looks forbidding on the chart, but we have been told that it has been dredged and that boats with drafts of not more than 5 feet should be able to enter through the privately marked channel. Proceed slowly; there is no telling how much this channel may have shoaled in. Once inside, you have 9 to 12 feet of water and are fully protected from all directions.

Antipoison Creek

Charts: 12225, **12235**

Legend has it that this creek is where Native Americans provided Captain John Smith with a poultice that counteracted venom from a stingray's dart, hence the name Antipoison.

Approaches. As you approach the mouth of Antipoison Creek, there is an enticing little cove inside North Point to port. Don't try it; there isn't any water inside.

Antipoison Creek is well marked, and the approach is easy. Honor the red "2" daymark west of North Point and swing wide of the red "4" flasher before you turn to head directly into the creek mouth. As you enter, favor the north side to avoid the small shoal to port. Once inside, you will find 8 to 10 feet of water almost to the head of the creek.

Anchorages. The entire creek is well protected from all directions. You can anchor anywhere; however, the best anchorages are in the first two coves to starboard after entering the creek. The first offers room for several boats to swing in 8 feet of water.

To get into the second cove, proceed far enough past the entrance so that you enter in the middle when you swing to starboard. This will ensure that you avoid the shoal on the east side of the entrance. The shoal is normally marked by a stick with a cloth tied to it, but don't depend on it. Inside, there are several other sticks—oyster bed stakes, not shoal markers. This anchorage offers pleasant, rural surroundings with little boat traffic. You won't find fuel or marina facilities here, but you can find some supplies on the north shore at the Little Bay Ice & Seafood Store, under an Amoco sign.

RAPPAHANNOCK RIVER

Charts: 12225, **12235**, **12237**

The northernmost of three major rivers that penetrate nearly 100 miles into Virginia's tidewater region, the Rappahannock River bears a strong resemblance to the Potomac. Both have a long point on the northern side of their mouths, the best cruising grounds in both are within 30 miles of the mouth, and both anchor their navigable headwaters in a sizable city (Fredericksburg for the Rappahannock).

Although the river is navigable for 95 miles of its length, extensive marshes begin just below the bridge at Tappahannock, 39 miles upriver. At that point the river begins to narrow, the marshes become more extensive, and there are no more marine facilities upstream.

When approaching the mouth of the Rappahannock, give a wide berth to Windmill and Stingray Points, on the north and south sides, respectively. When approaching from the north, you can cut inside Windmill Point Light by almost a mile and still be in 6 to 8 feet of water. The shoals come up rather suddenly. If you are not a very good judge of distance, hold close to the light. In addition, numerous fish traps and crab pots in the shallows of Rappahannock Spit drastically decrease the appeal of cutting inside the light.

Stingray Point Light, on the south side of the river's mouth, gives you no choice in approach. If you don't honor this mark, you may have to get out and walk.

Windmill Point

Charts: 12225, **12235**

Marinas & Restaurants. On the south side of Fleets Island, just inside the tip of Windmill Point, is Windmill Point Marine Resorts. If you like shoreside, resort-type facilities, this stop is a must. Simply honor the privately maintained markers to make your way into the dredged basin. The channel tends to shift, and if you draw 6 feet or more, entering can be a challenge. Forget any ideas of anchoring out. It's not that kind of harbor.

North Shore of the Rappahannock River:
Dividing Creek to Corrotoman River

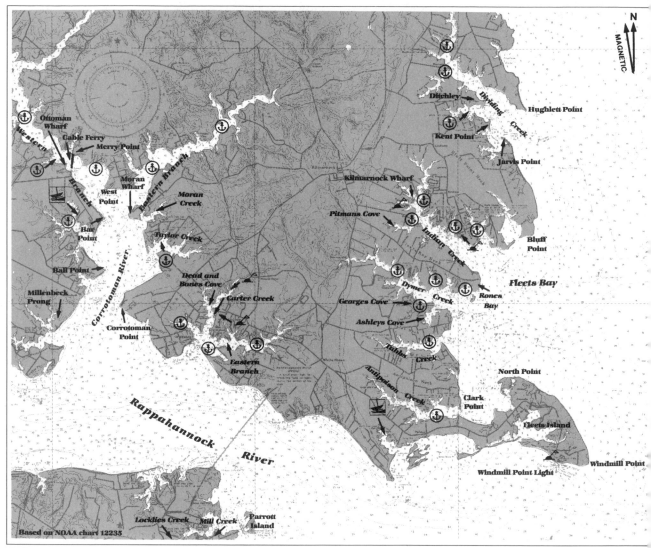

SCALE **1"** = **1.90** NAUT. MILES   ⚓ **Good anchoring**   ⚓ **Marina**   **Launching site**

The resort is nicely situated on a sloping beach overlooking the mouth of the Rappahannock and the Bay. It has tennis courts, golf, a pool, pedal boats, bicycles, and a nature trail. All this is in addition to the "standard" marina facilities and a motel. Many townhouses have been erected nearby, indicating that at least some people who have come here decided to stay. Dr. and Mrs. Wallace Atwood, who developed the original resort in the early 1970s, are in control once again and looking after their enterprise with tender loving care.

Don't try to enter any of the other inviting inlets between Windmill Point and Mosquito Point; not a one has any water.

Broad Creek (Deltaville)

  All facilities

Charts: 12225, **12235**

Just inside Stingray Point, on the south side of the mouth of the Rappahannock, is Broad Creek, a small harbor filled to capacity with boatyards and marinas. At last count I noted an even dozen.

Depths are reported to be 7 feet in the approach channel and 6 feet MLW in the harbor basin. All you have to do is pick up the first flashing 4-second green "1" channel marker (N37° 34.30′ W76° 18.48′) and follow the line of markers into the basin. The channel is narrow, so line up your course with the markers. Most of the marinas cater to transients as well as residents. There are no restaurants here, but transportation to nearby Deltaville is easy to arrange. Several area restaurants will send a car to pick you up.

This is a good spot for repairs or other marine services, but if you are looking for seclusion or an anchorage, try elsewhere.

Mill Creek

  No facilities

Charts: 12225, **12235**

The first navigable creek to appear on the south side of the Rappahannock River past Broad Creek, Mill Creek looks interesting at first glance. However, the entrance gets somewhat tricky after the initial set of markers. If you do attempt the entrance, don't try it in anything with a draft of much more than 3 feet; it is shoal inside.

The only boats that use this creek are the local fishing boats. There are no supplies for cruisers here.

The more adventurous may want to try the passage inside Parrott Island to approach Locklies Creek. You have to feel your way through, and few people would do it twice.

Locklies Creek

Charts: 12225, **12235**

Because of the shoals off Parrott Island, this creek is best approached by holding well out into the Rappahannock until you can line up the flashing 4-second, 14-foot green "9" marker near the south end of the Rappahannock River bridge and the flashing red "2" marker west of Parrott Island. A course that keeps you about 50 yards east of a line between these two markers will take you into the channel entrance.

Follow the markers at least to the first cove to starboard, which will serve as an anchorage for boats with less than a 5-foot draft. There are two small marinas in this area, but only the one by Locklies has gas and diesel fuel.

Past this point the creek shoals, and the chart doesn't give you much to go on. If you draw less than 3 feet, try it just to look. For spending the night, pass this creek by in favor of Carter Creek or the Corrotoman River.

Carter Creek (Irvington)

Charts: 12225, **12235**

Approaches. Just beyond the Rappahannock River bridge, on the north side of the river, the entrance to Carter Creek appears. No entrance instructions are necessary; just follow the markers. Past the entrance the creek fans out into a spray of coves or branches of the creek, one of the prettiest in the southern Bay. Yopps Cove and the Eastern Branch are to starboard; the main creek continues ahead until it forks into Church Prong and Dead and Bones Cove, and Carter Cove is to port. Take your pick!

Marinas & Restaurants. Carter Creek is a favorite with cruisers. In fact, its major drawback is that it draws too many boats! There are nine marinas in the main branch of the creek, including the luxurious Tides Lodge & Marina (804-438-6000) and the Tides Inn (804-438-5000), plus the friendly and informal Rappahannock River Yacht Club & Irvington Marina (804-438-5113). The latter has a tendency to attract big yachts. By the way, the Tides Lodge requires that men wear a jacket to the dining room after 6:00 P.M. and that women dress accordingly. There are several less posh restaurants right in the area, such as the Annabel Lee Restaurant and the River Café. A friend of ours reports that there is a "neat maritime antique store in nearby Irvington."

Anchorages. The creek offers complete security whether you tie up or anchor out, all the facilities and amenities you could ask for, and hospitable people. If you prefer relative privacy, put into Yopps Cove, to starboard just inside the entrance, or Carter Cove, to port, or head well up the Eastern Branch. A tour around the creek and its various branches clearly illustrates why it so attracts cruisers.

Corrotoman River

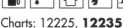

Charts: 12225, **12235**

Approach. About 3 miles past the Rappahannock River bridge, the Corrotoman River offers peaceful cruising grounds where you could easily spend several days exploring or simply enjoying the relatively unspoiled, thickly wooded shoreline. Poke around all parts of the Corrotoman to take in the scenery. The few protruding shoals are well marked. If you pay attention to where you are going, trouble will be hard to find. Nearly the entire length of the Corrotoman has plenty of water for most boats (7 feet or more). Plan to spend at least one day exploring it.

Anchorages. The first creek to port, just before you enter the Corrotoman River proper, is Whitehouse Creek. (This creek could be considered to be branching off either the Corrotoman or the Rappahannock, considering its location.) The Corrotoman has better anchorages, but this one recently became far easier to enter than it used to be after some locals installed private pilings, with the tops painted, to indicate the channel. The easiest way to enter is to depart from the lighted red "2" marker off Corrotoman Point on a course of 240 degrees. Use a depth-sounder to guide your way into the creek's mouth along the edge of the northern shoal until you can come to a due-south course into the main part of the creek. Here is a well-protected anchorage in 6 feet of water.

If your draft is 4 feet or less, you can also squeeze past the bar into Millenbeck Prong, which is to starboard as you are about to enter Whitehouse Creek. Because the area is still subject to shoaling, this is an exercise for the more adventurous.

As you clear the red "2" light Town Creek, the harbor at Millenbeck, becomes apparent to port. This appears to be a pretty harbor, but it is rather shoal and full of oyster stakes and crab floats. There probably won't be any room at the docks for your craft among the workboats. You might find some supplies in town, but it isn't worth the effort. If you need supplies, you are in the wrong river.

A course of 063 degrees from red "2" takes you to Taylor Creek, one of the good anchorages on the Corrotoman. The entrance appears to be formidable, with 2 feet indicated on the chart adjacent to the green "1" daymark at the creek entrance. However, there are rows of sticks, which you can use to guide you to the green "1" daymark close to the eastern shore. Be careful of the pile to port (probably capped by an osprey nest), hold close to green "1," swinging to port just as you clear it, and you should have 6 feet all the way in. Inside you will have a beautiful anchorage in 7 to 8 feet of water. Don't proceed past the point to the southwest where the creek forks since it shoals quickly.

Marinas. The next creek to port is Myer Creek, which lays claim to the only marina on the Corrotoman River, Yankee Point Sailboat Marina (804-462-5627), just inside the north fork of the creek. The marina has some limited marine supplies and a dockside sewage pumout facility for holding tanks. From here you should be able to arrange for transportation to a nearby store for other supplies.

Additional Anchorages. There is an excellent anchorage farther up this branch, about one bend past the marina. *Note: sailboats cannot go past the marina because of the overhead power line (clearance 35 feet) just beyond it.* No matter; one of the area's best anchorages is in the left fork of this creek in 7 to 8 feet of water. With a few homes tucked back in the wooded banks, this anchorage is serene and at least gives the impression of seclusion.

Moran Creek, the next creek to starboard, is an inveterate gunkholer's delight. Don't even attempt entry if your draft is 4 feet or more. The entrance is unmarked, and there are shoals on either side. The simplest approach is to take a course of 35 degrees from the red "4" daymark northeast of Ball Point and hold it until you are about 200 yards from the bank by Moran Wharf. Then swing to starboard and feel your way in around the sandbar to port, favoring the starboard side of the creek entrance. Just past the bar is a nice anchorage in 5 to 6 feet of water. You can explore nearly to the headwaters, but take it slow and feel your way.

Past Bar Point, 2 miles upstream from the river entrance, the Corrotoman forks into the Eastern Branch and the Western Branch, both of which are navigable for another 2 to 3 miles. Anchorages abound. Both branches are well protected from wind and wave. Pull to the side, out of the way of passing traffic, and drop your hook.

In the Eastern Branch only Hills and Bells Creeks offer a reasonable water depth past their entrances. The most favored anchorage in this branch is in the mouth of Bells Creek, off a nice sandy beach. Stay out of the other small tributaries as they shoal quickly.

The two significantly protruding shoals in the Western Branch, off West Point and the point opposite it, are well marked. These are the last navigational markers on this branch, but prudent cruisers need no more. Unlike in the Eastern Branch, most of the little tributaries in the Western Branch are navigable at least for a short distance past their entrances. The large bight to starboard just past West Point is an excellent hot-weather anchorage. Farther upstream are well-protected coves and tributaries if you feel the need for their additional shelter. Don't plan on proceeding more than ½ mile past Little Branch as the river quickly shoals.

You may still be able to get into John Creek, but I strongly advise against trying it due to the growth of the bar at its mouth—unless you are fond of dredging new channels. The same is true of Davis Creek, about a mile farther upstream. Lowrey Creek and both branches of Senior Creek offer tight refuges should you need one, but they are a little snug for hot weather. Anchoring in one of the many coves on the main part of this branch is normally preferable.

What to See & Do. One of the few remaining cable ferries on the Chesapeake still runs (since 1869) between Ottoman Wharf and Merry Point. If you approach while the ferry is in transit, leave plenty of room both ahead and astern of the ferry to avoid fouling the cable. One of the few free rides left in this day and age, there is no charge to ferry across the river. If you ever tour the area by car, try this interesting trip. Merry Point Mansion, built in 1767, is on its namesake point on the north side of the river. It isn't open to the public, but it is worth a look.

Urbanna Creek

 3

Chart: 12237

Like many rivers and creeks on the Bay, Urbanna has had many names. Its earliest recorded name was Nimcock Creek, but the source of that name is unknown. By 1680 the creek was known as Wormeley's Creek, after Ralph Wormeley, who built his estate, Rosegill, nearby. In 1705 the town of Queen Anne's City was established. The town's name was modified to Urbanna (Anne's City). It wasn't long before the creek assumed the town's name, both contracted into a single word, and so it remains today. Rosegill still exists, and we have been told that it is worth the 1-mile walk from the town to visit.

Approaches. Entering Urbanna Creek is simplicity itself, although the creek entrance may be a little difficult to see from the main part of the Rappahannock. The easiest way to find it is to run a course of about 290 degrees from the red "6" bell buoy off Towles Point until you can see the first marker, the red "2" light on the end of the jetty on the starboard side of the entrance to the creek. From there simply follow the markers on into the creek, favoring the starboard side after passing Bailey Point at the entrance.

Marinas, Restaurant, & Provisions. You will soon see the facilities offered by the four marinas there. The first one is really a restaurant, Windows, with 35 slips to accommodate transients. The other three are more conventional marinas, two of which, Urbanna Yachting Center (804-758-2342) and Dozier's Port Urbanna Yachting Center (804-758-2332), have dockside sewage pumpout facilities. The third marina is Jamison Cove Marina (804-758-0412). All three offer some transient slips. You can find nearly any kind of shoreside facility here.

Anchorages. For the best anchorage, go almost to the bridge, opposite Urbanna Boatyard. Although the creek is navigable for some distance beyond the fixed bridge, the vertical clearance of 21 feet sets the bridge as the head of navigation for all sailboats.

What to See & Do. During the Oyster Festival, normally the first weekend in November, don't expect to find any room anywhere in this creek. If you want to join this three-day party, make your reservation at one of the marinas early in the summer. During the rest of the year this is a quiet small town that prides itself on maintaining its character as a tidewater settlement. History buffs must tour the town. You can land just to the right of the grain elevators and walk in, or land at one of the marinas. The drugstore has great ice cream, and the Urbanna Inn offers excellent meals. The library used to be a tobacco warehouse, about 1777. About a mile inland are a supermarket and Rosegill. Urbanna's people are warm and friendly and willing to share tales of the town's history with you. Be sure to ask about Fort Nonsense, a favorite

tale of the spoofing of the British raiders during the War of 1812.

For the seclusion of a quiet cove, however, try elsewhere.

Robinson Creek

Chart: **12237**

One mile upstream from Urbanna Creek the dredged, 9-foot channel of Robinson Creek offers ready access to its two marinas. Unfortunately, the Joseph Conboy Shipyard went out of business long ago. For boats with drafts of less than 5 feet there is some anchorage room, but there are more interesting anchorages in the area.

Lagrange Creek

Chart: **12237**

Just above Robinson Creek is Lagrange Creek. A red daymark off Long Point gives promise of ready entrance to this 2-mile-long creek. Unfortunately, the water shoals quickly a short distance past the daymark, limiting access to shallow-draft (less than 3 feet) boats.

Just over a mile above the red daymark is Remlik Marine, offering gas, limited hardware, and inboard-outboard boat sales and repair.

This is a powerboat creek, so much so that cruising sailboats cannot even enter it.

Greenvale Creek

Chart: **12237**

On the east side of the Rappahannock about 2 miles above Lagrange Creek, Greenvale Creek offers the facilities of two marinas, where gas and ice are available. You must negotiate a well-marked, dredged, 6-foot channel to gain access to the creek.

Once you are inside, the creek opens out a little, allowing room to anchor between the two marinas.

Parrotts Creek

Chart: **12237**

Three miles farther upstream, just below Punchbowl Point, is the narrow, marked entrance to Parrotts Creek on the west side of the Rappahannock. Although facilities are available, this is day-trippers' country. Gas and ice are available at the Waterview Packing Company, but the water is too thin for comfort unless you are in a vessel that you can step out of and push. Cruisers should forget this creek.

Totuskey Creek

  No facilities

Chart: **12237**

The creek is on the east side of the Rappahannock, about 4 miles below the Tappahannock bridge. A long, narrow, well-marked channel, nominally 6 feet deep, stretches from the red nun "2" buoy about three-fourths mile off Waverly Point for a good 3 miles upstream.

Just outside the channel you can find some nice, secluded anchorages where local watermen make up most of the traffic. If you are a true gunkholer, try this one.

Piscataway Creek

  No facilities

Chart: **12237**

On the west side of the Rappahannock, about 2 miles below the Tappahannock bridge, Piscataway Creek offers an interesting anchorage to those with drafts of less than 6 feet. The entrance is unmarked but easy. Beware of a 5-foot spot just past the point at the entrance; from there to about 2 miles from the entrance you have 6 to 10 feet of water.

Just about anywhere after the first bend you can anchor fully protected from wind and wave. Not many cruising boats penetrate this far, but

those that do are likely to want to return. There are no marine facilities of any kind here, so plan accordingly.

Tappahannock & Upstream

Chart: **12237**

The town of Tappahannock is located on the west side of the Rappahannock River, just downstream from the bridge (fixed, 50-foot vertical clearance). Gas is available at the Haven Marina, a short distance up Hoskins Creek. The creek was dredged to 10 feet a few years ago, but check locally or with the Coast Guard to determine when the approach was last dredged since it frequently shoals in.

Boats with a draft of less than 4 feet can gas up at the Tappahannock Marina just above the bridge. Other supplies are available in town. There is no secure place to anchor, so unless you can take a slip at Haven or Tappahannock Marina, you probably should not try to spend the night here.

Although the river is navigable for another 50 miles above the Tappahannock bridge (all the way to Fredericksburg), this is normally about as far as cruising boats ever go. There are no marine facilities or even really good anchorages above this point, just the simple adventure of exploring the headwaters of this famous river. Should you try it, make sure that you have adequate fuel and other supplies for the round trip of more than 100 miles. Don't count on refueling at Fredericksburg or anywhere along the way; you will have to haul jerricans.

PIANKATANK RIVER
Charts: 12225, **12235**

For those running north or south on the Chesapeake Bay a favorite course is to follow the rhumb line between Smith Point and Wolf Trap Lights. This course neatly avoids most of the fish traps and crab pots by keeping you in 30 to 50 feet of water yet well out of the shipping lanes. By deviating about 5 miles from this course, you can easily enter the Piankatank River. It is one of the prettier tributaries on the Bay, with a wide selection of well-protected anchorages and plenty of marine facilities.

The entrance is broad and well marked, but don't try to cut inside any of the markers once you are into your approach. Some markers will let you get away with it, but many won't.

A course of 255 degrees from the flashing green "1" buoy should take you a good ¾ mile south of Stingray Point Light if you are approaching from the north. An extensive shoal extends to the east of Stingray Point.

If you are approaching from the south, head for the flashing green "3" marker about 1½ miles northeast of Cherry Point and come to the same course until you can pick up red "6." From here you can swing either to the northwest to enter Jackson Creek or sharply to the south to head upstream into the rest of the Piankatank. Be sure to honor the red "8" marker southeast of the tip of Stove Point—the bar between this point and the marker has caught more than one unwary captain! Watch out for fish traps during your initial approach.

The river is navigable for some 15 miles, from its entrance all the way to Freeport, but most larger cruising sailboats are stopped at about the 10-mile point by the 43-foot vertical clearance of the fixed bridge between Wilton Point and Dixie.

Jackson Creek

 ☆ 3 | 3 | *All facilities*

Charts: 12225, 12235

Approaches. At the apex of the angle formed by the southern shore of Stingray Point and the northern end of Stove Point Neck is Jackson Creek, the first of several excellent harbors off the Piankatank River and one of three areas rife with marine services. Looking at the chart, you may wonder whether you will have trouble negotiating the entrance. Indeed, the long shoal to port has snagged many a skipper who failed to notice the second pair of red and green daymarks ("3" and "4") close to shore almost due north of the first pair. The next two pairs ("5" through "8"), after you take a sharp turn to port beyond green "4," are also a little difficult to

pick out against the shoreline. However, with some forethought and attention to where you are and where you are headed, the entrance can be made without incident. There is at least 9 feet of water all the way in. Simply follow the markers and stay near the middle of the channel since the edges rise sharply.

Marinas. Past the entrance the creek splits into two forks. The right fork contains the Deltaville Marina (804-776-9812), offering a full set of marina services, including gas, diesel, ice, some marine supplies, and a self-service laundry. In the left fork is the Fishing Bay Yacht Club (804-776-2346). It tends to be crowded, and you must be a member of a yacht club with reciprocal privileges in order to use the facilities.

Anchorages. Both arms of the creek have good anchorages that are fairly well protected in most directions. Pick a spot out of the way of traffic, and make sure you have adequate room to swing. The area is rather built up, so you may have difficulty finding a place to land other than at the marinas.

Restaurants & Provisions. Deltaville, a nice, quiet little town, is less than a 1-mile stroll up the road from wherever you manage to land. In town are grocery stores, a hardware store, a bank, and a post office. There are at least three reasonably priced, informal restaurants in the middle of the three-block-long town: Taylor's (804-776-9611), Toby's (804-776-6913), and The Galley (804-776-6040). Taylor's will provide transportation if you call from a marina. I'm not sure about the other two.

This little harbor is a welcome refuge from bad weather as you can get into it quickly from the Bay. On the other hand, if you are looking for seclusion, head on up the Piankatank.

Milford Haven

 ☆ 3 | 3 | *All facilities*

Charts: 12225, 12235

Approaches. I have a little difficulty categorizing Milford Haven, other than as the body of water that makes Gwynn Island an island. The main entrance is from the Piankatank, past Narrows Point on the western tip of Gwynn Island and through the swing bridge connecting

Piankatank River

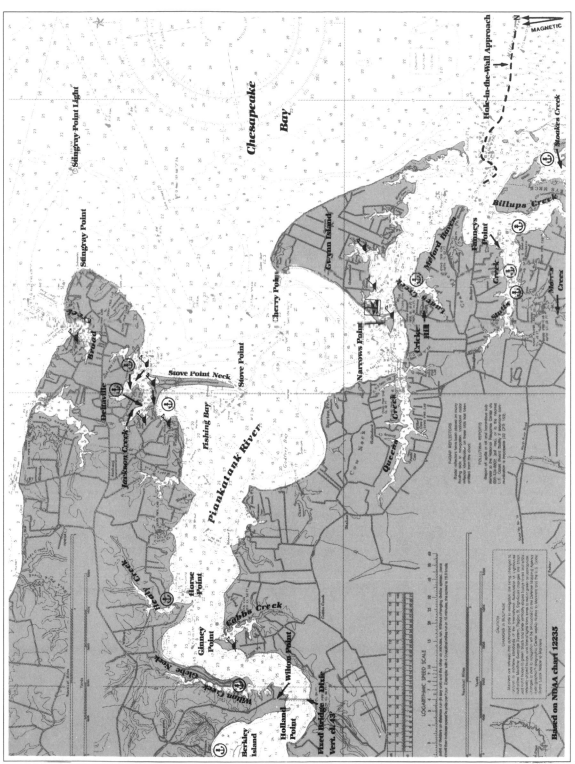

SCALE 1" = **1.31** NAUT. MILES   Good anchoring   Marina   Launching site

Based on NOAA chart 122235

the island to the mainland. This is the straightforward, "easy" approach.

Marinas. There is a cluster of marine facilities on both sides of the bridge on Gwynn Island. These marinas range from the full-service Narrows Marina, complete with motel, restaurant, pool, and self-service laundry, to the Gwynn Island Landing State Launching Ramp, which is just that.

Alternative Approach. Another entrance, locally called the Hole-in-the-Wall, is for gamblers. If you are heading north looking for a harbor or leaving the Piankatank heading south, the Hole-in-the-Wall offers a timesaving shortcut and a challenge to boatmen. If you draw less than 4 feet, give it a try, but go slowly and watch the markers carefully. Entering on a rising tide is recommended. Do not try this passage if you draw more than 4 feet. As you pass the red "6" light on the way in from the Bay, feel your way carefully, especially between red "8" and red "14."

Note that after you pass red "14" on the way in, the marker numbers in Milford Haven are referenced from the Narrows Point entrance, decreasing from "12" on down. So when entering from the Hole-in-the-Wall, keep the red markers to the right until you pass red "14," then keep red to the left as you head toward the Narrows Point entrance.

Once into Milford Haven, all you have to do is pay attention to the markers and keep an eye on the water itself. It is frequently clear enough for you to detect any shoals by glancing at the shelving edges. There is no excuse for going aground.

Anchorages. Anchorages abound, so you can veto tying up at any of the marinas near the bridge. Skip Edwards Creek unless you are heading for either Powell's Boatyard or the Edwards Railway here; other anchorages are less public.

One anchorage is just inside the mouth of Lanes Creek, where the depth starts to decrease from 7 feet. Barn Creek looks like another nice snug anchorage, but we haven't investigated it.

Stoakes Creek, just to the south of the Bay entrance to Milford Haven, calls to true-blue gunkholers as it is totally unmarked and the shoals on either side require that you feel your way in. Again, if you have a draft of 4 feet or

more, don't try it. No one should anchor here on hot, windless summer nights as the marshes are thick with mosquitoes and no-see-ums. The same holds true for Billups Creek, although the entrance is easier and there is 6 feet or more of water well into the creek.

Stutts Creek has the best anchorage just about anywhere upstream of the mouth of Billups Creek. This creek is navigable, with a depth of at least 6 feet, for a good mile past Fanneys Point, and you should explore it at least once. It is a pretty creek.

The more adventurous may decide to attempt to squeeze into Morris Creek, to the south. Owners of larger boats should plan to ask locally or sound the entrance from a dinghy as the entrance may have shoaled in. If you can get inside, I recommend a snug little anchorage in 6 feet of water just past the entrance. Sailboats should not go beyond the first bend because the water starts to get shallow and the overhead power cable has a 30-foot clearance.

History. Gwynn Island deserves some attention. With 1,500 acres, it is one of the larger islands in the Chesapeake. Unlike most of the other islands, it has had a remarkably slow rate of erosion, thanks to its relatively sheltered location on the west side of the Bay.

The island was originally settled by a Colonel Hugh Gwynn in 1634. The legend holds that the colonel and two of his servants were admiring the island, when they saw a sudden squall upset a small dugout canoe containing a young Native American girl. Upon rescuing the girl, they discovered her to be the daughter of the chief of the Piankatank tribe that inhabited the area. In gratitude, the colonel was given the island from which they made the rescue. He just as promptly managed to obtain an official grant to Gwynn Island from its English "proprietor."

Gwynn Island played a part in the Revolutionary War. After burning Norfolk, Lord Dunsmore, the Royal Governor of Virginia, assembled a fleet of more than 180 ships loaded with loyal Tories and some British troops, moved up the Bay, and took over Gwynn Island. Looting the island and devouring all the livestock, they then used the island as a base of operations, raiding other settlements, notably such Eastern Shore islands as Tilghman, James, and Sharps. Dunsmore's group was finally driven off by the local militia, which mounted cannon at Cricket Hill on the mainland. It is debatable whether it was the cannon or the outbreak of fever, which killed more than 500 of the Tories, that really drove Dunsmore and company off the island. Today a Coast Guard station occupies the site of the cannon batteries.

Until 1884, when a ferry started operating between Gwynn Island and the mainland, access was by individual boat only. The ferry has since been replaced by a modern swing bridge.

Much of Gwynn Island retains the flavor of an authentic turn-of-the-century fishing and seafaring community, despite the summer influx of tourists. The island has given the U.S. Navy and the maritime fleet many a ship captain.

Queens Creek

Charts: 12225, **12235**

Just west of Narrows Point on Gwynn Island is a narrow, marked channel leading into Queens Creek. A few years ago the controlling depth in this channel was 5 feet. It probably has filled in since then, so that the depth is probably something less than that now. If you carry more than a 3-foot draft, check the controlling depth with one of the local watermen before trying it. The creek opens up inside, providing a fair amount of anchoring room in a snug little harbor with 6 to 7 feet of water.

On the other hand, the shore is relatively built up, and the Queen's Creek Marina offers little for the transient. Go for the better anchorages farther upstream.

Fishing Bay

Charts: 12225, **12235**

Anchorage. The chart representation of Stove Point Neck resembles the head of a

pterodactyl. Beneath the dinosaur's neck and west of the thin peninsula forming its beak lies Fishing Bay, one of the most popular anchorages on the Piankatank. Unfortunately, save for the set of marinas located here, all the property is private. The marinas have put in a number of moorings recently, but there is still plenty of room in which to anchor. On a hot, windless, summer night this may well be the best place in the area to spend the night. It is well protected but still sufficiently open to the south and southwest to permit even the slightest breeze of southwesterly air (usually bug-free) to move over and through your boat.

Marinas. The marinas on the western side of Fishing Bay are sometimes a little difficult to pick out as you enter. You can find just about any marine facility you need, from ice to complete engine and hull repair. Fishing Bay Harbor Marina (804-776-6800) also has a pool (necessary if the nettles are in).

This is a nice but busy anchorage. For a snugger, more secluded harbor, investigate the remaining creeks and harbors upstream on the Piankatank.

Healy Creek

 No facilities

Charts: 12225, **12235**

Approach. Healy Creek, on the north shore of the Piankatank, is easier to enter than the chart might lead you to believe. Beware of the unmarked shoal on the east side of the approach to the creek entrance. Stay near the middle of the Piankatank until you can line up the first set of daymarks at the Healy Creek channel entrance. Do not confuse these with the red "14" Piankatank River daymark southeast of Horse Point. Once the entrance markers are lined up, head directly for them and be sure to keep them on the correct side of you. At the last marker, head directly for the opening, which should be clearly visible at this stage.

Anchorages. There is an exceptional anchorage just past the sandy hook at the entrance. You can anchor anywhere from just inside the entrance to the fork in the creek in about 7 feet of water. Here you will find a few slips belonging to the Horse Point Estate &

Marina and a couple of other boats already at anchor. The marina has no facilities for transients.

The whole creek is quiet and relatively secluded. It provides plenty of protection from wind and wave in a blow but is open enough to permit a cooling breeze in hot weather.

Cobbs Creek

Charts: 12225, **12235**

On the south shore of the Piankatank, just east of Ginney Point, is Cobbs Creek, offering an excellent, sheltered anchorage in 8 feet of water. The approach is straightforward, but be careful of the shoal north of the final red daymark. After you clear the sandy hook to port at the creek mouth you can drop your hook. Aside from a few watermen, you probably won't find much boat traffic.

Ginney Point Marina is located here, but all you are likely to obtain is ice or, possibly, a slip for the night. Most cruisers just anchor.

Wilton Creek

  No facilities

Charts: 12225, **12235**

This is our favorite anchorage on the Piankatank, partly because of the attractiveness of the creek itself and partly because of some special memories. It was here that our preschool daughters learned to row the dinghy by themselves. They insisted that they knew how, so we tied 100 feet of line to the painter of the dinghy and "cast them adrift." Within 15 minutes they had learned to row well enough to get the dinghy to take them more or less to where they wanted to go.

About that time a local resident rowed over and offered to let us land on his dock if we wanted to stretch our legs. Then he asked if we needed any ice or if he could drive us into town

Two young Shellenbergers fish from their dinghy. Wilton Creek is where they learned to row by themselves.

for supplies! Is it any wonder that we have a warm feeling for the place?

Approaches & Anchorages. Although unmarked, the entrance is easy. Swing wide around the southern tip of Glebe Neck and head directly into the mouth of the creek. There is 8 feet of water inside, gradually decreasing to about 5 feet a mile upstream. There are cliffs 10 to 20 feet high on either bank for a good portion of the creek's length. Anywhere in here is snug anchorage. The icing on the cake is the creek's north-south orientation, which allows a cooling breeze from the typical southerly in hot weather.

If you're looking for a snug, secluded anchorage in beautiful surroundings, stop here.

Wilton Point Bridge & Upstream

  No facilities

Charts: 12225, **12235**

Approach. The 43-foot vertical clearance of the fixed bridge between Wilton Point and Dixie makes this the head of navigation for most cruising sailboats. Some excellent cruising grounds await those who can get past the bridge. The overhead power lines just past the bridge have a vertical clearance of 68 feet, so they present no problem.

After passing under the bridge, swing wide around the tip of Wilton Point and head directly toward the east end of Berkley Island. This takes you past the unmarked shoal off Holland Point. The best anchorage is in 9 feet of water, north of Berkley Island. The island is uninhabited but has two docks, one on the north side, the other on the west side, which facilitate landing should you wish to explore.

Anchorages. The west side of the island is relatively high, tapering down toward the east until it ends in a long shoal extending to the southeast of the island. Holding is good, and the whole area is relatively wild. Since few cruising boats penetrate this far, this area offers seclusion.

The deep water continues for several miles upstream, all the way to Freeport. There are several potential anchorages, most of them comparatively exposed. By far the best is the one by Berkley Island. You have to contend with several unmarked shoals, but if you simply avoid all points of land, you should have no trouble.

You cannot get supplies in this part of the Piankatank.

Region 6

Region 7

WOLF TRAP LIGHT TO CAPE HENRY

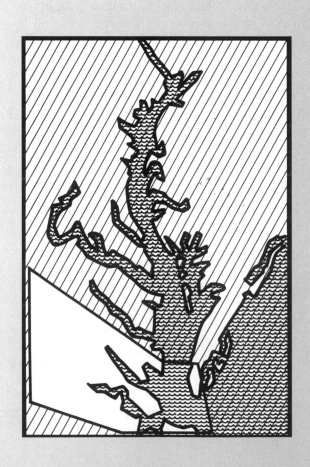

Wolf Trap Light to Cape Henry

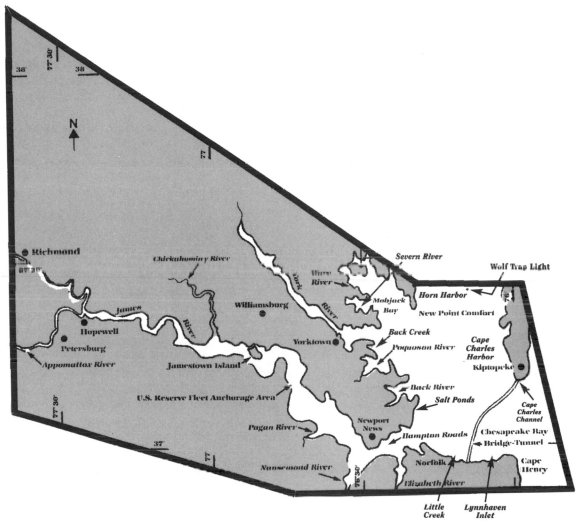

SCALE 1" = 15.5 NAUT. MILES

FROM WOLF TRAP LIGHT ON south, you are in the bottom of the Bay. Here the wave action is similar to that near the Atlantic coast in this latitude until the edge of the continental shelf. However, you are still in semiprotected waters, so you won't experience wave heights like those encountered in the open ocean. Until you proceed past the protection of Cape Henry and Cape Charles into the Atlantic Ocean proper you are still in the Chesapeake Bay.

Wolf Trap Light is placed to warn shipping traffic of the Wolf Trap Shoal. This shoal extends eastward from the Western Shore, approximately in the middle of a 10-mile stretch from the Hole-in-the-Wall entrance to Milford Haven (south of Gwynn Island) to the mouth of Mobjack Bay, which, with the possible exception of Horn Harbor, about 3 miles north of New Point Comfort, has no hospitable harbors. Wolf Trap Shoal takes its name from the British frigate HMS *Wolf*, which ran aground, thereby trapping itself on this shoal during the American Revolution. The frigate was captured by American revolutionaries, reputedly local watermen!

Each of the shores in the four cardinal directions in this part of the Bay has a distinct character. To the south is the cosmopolitan atmosphere of Norfolk, with the enormous ships docked or anchored by the Navy base. This is Hampton Roads, made famous by the classic battle between the first Union and Confederate ironclad ships, the *Monitor* and the *Merrimack* (renamed the *Virginia*). Here, too, is the entrance to the channels of the Intracoastal Waterway (ICW), leading all the way to Florida.

To the southwest and west are the cruising grounds of the York and James Rivers, as well as the numerous tributaries fanning off Mobjack Bay.

To the north is the entire balance of the Chesapeake Bay, with its fantastic collection of creeks, rivers, and harbors luring the cruiser.

To the east is the bottom of the Delmarva Peninsula, where there are only a few harbors to be found and explored by the cruiser, unusual for the Chesapeake.

EASTERN SHORE

South of Wolf Trap Light there are few harbors on the Chesapeake's Eastern Shore. The real cruising grounds are on the Western Shore. Only three sets of harbors are worth mentioning here: the cluster of three harbors around Cherrystone Inlet, Kiptopeke Harbor of Refuge, and Cape Charles Channel. A few other creeks are shown on the chart, but none is even close to navigable.

CAPE CHARLES HARBOR, KINGS CREEK, & CHERRYSTONE INLET

Charts: 12221, 12222, **12224**

These three harbors, the last natural ones on the Eastern Shore, are lumped together here because they share the same approach. The entrance is relatively long but well marked. Interestingly enough, you can safely ignore the first few markers in the entrance channel (all of those associated with Bar Channel) and directly approach the red "4" lighted spar near the beginning of Cherrystone Inlet Channel. From red "4" on, remain in the marked channel. At night there are ranges for each of these channels that bring you safely to the mouth of Cape Charles Harbor. Range A for Bar Channel, which runs from the Bay to the quick-flashing red "2" channel marker at the start of Cape Charles Harbor Channel, consists of a quick-flashing, 19-foot-high front range light and an equal-interval 6-second, 33-foot-high rear range light. Range B, from the quick-flashing red "2" channel marker to the entrance to Cape Charles Harbor Basin, consists of a quick-flashing red, 16-foot-high front range light and an equal-interval rear range light.

Cape Charles Harbor

Charts: 12221, 12222, **12224**

Approach, Anchorages, & Marinas. As you proceed through Cherrystone Inlet Channel the harbor basin appears off your starboard bow. Immediately to starboard as you enter the basin is the Cape Charles Refuel Dock, where ice, gas, and diesel fuel are available. Here is where you can arrange for a slip in the landlocked municipal basin behind the Coast Guard

National Geodetic Survey

Aerial view of Cherrystone Inlet, with Kings Creek at the bottom.

station. It is possible to tie up here at no charge long enough to go into town and return. Most of the bulkheads along the harbor basin are taken up by commercial clamming boats, so you are not likely to find space to tie up. You can anchor past the ferry slips provided that there is not a strong west wind.

Unless you rent a slip at the Cape Charles Town Harbor (757-331-2357), we recommend proceeding on to either Kings Creek or Cherrystone Inlet for the night. The harbor is open to the west, and there is only a little room to anchor.

Provisions & Restaurants. There are several stores on Cape Charles's main street where you can obtain supplies. There are also a couple of good restaurants and two hotels. Outside of the main street, the town is residential, with several stately old homes that are worth seeing.

331

Kings Creek

Charts: 12221, 12222, 12224

Kings Creek is still relatively unspoiled. The shore is lined with a marsh backed by pine trees with a few houses scattered among them. The only drawback is that it is currently unreachable by boats with drafts of 5 feet or more. If you draw less than 5 feet, you can find your way at least as far as Kings Creek Marina (757-331-2058), on the south shore just inside the entrance. *Note: Kings Creek Marina will be completely rebuilt and the channel dredged over the winter of 2001–2.*

There is an overhead power cable (vertical clearance 33 feet) well up the creek, but no cruising sailboat has any business going that far in; the water depth quickly drops to well under 4 feet, with 1 foot not uncommon.

Simply follow the markers into the creek, proceeding cautiously and checking the depth as you go. You will see the marina to starboard. Head into it just before reaching daymark "10." However, if you had trouble getting into the Kings Creek channel, you won't make it to the marina, nor will you get much farther upstream. Head back out and try Cherrystone Inlet.

Cherrystone Inlet

 No facilities

Charts: 12221, 12222, 12224

Approaches. To get into Cherrystone Inlet, just continue up the channel past Kings Creek and head for Wescott Point. Keep close to the spit making up Wescott Point to avoid the shoal to starboard. This shoal is frequently marked with bush stakes. If you see them, leave them to starboard.

Anchorages. This creek has a number of nice anchorages but no marine facilities or services of any kind.

You can anchor anywhere inside Wescott Point off a nice, sandy beach in good security. There is a large campsite on the opposite shore, below Mill Point, so you might want to continue upstream beyond Mill Point. There is at least 7

feet of water in Cherrystone Inlet for a distance of about 2 miles above Wescott Point. Proceed cautiously, as the band of deep water is not very wide. A shoal extends out from the western shore of the inlet about 2 miles into Cherrystone Inlet. The chart shows a house on the shoal; as you come up the inlet, the house appears to be sitting right in the middle of the waterway. Under no circumstances proceed beyond the house, for it marks the end of deep water, if 4 to 5 feet can be called "deep."

What to See & Do. To starboard just after you pass Kings Creek on the way in is Cherrystone Aqua Farms. Dr. Michael Pierson started raising clams there in 1984 and now markets several million each year. The facility is not open to the general public, but the occasional visitor, especially one by water, might manage to arrange a tour if he or she asks nicely.

To port, the first house on Savage Neck keeps several peacocks. You may not be able to see them from the water without glasses, but you will probably hear them on occasion. They were kept in "the old days" as intruder alarms.

Savage Neck is quite low, and there is little vegetation toward the end of the point, so that from your secure anchorage you can easily observe ships passing up or down the Bay. You couldn't ask for a better location to watch a beautiful sunset. After sundown it gets rather dark. The lack of shoreside lights tells you that you are in the country.

KIPTOPEKE BEACH

Charts: 12221, 12222, 12224

This title is not really the name of this harbor. Kiptopeke is simply the name of the nearest town. Kiptopeke Beach is indicated on the chart, but there is nothing there anymore. It used to be the terminal used by the Cape Charles ferry until it was replaced by the Chesapeake Bay Bridge-Tunnel. The old ferry slip is protected by a breakwater formed by the sinking of nine WWII-surplus ferrocement ships in a long row between the slip and the Bay.

Anchorages. There is an excellent barrier to wave action from the west, a little less from the north and south unless you anchor on the lee side of the old ferry slip itself. There is at least 6 feet of water on both sides of the ferry slip as long as you stay a prudent distance from the shore.

Approaches. One advantage of this spot is ease of approach. The two lines of concrete ships have plenty of water on all sides and can be made out from a considerable distance. As you approach, the apparently solid breakwater soon resolves itself into individual hulls with noticeable gaps between them. There is a white light on either end of the breakwater. The old ferry passage is right in the middle, where the northern line of four ships and the southern line of five ships overlap. It doesn't look like there is much room between the lines, but this is an illusion. After all, the ferries used to pass through here.

Kiptopeke Beach is now a Virginia state park, complete with a boat-launching ramp and a fishing pier but no slips. Boaters are asked to keep clear of the swimming beach to the north of the boat ramp. You will have to land by dinghy. You are not permitted to tie up at the dock, but there is room to anchor behind the concrete ships without too much disturbance from the boat ramp. This is usually a pleasant and popular anchorage; however, in a strong south to southeast wind it can be a rough ride. Freshwater and showers are available.

It is interesting to see the concrete ships, if only once. This is a different kind of Bay anchorage with comparative isolation. It seems to be a favorite spot for many boats out of the Hampton Roads area.

CAPE CHARLES CHANNEL
Charts: 12221, 12222, **12224**

This channel is little more than a shallow passage from Wise Point, on the Bay side at the southern tip of Cape Charles, to Magothy Bay, on the eastern side of the cape. Magothy Bay leads north to The Thorofare (another

Peter McClintock/Virginia Marine Resources Commission

Concrete World War II ships, sunk to form a breakwater to protect the old ferry dock, make a good harbor of refuge off a sand beach. The marina construction began in 1988.

one!), which eventually connects to Sand Shoal Inlet, on the Atlantic Ocean side of the Delmarva Peninsula.

The 40-foot vertical clearance of the fixed bridge stops just about all cruising sailboats.

Shallow-draft powerboats with an adventurous crew might attempt the channel passage to explore Magothy Bay after checking with a local regarding the current depth.

WESTERN SHORE

The Western Shore of the Bay from south of Wolf Trap Light to the mouth of the Bay is where this region's cruising traffic is concentrated. Excellent, attractive harbors ranging from the very popular to some that are rarely visited by cruisers pepper the area. I have chosen to treat the region from Hampton Roads to Cape Henry on the Atlantic side as part of the Western Shore cruising grounds, although technically this region is the southern shore of the Bay. A glance at the chart shows that it is for the most part contiguous to the Western Shore, and the dearth of anchorages in this region of the Eastern Shore increase the probability that you will approach Hampton Roads from the Western Shore. (Conversely, if you are entering the Bay at its mouth, you are more likely to proceed from the Roads up the Western Shore than to try the sparse offerings of the Eastern Shore here.)

HORN HARBOR
Charts: 12221, **12238**

Unless you count the extremely narrow, shallow, and twisting entrance to Winter Harbor (which nearly all sizable cruising boats should avoid) a couple of miles to its north, Horn Harbor is the first acceptable harbor in a long stretch of the Chesapeake's Western Shore as you head south from the vicinity of the Piankatank. This is not the snug little hurricane hole near the headwaters of the Great Wicomico River. This Horn Harbor is about 3 miles north of New Point Comfort, on the north side of the entrance to Mobjack Bay.

Approaches. The well-marked entrance was dredged in January 1990, making it readily accessible to boats drafting up to 6 feet. Deep-draft boats also can squeeze through the entrance channel as long as no northerly blow is expected (or in progress). The safest first-time approach to the channel entrance is a 288-degree departure from the Mo (A) "HH" buoy in the Bay to the red "2" light mounted on a peculiar-looking casement structure. The channel has shoaled somewhat from the north, and you should give the next marker, red "2A," a moderately wide berth. Then swing to pass close by the green "3." Take it slow through this area until you pass green "3" since the shoal tends to shift with the winter storms. This is the only tricky spot. From here on in, simply follow the markers. You may find that the markers do not agree with those shown on the chart. When there seems to be a conflict, honor the markers that are actually there and you should have no problem.

Anchorages. After you clear red "12" about ½ mile past Mill Point, the channel bends to the right, fairly well indicated by sticks. You will need to avoid the inevitable crab pots in the channel. Once you pass the red "4" daymark, you can anchor nearly anywhere in the creek or continue on past the next two bends to visit Horn Harbor Marina, where you will find gas, diesel fuel, ice, and limited hardware (mostly for powerboats). Shortly beyond the marina the water quickly thins. Near the marina is a good place to anchor in a blow.

MOBJACK BAY

Charts: 12221, **12238**, 12241

Mobjack Bay covers a considerable area. You can spend literally days exploring it. The mouth of this bay is 3½ miles wide from New Point Comfort to the edge of Guinea Marshes. From New Point Comfort the bay extends a good 7 miles to Ware Neck Point, where it divides into the North and Ware Rivers. Two-thirds of the way from the mouth of this bay to Ware Point, the East River splits off to the north, and the Severn River to the southwest. Four other anchorage areas are addressed below, but these four rivers are the principal tributaries of Mobjack Bay.

As you approach the mouth of the bay, beware of the extensive fish traps. This is defi-

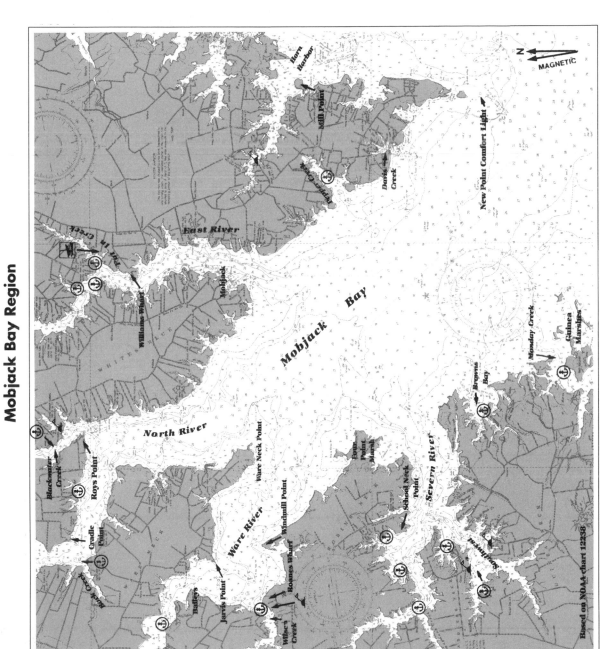

Mobjack Bay Region

SCALE 1" = **1.73** NAUT. MILES   Based on NOAA chart 12238

⚓ **Good anchoring**   ⚓ **Marina**   ⛵ **Launching site**

nitely working watermen's territory. At times the traps are so thick that there may seem to be no way through them. There is, but you have to take the time to find and follow the fairways, indicated by the black and white nuns (being replaced with yellow ones now). Needless to say, making your way through this maze of fish traps in the dark can be a nightmare. If you are not completely familiar with the area, do not approach at night.

One of the most prominent man-made landmarks in the area is the old New Point Comfort Lighthouse, off the southern tip of New Point Comfort. It is indicated on the chart by the notation "ABAND LT HO." This 63-foot-high sandstone structure, built in 1804, was replaced by a lighted buoy (or pair of buoys, depending on your perspective) in the early 1950s. However, the lighthouse remains a prominent structure, even as a ruin.

For ease of narrative, I cover the creeks and rivers in a counterclockwise direction around Mobjack Bay, starting with Davis Creek, just over a mile upstream from the New Point Comfort Lighthouse.

Davis Creek

Charts: 12221, **12238**

Approaches. On the chart Davis Creek appears to have a difficult, narrow entrance. Actually, even with a bit of sea running, it isn't hard for shoal-draft boats.

The first leg is almost due north. It is the longest and, with a channel width of about 50 feet (less than the 80 feet indicated on the chart), the most difficult leg because of the distance between the first two markers. After that the markers are much closer together and following the channel is easy. Be very cautious between red "4" and red "6," where you must negotiate your way between the outlying shoals before entering the creek proper. You should be able to see the shoals by the change in the color of the water (varying degrees of brown). To starboard, you can probably watch the assorted seabirds walk on the mud flats nearly up to the channel. The

controlling depth was 3 feet in 1986, and unless it has been dredged in the interim, only shoal-draft vessels should use this creek.

Once you pass between the two arms of land at the entrance, you will be able to stay in deep water even though the shoals to either side appear to be uncomfortably close.

Marinas & Dockage. Near the final marker in the creek a long dock extends nearly to the edge of the channel. This is the public landing, where you can tie up if you can find room. A little farther up is the Crabbers & Fishermans Wharf, a red building with white trim. I assume that the gas pumps here service the local watermen, as this creek does not even pretend to cater to cruising boats.

If you plan to explore Davis Creek, do it early in the day. Then if you can't find a place to tie up for the night, you'll have time to look elsewhere before nightfall. This is an interesting place to visit, but better and more attractive anchorages beckon cruisers farther into Mobjack Bay.

Pepper Creek

  No facilities

Charts: 12221, **12238**

Approaches. The entrance to Pepper Creek lies about 3 miles above New Point Comfort. The green "1" daymark at the outer end of the approach to this creek is a bit difficult to see until you are fairly close to it. The easiest way to start your approach is from the 15-foot-high flashing 4-second red "6" light in Mobjack Bay, southwest of Dutchman Point. From this light a course of 345 degrees takes you directly to Pepper Creek green "1." Leave this daymark a good 50 yards to port and head directly for the red "2" daymark, which looks like it is squarely in the middle of the creek entrance. Leaving red "2" close to starboard, swing to starboard and remain in the middle of the creek. Watch out for the 2-foot spot to port about 100 yards past the red "2" daymark.

Anchorages. Once inside, you can anchor nearly anywhere in the main part of the creek. Six feet of water is carried for half of its length, and then it starts to shoal to nothing. (Stay out of the first cove to starboard; it only has 1 foot of water.) Here you are protected from all but the southwest. Even from that direction the outlying shoals and the twist in the entrance channel moderate any waves. This is a pleasant anchorage, but the entire shoreline is marshy, so be prepared for mosquitoes.

East River

Charts: 12221, 12225, **12238**

The East River is perhaps the closest and most easily reached of the four main rivers off Mobjack Bay. It offers a number of nice anchorages in pleasant surroundings, but it doesn't offer much in the way of marine facilities.

Marinas. Just inside the mouth of the river, on the west side, is the town of Mobjack, where the large tanks and sizable fuel dock of the Tidewater Oil Company are clearly visible. These are strictly commercial docks. A narrow, well-marked channel just below Sharp Point leads to Mobjack Marina. The marina is for members only, but you can probably can get fuel and water there if you ask nicely. There is 7 feet of water at the bulkhead by the fuel dock.

Stay out of the inviting little coves along the way upriver. With the exception of Tabbs Creek, which has 5 feet of water well past its mouth, they are all shoal. Tabbs Creek has an overhead power cable (vertical clearance 40 feet), but water depths in that portion are so shoal that you are in trouble if you do pass under it. About 2 miles up the East River, just past Weston Creek on the east bank, is one of the last tide mills on the Chesapeake. Of course, it is no longer in operation, but it remains in a relatively good state of preservation. Consider stopping to visit. There is no dock, so you'll have to land by dinghy.

If you are in need of hull or engine repairs, try Zimmermans Marine, to port opposite Williams Wharf. No other facilities are available here.

Anchorages. The first good anchorage area is past Williams Wharf in Put In Creek. Stay in the middle as you enter the creek to avoid the shoals to either side. They are not extensive, but it is still better to avoid them. The creek carries at least 6 feet of water for a good mile past its entrance. You can anchor anywhere here that pleases your fancy, well protected from all directions.

Continuing past Put In Creek, the main branch of the East River from here to well past Woodas Point offers a number of choice anchorages. Perhaps the most attractive anchorages are in the mouth of Woodas Creek and tucked just below Woodas Point. The rest of the river beyond Woodas Point carries a minimum of 4 feet of water for another mile, at least in the middle, but the best anchorages are near the junction of Put In Creek with the East River.

North River

Charts: 12221, 12225, 12235, **12238**

With a width of about a mile, the first 3 miles of the North River past Ware Neck Point at its mouth are too broad for comfort, and there are no anchorages until you reach Blackwater Creek. Davis Creek, to port (not to be confused with the Davis Creek near the mouth of Mobjack Bay), may look like a possible stop until you notice the lack of water depth; pass it by.

Approaches & Anchorages. Blackwater Creek splits off to the north from the North River. In fact, the main river takes nearly a 90-degree turn to the west here, so if you don't turn sharply to port, you might enter Blackwater Creek accidentally. (In reality, you would have to try hard to do this.) Leave the red "2" light close to starboard, then favor the port side of the creek until Roys Point comes abeam. Thereafter, stay near the middle and you will find 7 to 10 feet all the way upstream to just short of the point where the creek forks for the last time. You can anchor nearly anywhere here. Perhaps the best anchorage is right in the mouth of Hampton Creek. Don't enter the creek itself as it shoals quickly. Oakland Creek, on the way in, provides a really snug anchorage for boats with a draft of less than 4 feet, if it hasn't shoaled in further. Proceed carefully.

Marinas. The only marine facilities on the North River are in Greenmansion Cove, just over ½ mile beyond the red "2" at the mouth of Blackwater Creek. Here Mobjack Bay Marina & The Yacht Yard (same place) offers gas, diesel, ice, limited hardware, and some transient slips. Just across from the marina is a large home called Greenmansion. Now a private home, at one time it was a summer resort. Whether the building got its name from the cove or vice versa, I don't know.

Additional Anchorages. Proceeding on up the main North River, the next really good anchorages occur after the river again bends to the north. Belleville Creek is a possible anchorage for powerboats with a draft of less than 3 feet, but the overhead power cable (clearance 30 feet) at its mouth prevents sailboats from even trying it. In fact, powerboats with high radio antennas also need to be careful.

At the northerly bend in the river, Back Creek offers an anchorage just inside its mouth for boats drawing less than 4 feet. Hold close to the green "7" daymark at the river's mouth and head for the middle of the creek mouth. Don't proceed past the second bend as the water gets shallow fast. Stay a good hundred yards or more to the east of the overhead power line there.

None of the other little creeks off the North River have much water, so stay out. You can anchor wherever you choose in the main river from Cradle Point to just past the unnamed point to starboard beyond Toddsbury Creek. Most cruisers choose to anchor in the vicinity of the cove between Auburn Wharf and Roys Point, but there is no particular reason not to proceed farther upstream for a bit more seclusion.

Ware River

  No facilities

Charts: 12221, **12238**, 12241

The third of the main rivers off Mobjack Bay, the Ware, offers no marine facilities for transient cruisers even though there is a tiny marina in Wilson Creek. The river does offer some nice scenery and very pleasant cruising.

Approaches. The approach to the Ware River is straightforward. Just swing well wide of the shoal off Four Point Marsh, especially the region northwest of Ware River Point, where there is a 1-foot spot well offshore. From here on in, simply honor the markers. There are a number of substantial shoals, but all are well marked. The biggest one to watch out for is the one extending to the southwest of Jarvis Point. The Jarvis Point red "6" lighted spar is well south of where you might expect to find it after clearing green "5" north of Windmill Point. There is no question of cheating and passing to the north of red "6"; you simply won't make it.

Anchorages. The first, and probably best, anchorage on the Ware is just inside Wilson Creek. There is a slight trick to entering this creek safely. Do not make your first attempt in poor visibility. The easiest approach is to take your departure from Jarvis Point red "6" on a course of about 305 degrees. Follow this course to within about 200 yards from the end of the long dock ahead. Then swing to port and parallel the shore until you can see the private aid with white arrows pointing to the channel. When you pass the red triangular private marker beyond what's left of Roanes Wharf, you will be in a snug, secure little anchorage. Simply anchor in the middle of the creek in 6 to 8 feet of water. The shore is full of docks tenanted by both the typical Bay workboats and a number of pleasure boats. Vessels with less than a 5-foot draft can continue on around the first bend in the creek. Deeper-draft boats shouldn't proceed much beyond the first little cove to port. Wilson Creek is a favorite spot for the lower Bay cruising clubs, and it is not unusual to find more than 30 boats anchored there on a summer weekend.

Should you elect to remain in the main river, continue around Jarvis Point and the next bend if you are looking for a more secluded area. You can anchor nearly anywhere past Baileys Point, but watch the depth as you move to the side of the river because the shoals are extensive. One other note of caution: The shoreline is marshy in much of this area, so expect to be visited by mosquitoes and no-see-ums at dusk.

Mobjack Bay, Severn River

Charts: 12221, **12238**, 12241

Seeing the name "Severn River" in conjunction with Mobjack Bay always gives me a little jolt. Granted, many different rivers and creeks on the Bay share the same names, but I can't help feeling that the Severn River of Annapolis and Naval Academy fame should be the only Severn on the Bay.

Approaches. I do not mean to slight this Severn River, which is very accessible and probably offers the best set of anchorages in the Mobjack Bay region. The entrance is easily found and negotiated. Simply pick up the 4-second flashing green "1" light located about midway between the marshy points on either side of the river's mouth.

Leave this marker to port and stay in the middle of the river until you select your anchorage. There are a few protruding shoals, but if you exercise prudence and pay attention to your chart and your position, they should present no problem.

Anchorages. Caucus Bay, to starboard beyond green "1" at the mouth of the Severn River, allows entrance to boats with less than a 4-foot draft. While negotiating this entrance, be sure to favor the western side to avoid the wide shoal to starboard. While interesting to poke into, Caucus Bay doesn't offer a good overnight anchorage as the eastern through southern part of this bay is wholly exposed to the long sweep of Mobjack Bay. In addition, the entire shoreline is a muddy marsh.

Whittaker Creek, also to starboard, offers a possible anchorage to boats with less than a 4-foot draft. Favor the western side of the approach from well out in the Severn River in order to avoid the 2-foot shoal extending a good distance into the river on the east side of the creek approach. Don't pass beyond the overhead power cable (clearance 30 feet) here unless you draw well under 3 feet; it shoals quickly. The shoreline is another muddy marsh, and there are better anchorages, so pass this one by too.

At Stump Point the river splits into the Southwest and Northwest Branches. The only marine facilities in the Severn River are found in the Southwest Branch.

Severn River, Southwest Branch

Charts: 12221, **12238**, 12241

Approaches. The Southwest Branch, to port, offers the first set of excellent anchorages on the Severn. The entrance is well marked and straightforward provided that you remember that you come to the Severn River green "3" light just before reaching the green "1" daymark at the entrance to the Southwest Branch. Leave them both to port and you'll have no problem. Swing sharply around the green "1" daymark and leave the red "2" daymark to starboard. All shoals from here on are well marked.

Anchorages. The small cove to starboard just past red "2" is an excellent anchorage if you don't try to go too far in. In fact, you can anchor anywhere in this branch as far up as ½ mile into either Willets Creek or Heywood Creek, the two forks of the Southwest Branch. The whole branch is well protected but still open enough to permit a welcome cooling breeze in hot weather. You can get a good fetch to the northeast, so watch the weather or be very selective in your anchorage.

Marinas. There are two marinas in the Southwest Branch, the only ones on the Severn River. However, the water depth is uncertain at both marinas for boats with a draft over 4 feet; ask first. The first is Holiday Marina (804-642-2528), on the south side, just beyond the entrance to Rowes Creek. Here you will find both gas and diesel fuel, ice, some hardware, pumpout, and a few slips for transient cruisers. The other is Glass Marine (really a builder of workboats), on the north side, at the entrance to Willets Creek. Gas and diesel, as well as some slips for transients, are available here.

Severn River, Northwest Branch

  No facilities

Charts: 12221, **12238**, 12241

The Northwest Branch offers a series of anchorages that are somewhat prettier than those of the Southwest Branch. It has a slightly higher shoreline and fewer marshes, and it pre-

Region 7

sents a generally more attractive set of surroundings. The lack of marine facilities and sources of supplies result in less traffic and more seclusion than in the Southwest Branch.

There is an excellent anchorage in the bight to the north, just past School Neck Point. This bight is actually the mouth of Free School Creek, which is only navigable to boats drawing less than 4 feet. The preferred anchorage is in the bight, in 7 feet of water.

Just to the west of Free School Creek is Bryant Bay, another excellent anchorage except for the considerable fetch to the southeast. As long as you don't proceed too far into the two forks to the west, you will find good holding in 5 to 7 feet of water. Be wary of the shoal extending to the east of the marshy point between these two forks.

Past Bryant Bay, simply pick an appealing spot. Most of the rest of the branch is reasonably well protected. If you are one of the more adventurous, consider feeling your way into Vaughans Creek. Don't try it with a draft of more than 5 feet.

Mobjack Bay, Browns Bay

Charts: 12221, **12238**, 12241

Approaches. Just south of the entrance to the Severn River, Browns Bay lies squarely in the middle of an extensive salt marsh. The entrance is well marked and easy to follow all the way into the little bay. Beyond the last marker, red "4," swing to starboard past the marshy point and you will find a nice little anchorage in 5 to 7 feet of water, unprotected only from due east. Even to the east the entrance shoals tend to break up and greatly reduce any waves, if not the wind, from that direction. Treat the white pole in the water just past red "4" as a red marker and leave it to starboard.

Marinas. A public dock is clearly visible as you enter. While cruisers are welcome, it is used almost totally by workboats (oyster, crab, and fish) to off-load their catch. There is nothing there for the visitor unless you are interested in buying fresh fish or perhaps some crabs as they come in. There is no marina, but there is a fuel

dock operated by Shackleford-Thomas Seafood, a wholesale fish house next to the public pier. The fuel dock has diesel fuel and gasoline.

If you choose to head for the public pier, take your departure from the white pole past the red "4" marker and head directly toward the end of the dock. There is 5 feet of water all the way to the pier and for most of the length of the pier. Be more careful approaching the fuel dock; ask about the water depth first, since there's less than you might expect.

Anchorages. In either case, don't plan to spend the night—or even any great amount of time—at the pier; anchoring out is definitely preferable. There will be some workboat traffic going in and out, but you can expect to be the only boat anchored there.

Pick your weather if you plan to stay overnight here. It's not a place to be locked into for several days during an extended blow, especially one from the northeast. However, if you enjoy observing the marsh wildlife in their natural habitat, you will be hard pressed to find a better location. Don't try to enter Johns West Creek, to the south of Browns Bay, in anything other than a dinghy. But if you are interested in seeing pristine marshland, by all means take out a dinghy and have a look at it. There's a lone "tree" marked on the chart about halfway up the creek, but don't look for it: either it has fallen or it isn't very large and is screened.

There are no supplies, restaurants, or much of anything else on or within walking distance of Browns Bay, just marsh and countryside. To us, that is its main attraction! Remember that *marsh* means lots of mosquitoes in the evening, so come prepared.

Monday Creek

  No facilities

Charts: 12221, **12238**, 12241

Everything said about the environment of Browns Bay holds true here except that here the channel is unmarked and you won't even see any workboat traffic. If you are looking for a secluded anchorage to observe marsh wildlife, this is it. The odds are that you will be the only boat for at least a mile in any direction.

Approaches. The approach to this creek is a gunkholer's delight! While there is plenty of water in the channel on the way in (7 feet minimum), the trick is to find and stay in the channel. There is no good reference in Mobjack Bay from which to take a reliable departure. The easiest way to enter is to start from a couple of hundred yards to the east of the red "2" daymark at the entrance to Browns Bay and travel due south until the water depth decreases to 6 to 7 feet. This should be the edge of the shoal on the west side of the approach. Continue sounding your way along, staying in 6 to 7 feet of water, until you find your way to a hard-to-see stake marking

the narrow part of the channel entrance. Leave the stake to starboard. From here, feel your way slowly into the creek, keeping in a water depth of 7 feet. The sides come up sharply in places, but if the water has any visibility at all, you can see the change in color where it shoals.

Anchorages. Anchor just past the point on the north side of Big Island in 7 feet. This is one of the few anchorages where you can look out into the main Chesapeake Bay from a harbor protected from waves, if not wind, in all directions.

VIRGINIA'S TRI-TOWN VACATIONLAND

Although most of the sites and attractions of the Chesapeake Bay are designed for easy access from the water, some of the major points of interest, clustered on the Gloucester Peninsula, are not.

The colonial town of **Williamsburg** is located near the geographical center of the Gloucester Peninsula, bounded on the northeast by the York River and on the southwest by the James River. It was established in 1632 as a small settlement, known as Middle Plantation, with a stockaded outpost to help defend Jamestown against Indian attacks. Unlike virtually all of the other settlements of that and the following century, Middle Plantation was not located with immediate access to a navigable body of water. The stockade was more than 6 miles inland from the banks of the James River and about the same distance from the shores of the York River.

In 1693 a charter granted by the king and queen of England established the College of William and Mary, named after them, at Middle Plantation.

In the fall of 1698 a fire destroyed the State House at Jamestown, although the colonists did manage to save all of the vital records. That fire, combined with the unhealthy and swampy conditions of the original Jamestown site, provided the incentive to relocate the capital of the colony to Middle Plantation. The town was laid out by Governor Nicholson in early 1699, and construction started almost immediately.

All of the buildings, residences and government buildings alike, were constructed in the style of the English homes and gardens popular during the reign of William and Mary, 1687–1709. The elegant Governor's Palace and formal gardens provided the centerpiece for what was to become perhaps the most beautiful colonial town established in this country.

With the move of the colonial capital from Jamestown to Middle Plantation in 1699, the town was renamed Williamsburg in honor of King William III. It quickly grew to be a fair-sized town with a population of about 1,800 people.

In 1780, during the Revolutionary War, the capital of the Virginia Colony was moved from Williamsburg to Richmond, considered a far safer location. With that, Williamsburg reverted to a quiet country town, although it was still the county seat.

Today the capital city of colonial Virginia is the largest restored 18th-century town in America. The public buildings and several exhibit homes are open to the public (admission fee), and there are displays and exhibits of colonial crafts, occupations, and gardens, as well as plentiful shopping, dining, and lodging for visitors. Maps are available at the Visitor's Center, which is open from 8:45 A.M. to 5:20 P.M. each day.

For more information, contact the Williamsburg Area Convention and Visitor's Bureau, *(continued next page)*

(continued from previous page)

P.O. Drawer GB, Williamsburg, VA 23187, 804-253-0192.

Amid Williamsburg's rolling hills is Busch Gardens, one of the most action-packed and diverse theme parks in the world. A visit to the 360-acre park with its European theme is reminiscent of old-world Europe, complete with quaint villages, exciting rides, exquisite cuisine, and an array of entertainments and shops. The Old Country is open from April through October and consistently ranks as one of the state's most popular tourist attractions.

For the latest information on admission fees and hours, call 804-253-3350.

Next, follow the Colonial Parkway to **York-town**, where American and French troops forced Cornwallis's British troops to surrender in 1781. Points of interest include the Yorktown Victory Center and surrounding battlefields; Waterman's Museum, a unique tribute to the life of Chesapeake Bay watermen; and On the Hill, an arts center focusing on the visual arts that contains the work of a 30-member cooperative, as well as displays by regional guest artists. For more on Yorktown, see the main text.

The third corner of the historic triangle is occupied by **Jamestown**, the first permanent English colony in America. At Jamestown Settlement guests can board full-size replicas of the *Susan Constant*, the *Godspeed*, and the *Discovery*, the small ships that brought the colonists to the New World in 1607. Jamestown is also covered at length in the main portion of the text.

YORK RIVER

Charts: 12221, **12238**, 12241, 12243

Together with the James River, the York River forms one of the borders of the famous Gloucester Peninsula, on which a significant portion of this nation's early history was made. On this peninsula can be found the historic towns of Yorktown, Williamsburg, and Jamestown, not to mention Newport News at the tip of the peninsula. The latter two are covered in the section on the James River, but a cruise up the York River makes a visit to Yorktown and Williamsburg relatively easy. Yorktown has an information center, where you can arrange for tours of Yorktown, as well as more-extensive excursions to Jamestown or Williamsburg.

While there is deep water at Yorktown, the docks do not lend themselves to tying up, nor are there any marine facilities. Because of the water depth off the town (50 to 80 feet), anchoring is not very convenient either. A better course of action is to anchor or take a slip at one of the marinas in Sarah Creek, across the river from Yorktown. From there you can take a 2-mile walk to Yorktown or arrange for transportation at one of the marinas.

As with many of the broad-mouthed rivers fronting on the Bay, there is more than one way to approach the York River entrance. If you are approaching from the south, it is essential to stay more than 2 miles offshore from Big Salt Marsh in order to avoid the outer reaches of Poquoson Flats. Save for the black and white fish-trap-area markers, these shoals are unmarked. The safest approach from the south is to either follow the fish-trap markers until you can parallel the York River entrance channel or to pick up and follow this shipping-channel well offshore. The alternative is to keep a close watch on your depth sounder and be constantly aware of your exact location until you enter the York River proper. Once you are clear of Poquoson Flats, the rest of the approach is easy.

From the north there are two approach routes, the easy one and the short one. A long shoal extends well to the east of Guinea Marshes on the north side of the York River entrance. This shoal hooks to the south for another 2 miles past Swash Channel Light, which itself is a good mile offshore. The safe passage is to continue south until you can pick up the last pair of lighted red and green buoys marking the end of the York River channel, then swing to starboard to enter the York River. The shorter route is to use Swash Channel, a natural channel through the middle of the shoal. This approach really isn't hard and can save you a couple of miles. Simply take a departure from the red "3" light southeast of New Point Comfort on a course of

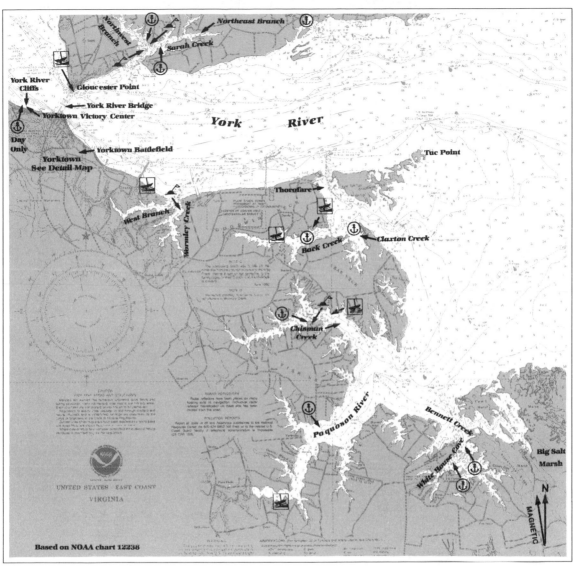

Northwest Branch

Northeast Branch

Sarah Creek

York River Cliffs

Gloucester Point

York River Bridge

Yorktown Victory Center

York   River

Day Only

Yorktown Battlefield

Yorktown See Detail Map

Tuc Point

Thorofare

West Branch

Wormley Creek

Back Creek

Claxton Creek

Chisman Creek

Bennett Creek

Poquoson River

Big Salt Marsh

White House Cove

N MAGNETIC

UNITED STATES   EAST COAST

VIRGINIA

Based on NOAA chart 12238

SCALE **1**″ = **1.57** NAUT. MILES   ⚓ **Good anchoring**   ⚓ **Marina**   **Launching site**

248 degrees. This course, which includes a dog-leg to the north to avoid the north end of the shoal south of the channel, takes you to the green "3" Swash Channel light, which you must leave to starboard. Hold about 100 yards east of Swash Channel Light and swing to port to a course that leaves the red "2" daymark south-southwest of the green "3" light to port. (A good look at the chart shows the reason for this anomaly.) Once past red "2," you can easily run to green "1" and enter the rest of the York River.

Perrin River

Charts: 12238, **12241**

The first harbor on your way upstream from the Bay is the Perrin River, on the north shore of the York. A cursory glance at the chart may give those with deeper-draft vessels some pause. Actually, those with drafts up to 6 feet

Region 7

will have no problem negotiating the entrance channel and finding a good place to anchor.

Approaches. As you make your approach, keep the red "2" nun well to starboard to avoid the extensive shoal off Sandy Point. Come close to the red "4" light on a spar before swinging to port and following the rest of the markers into the river. Favor the west side of the channel, especially as you pass the "No Wake" sign to starboard.

Dockage, Facilities, & Provisions. Stay out of the inviting cove to port as you enter the river; it has less than 2 feet of water in its deepest part. Ahead to starboard are the docks of Cook's Landing Marina, where you will find plenty of marine facilities, including transient slips, fuel, ice, some marine supplies, a swimming pool, and a dockside sewage pumpout facility.

Marinas. The best place to anchor is just past the place where the Perrin makes a sharp turn to the west, right after the green "11" daymark. Here you will have good holding in 6 feet of water with plenty of room to swing. Boats with less than a 6-foot draft can proceed upstream several hundred yards past where the river bends back to the north. Proceed slowly, and watch your depth. Like most parts of the Bay, this area is subject to silting in.

Although it is a satisfactory harbor, the Perrin River is not the area's best, at least not when compared with Sarah Creek, farther up the York.

Wormley Creek

Charts: 12238, **12241**

Approaches. Generally overlooked by cruising boats, Wormley Creek is on the south shore of the York, about 2 miles downstream from Yorktown. A large generating plant with several huge smokestacks dominates the area. While these stacks serve as an excellent guide to the creek's entrance from a long way off, they aren't nearly as noticeable once you are in. The entrance to Wormley Creek is just past the piers belonging to the power plant. The rest of the approach is easy: simply line up the entrance markers and follow them on in. There is at least 5½ feet in the channel at mean low water.

Y O R K   R I V E R

344

Marinas. The one marina on the creek, Wormley Creek Marina (757-898-5060), is to port just inside the entrance. There is a 6-foot depth at the marina, and although transients are rare, they are always made welcome. The marina offers slips for transients, gas, diesel, and a dockside sewage pumpout facility. Ice doesn't seem to be available. Incidentally, this marina is also the only place in the creek where you can stay for the night. There isn't much room here to anchor.

Just past the marina, the dredged channel turns to the west, into the West Branch of the creek. Stay out of the main branch; it's too shoal. The channel continues for about ½ mile, terminating at the docks of the U.S. Coast Guard Training Center. Follow the channel at least once, if only to satisfy your curiosity.

For a secluded anchorage, try elsewhere.

Sarah Creek

Charts: 12238, **12241**

This creek is the most popular harbor on the York River, with good reason: The entrance is easy, there is good water depth, the surroundings are pleasant, and you can either anchor out or visit the excellent marine facilities here. Creek depths range from 7 to 14 feet throughout most of the creek, facilitating exploration.

Approaches. Make your approach by leaving the first Sarah Creek marker, the red "2" light, to starboard. From there simply honor the remaining markers. Hold close to the sand spit to port as you first enter the creek; there is an unmarked shoal to starboard.

Marinas & Restaurants. Immediately past this sand spit is the York River Yacht Haven (804-642-2156), in the small bight to port. Here you can find just about all the marine facilities you could need, including a ship's store, a pool, bike and car rental, a dockside sewage pumpout facility, a self-service laundry, some groceries, a courtesy car, and four nearby restaurants. In addition, slips are available for transients. There is even a sail loft, which replaced their restaurant.

Two more marinas, Jordan Marine Service (804-642-4360) and Gloucester Point Marina

(804-642-6156), are located well up the Northwest Branch of the creek. The former caters primarily to workboats and doesn't offer much for the transient cruiser, but Gloucester Point has gas, diesel, ice, some marine supplies, and transient slips.

Anchorages. You can anchor just about anywhere in Sarah Creek. It is all well protected, and the surroundings are pleasant. Try to stay to the side so you don't block the passage of other boats. The most popular anchorage is in 9 feet of water just inside the Northeast Branch of the creek. Stay out of the little tributaries to the north and south of this anchorage area if you have more than a 4-foot draft.

Sarah Creek is probably the ideal place to leave your boat if you plan to visit historic Yorktown, the scene of the surrender of the British General Cornwallis at the close of the Revolutionary War. Alternatively, you may want to rent a car or arrange for some other transportation to visit Williamsburg or Busch Gardens, just a few miles farther away. Whether you take a transient slip or anchor out, you can leave your boat here and expect to find it safe and secure when you return. Any of the marinas will be happy to help you to plan these excursions and assist in arranging transportation. For the hardier souls, it is only about a 2-mile walk into Yorktown from any of the marinas on Sarah Creek.

Yorktown

 No facilities

Charts: 12238, **12241**, 12243

This is the Yorktown of Revolutionary War history. But there is more to the story than the victory of the Continental army.

History. The town was established in 1691 on the bluffs above the river. A mere 6 years later it became the county seat, and it developed as a thriving business center for the area. It also became a major port for the tobacco trade. By the mid-18th century the center of tobacco production had moved farther south, as the soil in the Yorktown area had been exhausted. Yorktown began to decline, and by the time of the Revolution it was no longer a major port.

Prior to and during the Revolution the majority of the residents and town leaders supported the patriot cause. In fact, they held their own "tea party" in December 1774. Although the town provided many troops to the cause, it saw little of the war until the British troops under General Cornwallis occupied the town in August 1781, driving out the small colonial garrison.

Region 7

The French general Jean Rochambeau saw a chance and persuaded General Washington to delay his attack on New York to make a concerted effort to stop Cornwallis at Yorktown. The plans were laid: The French Admiral de Grasse would engage the British fleet and take control of the Chesapeake Bay and the York River to prevent the resupply or withdrawal of Cornwallis by sea. The Marquis de Lafayette, with a combined French and American force, would prevent Cornwallis from withdrawing by land until Washington and his army could join Lafayette to launch a combined attack. As we know, the plan worked. By late September, General Cornwallis was effectively surrounded and outnumbered.

On 3 October 1781 the fighting began. By 17 October the British had lost several key positions. Cornwallis finally realized that his position was hopeless and raised a flag of truce. Two days later, on 19 October, Cornwallis accepted the surrender terms, and for all practical purposes the war was over. Some desultory fighting continued until the Treaty of Paris, signed on 3 September 1783, formalized the peace between Great Britain, France, and what was to become the United States of America.

The surrender of Cornwallis gave Yorktown an immortal place in history, but the siege devastated the already diminished town. It never recovered its prerevolutionary size and activity. Today it is a small, peaceful town that looks with pride on its historic battlefield. (The Yorktown Victory Center tells the tale of those historic days.)

Anchorages. A visit to Yorktown involves a few complicating factors regarding access by boat, however. The town is no longer a port, and there are no docking facilities. The water off the town is deep, about 80 feet, and the bottom rises abruptly near shore, making anchoring difficult. If you plan to spend the night, put into Sarah Creek, directly across the York River, and either walk the 2 miles to Yorktown or arrange transportation at one of the marinas.

Yorktown

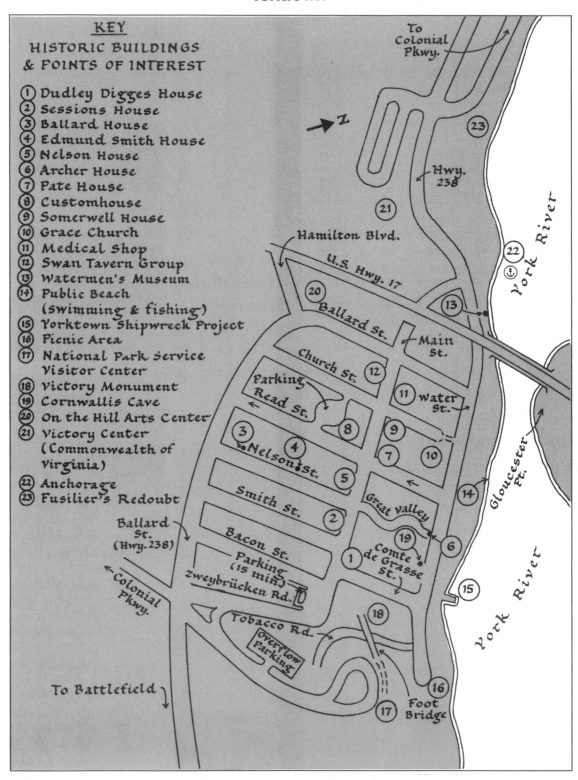

KEY
HISTORIC BUILDINGS & POINTS OF INTEREST

1. Dudley Digges House
2. Sessions House
3. Ballard House
4. Edmund Smith House
5. Nelson House
6. Archer House
7. Pate House
8. Customhouse
9. Somerwell House
10. Grace Church
11. Medical Shop
12. Swan Tavern Group
13. Watermen's Museum
14. Public Beach (swimming & fishing)
15. Yorktown Shipwreck Project
16. Picnic Area
17. National Park Service Visitor Center
18. Victory Monument
19. Cornwallis Cave
20. On the Hill Arts Center
21. Victory Center (Commonwealth of Virginia)
22. Anchorage
23. Fusilier's Redoubt

To Colonial Pkwy.

Hwy. 238

York River

Hamilton Blvd.

U.S. Hwy. 17

Ballard St.

Main St.

Church St.

water St.

Parking

Read St.

Nelson St.

Smith St.

Great valley

Ballard St. (Hwy. 238)

Bacon St.

Parking (15 min.)

Zweybrücken Rd.

Comte de Grasse St.

Colonial Pkwy.

Tobacco Rd.

Overflow Parking

To Battlefield

Foot Bridge

Gloucester Pt.

York River

YORK RIVER

SCALE 1" = 680 FEET

Waterman's Museum Pier with the York River Bridge to the northeast. This beach is a good spot for landing a dinghy to tour Yorktown.

If you wish to visit Yorktown just for the day in fair weather, there is another choice. There is an area just above the York River bridge where you can pull near shore, by the York River Cliffs, to anchor in 7 to 10 feet of water. You have to land by dinghy; there is no place for larger boats to tie up. The York River bridge presents no obstacle to navigation. It is composed of two swing bridges, which have a vertical clearance of 60 feet when closed. The only problem is that the area is open for the entire sweep of the river in both directions and is not a good place to be in a blow. There is some serendipity in anchoring here. First, you can land just a little downstream, at the Waterman's Museum dock, and visit the museum. Then turn right on the road by the museum and walk a little way up the hill to visit the Yorktown Victory Center or turn left and walk through the town itself up to the Yorktown Battlefield Park and its fabulous Visitor Center.

What to See & Do. The Waterman's Museum is dedicated to telling the story of Virginia's working watermen—crabbers, oyster tongers and dredgers, net fishermen, menhaden fishermen, and boatbuilders—from the Native Americans up to today's watermen. Inside the building there are assorted models and displays about fishing, crabbing, clamming, and oyster-

ing. Outside there are displays of workboats and the oystering tools used. The dock by (or on) which you landed is a replica of an old tobacco wharf. Here you can also try your hand at tonging for oysters.

The Waterman's Museum is open Monday and Thursday through Saturday from 10:00 A.M. until 4:00 P.M. and on Sunday from 1:00 to 4:00 P.M., from Memorial Day to Labor Day.

Your next stop should be the Yorktown Victory Center (admission $7.75 adult, $3.75 children), a short walk west along the road to the top of York River Cliffs. Here, you walk down an indoor multimedia re-creation of an 18th-century lane where voices and figures recount major events leading up to and including the American Revolution, culminating with a showing of the video *The Road to Yorktown* in the museum theater. This film depicts the crucial sea battle between the French and British fleets and the siege of Yorktown that led to the British surrender. Outside is an 18th-century military encampment where you can speak with both soldiers and camp followers, who relate stories of life in the period. A proper tour of the Victory Center takes at least 2 hours. By the time you leave, you will have a far better understanding of the events leading up to and including the siege of Yorktown—brought home even

347

more by a tour of the redoubts on the actual battlefield. The Yorktown Victory Center is open daily from 9:00 A.M. to 5:00 P.M. year-round, except Christmas and New Year's Day. For more information, contact Yorktown Victory Center, P.O. Box 1976, Yorktown, VA 23690, 804-887-1776.

As you retrace your steps back along the road, continue east on Water Street for just under a mile to where the road turns up a hill to the east of the town, on Compte de Grasse Street. A little beyond the top of the hill, you will come to the Victory Monument. It's big—you can't miss it! By the monument is a footbridge that takes you directly to the National Park Service Visitor Center (no charge), on the actual battlefield. Here you can see the original field tents used by Washington, walk through a re-creation of about one-quarter of an 18th-century ship of the line right in the building, see the 12-minute video *The Siege of Yorktown*, and go to the observation deck for an elevated view of the battlefield. A driving tour has been laid out, complete with a tape cassette and recorder that you can rent at the Visitor Center bookstore. Unfortunately, the whole battlefield is far too large to tour on foot. However, adjacent to the visitor center are the British Inner Defense Line and Hornwork, an untouched British redoubt, part of the Second Allied Siege Line, and a French artillery emplacement. Two more redoubts are located near the cliffs overlooking the York River. Free maps are available at the visitor center.

As you return to your boat, walk along Main Street to take a look at the stately homes, many of which date back to the 18th century.

Finally, should you be cruising in the area in October, 19 October is celebrated as Yorktown Day, the day of the British surrender. The celebration includes a parade, wreath-laying ceremonies, military drills, colonial music, and a traditional Brunswick stew luncheon.

Don't miss a visit to Yorktown.

Upper York River

 No facilities

Charts: 12241, **12243**

The York River is navigable as far as West Point, where it divides into the Mattaponi River

to the northwest and the Pamunkey River to the west. However, the more than 20 miles between the York River Bridge and West Point are relatively uninteresting. There are no suitable safe harbors, and the shoreline is low and marshy. West Point has a paper and pulp plant, the "fragrance" from which does little to enhance the surroundings. There are no marine facilities, except launching ramps. In short, don't bother going upstream beyond Yorktown except to be able to say that you've "been there." The restricted area in the York River restricts anchoring, but only ships would even consider anchoring here—it is too exposed for small craft. The Naval Weapons Station on Stony Point is a supply depot, so you might see some sizable Navy ships tied up there.

BACK CREEK TO SALT PONDS

Charts: 12221, **12222**, **12238**, 12241

Back Creek

Charts: 12221, **12238**, 12241

Not to be confused with the Back *River* about 8 miles to the south (see page 350), this particular Back *Creek*, one of close to a dozen on the Bay with this name, is located just south of the mouth of the York River.

Approaches. Unlike any other Back Creek, this one has a "back door" called the "Thorofare," which allows a direct access from the York River for some boats. Unfortunately, the Thorofare has silted in recently, and the controlling depth is debatable. Don't even think about it if you draw more than 3 feet. If you still want to try it, ask a local waterman or sound it by dinghy first. Better yet, wait for low tide and then land and wade the channel in the critical region between markers "10" and "14." There certainly can be no surer way to determine the true condition of the channel.

Back Creek itself presents easy access from the Bay through a well-marked channel, but give the shoal east of Tue Point a wide berth during your approach. Start your entrance from the flashing 5-second red "2" light. Actually, you can cut a couple of hundred yards inside red "2," but watch out for the 4-foot shoal directly north of it. From there just follow the markers. If you continue more or less straight past green "7," you may find yourself in the entrance to the Thorofare, with shoals closing in on all sides! Swing to the left as you pass the green "7" daymark off Green Point to head into the main part of Back Creek.

Marinas. The numbers on the markers up to this point are referenced to The Thorofare, continuing in ascending order into the York River. As you proceed into Back Creek past green "7," the next marker is the Back Creek green "1" daymark. Ahead to port are the docks of Mills Marina, which offers gas, diesel, ice, and some limited groceries. The marina also can provide some transient slips, but prior reservations are strongly recommended if you prefer to tie up at a marina.

Anchorages. Just to port midway between green "7" and Back Creek green "1" is the unmarked entrance channel to Claxton Creek. Sound your way in carefully, staying near the middle, and you will find a nice anchorage in 5 to 6 feet of water. Although the shore is low and marshy, "bugs" aren't much of a problem as long as there is some wind. On the plus side, you will probably be all alone in a serene, secluded anchorage, well protected from waves in all directions.

A little farther on, to starboard, is the Back Creek Park, a 26-acre area donated to the county by Amoco Corporation. There are a couple of floating docks, launching ramps, a playground and picnic area, and six tennis courts.

Back Creek is a pleasant creek, which may be why it is rapidly filling up with homes and docks. You can anchor nearly anywhere here provided you pull out of the main channel so as not to block traffic. The creek has at least 7 feet of water up to about 200 yards past green "3," a little short of where the creek forks. There is 5 feet of water in most of the north fork of the creek, but it is unmarked, so sound your way in. Be sure to take into account the state of the tide, which can range up to 3 feet in this area.

Poquoson River

Charts: 12221, **12238**

Approaches. There is only one approach to the Poquoson River. Poquoson Flats, on the south, and the shoal off Tue Point, by the mouth of the York River, to the north, dictate that a course parallel to, if not within, the channel, marked by the pairs of buoys starting in the middle of the approach to the York River, be followed.

As you approach York Point, on the north side of the entrance to the Poquoson, you need to make a choice. The Poquoson River itself has

Poquoson, on the river of the same name, is home port for many watermen.

Virginia Division of Tourism

little to attract the cruiser, quickly becoming shoal before there is much in the way of protection. However, two creeks off the river are worth looking into. The first of these, Bennett Creek, has its entrance just to the southwest of the green "11" light between York Point and Cow Island. The other, Chisman Creek, curves to the north after you round the red "14" marker just south of York Point.

Anchorages & Marinas. Bennett Creek offers some protected anchorages, four marinas, and an interesting challenge to the gunkholer with the nerve to explore it. After rounding the Poquoson green "11" light, hold close to the Bennett Creek green "1" daymark and head directly for the red "2" marker ahead. Ignore the first cove to starboard, Lyons Creek, which is too shoal to be useful.

The next cove to starboard is White House Cove, where there are some protected anchorages as well as three marinas, at least two of which offer restaurants and slips to transients. Fuel is available only at the York Haven Marina (804-868-4532). The channel is well marked. Just honor the markers. Don't proceed past the last marker into either fork of this cove as the forks shoal quickly.

If you continue past White House Cove, you will find some secluded anchorages in 8 feet of water, provided you don't go too far and enter any of the five coves splitting off at the end of Bennett Creek. The shore is low and marshy, which means mosquitoes in the evening hours.

For the adventurous there is a narrow, unmarked channel directly opposite Lyons Creek, leading between Cow and Marsh Islands. This channel holds 6 to 7 feet of water through the marshes, all the way to Lloyd Bay. In truth, there is little to attract most cruisers. There are no good anchorages, and there is no attractive scenery, just marshland. However, for those who like the challenge of finding a passage that no one save another gunkholer would appreciate, this one is a real novelty.

Additional Anchorage & Facilities. In Chisman Creek, on the north shore of the Poquoson, there are three marinas, none of which advertises slips for transients. They do have most of the other marine facilities that you may need, except diesel fuel. The best anchorage is in the main creek, just past the mouth of Goose

Creek and the two marinas on the south shore. Stay out of Goose Creek and the inviting coves near the entrance, first to starboard and then to port; they don't have much water.

While the Poquoson is interesting to visit at least once, there is little on it or its tributaries to cause a cruiser to seek them out more than once.

Back River

Charts: 12221, **12222**, 12238

This is Back *River*, located about midway between the mouths of the York and James Rivers, not the Back *Creek* at the mouth of the York (see page 348). There are well over a dozen Back Creeks, Rivers, and so on, on the Bay, possibly as many as two dozen. I don't think that anyone has ever taken the trouble to make an exact count.

In any event, *this* Back River can provide a harbor of refuge in a blow but is not likely to be sought as an anchorage by choice. It is now home to several marinas, at least two of which offer slips for transients and most of which offer the usual marine facilities sought by cruisers, with the exception of a restaurant. There are dredged channels to the marinas, most of them located on the south shore, just inside the river entrance.

Approaches. Follow the markers on the way in, holding close to Northend Point as you enter the river. Immediately after passing Northend Point, swing hard to port to enter the channels to the marinas. Head directly for the green "1" daymark ahead. If you proceed too far past Northend Point before making your turn, you may "survey" an unmarked shoal.

Anchorages. If you are looking for an anchorage, proceed up the river and on into either the Northwest or the Southwest Branch. In the Northwest Branch, anchor just west of the tip of Tin Shelf Point, near the western shore. Don't continue beyond Tabbs Point if you draw more than 4 feet. In the Southwest Branch, favor the western shore and anchor wherever you find a presentable spot. Beware of the underwater cable area near the white-orange can "A" by the tanks on the shore.

Back River

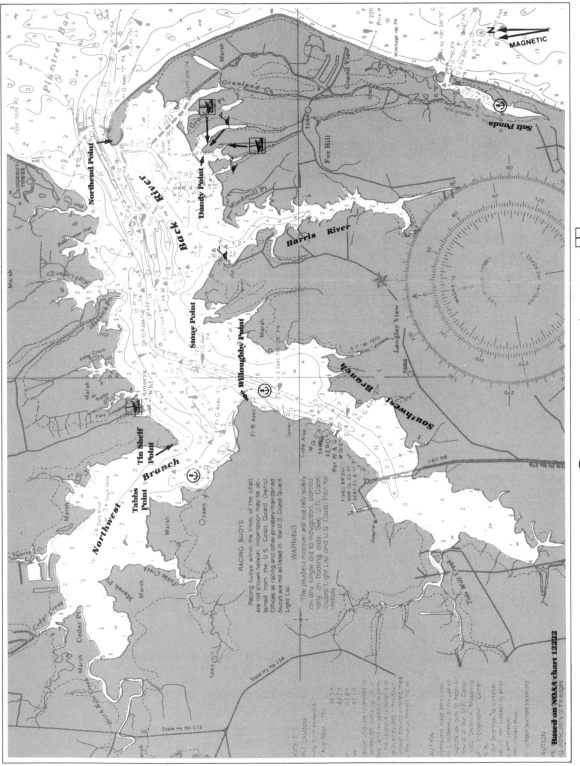

SCALE 1" = **0.80** NAUT. MILES

⚓ **Good anchoring**   ⚓ **Marina**   🚤 **Launching site**

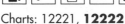

You soon will discover that Langley Air Force Base is located nearby. The noise of the planes may force you to look for a more peaceful harbor.

Region 7

Salt Ponds

Charts: 12221, **12222**

Salt Ponds is located about midway between Back River and Old Point Comfort.

Approaches. The easiest way to find the entrance to Salt Ponds is to pick up the Fl G 2.5s "3" light (N37° 03.23′ W76° 15.66′) just over 1 mile offshore and run up Horseshoe Channel, the rows of markers denoting a fairway through the designated fish-trap areas on Horseshoe Shoal, until you can pick up the pairs of privately maintained entrance daymarks leading to the stone jetties of the entrance to Salt Ponds. The channel has a bad habit of shoaling in at the ends of the stone jetties, especially on the north side. It was supposed to be dredged in 1987, and it has probably been dredged more recently, but enter cautiously anyway. There normally is a sort of yardstick on the south side of the entrance that is helpful in indicating the water depth in the channel at different stages of the tide. We hope that it has been kept up to date.

Marina. Inside the entrance are markers leading to a canal on the west side where there is a residential community, as well as the excellent Salt Ponds Marine Resort (888-881-0897). The marina is now in full operation, with 255 slips, floating docks, a pool, a restaurant, and a sewage pumpout facility.

Don't try to anchor or tie up in the canal. Continue past the last marker, checking the depth as you go until you can anchor. There is room for perhaps five boats, although the area is becoming more crowded. Land by dinghy on the east side to walk over and explore the Bay side.

BACK CREEK TO SALT PONDS

HAMPTON ROADS

Charts: 12206, 12207, 12221, **12222**, 12253, 12254, 12256

Every schoolchild has heard of Hampton Roads, the scene of the battle between the Civil War ironclads the *Monitor* and the *Virginia* (the *Merrimac* to unreconstructed Yankees). This battle was fought in sight of Fort Monroe, located on Old Point Comfort. The fort has been in continuous existence and use since 1823 and is currently the home of the Casemate Museum and headquarters of the U.S. Army Training and Doctrine Command.

Many think of Hampton Roads as a bay or a wide river mouth where the Union blockade formed a picket line of warships. In reality, Hampton Roads is neither a river, a creek, or a bay; it is a region, and a relatively small region at that. It comprises only about the last half-dozen miles between the mouth of the James River and the Chesapeake Bay, but in that distance it encompasses Fort Monroe, the Hampton River, Willoughby Bay, the entrance to the Elizabeth River, the huge Norfolk Naval Base, and the Nansemond River.

There is a certain amount of argument over whether Hampton Roads should be considered an entity or a part of the James River. Certainly there is justification for both viewpoints. From a chart it is easy to conclude that the major river in the area, the James, continues its sweep down to the Bay, including the Hampton Roads region within its lower reaches and mouth. Hampton Roads has traditionally been considered the junction of several rivers, including the James, and looked upon more as "Hampton Roads Harbor" than anything else. I have chosen to go with tradition and treat Hampton Roads as itself a major entity. We shall define the start of the James River as the region between the tip of the point at Newport News on the north side and the western bank of the mouth of the Nansemond River. The rest of the area down to the Bay is defined as Hampton Roads.

Almost in the middle of Hampton Roads the Elizabeth River splits off to the south to lead into the docks of Norfolk and Portsmouth and the entrance to the Intracoastal Waterway. A short distance to the east, beyond the long Bay Bridge-Tunnel, lies the Atlantic Ocean. To the north is

Hampton Roads Area

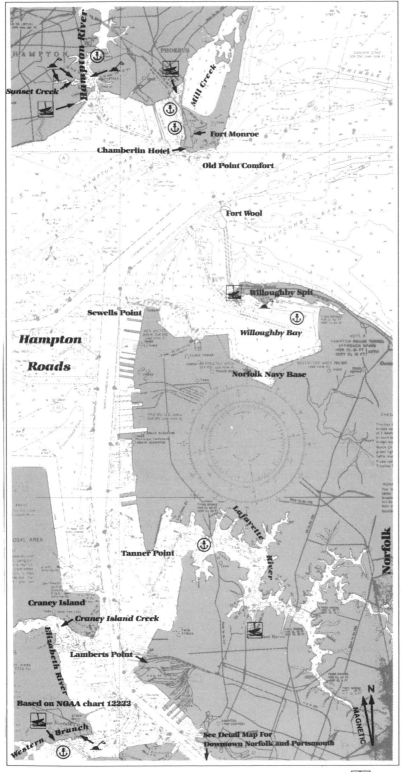

HAMPTON

Hampton River

Sunset Creek

PHOEBUS

Mill Creek

Fort Monroe

Chamberlin Hotel

Old Point Comfort

Fort Wool

Willoughby Spit

Sewells Point

Willoughby Bay

Hampton

Roads

Norfolk Navy Base

Lafayette River

Tanner Point

Craney Island

Craney Island Creek

Lamberts Point

Elizabeth River

Based on NOAA chart 12222

Western Branch

Norfolk

N

MAGNETIC

See Detail Map For
Downtown Norfolk and Portsmouth

SCALE 1" = 1.41 NAUT. MILES   ⚓ **Good anchoring**   ⛵ **Marina**   🚤 **Launching site**

the entire expanse of the Chesapeake Bay, and to the west is the entire length of the James River.

Mill Creek

Charts: 12221, **12222**, 12245, 12256

Of the more than a dozen Mill Creeks on the Bay, this one is probably the easiest to locate and enter but also the least attractive as an anchorage. The primary redeeming factor, which makes this creek well worth a visit, is the traditional star-shaped fort of Fort Monroe, on Old Point Comfort, just east of the anchorage on Mill Creek.

Approaches. The massive, seven-story, redbrick Chamberlin Hotel, on the tip of Old Point Comfort, is an unmistakable landmark, visible for miles, which makes locating and entering Mill Creek simplicity itself. Head for the hotel until you can see the large concrete abutments of the northern terminus of the Hampton Roads (Hampton to Norfolk) Tunnel to the west of the Chamberlin. The approach to Mill Creek lies directly between these two landmarks. Be sure to honor the green "3" daymark to port as you enter. It marks the end of a shoal extending from the tunnel abutments. Once past green "3," you can leave the marked channel and pick a spot to anchor.

In fact, you never truly enter Mill Creek! The navigable portion is really the approach, bounded on the east by Old Point Comfort and on the west by the causeway approaching the tunnel terminus. You can look under the low causeway toward the western part of Hampton Roads, although the causeway provides fair protection from wind and wave. A fixed bridge with a vertical clearance of only 6 feet effectively prevents all but dinghies and runabouts from entering the true mouth of Mill Creek. Even those are pretty much stopped by the shoal waters beyond the next bridge, a couple hundred yards farther on.

Anchorages. There are only two choices for anchoring here. The maximum protection is near the fixed bridge by the fishing-boat docks ahead, but be sure that you don't block

the fishing trawlers' access to the locks, for obvious reasons. Just past the fixed bridge is Sam's Seafood Restaurant. By all means take your dinghy under the bridge, tie up to Sam's piers, and have a meal there if you can. Ice and groceries are also available at Sam's.

The other anchorage area is just off the Fort Monroe Marina, just inside the tip of Old Point Comfort. Only Fort Monroe military personnel can tie up at the marina, but you can anchor off and land at the dinghy dock to visit Fort Monroe for the day or to have dinner in one of the magnificent dining rooms of the sumptuous Chamberlin Hotel. For that matter, just take a stroll through the huge lobby and visit the gift shop and small museum, which has relics of the "old days" of the Chamberlin and its predecessor from the days of steamboats. That by itself is worth the trip!

What to See & Do. Fort Monroe, the largest stone fort ever built in the United States, was named in honor of President James Monroe. Its construction was started in 1819, and it has been continuously occupied since 1823. Today the installation is a National Historic Landmark and serves as the headquarters for the U.S. Army Training and Doctrine Command. The star-shaped fort and the Army post that surrounds it make up an active military installation, and most of the buildings are either residences or offices. Be sure to respect their privacy and work areas.

To get to the fort from the marina, walk to the far end of the Chamberlin Hotel and turn left on Ingalls Road. A short distance ahead is a pedestrian bridge over the moat that surrounds the entire fort, leading to a small sally port through the ramparts. As you pass through the sally port, turn right and you will be at the entrance to the Casemate Museum, housed directly within the walls of the fortification. This should definitely be your first stop at Fort Monroe. Allow about 1½ hours to complete a walking tour of all the sights indicated in a pamphlet guide available at the Casemate Museum.

Casemates are rooms within the walls of a fortification. Many of those at Fort Monroe were used as living quarters from the time the fort was built until the end of the Civil War. Bachelors were given one room, and families were given two. On occasion, some of the case-

Fort Monroe. Built in the 1820s, this is still an active fort, home of the Training and Doctrine Command Headquarters of the U.S. Army. It represents the epitome of "Star Fort" construction.

Old Point Comfort Lighthouse, just outside the Fort Monroe moat.

HAMPTON ROADS

mates were made into cells. One such cell was used to imprison the Confederate president Jefferson Davis after the Civil War. His cell, sample living quarters, gun emplacements, and many other exhibits about Fort Monroe and the Coast Artillery Corps are included in the museum. Admission is free, and the museum is open daily from 10:30 A.M. to 5:00 P.M.; closed Thanksgiving, Christmas, and New Year's Day.

The building directly opposite the Casemate Museum served as the quarters of the then Lieutenant Robert E. Lee when he was stationed at Fort Monroe (1831–34). The house is a private military residence and is not open to the public.

Turn right on exiting the museum and head up the steps to the Jefferson Davis Memorial Park, at the top of the ramparts, for a view of the lower Chesapeake and Hampton Roads. A mile away, on the other side of the entrance to Hampton Roads, is Fort Wool, began in 1819 (but not completed until 1834) as a sister fort to Fort Monroe to protect Hampton Roads and the James River. A stroll counterclockwise along the ramparts takes you past the rear of the imposing General Officers' Quarters to the Old Point Comfort Lighthouse, all located just outside the moat.

The Old Point Comfort Lighthouse has been in continuous operation since 1802. The classic lighthouse and adjacent lighthouse keeper's cottage are worth investigation, but they can be viewed only from the outside; visitors are not permitted inside either structure. The lighthouse is still in operation, and the old lighthouse keeper's cottage is now used as military housing.

After descending the ramparts you can either exit the fort through the eastern sally port and return past the Chamberlin Hotel along the seaside walkway or take a shortcut through the parade ground within the fort to return the way you came in. If you choose the latter, be sure to take a look at the Lincoln Gun, the first 15-inch Rodman gun ever made. It was cast in 1860, inspected by President Lincoln in 1862 (when it was named for him), and used to bombard Confederate batteries near Norfolk during the Civil War.

Across the street from the main sally port, the YMCA offers refreshments and snacks for the hungry and thirsty—it's a good stopping place before you return to your boat.

For more information contact Casemate Museum, P.O. Box 341, Fort Monroe, VA 23651, 804-727-3391.

HAMPTON ROADS

356   *The main sally port entrance over the moat to Fort Monroe.*

Fort Monroe's Casemate Museum contains exhibits of seacoast articles and the cell in which the Confederate president Jefferson Davis was imprisoned after the Civil War, and exhibits depicting the fort's history.

Hampton River

 3 *All facilities*

Charts: 12221, **12222**, 12245

Approaches. The entrance channel to the Hampton River is located on the north side of the entrance to Hampton Roads, just to the west of the massive concrete structure west of Old Point Comfort where the Hampton Roads (Hampton to Norfolk) Tunnel dives under the surface by Old Point Comfort. Even if you have trouble locating that, you can't miss the massive Chamberlin Hotel, described above. The well-marked channel leads to a snug harbor with a variety of marine services.

Anchorage & Marinas. You may not be able to find a good place to anchor here except near the Settlers Landing Bridge upstream. The channel is too narrow in most places. However, you should have little trouble finding a slip for the night at one of the many marinas. Hampton Roads Marina (757-723-6774), in Sunset Creek, to port just past the river entrance, advertises transient slips, as does the Bluewater Yacht Yard (757-723-0793). Hampton Roads Marina also offers a courtesy car. Joy's Marina,

to starboard, seems to have no transient facilities. For those with a membership in a recognized yacht club, the Hampton Yacht Club (757-722-4000), to port just beyond Sunset Creek, is most hospitable and will help visitors find a slip. Hampton Creek Marina (757-723-0998), just past the Hampton Yacht Club, also offers transient slips.

What to See & Do. Stop at the Hampton Visitor's Center, to port just before the bridge at the head of navigation. The center has a dock, the Hampton Public Piers (757-727-1276), and will provide you with more information on the area than you can use. The center may also have information about possible areas to anchor. Be sure to visit the new Air & Space Science Museum in downtown Hampton. Next to the museum is one of the few remaining merry-go-rounds with wooden horses, a relic from the old Buckroe Beach Amusement Park.

The large white bridge a little beyond the Visitor's Center marks the head of navigation for sailboats. Even if a sailboat can clear the bridge, the shoal water on the other side stops everything except shoal-draft vessels and waders.

HAMPTON RIVER: AN IGNOBLE END FOR THE INFAMOUS BLACKBEARD

Whether Captain Edmund Teach, better known as Blackbeard for his long, black beard, was truly the fiercest and most cold-blooded pirate in history or simply the best showman, he represents the epitome of the classic pirate, inspiring fear in his victims, his foes, and even his own crew. A huge, powerful man, he was the very image of a nightmare incarnate.

Operating mostly in the Carolinas, Blackbeard blockaded the port of Charleston through most of 1717 and 1718. Some said that he even blockaded the mouth of the Chesapeake. However, since by that time nearly every act of piracy in the vicinity was being attributed to Blackbeard, the latter is doubtful. Carolina's Royal Governor, Charles Eden, tolerated and accommodated him there, probably lining his own pockets in the process.

Governor Spotswood of Virginia finally caused the demise of this notorious pirate, appointing the British navy lieutenant Robert Maynard, commanding two sloops of war, the *HMS Jane* and the *HMS Ranger*, to seek out and destroy this menace. This he did, tracking the pirate to his lair in the Carolina Outer Banks and engaging the larger and better-armed *Adventure* of Blackbeard. Maynard actually won by a ruse, sending nearly all of his crew below and tricking Teach into boarding the *Jane*, thinking all were dead. Then Maynard's men swarmed out, and the final battle began.

The battle of Ocracoke Inlet lasted only a few minutes, but casualties were high on both sides. Blackbeard fell dead only after sustaining at least twenty-five wounds.

On 3 January 1719 Maynard arrived in Hampton Roads aboard the captured pirate ship *Adventure* with the severed head of Edward Teach hanging under its bowsprit, a grisly trophy to be presented to the colony of Virginia.

Willoughby Bay

Charts: 12206, 12221, **12222**, 12245, 12254, 12256

Approaches. Willoughby Bay is a well-protected, sizable harbor that, although lacking in attractiveness, offers plenty of anchoring room and is an easily entered harbor of refuge. It is to the south, immediately inside the entrance to Hampton Roads after you clear Fort Wool. Be sure to honor the first pair of markers as you enter this bay's channel because of the pincerlike shoals at its mouth. Once you pass the second green daymark, you need not worry too much about the rest of the markers, provided you err to the west, not the east, should you drift out of the channel. There can be a fair tidal current that tends to push you out of the channel, so keep tabs on your position and the markers fore and aft.

Marinas. As you clear the last set of entrance-channel markers, there are three marinas to port, followed by the municipal boat ramp with 150 feet of dockage. The depth at the municipal dock is not certain, so feel your way. Sailboats should avoid the area around the municipal boat ramp because the water is very shallow with several shoals. The marinas are clustered inside the curl at the tip of Willoughby Spit. Willoughby Bay Marina (804-583-8223) and Willoughby Harbor Marina (804-583-4150) offer transient slips, and the latter even has a self-service laundry. Rebel Marine Service (804-588-6022) has a towing service with a salvage crew and divers on call, a fairly unique service on the Bay. It also has an unadvertised paperback book library, where you can exchange your paperbacks for others at no cost. This is something we would like to see more of on the Bay! Rebel Marine is the home of a rather unique vessel, the auxiliary sail-powered 51-foot Tugantine, the *Norfolk Rebel*. If it is in port, go take a look.

Anchorages. If you choose to anchor, Willoughby Bay is somewhat open to the northwest, but the entrance shoals minimize the wave action, and you can tuck into the northeast corner of the bay and find reasonably good shelter even from that direction.

As stated earlier, this is not a pretty anchorage. Interstate 64 emerges from the Hampton Roads Tunnel and runs along a causeway for the entire length of Willoughby Spit, so you should expect constant road noise. Save for the marinas, the area borders on being barren. All of the southern and eastern shoreline of this bay is a restricted area belonging to the Norfolk Navy Base. Landing or even anchoring close to these shores is prohibited. (Have you ever been chased away by a helicopter?) Many charts show a seaplane-landing lane down the middle of Willoughby Bay, but its use has been discontinued.

Willoughby Bay is fine as a harbor of refuge or a place to stop for a lunch break or a visit to a marina or restaurant. If you are coming out of the James or heading north from the Intracoastal Waterway, it serves as a good jumping-off place for a cruise up the Chesapeake or out into the Atlantic. But if you are looking for a secluded, quiet anchorage, go elsewhere.

FORT WOOL

In the mouth of the James River, about a mile south of the tip of Old Point Comfort and the bastions of Fort Monroe, is a totally man-made island with a somewhat checkered history. The island came into being as a result of decades of dumping ship ballast on a shoal, long before any conscious efforts to stabilize the resulting pile of stones into an island that could be used for anything.

Although Fort Monroe, constructed on Old Point Comfort, was intended to defend the mouth of the James River, the artillery of the day wasn't quite up to the task. In an effort to better protect the mouth of the river, in 1819 construction of an island began on the site of the ballast pile (or riprap), to be followed by the construction of a fort. For several decades it was called Fort Calhoun, in honor of John C. Calhoun, then President Monroe's secretary of war.

Stabilizing the island with fill so a foundation could be laid turned out to be more difficult than anticipated, and the cornerstone of the fort wasn't laid until 1826. The fort was solid, built to withstand even cannonballs. Nature's assault was another story.

Even after the fort was completed, the island was not stable. The weight of rock and masonry caused the island to continue to sink into the mud. During his tour of duty at Fort Monroe a young lieutenant of engineers, one Robert E. Lee, was assigned the onerous task of stabilizing the island. This he accomplished by adding more rock, finally succeeding in the last three months of his 1831–34 tour there.

At times the fort was used as a summer resort by government dignitaries, notably Presidents Andrew Jackson (in 1831 and 1833) and John Tyler (in 1842). During the Civil War, prisoners of war and other federal convicts were sent to the fort for punishment.

President Lincoln visited Fort Wool (so renamed for a former commandant) in May 1862 to observe an artillery bombardment of Confederate batteries on Norfolk's Sewells Point. This was also the occasion of the testing of the experimental Sawyer rifled cannon, now displayed on Fort Monroe as "The Lincoln Gun." The last active bombardment by guns on Fort Wool ended with the landing of Union forces on a Norfolk beach and the surrender of Norfolk on 10 May 1862.

Fort Wool remained in active federal service, with no further significant activities, until it was abandoned by the Army in 1967. Today only pigeons and seagulls (and perhaps a few ghosts) inhabit the island, but it is worth a visit to walk around the remains of the fort and muse about the conditions endured by the soldiers assigned to such a barren place in days long gone by. In spite of its closer proximity to Willoughby Spit, off the shores of Norfolk, the 15-acre, kidney-shaped island is now a park owned and operated by the city of Hampton, visited daily by tour boats based in that city.

HAMPTON ROADS

ELIZABETH RIVER (NORFOLK & PORTSMOUTH)

Charts: **12206**, 12207, 12221, 12222, 12245, 12253, 12254

Exactly where the Elizabeth River begins is probably arguable. For purposes of continuity and description, we locate the entrance to the Elizabeth River just to the west of Sewells Point, down the large, clearly marked, north-south-oriented channel. You probably won't notice Sewells Point because you will be too busy gawking at the huge Navy ships, aircraft carriers, and the like, berthed at the piers all along the eastern side of the channel from Sewells Point to Tanner Point. (For information about guided tours of the Norfolk Navy Base, call 804-627-9291.) You may also find yourself dodging other shipping traffic if you pick an inopportune moment to enter this channel. As a matter of fact, you don't have to remain in the shipping channel. It is smarter to parallel its path just to the west of the line of red markers, where the water depth

U.S. Navy

The Elizabeth River channel is busy; you will be dodging shipping traffic and huge Navy ships, carriers, and the like. The Norfolk Navy Base piers extend from Sewells Point to Tanner Point on the eastern side of the channel.

U.S. Navy

ELIZABETH RIVER (NORFOLK & PORTSMOUTH)

averages 15 feet. Don't even think of stopping in this region. The first place you can get out of the traffic pattern is at the Lafayette River.

For about the first 15 miles the Elizabeth River is bounded on the east by the city of Norfolk, founded in 1680 by an act of the Virginia Assembly that set aside 50 acres on the banks of the Elizabeth River to establish a town. From then on the town has continued to grow, and it is still trying to do so today (just ask any Virginia Beach resident!).

This growth has not been unimpeded. At the beginning of the American Revolution, on 1 January 1776, a British fleet under Lord Dunsmore bombarded the town. What was left after the bombardment was burned to the ground by the patriots to prevent British occupation, an extreme but effective measure. The sole survivor from that time is the St. Paul's Episcopal Church, still an active parish, which holds one of Lord Dunsmore's cannonballs embedded in one of its walls to this day.

Norfolk quickly recovered from this disaster, and by the end of the 18th century it was booming with shipbuilding and maritime activities. But it had two more severe blows to absorb. In 1855 a yellow-fever epidemic devastated the population and brought shipping activities to a halt. Less than 10 years later the city was occupied by Union troops as the *Monitor* and the *Merrimac* clashed in Hampton Roads during the Civil War.

Today, as in the beginning, Norfolk relies heavily on the shipping industry (it is one of the country's two largest ports) and a growing U.S. Naval presence (it has the largest Navy base in the world). Downtown Norfolk, once a dingy area of wharves and shady establishments, has been revitalized and now sparkles with life and activities. (See under Downtown Norfolk, pages 362–66, for more details.)

Across the Elizabeth River from downtown Norfolk is the city of Portsmouth. Sometimes thought of as a suburb of Norfolk, Portsmouth, founded in 1752, has a separate identity and is undergoing its own renovation. Surrounded by water on three sides, this city has always been associated with ships and the sea.

The Norfolk Naval Shipyard, the oldest naval shipyard in the United States and the largest ship-repair yard in the world, is located

in Portsmouth, not Norfolk, and is Portsmouth's largest employer. The first cruiser, the first battleship, and the first aircraft carrier of the U.S. Navy were all built here. The first drydock, built here in 1831, is still in use, along with more modern ones. The first ironclad, the *Merrimac* (renamed the *Virginia*) was fitted out in the Portsmouth shipyards prior to its successful engagement with the blockading wooden vessels of the U.S. Navy and the fateful, if inconclusive, battle with the *Monitor*.

Commercial shipping commands its share of attention. Container ships regularly visit the docks between Pinner and Love Points.

The city itself has much more to offer than just its shipping, however. It caters to private boats as well as to visitors arriving by land, and there is plenty to see and do. Like downtown Norfolk, Portsmouth's Olde Towne has been revitalized and certainly is not to be missed. (See under Portsmouth, pages 367–68, for more details.)

Beyond Norfolk and Portsmouth is the entrance to the Intracoastal Waterway, the main "inside" route to the southern waters all the way to Florida (the passage through the ICW, a story all its own, is beyond the scope of this book).

Lafayette River

Charts: 12206, 12207, 12221, **12222**, 12245, 12254

Approaches. The entrance to the Lafayette River is directly opposite the northern tip of Craney Island, the first solid piece of land to starboard as you proceed south on the Elizabeth River. From Craney Island, head due east to pick up the lighted red "2" marker at the entrance to the channel leading into the Lafayette River. This channel is relatively narrow but well marked. Simply follow the markers.

Marinas. The Norfolk Yacht & Country Club is just outside the first bridge. The club offers reciprocal privileges to members of recognized yacht clubs, and service is available on a 24-hour basis. Gas, ice, and water are available at the dock, and slips are often available.

The 26-foot vertical clearance of the Route 337 (Hampton Boulevard) fixed bridge makes this the head of navigation for nearly all cruising sailboats, even though there is a minimum of 7 feet of water in the channel for another 1½ miles. There are a couple of small powerboat marinas on the south shore, about a mile past the Route 337 bridge and a little before the next bridge, the Route 460 (Granby Street) bridge, but their facilities are limited.

Anchorages. There is some room to anchor near the red "14" marker just short of the bridge. Be careful as you head south out of the channel; it shoals quickly. The permanent moorings in this area serve as a reference. Past the bridge there is little, if any, room to anchor outside the channel, except for shallow-draft boats. For sailboats it is the yacht club or nothing if you can't find anchorage space near red "14."

Craney Island Creek

NO RATING

Charts: 12206, 12221, **12222**, 12245, 12253
Just south of Craney Island is a marked channel leading west to the U.S. Coast Guard station there. Even though the only land battle won by the Americans during the War of 1812 was fought on Craney Island, there is nothing to see. (The Battle of New Orleans was fought after the conclusion of the war.) The Coast Guard station is all that is there.

Western Branch

Charts: 12206, **12221**, 12222, 12245, 12253
Below Lamberts Point the marked channel of the Western Branch of the Elizabeth River leads out of Port Norfolk Reach, to the southwest. Three marinas are clustered on the north side of the fixed bridge, two before and one after the bridge. The vertical clearance of the bridge is 45 feet. If you are in a sailboat whose mast, including any antennas, is taller than that, you have reached the head of navigation.

Even if you are able to get past the first bridge, the next one has a vertical clearance of only 28 feet. The area between these two bridges is the only area in which you may try to anchor on this branch of the Elizabeth River. It is fairly well protected, except from the east. The bottom provides good holding in soft mud, and it should be relatively peaceful.

If you are unable to clear the first bridge, forget this one, except for a possible trip to the marinas for resupply or to rent a slip.

Scotts Creek

Charts: 12206, **12221**, 12253
South of the Western Branch and north of Hospital Point, Scotts Creek opens to the west off the Elizabeth River. Scotts Creek Marina (757-399-2628), a full marina with a marine store, provides a shuttle service to Waterside, across the river in Norfolk. The city of Portsmouth has approved the dredging of the length of Scotts Creek and has plans for a marine-related business park on the north shore. At present the Portsmouth Boating Center (757-397-2092) is open, with fuel, a pumpout facility, and a few transient slips.

Downtown Norfolk

Charts: 12221, 12222, 12253, **12254**, 12256
The Main Branch of the Elizabeth River continues for about 2 miles past the junction with the Western Branch. Then, a short distance past Town Point, it forks again into the Southern Branch and the Eastern Branch. The Southern Branch leads to the Intracoastal Waterway. The Eastern Branch holds little of interest to the cruiser save a couple of marinas.

This section of the Main Branch of the Elizabeth River, between the junction with the Western Branch and the split to the south, is the region of primary interest to cruisers and many others as well. Here the attractions of downtown Norfolk on one side and the Olde Towne of Portsmouth on the other are located.

ELIZABETH RIVER (NORFOLK & PORTSMOUTH)

Region 7

Just before the fork in the river, on Town Point itself, the city of Norfolk has made a much-heralded attempt to revive downtown Norfolk, pumping millions of dollars into the project to clear the old waterfront, build a pretty riverside park, construct a spacious parking garage, and underwrite the $13.5 million Waterside pavilion.

Marinas, Restaurants, & Provisions. Norfolk's Waterside Festival Marketplace, a conceptual replica of Baltimore's Harborplace, is located behind the breakwater of City Marina at Waterside, just past Town Point Park. You can sail right up to the pavilion and dock, although reservations for a slip or dock space are virtually a necessity during the main boating season. (The City Marina at Waterside monitors VHF-FM channels 16 and 68, or you can phone 757-625-2000.) There is always someone eager to take your lines, and not necessarily marina personnel!

Within the pavilion are more than 120 shops offering a wide variety of items for sale, including a fantastic assortment of food in numerous stands and restaurants. (There is a fudge-making concession that demonstrates its technique in a singularly entertaining manner. You have to see it—I can't explain properly.) Waterside draws people from outlying areas who otherwise might have little reason to go to downtown Norfolk. It seems that Norfolk, like Baltimore, is having a great deal of success in the renovation and revitalization of its waterfront. Open seven days a week, Waterside has become almost as much a gathering place as a marketplace.

What to See & Do. It isn't a coincidence that a variety of festivals, concerts, theater presentations, celebrations, and assorted other entertaining activities are featured, usually free of charge, in the adjacent Town Point Park. This 6½-acre waterfront park includes a brick promenade that runs the length of the waterfront (including past Waterside), an "activities area," and a 5,000-seat amphitheater-on-the-grass. Beyond the amphitheater is the Nauticus Maritime Center (757-664-1001 or 800-664-1080), a hands-on maritime museum housed in a building designed to look like a ship. In 1999, Nauticus added an 888-foot-long floating exhibit, the battleship USS *Wisconsin*. The ship remains on the Naval Vessel Register, which means that in the event of hostilities it could be reactivated. Built

Deborah Wakefield / Norfolk Convention & Visitors Bureau

Waterside Festival Marketplace. You can cruise right up to the pavilion and dock. Inside the pavilion houses more than 120 shops.

ELIZABETH RIVER (NORFOLK & PORTSMOUTH)

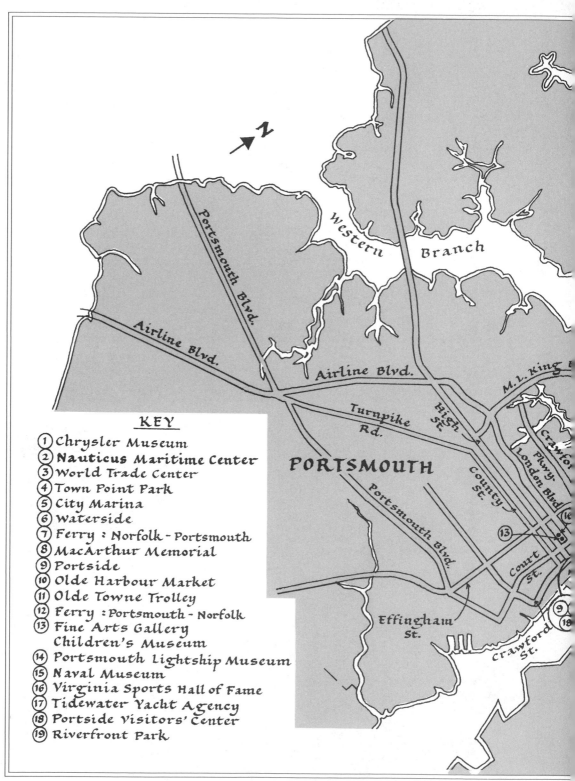

Western Branch

Portsmouth Blvd.

Airline Blvd.

Airline Blvd.

Turnpike Rd.

High St.

M.L. King

Crawford Pkwy.

London Blvd.

County St.

PORTSMOUTH

Portsmouth Blvd.

Court St.

Effingham St.

Crawford St.

KEY

1. Chrysler Museum
2. **Nauticus Maritime Center**
3. World Trade Center
4. Town Point Park
5. City Marina
6. Waterside
7. Ferry : Norfolk - Portsmouth
8. MacArthur Memorial
9. Portside
10. Olde Harbour Market
11. Olde Towne Trolley
12. Ferry : Portsmouth - Norfolk
13. Fine Arts Gallery
    Children's Museum
14. Portsmouth Lightship Museum
15. Naval Museum
16. Virginia Sports Hall of Fame
17. Tidewater Yacht Agency
18. Portside Visitors' Center
19. Riverfront Park

SCALE **1"** = **0.20** NAUT. MILES

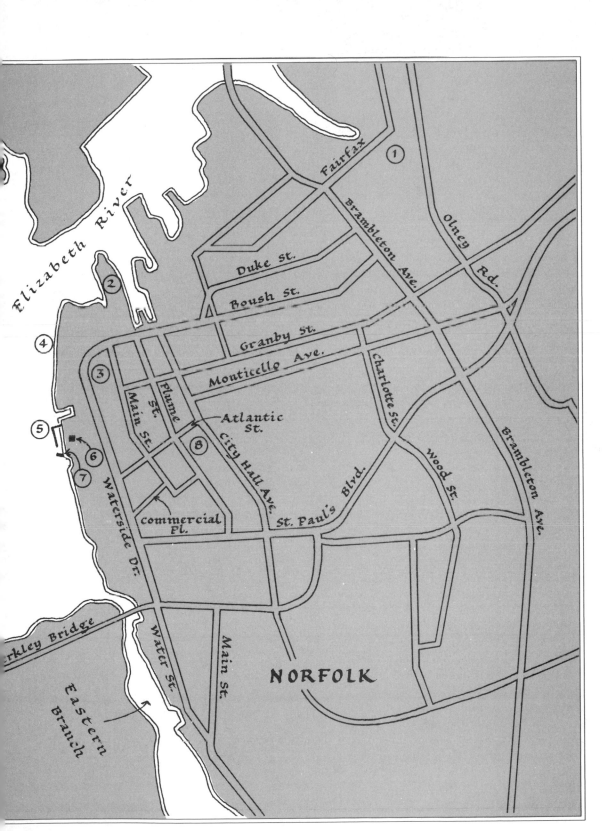

Elizabeth River

Fairfax

①

Brambleton Ave.

Olney Rd.

②

Duke St.

Boush St.

④

Granby St.

③

Monticello Ave.

Charlotte St.

Plume St.

Main St.

Atlantic St.

⑤

⑧

City Hall Ave.

⑥

St. Paul's Blvd.

⑦

Wood St.

Brambleton Ave.

Waterside Dr.

commercial Pl.

...rkley Bridge

Water St.

Main St.

NORFOLK

Eastern Branch

in Philadelphia in 1943, the *Wisconsin* saw action in World War II, the Korean War, and the Persian Gulf War.

Behind and to the north of the Waterside pavilion is the World Trade Center. Behind that is the W. T. Brownley Company, which specializes in nautical instruments and charts. It also has a compass-adjusting service.

Slightly farther afield, south of the junction of Plume and Bank Streets, is the Douglas MacArthur Memorial, composed of four buildings. The one to visit first is the Theatre, which contains several displays and continuously shows a 22-minute compilation of newsreels featuring General of the Army Douglas MacArthur. The Library and Archives houses MacArthur's 4,000-volume book collection and more than 2 million assorted documents. The Gift Shop, in addition to the obvious, displays MacArthur's 1950 Chrysler Imperial limousine. The Memorial, where the General is entombed in a large rotunda, is a conversion of the 19th-century Norfolk city hall. The basic theme is MacArthur's creed: "Duty, Honor, Country."

Also in the vicinity is the Chrysler Museum, rated by the *Wall Street Journal* as one of the top 20 art museums in the country. Named for Walter P. Chrysler, of automotive fame, the collection includes not only Roman, Greek, Oriental, and pre-Columbian American art but also paintings and sculpture from major periods of European and American art.

For ranging farther afield, there is a Norfolk Express Trolley Tour, which takes you around downtown Norfolk and over to the Norfolk General Hospital and Fort Norfolk area. A guide aboard the trolley regales you with tales of the sites and the city along the way. The trolley stops at a substantial number of the sights, where you can disembark and explore and then board the next trolley that comes along to continue the tour. In 2001 the fare was $3.50 a person, $1.75 for senior citizens and children. It runs from 10:30 A.M. to 3:00 P.M. from May to September and from noon to 3:00 P.M. in September.

One more item that I should mention: early each June, Norfolk conducts a three-day-long Harborfest, centered on Waterside, featuring all kinds of activities and entertainment. If you plan to arrive during that time, make your reservations well in advance! For more infor-

mation, contact the Norfolk Convention and Visitors Bureau, 236 E. Plume Street, Norfolk, VA 23510, 804-441-5266.

Speaking of trips, you can leave your boat where it is and take the *Carrie B.*, a replica stern-wheel riverboat ferry, from the dock in front of Waterside across the Elizabeth River to visit Portside and the city of Portsmouth. The ferry departs Waterside every half-hour at quarter after and quarter before the hour. It returns from Portside, departing every half-hour at the hour and half-hour. The 15-minute ride costs a staggering $1.50 per person (as of 2001), and senior citizens get a 50 percent discount on the fare, so there's no excuse not to try it. It provides a new perspective as well as an interesting trip, and it's the easy way to get to and from Portside.

You can cruise the Elizabeth River on the *American Rover*, a 135-foot, three-masted topsail schooner modeled after Chesapeake Bay cargo schooners of the past century. It is the largest such passenger-carrying schooner under U.S. flag. The *American Rover* departs from Waterside Marina; for information or reservations, call 804-627-SAIL. The *American Rover* offers daily 2- and 3-hour tours of Hampton Roads nautical landmarks, allowing you to see the sights and let the captain worry about the shipping and naval traffic. In 1992 the futuristic-looking *Spirit of Norfolk* began offering lunch, dinner, and moonlight cruises.

The Elizabeth River ferry runs between Norfolk and Portsmouth. The 15-minute ride provides a low-fare easy passage between cities.

Portsmouth

  All facilities

Charts: **12206**, 12221, 12222, 12245, 12253

Just across the Elizabeth River from Waterside is Portside, Portsmouth's complement. You can lay alongside the quay opposite the Portside-Waterside Ferry landing at no charge for at least two hours. However, you may find the climb up to the top of the quay a bit arduous.

Anchorages. There is a possible anchorage off either side of Hospital Point, but you have to stay well out, not far from the channel, because of shoaling. It is exposed to wakes from passing traffic and you still have the problem of landing. Finding a place to take a dinghy in and leave it is not insurmountable, but you really don't need another nuisance here.

Marinas. A far better idea is to put into the Tidewater Yacht Marina (757-393-2525), a couple hundred yards to the north of Portside, behind a large wooden breakwater. Here are all the marine facilities you have dreamed of, including a dockside sewage pumpout facility and a self-service laundry. Take a slip here, and you can wander Portsmouth and Norfolk to your heart's content, assured that your boat is in good hands.

What to See & Do. Be sure to make your first stop the large Visitor's Center, just above the ferry landing, to collect all manner of information and brochures on the area. Rest rooms, as well as the ticket counter for a trolley tour, a counterpart to the one in Norfolk, are located here.

Open from spring through early fall, Portside offers a dozen open-air shops with everything from plants to seafood (the Olde Harbour Market), a variety of entertainment on its floating stage (free), and roving entertainers (the Portside Players). Nearby is the starting point for a 45-minute trolley tour of Olde Towne, with its collection of historical houses and at least six museums (the Children's Museum, the Fine Arts Gallery, the Virginia Sports Hall of Fame, the Naval Shipyard Museum, the Museum of Military History, and the Lightship Museum). In all, more than 50 points of interest are highlighted. Actually, all are within easy walking distance of Portside, but the narrated tour by trolley makes a good introduction to the whole area with little effort on your part. The fare is only $3.50 a person, half-price for senior citizens and children.

Region 7

Portside, the Portsmouth complement to Norfolk's Waterside, and the ferry docks. You can lay alongside the quay (not shown) opposite this landing for two hours at no charge.

ELIZABETH RIVER (NORFOLK & PORTSMOUTH)

367

A 45-minute trolley tour of Old Towne (Portsmouth) includes a guide whose talk serves as an introduction to the historic district and area museums.

To the north is Hospital Point, with the large Portsmouth Naval Hospital. Nearly everything else to see is to the south and west of the Visitor's Center.

On the quay, just a little south of the ferry-landing area, is the Portsmouth Lightship Museum. The museum is an actual 1915 Coast Guard lightship, *Lightship Charles*, which you can board and examine, together with exhibits and artifacts that describe the era of lightships.

Next, just a little farther down Water Street, past Riverside Park (the only open space left in Portsmouth), is the Naval Shipyard Museum, where "Naval history comes alive" with displays of weapons, ship models, flags, and pictures. Some of the guns there were actually used by the British during the Revolution in the shelling of Norfolk from Portsmouth.

From there, turn down High Street to visit the Children's Museum and the Fine Arts Gallery, both located in the 1846 Portsmouth courthouse. The exhibits in the Children's Museum are out in the open, and touching or working with them is encouraged. Next door is the Virginia Sports Hall of Fame, with exhibits from major sports figures from the entire state.

There is so much more that I won't even attempt to address it all. For information on where else to go and what else to see in the area, get a copy of the *Olde Towne Lantern Tour* pamphlet from the Visitor's Center. This pamphlet provides more details and anecdotes on the sights visited on the trolley tour, but now you can take your time. You will find a warm welcome everywhere you go.

For more information, contact the Department of Economic Development, 801 Crawford Street, Portsmouth, VA 23704, 757-393-8804. Visitor information is also available at the kiosk at High and Water Streets (High Street Landing), 757-393-5111, or at the front desk of the Museum of Military History, 701 Court Street, 757-393-2773.

Eastern Branch

Charts: 12206, **12207**, 12221, 12253

There is little to say about the Eastern Branch of the Elizabeth River. Although it is navigable for a few more miles, it has no particular points of interest and is not an especially attractive route to take. Pass it by.

Southern Branch (ICW)

  All facilities

Charts: **12206**, 12207, 12221

Approaches. The Southern Branch of the Elizabeth River leads to both branches of the Intracoastal Waterway: the Albemarle and Chesapeake (A&C) Canal and the Great Dismal Swamp Canal.

The A&C Canal is shorter, wider, and deeper, but there is a long stretch down the Currituck Sound and then across Albemarle Sound at the southern end of it that seems to be rather uncomfortable as a general rule.

The Dismal Swamp route is longer but more interesting. It runs straight as an arrow, except for one bend, for 22 miles with a controlling depth of 6 feet and terminates at the village of South Mills in North Carolina. Those planning to take the Dismal Swamp Canal should check with the Coast Guard to ascertain the current controlling depth in the canal and, if the weather has been dry, whether it is even open.

Marinas. If you expect to need any marine facilities along the way, take the first route. If you want a more interesting trip and can hold out for any marine facilities until you reach Elizabeth City, North Carolina, take the second one.

Unless you plan to take the ICW, at least as far as Lake Drummond on the Dismal Swamp route, this branch of the Elizabeth River holds little interest.

Nansemond River

Chart: **12248**

Although readily accessible from Hampton Roads, the Nansemond River is permanently spoiled for cruisers. Aside from the marshy shores, which can be a plus, the area is heavily commercial, and oil and gravel barges frequently ply the channel.

Anchorages are effectively nil because of shoals outside the marked channel. Bennett Creek Marina, on the south shore just before the drawbridge at Town Point, offers some facilities for powerboats. Brady Marina is ½ mile up the shallow Western Branch, which is more than 10 miles up the Nansemond River from its mouth. Eight feet of water is carried in the channel of the Nansemond all the way to Suffolk, but I don't recommend the trip unless you just want to take a look.

JAMES RIVER

Charts: **12221**, **12248**, 12251, 12254

The James River has its origins west of Virginia's Blue Ridge Mountains. From there it meanders through the Piedmont, passing names notable in the history of this country: from the Blue Ridge, through Lynchburg, over the Piedmont Plateau, past Richmond, joining with the Appomattox River (which passes nearby Petersburg), swelling in size to flow by the stately plantations of Shirley, Westover, Berkeley, Brandon, and others, on past the Jamestown Colonial National Historical Park, by Newport News, to Norfolk and the famous Hampton Roads, where it empties into the Chesapeake Bay. Admittedly, urban and industrial development has made its impact on the river's scenery. For instance, more than 10 years ago there was a large industrial spill (some say deliberate dumping) of the toxic chemical kepone that polluted a large portion of the James

River, causing a prohibition of harvesting of all marine life from most of the James River for several years. The chemical sank to the bottom and remains there, slowly being buried in silt but retaining its toxicity for years to come. I am not sure of the current status of the restrictions, but I believe that most of them have now been lifted. While this and similar events of the recent past give one pause, the names associated with this river and the history these names bring to mind continue to stir our imaginations, and the basic beauty of the river itself in most of its reaches still remains to draw the cruiser.

The James River bridge, at Newport News, is a minor obstacle to some ships due to its 65-foot vertical clearance when the lift bridge is closed. There normally is an operator on duty, and the clearance is 145 feet with the lift raised. The James is navigable for about 90 miles, all the way to Richmond, although few choose to cruise that far. As with many Bay rivers, the best cruising grounds are near its mouth.

But the James is a unique Bay river in that above its junction with the Chickahominy twists and turns and islands split the channel, making it more reminiscent of tales of the Mississippi River than of Chesapeake Bay cruising. Beyond this junction the river cruising is more like wilderness trekking on the water than you will find on any other river with direct, navigable access to the Bay. Few cruisers proceed upstream of the junction with the Chickahominy, feeling that the trip is not worth the trouble. But if you are looking for something very different from the ordinary Bay cruising, try making the trek to Richmond. If you do, allow

The James River bridge has a closed vertical clearance of 65 feet.

J AMES R IVER

369

Lower James River

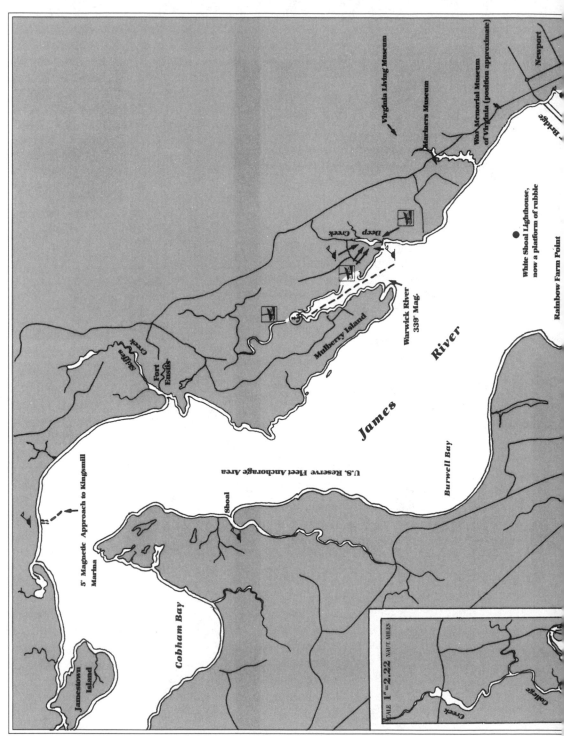

Virginia Living Museum

Mariners Museum

War Memorial Museum
of Virginia (position approximate)

Newport

Bridge

Deep Creek

Deep Creek

White Shoal Lighthouse,
now a platform of rubble

Rainbow Farm Point

Warwick River
339' Mag.

Mulberry Island

James

River

Skiffes Creek

Fort
Eustis

U.S. Reserve Fleet Anchorage Area

Burwell Bay

5' Magnetic Approach to Kingsmill
Marina

Shoal

Cobham Bay

Jamestown
Island

SCALE 1" = 2.22 NAUT. MILES

College

Creek

plenty of time to poke into the bights where the river has changed its course, creating islands such as Turkey, Jones Neck, and Hatcher. Bear in mind that in the upper reaches you must navigate a relatively narrow channel where there is occasional shipping traffic.

Newport News

Charts: 12221, 12248, **12254**

While not exactly the best cruising country, the city of Newport News offers some attractions that are well worth the trip. The difficulty lies in finding a secure place to leave your boat in reasonable proximity to the points of interest. For a day stop in fair weather, anchor in the James River near the shore and land by dinghy. For an overnight stay there is little choice other than to take a slip in one of the marinas.

Marinas, Restaurants, & Provisions. Although Newport News Creek, at the southern tip of the point, looks like a potential anchorage on the chart, this is not an attractive harbor for cruising boats. It is crowded with commercial boats and is distinctly unappealing to cruisers. It is also well beyond walking distance from the prime points of interest. Three marinas are located here. Crockett's Marina and Davis Boat Works offer dockage, which would be smart if you stay here. Anchoring in the harbor doesn't seem to be a good idea.

The Municipal Marina–Peterson Yacht Basin is located roughly midway between Newport News Creek and the Hampton River, but it is restricted to smaller boats because of a fixed bridge with a 12-foot clearance.

A better choice for those wishing to visit Newport News and its many attractions would be to put in to the Leeward Marina, located behind a breakwater just south of the James River bridge (Route 17). Simply head for the base of the bridge, and daymarks will guide you to the opening in the breakwater. This marina, opened by the city of Newport News in mid-1988, is operated by the city's Parks & Recreation Department. Ice is available at the marina and grocery stores; restaurants and two large shopping malls are within walking distance.

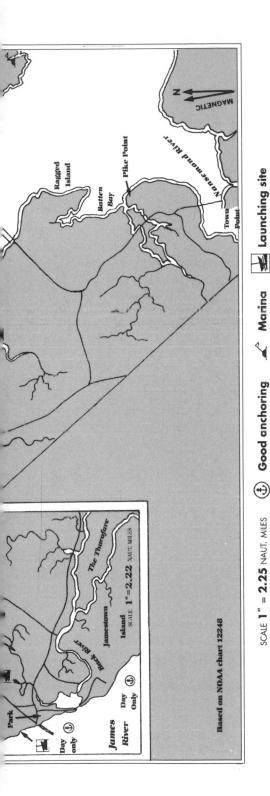

SCALE **1" = 2.25** NAUT. MILES

⚓ Good anchoring   ⚓ Marina   🚤 Launching site

Newport News Shipbuilding & Dry Dock Co.

The Newport News Shipbuilding & Dry Dock Company is the largest privately owned shipyard in the nation. Shown here is the Dorothy, *the company's first vessel. The 90-foot tugboat worked the New York Harbor until 1912.*

What to See & Do. The Mariners' Museum (admission fee) is probably the prime attraction for cruisers in this area. Located on a 550-acre park and wildlife sanctuary about 2 miles north of the James River bridge, the museum has an extensive collection of figureheads, navigation instruments, whaling equipment, lighthouse and lifesaving devices, numerous ship models, marine paintings, and temporary special exhibits. A Chesapeake Bay wing opened in the fall of 1989. The museum is open year-round except Christmas Day. The hours are Monday through Saturday from 9:00 A.M. to 5:00 P.M. and Sunday from noon to 5:00 P.M. (For more information, contact Mariners' Museum, Newport News, VA 23606, 757-595-0368.)

Just north of the bridge is the War Memorial Museum of Virginia, which is dedicated to U.S. military history from 1775 to the present. The collection contains more than 30,000 artifacts, including uniforms, weapons, artwork, aircraft, vehicles, and other materials that relate to every U.S. military involvement from the Revolution to Vietnam. Special programs are also available.

For more information, call 757-247-8523.

A little harder to get to but still worth a visit is the Virginia Living Museum, on J. Clyde Morris Boulevard. Formerly the Peninsula Nature and Science Center, it has been transformed into a combination natural history museum, zoological park, aquarium, and planetarium. It is open seven days a week. Summer hours (mid-June to Labor Day) are Monday through Saturday from 9:00 A.M. to 6:00 P.M. and Sunday from 10:00 A.M. to 6:00 P.M. Winter hours (Labor Day to mid-June) are Monday through Saturday from 9:00 A.M. to 5:00 P.M. and Sunday from 1:00 to 5:00 P.M. The museum is also open every Thursday evening from 7:00 to 9:00. For more information, contact Virginia Living Museum, 524 J. Clyde Morris Boulevard, Newport News, VA 23601, 757-595-1900.

Batten Bay & Chuckatuck Creek

 3 *No facilities*

Charts: **12248**, 12254

Here's a bit of a gunkholer's challenge! Both Ragged Island Creek and Chuckatuck Creek split off from Batten Bay, but only Chuckatuck Creek offers any possibility of entry—and don't try it with a draft of 4 feet or more.

Approaches. To approach the first marker of the channel through Batten Bay, you should be on a course of about 270 degrees toward the southern tip of Ragged Island. As soon as you are able to see the red "2" daymark, the southernmost of the cluster of red and green markers, head directly toward it. Leaving red "2" close to starboard, swing to leave the next marker, the lighted green "3," close to port. Leave the rest of the green markers close to port until you reach green "7." At this marker swing hard to port to line up with the opening to the creek just north of Pike Point. You should be able to see the lighted red "8" marker, which you should leave close to starboard, ahead.

Anchorages. Once past the red "10" daymark beyond Pike Point, you can anchor near the southern shore in the mouth of the second cove to port.

The drawbridge has 21 feet of vertical clearance when closed. It may require prior notice to have the bridge opened, and it probably isn't worth the effort; there are no good anchorages past the bridge, and the creek shoals to less than 4 feet in about a mile.

Try it for the experience, but it is unlikely that you will want to do it again.

Pagan River

Chart: **12248**

Approaches. A little over 2 miles beyond the James River lift bridge you should be able to see the channel markers for the Pagan River to port. The first set of markers is southwest of the abandoned White Shoal Lighthouse (nothing is left of the lighthouse but rubble on a platform) on the downstream side of White Shoal in the middle of the James River. The channel has a controlling depth of 6 feet and is well marked and easy to follow. Don't stray far from the markers as the channel has a nominal width of

only 80 feet. For those with a draft of less than 4 feet it may be tempting to make some short-cuts. This is a bad idea due to the numerous fish and oyster stakes outside the channel, many of which are barely at or below the surface.

Marinas. As you pass Rainbow Farm Point, Jones Creek opens to port. This creek leads to the limited marina facilities at Rescue, about ½ mile up the creek. As you pass Battery Park (featuring the Battery Park Fish & Oyster Company) remain in the middle and honor any of the private markers you encounter. Consider the fixed bridge at Rescue to be the head of navigation. The vertical clearance of 10 feet may allow some powerboats to pass, but the ½- to 1-foot shoal on the other side quickly discourages those who try to continue upstream.

Anchorages. The place in the Pagan River where the channel opens out past the first bend beyond Battery Park used to be a reasonable spot to anchor. That is now taken up by the Gatling Pointe Yacht Club, a private facility associated with a new housing development. There is a possible anchorage in a small bight in the first creek to port beyond the yacht club. Don't go too far in as it shoals rapidly! The shores in this region are low and marshy, promising mosquitoes, and you won't find anyplace to land except in mud. If you plan to go ashore, continue on. There really is no good place to anchor on the Pagan River until you reach Smithfield.

The narrow Bob Shoal Channel on the Pagan River begins about 1½ miles past the mouth of Jones Creek. It runs for just over ½ mile and is reputed to have a controlling depth of only 4 feet. If you draw more than that, you are on your own!

What to See & Do. The town of Smithfield (of Smithfield Ham fame) lies about 2 miles upriver from Battery Park. Here you can tie up at the dock of the Smithfield Station, a combination marina, restaurant, hotel, and river-cruise station. The 35-slip marina can accommodate boats up to 70 feet LOA. Rates vary according to the length of stay. From here it is a short walk to tour Smithfield's historic district, do a little shopping (remember those hams?), or just relax and enjoy your stay in a quiet country town. Smithfield was settled in 1752, primarily by British merchants and ship captains. Ten of the houses in town predate the Revolutionary War. After the Civil War it was a center for the flourishing peanut industry, resulting in the construction of a number of elaborate Victorian houses with turrets, towers, and stained-glass windows. Smithfield is the main reason for any cruising boat to enter the Pagan River. (Note: the Pagan River in this area can have a tidal current flow as high as 4 knots: be prepared for it when anchoring or maneuvering.)

The fixed bridge at Smithfield has a vertical clearance of 15 feet. If you can pass that obstacle and the bridge ½ mile beyond it (vertical clearance 16 feet), the river is navigable for about another 2 miles for those boats with less than a 4-foot draft. This part of the river wanders through some very sparsely settled territory—a real draw for gunkholers.

Deep Creek

Chart: **12248**

Deep Creek is on the eastern shore of the James, about 2 miles due north of the upstream end of White Shoal.

Approaches. The inviting basin in Deep Creek is accessible through a mile-long, well-marked channel. The approach is a little deceptive as the channel initially appears to lead into the mouth of the Warwick River, directly to the north. It soon bends to the right, leading to the entrance to Deep Creek, just visible between a grassy knoll on the starboard side and a white building (city jail) on a small bluff to port. Unfortunately, the controlling depth in the channel is uncertain. If you have a draft of 4 feet or more, check locally before attempting the channel. (The James River Marina advertises that it monitors VHF-FM channel 16.)

Marinas & Restaurants. As you pass between these two "landmarks" the basin inside opens out. The city dock is beside the spit, but it is usually cluttered with commercial boats. Easily visible are the three marinas and the Warwick Yacht & Country Club. Most of the marine facilities you need are there, including a dockside sewage pumpout facility at the Menchville Marine Supply Corporation. Transient slips are not advertised but are probably

available for the asking. Herman's Harbor House Restaurant is also right on the water.

Anchorages. For anchoring, try the bight to starboard beyond the city dock, just short of several workboat tie stakes. Do not go beyond the range mark unless you are in the channel leading to the Warwick Yacht & Country Club. The rest of the area is shoal.

This harbor may not be secluded, but it is secure if you can get into it.

Warwick River

  No facilities

Chart: **12248**

Approaches. It is possible to get into the Warwick River if you have less than a 4-foot draft, but the channel is not well marked and there are extensive shoals. Start your approach in the same channel that leads into Deep Creek. Instead of turning to starboard at the channel dogleg, swing about 20 degrees to port and head directly for the red "2" daymark ahead. Leave this daymark and all following red markers close to starboard. Be very careful just before and after red "8" as there are shoals just under the surface in that vicinity. Feel your way past this marker slowly.

Anchorages. As you pass the two marshy points, swing to starboard to leave the green "11" daymark to port. You can anchor in 6 to 8 feet of water toward the middle of the river in this region. It is possible to proceed for nearly another mile if you feel your way carefully past the next bend in the river. Fort Eustis covers the entire Mulberry Island peninsula, to port as you enter the river. There are no marine facilities anywhere on this river and nothing in particular to attract the cruiser, with the possible exception of the U.S. Army Transportation Museum at Fort Eustis, which, however, is not readily accessible from the shores of the Warwick River. Skiffes Creek is a far better choice for an anchorage.

Cruising into the Warwick River offers an interesting challenge to the gunkholer, but repeat visits are unlikely.

U.S. Reserve Fleet

NO RATING

Chart: **12248**

As you proceed up the James River, you will see what appears to be an enormous fleet of ships anchored along the western side of the river. This is the "mothballed" reserve fleet. Be advised that the Maritime Administration, which has jurisdiction over this fleet, has designated the anchorage as a restricted area with the following admonition: "No vessels or other watercraft, except those owned or controlled by the U.S. Government, shall cruise or anchor between Reserve Fleet units, within 500 feet of the end vessels in each unit, or within 500 feet of the extreme units of the fleet, unless specific permission to do so has first been granted in each case by the enforcing agency."

Keep your distance, but get a good look at you go by. It's an impressive sight.

Skiffes Creek

 No facilities

Chart: **12248**

Past the northern end of the Reserve Fleet, just before the James makes a 90-degree left turn, a deep (11 feet), well-marked channel leads into Skiffes Creek. While all facilities in this region are the property of Fort Eustis, you may be allowed to tie up temporarily while you visit the U.S. Army Transportation Museum, located in Building 300, Washington Boulevard, on the post, about a mile away.

The museum is the only one of its kind. Its complete display of military transportation depicts more than 200 years of U.S. Army history. The displays include aircraft, helicopters, trains, marine vessels, and one-of-a-kind experimental vehicles, such as the Aerocar Flying Saucer. Admission is free.

Although entrance to this creek is not specifically restricted, we recommend skipping this one except to visit the museum.

Kingsmill

Chart: **12248**

This is not a creek, a river, nor a cove. Neither is it an anchorage. It's a marina, and a private one at that. So why am I singling out this marina in a book on harbors and gunkholes? There are two main reasons.

Marinas & Restaurants. First of all, it's the only refuge for a considerable distance on this part of the James, with the possible exception of Skiffes Creek, which is described above. Kingsmill, developed by Anheuser-Busch, is really both a resort and a residential community. The marina is privately owned, but it does reserve a few transient slips (perhaps as many as 10), which can accommodate boats as large as 50 feet. The Kingsmill Restaurant is within walking distance. (I'm told that men are supposed to wear jackets and reservations are a must.) A van is available to take you to the Kingsmill shops or even to Busch Gardens, a few miles away. Reservations for slips at the marina are recommended (757-253-3919). The resort offers vacation packages; the toll-free number is 800-832-5665.

What to See & Do. Second, it gives me the opportunity to mention the starting (or ending) point for a unique cruise either in your own hull or aboard one of the cruiser boats out of Richmond. Operated by Harbor Cruises of Newport News, these boats regularly cruise between Richmond and Kingsmill, providing a guided tour of the upper reaches of the James and a long series of great plantations. The tour could never be achieved by land in like manner. If you don't want to tackle the rest of the James in your own hull, this cruise is a good alternative. The trip takes about six hours. At the terminus are buses that will return you to your starting point.

Approaches. To get to Kingsmill, follow the shipping channel from the vicinity of Skiffes Creek to the point where it bends to head west. Take your departure from buoy red "38" on a course of 310 degrees or from red "40" on a course of 352 degrees. The jetties at the entrance quickly become apparent. The final approach to Kingsmill can be a little nerve-racking if you haven't been there before because of the wide shoals on either side of the entrance jetties. Don't worry about it; simply head straight between the jetties and you will find yourself in the sheltered waters of the marina.

For a jumping-off place to somewhere else or to stay at the marina overnight, this is a great spot. If you like to anchor out in seclusion, forget it; this is not an anchorage.

Jamestown

  No facilities

Charts: **12248**, 12251

History. Not far from the western tip of Jamestown Island is a monument to commemorate the establishment of the first English colony in the New World. The inscription at the base reads:

"Jamestown, the first permanent colony of the English people. The birthplace of Virginia and of the United States. May 13, 1607." The island is administered by the National Park Service and is classed as a National Monument.

Here, too, are a statue of the indomitable Captain John Smith and a monument to Pocahontas, the Native American princess who pleaded with her father, Powhatan, for Smith's life.

These landmarks are relatively recent, all constructed in the 20th century. Only one landmark dates back to the original Jamestown: the Jamestown Church Tower, constructed in 1639. A walking tour leads to the remains of the other structures that have been unearthed in a continuing excavation program.

Anchorages. There is no place to tie up a boat to land on Jamestown Island. The Thorofare, a wide passage of water that leads to the north of Jamestown Island and connects into

National Park Service

The Jamestown Church Tower dates back to the 1640s. It is the one landmark on Jamestown Island from the original settlement. (The church behind it is a reconstruction built on the original foundation.)

JAMES RIVER

the Back River, making it truly an island, is too shoal to even consider entering in anything you won't be able to step out of and push. Stay out of it! Your only choice if you are in a sailboat is to anchor out in the James and land by dinghy. The best place is about 500 yards downstream of the "monument" indicated on the chart, where there is a section of 9 to 15 feet of water. Other than that, the river is either too deep or too shallow to anchor comfortably.

What to See & Do. In 1957, on the bank of the James River just north of James Island, the state of Virginia constructed a replica of the first stockade built by the colonists, as well as a number of buildings that were used during the Jamestown Exposition that year. All of these remain and are open to visitors. They are now designated Jamestown Settlement, a living-history museum that depicts life in America's first permanent English settlement. Moored at the dock below the buildings are three ships, replicas of the *Susan Constant*, the *Godspeed*, and the *Discovery*, which carried the 105 colonists who settled Jamestown in 1607. All three faithful reproductions were built in Norfolk and launched in 1984; and they are worth a visit. If you do visit the settlement, plan to spend 1½ to 2 hours simply wandering around the indoor and outdoor exhibits. Take your time and get the flavor of the place.

Visiting Jamestown Settlement or the ships by boat—"Aye, there's the rub!" as William Shakespeare put it. The problem is that unless you are in a shoal-draft boat (2-foot maximum draft) your only choice is to anchor out in the James River and land by dinghy or to put in to another harbor and visit by car. Under no circumstances tie up to the ferry dock as it is in use and you could find yourself in real trouble.

Landing at Jamestown Settlement by dinghy may present a slight problem of a different sort. The settlement is not set up to receive visitors by water, and there is an admission fee ($10.25 adult, $5 for children).

Shoal-draft boats with a vertical clearance of less than 12 feet can pass under the bridge between Jamestown Island and the exposition area on the mainland into Powhatan Creek. There are two marinas about a mile upstream from the bridge. The problem is getting by the shoal area just inside the bridge, between day-

Replicas of the Susan Constant, *the* Godspeed, *and the* Discovery *at the Jamestown Settlement. Visitors can board and tour the* Susan Constant, *the largest of the three.*

marks red "10" and green "11." Don't try it in any vessel that you can't get out of and push.

In any event, be sure to visit Jamestown Island and Jamestown Settlement. If you can't make it by water, go by car from wherever you do make port.

Grays Creek

Chart: **12251**

Approaches. Grays Creek is located on the southwestern shore of the James River, almost directly opposite the Jamestown Church Tower, on the western tip of Jamestown Island. The easiest approach is to head on a course of 230 degrees from the red "55" marker in the James River. This will take you to the first of a set of three pairs of red-green markers that will guide you into the creek. You need to negotiate the entrance carefully because the creek is full of assorted snags, obstructions, and submerged pilings outside the channel. The channel has

6 to 7 feet of water over a muddy bottom, and there is deeper water once you are past the 2-foot bar at the creek mouth. Favor the port side and feel your way in slowly as the shoals have a tendency to shift.

Anchorages. Once you get in, there is plenty of water in the creek for a distance of more than 2 miles. Grays Creek Marina is to port just past the first bend in the creek. This marina's down-home atmosphere makes it well worth stopping by, if only to chat with the owner for a bit. You can lay alongside the fuel dock for fuel and supplies, perhaps even overnight; however, we recommend anchoring somewhat beyond the marina in 12 to 15 feet of water, where you will be well protected from weather by the high banks to either side.

Understandably, there is little traffic on this creek, so it will be quiet. The shores are marshy, which means mosquitoes after dark. Be prepared for them.

From the marina it is just a short walk into Scotland (a little over ½ mile). You can take the ferry from Scotland directly to the landing just above Jamestown Settlement, secure in the knowledge that your boat is safe.

Chickahominy River

Chart: **12251**

About 4 miles above Jamestown lies the entrance to the Chickahominy River, the first James River tributary worth exploring to any extent in its own right. From Barrets Point, at the entrance to the Walker Dam Lock, 18 miles upstream, the river winds its way through the countryside. Aside from the main river, there are a number of narrow but navigable creeks to poke into. The river is used only by pleasure craft and a scattering of local fishermen. Unlike on the James, there is no commercial traffic to contend with.

Approaches. The approach to the Chickahominy is easy, at least from downstream on the James. The channel through the flats at its entrance is well marked, and the few shoals beyond the Barrets Ferry swing bridge have strategically

located daymarks. The sole exception is Buzzard Bay, which is unmarked, but stay out unless you intend to walk!

Marinas & Provisions. The Riverside Resort is to starboard just beyond the bridge. There is no fuel available, but you can get ice, some groceries, and beverages. There is also a self-service laundry. There are no more marinas until you reach Old Neck. From there to the Walkers Dam Lock six marinas are scattered along the river. They are evident as you pass by. None carry diesel fuel, however.

Anchorages. There are numerous places to anchor along the Chickahominy. Simply pick a spot off to one side of the river, taking advantage of the twists and bends to minimize the fetch from any direction, and drop the hook. Gunkholers may prefer to pull into one of the creeks along the way to find a snug anchorage, but it isn't really necessary.

The first of the navigable creeks to appear is Gordon Creek, less than ½ mile to starboard past the swing bridge. If you can squeeze past the shoal encroaching from the north just beyond the first bend, you will find a minimum depth of 5 feet all the way to Nayses Bay, about 2 miles upstream. If you are looking for a secluded anchorage, this one will be hard to beat! The creek carries 5 feet for about another ½ mile beyond Nayses Bay, but sailboats had better watch out for the overhead cable at the first bend, which has a vertical clearance of only 40 feet. The cable makes this bend in the river the head of navigation in Gordon Creek for most cruising sailboats.

Next to appear, to port, is Morris Creek, with its 10-foot-deep entrance appearing between the marshy banks of Pig and Blank Points. Although the creek carries a minimum depth of 8 feet for a distance of more than 2 miles past its entrance, exploration of this creek is limited to smaller powerboats without tall radio antennas because of an overhead power cable with a vertical clearance of only 15 feet about 100 yards inside the entrance.

Nettles Creek, to starboard, is extremely narrow but has at least 5 feet of water to just beyond its first bend, where there is a 4-foot spot. It may be intriguing, but don't proceed beyond the second bend or you may run afoul of the snag reported there. *(continued page 382)*

Chickahominy River

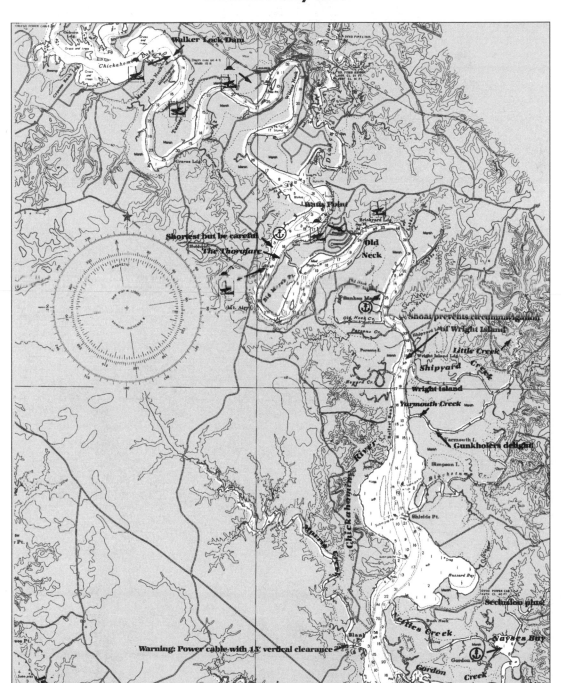

Walker Lock Dam

Wards Point

Brickyard Ldg.

Shortest but be careful

The Thorofare

Old Neck

Shoal prevents circumnavigation of Wright Island

Little Creek

Shipyard Creek

Wright Island

Yarmouth Creek

Gunkholer's delight

Shields Pt.

Buzzard Bay

Seclusion plus

Warning: Power cable with 13' vertical clearance

Nayses Bay

Gordon Creek

Barrets Ferry Swing Bridge

Based on NOAA chart 12251

Barrets Point

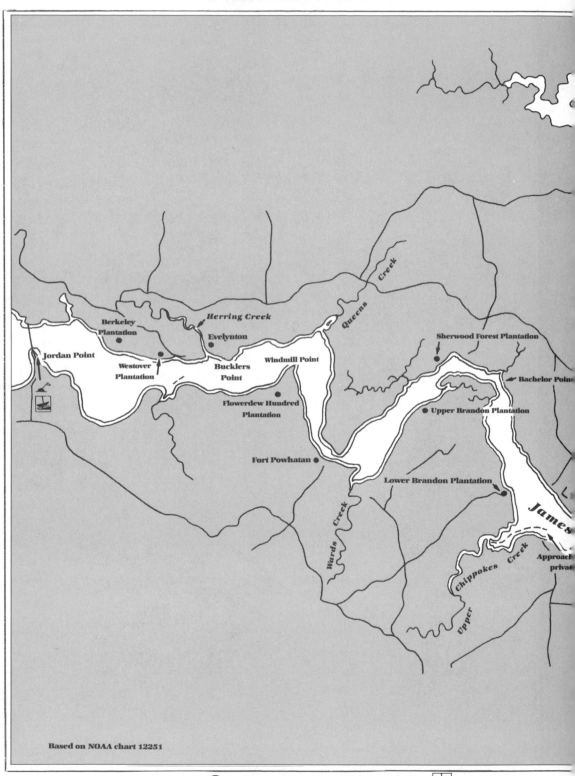

Berkeley Plantation

Herring Creek

Evelynton

Jordan Point

Westover Plantation

Bucklers Point

Windmill Point

Queens Creek

Sherwood Forest Plantation

Bachelor Point

Flowerdew Hundred Plantation

Upper Brandon Plantation

Fort Powhatan

Lower Brandon Plantation

James

Wards Creek

Approach private

Upper Chippokes Creek

Based on NOAA chart 12251

SCALE **1″** = **2.33** NAUT. MILES ⚓ **Good anchoring** ⚓ **Marina** **Launching site**

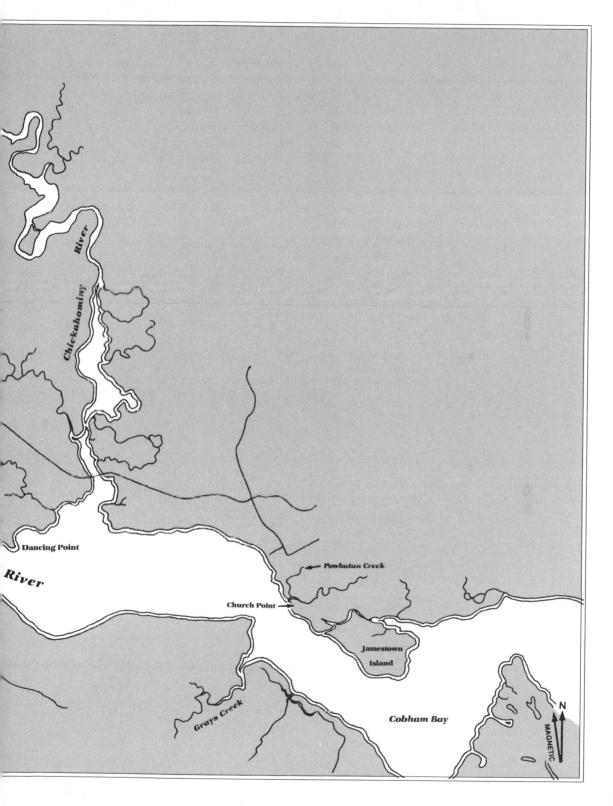

Region

Chickahominy *River*

Dancing Point

River

Powhatan Creek

Church Point

Jamestown Island

Grays Creek

Cobham Bay

N
MAGNETIC

(continued from page 378)

Yarmouth Creek is the next navigable creek. If you can get past the 4-foot bar at its entrance, you can almost circumnavigate Wright Island by swinging to port at the junction with Shipyard Creek. Unfortunately, a 2-foot bar just inside the mouth of Shipyard Creek prevents direct access to the Chickahominy for most boats. That's why I say, "*almost* circumnavigate." Yarmouth Creek has 5 to 10 feet of water as far as its junction with Little Creek, just less than ½ mile beyond Shipyard Creek. Don't try to proceed beyond this junction as the creek shoals rapidly.

Beyond Shipyard Creek the Chickahominy narrows somewhat and begins a series of twists and turns, which make for an interesting trip. Sailboats should beware of the overhead power cable across the river about midway between Old Neck and Big Marsh Points, less than ½ mile past the Chickahominy Marina, to starboard. It has a vertical clearance of only 44 feet. Most cruising sailboats have to consider this cable the head of navigation on the Chickahominy.

There are no navigable creeks off the river beyond this point, with one possible exception. The adventurous might attempt the shortcut through Big Marsh Point via The Thorofare to cut more than 1½ miles off the trip upstream. It is supposed to have a controlling depth of 5 feet, but that probably should not be believed.

Just short of Watts Point, beware of a shoal in the middle of the river, indicated by green daymarks at either end. Be sure to honor them.

The rest of the way to Walker Dam Lock, you are really into river cruising. If you exercise a little prudence, you'll have no problems as there is plenty of water nearly from shore to shore, save for a few fairly evident shoals. It may be possible to proceed past Walker Dam Lock and on into Chickahominy Lake, but since we have no information on it, we can't recommend the passage.

Upper Chippokes Creek

 ☆ 3 *No facilities*

Chart: **12251**

Approaches. About 5 miles up the James from the mouth of the Chickahominy is the hard-to-find entrance to Upper Chippokes

Creek. The entrance channel, marked by private poles or stakes, is close to the southern side of the creek mouth. The channel is narrow and winding with a controlling depth of 5 feet. If you do manage to make your way in, you can find an anchorage beyond the long, marshy point that looks like a finger pointing north. The creek is navigable for at least 3 miles and offers some good gunkholing but little else.

Marina & Restaurant. Just below the mouth of the creek, on the south shore of the James River, is Claremont Beach Campgrounds. There are no docking facilities, but ice, showers, and a restaurant are available. You can also get gasoline, but you will have to carry it in jerry cans.

Powell Creek

 ☆ 3 *No facilities*

Chart: **12251**

Approaches. Fourteen miles above Upper Chippokes Creek is an extremely narrow but deep little creek that is rarely visited by cruising boats. Two poles mark the entrance to Powell Creek's 9-foot-deep channel through the marshy delta. If you make your approach at or near low tide, you should easily be able to see the channel—it's where the water is and the grass or mud isn't!

Once inside, you can follow this winding creek for almost 2 miles before the water depth decreases to less than 8 feet. This happens shortly after you reach the marsh to starboard at a sharp bend in the creek. Call a halt as soon as the water depth starts to decrease as it shoals relatively abruptly a little farther along.

This is not a cruising area for the faint-hearted. The narrow, winding stream between the comparatively high banks can be somewhat claustrophobic for those in larger boats, in spite of the deep water. On the other hand, isn't this exactly what a gunkholer finds most intriguing?

Appomattox River

 ☆ 2

Chart: **12251**

Approaches. From Powell Creek on up-stream, pay careful attention to the chart and don't stray too far out of the marked channel even to avoid passing commercial traffic. The James shoals quickly outside of the marked channel.

About 3 miles above the Benjamin Harrison Bridge over the James River at Jordan Point, the Appomattox River branches off to the west. The fixed Route 10 bridge, at Hopewell, right at the mouth of the Appomattox, has a vertical clearance of only 40 feet, which denies most cruising sailboats access to the river. A mile beyond that bridge is a swing railroad bridge with a vertical clearance of 12 feet when closed. (Presumably it opens on demand, but I am not sure.) If you can clear the bridge, there is a well-marked channel most of the way to Petersburg. The controlling depth is 6 feet to the Lone Star Company Basin, about two-thirds of the way past Gatling Island, just under 8 miles from the James River. The controlling depth then drops to 2 feet for the ½ mile, to the Appomattox Small Boat Harbor, just past the tip of Gatling Island. You can't quite make it all the way to Petersburg. If you want to tour the Petersburg area, you'll have to rent a car or find some means of motor transportation. Touring on foot is not feasible.

What to See & Do. The city of Hopewell is located on the south side of the junction of the James and Appomattox Rivers. It is possible to land on City Point, but only from the James River side, where there are piers to lay alongside of. The Appomattox River side is barred by a 1-foot shoal that extends nearly ½ mile into the Appomattox from the James River to the Route 10 bridge. Here, the City Point Historic District offers a walking tour of about two dozen homes, many of which were used by the Union Army during the Civil War. General Grant was headquartered on the grounds of Appomattox Manor, now the City Point Unit of the Petersburg National Battlefield Park. The manor house and grounds, together with Grant's cabin, are open to the public daily from 8:00 A.M. to 4:30 P.M. Admission is free.

For those who can make it past the Route 10 bridge, one of the few plantation houses left on the Appomattox, Weston Manor, is accessible. Built before the American Revolution, is an excellent example of late Georgian plantation architecture. *(continued page 387)*

Region 7

Lower Appomattox River

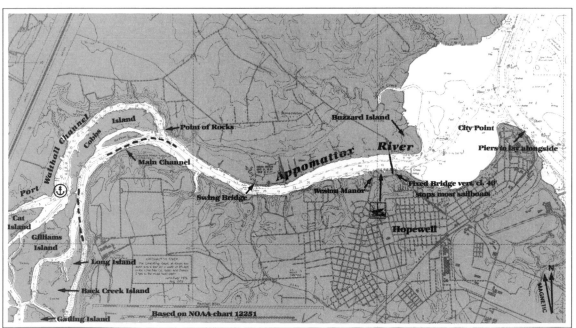

SCALE **1"** = **0.84** NAUT. MILES ⚓ **Good anchoring** ⚓ **Marina** 🚤 **Launching site**

JAMES RIVER

JAMES RIVER PLANTATIONS

Between the intersection of the Chickahominy and James Rivers and just above the Appomattox River are a series of prominent, historic Virginia plantations that are well worth seeing even if you don't or can't tour them. In most cases, shoals on the river prevent a close approach to shore, and the buildings are generally placed some distance from the riverbank. A good pair of binoculars and a telephoto lens for your camera are a must.

Although Powell Creek and the Appomattox River are interspersed between the plantation locations on the James River, the plantations are listed sequentially here for ease of presentation.

Tettington. Just past the entrance to the Chickahominy River, by Sandy Point on the north side of the James River, is the old Lightfoot home, Tettington. The chief points of interest are its beautiful lawn and garden, which center on the boxwood shrubbery. This is a private residence, not open to the public, but be sure to take a good look as you go past.

Brandon. On the south side of the James, at the next bend on the river upstream from Tettington, are two famous homes, Lower Brandon and Upper Brandon. Lower Brandon is the original residence of the Brandon Plantation, which was granted to a John Martin, a compatriot of the Captain John Smith of note and, later, a member of "His Majesty's first council in Virginia." The present house at Lower Brandon was built in the mid-1700s, and the house at Upper Brandon was built in the 1820s. Neither estate is open to the public.

Sherwood Forest. Sherwood Forest Plantation is located on the south side of the James River, at the top of the bend in the river opposite the Brandon Plantation.

The manor house on Sherwood Forest Plantation—a working plantation for more than 250 years and the home of two U.S. presidents, William Henry Harrison and John Tyler—is not like the other plantation houses in the area. The white frame building is 300 feet long. The original building was constructed in 1730.

The estate is a National Historic Landmark, and the grounds are open to the public daily from 9 A.M. to 5 P.M. (admission $9 adults,

Sherwood Forest Plantation.

Virginia State Travel Service

$6.50 children). Tours of the mansion can be arranged by calling 804-829-5377.

Flowerdew Hundred. Located on the south side of the James River, at the top of the bend in the river opposite Charles City, is the site of one of the earliest English settlements in Virginia. Today the culture and history of the region is studied and interpreted here.

There is a museum shop and bookstore, where reproductions and cornmeal ground at the windmill are for sale. Hours are Tuesday through Sunday from 10:00 A.M. to 4:00 P.M., April through December 15 (admission $6.00 for adults and $3.00 for children). It is operated by the Flowerdew Hundred Foundation, a nonprofit organization, which you can contact at 1617 Flowerdew Hundred Road, Hopewell, VA 23860, 804-541-8897.

Evelynton. Between Charles City and the Benjamin Harrison Bridge, on the north side of the James River, are three plantations—Evelynton, Westover, and Berkeley—each of which has its own story to tell. The first of these as you proceed upstream is Evelynton, originally a part of William Byrd's colonial Westover Plantation and named after his daughter, Evelyn.

In 1862 Union troops almost completely destroyed the plantation, burning the house and slave quarters and destroying the largest trees. In 1864 Evelynton was purchased by the Ruffin family, in whose hands it has remained. The present house, a Georgian manor, is built atop the original foundation and constructed of 250-year-old brick.

The house, grounds, and gardens are open to the public from 9:00 A.M. to 5:00 P.M. daily (admission $9 adults, $6.50 children). There is also a gift shop and a nursery.

Westover. Just the other side of Herring Creek from Evelynton is the stately mansion and plantation of Westover, built by William Byrd II in 1730. The house is probably one of the finest examples of Georgian architecture in the country, complemented by a long sweep of lawn down to the James River and an abundance of 100- to 150-year-old tulip trees.

The grounds, outbuildings, and garden are open year-round 9 A.M. to 6 P.M. (admission $2.00 adults, 50¢ children). The main house is not open to the public.

Berkeley. On the north shore of the James River, just downstream of the Benjamin Harrison Bridge, is the beautiful Berkeley Plantation. Built by Benjamin Harrison IV in 1726, the Georgian mansion, which is said to be the oldest three-story brick house in Virginia, sits on a small hilltop overlooking the river. Ten acres of formal, terraced boxwood gardens and lawn extend from the mansion for ¼ mile down to the James River.

The plantation is open daily from 9:00 A.M. to 5:00 P.M. (admission $9.50 adults, $8.55 seniors, and graduated children's rates). For more information, contact Berkeley Plantation on Route 5, Charles City, VA 23030, 804-829-6018.

Shirley Plantation.

Shirley. Shirley Plantation lies on the east side of the James River, just around the next point after the Benjamin Harrison Bridge, about 1½ miles past the mouth of the Appomattox River. This is the oldest plantation in Virginia, founded a mere six years after the arrival of the first permanent English settlers at Jamestown in 1607. Unique to this country, a complete set of 18th-century brick buildings form a classic Queen Anne forecourt.

The plantation is designated as a National Historic Landmark, and it is no exaggeration to state that a visit to Shirley is a bit like stepping into American history. Shirley has been the home of the Carter family since 1723; home to Ann Hill Carter, mother of Robert E. Lee, it is owned and operated by the ninth generation of the family. Shirley is open to the public year-round, except Thanksgiving Day and Christmas Day, from 9:00 A.M. to 5:00 P.M. The admission fee ($9 adults, $6 youths, $5 children) helps to preserve and improve the plantation. For more information, contact Shirley Plantation, Charles City, VA 23030, 804-829-5121.

Berkeley Plantation.

JAMES RIVER

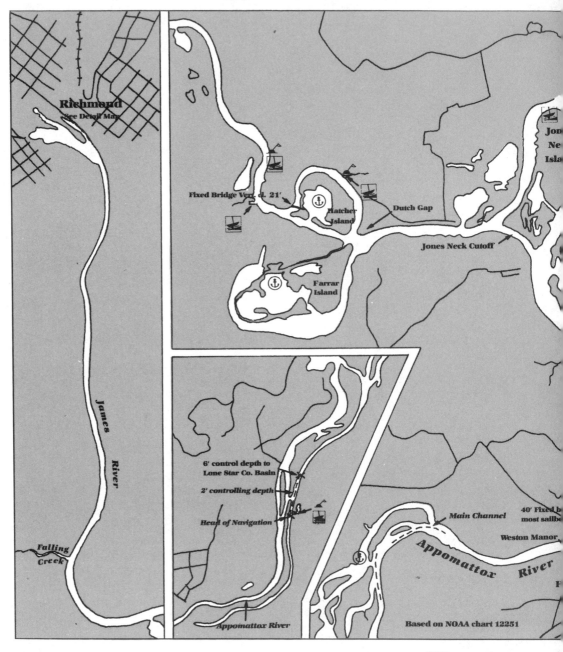

Richmond
See Detail Map

Fixed Bridge Vert. cl. 21'

Hatcher Island

Dutch Gap

Jones Neck Cutoff

Jon
Ne
Isl

Farrar Island

James River

6' control depth to
Lone Star Co. Basin

2' controlling depth

Head of Navigation

Main Channel

40' Fixed b
most sailbo

Weston Manor

Appomattox River

Falling Creek

Appomattox River

Based on NOAA chart 12251

SCALE **1"** = **1.28** NAUT. MILES ⚓ **Good anchoring** ⛵ **Marina** 🚤 **Launching site**

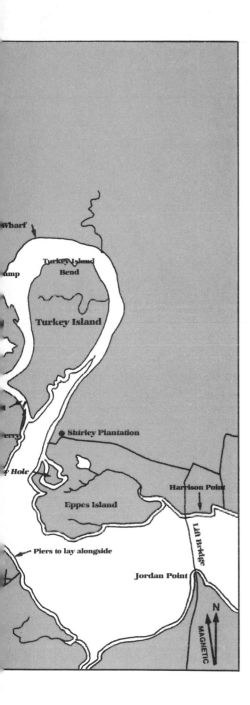

(continued from page 383) Weston Manor still retains much of its original furnishings. You can tie up to some of the piers below the manor, but you must ask permission first. The manor itself is located at 21st Avenue and Weston Lane. For information on Hopewell, contact the Hopewell Visitors Center, 201-D Randolph Square, Hopewell, VA 23860, 804-541-2206.

One mile past the railroad bridge a cluster of islands center in the river, starting at Point of Rocks, at the tip of Cobbs Island. The left fork leads on up the Appomattox. The right fork leads to Port Walthall Channel, which is navigable for another 2 miles, opening the potential for exploring and gunkholing. There are high banks to starboard on the mainland and Cobbs Island; to port is low and swampy. The channel forks again at Cat Island. Only the right (west) fork is navigable, leading to Swift Creek and the head of navigation for the Port Walthall Channel.

The main channel of the Appomattox splits again at Long Island. The right fork is the "Old Channel," which is no longer navigable, although it is possible for shoal-draft boats with strong-nerved skippers to make it all the way past Back Creek Island to the tip of Gatling Island. However, you can't make it back into the main channel without retracing your course. This one is reserved for gunkholers.

Anchorages & Marinas. In spite of the historical perspective of the area and the undeniable appeal of gunkholing around the cluster of islands, the Appomattox River does not have great appeal to cruisers. Although it is quite feasible to simply anchor to one side of the river, there are no good harbors and no marine facilities catering to cruising boats, with the possible exception of Appomattox Small Boat Harbor, near Prince George. This marina caters mostly to small boats (runabout class), although it does have a 50-ton marine railway and the only shower facility in the area accessible to cruisers.

Upper James River to Richmond
Chart: **12251**

Once you proceed beyond the junction of the Appomattox River with the James, the river changes again. Now you are truly into river cruising of a different sort than anywhere else in the Chesapeake Bay area. The river takes three big loops, each of which is cut off by the main commercial channel to form islands. Here are harbors and cruising grounds for you to explore at your leisure with no concern for the commercial traffic that threatens in the main channel. This is the prime reason for venturing so far up the James River.

Turkey Island

 ⭐ 3 *No facilities*

Chart: **12251**

Approaches. One and a half miles above the Appomattox River, the James makes a big loop around Turkey Island. The commercial traffic follows Turkey Island Cutoff, to the south of the island, leaving a stretch of nearly 6 miles for you to explore in peace. There is farmland on the southern third of the island, reached by a cable ferry in the middle of the cutoff. The rest of the island is covered by the uninhabited Presque Isle Refuge, which is a swamp, and the marsh in Turkey Island Bend.

Favor the mainland side of the river on your way around the island, especially around Turkey Bend on the north side of the island. Favor the island side along the southwestern half of the island, by the steep bank, to avoid the shoal on the mainland side by Curles Swamp. Circumnavigation of the island is easy and worth the trip.

Anchorages. Should you choose to spend the night, simply pick your spot. But remember that this is an area with swamps and marshes, which means that you should expect mosquitoes and other insects, so come prepared.

Jones Neck Island

⭐ 3 *No facilities*

Chart: **12251**

Approaches. Two miles above Turkey Island the James makes its next big loop, around Jones Neck. Jones Neck Cutoff makes Jones Neck into a true island. The eastern half of the island is a marsh, and the western half is farmland. How the farmers managed to get vehicles onto the island is not apparent, but somehow they did it. There is what appears to be a chan-

nel into a basin in the middle of the island on the eastern side, but the depth is uncertain. Don't try it in anything but a dinghy, and be prepared to get out and push.

Anchorages. Circumnavigation of the island is easy, as is finding a nice spot to anchor for the night. There is a public launching ramp directly north of the island, so you can expect some local rowboat and runabout traffic. At dusk the traffic disappears, leaving you alone in a quiet, peaceful anchorage.

Just west of Jones Neck, at Varina Farm, there is a basin off the north side of the James. It looks intriguing, but there is no information on it, and it may well be private. Leave it alone.

Farrar Island

⭐ 3 *No facilities*

Chart: **12251**

Approaches. Directly opposite the point labeled "Dutch Gap" on the chart, about 2 miles upriver from the west end of Jones Neck Island, is the 400-yard-long false mouth of the waterway leading to an interesting basin in the middle of Farrar Island.

The deceptively wide mouth quickly necks down to the true entrance, marked by the quick-flashing green marker on the east side of the entrance. Be sure to leave this marker to port as you head southwest into the "creek." There is a quick-flashing green "151" James River marker almost onshore at the west side of the entrance. Hold a course between these two markers, then remain about in the middle until the creek starts to curve to the west, about ¾ mile from the entrance. At that point, hold close to the western shore, guiding carefully between the zero-foot shoal and the main part of the island until you can enter the narrow channel leading into the basin.

Anchorages. When the channel opens out into the basin, remain in the northern quarter of the main basin to anchor.

There were some buildings on the point protruding into the basin from the west side, but the access bridge to them is in ruins, and they must be abandoned by now. Several underwater wrecks are scattered throughout the basin, and there is a shoal in nearly the geometric center of the basin, all to be avoided. The rest of the basin is a gunkholer's delight.

If you are looking for a private, secure, secluded anchorage, try this one. However, you will be surrounded by swamp and marsh, so be prepared for mosquitoes.

Hatcher Island

Chart: **12251**

Approach. Just past the entrance to Farrar Island the James makes its last big loop before the long, barren stretch to Richmond. At Dutch Gap the river makes a 1½-mile loop to the north around Hatcher Island.

Favor the mainland side of the river as you circumnavigate the island, except on the western side, where you should favor the island side.

Marinas. Here is the only marina to offer gas and some repairs on this part of the James, Richmond Yacht Basin. Little else in the way of marine facilities is available to transient cruisers.

Anchorages. One unique feature of Hatcher Island is the large, navigable basin right in the middle that offers an excellent anchorage in 7 to 23 feet of water. Stay in the center as you enter from Dutch Gap Cutoff and anchor anywhere in the eastern half of the basin. There is a marsh to the east, but you can anchor far enough out that insects should be only a minor problem.

James River above Hatcher Island

Chart: **12251**

Above Hatcher Island you are well advised to remain in the main channel of the James for the entire 18 miles to Richmond. Except for King's Landing, about a mile past Hatcher Island, and Falling Creek Marina, at the entrance to Falling Creek, which offers only engine repairs, there are no facilities upriver. It is not an unpleasant trip, but it can be a bit tedious. The only rea-

son to make it is to visit Richmond by water. You need to look at the chart carefully in this area. A cable crossing the James might be mistaken for the fixed bridge (21-foot vertical clearance) that connects Hatcher Island to the mainland. The bridge does not cross the James, and the cable is high enough to present no problem for you to pass beneath.

The channel ends at Richmond, just past the railroad marshaling yard, a few hundred yards before the first bridge over the James. If you pass the docks at Shiplock Park where the James River Cruise Boats dock, stop! You run out of water very quickly because you have reached the head of navigation of the James River.

Richmond

Chart: **12251**

History. The city of Richmond's location is very much due to a quirk of nature. Seven miles of falls 125 miles above the mouth of the James River form the upper limit of navigation on the river and block access to the more than 200 miles of the James River that extend into the interior of the country. Early settlers recognized the commercial opportunities presented by the falls' blocking navigation on the river and soon formed a settlement there. Richmond's history is one of steady growth, greatly enhanced by its selection as the state capital. The establishment of the big tobacco companies and heavy industry also contributed to its growth.

During the Civil War, Richmond was the capital of the Confederate States of America, as well as the South's largest industrial center. The city has a substantial national military park along its eastern perimeter, most of it the result of seven major attempts by Union forces to capture the city, which the Confederates successfully repelled. Richmond fell only after the capture of Petersburg, following a 10-month siege, broke the Confederacy's defenses.

The defeat of the Confederacy, while immediately traumatic, was only a temporary setback to Richmond's growth. Today Richmond is a

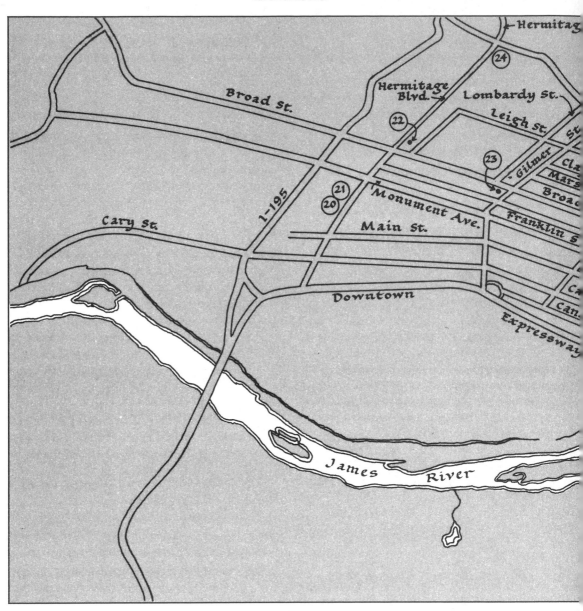

KEY

1. Annabel Lee Riverboat
2. Shiplock Park
3. Kanawha Locks
4. Edgar Allen Poe Museum
5. Farmer's Market
6. Kanawha Locks
7. Shockoe Slip
8. Governor's Mansion
9. State Capitol
10. Bell Tower
11. St. Paul's Church
12. Old City Hall

SCALE **1"** = **2.85** MILES

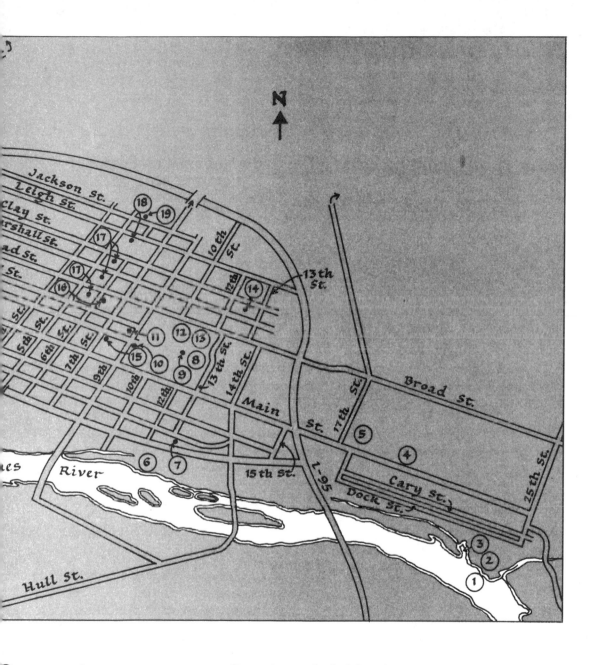

N

Jackson St.
Leigh St.
Clay St.
Marshall St.
ad St.
St.
10th St.
13th St.
12th St.
13th St.
14th St.
15th St.
River
Main St.
Broad St.
17th St.
Cary St.
Dock St.
25th St.
Hull St.
I-95
15th St.

③ State Library
④ Museum of the Confederacy
⑤ Lee House
⑥ Carpenter Center
⑦ 6th St. Marketplace
⑧ Coliseum

⑲ Richmond Children's Museum
⑳ Virginia Museum of Fine Arts
㉑ Virginia Historical Society
   (Battle Abbey)
㉒ Science Museum of Virginia
㉓ American Hist. Foundation Museum
㉔ Metro Richmond Visitors' Center

busy, bustling city, the cultural leader of the state, with a suburban region extending most of the 23 miles south to Petersburg, forming a sort of megapolis much like the one between Baltimore and Washington, D.C., in Maryland.

What to See & Do. The waterfront area, known as Shockoe Slip, was once a bawdy, low-class district, avoided by the "better class" of citizens. Today it is an attractive area of shops and restaurants with a terminal for James River Cruise Boats and a city dock where private craft can tie up (on a space-available basis) to visit the city. Some of the points of interest are within easy walking distance, but many require some form of motor transportation. Both bus tours and self-guided car tours are available. I mention only a few of those points within walking distance from the city dock.

Perhaps the best place to start is at Chimborazo Park, to the east of the city dock, where the Richmond National Battlefield Park Visitor's Center is located. Dedicated to the battlegrounds that were the setting of the 1861–65 defense of Richmond, the center offers exhibits, an audiovisual program, and maps for a 97-mile tour through the battlefield sites. Needless to say, you aren't going to walk all of that one.

As you leave the visitor's center, head west along Broad Street to stop at St. John's Church. Built in 1741, this church was the site of the 1775 Revolutionary Convention, during which Patrick Henry gave his famous "Give me liberty or give me death!" speech. On summer Sunday afternoons there is a reenactment of his speech.

Head down 24th Street until you reach Main Street, turn right, and go about five blocks to find the Edgar Allan Poe Museum, which is housed in the Old Stone House, built in 1737, believed to be Richmond's oldest surviving stone building. The museum contains Poe memorabilia and artifacts from the days when he lived, wrote, and romanced there. It is open daily.

A jaunt up 19th Street and left on Broad Street soon takes you to a cluster of sights. To the right on 12th Street is the Museum of the Confederacy, containing the world's largest collection of Confederate memorabilia. Jefferson Davis's home during the war, the White House of the Confederacy, is right next door.

Two blocks west is the Valentine Museum,

presenting the life and history of Richmond up to the present.

Three blocks south is Capitol Square, site of the beautiful Virginia State Capitol. Designed by Thomas Jefferson in 1785, this was the first building in America to be constructed in the form of a classic Greek temple. This is the home of the oldest known legislative body in the Western Hemisphere, the Virginia legislature. It also houses Jean-Antoine Houdon's statue of George Washington.

Continue south from Capitol Square on 12th Street to return to the waterfront and the site of the Kanawha Canal Locks, two locks remaining from the first canal system built in America. At one time the canal extended from the bottom of the falls at Richmond, past Lynchburg, to Buchanan on the far side of the Blue Ridge Mountains. Started due to the efforts of George Washington in 1784, the canal was finally completed in 1851. It served well until the railroads superseded it, as they did virtually all of the canals in the country. A narrated audiovisual presentation describes the history and significance of the old Kanawha Canal. I recommend visiting it.

There are many other points of interest in Richmond. Most lie a bit farther afield and are beyond the scope of this book. For all practical purposes, the falls at Richmond mark the end of cruising the James River by any vessel that you can't pick up and carry.

HAMPTON ROADS TO CHESAPEAKE BAY BRIDGE

Charts: 12205, 12207, 12221, **12222**

Just 2 miles west of the south end of the Chesapeake Bay Bridge-Tunnel is the entrance to Little Creek, the last good, easily entered harbor before you leave the Bay and enter the Atlantic Ocean.

Little Creek

  All facilities

Charts: 12205, 12207, 12221, **12222**
Approaches. The approach is wide open, and the broad entrance channel is readily located by

the 70-foot-high, lighted green "1" beacon on the end of the east jetty. Depth is no problem; it's 20 feet all the way into the basin.

As you enter the channel into the creek, you can't help but notice the Coast Guard station and the Navy Amphibious Base (part of the Atlantic Fleet); they take up most of the harbor area, and assorted good-sized vessels are frequently moored there. You are free to take a swing around the harbor and look at these boats, but tying up at any of the docks belonging to these facilities is not permitted.

Marinas, Restaurants, & Provisions.
All of the marina facilities in Little Creek are in the first (western) branch to starboard, just past red "8" as you enter. Favor the south side of this branch as there is some shoaling on the north side, especially past the green "3" daymark. There are five marinas on this branch. Together, they offer every marine facility. You should have no problem finding an overnight slip. A large shopping center less than a mile from any of the marinas includes a supermarket and a large department store, as well as assorted other shops. Any of the marinas can help you find transportation if you aren't up to the walk.

This is not a harbor where you can expect to anchor out, let alone in seclusion. It's a busy, crowded place, but it is the closest reasonable jumping-off place for a trip offshore. If you prefer to anchor out, head back inside Hampton Roads to Willoughby Bay, a distance of about 9 miles from Little Creek. Boats that can clear

an overhead limit of 35 feet might consider Lynnhaven Inlet, 4 miles to the east.

Lynnhaven Inlet

Charts: 12205, 12207, 12221, **12222**

The entrance to Lynnhaven Inlet is just 2 miles east of the Chesapeake Bay Bridge-Tunnel and 4 miles west of Cape Henry Light. It leads to an interesting series of inland waterways and bays, providing a "back door" to Virginia Beach. Unfortunately, the use of this entire area is limited to powerboats or small sailboats that can pass under the series of fixed bridges (vertical clearance 35 feet) at its entrance.

Approaches. Because of its fairly exposed position, the entrance channel to the ocean shifts constantly. Buoys are moved regularly to correspond to the channel shifts, but for obvious reasons we don't recommend trying the passage under rough conditions with an onshore wind. There is also a strong tidal current, especially under the bridges. Considerable caution is advisable except in slack water. The controlling depth in the channel usually is not a problem; it's at least 6 feet.

You could proceed for about a mile south-southeast into the Lynnhaven River or follow markers from the Lynnhaven River into the

Lynnhaven Inlet (foreground) with Chesapeake Bay Bridge-Tunnel in the background.

Western Branch, but there are no good anchorages or marine facilities. The other route is far preferable.

Marinas. Once past the bridges, turn to port and follow the markers to the east into Long Creek (actually a canal for the first mile). This is where most of the marinas, with plentiful facilities, are located, and it is the start of the passage to Virginia Beach. Lynnhaven Municipal Marina also has a dockside sewage pumpout facility.

Anchorages. The first anchorage is in Broad Bay, reached by following the markers to the east until the waterway opens into the bay. You can anchor here or proceed through The Narrows into Linkhorn Bay. Linkhorn Bay offers a number of little coves, especially along its western shore, which seem to offer more attractive anchorages than Broad Bay. If you choose to anchor in either Broad Bay or Linkhorn Bay, be careful of submerged piles as you approach the shore.

Additional Marinas. If you want to visit Virginia Beach, head up the east fork of Linkhorn Bay and take a slip at the White Heron Motel & Yacht Club or anchor nearby and land by dinghy. The Barco Marine Railway, in the same vicinity, has 10 service slips, and it may be possible to rent one overnight.

CAPE HENRY
Charts: 12205, 12207, 12221, **12222**

There are two lighthouses on Cape Henry within a few hundred yards of each other. The old lighthouse was built in 1791. Although it is no longer in service, it is in good enough condition that visitors are allowed to climb to the top for an excellent view of Virginia Beach and the entrance to the Chesapeake. The oldest federal lighthouse in the country, it was authorized by the first Congress of the newly formed United States. It served well for almost 90 years, until 1881.

The nearby new lighthouse is new only in comparison. Built in 1879, it now houses one of the world's most powerful lights, visible from 20 miles out.

Near the base of the old lighthouse stands a stone cross marking the site of the first landing,

in 1607, of the colonists who went on to found Jamestown. Adjacent to the cross is a commemorative placard that reads in part:

> On April 26, 1607, three small ships approached the Chesapeake Bay from the southeast and made their landfall at Cape Henry, the southernmost promontory of that body of water. The Virginia Company expedition had set sail from England in December, 1606. Released from their four month confinement, the colonists, led by the Reverend Robert Hunt, gave thanks to God for their safe voyage. Before them lay the vast American wilderness known as Virginia.

Here, where it all began, we now leave the Land of Pleasant Living, the Chesapeake Bay, and move on to address the less hospitable waters of the Atlantic coast and the Delaware Bay and River.

The new and old Cape Henry lighthouses. The new tower houses a powerful light, visible 20 miles at sea. Visitors can climb to the top of the old tower for a view of Virginia Beach.

Region 8

CITY ISLAND TO SANDY HOOK

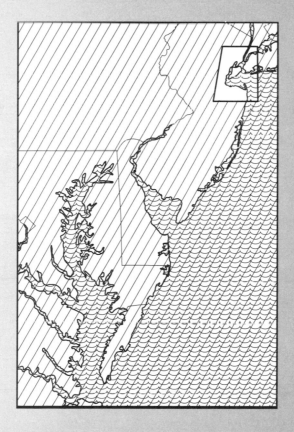

City Island to Sandy Hook

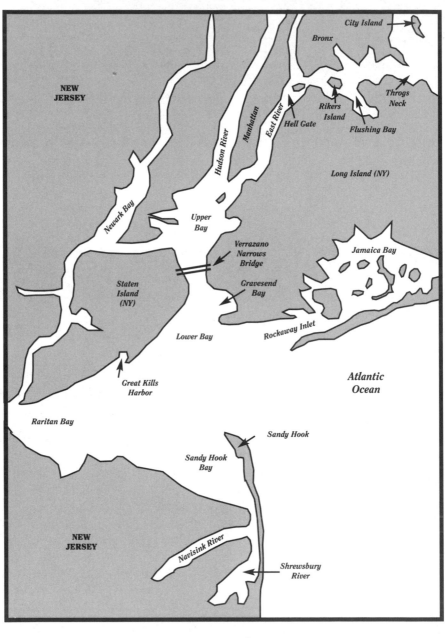

statute miles

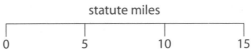

0   5   10   15

At the Long Island Sound end of the East River there are many harbors available to the cruiser. With the exception of City Island, these are all beyond the scope of this book.

Some consider the entrance to the East River at Throgs Neck to be the real northern terminus of the ICW. That seems to be a matter of opinion, but as you head north or south the section from City Island through the East River into New York Harbor and through the Verrazano Narrows into Sandy Hook Bay permits a full day's travel in semiprotected waters or better. Unfortunately, good harbors are only available at either end of this leg. Once you start into the East River heading south or pass the Verrazano Narrows headed north you are committed. Especially in the East River the current will not permit you to change your mind readily once you are well under way.

The passage through the East River is an interesting trip. The fantastic number of skyscrapers on the north side is even more impressive when you are traveling by water. Of course, New York Harbor is full of must-see sites, many of which are actually best seen from the water. (The skipper may be a bit too busy dodging commercial traffic to do much sightseeing.) A few marinas in the harbor area may offer transient berths. Other than that, there are no places to anchor, let alone sheltered harbors for cruising boats.

As you pass out of the Verrazano Narrows into Sandy Hook Bay, several secure harbors become available. To the northeast is Jamaica Bay, at the mouth of the Hudson River. To the southeast is Sandy Hook Bay proper. The first and closest harbor is the fully protected Great Kills Harbor, on Staten Island, immediately to the south of the Verrazano Narrows. Three more harbors in the southeast corner of Sandy Hook Bay— Horseshoe Cove on Sandy Hook, Atlantic Highlands Yacht Harbor, and the entrance to the Shrewsbury River and points beyond—provide good jumping-off points for those planning either to head northwest for New York City and points beyond or to proceed out into the Atlantic northeast toward the tip of Montauk Point or Block Island or south down the New Jersey coast.

CITY ISLAND TO NEW YORK HARBOR UPPER BAY

Charts: 12327, 12333, **12334**, **12335**, **12339**, 12363, **12364**, 12366

City Island

Charts: 12363, **12364**, 12366

City Island, which really is an island, is a small community at the edge of New York City surrounded by the waters of Long Island Sound and Eastchester Bay. Execution Rocks Lighthouse is to the northeast, and Stepping Stones Lighthouse is to the south. The fixed bridge connecting City Island to the mainland was built in 1897 using recycled steel from the battleship *North Carolina*. Its vertical clearance is only 12 feet, prohibiting circumnavigation of the island by all except small powerboats or skiffs.

First established as an English settlement in 1685, City Island became an important shipbuilding and yachting center during the 18th and 19th centuries. During World War II, PT boats, submarine chasers, landing craft, tugs, and minesweepers were built here. Yachting revived after the war, and today City Island is teeming with yacht clubs, marinas, sailmakers, sailing schools, fishing boats, and marine supply and repair shops. There are also two self-service laundries that are a boon to the cruiser.

City Island is an excellent jumping-off point for the trip through the East River into New York Harbor and beyond, as well as a stopover for the trip out toward Long Island Sound and beyond.

Approaches. The waters around City Island are sheltered from the east (i.e., from Long Island Sound) by Hart Island and from the west by the mainland. As a result, both the east and west sides of the island are lined with moorings, marinas, and yacht clubs, plus some anchorage room. If you are headed for the harbor

City Island Area
73°47′

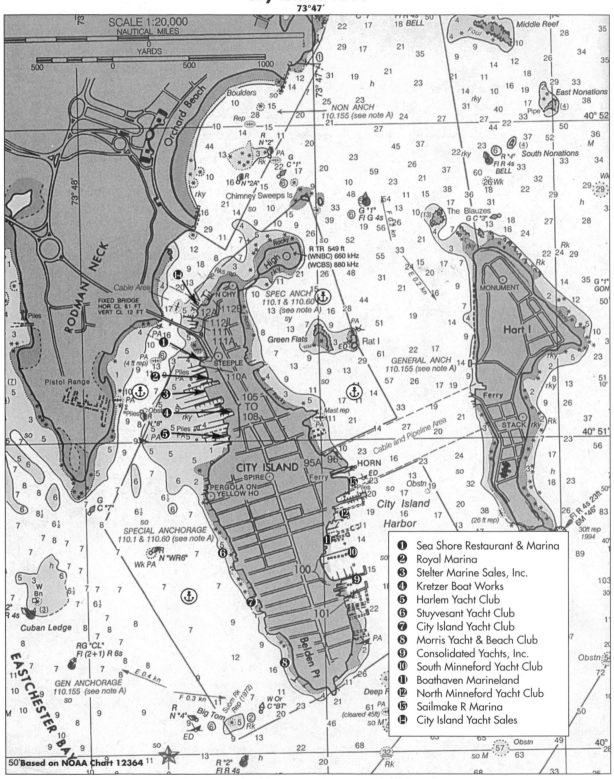

Based on NOAA Chart 12364

Legend:
1. Sea Shore Restaurant & Marina
2. Royal Marina
3. Stelter Marine Sales, Inc.
4. Kretzer Boat Works
5. Harlem Yacht Club
6. Stuyvesant Yacht Club
7. City Island Yacht Club
8. Morris Yacht & Beach Club
9. Consolidated Yachts, Inc.
10. South Minneford Yacht Club
11. Boathaven Marineland
12. North Minneford Yacht Club
13. Sailmake R Marina
14. City Island Yacht Sales

⚓ Good anchoring ⚓ Marina Launching site

Freda Gandy

Stepping Stones Light, southeast of City Island, warns of a collection of rocks between the light and Elm Point on the mainland.

on the east side of the island and approaching from the direction of Long Island Sound, you may pass to either the north or the south of Hart Island. If you are heading for the harbor on the west side, the only approach is from the south end of Eastchester Bay along the southwest shore of City Island.

The shortest route from Long Island Sound to the harbors on the east and northwest sides of the island is the rock-strewn but passable and well-marked route north around Hart Island. Go slowly and follow the navigation markers. As you pass north of Hart Island, be sure to stay between green can "3" and the flashing red 4-second red "4" at the South Nonations, then swing north and wide of The Blauzes. *(Note: Under no circumstances should you pass between the South and East Nonations or between the Blauzes and Hart Island. The water there is not only very thin but also lumpy!)* If you are heading for any of the marinas in the northwest corner of the island, north of the bridge to the mainland, you will find plenty of water, but the channel is un-

marked. From red "2A" off Orchard Beach, aiming for the center of the bridge will keep you in midchannel until you reach the longest of the piers there. The pier extends all the way to the channel.

The other approach from the east is around the south end of Hart Island, a wide-open, easy route with few obstructions. As you approach the northeast corner of City Island, beware of the unmarked shoal, Green Flats, to the northwest of Rat Island. It extends more than halfway from Rat Island toward City Island.

When approaching the harbors on the west side of the island, especially from the east, beware of Big Tom, a rock lying to the southwest of the southern tip of City Island. It is positioned roughly in the middle of a triangle formed by N "4," Fl R 4s R"2," and W Or C "BT." Unfortunately, during the prime boating season, especially on weekends, there may be so many boats in this area that you may have trouble seeing these buoys. Remain on a course that will take you at least ¼ mile south of the tip of

City Island until you can pick up red "2." From there a course of roughly 315 degrees will bring you to the west of nun "4" and clear of Big Tom. You also need to be wary of nun "WR6" marking a 3-foot spot about ¼ mile off the middle of the west side of the island. In the center of Eastchester Bay lies Cuban Ledge. The Fl R 4s R"2" due south of Rodman Neck marks the west side of the ledge, and there is a white beacon at the shallowest point of the ledge. If you pass to the east of Fl (2+1) RG "CL" on a north-northeast course toward the anchorage area between Rodman Neck and City Island, you will keep well clear of the ledge.

Anchorages. If you look on a chart, you will see Special Anchorage Areas indicated down both sides of City Island. That may well translate to "mooring fields," as these areas are nearly completely filled with moorings. Even so, room can usually be found to anchor, although renting a local mooring may make you feel more secure. No matter where you moor or anchor, you will have plenty of company.

The most popular and best-protected anchorage is between the northwest corner of City Island and Rodman Neck, south of the fixed bridge that connects City Island to the mainland. Be sure not to block the channel leading to the bridge as it is in frequent use by local powerboats. Watch the depth as you approach either shore and be sure to allow for the tide. There are several 3- to 4-foot areas at MLW toward the shores on either side. The current here can run up to 2 knots in the vicinity of the bridge, and it drops rapidly the farther south of the bridge you anchor. There is a New York Police Pistol Range on Rodman Neck, and you will frequently hear the range commands, followed by a fusillade of shots. Don't worry. They are not shooting at you.

The area east of City Island, labeled "City Harbor" on the chart, is somewhat better protected from southerly winds, but the holding in some parts may be a bit iffy. You should be able to find anchorage room both north and south of Green Flats and Rat Island, although the southern location is better. In a northeast wind the area north of Rat Island can get rather lumpy, whereas Hart Island and Rat Island shelter the area south of Rat Island. Beware of a wide cable and pipeline area extending be-

tween the middle of City Island and the middle of Hart Island: do not anchor there! It is easily identified, as it runs between the ferry docks on City Island and Hart Island, directly across from each other.

It is also possible to anchor off the southwest side of City Island, but this area is the least protected from wind, wave, and wakes.

Marinas & Restaurants. Most of the residential areas are clustered on the west side of the island, but you will also find the Harlem, Stuyvesant, City Island, and Morris Yacht Clubs here. The northwest corner of the island holds numerous boatyards and marinas, most of which are more suitable for powerboats. The entire eastern side of the island is full of boatyards, marinas, and outfitters. Kretzer Boat Works (718-885-3600), just short of the bridge on the west side of the island, is the only place that offers both gasoline and diesel fuel. On the east side of the island, City Island Yacht Sales (718-885-2300) offers gasoline, and Sailmake R Marina (718-885-2700) is the only place that currently has a pumpout facility.

There are nearly two dozen restaurants on the island, most of them along the main street. There are also several places for obtaining provisions, including an IGA grocery. It only takes about 30 minutes to walk the entire length of the island, so everything is nearby.

The Harbor Restaurant (718-885-1373), the Sea Shore Restaurant & Marina (718-885-0300), and the City Lobster House (718-885-1459) all offer dockage for patrons.

What to See & Do. While City Island is not exactly a sightseeing hot spot, a trip to the City Island Museum is worth making. The museum is located in one of the area's most picturesque historic buildings, the old Public School 17, built in 1897 on a former Indian burial ground at one of the highest points on the island. When the school building was sold for development in 1986, the city reserved space for use by the City Island Historical Society and the community center. Several of the old schoolrooms now serve as galleries for the museum. Located at 190 Fordham Street, roughly in the middle of the island, the museum is open Sundays and Wednesdays from 1:00 to 5:00 P.M. and by appointment.

The North Wind Museum, on City Island

Avenue, houses whale exhibits and a collection of nautical art. Its interesting front yard is a museum of sorts in itself.

The New York Botanical Gardens and the Bronx Zoo are only a bus or a short cab ride away.

Flushing Bay

Chart: **12339**

Flushing Bay, on the south side of the East River about 3 miles west of Throgs Neck, extends southeast between the town of College Point and La Guardia Airport. It is not really an area we would choose as a stopover point, but there are marinas inside that do offer some facilities, notably fuel and some transient slips, should you need them. Flushing Bay contains old factories and sanitation plants. Off College Point you may have to be careful of barges approaching the sanitation plant. Aircraft from La Guardia Airport create a racket loud enough to wake the dead.

Although not exactly attractive, Flushing Bay does offer a sheltered location from all directions but the northeast. The World's Fair Marina, at the head of the bay, even offers protection from that direction, as well as transient slips and a large restaurant.

Approach. A dredged channel marked by buoys and lights extends from the East River through the bay to the mouth of Flushing Creek and upstream for about 0.8 mile to the IRT (Roosevelt Avenue) railroad bridge. A 0.6-mile-long dike, covered at high water and marked at each end by a light, runs along the west side of the channel to within 0.3 mile of the head of the bay. There is a turning basin on the west side of the dredged channel at the entrance to Flushing Creek. A small-craft basin extending northwest from the turning basin is protected by an earthen dike that extends from the west side of the bay. Depths of up to 7 feet, with some shoaling, are reported in the small-craft basin.

Marinas & Restaurants. The marinas on College Point have limited transient slips and provide access to a few restaurants and pizzeria-type establishments resembling pubs. The main

street, College Point Avenue, provides restaurant choices ranging from McDonald's to a number of Chinese and Thai restaurants. Incidentally, Frank Tiborsky Marine (718-353-2653) is the only marine facility on College Point that advertises moorings (5) for transients.

The World's Fair Marina (718-478-0480), in the anchorage basin, claims depths of at least 11 feet inside. It offers gas, diesel, transient berths, electricity, water, ice, and limited electrical and engine repair. The Grand Bay Restaurant (718-898-3663) is located on the premises of the marina. Any other restaurant will require a taxi ride into Queens or at least around to College Point.

What to See & Do. The World's Fair Marina got its name from the 1964 World's Fair, the site of which is only a short walk away. Flushing Meadows Corona Park, where Shea Stadium, the home of the New York Mets, is located, also has ball fields and basketball and tennis courts. On the old World's Fair grounds is the Hall of Science (718-669-0005), which was built as the Science Pavilion for the fair and is now a hands-on museum of science and technology.

A taxi ride will take you to the Aqueduct Race Track or Belmont Park Race Track.

East River to New York Harbor

Charts: 12327, 12333, **12334**, **12335**, **12339**

The East River is a 14-mile-long strait that connects the Upper Bay, the portion of New York Harbor between The Narrows and The Battery, with Long Island Sound (multiple charts needed here for full coverage). The entrance from Long Island Sound is between Throgs Neck and Willets Point. The entrance from the New York Harbor Upper Bay is between The Battery on the southern tip of Manhattan Island and Governors Island. Hell Gate, located about halfway between Throgs Neck and The Battery, is notorious for its strong tidal currents and eddies, making for a rough and hazardous passage if you do not time it properly.

The Narrows connects the Upper and Lower Bay portions of New York Harbor. The Verrazano Narrows Bridge, a fixed suspension bridge linking Staten Island and Brooklyn between Fort Wadsworth and Fort Hamilton, indicates its narrowest point. The bridge presents no impediment to any form of water traffic as it has a vertical clearance of 215 feet and a mid-channel width of 2,000 feet. There is a fog signal on the eastern end of the bridge.

Tides & Current. In the East River the flood current sets eastward and the ebb sets westward. This is directly the reverse of conditions in Long Island Sound, where the flood is generally westward and the ebb is generally eastward. The nominal peak current through the East River is 0.7 knot at Throgs Neck, 1.6 knots at Port Morris, 4 knots in Hell Gate, 3 knots at the Brooklyn Bridge, and 1.5 knots north of Governors Island. Note that in Hell Gate the flood current (eastward) is 3.4 knots and the ebb (westward) current is 4.6 knots. Unfortunately, the currents in Hell Gate also tend to deviate significantly from the published predictions, so it is very important to plan your passage through the East River so that you pass through Hell Gate at or very close to slack water. The apocryphal stories you may hear about whirlpools that swallow vessels are just that—stories. Even so, it is true that this area can become rather unpleasant when the current is high.

The mean range of tide in the East River is 7.1 feet at Willets Point, 5.1 feet at Hell Gate, and 4.6 feet at The Battery. The tidal range will present no problems to the cruiser; it's the current that you have to watch.

Approach & Hazards. Regardless of whether you are heading west from Throgs Neck toward the Upper Bay or the reverse, it is extremely important to plan your passage to arrive at Hell Gate at near slack water. If you are departing from Throgs Neck, the ideal would be to make your passage while the current is still slightly against you, arriving at Hell Gate at or just before slack water and proceeding the rest of the way after the current change. This way, the current would be in your favor through the rest of the East River, where the current is higher. This is especially important for those in a low-powered craft such as a sailboat.

During your transit, it is advisable to maintain a listening watch on VHF-FM channel 13 so that you will have advance warning of the presence of any commercial traffic, especially tugs with barges. It would also be wise to stay to your starboard side of the passage and avoid the center when possible. Not only will this help you to avoid commercial traffic but the currents tend to run slower out of the center. The water remains deep quite close to the shore, but beware of old pilings there.

Hell Gate Bridge, looking east. Plan your arrival for slack water here to avoid several problems.

Seaplane landing in the East River near Skyport Marina.

On your departure from Throgs Neck, the channel remains deep and nearly ½ mile wide all the way to Rikers Island, where the waterway narrows. You need to leave Rikers Island to the south (port). Just beyond it are the North Brother and South Brother Islands. Although there is a channel between the them, a wiser course is to round North Brother Island by leaving both islands to port (south). After you round North Brother Island, it's a straight shot of about 1.5 nautical miles to the Hell Gate Bridge. Simply guide along the north shore to the bridge to avoid confusion. As you pass under the Hell Gate Bridge you'll make a blind S-turn through Hell Gate. Ordinarily, you would leave the well-marked Mill Rock to starboard. However, should a large commercial vessel "suddenly" appear, you may want to leave it to port to stay away from the oncoming monster. If you are in a sailboat, be sure to leave Roosevelt Island to the south. That is, pass between Roosevelt Island and Manhattan Island. On the other side is a lift bridge with a vertical clearance of 40 feet in the down position. You can't be sure of getting the bridge to lift in time if that is necessary, and if the current is pushing you,

you may not be able to turn around in time. (The current can reach 4 to 5 knots here!) Clearing any of the other bridges is no problem. They all provide 130 feet or more of vertical clearance. Once you are past Roosevelt Island, the rest of the passage is easy all the way to Governors Island and New York's Upper Bay.

Marinas & Restaurants. Marinas and restaurants readily accessible by boat in this vicinity are relatively few and far between. In fact, I know of no restaurants here where you can tie up directly. The whole harbor area is so heavily commercial that you probably wouldn't want to do so anyway. Of course, there are restaurants galore once you get ashore.

If you want to spend some time in New York City or to visit any of the sights in the area, your only real choice is to take a slip at one of the scarce marinas. From most of them you can take a cab, a subway, a bus, a rental car, or a ferry to the shoreside attractions.

The Skyport Marina, on the Manhattan side of the East River, about midway between the eastern tip of Roosevelt Island and the Williamsburg Bridge, has five transient slips, but I don't think that I would like to contend with the cur-

403

The Brooklyn Bridge spans the East River, connecting Manhattan and Brooklyn. Here, we look south.

rent in that area, even in a slip. The marina does have diesel fuel, gasoline, and water.

There are seven marinas in the 8-mile stretch of the Hudson River from Governors Island to the George Washington Bridge; all have facilities for transient boats. Half of them are on the New Jersey side of the river, and all are located on the Hudson River north of The Battery.

1. Liberty Harbor Marina. This is the first marina of note and probably the most useful for the cruiser passing through the area. It is located on the north side of the Morris Canal Basin, whose entrance is about ½ mile north of Ellis Island. This basin is all that is left of the old Morris Canal. On the north side of the entrance is buoy "WR2" (N40° 42.6′ W74° 02.0′), which marks a wreck. Be sure to leave it to starboard on your way in. One of the ferries also is located on the south side of the basin entrance. Be wary of them as you approach the entrance.

2. Newport Yacht Club & Marina. This facility is located in Jersey City, about 0.8 mile north of the entrance to the Morris Canal Basin, not far from another ferry terminal.

3. Lincoln Harbor Yacht Club. About 4.3 miles north of Ellis Island (N40° 46.1′ W74° 00.7′), this Weehawken yacht club offers some transient slips and other amenities.

4. Port Imperial Marina. This marina is also located in Weehawken, about 5 miles north of Ellis Island (N40° 47.3′ W73° 59.9′).

5. North Cove Yacht Harbor. Located on Manhattan, just upstream of The Battery, in the shade of the World Trade Center buildings, this marina advertises 26 slips available to the transient. The marina has fresh water but no fuel.

6. Surfside 3 Marina. This marina is located at Chelsea Piers, about 2 miles upstream of The Battery, due south of the Empire State Building. It offers not only 30 slips for transients but access to the restaurants in the Chelsea Pier complex. No fuel is available here, however.

7. 79th Street Boat Basin. Located about 6 miles north of The Battery, this marina offers easy access to public transportation within the city and is within walking distance of Central Park. It has 9 slips and 10 moorings available to transients, the only marina in the area to offer moorings. No fuel is available here.

New York Harbor

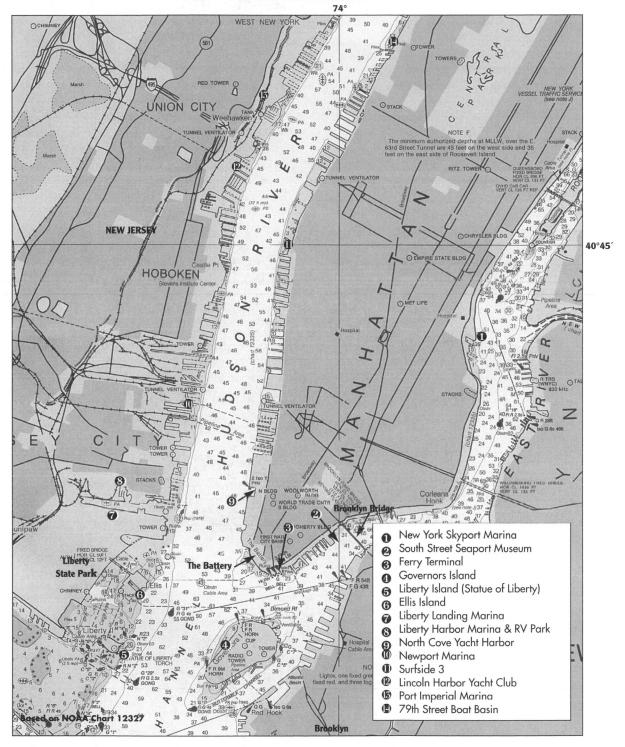

74°

40°45′

1. New York Skyport Marina
2. South Street Seaport Museum
3. Ferry Terminal
4. Governors Island
5. Liberty Island (Statue of Liberty)
6. Ellis Island
7. Liberty Landing Marina
8. Liberty Harbor Marina & RV Park
9. North Cove Yacht Harbor
10. Newport Marina
11. Surfside 3
12. Lincoln Harbor Yacht Club
13. Port Imperial Marina
14. 79th Street Boat Basin

SCALE **1.13″ = 1** NAUT. MILES   **Good anchoring**   **Marina**   **Launching site**

What to See & Do. *NEW YORK CITY.*

I can describe only a few of the many attractions of New York City here. If you don't choose to tie up at one of the marinas on the Manhattan side of the Hudson River, access to Manhattan from the New Jersey side of the river is quite quick and easy. New York Waterway (800-53-FERRY) has ferries that run from Jersey City and Weehawken to West 38th Street and the World Financial Center, with free connecting buses to Chelsea Piers. If you are located at the Newport Yacht Club, you can hop aboard a PATH train (800-234-PATH) to ride into Greenwich Village, in the heart of Manhattan. The New York Convention & Visitor's Bureau is located at 59th Street and Columbus Circle. If you are unfamiliar with New York, this would be a good place to begin.

If you want to tour the harbor, but not in your own hull, try taking a round trip on the Staten Island Ferry (718-390-5253). It departs from a terminal at South and State Streets near The Battery. For about 50¢ it offers an excellent view of New York's skyline and the harbor. The Circle Line offers a more expensive but guided and inclusive tour. Departing from Pier 83 at the end of West 42nd Street, it has several cruises each day that circumnavigate Manhattan, something you probably would rather not do in your own hull anyway.

SOUTH STREET SEAPORT MUSEUM. Located between The Battery and the Brooklyn Bridge, the South Street Seaport Museum is built on the site of what once was the country's leading port, now an eleven-square-block historic district in lower Manhattan. Founded in 1967, the museum has as its mission to trace the history of the port of New York and its commercial and cultural impact on the city, the state, and the nation. In addition to inside exhibits, there are several ships that serve as floating exhibits. Perhaps the most impressive of these is the tall ship the *Peking*, noted in the China trade and featured in a famous film made by Irving Johnson on one of the vessel's trips around Cape Horn.

Unfortunately, there is currently no place where you can tie up to visit the museum, but you certainly can pause to get a glimpse into the past as you cruise past the historic ships berthed there. Should you decide to visit Manhattan, the South Street Seaport Museum is

CITY ISLAND TO NEW YORK HARBOR UPPER BAY

406 *The South Street Seaport Museum is not accessible by water, but you can get a good look as you pass.*

well worth a stop. Admission is $6 for adults, $5 for seniors, $4 for students, and $3 for children.

GOVERNORS ISLAND. Governors Island marks the western entrance to the East River. Formerly a U.S. Army installation, it is now a U.S. Coast Guard support center (fairly inactive at present). Fort Columbus is on the northeastern portion of the island, and Castle William is at its northwestern end. There is a small marina located on the island, but unless you are a member of the U.S. military, tying up and landing on the island is prohibited.

LIBERTY STATE PARK. Formally opened on Flag Day, 14 June 1976, most of this 1,122-acre park is open space, with approximately 300 acres developed for public recreation.

The Liberty Science Center, located on Phillip Street, has three floors of interactive exhibits that focus on invention, health, and the environment. It also holds the Kodak OMNI Theater, with the largest IMAX dome screen in the world.

The Interpretive Center & Designated Natural Area, located on Freedom Way, is an environmental and historical education facility. Adjacent to the center is a 60-acre natural area

The Staten Island Ferry arriving at the terminal by The Battery in Lower Manhattan.

The impressive Manhattan skyline seen from New York Harbor. The East River and Brooklyn are to the right.

The Statue of Liberty and Liberty Island are accessible only by ferry.

consisting mostly of salt marsh, with nature trails and observation points.

Pool facilities are available to the public at a nominal charge from Memorial Day to Labor Day, including showers, rest rooms, a changing area, and a first-aid station.

The Circle Line Statue of Liberty Ferry service from Liberty Park to Ellis Island and the Statue of Liberty is available throughout the year. The ferry sails every day but Christmas Day, weather permitting. Ferries run every 20 minutes from 8:30 A.M. to 7:00 P.M. (fee $7 adults, $3 children, and $6 seniors, children under 3 years ride free. Note: If you want to climb to the crown of the Statue of Liberty, you must take the 8:30 A.M. ferry.

STATUE OF LIBERTY. Rising some 300 feet in the harbor, Lady Liberty is an international symbol of freedom. Most people are unaware that the statue was officially a lighthouse from 1886 to 1902. It was the first lighthouse in the country to use electricity, produced by a specifically made dynamo plant on the island. The beam was visible from more than 25 miles

out to sea. The Statue of Liberty was designated a National Monument in 1924 and a World Heritage Site in 1984. It now shines brighter than ever, lit from below by floodlights, a spectacular view at night.

Unfortunately, landing on the shore is prohibited. The only access to the island is via the Circle Line ferries, which operate out of three locations: the nearby Liberty State Park in New Jersey, lower Manhattan, and Hoboken, New Jersey. If you really want to visit the Statue of Liberty, your best bet is to call for a transient slip at Liberty Landing Marina in Jersey City (201-985-8000), about a mile north of Liberty Island. From there it is only a short walk to the ferry terminal in Liberty Park, where you can take the Circle Line Statue of Liberty Ferry to Liberty Island.

ELLIS ISLAND. More than 40 percent of the U.S. population descends from the 17 million immigrants who passed through Ellis Island from 1802 to 1954, now Ellis Island National Monument. The three-story Ellis Island Immigration Museum is in the same building that the immigrants came through. The Circle Line ferry will take you from Liberty Park to Ellis Island with an option to visit the Statue of Liberty. (See under Liberty State Park, above, for ferry details.) There is also a foot causeway from the mainland to Ellis Island for the hardy visitor. There is no charge to use the causeway.

GRAVESEND BAY TO JAMAICA BAY

Charts: 12326, 12327, **12350**, **12402**

Gravesend Bay
(Coney Island Creek)

Charts: 12326, 12327, **12402**

Gravesend Bay is located on the west side of Coney Island, just a couple miles below the Verrazano Narrows Bridge. Gravesend Bay itself offers little or no shelter for the cruiser except in the marina located there. Marine Basin Marina (718-372-5700), on the Brooklyn side of the mouth of Coney Island Creek, is a well-protected facility with floating docks, deep water, and a watchman-protected property. They offer up to 10 slips for transients, diesel fuel, gasoline and fresh water.

Taking a slip at the marina is really your only choice if you want to stop over in Gravesend Bay. On charts Coney Island Creek seems to be a possible anchorage for those heading south from the vicinity of New York City or awaiting favorable current conditions to transit the East River northbound. You might even think it is possible to take advantage of proximity to the Coney Island Amusement Park to pay the park a visit. It is not!

Although easily entered and well buoyed, Coney Island Creek is a mess. What is left of a marina on the west side of the creek is a wreck, literally. There are powerboats heaped atop one another on the shore as if dumped there by a hurricane. The remaining piers are crumbling, although a few boats may still be tied up there.

The rest of the land on that side looks rather unattractive. The water, which was at least 10 feet deep, was full of trash, including an incredible number of used condoms, the last time we were there. The land on the other side is even more dismal, full of decrepit buildings and high-rise apartments. To our eyes, it also looks like a bad place to be at midday, let alone at night.

This definitely is not a place to be recommended, even to anchor out. Pass it by.

Rockaway Inlet & Jamaica Bay

Charts: 12326, 12327, **12350**

Jamaica Bay is on the south shore of Long Island, about 15 miles southeast of The Battery on Manhattan. Rockaway Beach forms the south shore of the bay. This bay is rife with meadows, hassocks, and marshes. The north and east shores are bordered by marshlands that extend inland for some distance. Channels

Region 8

Steve Anderson

Sunset over the Verrazano Narrows Bridge at the entrance to New York Harbor.

GRAVESEND BAY TO JAMAICA BAY

and basins have been dredged to depths of 12 to 20 feet throughout the bay. The bay is about 7 miles long by 3½ miles wide, an area of about 22 square miles.

The mean range of tide at Rockaway Inlet is about 5 feet. The entrance channel near Rockaway Point has a peak ebb current velocity of more than 3 knots; the flood current is not as strong. (See the *Tidal Current Tables* for predictions.)

Approach. Rockaway Inlet, the entrance to Jamaica Bay, is between Rockaway Point on the southeast side and Manhattan Beach and Barren Island on the north side. There are two approaches to Jamaica Bay, a northern channel along Coney Island and a southern channel starting at the tip of Rockaway Point.

If you are approaching from New York Harbor or Sandy Hook Bay, you can most easily use the northern channel or Coney Island Channel. (Note: This channel is referenced to New York Harbor, not Jamaica Bay. When entering Jamaica Bay, leave the red markers to port and the green markers to starboard until you reach the middle of Coney Island. Thereafter, the markers revert to reference to Jamaica Bay or its assorted tributaries.) Simply head for the west end of Coney Island until you can see the channel markers, then follow them along the south shore of Coney Island into Jamaica Bay.

Use the southern entrance channel when approaching from offshore. A jetty extends from the tip of Rockaway Point, marked by a light on its outer end. On the west side of the entrance channel is a shifting sandbar, with depths of less than 1 foot and marked by breakers, that often makes its presence known to the unwary. This channel is referenced to Jamaica Bay, so leave the red markers to starboard and the green to port.

Anchorage & Marinas. Sheepshead Bay, located on the north side of the east end of Coney Island and north of Manhattan Beach, is well protected and used by numerous pleasure and fishing vessels. The well-marked channel has a depth of 12 to 14 feet to the bay entrance. Inside the bay, the depths range from 6 to 10

feet to the bridge near the head of navigation, except for shoaling along the edges. The small-craft facilities in the bay offer gasoline, diesel, water, ice, marine supplies, berths, and electricity. Limited engine repairs and a 1.5-ton lift are also available.

Plumb Beach Channel, leading to Gerritsen and Shell Bank Creeks, is only accessible to vessels that can pass under the fixed bridge with a vertical clearance of 35 feet. If you can clear the bridge, Shell Bank Creek leads westerly and Gerritsen and Mill Creeks lead northwesterly. Passing beyond the ruins of the old fixed highway bridge over Mill Creek is not recommended because so many pieces of the bridge structure have fallen into the water. Small-craft facilities on Shell Bank Creek offer gasoline, diesel, water, ice, marine supplies, and complete engine and hull repairs.

Dead Horse Bay, off Plumb Beach Channel just before the fixed bridge, leads into the southwest side of Barren Island. A marina on the north side of the bay offers both berths and moorings. There also appears to be some anchorage room among the moorings in 10 to 13 feet of water with a mud bottom.

The Gil Hodges Memorial (Marine Parkway) Bridge, crossing Rockaway Inlet between Rockaway Point and Barren Island, is a vertical-lift span with a vertical clearance of 55 feet down and 152 feet up. The Rockaway Coast Guard station is on Rockaway Point, just west of the bridge. Past the bridge are multiple basins and areas where you can anchor in reasonable security. The area is filled with marshes and meadows laced with channels that you may explore to your heart's content. Running aground here is reminiscent of the same in the Chesapeake. The soft mud bottom makes grounding largely a so-what affair unless you manage to do so at extreme high tide.

Cross Bay Memorial Bridge, crossing Beach Channel at Rockaway Beach, is a fixed span with a vertical clearance of 55 feet. If you cannot clear that, you have reached the head of navigation. If you can, there are many more areas to explore beyond it.

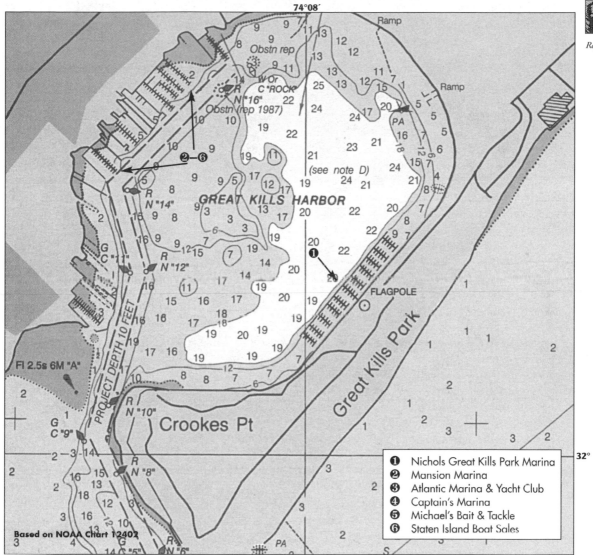

Region 8

74°08′

Ramp

Ramp

Obstn rep

W Or C "ROCK"

Obstn (rep 1987)

GREAT KILLS HARBOR

(see note D)

N "16"

N "14"

N "12"

G C "11"

N "12"

FLAGPOLE

Great Kills Park

Fl 2.5s 6M "A"

PROJECT DEPTH 10 FEET

R N "10"

G C "9"

Crookes Pt

R N "8"

Based on NOAA Chart 12402

R N "6"

G C "5"

PA

32°

❶	Nichols Great Kills Park Marina
❷	Mansion Marina
❸	Atlantic Marina & Yacht Club
❹	Captain's Marina
❺	Michael's Bait & Tackle
❻	Staten Island Boat Sales

SCALE **5.85"** = **1** NAUT. MILES   ⚓ **Good anchoring**   **Marina**   **Launching site**

WESTERN LOWER BAY
Charts: **12324**, 12327, **12331**, **12401**, **12402**

Great Kills Harbor, Staten Island

Charts: 12327, 12331, **12402**

Great Kills Harbor, on the south side of Staten

Island northwest of Old Orchard Shoal Light, is used strictly by pleasure boats. It offers a secure harbor with a terrific view of the Verrazano Narrows Bridge, especially at night, when the bridge is lit up like a Christmas tree. It's a handy stopover point for awaiting the proper weather and tide conditions to begin the trek through the East River to Long Island Sound or around Sandy Hook on the passage south down the New Jersey coast. It also offers an opportunity for you to stretch your legs in this part of the Gateway National Park System.

Approach. If you are approaching from the Verrazano Narrows, it may be advisable to head for the Old Orchard Shoals Light (N40° 30.7′ W74° 05.9′) in order to avoid the shoals off the Staten Island shore. From there it's about 1½ miles to Great Kills Light. Great Kills Light (N40° 31.3′ W74° 07.9′) is a 35-foot-high skeleton tower with a red and white, diamond-shaped daymark on a red concrete base, located to the east of the harbor channel entrance. Leave the light to starboard and follow the well-marked channel into the basin. The buoyage system continues along the northwest side of the harbor, but once you have cleared Crookes Point at the entrance, you can pretty much ignore the markers. However, you do have to be careful of the 3-foot spot in the center of the harbor among the mooring field. The mean-tide range here is about 5 feet.

Anchorage. At first glance, it may appear that there is no room to anchor among the moorings; there is some room, but you will have to search for it. If you have a shoal draft, you will find an empty spot among the moorings where the 3-foot shoal lends itself only to boats with a lesser draft than that or boats that don't mind grounding at low tide.

Marinas & Restaurants. As you enter the basin, a half-dozen marinas and yacht clubs are lined up to port. Staten Island Boat Sales (718-984-7676) and Mansion Marina (718-984-6611) offer transient slips (reservations recommended), repairs, diesel, and gasoline. Staten Island Boat Sales also has a marine store.

Michaels Bait & Tackle, immediately past Staten Island Boat Sales, has a 100-foot gas dock offering diesel and gasoline. However, you may have to tie up and walk a couple of blocks inshore to get someone to come to the dock and turn on the pump.

To starboard on the east side of the basin is Nichol's Great Kills Park Marina (718-351-8476), offering transient slips, partial engine repairs, and some marine hardware. It also provides convenient access to Great Kills Park.

Apparently, all of the moorings in the basin belong to the assortment of yacht clubs. I don't know whether any are available to transients, but it wouldn't hurt to ask.

Inshore behind the marinas and yacht clubs are several restaurants.

What to See & Do. The Staten Island Unit of the Gateway National Park extends along the south shore of the island. It includes Fort Wadsworth, Miller Field, Great Kills Park, and Hoffman and Swinburn Islands.

Fort Wadsworth is one of the oldest military installations in the United States, first used during the Revolutionary War. The military closed the site as a military installation in 1994. Visitors who wish to explore the site can view exhibits and an introductory video in the Visitor's Center, then walk along a 1½-mile trail around the major fortifications of the site. The Visitor Center is open Wednesday through Sunday from 10:00 A.M. to 5:00 P.M.

Miller Field, a former U.S. Army base, contains two post–World War I military aircraft hangers, 64 acres of athletic fields, picnic areas, a community garden, and the Swamp White Oak Forest.

Great Kills Park has a seasonal swimming beach, athletic fields, a public boat-launching ramp, nature trails, a model-airplane field, and miles of trails for jogging and walking.

Hoffman and Swinburn Islands were constructed in 1872 to serve as a quarantine station and crematorium for immigrants entering the United States. These islands now serve as nesting sanctuaries for many bird species and are not open to the public.

Horseshoe Cove, Sandy Hook

  No facilities

Charts: 12324, 12327, **12401**

Horseshoe Cove, on the west side of Sandy Hook, is a suitable anchorage except when there is a strong southwest wind, at which time it may well become a little roily. Shoaling has been reported in recent years, so proceed into the cove with caution. However, Horseshoe Cove is probably the only place where you can anchor if you want to visit Sandy Hook National Park, part of the Gateway National Park System. The park is open daily from sunrise to sunset.

Because of its location overlooking the entrance to New York Harbor, Sandy Hook has played a major role in both navigation and coastal defense. In 1870 the first U.S. Army proving ground began testing weapons here, and in 1895 Fort Hancock was established as part of the defenses for New York Harbor. Today the buildings and fortifications of Fort Hancock are preserved and open to the public, as is Sandy Hook Lighthouse. Both are less than a mile from Horseshoe Cove.

Approach & Anchorage. If you are entering Sandy Hook Bay from the ocean, be sure to remain in the well-marked Sandy Hook Channel until well into the bay. Don't hug the shore, as the shoals tend to extend farther out than the charts seem to indicate. From anywhere else in Sandy Hook Bay it's a direct path to the Horseshoe Cove entrance. Guide around the sandy point and swing north into the sheltered area behind it. There are sticks in the water to mark fishnets. Stay away from them. There is plenty of room to anchor outside of them.

What to See & Do. Sandy Hook includes 6 miles of ocean beaches, salt marshes, the waters of Sandy Hook Bay, and the historic site of Fort Hancock. Hiking, fishing, birding, and beach-combing are common activities throughout the year. Lifeguards are on duty at the ocean beaches during the summer months. The Sandy Hook Visitor's Center, housed in the 1894 U.S. Life-Saving Station, features exhibits and a bookstore; it is open daily from 10:00 A.M. to 5:00 P.M. Visit the center for information on the attractions and the best way to see the park. The mile-long Old Dune Trail begins nearby.

Fort Hancock Museum, housed in the former post guardhouse, is only about a ½-mile walk from Horseshoe Cove. It contains a bookstore, exhibits, and dioramas about Fort Hancock. It is open on weekends from 1:00 to 5:00 P.M.

History House, close to the museum, is a restored 1898 lieutenant's residence on Officers Row, overlooking Sandy Hook Bay. Its exhibits illustrate everyday life at Fort Hancock. Volunteers staff the building. Like the museum, it is open on weekends from 1:00 to 5:00 P.M.

The Sandy Hook Lighthouse, the oldest continuously working lighthouse in the country, still guides ships along the New Jersey coast and into the harbor. It was commissioned by George Washington and built in 1764 by Isaac Conro to aid mariners entering the south end of the approach to New York Harbor. The New Jersey Lighthouse Society conducts tours of the light from spring through the fall on Satur-

day and Sunday from 12:00 to 4:00 P.M. The grounds are open daily all week.

Battery Potter is the oldest gun battery at Fort Hancock. Check the program listing from the Visitor's Center for weekend tours.

Atlantic Highlands Yacht Harbor

Charts: **12324**, 12327, **12401**

Approach. This artificial harbor is located about a mile west of the entrance to the Shrewsbury River, far enough so that even its eastern approach is out of any significant current in or out of the river. A long breakwater protects the basin. The normal entrance is on the east side of the breakwater. It is difficult to see the breakwater, let alone the marker on its east end until you are within a mile of it. The easiest way to make your approach is to head midway between a gray concrete high-rise building on top of The Highlands to the east and a red and white radio tower to the west. The end of the breakwater is almost exactly midway between these two structures. As you round the end of the breakwater, the whole basin opens before you, with a wide entrance impeded only by the need to avoid the numerous boats on moorings.

An entrance at the other (west) end of the breakwater is not obvious on the chart. We were told that boats with close to a 6-foot draft or more should not attempt to pass through this entrance at anywhere near low water. However, it seems that all the commercial boats do exit this way. When we made our exit from Atlantic Highlands Yacht Harbor through the west opening in the breakwater at extreme low water, the controlling depth was no less than 5 feet. Ruins of pilings from an old dock immediately ahead of the opening require a 90-degree turn to the north to exit. At high water the collection of pilings may well be submerged. That's something to remember!

Anchorages. As you enter the basin through the main (east) entrance, there's an anchorage area on the inland side that is deliberately kept clear of moorings. Watch your depth if you choose to anchor here, and don't forget

413

Sandy Hook Bay

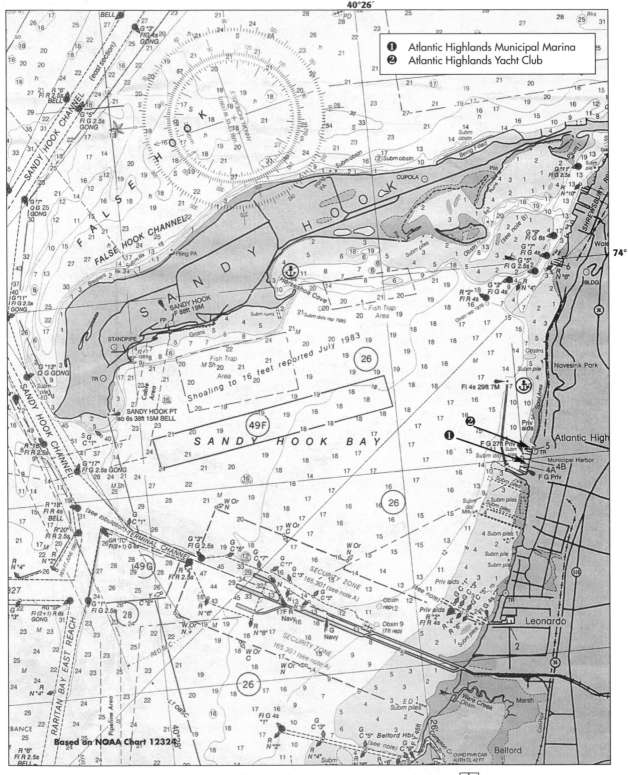

40°26′

❶	Atlantic Highlands Municipal Marina
❷	Atlantic Highlands Yacht Club

SANDY HOOK CHANNEL (east section)

FALSE HOOK CHANNEL

S A N D Y   H O O K

CUPOLA

Horseshoe Cove

SANDY HOOK
F 88ft 19M

STANDPIPE

SANDY HOOK PT
Iso 6s 38ft 15M BELL

Fish Trap
Area

Shoaling to 16 feet reported July 1983

S A N D Y   H O O K   B A Y

49F

SANDY HOOK CHANNEL

TERMINAL CHANNEL

SECURITY ZONE
165.301 (see note A)

SECURITY ZONE
165.301 (see note A)

RARITAN BAY EAST REACH

Pipeline Area

Navesink Park

Atlantic High

Municipal Harbor

Leonardo

Ware Creek

Belford Hbr.
(see note)

Belford

Marsh

Based on NOAA Chart 12324

SCALE **1.36″** = 1 NAUT. MILES   ⚓ **Good anchoring**   ⚓ **Marina**   ⛵ **Launching site**

the state and range (5 feet) of the tide. There is also room to anchor between the end of the breakwater and the first set of moorings. Like the rest of this harbor, the anchorage area is well protected and in easy reach of the shore facilities by dinghy.

Marinas & Restaurants. The harbor is filled with moorings, all cared for by the Atlantic Highlands Municipal Marina even though many of them belong to the Atlantic Highlands Yacht Club (AHYC). The AHYC is located on the top floor of the Shore Casino in the middle of the parking lot. Transients are welcome, and you should be able to find a slip or a mooring here, although you may have to tie off to the end of a pier. Moorings are assigned by the AHYC, and slips and pier-end assignments are made by the marina. If you wind up at the end of a pier, adjust spring lines carefully to keep your bumpers properly positioned against the raw pilings as the tide rises or falls. A fender board will prove very useful.

There are two restaurants in the pier area. A short walk to the west will take you to the town's main street, where you will find several more restaurants, a self-service laundry, and a Foodland supermarket. The supermarket is across the alternate shore route, where there is very heavy traffic, although a stoplight will permit you to cross in one piece. The Skipper's Shop, a marine store, carries an impressive array of marine supplies, though sailboat equipment is scarce.

What to See & Do. Unless you are interested in seeing a substantial collection of Victorian-style houses, there's not much in the way of conventional shoreside attractions. However, it's a lovely little town, and you really should take the time to stroll through it.

There is a nice, sandy beach that stretches for more than ¼ mile to the east of the marina. At low tide, especially, the beach offers wonderful opportunities for strolling, beach-combing, wading, and possibly even clamming. Even at high tide there is plenty of beach for most purposes.

Shrewsbury & Navisink Rivers

Charts: **12324**, 12327, 12401

Approach. The entrance to the Shrewsbury River is a narrow passage in the southeast corner of Sandy Hook Bay. Set your course for the Fl 4s R"2" (N40° 25.2´ W74° 00.3´), which is just to the east of the breakwater protecting the Atlantic Highlands boat basin. From there simply follow the buoys into the mouth of the Shrewsbury River. This leads between Sandy Hook and the Highlands and past the ruins of an old railroad bridge and the Route 36 drawbridge, with a closed vertical clearance of 35 feet.

Beyond that passage the Navisink River forks to the west and the Shrewsbury River continues due south into a very narrow channel. Follow the marked channel carefully and keep a depth-sounder. You have to be very careful to remain in the channel: it has a nasty habit of changing its location due to storms, and even the markers may not always be in the correct location. At low tide many but not all of the mud flats will be visible. Even small powerboats with outdrives can get into trouble if they stray out of the marked channels.

If you proceed up the Navisink River, there is one more drawbridge to negotiate, with a closed vertical clearance of 35 feet. Past this bridge the channel opens up for about 1½ miles, then narrows again for the rest of the way to Red Bank, 3 miles past the bridge. For all practical purposes Red Bank is the head of navigation because the Route 35 fixed bridge has a vertical clearance of only 8 feet.

The Shrewsbury River quickly reduces to a very narrow, marked channel that runs south to Long Branch. This is predominantly small powerboat country. Outside this channel there are no facilities, and there is precious little water. Cruisers are advised to pass it up.

Anchorage. Don't expect to find many convenient anchorages; with only a few exceptions the mud flats restrict passage to the narrow channels on the Navisink River. I know of no place for a cruising boat to anchor on the Shrewsbury River beyond its junction with the Navisink.

Once you clear the first bridge on the Navisink River, the channel opens up and you can find several places to anchor under the bluffs. Just make sure that you are clear of the channel and that you anchor in enough water to keep you afloat at low tide. The tide range here is about 4 feet.

Marinas & Restaurants. For all practical purposes, there are no useful facilities for transient cruising boats on the Shrewsbury River other than right at its entrance from Sandy Hook Bay. Just as you enter the channel into the Shrewsbury River, a string of small marinas appears to starboard. The first is Sandy Hook Bay Marina, offering transient slips and an excellent restaurant. Next come Captain's Cove Marina and the Marina on the Bay Yacht Club, which offer some transient slips and little else for the cruiser. Schupp's Pier, on the eastern end of the point formed by The Highlands, offers diesel and gasoline. Next to Schupp's Pier is Bahrs Landing, offering transient slips, diesel, gasoline, and a restaurant. There are other marinas in this vicinity, but they appear to offer little to the transient cruiser.

Up the Shrewsbury River, past the Route 520 drawbridge, the river appears to widen out and is rather attractive. However, you are still constrained to a narrow channel. There are a few small marinas here, mostly catering to powerboats. We find other areas more appealing. Pass this one by.

If you follow the Navisink River to its effective head of navigation, you will arrive at Red Bank, where you will find a substantial collection of shops, restaurants, and bars. The town-owned Marine Park has a shallow pier that doesn't lend itself to cruising boats of any size. However, there are several marinas nearby that are more accessible.

Located on the south bank by the Route 35 bridge is the famous Molly Pitcher Inn & Marina. It was designed to resemble Philadelphia's Independence Hall and is named for the legendary heroine of the Revolutionary War battle of Monmouth, Molly Pitcher. The marina, immediately below the inn, claims to maintain 16 slips for transients.

From any of the marinas it is only a short walk to the stores in town.

Region 9

SANDY HOOK TO CAPE MAY

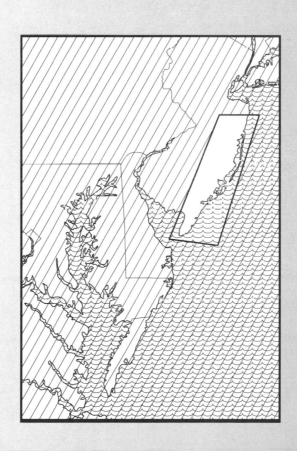

Sandy Hook to Cape May

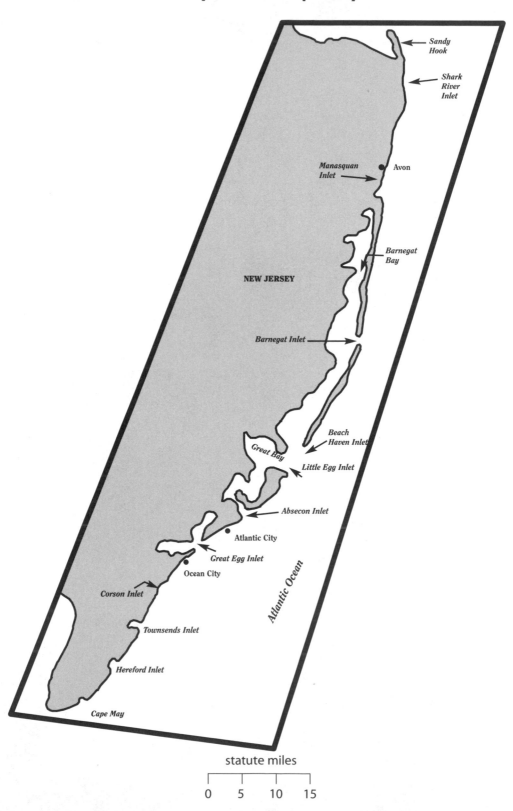

Sandy Hook

Shark River Inlet

Manasquan Inlet · Avon

Barnegat Bay

NEW JERSEY

Barnegat Inlet

Great Bay

Beach Haven Inlet

Little Egg Inlet

Absecon Inlet

· Atlantic City

Great Egg Inlet

· Ocean City

Atlantic Ocean

Corson Inlet

Townsends Inlet

Hereford Inlet

Cape May

statute miles

0   5   10   15

THE NEW JERSEY COAST extends in a generally southerly direction for 44 miles from Sandy Hook to Barnegat Inlet. From there it goes southwesterly for about 66 miles to Cape May Point.

There are an even dozen inlets along New Jersey's 120-mile Atlantic coastline. However, half of them are problem inlets that require recent local knowledge to even attempt to enter. Some of these are not recommended to the transient under any circumstances, let alone rough weather. The remaining inlets provide relatively safe passage, but even most of these require extreme caution when entering in other than benign conditions. In most cases the navigational aids marking the inlets are not shown on the charts because they are frequently moved due to changing conditions.

Cruising southward down the Atlantic coast, the safest inlets are Shark River, Manasquan, Barnegat, Absecon, Great Egg, and Cape May Inlets. Even these relatively safe inlets can offer a very rough transit and may even become impassable under certain conditions of weather, wind, and tide. As always, whether to enter (or exit) an inlet is a judgment call by the skipper of the vessel, taking into account the current conditions, the type and size of the vessel, and the skill of the crew.

Although it should be obvious, it is worth stating that it is critically important to be sure that the inlet you are attempting to enter is really the inlet you think it is *before* making your approach. Even then, I strongly advise a call to the local Coast Guard station to verify entrance and channel conditions before starting your approach.

Shark River Inlet

Charts: **12324**, 12326

About 20 miles south of the tip of Sandy Hook, between the towns of Avon and Belmar, the Shark River Inlet is one of the easier inlets to enter on the New Jersey coast. Many recreational vessels use it year-round, but its heaviest use is by charter and party fishing boats, the majority of which seem to operate out of the Belmar Municipal Boat Basin.

The mean range of tide here is approximately 4 feet.

Approach. A pair of jetties, with appropriate lights mounted on their seaward ends, protect the inlet. In addition, a fog signal is mounted at the end of the north jetty. The Shark River Coast Guard station is located on the north side of the inlet, about ¼ mile inside the jetties.

The inlet is best entered by approaching from the bell buoy off the mouth of the inlet. Do not hug the north jetty entrance; a large number of fallen rocks are located in this vicinity. In rough weather, especially with an onshore wind and outgoing current, serious consideration should be given to entering Manasquan Inlet instead of this one. Aside from the wave action, wind and current can push you to one side or the other as you approach, causing a distinct increase in your laundry bill. However, once you are inside the mouth of the inlet, things will calm down.

There are two sets of bridges to be negotiated as you proceed to the majority of the facilities on the Shark River. The first of these, located immediately inside the jetties, is the Ocean Avenue Bridge, which has a reputation for being somewhat unresponsive to requests to open the drawbridge unless you call on channel 13 specifically to the Ocean Avenue Bridge, not the Shark River Bridge.

The remaining set of three bridges, one of which is a railroad bridge, will open in concert. However, if there is any rail traffic in the offing, you will have to hold position and wait for it to pass. (Trains really don't stop as readily as automobiles.) Call the Route 35 bridge at Shark River to request an opening. The bridgetender will arrange for all three bridges to open. A sign posted on the bridges indicated that the bridges need open only on the hour and half-hour, but the bridgetender may be more accommodating if rail and other traffic permits. Supposedly, there is a project under way to replace the Route 35 lift bridges with a fixed bridge having the standard 65-foot MHW clearance. As I write this, I do not know its status or whether there are plans to do the same with the railroad bridge.

Anchorages. Anchorage room here is at a bit of a premium. Boats with a draft of more than 4 feet need not apply unless they are willing to take the risk of anchoring in the river, with its reversing current and the possibility of impeding other traffic.

It is possible to anchor just past the Municipal Marina, to port beyond the last set of bridges,

provided you can find room. If you do, it is possible to land at the gas dock and then walk a block down 10th Avenue to where the downtown area offers restaurants and provisions.

Those who have less than a 4-foot draft or are willing to go hard aground at low tide can anchor in the basin at the end of the channel around Shark Island. The chart indicates 5-foot

Shark River

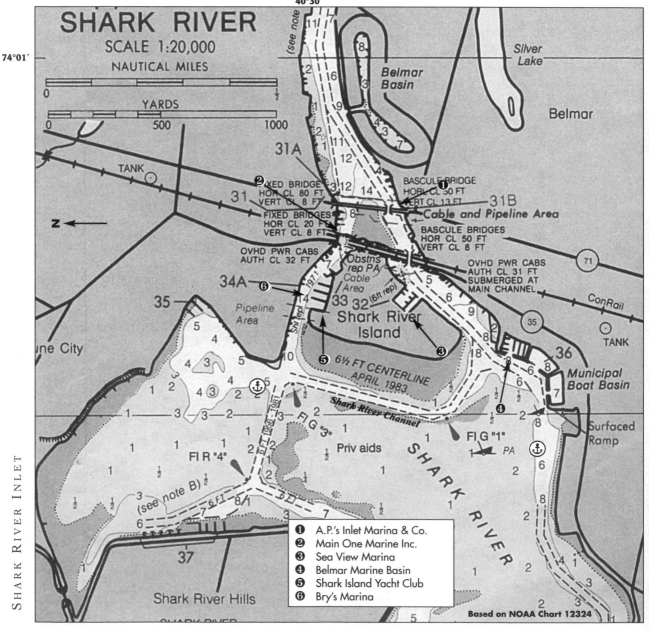

❶ A.P.'s Inlet Marina & Co.
❷ Main One Marine Inc.
❸ Sea View Marina
❹ Belmar Marine Basin
❺ Shark Island Yacht Club
❻ Bry's Marina

Based on NOAA Chart 12324

⚓ **Good anchoring**   ⚓ **Marina**   🚤 **Launching site**

depths at MLW in this basin. It lies! Except for a short segment of the Shark River Channel just past the last set of channel markers, there is only 3 feet or less of water at MLW. In that short segment it is possible to anchor in 6 feet of water at MLW, but you run the risk of swinging into the Shark Island Channel on a falling tide or bumping the bottom in the other direction as the tide starts to come in. Also, there is probably only room for one boat.

We anchored there once and didn't get it quite right. We found ourselves hard aground with a very stable view of uncovered flats all around us as we waited for the tide to come back in. What looked like a piling coming out of the water as the tide fell turned out to be the center console on what was left of a small wooden boat. We saw lots of clam spouts on the flats, but we didn't see anyone actually engaged in clamming.

Marinas & Restaurants. A. P.'s Inlet Marina (908-681-3303) is located to port just before you reach the second bridge. Although it is a small facility, it claims to offer transient slips, diesel, gasoline, and water.

The Belmar Municipal Boat Basin (908-681-2266) is located to port just past the second set of bridges. You may be able to find a transient slip there, but they are a bit scarce. Diesel and gasoline are also available. From the marina it is only a short walk down 10th Avenue to the restaurants and food stores in the bustling downtown area.

If you can negotiate the narrow channel past Shark Island, the hospitable Shark Island Yacht Club (908-502-0094) welcomes transients when there is room. No fuel is available there.

What to See & Do. Save for summer cottages, this is not exactly a tourist area. We saw no reason even to get off the boat to land, as there appears to be nothing to see. There is one exception, however.

The collection of houses lining both shores between the two sets of bridges is rather unique. There are Cape Cod cottages, ranch houses, mansion-size houses in the style of cottages, even a Mexican-style house. Unlike most neighborhoods, individuality reigns supreme here.

Tom McGuire

Aerial view of Shark River Inlet, looking west-southwest.

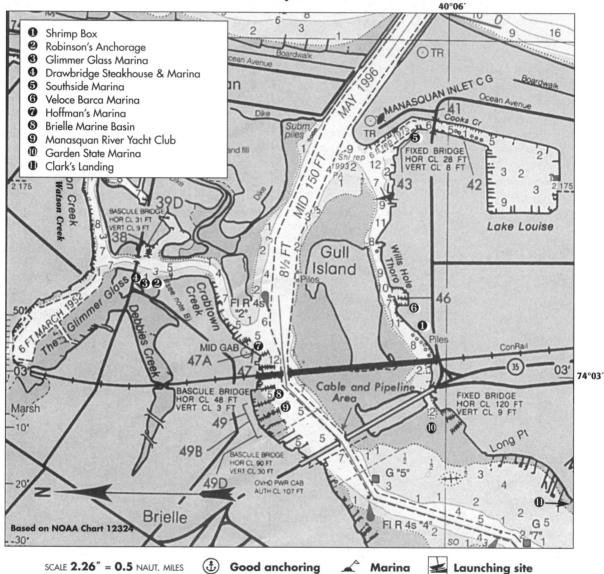

1. Shrimp Box
2. Robinson's Anchorage
3. Glimmer Glass Marina
4. Drawbridge Steakhouse & Marina
5. Southside Marina
6. Veloce Barca Marina
7. Hoffman's Marina
8. Brielle Marine Basin
9. Manasquan River Yacht Club
10. Garden State Marina
11. Clark's Landing

Region 9

40°06′

74°03′

03′

Based on NOAA Chart 12324

SCALE **2.26″ = 0.5** NAUT. MILES   ⚓ **Good anchoring**   ⚓ **Marina**   🛥 **Launching site**

Manasquan Inlet

Charts: 12323, 12324

About 5½ miles south of Shark River Inlet is Manasquan Inlet, a well-marked inlet considered to be one of the easiest to enter on the New Jersey coast. It serves both as the entrance to the Manasquan River and as the northern terminus of the New Jersey portion of the Intracoastal Waterway. As a direct result, traffic is

often *extremely* heavy. A large charter fishing fleet is based here, and there are many large, private powerboats. Be careful!

Approach. Bordered on the north by the town of Manasquan and on the south by Point Pleasant Beach, the inlet is subject to frequent dredging. Unlike the entrances to most New Jersey inlets, its entrance is unimpeded by bars. The safest approach is to take a departure to the entrance from the Manasquan Inlet lighted bell buoy red "2M" (N40° 05.5′ W74° 00.8′). However, under most conditions you can head directly for the pair of entrance jetties (N40°

Tom McCuire

Aerial view of Manasquan Inlet, looking northwest.

06.1′ W74° 01.9′), marked with lights on each end. If you enter cleanly and proceed as near to the middle of the channel as other traffic will allow, you should have no problems under normal conditions. Regular users of the inlet tend to cut rather close to the rock piles with no problems.

Although conditions in the inlet are usually favorable, the Manasquan Coast Guard station personnel caution that there are times when the inlet demands a great deal of respect. Conditions to look out for include heavy weather at the mouth of the inlet, especially under conditions of onshore winds, outgoing current, and a following sea. Certain wind and current conditions may push your boat to one side of the inlet or the other. Do not follow other boats too closely, and allow even more of a buffer space when the weather becomes increasingly heavy.

A marked, dredged channel leads from the inlet for about 5 miles up the Manasquan River. About 2 miles from the inlet is the entrance to the Point Pleasant Canal, the real starting point of the New Jersey ICW. However, most of this passage is best left to powerboats. Although the passage is quite possible, because of the numerous bridges, shoal waters, and currents, cruising sailboats of any size are better off taking the coastal route.

Anchorages. There is virtually no room to anchor in the Manasquan River. Your only choice is to find some place to tie up or to proceed about 2 miles west into the Point Pleasant Canal and 2 more miles, through two lift bridges and west of Herring Island, into the Metedeconk River. There it is possible to anchor off the marsh at the mouth of the Metedeconk River by the flashing green "1." *(Note: Currents in the Point Pleasant Canal can reach 4 to 6 knots and may be quite turbulent in the vicinity of the two lift bridges. Low-powered vessels, especially, are advised to wait for near slack water before attempting the passage.)*

Marinas & Restaurants. There are about a dozen marinas in the Manasquan River. Most have at least a few transient slips, but only a couple are likely to have an available transient slip in the prime boating season.

Brielle Marine Basin (732-528-6200), to starboard immediately past the railroad drawbridge, claims to hold 15 transient slips available and can handle boats up to 100 feet LOA. It has diesel, gasoline, and a marine store.

The Shrimp Box restaurant (732-899-1637), in Wills Hole Thorofare, to the south immediately after you enter the inlet, offers free dockage alongside the bulkhead for those dining there and can also provide overnight dockage.

The Drawbridge Steakhouse & Marina (732-223-8434) is to starboard in Crabtown Creek, just before you reach the drawbridge over that creek. It has a couple of transient berths that may be used by customers while dining. Overnight accommodation is uncertain, at best.

The Garden State Marina (732-892-4222), to port just beyond the railroad and Route 35 drawbridges, claims to offer 10 transient slips with 6 feet of water at MLW. No fuel is available there.

What to See & Do. The area around Manasquan Inlet is composed of residential communities, which means that it is pretty quiet. If you are looking for amusements, the usual seaside attractions, including a nice sandy beach, are available along the oceanfront.

Barnegat Inlet

Charts: 12323, **12324**

Not long ago Barnegat Inlet was one of the most notorious of the inlets on the Atlantic coast in spite of repeated efforts by the government to keep it accessible. Then, in 1988 a three-year, multimillion-dollar project was initiated to change the alignment of the inlet from its previous arrowhead configuration to one with parallel jetties and to significantly extend the south jetty to seaward. Completed in 1991, the new south jetty juts out almost ½ mile into the ocean, and sand has filled in the area between the old and new south jetties. The ocean ends of both jetties are well lighted, although the outer part of the north jetty is at least partially submerged at high water. It was hoped that the long, parallel design of the jetty pair would provide a

tidal-flushing action that would help to deepen and maintain the inlet, reducing the previous problems with shoals and breaking seas. Within the jetties this appears to be working.

Even so, until 1995 Barnegat Inlet was considered a bit on the iffy side if there was any sea running. Even the Coast Guard vessels would often divert to Manasquan Inlet when the current, wind, and sea combined to make "interesting" conditions. The offshore approach to the inlet was serpentine, and the channel was constantly changing, with a few uncomfortably shallow spots to catch your attention. With any significant sea making up, the danger of broaching while trying to stay in the channel was quite real.

Then, in 1995 the seaward side of the inlet was dredged and the entrance channel widened and realigned to a straight-in approach, adding Barnegat Inlet to the ranks of the more easily accessible inlets. In fact, in June 1995, while returning from a cruise to New York, we had no problem entering Barnegat Inlet in a pea-soup fog, visibility about 50 yards, without radar. A year earlier, before the dredging, I wouldn't have even tried it.

Located roughly midway between Cape May and Sandy Hook, Barnegat Inlet now offers an excellent and convenient stopover point for a passage up or down the New Jersey coast. Once a notorious, often treacherous inlet, it is now easily entered, leading to a pleasant anchorage or excellent marina facilities. Those who may have shunned it in the past should definitely give it a try.

Approach. Barnegat Lighthouse makes an excellent landmark for locating the inlet from well over 5 miles off (unless, of course, there is fog). The safest approach is to take your departure toward the outer set of buoys marking the entrance channel from the Barnegat outer buoy red-white Mo(A) (N39° 44.5′ W74° 03.7′). From red-white Mo(A) a course of 310 degrees magnetic will take you directly to the first set of channel buoys. The ocean ends of the jetties are well lighted and easily identified from seaward, and the approach channel to the inlet is well buoyed.

Make sure that you remain within the channel marked by the buoys unless advised otherwise by local information. There are sandbars

Barnegat Inlet

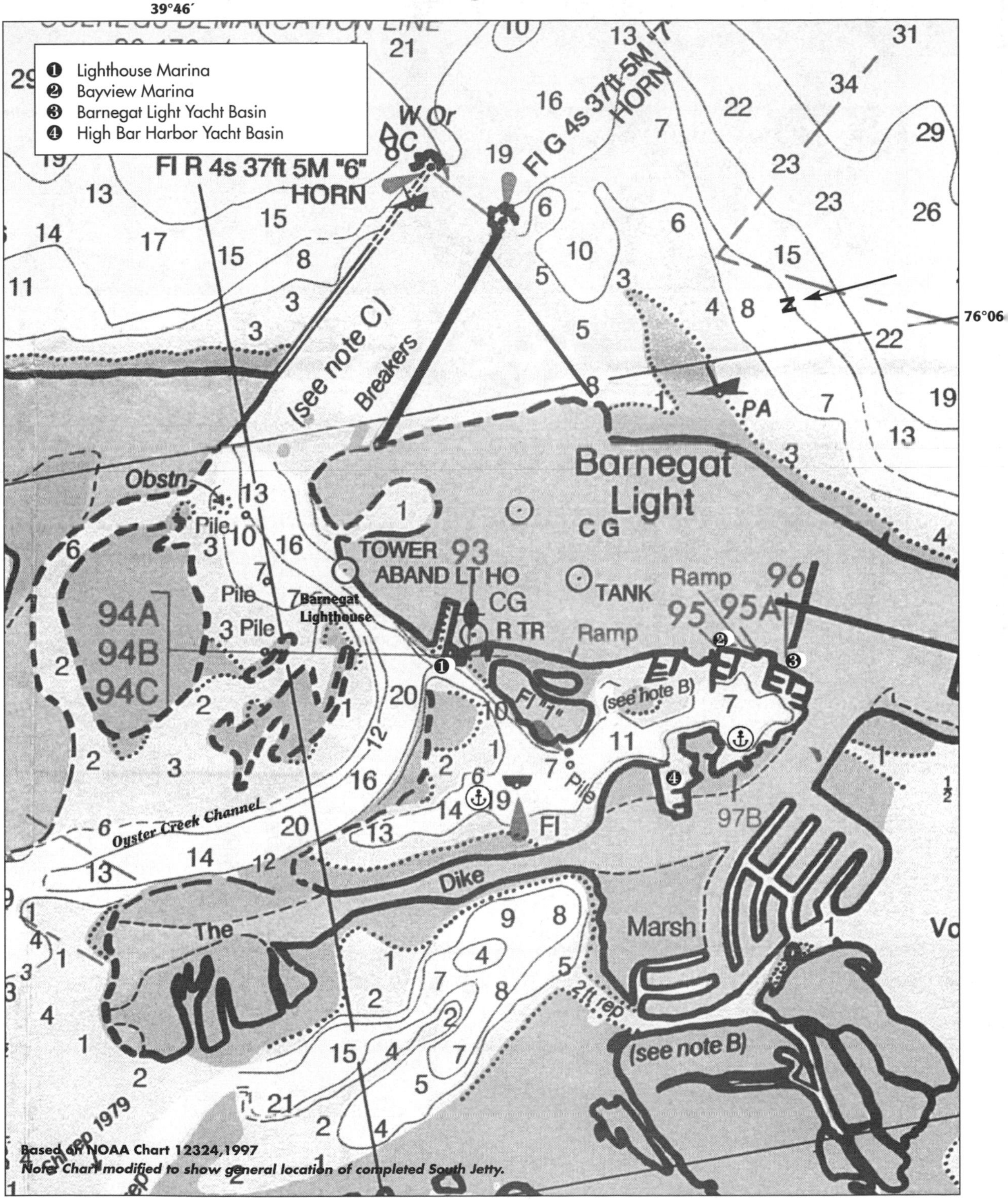

39°46′

❶	Lighthouse Marina
❷	Bayview Marina
❸	Barnegat Light Yacht Basin
❹	High Bar Harbor Yacht Basin

Fl R 4s 37ft 5M "6"
HORN

Fl G 4s 37ft 5M "7"
HORN

W Or
C

(see note C)

Breakers

Obstn

Pile

Pile

Pile

3 Pile

94A
94B
94C

Barnegat
Lighthouse

TOWER 93
ABAND LT HO
CG
R TR

Barnegat
Light
CG

TANK

Ramp

Ramp

95 95A

96

Fl "1"

(see note B)

Oyster Creek Channel

Fl

Pile

97B

Dike

The

Marsh

(see note B)

Va

76°06′

PA

Based on NOAA Chart 12324, 1997
Note: Chart modified to show general location of completed South Jetty.

SCALE **3.35″** = 1 NAUT. MILES   ⚓ **Good anchoring**   ⚓ **Marina**   🚤 **Launching site**

Aerial view of Barnegat Inlet, looking southwest.

Tom McGuire

on both sides that shift whenever there is a violent storm, and shoals often can be found inside the jetties, particularly on the south side. So far, they have not hindered navigation. The outer section of the north jetty is often partially submerged, and particular attention should be paid to the state of the sea when approaching the inlet, as is true of any ocean inlet. Under no circumstances should you attempt to pass between the north jetty light and the mainland. The rocks there are very unfriendly.

At this writing the approach channel is straight in from the outer seaward buoy, making the entrance quite easy. I am told that the authorities intend to keep it that way. Even so, the prudent mariner making a first-time approach will contact the Barnegat Light Coast Guard station to verify the status of the channel.

After you enter between the jetties and Barnegat Lighthouse is abeam, swing hard to port and keep close to the shore to port as you head past the Coast Guard station. Beware of the split in the channel just off the station. The

Oyster Creek Channel that leads into Barnegat Bay requires a sharp turn to starboard at an RG junction buoy as it heads between a set of shoals toward the bay. The channel to the marinas and anchorages at Barnegat Light leads straight ahead, close to the eastern shore here. Make note of the location of the channel in this vicinity as you enter. If you miss it on the way out, you will find yourself hard aground on the huge sandbar directly to the west of the Coast Guard station.

Beware of powerboat traffic in this area, especially some very large sightseeing and fishing headboats, which tend to roar in and out once they are outboard of the Coast Guard station by the lighthouse.

Anchorages. If you are not the type to tie up at marinas or simply want to anchor out, there is a super anchorage to the southwest of the Coast Guard station, roughly halfway between the station and the High Bar Harbor Yacht Club. Anchor there in relatively pristine conditions in 6 to 20 feet of water. (Just be sure to go *around* the bar directly west of the Coast Guard station.)

It's also possible to anchor on the west side of the basin just past the High Bar Harbor Yacht Club.

Marinas & Restaurants. At least four marinas in Barnegat Light accept transients; Lighthouse Marina, Ed's Boat Rentals (up to 30 feet), High Bar Harbor Yacht Club, and Barnegat Light Yacht Basin. All four are in the vicinity of the town of Barnegat Light, and except for High Bar Harbor Yacht Club, they apparently cater primarily to powerboats.

The Lighthouse Marina (609-494-2305) is the first one you will encounter on your way in. As you would expect from the name, it is quite close to Barnegat Lighthouse. It offers transient slips, if available, and the most convenient place in the area to obtain diesel fuel or gasoline.

Ed's Boat Rentals, immediately past the Lighthouse Marina, caters mostly to smaller powerboats and also offers a place to tie up a dinghy and go ashore in Barnegat Light. Gasoline is also available.

In the early 1990s an attractive, new, 175-slip marina, the High Bar Harbor Yacht Club (609-494-8801) was built just inside the inlet to the southwest, about ¼ mile past the Coast Guard station. Although set up for condominium slips, it welcomes transients. It also appears to be the only marina in the area where you will find sailboats tied up. A unique floating breakwater almost totally prevents any waves from reaching the floating docks of the marina, including wakes created by passing traffic. There are full, private bath facilities, a laundry center, a pool, and even an exercise room. No fuel is available here. The marina is only a short dinghy trip across a small body of water from the town of Barnegat Light.

At the head of navigation is Barnegat Light Yacht Basin (609-494-2369), offering some transient slips and diesel fuel. This is also the home of a considerable number of charter boats and a couple of large fishing "head" boats (i.e., per-head fee).

There are several restaurants in town. At least one of these, Kubel's, will provide transportation to those wishing to dine there. We have had a car from Kubel's pick us up at the High Bar Harbor Yacht Club many times, and the staff have gone out of their way to make it a pleasant experience. Unfortunately, I cannot speak for any of the many other restaurants from personal experience.

What to See & Do. Recreational facilities include oceanside bathing beaches and a tennis court and a basketball court on West 10th Street. There is now a beach tram to the three northernmost beach accesses.

Of course, Barnegat Lighthouse is a major attraction. Visitors can climb to the top of the lighthouse to get a bird's-eye view of the area. A link fence has been installed around the top to keep birds from crashing into the glass of the lighthouse. The area southeast of the lighthouse is fenced off for endangered shore-nesting birds every spring and summer. The Barnegat Light Historical Society Museum, located between 5th and 6th Streets on Central Avenue, houses the original lighthouse lens. Behind the museum are the beautiful Edith Duff Gwinn Gardens.

From the lighthouse you can walk a long way out on the southern breakwater at the inlet. This walk seems to give you a better perspective of the passage you made through that inlet. While actually negotiating the inlet you are usually too busy to pay much attention to your surroundings. This provides you an excellent view of the inlet and the ¾-mile-long beach south of the jetty, as well as bird-watching opportunities.

The Barnegat Light Coast Guard station is located at the bay end of 6th Street.

At 18th Street are numerous charter boats available for sightseeing and fishing, as well as the Viking Village shops.

Beach Haven Inlet

   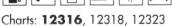

Charts: **12316**, 12318, 12323

Seventeen miles south of Barnegat Inlet is the entrance to Beach Haven Inlet. As in the case of most of the inlets along the New Jersey coast, the buoys are not charted and are frequently relocated to mark the best water in the entrance. The inlet is usually adequately marked, but some of the buoys may be submerged due to a combination of adverse current and wind conditions. The worst sea conditions result from prolonged southeast winds.

Entering this inlet requires checking with locals about current conditions due to the shifting shoals. Beach Haven Inlet can be used under favorable conditions, as indicated by the traffic it enjoys from knowledgeable local skippers. However, even under favorable conditions, the transient skipper without a local guide or current knowledge of the entrance is well advised to bypass this inlet in favor of Little Egg Inlet about a mile farther south.

Little Egg Inlet

Charts: **12316**, 12318, 12323

Just south of Beach Haven Inlet is Little Egg Inlet. Considerable care should be taken to identify which of these inlets you are approaching. If you mistakenly enter Beach Haven Inlet thinking you are in Little Egg Inlet, you are in serious trouble.

Although we do not recommend Little Egg Inlet for transients, either, if you insist on using an inlet in this area, Little Egg Inlet is the far better choice.

If there is any significant sea, breakers will appear all across the bar at the entrance to Little Egg Inlet, making the approach both hazardous and difficult to recognize. Even worse, they will often be on your beam. In other than calm and benign conditions, you should avoid this inlet completely.

In spite of this, those with local knowledge consider Little Egg Inlet relatively safe. This is another inlet where you must be extremely alert to buoy locations. The inlet channels and shoreline are constantly changing, and the positions of the buoys frequently shift, so none of them are charted.

Approach. Start your approach from the Little Egg Inlet outer lighted buoy Mo(A) (N39° 27.8′ W74° 16.6′). The first of the channel buoys should be less than a half-mile to the northwest of this buoy. On your approach to

this inlet, another surprise awaits you. Although the inlet is well buoyed, the buoys are center-channel buoys, not the lateral aids you will find elsewhere. These are vertical red and white striped buoys containing sequential letters (not numbers) that start with "A" at the seaward end of the channel. The entrance channel is about two-miles long and is quite likely to contain several dogleg turns that might easily be overlooked.

Once through the entrance channel, you will connect with the New Jersey ICW at lighted marker "120." Turn north (to starboard) to follow the New Jersey ICW inside the barrier island to Sea Isle City.

If you turn south on the ICW after clearing the inlet, you will find yourself in a narrow, restricted channel with no anchorage room and no facilities within a reasonable distance.

Marinas & Anchorages. On clearing the inlet channel, turn north (to starboard) and follow the New Jersey ICW for about 2 miles. The first marina you will reach is Pirates Cove Marina, which offers no facilities for transients. The second marina you will come to is Penna's Marina, which welcomes transients. If you have a shoal draft and a LOA less than 47 feet, you can probably find a slip there for the night. Penna's also offers diesel and gasoline. From there on, you are on your own. While there are well over a dozen more marinas in the Beach Haven area, they all cater to powerboats with a 36-foot LOA or smaller, mostly much smaller.

If you pass farther up this part of the ICW and enter Little Egg Harbor, you may be able to anchor, but there will be little protection from either wind or wave.

Brigantine Inlet

Charts: **12316**, 12318

Located 2.6 miles south-southwest of Little Egg Inlet, this inlet is not buoyed and has a tendency to shoal almost completely. Although there is a significant amount of local small-powerboat traffic, the transient should avoid this inlet completely in favor of Absecon Inlet, six miles farther south. Be sure to hold well offshore while passing this area. Brigantine Shoal extends well offshore and can offer a rough passage if there are any waves making up.

Absecon Inlet (Atlantic City)

Charts: **12316**, 12318

Since Donald Trump initiated the construction of a large number of casinos, few individuals don't know something about Atlantic City even if they have no personal knowledge of the famous boardwalk and its associated attractions. But Atlantic City has been a resort and boating destination long before casinos proliferated, although it had been getting a little tattered.

Approach. Absecon Inlet is easy to find. You need only to locate the high-rise buildings all along the beach and head just to the north of them. A large, green-sided building makes a good landmark for locating the mouth of the inlet. Absecon Lighthouse is near this green-sided building, but you will find it hard to see among the high-rise buildings.

The inlet is well buoyed with relatively deep water, and because it is widely used by both commercial and recreational vessels, it receives frequent maintenance. The entrance is well protected by jetties and should present no problems to the prudent skipper. As with all inlets on the coast, be aware of the current and wave conditions before entering or exiting. An outgoing current against even moderate waves can produce some rather nasty conditions. There have been reports of currents in excess of 2.5 knots in the inlet.

You may often find a pod of dolphins cavorting in the outer reaches of this inlet. They seem to think that they have been appointed a welcoming committee, and they sometimes come quite close to passing boats.

One mile northwest of the south jetty light is Clam Creek, on the south side of the inlet. On the south side of this creek are Gardner Basin, Snug Harbor, and Delta Basin, and the excellent Senator Farley State Marina is on its north side.

The Brigantine Boulevard Bridge, 1½ miles above the entrance to Absecon Inlet, is a fixed span with a vertical clearance of 60 feet. It is quite possible to proceed a considerable way beyond the bridge. However, with all the attractions near the mouth of the inlet, not many will bother.

Anchorages. The anchorage of choice is on the south side of the inlet, between the entrance to Clam Creek and the highway bridge. There is a strong reversing current here and, especially on weekends, a great deal of powerboat traffic, which keeps the anchorage rather lumpy.

You can proceed past the bridge and find a more secluded anchorage among the marshes if you like. Almost exactly a mile past the bridge, Absecon Channel branches off to port. It dead-ends in a marsh 1.8 miles down the channel, which means that you can probably find an anchorage all to yourself with only occasional small powerboats going by. If you do so, remember that you are in the middle of a marsh; the New Jersey mosquitoes in this area are reputed to carry off cattle!

Marinas & Restaurants. Immediately inside the inlet are two private marinas and the state-owned Senator Frank S. Farley Marina. Both the Senator Farley Marina and Kammerman's Atlantic City Marina can easily be reached by turning south into Clam Creek a short distance past the jetties. The third, Harrah's Atlantic City Marina, is located just west of the Brigantine Boulevard Bridge.

The Senator Farley Marina (609-441-8482) is by far the largest. Although owned by the state of New Jersey, it is managed by Trump Marina & Associates. (Trump Marina is the large casino across the street from the marina.) It holds 166 slips for transients and provides just about all the amenities that you might need, including a marine store, gasoline, diesel, a pumpout station, and a self-service laundry. Contact the dockmaster on VHF-FM channel 65. The marina does not appear to monitor channel 16 or 9, although that may change. There is a restaurant on the premises with patio dining, including entertainment, and the Trump Marina Casino across the street contains several restaurants.

Kammerman's Marina (609-348-8418) is on the east side of Clam Creek, opposite the state marina. It offers slips for transients up to 75 feet LOA, a marine store, gasoline and diesel fuel, and free land transportation to anywhere in Atlantic City. It monitors VHF-FM channel 16 and will direct you to a working channel after you make contact.

Harrah's Atlantic City Marina (609-441-

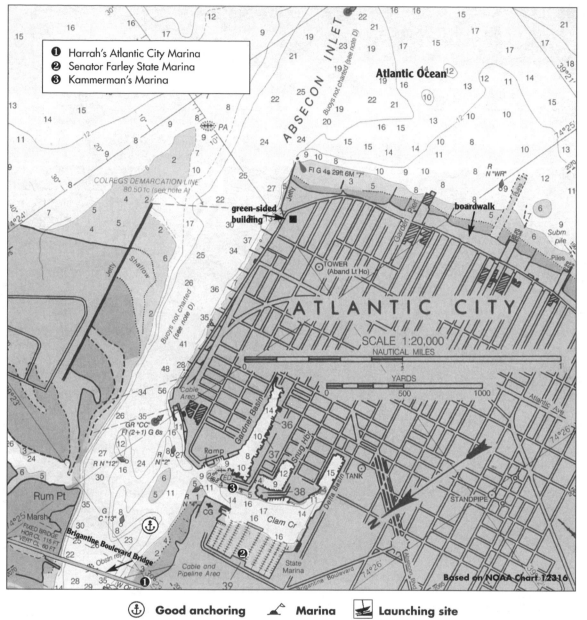

Region 9

❶ Harrah's Atlantic City Marina
❷ Senator Farley State Marina
❸ Kammerman's Marina

⚓ **Good anchoring**   ⚓ **Marina**   ⛵ **Launching site**

5315) is easy to find. Just look for the huge neon sign on Harrah's Casino and turn to port to enter the marina immediately after passing the Brigantine Boulevard Bridge. Harrah's monitors channels 16 and 9 and will direct you to a working channel after you make contact. No fuel is available here, but water, showers, and laundry are included in the price of the slip. You can even order a meal to be delivered di-

rectly to your boat. The only problem is that the slips are subject to the tidal current, which can make maneuvering into a slip an "interesting" experience if your timing is off and you don't arrive at or near slack water. Harrah's Casino has several restaurants.

What to See & Do. Jitney buses are available from the marinas to any of the twelve casinos, as well as to the 4-mile-long board-

Aerial view of Atlantic City, looking southwest. Absecon Inlet is in the foreground.

Tom McGuire

walk. As of 1999 the charge was $1.50 a person. By all means take the jitney if you are heading for the boardwalk area. It eliminates a 2-mile walk through areas that are generally considered unsafe.

Constructed in 1870 and the first of its kind in the world, the 4-mile-long Atlantic City boardwalk is crammed with small shops, food vendors, and assorted amusements. Immediately in front of the Taj Mahal Casino is the Steel Pier, devoted to rides and other forms of carnival amusements. Ocean One Pier, just north of the Convention Center at the end of Arkansas Avenue, is actually a mall, complete with restaurants and stores.

The biggest attractions in Atlantic City today are the huge casinos, along the boardwalk and near the marinas. In addition to offering gambling, these casinos are almost cities in themselves, with hotel facilities, shops, numer-

ous restaurants, and big-name shows. They are open around the clock, and you could well spend 24 hours in them, totally losing track of time.

Great Egg Inlet (Ocean City)

Charts: **12316**, 12318

Six and a half miles to the south of Absecon Inlet is Great Egg Inlet. There is some debate about the advisability of using this inlet. It depends entirely on the state of the current and especially the sea conditions. If there is any sea making up, you would be wise not to attempt the entrance. Even under benign conditions, I do not recommend transiting the inlet during any ebb current, and I definitely don't recommend it when the current is near its peak. A bar about midway across that the inlet creates some nasty conditions even when there is only a very small sea swell.

Once in the late 1990s I failed to follow my own advice and exited the inlet while the ebb current was still flowing. Although the sea swell offshore was less than 1 foot, we twice took solid green water over the bow before we could cross the bar. The water somehow managed to find its way through our forward ventilator and turned the forward V-berth into a small pond! I guess some lessons still have to be learned the hard way.

Approach. Take your departure from the Great Egg Harbor lighted buoy RW Mo(A) (N39° 16.2′ W74° 31.9′). The first channel marker should be visible about ¼ mile away on a bearing of about 345 degrees magnetic from Mo(A). Simply follow the buoys in through the inlet until you have the Ocean City to Longport drawbridge, to port, roughly abeam.

Once you have negotiated the inlet, turn to port (south) and call the bridgetender on VHF radio if you need to have the drawbridge raised. He is normally quite responsive but may not actually be in the control station at the time you arrive. Plan to keep your distance from the bridge until you see it actually begin to lift.

(Note: As of 2000, the Coast Guard "Local Notice to Mariners" states that work is in progress to replace this bridge with a fixed bridge. The main navigational channel will be relocated approximately 1,000 feet north of the existing channel and will provide a vertical clearance of 65 feet with a 150-foot navigational channel between piers. The replacement project is expected to be completed by July 2001. The northernmost portion of the old bridge will be converted to a public fishing pier; the rest will be removed. Please exercise caution while transiting this area.)

Past the bridge the area opens up and there is lots of room to maneuver. You have several choices at this point. You can hold to port and negotiate the next bridge to move farther down this portion of the New Jersey ICW (for you have now rejoined a part of it); you can head for the low fixed bridge ahead to anchor; or you can bear off to starboard toward some of

the marinas located about a mile away. However, beware of the unmarked shoals in this area, especially between the drawbridge and fixed bridge that will be visible to the south.

Anchorages. The best place to anchor in this vicinity is close to the fixed Route 52 bridge west of Ocean City. From the south end of the Ocean City to Longport drawbridge follow a course toward the center of the fixed Route 52 bridge. Watch your depth-sounder carefully so that you don't get too close to the shoals on either side as you approach the area of the bridge. Anchor anywhere here. You will find that you are not only sheltered from the wind and wave to a surprising extent but also far enough in to be away from the personal watercraft rental facility at Ocean City and out of the mainstream of the loops where the PWCs buzz around.

If you bear to the northwest and proceed through the Route 52 drawbridge at Somers Point, you will find anchorage room off the marshes in Great Egg Harbor. Continue on and pass under the fixed bridges of the Garden State Parkway and you will also have access to the Great Egg River and the Tuckahoe River. These rivers are navigable for 13 and 7 miles, respectively, wending their way through the fairly unspoiled pine barrens.

Marinas & Restaurants. Ocean City has several marinas, but finding one that welcomes transients is a little harder than you might expect. The majority of the marinas have been converted into residential or condominium marinas and no longer offer public facilities. Your best bet for transient facilities is the Harbor House Hotel & Marina (609-399-8585), located roughly halfway between the Ocean City to Longport Bridge and the next bridge to the south on the ICW. In addition to transient slips, it has gasoline, diesel, a swimming pool, and a restaurant.

Many more marine facilities are located on the mainland at Somers Point. Bear to the northwest and follow the marked channel about 2 miles to Somers Point. Do not take the waterway to the north *immediately* past the bridge. That's the ICW northbound. At Somers Point you will find a number of small-craft facilities with fuel, shops, restaurants, and repair facilities.

What to See & Do. The 2-mile-long boardwalk at Ocean City is lined with shops, restaurants, movie theaters, "adventure" golf

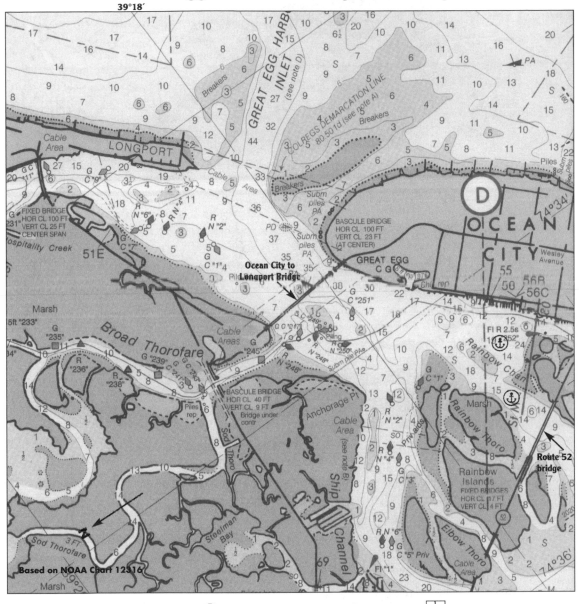

SCALE **1.80"** = **1** NAUT. MILES   ⚓ **Good anchoring**   ⚓ **Marina**   🛥 **Launching site**

courses, amusement rides, and a sizable water-park. The Ocean City Pops is booked at the Music Pier all summer long.

The Ocean City Historical Museum is filled with exhibits that enable the visitor to experience more or less firsthand the evolution of this seaside resort.

Near the museum is the Ocean City Arts Center, featuring sculptures, paintings, drawings, and photography by local artists.

Incidentally, Ocean City is still a dry town: no alcoholic beverages are sold, and public consumption of alcohol is prohibited.

Corson Inlet

This inlet is another of those that should be scrupulously avoided by the transient and possibly even by local skippers except under the most benign conditions. Pass it by in favor of

Great Egg Inlet to the north or Cape May Inlet or Townsends Inlet to the south.

Townsends Inlet

Charts: 12316, 12318

Townsends Inlet was once an inlet to be avoided except for those with the critical local knowledge, but fairly recently the borough of Avalon has attempted to convert it into one of the better inlets along the New Jersey coastline. The inlet has been dredged to a depth of 22 feet for a width of 300 feet along a 1,000-foot channel. As part of a five-year plan the channel was maintained in 1993, and the intent is to keep it in its present condition or better. In fact, the primary entrance caution is to remain clear of the rock jetty when entering from seaward. Study your chart carefully before starting your approach.

Approach. The drawbridge just inside the entrance is manned 24 hours a day and should present little difficulty if you contact the tender by radio a reasonable period of time prior to your approach. Beware of currents and possibly some eddies in the vicinity of the bridge.

The hard part is to find the start of the inlet entrance from seaward. Take your departure from RW lighted buoy Mo(A) (N39° 06.01′ W74° 41.38′). From Mo(A) a course of approximately 310 degrees magnetic for about ½ mile will take you to the first of the actual channel buoys. These are lettered, not numbered, and they start with RW "B." Follow them carefully. The approach will take you uncomfortably close to the beach, and you will have to follow that course nearly all the way to the highway drawbridge. You will see breakers to your right and left all the way in, which certainly makes for a tense time of it.

The drawbridge, attended 24 hours a day, has only a 23-foot vertical clearance when closed. Be sure to call the bridgetender in plenty of time for the bridge to open. There is little room to turn around or hold position to await a delayed opening. As with any of the coastal inlets, beware of the current, especially in the vicinity of the bridge.

Once past the drawbridge, you will find yourself in another segment of the New Jersey ICW.

Anchorages. If you turn north on the New Jersey ICW and proceed for 1 mile, Townsends Channel will branch off to the west. There you will find plenty of room to anchor in relative seclusion, save for assorted small private fishing boats and perhaps a few runabouts.

If you turn south on the ICW, bear to the west and anchor in the mouth of South Channel. In either cases you will be surrounded by marsh, so be prepared to fend off the flying vampires as night falls and perhaps even during the day.

Marinas & Restaurants. Immediately to the north of the bridge on the ICW is the small Pier 88 Marina, which welcomes transients and offers diesel and gasoline. There is a restaurant nearby.

About 3 miles north on the ICW is the Minmar Marine Basin, which also welcomes transients measuring up to 50 feet LOA. No fuel is available at Minmar. Larsen's Marina, next door to Minmar, offers gasoline and diesel but no transient slips. Both are located in Sea Isle City, only a short distance from the ocean beach and an assortment of restaurants and other stores.

About ½ mile south of the bridge on the ICW is Avalon Pointe Marina, which offers slips for transients up to 70 feet LOA but no fuel.

Hereford Inlet

Charts: 12316, 12318

Local knowledge is an absolute necessity for those using Hereford Inlet. This inlet is one of the most "restless" on the coastline in terms of the location of the usable channel. Even local skippers are advised not to attempt entry with a following sea of any magnitude. Pass it by.

Cape May Harbor

Charts: 12214, 12304, 12316, 12317, 12318

This is perhaps the best inlet on the New Jersey coast. Cape May Harbor serves as an excellent stopover point for the cruiser awaiting appropriate weather for the offshore run north or south or for a favorable tide and current state before jumping off on the inside leg up the

Delaware Bay to the Chesapeake & Delaware Canal and beyond. The harbor may be entered or exited either through the inlet on the Atlantic side or, if your vessel requires less than a 55-foot vertical clearance, through the Cape May Canal from Delaware Bay. For those rare few whose timing is superb, it can even serve as a shortcut, saving several miles over the trip around the end of Cape May to head up Delaware Bay.

The mean range of tide is 4.4 feet in Cape May Harbor, and the current velocity in Cape May Inlet can exceed 2 knots.

Cape May Inlet Approach. Like most ocean inlets, Cape May Inlet may be impossible to enter under certain conditions, notably when there is heavy surf, especially with an opposing current and wave situation. In fact, in really rough conditions some boats heading for Cape May Harbor may be forced to bypass the inlet, circle around the end of Cape May, and enter the harbor through the Cape May Canal from the Delaware side.

This deepwater inlet is kept viable by frequent dredging. There is at least 20 feet of water on the approach to the entrance between the lighted jetties at the mouth of the inlet, although the preferred approach is to round the flashing 4-second bell buoy, red "2CM" (N38° 55.8′ W74° 52.3′), about ½ mile southeast of the jetties. From red "2CM" it is a straight shot into and through the inlet. Be aware that there is usually a fair amount of traffic coming and going here, and note that the jetty lights are to seaward of the end of the submerged ends of the jetties. A lighted range marks the channel between the jetties.

Immediately after you clear the inlet a section of the New Jersey ICW extends to starboard, easily identified by the U.S. Route 9 drawbridge. The buoyed channel leading to Cape May Harbor is to port.

Cape May Canal Approach. From the southern end of Cape May Harbor, the Cape May Canal runs west for about 4 miles to Delaware Bay. Traffic entering the canal from Cape May Harbor is supposed to be controlled by red and green lights. However, most people claim to pass through the canal without ever seeing these lights.

The tidal current through the canal can be substantial, frequently exceeding a normal peak

of about 2.5 knots. However, since you normally would time your passage out through the canal for shortly prior to the flood current in the mouth of Delaware Bay, you will rarely encounter much of this current. The same is typically true for arrivals at the canal, although this is more problematic.

The speed limit in the canal is 6 knots (posted as 6½ statue miles per hour). This can sometimes be a nuisance to powerboats trying to clear the canal before the start of the flood tide in Delaware Bay, but you had better heed it.

The range of tide is typically 4 feet with a controlling depth in the canal of at least 6 feet MLW. Sailboats with a draft approaching 6 feet should contact the Corps of Engineers for the latest controlling depth in the canal. The Coast Guard station at Cape May Harbor also should have that information.

Additional potential problems (at least for larger sailboats) are two fixed highway bridges with vertical clearances of 55 feet MHW and a swing railroad bridge that has a mere 4-foot vertical clearance when closed. No one of our acquaintance has ever seen the railroad bridge in its closed position. The Coast Guard "Local Notice to Mariners" has repeatedly stated that the bridge is in operation, but the hours when it is closed appear to be relatively few. In any event, it presents no real problem.

Just inside the mouth of the canal at Delaware Bay is the northern terminus of the Cape May–Lewes Ferry. If you see the ferry coming or notice significant activity aboard the ferry as it prepares to depart its dock, give it plenty of room.

The canal exits through two lighted jetties into Delaware Bay. From there a course of 322 degrees magnetic will take you to Miah Maull Shoal Light, shorter than the route around Brandywine Shoal Light. However, when approaching the canal from the Delaware, beware of the start of the flood current, which will set you a surprising distance to the north if you are not careful.

Anchorages. The 1½-mile-long Cape May Harbor is oriented on a north–south axis and has a width of approximately ¼ mile. In spite of its size, anchorage space is scarce, mainly because of shoaling outside of the channel. There are plenty of marinas around the harbor with all

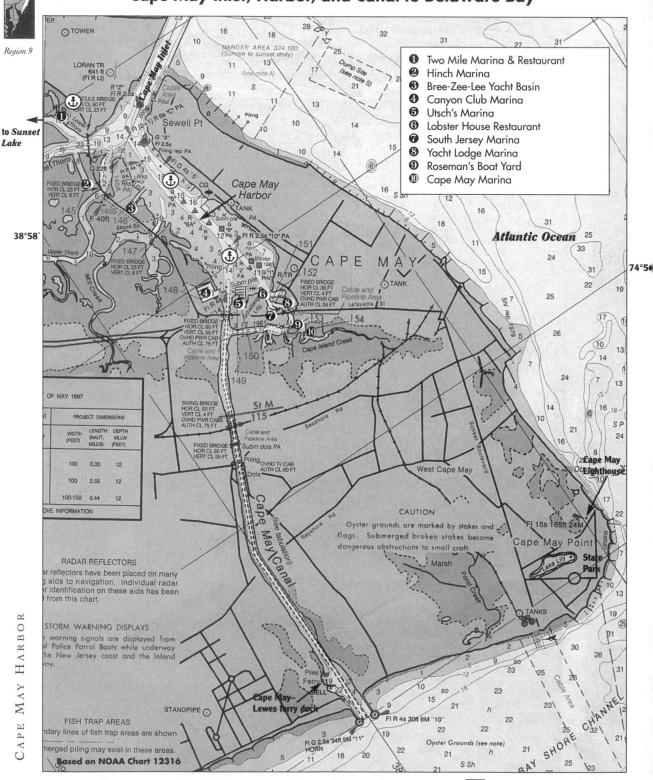

Cape May Inlet, Harbor, and Canal to Delaware Bay

❶ Two Mile Marina & Restaurant
❷ Hinch Marina
❸ Bree-Zee-Lee Yacht Basin
❹ Canyon Club Marina
❺ Utsch's Marina
❻ Lobster House Restaurant
❼ South Jersey Marina
❽ Yacht Lodge Marina
❾ Roseman's Boat Yard
❿ Cape May Marina

to *Sunset Lake*

38°58′

74°5

Atlantic Ocean

CAPE MAY HARBOR

RADAR REFLECTORS
ar reflectors have been placed on many
g aids to navigation. Individual radar
r identification on these aids has been
from this chart.

STORM WARNING DISPLAYS
n warning signals are displayed from
of Police Patrol Boats while underway
he New Jersey coast and the Inland
vay.

FISH TRAP AREAS
ndary lines of fish trap areas are shown

merged piling may exist in these areas.
Based on NOAA Chart 12316

OF MAY 1997

PROJECT DIMENSIONS		
WIDTH (FEET)	LENGTH (NAUT. MILES)	DEPTH MLLW (FEET)
100	0.35	12
100	2.55	12
100-150	0.44	12

OVE INFORMATION

CAUTION
Oyster grounds are marked by stakes and
flags. Submerged broken stakes become
dangerous obstructions to small craft.

Cape May—
Lewes ferry dock

Cape May Lighthouse

Cape May Point
State Park

SCALE **1.49″** = 1 NAUT. MILES   ⚓ **Good anchoring**   ⚓ **Marina**   **Launching site**

of the facilities you are likely to need or want. There is at least 7 feet of water throughout the channel down the middle of the harbor, opening out somewhat at the southern end.

The southeast corner of Cape May Harbor is the primary mecca for transient cruising boats. Once you are a few hundred yards south of the "Tank" shown on the chart beyond the Coast Guard station on the east side of the harbor, simply pull out of the channel and find a spot to drop the hook. This may not be easy as you will have plenty of company much of the time. Beware of old pilings in the water toward the vicinity of the tank.

As stated, anchorage space in Cape May Harbor itself is fairly scarce. If you would rather anchor out than take a slip at one of the marinas and aren't interested in the facilities or hustle of the town, try heading up the New Jersey ICW to Sunset Lake. This is a nice little basin located a little less than 3 miles north of the Route 9 drawbridge near Cape May Inlet. (You will have to negotiate the Route 9 drawbridge just north of the inlet.) Here you will find a good-sized, well-protected anchorage with water depths of between 7 and 29 feet. Unfortunately, a PWC-rental facility located on

Sunset Lake means that PWCs will be buzzing around and around the lake from before 10:00 A.M. until at least 5:00 P.M. during the summertime. Another possibility for one or two boats is in the Lower Thorofare, to the east immediately after passing north through the Route 9 drawbridge.

Marinas & Restaurants. All of the marinas in the vicinity of the entrance to the Cape May Canal are within easy walking distance of several restaurants.

The Canyon Club Marina (609-884-0199) is located on the north side of the entrance to the Cape May Canal from the harbor. Transients are welcome, and gasoline and diesel fuel are available. This is a large facility with a deep, easy entrance; its markers become obvious as you approach the east side of the first bridge over the canal.

Utsch's Marina (609-884-2051) is located on the south side of the entrance to the Cape May Canal. At low tide it is necessary to follow the channel into the main harbor from the canal and swing to starboard, as if heading into Schellenger Creek. Pass about 50 yards south of the red "2" daymark, then swing to port and head directly for the entrance to the marina. You'll

Entrance to the Cape May Canal from Delaware Bay.

CAPE MAY HARBOR

find at least 5 feet of water all the way in. At high tide you can head directly in from virtually any direction. Utsch's welcomes transients and offers gasoline and diesel fuel, as well as other amenities such as showers and a marine store.

The Yacht Lodge Marina (609-884-5224) and the South Jersey Marina (609-884-2400) are located in Schellenger Creek, to the south of Cape May Harbor. Both offer slips for transients, showers, a marine store, and gasoline and diesel fuel. The Yacht Lodge Marina also has a self-service laundry. Unless you are using a large-scale chart of the harbor, you may not find Schellenger Creek marked on your chart. It's the little creek that runs directly from the extreme south end of the harbor east through a bridge to rejoin the Cape May Canal.

In addition to the marinas on this creek, the Lobster House Restaurant (609-884-8296) is located on the old fish dock at the creek entrance. Temporary dockage is available to restaurant patrons, although space tends to be at a premium in peak season. There can be a substantial current through Schellenger Creek. Be careful when you try to come alongside or enter a slip.

Two Mile Marina & Restaurant (609-522-1341) is located in Lower Thorofare, extending east of the New Jersey ICW, just north of the drawbridge adjacent to the entrance to the harbor from Cape May Inlet. The only drawback to this location is that the ebb or flood current can make tying up at the piers an "interesting" exercise at times other than slack water. The excellent restaurant is well worth a visit. You can tie up at the pier at no charge if dining there.

What to See & Do. Cape May has been designated a National Historic Landmark because of its fantastic collection of Victorian architecture, having changed little since the end of the 19th century. A walk down Washington Street, with stately Victorian homes on both sides, will bring you to the 3-block-long Washington Street Mall. This outdoor pedestrian mall was established by closing this segment of Washington Street to traffic.

From the mall it is only a short walk to the ocean beach.

Although a bit far to walk, a trip to Cape May Point State Park is well worth the effort. It's about 5 miles from the harbor down Sunset Boulevard and to the end of Lighthouse Road. The park is the location of the Cape May Lighthouse, which is open to the public. The view from the top is nothing short of spectacular. The Atlantic Ocean is to one side, Delaware Bay to the other, and Cape Henlopen is 17 miles due south. On a clear day you can see the opposite shore.

The park has 3 miles of nature trails and boardwalks. Guided tours are available, and information for self-guided tours is available at the park office. Just offshore is a concrete World War II artillery bunker, built in 1942 to protect the mouth of Delaware Bay, together with its twin on Cape Henlopen. When constructed, it was on a sand dune almost ¼ mile inland from the ocean. With the moving shoreline, it is located farther offshore each year.

If you walk along the beach, keep an eye peeled for small, quartz, semiprecious stones called Cape May diamonds. If you can't or don't want to find any on your own, many of the stores sell them in various forms, mostly cut, polished, and set in jewelry.

The Cape May Historical Museum is located at the Cape May Courthouse on Route 9.

If you have access to transportation, there is a 128-acre zoo in the Cape May County Park, about 10 miles north of the town of Cape May.

Region 10
DELAWARE BAY & RIVER

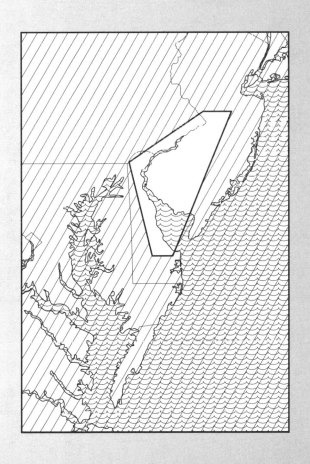

Delaware Bay & River

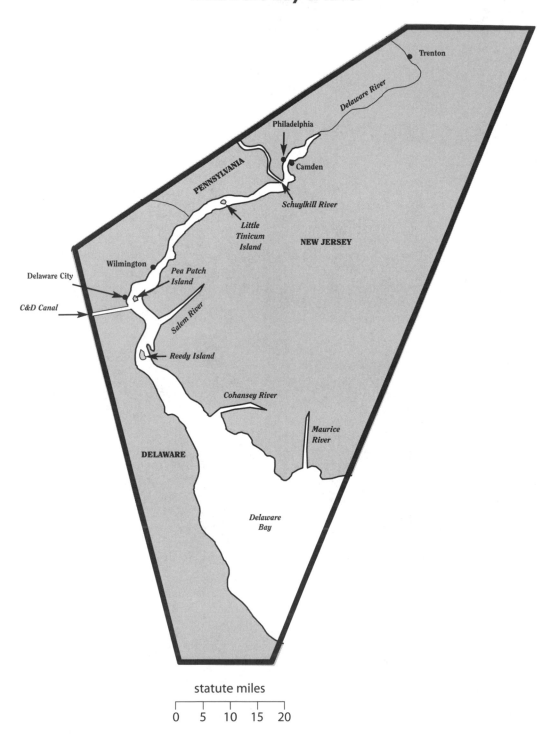

statute miles

0   5   10   15   20

EW PEOPLE CRUISE THE Delaware Bay for pleasure. It is normally something to endure in order to reach the Chesapeake Bay or, conversely, Cape May in preparation for the Atlantic passage north. A rare few may head up the Delaware River to Philadelphia or beyond.

However, this passage of less than 50 miles between Cape May and the Chesapeake and Delaware (C&D) Canal is a vital link in the much-to-be-enjoyed inside route of the ICW, through the cruising grounds of the Chesapeake Bay, to the southern links with the routes south to escape the winter (or the path north for the summer).

The mean range of tide in Delaware Bay is 5 to 5½ feet. The resulting currents, together with the shallowness of the bay and the flow of the Delaware River, can combine to make some fairly uncomfortable conditions on the bay, especially when the current and winds oppose each other and you are headed into a strong wind. Currents can range from a low peak of about ⅓ knots to well over 2 knots at times, and crosscurrents and eddies can combine to throw the unwary well off course.

On the other hand, if your timing is good, you can take advantage of the current to give you a boost either up or down the Delaware Bay. If your vessel can make 6 knots or more, you can ride the current most, if not all, of the way from Cape May to the C&D Canal or vice versa. Slower vessels should start before the beginning of the flood when departing Cape May and before the beginning of the ebb when departing from the C&D Canal to maximize the boost and minimize the adverse current, especially in the upper reaches.

It is preferable, but by no means essential, to transit Delaware Bay during daylight. You can save considerable distance by heading directly between the Cape May Canal and the Miah Maull Shoal Light, a course of 322 degrees from the canal. This is a distance of about 17 miles, during which you will pass no intermediate markers or reference points until you intersect the shipping channel. The red, occluding, 4-second light of the 59-foot-high Miah Maull Shoal Light serves as a good target as soon as you are able to locate it. Once you find the shipping channel, navigation the rest of the way to the C&D Canal is easy; simply run the outside edge of the channel from buoy to buoy. There is plenty of room to parallel the channel outside of the buoys. This neatly keeps you on course and well away from any shoals or ledges, with one possible exception: if you are running at night, beware of Cross Ledge Shoal to the east of your course, especially the ruins of the abandoned lighthouse at the south end of Cross Ledge.

The presence of large ships heading up or down the channel is a far greater danger than any possibility of grounding. Stay out of the shipping channel itself as a matter of course, especially if a ship is anywhere in sight. Even if a ship does see you on its radar (not necessarily a high probability), it will have little choice for any kind of course change, and it will not be able to stop should you become disabled within the channel (or simply get careless). Although there is a lot of shipping activity on the Delaware, wakes from even large ships are seldom a problem because they tend to keep their speed down on this passage.

On occasion there is fog, especially in the fall and in the area of Brandywine Shoal and below. Normally it burns off by noon, but it frequently lasts for a day or more. If you do travel in fog on Delaware Bay, do so only with the instrumentation that will permit you to keep close to your planned course and stay out of the shipping channel.

Between Cape May and the C&D Canal, harbors are few and far between. In fact, there really is only one, the Cohansey River, which bears much consideration. The one other possibility, the Maurice River, is too far out of the way, except to take shelter from a northwest blow that comes up after you are well under way toward the C&D Canal. (Frankly, we would prefer to head back to Cape May.) Both of these rivers are on the New Jersey shore. Other than Breakwater Harbor, inside Cape Henlopen, or the C&D Canal itself, there are no harbors on the Delaware shore worth mentioning for cruising boats. (See region 11, Delmarva Peninsula, for details on Breakwater Harbor.)

DELAWARE BAY

Charts: **12304**, **12311**

Maurice River

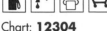

Chart: **12304**

Approach. The entrance channel to the Maurice River is located a good 7 miles off any normal route you may plan to take between the C&D Canal and Cape May. The approach takes you over Egg Island Flats in water 7 to 12 feet deep. With a strong wind from anywhere in the southwest quadrant it will be rough!

A red-roofed lighthouse near the entrance is visible from several miles away. As you get closer, look for the flashing green "3" marker paired with a red "2" nun at the entrance to the 2½-mile-long channel into the river. Take a course from green "3" to the green "5" marker, then swing to port to head for the west side of the mouth of the river. Don't be misled by the green "11" marker on the east side; a long shoal extends from East Point nearly into the river's mouth. There is reputed to be as much as 7 feet of water in the channel, but if your draft comes anywhere near that, we suggest you stay out.

Anchorages, Marinas, & Restaurants. The town of Bivalve, a little way upriver, is the most convenient stopping place. Be sure to follow the channel on the way to Bivalve; there are plenty of stakes in the river, many of them broken off and just underwater. As the name indicates, this is an oystering port, probably the busiest on the Delaware. Don't look for typical pleasure-boat facilities—there aren't any. However, you may be able to find dock space on either shore where you can tie up. Anchoring space is debatable at best. Groceries and boat supplies are available nearby, but remember that this is a working waterman's harbor, so yacht supplies are likely to be unavailable.

Port Norris, farther upstream, is reputed to have similar facilities.

Cohansey River

Charts: **12304**, 12311

About 30 miles above Cape May, or less than 20 miles below the C&D Canal and about 2 miles northeast of the shipping channel near Ship John Shoal, is the Cohansey River, perhaps the only reasonable harbor for the transient on the passage between these two end points.

Approaches. The land is all low and marshy, making it difficult to see the entrance until you are almost upon it. The easiest way to find it is to take a bearing from Ship John Shoal Light or another channel marker and follow that course, frequently checking your back bearing until you are within visual range. Err on the side of the Cohansey Light so that you will know which way to turn if you have to search for the entrance.

There are two entrances to the Cohansey: one is the unmarked passage through Cohansey Cove to the south of Cohansey Light; the other is through the dredged "canal" just to the northwest of the light. Of the two entrances the latter is a better choice; the canal is nearly 20 feet deep, and the approach is supposed to be marked by range lights. However, as of 1999, the second light, green "3," was missing. In fact, there was no sign that it had ever existed. If it is still missing, simply head for the first light, green "1," on a bearing of 42 degrees magnetic, favoring the north side of the entrance, and you will enter easily. By the way, this entrance bears no resemblance to anything you may think of as a canal, but that is what it is called locally.

Anchorages. As soon as you are inside the two points of land at the entrance, the best anchorage is in the bend just southeast of the canal with around 30 feet of water. The current reverses here and can get quite strong. Be sure to allow for it when you anchor. The shoreline is marshy and uninhabited (by people). It will be fairly quiet and peaceful as nearly all of the traffic through the canal will be from or to the upstream reaches, and even that should be light. Beware of a set of old pilings along the southwest shore here; some of them may be below the water.

Cohansey River

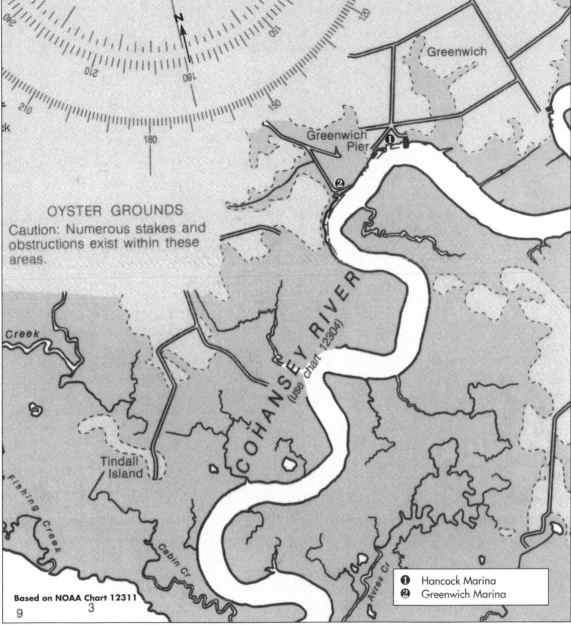

75°21'

39°23'

Greenwich

Greenwich Pier

OYSTER GROUNDS
Caution: Numerous stakes and obstructions exist within these areas.

COHANSEY RIVER
(use chart 12304)

Creek

Tindall Island

Fishing Creek

Cabin Cr

Ayres Cr

❶ Hancock Marina
❷ Greenwich Marina

Based on NOAA Chart 12311

9   3

SCALE **2.20"** = **1** NAUT. MILES   ⚓ **Good anchoring**   ⚓ **Marina**   🚤 **Launching site**

Other anchorages may be found in any of the many bights of the river as you head upstream. All are in good holding, but you will be subject to a strong reversing current. Be sure to use a Bahamian moor or an anchor, such as a plow or Bruce, which will hold or readily reset when the current changes. It's also a good idea to set your helm to one side so that you will not run over your anchor line when the current reverses or when the wind opposes the current. The latter is a lesson we learned the hard way when our anchor rode snagged on our keel and chafed through at 2:00 A.M. on a pitch-black night!

DELAWARE BAY

443

Remember, you are in a marsh, so in warm weather be prepared to deal with flies and no-see-ums by day and mosquitoes by night.

Marinas & Restaurants. There are two marinas 2 to 3 miles upriver from the canal, both on the west (or is it north?) side of the river, where you can obtain most of the marine facilities you may require.

The first one you will reach is Hancock Marina. You can lay alongside the floating dock wherever you can find room, but keep clear of the fuel-dock portion unless you are taking on fuel. Both sides of a work shed and both fuel tanks are decorated by excellent orca paintings by Dan DunLeavy, a young artist who also painted the marine scene on the convention center at Cape May. The Bait Box Restaurant is also located on the grounds of the marina.

The Greenwich Marina is about ¼ mile farther upstream, also to port. It too has a floating dock plus some slips. Unfortunately, the restaurant located there has been closed for some years, pending a new owner, which may never happen.

What to See & Do. The village of Greenwich is only about ½ mile inland from Greenwich Marina. If you have the time and any interest at all in American history, be sure to visit it. There are several colonial homes here, all identified by plaques near their doors. They are occupied, so don't expect to walk in.

The Greenwich Country Store, at the corner of Maple and Ye Greate Streets, has a delicatessen that makes great sandwiches. The Down Jersey Sub, composed of turkey, dressing, and cranberry sauce, is excellent.

Artificial Island

Chart: **12311**

Less than ⅓ mile off the northwest corner of Artificial Island in Delaware Bay, where the Salem Nuclear Power Plant is located, and approximately 4 miles south of the eastern entrance to the C&D Canal are mooring floats composed of 55-gallon steel drums floating mostly submerged. This is a commercial anchorage area for vessels servicing the nuclear power plant, but these drums definitely are a hazard for anyone transiting the vicinity. They are difficult to see in the daytime, especially

when a current is running strong. At night they are virtually invisible.

If transiting this area in conditions of poor visibility, be sure to remain close to the shipping-channel markers to avoid ruining your entire day.

Reedy Island

  No facilities

Chart: **12311**

The area between Reedy Island and the Delaware shore offers a nice stopover spot for vessels making the trek to or from Cape May and the Chesapeake Bay or the upper reaches of the Delaware River. While there is almost no protection from wind, the island and the breakwater that runs between the collection of little islands and other shoals in this vicinity provide considerable protection from wave action from the main part of the Delaware River.

Formerly the sight of a federal quarantine and detention station, Reedy Island is currently uninhabited, and no vestiges of any structures can be seen. A submerged rock dike extends 3 miles southward from Reedy Island and roughly parallels the mainland shore. The dike is marked by both lights and unlighted seasonal warning buoys. Do not attempt to cross over this dike, even at high water. At low water it usually can be seen, or it will at least be awash.

Port Penn is a village on the western shore opposite Reedy Island. The landings at the village are unusable for all practical purposes. Don't try them.

Approaches. There are two approaches to the anchorage area behind Reedy Island: the somewhat dicey, unmarked northern approach through the shoals between the upper island and the entrance to the C&D Canal, and the much more prudent, well-marked entrance through the breakwater just downstream of Reedy Island proper.

Although we have successfully negotiated the northern approach with no problems, I will not offer directions for this approach here. It's a little too tense for any but the inveterate gunkholer who doesn't mind bumping bottom or dredging new channels.

The entrance through the breakwater south

of Reedy Island is identified by a pair of red and green navigation markers mounded on either side of the entrance. There is at least 10 feet of water in the entrance at MLW. Simply pass through the center of the opening, continue for at least 50 yards beyond the entrance, and then turn either north or south to anchor in the shelter of either island.

Anchorage. There is good holding in mud, but there is a reversing current that is stronger than you might expect in this relatively sheltered area. If the wind opposes the current, you may find your boat pushed up over the anchor rode, where it may foul your prop or keel, with the attendant fuss and feathers. If you lash your helm to one side, you will lay comfortably to one side of your anchor rode in full security, neatly avoiding entangling your rode with any protruding parts of your boat.

Do not anchor in the cable area between the middle of Reedy Island and Port Penn. It is clearly marked on both the mainland and the island if you look for it.

Chesapeake & Delaware Canal
Chart: **12277**

Actually, finding the entrance to the C&D Canal is not difficult. The readily visible entrance will appear to port about 6 miles after you pass the obvious towers of the Salem Nuclear Power Plant on Artificial Island, on the Jersey shore to starboard. Simply honor the markers to port to avoid the extensive shoal on the Delaware side and you will enter the canal easily. At night, the floodlights lining the canal make it unmistakable.

For more information on the canal itself, see region 1, Chesapeake & Delaware Canal, pages 93–96.

Salem River

Chart: **12311**

Across the Delaware River from the entrance to the C&D Canal is the Salem River. Although the river itself is fairly deep and leads into some interesting marshlands, offering opportunities for exploring and gunkholing, unless you are desperate for fuel, we really don't see any good reason for cruising boats to enter this river.

Approach. Although the river itself is directly across the Delaware River from the entrance to the C&D Canal, the entrance to the river channel is 1¼ miles downstream, starting at Fl R 4s R"2" (N39° 32.6´ W75° 32.2´) off Elsinboro Point. From there the channel, although narrow, is well buoyed, and the water on either side is very shoal. Inside the river proper the water is quite deep. As you pass the southern tip of Hickory Island the river splits; the main river takes a long loop to the north, and a cut directly ahead offers the shortest course to the Route 49 drawbridge.

Anchorages & Marinas. If you take the loop to the north, not only will you be able to find room to anchor but the Penn Salem Marina will be to port. The marina offers gasoline, diesel, complete engine and hull repairs, and a dockside pumpout station, as well as transient slips.

At the end of the cut, just before the drawbridge, is Barber's Boat Basin, offering transient slips, a marine store, and gasoline.

The tidal range here is 5.6 feet. At the entrance to the river the peak current is about 1.6 knots, but it may be as high as 3 knots in the cut.

What to See & Do. This is not exactly a tourist area, so don't look for much of anything along that line. However, if you are looking for a place to do some quiet gunkholing, proceed past the drawbridge and either explore the main part of the river for several miles in your primary vessel or anchor and explore the numerous little tributaries through the marsh in your dinghy. As with any marsh, be prepared for flies by day, no-see-ums in the evening, and mosquitoes at night.

Delaware City

Chart: **12311**

About 1.6 miles upstream of the mouth of the C&D Canal is the entrance to Delaware City, Delaware. This body of water is actually the Delaware River terminus of a previous incarnation of the C&D Canal, although it no longer serves that role in any way. In addition to providing shelter for the night, Delaware City offers a convenient place for reprovisioning. A miniature old town with attractive colonial buildings, many of which have been restored, it's also a pleasant stop in its own right. Everyone we met was friendly and helpful, and the whole place was well kept and clean.

Approach. The easy-to-find entrance may be reached from Bulkhead Shoal Channel, the western channel past Pea Patch Island, in the Delaware River. The entrance is clearly indicated by the Fl G 4s green "1" marker (N39° 34.8′ W75° 35.1′). The controlling depth of 7 feet MLW provides access to most cruising boats.

Anchorage & Marina. Don't try to anchor in the small basin just inside the entrance. There isn't much room in the basin, and the town dock is suitable only for dinghies, except near high tide.

Aerial view (looking west) of the Delaware entrance to the C&D Canal, Delaware City, and Pea Patch Island.

DELAWARE RIVER

National Geodetic Survey

Aerial view of Fort Delaware on Pea Patch Island.

A little farther in is the Delaware City Marina, which usually has some room for transients along its floating dock. Be warned that there is a reversing current here. Although it isn't very strong, you do need to prepare for it when you tie up. There's lots of marsh around, so be prepared to fend off the flying vampires as sunset approaches, and be sure that you have a good set of screens on all openings to your boat.

What to See & Do. From the marina it is only a short walk into town, where you'll find a drugstore, a couple of grocery stores, a deli, a pizzeria, a restaurant, and a liquor store.

There is also a ferry dock that provides passenger service to Fort Delaware on Pea Patch Island. However, the ferry operation is restricted to weekends and holidays from the end of June to the end of September, plus Wednesday through Friday from mid-June to the beginning of September.

Pea Patch Island

  No facilities

Chart: **12311**

Pea Patch Island is the site of Fort Delaware State Park, one of Delaware's first state parks, created in 1951. A Union fortress dating from 1859, Fort Delaware once served as an infamous prison for Confederate prisoners of war.

There is no place for private vessels to tie up to visit the island. While it is possible to anchor off the New Jersey side of the island, there is virtually no protection from wind or wave, and there are many rocks near the shore. A far better way to visit the island is to take the ferry

from Delaware City. Then you can enjoy your visit without having to worry about the security of your anchored vessel or even the difficulty of landing by dinghy in the first place.

A half-mile ferry ride from Delaware City will land you at the dock about a mile from Fort Delaware. From there a jitney will take you to the fort and back.

From the end of April to the end of September the Fort is open Saturdays, Sundays, and holidays from 11:00 A.M. to 6:00 P.M. From mid-June through Labor Day it is also open Wednesday through Friday from 11:00 A.M. to 4:00 P.M. There is a charge for boat transportation in lieu of a park user fee. Tours of the fort include visits to museums containing artifacts from the island's past. Civil War living-history presentations are performed daily, and there are frequent special events and other programs here.

Pea Patch Island is also a summer home to nine different species of herons, egrets, and ibis. A hiking trail and observation tower provide opportunities for photography and nature study.

Christina River (Wilmington)

Charts: **12311**, 12312

It is unfortunate that a city as pleasant and interesting as Wilmington has effectively no facilities for pleasure craft. There used to be a couple of small marinas several miles up the Christina River, but they are now defunct and overgrown. The river is strictly commercial, although it is a bit of a study in contrasts. At the mouth of the Christina River the south shore is heavily industrial and centered on the Wilmington Marine Terminal. Directly across from the Marine Terminal, on the north shore, is a comparatively pristine area that is home to a large variety of wildfowl. As you head upstream, you will find yourself among a strange mix of modern, glass-covered office buildings and 19th-century buildings, many of which are in the process of being renovated. The river runs through the city of Wilmington and to the towns of Newport and Christiana. The controlling water depth to Newport is about 5 feet.

DELAWARE RIVER

447

Newport, nearly 7 miles above the mouth, is the head of practical navigation.

Approach. Entering the Christina River is easy. One and a half miles upstream of the Delaware Memorial Bridges you will come to the 36-foot-high flashing green "1" light at the end of a stone jetty. This marks the south side of the entrance to the Christina River. A red bell buoy, R"2," marks the end of the shoal on the north side. There are no other navigational markers, but they are not needed. There is about 12 feet of water for the next four miles, farther than you are likely to go due to the obstruction of bridges.

The first bridge, at Route 450, about a mile upstream, has a vertical clearance of 60 feet. The railroad bridge, next, is permanently open. The series of three drawbridges after that, with vertical clearances of 20, 19, and 8 feet, respectively, will effectively stop most cruising boats. All three require at least 8 hours' notice before opening. It's not worth the trouble.

What to See & Do. At present there is not much on the Christina River to entice cruisers. The city is in the process of renovating at least some of the waterfront, but it has a long way to go, and things do not seem to be proceeding

The Kalmar Nyckel *is a replica of the pinnace that brought the first colonists to the Wilmington area in 1638.*

DELAWARE RIVER

Kalmar Nyckel Foundation

rapidly. There are plans for a theater, shops, a museum, a park, and a 2½-mile river walk on the northern shore. However, there seem to be no plans to provide any real boater access.

The *Kalmar Nyckel* is a reproduction of the Swedish-owned, Dutch-built, three-masted armed pinnace that brought the first permanent European settlers to the Delaware Valley in 1638. The original *Kalmar Nyckel* departed from Göteborg, Sweden, in November 1637 with 24 settlers from four countries onboard. It landed on the banks of the Christina River. When the ship returned a year later, all the settlers were alive and well, something that simply did not happen at most of the other settlements of the time. All in all, the ship made four round trips, more than any other "settler" ship of the era. It was finally lost in the late 1600s. The replica of the *Kalmar Nyckel*, constructed at a shipyard adjacent to the original landing site, was launched on 28 September 1997 and commissioned on 9 May 1998. Today she is a fully functional sail-training vessel and has represented Delaware at festivals from Virginia to New York. The ship is berthed at her own compound on the north side of the Christina River, immediately past the junction with Brandywine Creek. There is a small floating dock near the ship's dock, where transients may tie up to visit the vessel. (For more information, call the Kalmar Nyckel Foundation, 302-429-7447)

Just below the *Kalmar Nyckel* is the main attraction to cruisers on the Christina River, the Up the Creek Restaurant, located at the junction of the Christina River and Brandywine Creek, about 1½ miles above the Wilmington Marine Terminal. It has a floating dock for transients that appears to have been designed for smaller boats. Some oddly designed mooring stanchions hinge down to secure boats. Larger cruising boats may have some problems with them. The ambiance of the restaurant is a little strange (you will have to see for yourself), but the food is good.

Riverfront Park, a bit farther upstream, is well bulkheaded, but there is no fender system, and there are no mooring bitts of any kind. There is also a kind of fence blocking the park off from the river. Access to the park is available through a gated entry well downstream by the mooring dolphins for the *Kalmar Nyckel*.

Philadelphia & Upriver
Charts: **12312**, **12313**, **12314**

Essington (Little Tinicum Island)

Chart: **12312**

About 2½ miles above the Commodore Barry Bridge, RG buoy "TS" (N39° 51.0′ W75° 19.6′) divides the channel into the main channel, to starboard, and the port channel to Darby Creek and behind the 2-mile-long Little Tinicum Island. You will find several marinas along the mainland behind Little Tinicum Island, right off the end of one of the runways of Philadelphia International Airport. Although these facilities can provide fuel and supplies, few transients will want to take advantage of the slips available, if only because of the aircraft noise. Don't plan on anchoring here.

The channel between the island and Essington is unmarked but presents no problem until you reach the upstream end of the island. Because of flats and shoals to both sides, remaining in the channel until it rejoins the main river channel is somewhat precarious. A better course is to head back and round the downstream side of the island to rejoin the main channel.

Schuylkill River

  No facilities

Charts: **12312**, **12313**

A casual glance at a chart would lead you to believe that the Schuylkill River, which runs right through the city of Philadelphia, offers places to anchor or tie up in order to visit the city. Unfortunately, this is not true. The Schuylkill River wharves and piers are mostly used to handle bulk petroleum products. This river is also home to the old Philadelphia Navy Shipyard, on League Island, now closed. In other words, it is completely industrial. There are no facilities for private vessels of any sort. Cruising boats should enter only to take a short sightseeing trip.

Philadelphia

Charts: 12312, **12313**

It is impossible for me to think of Philadelphia without remembering the famous quote from W. C. Fields regarding the prize for a mythical contest: "First prize is one week in Philadelphia. Second prize is two weeks in Philadelphia." Even when he made it, the comment was neither fair nor true. Philadelphia is definitely an interesting place. The only problem is getting there.

For a city with an excellent waterfront, Philadelphia does not do much to attract pleasure craft. If you don't know where the marinas are located, you may never find them. Even publicity for the main waterfront attraction, Penn's Landing, doesn't mention how to get there by water or even that slips are available for pleasure craft.

The waterfront's old commercial terminals are slowly being replaced by people-oriented facilities. Currently, the waterfront area of interest to the visitor extends roughly from the Museum & Independence Seaport, just south of Penn's Landing, to a few blocks upstream of the Benjamin Franklin Bridge, which runs between Philadelphia and Camden, New Jersey. The rest of the points of interest are farther inland.

Approach. Proceed up the Delaware River almost to the Benjamin Franklin Bridge. Then look for the collection of ships and head between them and the base of the bridge until you enter the marina at Penn's Landing or the Pier 5 Marina, by the bridge.

Anchorage & Marinas. For all practical purposes, there is no place to anchor in this area. Although the water depth does not preclude anchoring, there is a lot of commercial traffic, and you will have problems getting ashore.

Penn's Landing Marina (215-923-9129) is located in the middle of the public park at Penn's Landing. Adjacent to the marina is the ferry to Camden, New Jersey, across the river. The marina basin is protected from wakes and other wave action by a huge concrete breakwater. This is probably the optimum location for a visit to both Philadelphia and the New Jersey State Aquarium, across the river in Camden.

The old Philadelphia Navy Yard is at the junction of the Schuylkill and Delaware Rivers.

Philadelphia, Pennsylvania, and Camden, New Jersey

75°09′

Region 10

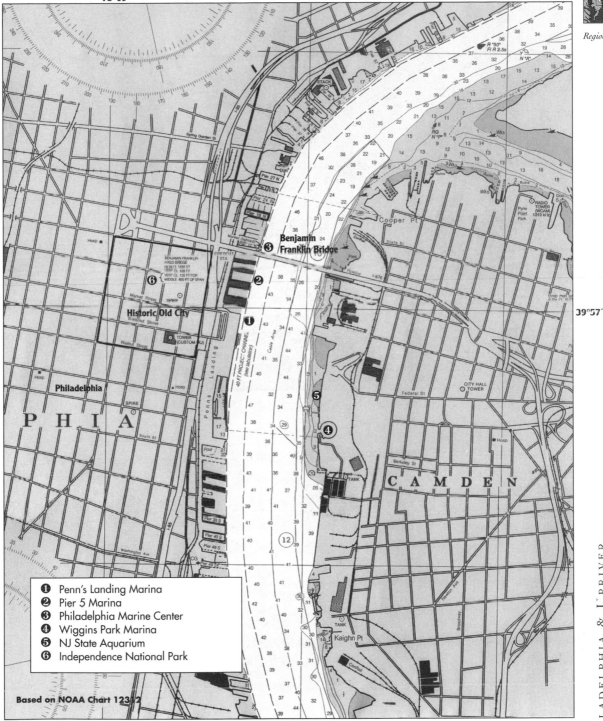

Benjamin Franklin Bridge

Cooper Pt

Historic Old City

Philadelphia

P H I A

C A M D E N

39°57′

❶ Penn's Landing Marina
❷ Pier 5 Marina
❸ Philadelphia Marine Center
❹ Wiggins Park Marina
❺ NJ State Aquarium
❻ Independence National Park

Based on NOAA Chart 12312

SCALE **1.34″** = **0.5** NAUT. MILES   ⚓ **Good anchoring**   ⚓ **Marina**   ⛵ **Launching site**

PHILADELPHIA & UPRIVER

451

Philadelphia (left) and Camden (right) waterfronts. The Benjamin Franklin Bridge connects the two cities.

National Geodetic Survey

If there is no room at Penn's Landing, go to the Pier 5 Marina (215-351-4101), almost at the base of the bridge. The facilities there are comparable to those at Penn's Landing. The Pier 5 Marina also has a marine store, groceries, a swimming pool, and a restaurant on the premises.

Past the bridge but almost in its shadow is the Philadelphia Marine Center (215-931-1000). The facilities are quite sheltered, and there are a couple of restaurants almost on the premises, as well as limited groceries. This is the only marina of the three that offers diesel fuel and gasoline, and it also has a self-service laundry.

At Camden, directly across the Delaware River from Penn's Landing is Wiggins Park Marina (609-541-7222), offering transient slips for both power and sail. It is within walking distance of the ferry to Philadelphia and adjacent to the New Jersey State Aquarium.

What to See & Do. All of the marinas mentioned above are close to most of Philadel-

phia's major attractions. Right at Penn's Landing is the Museum & Independence Seaport, featuring the submarine *Beguna* and Admiral Dewey's flagship from the Great White Fleet, the battleship *Olympia*.

Also at Penn's Landing is the square-rigger and floating restaurant *Moshulu*.

It's a short ferry ride to the New Jersey State Aquarium, in Camden. An aerial tram under construction in 2000 should be completed by now. The pedestrian tram will run from Penn's Landing to the Camden waterfront via cable cars or gondolas. This aquarium is one of only two in the country that have tanks large enough to accommodate tuna, which swim up to 35 mph while making sharp, sudden turns. There are seal shows, dive presentations, and other events in addition to the fantastic displays, such as a 760,000-gallon open ocean tank.

If you plan to tour the historic district of Philadelphia, your first stop should probably be at the National Park Visitor Center, just a few

Penn's Landing is a waterfront recreation area open year-round.

blocks from the waterfront, at the intersection of Chestnut and 3rd Streets, where you can pick up brochures on the various attractions. Of course, the Philadelphia historic district is the location of Independence Hall (a World Heritage Site) and the famous Liberty Bell, both part of Independence National Historical Park, the Philadelphia U.S. Mint, and more. Enjoy touring the historic buildings and watching the friendly, helpful costumed characters wandering about the area. Show toleration for these characters' ersatz English accents; it's all part of the game.

Delaware River above Philadelphia

 2 *No facilities*

Charts: 12313, **12314**

Above Philadelphia the Delaware River is navigable for another 30 miles, all the way to the fixed railroad bridge at Trenton, New Jersey. The bridge has a vertical clearance of 12 feet, and, even if you can get through that, a short distance upstream are rapids that will halt all boats except those small enough to portage. There is little above Philadelphia to draw the cruiser and little reason to make the trip, except, perhaps, simply to have done it. For those with enough ambition or curiosity to make the 25- to 30-mile trek beyond Philadelphia, the following is a thumbnail sketch of what you can expect to find.

The Conrail railroad bridge that crosses the Delaware between Bridesburg, Pennsylvania, and Delair, New Jersey, is a vertical-lift span with a vertical clearance of 49 feet when down and 135 feet when up. Two and a half miles past the railroad bridge, the highway drawbridge between Tacony, Pennsylvania, and Palmyra, New Jersey, has a vertical clearance of 53 feet when down. Gasoline and some supplies are available at a small boatyard on the west side of the bridge at Tacony.

Three miles above the Tacony–Palmyra bridge and just short of Rancocas Creek is Dredge Harbor, on the New Jersey side. This is a base for both sand- and gravel-dredging

PHILADELPHIA & UPRIVER

453

equipment and pleasure boats. The sand-and-gravel facility is on the northeast side of the harbor. Beyond the sand-and-gravel company wharves are four marinas, offering transient slips, diesel, gasoline, marine supplies, and restaurants. The Dredge Harbor Marina also has a swimming pool and a recreation area.

Rancocas Creek has some sand- and gravel-barge traffic as far as the first bridge. Beyond the two swing bridges only pleasure boats use the creek. Water depths run about 5 feet as far as Centerton and 6 miles above the creek mouth. There are small-craft facilities near the first bridge and at Bridgeboro. Transient slips, marine supplies, and restaurants are available. Rancocas Marine is the only one offering gasoline. No diesel is available.

Upstream and on the Pennsylvania side of the river, Poquessing Creek forms the upper boundary of the city of Philadelphia. The Delaware River Yacht Club, just below the mouth of the creek, has a float landing, where gasoline may be obtained. Just above the mouth of the creek is Mud Island, a mud flat that is partly submerged at high water. The lower part of the channel between the island and the Pennsylvania mainland is often used as a small-boat anchorage.

Neshominy Creek, at Croyden, Pennsylvania, has depths of about 7 feet as far as the fixed highway bridge (vertical clearance 9 feet). Transient slips, marine supplies, restaurants,

and showers are available, but there is no fuel.

The Burlington–Bristol highway bridge is a vertical lift span with a vertical clearance of 62 feet when down and 134 feet when up. It will present no problem to most cruising boats.

Just above the bridge, the channel splits at Burlington Island. The main channel, to port, is the better choice if you are continuing on up the Delaware River. The other channel, designated the auxiliary channel, is quite passable to cruising boats, but at the upstream end unmarked shoals to either side can trap the unwary. Curtain Marina, in the mouth of Assiscunk Creek off the auxiliary channel, offers transient slips, repairs, marine supplies, a restaurant, and gasoline.

Bordentown, New Jersey, on the southeast side of the entrance to Crosswicks Creek, was the terminus to the Delaware and Raritan Canal, which was abandoned in 1933. There is a trio of yacht clubs in the mouth of Crosswicks Creek where you may be able to obtain a transient slip and possibly gasoline.

Above Bordentown you are advised to stay in the dredged channel the rest of the way to Trenton (about 5 miles). Shoals and rocky ledges border the channel. For all practical purposes, there are no pleasure-craft facilities upstream of Bordentown. Once you reach Trenton, you have little recourse but to turn around and head back downstream. There is no place to tie up and no room to anchor.

Region 11

DELMARVA PENINSULA

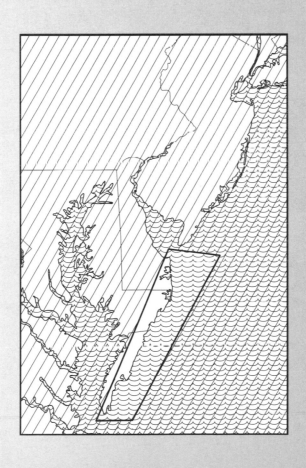

Delmarva Peninsula

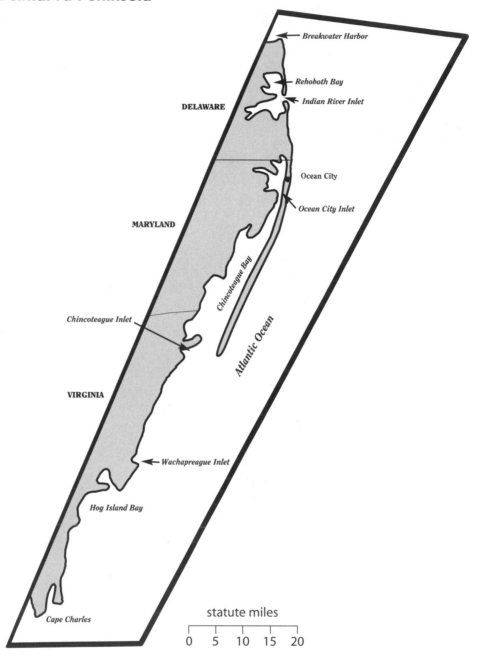

Breakwater Harbor

DELAWARE

Rehoboth Bay

Indian River Inlet

Ocean City

Ocean City Inlet

MARYLAND

Chincoteague Bay

Chincoteague Inlet

Atlantic Ocean

VIRGINIA

Wachapreague Inlet

Hog Island Bay

statute miles

0   5   10   15   20

Cape Charles

F OR THOSE HEADED SOUTH toward
Florida the main advantage of the approximately 115-mile-long outside route between Cape May and Norfolk is that it is less
than half as long as the inside trek up the
Delaware Bay, through the Chesapeake and
456 Delaware Canal, and down the Chesapeake

Bay. For most cruisers that's about the last good
thing that may be said about it. If your boat is
not sturdy enough in design and properly
equipped for an offshore ocean passage, don't
even think about taking the outside route. Although it is not normally a difficult overnight
run for a capable boat, especially in the summer,

a storm can come up fairly quickly, so choose your weather and time your trip carefully! If a storm is on the way and you are not absolutely sure of being able to enter one of the scarce sheltering inlets well before it arrives, head offshore or don't start.

The last good, all-weather harbor between Cape May and Norfolk is behind the artificial breakwater inside Cape Henlopen, on the south side of the mouth of Delaware Bay. Even though there are four or five navigable inlets along the Delmarva coast, you cannot depend upon being able to enter even the best of them under deteriorating conditions, especially against opposing ocean waves and an outgoing tidal current. All have shifting shoals, and at any given time the channel may not be where the buoys indicate. In fact, negotiating narrow oceanside inlets anywhere is something of an art in itself, and books have been written on the subject.

For better or worse, the following are the prime points of interest for a cruiser taking the outside route from Cape May to the Norfolk area.

Breakwater Harbor
(Lewes, Delaware)

Charts: 12214, **12216**, 12304

Strictly speaking, both Breakwater Harbor and Lewes (pronounced *Lewis*) are technically inside the mouth of Delaware Bay. However, from a logistical standpoint, it makes more sense to group them with the rest of the harbors and inlets along the Delmarva Peninsula. With the possible exception of Ocean City Inlet, Maryland, this is the last all-weather harbor on the long stretch between Cape Henlopen and the entrance to the Chesapeake Bay. This makes it an excellent jumping-off point for those heading south down the coast or taking a trip "round the horn" to circumnavigate the Delmarva Peninsula.

Approach. Tucked just inside Cape Henlopen, about 17 miles south of Cape May Inlet, and protected by a pair of long breakwaters is the appropriately named Breakwater Harbor.

Enter the harbor on either side of the 2-mile-long outer breakwater, whose west end is a good 2 miles offshore. The east end is still about a mile offshore.

There is no need to hold to the channel on the west side; there is at least 9 feet of water for a mile to either side of it. In fact, it may be better to stay out of the channel if the Cape May–Lewes Ferry (whose terminal is located in the southwest corner of the harbor) is operating.

The east channel also has plenty of room, but stay well off the Cape Henlopen shore; it shoals a long way out. (Notice the ½-mile length of the first pier in the southeast corner of the harbor.)

Anchorage, Marinas, & Restaurants. The best protection for anchoring is inside the inner breakwater, near the ferry terminal. A touristy store and a small restaurant are located inside the terminal building.

If you are looking for fuel, water, or other marine supplies, enter Roosevelt Inlet to the Lewes and Rehoboth Canal (west of Breakwater Harbor) and proceed 1½ miles to Lewes. The canal's controlling depth is a well-maintained 8 feet. The public dock and the Inn at Canal Square are just before the drawbridge, which opens on demand. The next bridge is fixed and has a 35-foot vertical clearance, which will stop all sailboats.

The Lewes Yacht Club, just inside the canal entrance, offers gasoline and diesel fuel. Just short of the drawbridge on opposite sides of the canal, Lewes Boat Yard and the Angler Restaurant offer transient slips. Immediately past the drawbridge is Lewes Harbor Marina, offering gasoline and diesel fuel but no transient dockage.

What to See & Do. Settled by the Dutch in 1631, Lewes is Delaware's oldest settlement. The town is the site of an enclave of historic buildings and homes, many carefully restored and moved (yes, moved!) to the town. The Lewes Historical Society (302-645-7670) offers tour tickets for the Lewes Historic Complex.

The Zwaanendael Museum is worth a visit. Among other exhibits, it contains many of the treasures recovered from the 18th-century British brig, the HMS *DeBraak*, discovered in the late 1960s off the coast by divers. The design of the building is based on the City Hall in Hoorn, Netherlands.

Lewes, Delaware, and Breakwater Harbor

75°07′

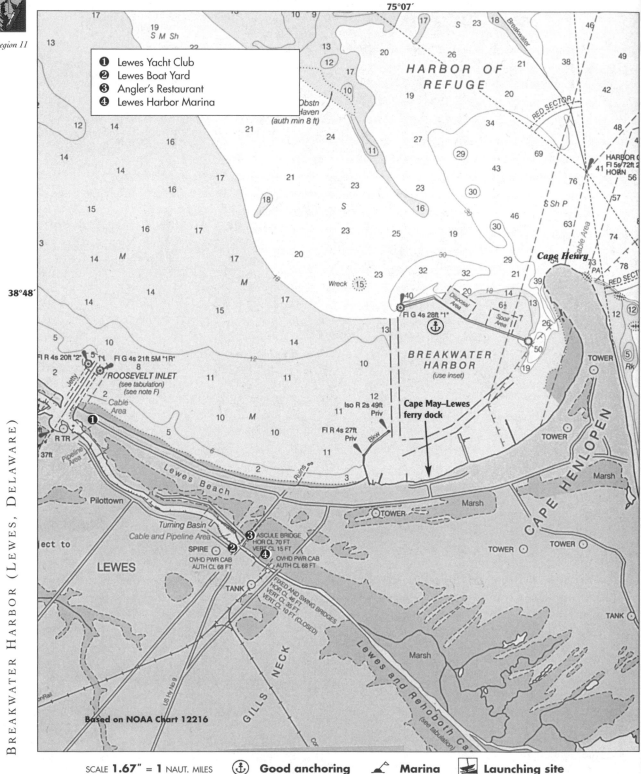

❶ Lewes Yacht Club
❷ Lewes Boat Yard
❸ Angler's Restaurant
❹ Lewes Harbor Marina

HARBOR OF REFUGE

Obstn Haven
(auth min 8 ft)

Cape Henry

BREAKWATER HARBOR
(use inset)

Cape May–Lewes ferry dock

Fl G 4s 28ft "1"

Fl R 4s 20ft "2"
Fl G 4s 21ft 5M "1R"
ROOSEVELT INLET
(see tabulation)
(see note F)

Cable Area

Iso R 2s 49ft Priv

Fl R 4s 27ft Priv

Lewes Beach

Pilottown

Turning Basin
Cable and Pipeline Area

LEWES

SPIRE

TANK

BASCULE BRIDGE
HOR CL 70 FT
VERT CL 15 FT

OVHD PWR CAB
AUTH CL 68 FT

OVHD PWR CAB
AUTH CL 68 FT

FIXED AND SWING BRIDGES
HOR CL 46 FT
VERT CL 35 FT
VERT CL 10 FT (CLOSED)

GILLS NECK

CAPE HENLOPEN

TOWER

TOWER

TOWER

TOWER

TANK

Marsh

Marsh

Marsh

Lewes and Rehoboth Ca.
(see tabulation)

Based on NOAA Chart 12216

SCALE **1.67″** = **1** NAUT. MILES   ⚓ **Good anchoring**   ⚓ **Marina**   🚤 **Launching site**

Lewes is also the site of the University of Delaware College of Marine Studies (302-645-4346), which gives tours by reservation on Fridays during the summer.

Breakwater Harbor is the terminus of the Cape May–Lewes Ferry (800-64-FERRY, 800-643-3779), which offers a 70-minute cruise across the mouth of Delaware Bay to Cape May, New Jersey, providing food and occasional entertainment to foot passengers, bikers, and those traveling by automobile.

Indian River Inlet

Charts: 12214, **12216**

Twelve miles south of the tip of Cape Henlopen is the first inlet on the Delmarva Peninsula. Indian River Inlet provides a passage through the strip of beach separating Rehobeth and Indian River Bays from the ocean. Unfortunately, the 35-foot vertical clearance of the fixed bridge over the inlet bars entrance to virtually all cruising sailboats. Although it is accessible to cruising powerboats, they rarely use it, partly because of the shifting channels inside the inlet and the shallow waters of both bays.

Approach. Local powerboats and fishing boats are the primary users of this inlet. Use by these boats is evidently heavy enough to make it worthwhile to maintain a buoyage system, including lights on the jetties. (Radio beacon R Bn-308 has been discontinued.) There is also a Coast Guard station located nearby.

Marinas. An assortment of marinas on the Indian River provide virtually all the marine services that you may need. In addition, two marinas at the north end of Rehobeth Bay offer most marine services except diesel fuel.

The Cape May–Lewes ferries cross the mouth of the Delaware Bay hourly, passing each other midway across.

Cape May–Lewes Ferry Authority

Ocean City Inlet

Chart: 12211

Thirteen miles south of Indian River Inlet is Ocean City Inlet, the only one of the navigable inlets that merits serious consideration by cruising boats. Except in the case of moderate to heavy onshore winds, this inlet is relatively easy to negotiate.

Approach. Under other than benign conditions, obtain recent local knowledge or bypass the inlet entirely (unless you are feeling lucky). A tidal current well upward of 3 knots at peak can be encountered if you hit it at the wrong time. Check the tide tables for the probable slack-water times to make your entrance. Do not attempt to negotiate the inlet, especially in a sailboat, under conditions of an outgoing current and onshore winds of much over 15 knots. At best, you won't like it. At worst, you may broach, founder, or hit an obstruction, any of which will definitely ruin your day.

The entrance is clearly marked with high stone jetties and buoys to seaward. (Radio beacon 293, once located on the north side of the inlet, has been discontinued.) Some sort of obstruction, marked by a white-orange buoy, is located a bit to the southeast of the inlet. Do not depend on the seaward buoys to properly mark the channel as storms can readily change the channel's actual location and depth.

There is a Coast Guard station at the west end of the entrance, on the north side. A VHF-FM radio call to the station to obtain information on the channel's location and controlling depth prior to negotiating this inlet is a good idea for the first-timer. Even better, ask the advice of a local boat or get one to lead you through the inlet.

Anchorages, Marinas, & Restaurants. Inside the inlet, the Ocean City Channel leads northward to an assortment of marinas and charter-boat facilities where you can obtain virtually any marine services or supplies that you might need. Nearly all the marinas useful to the transient are located just inside the inlet. There is little reason to proceed through the drawbridge if you are in need of fuel, supplies, or a slip for the night.

Past the drawbridge the channel eventually leads to Isle of Wight Bay. Beyond Isle of Wight Bay are Assawoman Bay and the St. Martin River. Should you choose to head toward these bays, be sure to follow the channel carefully unless you plan to get out and walk!

A channel to the south of the inlet may permit anchoring in the more pristine region of the north end of Sinepuxent Bay, a little past the commercial fish harbor on the mainland side. The channel continues behind Assateague Island all the way to Chincoteague Bay, but it tends to be shallow and subject to frequent shifting—it may not be where the buoys indicate. Although the controlling depth is reputed to be about 4 feet, if you can't get out and push your boat or you object to grounding, better forget it.

What to See & Do. It seems almost redundant to attempt to describe the attractions of Ocean City. The primary attraction of this resort town is, of course, the 2.6-mile-long boardwalk, which is lined with all of the typical seaside fare, including carnival-like amusements, restaurants, food stands, souvenir shops, and assorted other attractions, including a 1902-vintage carousel and other rides. There is also the Ocean City Wax Museum, which somehow seems like an odd thing to find at a seaside resort.

Right at the inlet is the Ocean City Lifesaving Museum (401-289-4991), which depicts the life-saving service in the Delmarva region.

On the Isle of Wight Bay side, Bay Cruises (410-213-0926) offers some interesting cruises: a 3-hour nature cruise featuring offshore marine animals, a 1-hour Ocean City overview cruise, and a 24-hour "tuna trip" aboard the *Ocean City Princess*.

The rest of Ocean City is filled with the typical tourist-trap establishments, shops, and restaurants, not to mention the superb sandy beach that extends for miles.

Ocean City, Maryland, and Ocean City Inlet

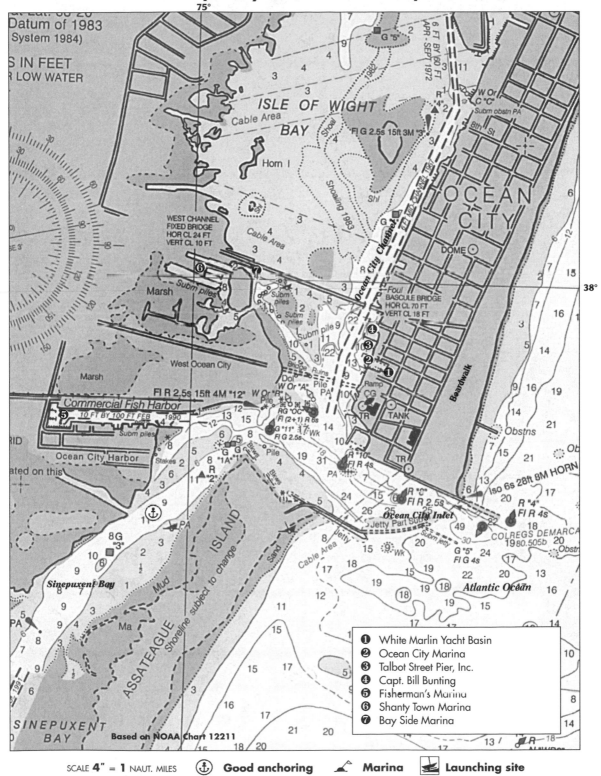

Legend:
1. White Marlin Yacht Basin
2. Ocean City Marina
3. Talbot Street Pier, Inc.
4. Capt. Bill Bunting
5. Fisherman's Marina
6. Shanty Town Marina
7. Bay Side Marina

SCALE **4" = 1** NAUT. MILES ⚓ **Good anchoring** ⚓ **Marina** **Launching site**

462 *Aerial view (looking north) of Ocean City Inlet.*

Chincoteague Inlet

  No facilities

Charts: **12210**, 12211

A little more than 34 miles south of Ocean City Inlet is the winding and changeable inlet to Chincoteague Channel. While the entrance channel is buoyed, it is quite undependable and is not recommended for use by anyone without recent local knowledge of the channel and its approaches.

If you do manage to negotiate the entrance, the channel winds through marshes and plentiful shoals inside of Chincoteague Island, past a swing bridge, to Chincoteague Bay.

Chincoteague Island is the setting for Marguerite Henry's beloved children's book, *Misty of Chincoteague*, but I find little else to recommend it, especially in light of the iffy inlet and channel.

Wachapreague Inlet

Chart: **12210**

Approximately 20 miles south-southwest of Chincoteague Inlet is the highly dubious Wachapreague Inlet. Although the entrance is marked with a lighted bell buoy and assorted unlit buoys, it should be attempted only by boats with less than a 4-foot draft and under benign conditions.

If conditions are rough, it is too dangerous to attempt, especially for a stranger. Under calm conditions, why bother? If you try it anyway, be sure to check the tide tables for the approximate time of slack water to avoid strong currents.

WACHAPREAGUE INLET TO CAPE CHARLES

Charts: 12210, 12221, **12224**, 12225

There are several other inlets on the 40 miles of Virginia coastline between Wachapreague Inlet and the entrance to the Chesapeake Bay. All have channels and shoals that shift frequently, making them virtually unusable to cruisers. Cruisers are well advised to steer a course well off the entire coastline in this region; a minimum of 3 miles seems prudent. It

takes only a glance at the chart to confirm this blanket comment.

One possible exception is worth mentioning. If they have the skill and nerve to negotiate the fairly treacherous Sand Island Inlet into Cobb Bay, power cruisers with less than a 3-foot draft can take an inland waterway route through Sand Shoal Channel and Mockhorn Channel to Magothy Bay and then through Cape Charles Channel into the Chesapeake (see Cape Charles Channel, pages 333–34). This trek is only for the truly adventurous. If occasional grounding bothers you, forget it.

On approaching the mouth of the Chesapeake, beware of Nautilus Shoal, which extends 2 to 4 miles southeast of Fishermans Island, just south of Cape Charles. In calm weather some rudimentary navigation and prudence can permit you to save considerable distance by passing between Nautilus Shoal and Fishermans Island. However, if there is any sea making up or any uncertainty about your exact location, a wiser course is to remain well offshore until you can pick up nun "2" southeast of Nautilus Shoal or one of the shipping-channel buoys before changing course to enter the Bay.

CHESAPEAKE BAY ENTRANCE

Charts: **12221,** 12222, 12224

The mouth of the Chesapeake Bay, between Cape Henry to the south and Fishermans Island, off Cape Charles, to the north, is 10 miles wide. The Chesapeake Bay Bridge-Tunnel, which spans the mouth of the Bay from Lynnhaven Roads, 5 miles inside Cape Henry, to Cape Charles, divides the entrance into three channels. Thimble Shoal Channel passes between trestles "A" and "B" in the south; Chesapeake Channel, in the middle, passes between trestles "B" and "C"; and the North Channel passes under a pair of fixed bridges with vertical clearances of 75 feet less than a mile southeast of Fishermans Island. Which channel you choose depends mostly upon where you are coming from and where you are going and, of course, the weather conditions. In any conditions you need to be aware of the tidal current. It can easily exceed 2 knots at peak, not only throwing you off course but greatly affecting

Chesapeake Bay Entrance

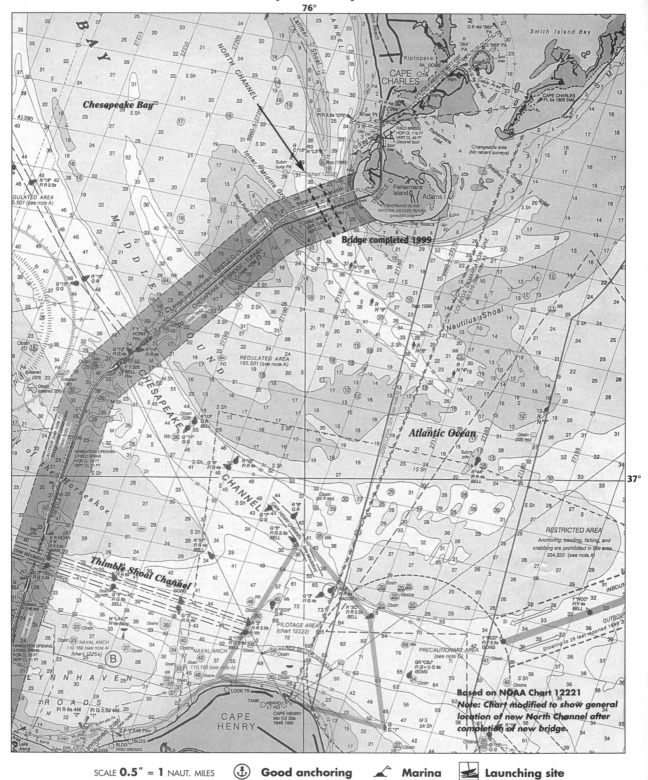

SCALE **0.5" = 1** NAUT. MILES   ⚓ **Good anchoring**   ⚓ **Marina**   🚣 **Launching site**

your passage through any of the Bay-Tunnel channels.

If you are heading for the James River area, follow the Thimble Shoal Channel. For the York River or Mobjack Bay, Chesapeake Channel is the shortest course. For all other points north on the Bay, use the North Channel unless there is heavy wave action, in which case stay farther away from the breakers on Nautilus Shoal south of Cape Charles. (See region 7, Wolf Trap Light to Cape Henry, for details on harbors in the vicinity.)

There are additional openings for small craft in trestles "A" and "B," each composed of a group of three spans with a vertical clearance of 21 feet and a horizontal clearance of 70 feet. Fixed green lights mark the centerline of each span, and fixed red lights mark the outermost bridge support pilings on each side of the openings. Note: Sailboats and power cruisers of any substantial size should not attempt these openings.

Northern Approach. If you are proceeding down the Delmarva Peninsula south of the Ocean City Inlet, you should remain a minimum of 3 miles offshore, preferably farther. This will allow you to maintain your course near or outside of the 3-fathom line and away from the protruding shoals. As you approach Sand Shoal Inlet and the Cape Charles area, a more prudent distance would be 4 miles or more offshore.

Near Sand Shoal Inlet, use the Sand Shoal Inlet RW "A" Mo(A) Whistle Buoy (N37° 17.8′ W75° 41.2′) as a convenient waypoint. From there continue down the coast, maintaining a 4-mile minimum distance offshore. In rough conditions you should get farther offshore and use the Cape Charles Fl R 4s R"14" Bell Buoy (N37° 07.4′ W75° 50.0′), about 7 miles offshore, as a waypoint to avoid the collection of shoals off of Cape Charles.

From red "14" a course of 250 degrees magnetic will take you to the first unlighted buoy, nun "2," of the North Channel entrance to the Bay. This channel passes between Nautilus Shoal and an unnamed shoal to the south of the channel. Note that none of the buoys marking this channel are lit. In rough conditions or at night you would be well advised to bypass this entrance channel in favor of the Chesapeake

Chesapeake Bay Bridge & Tunnel District

Northern end of the Chesapeake Bay Bridge-Tunnel at Fishermans Island. The North Channel passes under the two fixed bridges.

Channel (middle channel). Although cruising boats are unlikely to run aground on either shoal, they can produce breakers in rough conditions or a sizable swell.

If you are heading for the York River or Norfolk area, continue past North Channel nun "2" on the same course of 250 degrees magnetic for 1.8 miles to Middle Ground South Entrance Bell Buoy Fl R 4s R"4A" (N37° 01.3′ W75° 54.1′). From red "4A" you can easily pick up the buoys of Chesapeake Channel or Thimble Shoals Channel to pass through the Chesapeake Bay Bridge-Tunnel into the Chesapeake.

Southern Approach. Those with a capable boat and crew and with limited time to make the trip between the Chesapeake and points south will normally opt for the ocean passage well offshore around Cape Hatteras. Since you can keep going 24 hours a day offshore,

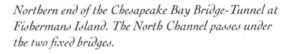

CHESAPEAKE BAY ENTRANCE

465

Southern end of the Chesapeake Bay Bridge-Tunnel, looking north from Thimble Shoal (south) Channel. The fishing pier is in the center left.

Chesapeake Bay Bridge & Tunnel District

whereas you can normally travel the ICW only during daylight, the outside route obviously takes only a fraction of the time an ICW trip would take. Of course, the strain on the crew and the hazards of a storm are also significantly greater offshore. Details for such a passage are well beyond the scope of this book. Here we address approaching and entering the Chesapeake Bay.

The southern approach to the Chesapeake Bay involves few hazards. Ordinary prudence would dictate a passage well to seaward of Cape Hatteras, which would normally put you on a course to the Chesapeake Bay entrance that would keep you away from trouble with the few outlying shoals near its mouth.

Fourteen miles east of the tip of Cape Henry is the Fl(2) W 15s Chesapeake Light (N36° 54.3′ W75° 42.8′). This is a Texas tower with a white superstructure and a blue base. Rising 117 feet above the water on four piles, it is the primary reference point for entrance into the Bay from the south through the east. There is no chance of mistaking it for something else. The name "Chesapeake" is emblazoned in white on all sides of the structure.

From Chesapeake Light, a course of approximately 295 degrees (plot your own course more precisely) will take you to the Bay entrance. It won't be long before you run across the strings of buoys marking the shipping channels. Follow them if you wish, but stay out of the channel if there is a ship in sight.

CHESAPEAKE BAY ENTRANCE

Appendices

1. VHF-FM CHANNELS

As a result of an action by the Federal Communications Commission (FCC) in September 1985, there is one less VHF-FM "chatter" channel available for our use. The FCC has limited the use of channel 70 to automated calling only. Recreational use is now prohibited.

A new transmitting technology called *digital selective calling* (DSC) allows the equivalent of direct dialing on channel 70; when the channel receives a coded signal, the radio will automatically switch to another channel for the message. This is also due to become part of the Future Global Maritime Distress and Safety System (FGMDSS), just becoming operational. The cost of DSC equipment will likely initially limit its use to commercial ships, until the cost drops.

Although the uninformed continue to use channel 70 for chatter, its reclassification is official. Use of this channel can result in a "nasty-gram" and fine from the FCC. Stay off it!

Recreational boaters may use channels 9, 68, 69, 71, 72, and 78 as working channels. Channel 72 is for ship-to-ship use only, and channel 9 is shared with commercial vessels.

Note: All Marine Radiotelephone operators (channels 24–28) and bridge operators (channel 13) are to be called directly on their assigned working channels. All others must first be contacted on channel 16 before switching to a working channel.

The following are VHF-FM radiotelephone channels that are pertinent to pleasure craft (arranged by functional priority). With few exceptions, all other channels are restricted to commercial or government purposes and are not for recreational boaters' use. BOAT/US offers a free FCC publication regarding the use of VHF-FM radios to its members. It also offers the *Maritime Radiotelephone User's Handbook* for under $5.

Channel 16. For distress and calling. In anything short of a Mayday situation, shift to a working channel as soon as possible.

Channel 9. An alternate calling channel to channel 16. May be used as a working channel, but shift to another working channel as soon as contact is made.

Channel 6. Reserved for ship-to-ship safety purposes, not to be used for general conversation. Often employed in search-and-rescue operations.

Channel 13. Bridge-to-bridge frequency for commercial craft. Also used for contact with drawbridge operators and C&D Canal Control.

Channel 22. Primary Coast Guard working channel. Contact the Coast Guard on channel 16 first; the Coast Guard doesn't monitor channel 22.

Channel 81. Secondary Coast Guard working channel.

Channels 25 and 26. Baltimore (Maryland) and Beach Haven (New Jersey) marine operator.

Channels 25–27. Norfolk (Virginia) marine operator.

Channel 26. Point Lookout and Ocean City (Maryland) and Atlantic City (New Jersey) marine operator.

Channel 27. Prince Frederick (Maryland), Lewes (Delaware), and Toms River (New Jersey) marine operator.

Channel 28. Wilmington (Delaware), Cambridge (Maryland), Staten Island (New York), and Washington (D.C.) marine operator.

Channel 84. Dover (Delaware) marine operator.

Channel 86. Bethany Beach (Delaware) marine operator.

Channels 68, 69, 71, 72, and 78. Noncommercial ship-to-ship, general communications (chatter channels).

Channel 70. Reserved for DSC (since 1986). Do not use!

WE-1, WE-2, and WE-3. NOAA weather broadcast.

2. U.S. COAST GUARD MARINE INFORMATION & COASTAL WEATHER BROADCASTS

The Fifth Coast Guard District stations listed below announce all Broadcast Notices to Mariners (initial call-up) on 2182 kHz (single-side band, or SSB) and/or 156.8 MHz (channel 16 VHF-FM) and shift to 2670 kHz (SSB) and/or 157.1 (channel 22 VHF-FM) where the complete broadcast text is read. These stations broadcast marine and weather information upon receipt as follows:

STATION	FREQUENCY	TIME (GMT)	WEATHER	NOTICE TO MARINERS
Coast Guard Group, Atlantic City	Ch 2	2303, 1103	yes	yes
	2671.4 (2670) kHz	2303, 1103	yes	yes
Coast Guard Group, Philadelphia	Ch 22	0035, 1235	no	yes
Coast Guard Group, Baltimore	Ch 22	0130, 1205	no	yes
Coast Guard Group, Eastern Shore	Ch 22	0200, 1145	no	yes
	2671.4 (2670) kHz	0233, 1403	yes	yes
Coast Guard Group, Hampton Roads	Ch 22	0230, 1120	no	yes
	2671.4 (2670) kHz	0203, 1333	yes	yes
Coast Guard Group, Cape Hatteras	Ch 22	0100, 1055	no	yes
	2671.4 (2670) kHz	0133, 1303	yes	yes
Coast Guard Group, Fort Macon	Ch 22	0130, 1030	no	yes
	2671.4 (2670) kHz	0103, 1233	yes	yes
Coast Guard	448 kHz	0020, 1520	yes	yes
CAMSLANT Chesapeake (NMN)	518 NAVTEX "N"	0130, 0730, 1330, 1930	yes	yes
	4426.0/6501.0/ 8764.0 kHz	0400, 1000, 0530	yes	no
	6501.0/8764.0 kHz 13089.0 kHz	1130, 1600 2200, 2330	yes	no
	8764.0/13089.0/ 17314.0 kHz	1730	yes	no

3. USEFUL WAYPOINTS

With the advent of low-cost LORAN and Geo-Positioning System (GPS) units, not only off-shore navigation but also coastal piloting has changed dramatically. In order to get from point A to point B, you still need to lay out a course and distance and obtain a course to steer, applying "Kentucky windage" to correct for the effect of current. But now there are tools to perform the necessary calculations. All you need to do is key in sets of geographical coordinates for reference points on the surface of the earth, called "waypoints," and "connect the dots" to establish a series of courses, or "routes." The navigational unit will tell you not only which way to steer but also how far off the planned course you actually are and how to steer to correct for it. Isn't that wonderful!

Of course, the prudent navigator will also remain fully aware of his or her position and be prepared to revert to dead reckoning to maintain course in the event that gremlins get into the works and the electronic navigator fails. (You weren't relying on electronic charts to the point that you had no appropriate paper charts aboard, were you?)

The following table contains a set of waypoints for the area covered by this book. They are intended to serve only to help you locate some of the more interesting or hard-to-locate places. You, of course, will calculate your own waypoints to lay out proper routes to follow as you pilot your vessel from place to place. (I certainly would not rely on someone else's way-points without checking to make sure that they are at least roughly correct.) By the way, I feel that providing waypoint coordinates obtained from a chart to two decimal points of minutes is somewhat like measuring a sponge with a micrometer. With that degree of resolution, if you make the measurements five times, you will probably come up with five different answers. No matter. Any of the values will be close enough for all practical purposes.

One other caveat: some of the waypoints in this table are for markers that are placed on land. For example, if you attempt to sail directly up to the Fort Wool Light in the entrance to Hampton Roads, you will have to debark from your grounded boat and walk the rest of the way.

In accordance with the layout of the regions in this book, the sequence of waypoints is generally from north to south or from the mouth of a body of water, such as the Delaware River, upstream.

Chesapeake Bay Waypoints

Waypoint Name	Light Characteristics	Latitude/Longitude
Susquehanna R. Ent. Sandy Point G "1"	Fl G 2.5s	N39° 27.80′ W76° 02.90′
Sassafras R. Ent. R "56"	Fl R 4s	N39° 22.72′ W76° 06.12′
Pooles I. Bar Light	Fl W 2.5s	N39° 15.78′ W76° 16.65′
Love Point Light (Chester R.)	Fl W 6s	N39° 03.42′ W76° 17.00′
Queenstown Cr. N "2"	—	N39° 00.30′ W76° 10.40′
Kent Narrows North Ent. R "2K"	Q Fl R	N38° 59.22′ W76° 14.78′
Kent Narrows South Ent. G "K"	Fl G 4s	N38° 57.30′ W76° 14.60′
Bodkin Point G "3"	Fl G 4s	N39° 08.18′ W76° 25.05′
Baltimore Light (Magothy R. Ent.)	Fl W 2.5s	N39° 03.56′ W76° 23.95′
Lake Ogleton G "1" (Severn R.)	Fl G 4s	N38° 57.12′ W76° 27.48′
Whitehall Bay R "2"	Fl R 4s	N38° 59.23′ W76° 26.30′
Bloody Point Bar Light (S. Kent I.)	Fl W 6s HORN	N38° 50.03′ W76° 23.52′
Wye River C "3"	—	N38° 50.54′ W76° 12.50′
Knapps Narrows (Bay side) G "1"	Fl G 4s	N38° 43.27′ W76° 20.78′
Knapps Narrows (Choptank side) G "3"	Fl G 4s	N38° 42.56′ W76° 19.43′
Choptank R. Light	Fl W 4s	N38° 39.35′ W76° 11.10′
Little Choptank R. G "1"	Fl G 2.5s	N38° 33.22′ W76° 19.26′
Drum Point (Solomons), Patuxent R. R "4"	Fl R 2.5s	N38° 19.14′ W76° 25.25′
St. Leonard Cr., Patuxent R. G "1"	—	N38° 23.07′ W76° 30.15′
Point No Point Light	Fl W 6s HORN	N38° 07.66′ W76° 17.40′
Hooper Island Light	Fl W 6s HORN	N38° 15.35′ W76° 15.00′
Holland Island Bar Light	Fl W 2.5s HORN	N38° 04.12′ W76° 05.76′
Smith Island East Ent G "1"	Fl G 2.5s HORN	N37° 58.40′ W75° 58.77′
Smith Island West (Bay) Ent. G "1"	Fl G 4s	N38° 00.00′ W76° 03.37′
Janes Island Light (Crisfield App.)	Fl W 4s HORN	N37° 57.80′ W75° 55.10′
Tangier Island East Ent. G "1"	Fl G 2.5s HORN	N37° 50.40′ W75° 58.30′
Tangier Island West Ent. G "1"	Fl G 2.5s	N37° 49.90′ W76° 00.25′
Point Lookout Light (Potomac R.)	Fl W 5s HORN	N38° 01.50′ W76° 19.40′
St. Marys R. Mouth RG	Fl R(2+1) 6s	N38° 04.52′ W76° 26.03′
Coan River G "5"	Fl G 4s	N38° 00.10′ W76° 27.08′
Yeocomico River R "2"	Fl R 4s	N38° 02.45′ W76° 30.05′
Smith Point Light	Fl W 10s HORN	N37° 52.80′ W76° 11.00′
Great Wicomico River Light	Fl W 6s	N37° 48.24′ W76° 16.10′
Onancock Creek G "1"	Fl G 4s	N37° 43.46′ W75° 51.05′
Windmill Point Light, Rappahannock R.	Fl W&R 6s	N37° 35.80′ W76° 14.15′
Piankatank R. Ent. G "3"	Fl G 4s	N37° 32.32′ W76° 16.70′
New Point Comfort, Mobjack Bay Ent. R "2"	Fl R 2.5s	N37° 17.75′ W76° 15.70′
Back River Channel Ent. G "1BR"	Fl G 4s	N37° 05.60′ W76° 15.00′
Kiptopeke Breakwater Center Ent.	—	N37° 09.90′ W75° 59.60′
Fort Wool Light (Hampton Roads)	Fl W 4s	N36° 59.25′ W76° 18.15′
Little Creek G "1"	Fl G 4s	N36° 55.95′ W76° 10.70′

Atlantic Coast Waypoints

Waypoint Name	Light Characteristics	Latitude/Longitude
Stepping Stones Light, L.I. Sound	Oc G 4s	N40° 49.45′ W73° 46.50′
City Island R "2"	—	N40° 49.90′ W73° 47.60′
Rockaway Point Light	Fl W 4s HORN	N40° 32.50′ W73° 56.50′
Great Kills Light	Fl W 4s	N40° 31.28′ W74° 07.94′
Old Orchard Shoals Light	Fl W 6s HORN	N40° 30.72′ W74° 05.95′
Atlantic Highlands Harbor E. Breakwater	Fl R 4s	N40° 25.10′ W74° 01.10′
Sandy Hook Channel Gong R "9"	Q Fl G GONG	N40° 28.74′ W73° 58.87′
Sandy Hook Sea Buoy "S"	Fl W 2s HORN	N40° 26.52′ W73° 55.04′
Sea Bright Sea Bell R "1"	Fl R 2.5s BELL	N40° 20.47′ W73° 55.60′
Shark River Inlet Approach Bell RW	Mo(A) BELL	N40° 11.10′ W74° 00.00′
Manasquan Inlet Approach Bell R "2M"	Fl R 4s BELL	N40° 05.50′ W74° 00.80′
Barnegat Inlet Approach Bell RW	Mo(A) BELL	N39° 44.75′ W74° 04.40′
Absecon Inlet Entrance R "2"	Fl R 2.5s	N39° 21.50′ W74° 23.90′
Great Egg Inlet RW "GE"	Mo(A) BELL	N39° 16.20′ W74° 31.90′
Cape May Inlet R "2CM"	Fl R 2.5s BELL	N38° 55.77′ W74° 51.31′
West Breakwater Light (Lewes) G "1"	Fl G 4s	N38° 48.03′ W75° 07.00′
Ocean City Inlet Approach, MD, R "2"	Fl R 4s BELL	N38° 19.48′ W75° 03.68′

Delaware Bay & River Waypoints

Waypoint Name	Light Characteristics	Latitude/Longitude
Cape May Canal Ent. (DE) R "8"	Fl R 2.5s	N38° 58.00′ W74° 58.76′
Brandywine Shoal Light	Gp Occ 12s HORN	N38° 59.20′ W75° 06.80′
Miah Maull Shoal Light	Occ 4s HORN	N39° 07.60′ W75° 12.50′
Cross Ledge Light	E Int 6s HORN	N39° 10.90′ W75° 16.05′
Ship John Shoal Light	Fl W 6s HORN	N38° 18.30′ W75° 22.60′
Cohansey River Ent. G "1"	Fl G 4s	N39° 20.70′ W75° 22.00′
Reedy Point, C&D Canal RG "CD"	Fl R(2+1)s	N39° 33.80′ W75° 33.15′

4. PARTIAL LISTING OF CHARTER SERVICES ON THE CHESAPEAKE

KEY

S	Sailboat Charters
P	Powerboat Charters
F	Fishing Charterboat Service
H/B	Fishing Headboat Service
H	Houseboat Charters
C	Crewed Cruises
	(Medium to Large Cruise Boats)

Numerous charter services are available in the Chesapeake. This list is designed to provide a reasonable starting point. The services are listed by region and body of water, in the same order as in the text. While the name or office of the charter service may actually differ from what is given here, the location should be correct. In most cases, the name given here is that of the marina where the service is located, not necessarily the name of the service itself. (Services can relocate or change hands; marinas can change hands but tend to stay put.) Regardless of these differences, the names and telephone numbers given here should allow you to contact the charter services.

Region 1

HEAD OF BAY TO POOLES ISLAND

S   HAVRE DE GRACE MARINA
Water St.
Havre de Grace MD 21078
410-939-2161

S, P   SKIPJACK COVE MARINA
P.O. Box 208
Georgetown MD 21930
410-275-2122

S   SAILING ASSOCIATES, INC.
P.O. Box 6
Georgetown MD 21930
410-275-8171

S   LA VIDA YACHTS, INC.
22174 Great Oak Landing Road
Chestertown MD 21620
(Fairlee Creek)
410-778-0329

Region 2

POOLES ISLAND TO BAY BRIDGES

S   TOLCHESTER MARINA
P.O. Box 503, RR 2
Chestertown MD 21620
410-778-1400

S SWAN CREEK MARINA
Yard A, Gratitude Point
Rock Hall MD 21661
410-639-7813

S GRATITUDE BOAT SALES, INC.
Lawton Ave.
Rock Hall MD 21661
410-639-7111

S THE HAVEN CHARTERS
Gratitude Rd.
Rock Hall MD 21661
410-639-7140

S GREAT RIVER YACHT CHARTERS
5649 Walnut St.
Rock Hall MD 21661
410-639-2166 or 800 677-2166

S THE SAILING EMPORIUM
Green Lane
Rock Hall MD 21661
410-778-1342

F ROCK HALL SEAFOOD
Rock Hall MD 21661
410-639-2261

S, P WILD DUCK CHARTERS
Piney Narrows Yacht Haven
210 Piney Narrows Rd.
Chester MD 21619
410-643-7200

S MARYLAND MARINA CHARTERS
3501 Red Rose Farm Rd.
Baltimore MD 21220
410-335-3898

S, P NANTICO MARINE CENTER
402 Key Highway
Baltimore MD 21230
410-962-1171

S, P, C CHESAPEAKE CHARTERS
418 E. 31st Street
Baltimore MD 21218
410-235-7224

C THE BALTIMORE PATRIOT
Pratt & Light Sts.
Baltimore MD 21230
410-685-4288

C CLIPPER CITY, INC. (Tall Ship)
1003 Old Philadelphia Rd.
Baltimore MD 21230
410-539-6277

C SCHOONER NIGHTHAWK
CRUISES
1715 Thames St.
Baltimore MD 21230
410-327-7245

S CHESAPEAKE CRUISES
White Rocks Yachting Center
1402 Colony Rd.
Pasadena MD 21122
410-437-2123

S GIBSON ISLAND YACHT BASIN
487 New York Ave.
Pasadena MD 21122
410-255-3488

Region 3

BAY BRIDGES TO LITTLE CHOPTANK RIVER

S LIPPINCOTT CHARTERS
Rt. 1, Box 545
Grasonville MD 21638
410-827-9300

S, P C&C CHARTERS
Mears Pointe Marina, Box 535AA
Grasonville, MD 21638
410-827-7888

S, P EASTERN SHORE YACHT
CHARTERS
Box 589
Oxford MD 21654
410-226-5000

S MEARS YACHT HAVEN
502 E. Strand, P.O. Box 130
Oxford MD 21654
410-226-5450

S, P   AMERICAN POWERBOAT
SCHOOLS
125 Riverview Ave.
Annapolis MD 21403
410-721-7517

S, P   ANNAPOLIS BAY CHARTERS
Box 4604
Annapolis MD 21403
410-269-1776

S, P   ANNAPOLIS CITY MARINA
410 Severn Ave.
Eastport, Annapolis MD 21403
410-268-0660

S   AYS CHARTERS & SAILING
SCHOOL
7416 Edgewood Rd.
Annapolis MD 21403
410-267-8181

S   BIGHT SERVICES, INC.
Annapolis Landing Marina
992 Klakring Rd.
Annapolis MD 21403
410-268-2414

S   CHESAPEAKE & POTOMAC
YACHT SERVICE
301 Burnside St.
Annapolis MD 21403
410-263-7224

S, P   PIER 4 MARINA
301 Fourth St.
Annapolis MD 21403
410-268-2987

S   LILLY BROS. YACHT YARD
726 Second St.
Eastport, Annapolis MD 21403
410-263-8881

S   NORTH-EAST-WIND
CHARTER, LTD.
306 Second St.
Annapolis MD 21403
410-267-6333

S   HORN POINT HARBOR MARINA
121 Eastern Ave.
Annapolis MD 21403
410-263-0550

S, P   ATLANTIC SAILING YACHTS
7078 Bembe Beach Rd.
Annapolis MD 21403
410-268-4680

S   CHESAPEAKE SAILING SCHOOL
Port Annapolis Marina
7074 Bembe Beach Rd.
Annapolis MD 21403
410-269-1594

P   CHESAPEAKE BAY TRAWLERS
690 Fairview Ave.
Annapolis MD 21403
410-263-2838

C   CHESAPEAKE MARINE
TOURS, INC.
Box 3350
Annapolis MD 21403
410-268-7600

S   MOONSHADOW YACHT
CHARTERS
Box 6529
Annapolis MD 21403
410-266-9060

S, P   PARADISE BAY YACHT
CHARTERS
215 Severn Ave.
Annapolis MD 21403
410-268-9330

S, P   HIGHSPIRE YACHT SERVICES
P.O. Box 4249
Annapolis MD 21403
410-263-2838

S, P   CRUISING YACHT CHARTERS
Liberty Marina
410 Westbury Dr.
Riva MD 21140
410-956-5530

H   OAK GROVE MARINA
Rt. 2
Edgewater MD 21037
410-266-6696

F   BAY VIEW MARINA
1061 Turkey Point Rd.
Edgewater MD 21037
410-269-6887

F   BLUE WATER MARINA
1024 Carrs Wharf Rd.
Edgewater MD 21037
410-798-1232

S, P   WEST RIVER YACHT
HARBOUR
Box 125
Galesville MD 20765
410-867-0650

S   HARTGE CHESAPEAKE
CHARTERS
Church Ln.
Galesville MD 20765
410-867-7240

F   DEALE MARINA
485 Deale Rd.
Deale MD 20751
410-261-5220

F   HAPPY HARBOUR MARINA
Deale MD 20751
410-867-0949

F   HERRINGTON HARBOUR
Rose Haven on the Bay, Rt. 261
Friendship MD 20758
410-741-5100

F   SEASIDE CRAB HOUSE
Chesapeake Beach MD 20732
410-257-7269

F, H, B   ROD 'N' REEL DOCK
P.O. Box 99
Chesapeake Beach MD 20732
410-257-2191

Region 4

LITTLE CHOPTANK RIVER TO POTOMAC RIVER

F   QUEEN ANNE MARINA
410 Congressional Dr.
Stevensville MD 21666
410-643-5065

F   KNAPPS NARROWS MARINA
Bay Hundred Restaurant
P.O. Box 279
Tilghman MD 21671
410-886-2622

F   CAP'N BUCKS SEAFOOD
Tilghman MD 21671
410-886-2244

F   HARRISON'S CHESAPEAKE
HOUSE
Tilghman MD 21671
410-886-2123

S   DICKERSON BOATBUILDERS, INC.
RR 2, Box 92
Trappe MD 21673
410-822-8556

S   MADISON BAY MARINA
P.O. Box 41
Madison MD 21648
410-228-4111

S, P   SPRING COVE MARINA
Box 160
Solomons MD 20688
410-326-2161

F   BUNKY'S CHARTER BOAT
MARINA
Main St.
Solomons MD 20688
410-326-3703

F   RIPPON BROS.
Hoopersville MD 21642
410-397-3200

F	**TOWN CREEK MARINA** Rt. 2, Box 62 California MD 20619, 410-862-3553
F	**CLARKE'S LANDING** Rt. 1, Box 891 Hollywood MD 20636 410-373-9819
F	**SCOTT'S COVE MARINA** Chance MD 21816 410-784-2363
F, H, B	**CRISFIELD FISHING CENTRE, INC.** Jersey Island Crisfield MD 21817 410-968-3162

Region 5

POTOMAC RIVER

H, B	**POINT LOOKOUT STATE PARK** Scotland MD 20687 410-872-5688
F	**SWANN'S PIER** Piney Point MD 20674 410-994-0774
F	**YEOCOMICO MARINA** P.O. Box 38 Kinsale VA 22488 804-472-2971
F	**KRENTZ MARINE RAILWAY** Harryhogan Point VA 22435 804-529-6800
S	**FORT WASHINGTON MARINA** 13600 King Charles Terrace Fort Washington MD 20744 410-292-7700
C	**ELENA—QUEEN OF HEARTS** (paddlewheeler) 600 Water St. Washington DC 20024 202-488-1249

C	**POTOMAC RIVERBOAT CO.** (paddlewheeler) 205 The Strand Alexandria VA 22314 703-684-0580

Region 6

POTOMAC RIVER TO WOLF TRAP LIGHT

F	**SMITH POINT MARINA** Rt. 1, Box 312 Little Wicomico River Reedville VA 22539 804-453-4077
C	**BUZZARD'S POINT MARINA** Reedville VA 22539 804-453-3545
S	**RAPPAHANNOCK YACHTS, INC.** Irvington VA 22480 804-438-5353
S, P	**IRVINGTON MARINA** Irvington VA 22480 804-438-5113
F	**LOCKLIES MARINA** Topping VA 23169 804-758-2871
S	**DOZIER'S DOCKYARD, INC.** Rt. 33 & Broad Creek Deltaville VA 23043 804-776-6711
F	**BURRELL'S MARINA** P.O. Box 203 Urbanna VA 23175 804-758-5016
S	**URBANNA MARINE CORP.** P.O. Box 520 Urbanna VA 23175 804-758-2342

WOLF TRAP LIGHT
TO CAPE HENRY

F   GARTZ MARINA
     127 East River Rd.
     Poquoson VA 23662
     804-868-6821

H, B CHESAPEAKE CHARTER
      SERVICE
      Jones Marina
      519 Bridge Rd.
      Hampton VA 23669
      804-723-0998

F   LITTLE BOAT HARBOUR SUPPLY
     201 Jefferson Ave.
     Newport News VA 23601
     804-245-7796

F, H, B SHORE DRIVE MARINA
         8180 Shore Dr.
         Norfolk VA 23518
         804-463-8800

F   COBB'S MARINA
     4514 Dunning Rd.
     Norfolk VA 23518
     804-588-5401

F   BUBBA'S MARINA & BOAT RAMP
     3323 Shore Dr.
     Virginia Beach VA 23451
     804-481-9867

F   LYNNHAVEN MUNICIPAL
     MARINA
     3211 Lynnhaven Dr.
     Virginia Beach VA 23451
     804-481-7137

F   D&M SPORT FISHING CENTER
     3311 Shore Dr.
     Virginia Beach VA 23451
     804-481-7211

5. DOCKSIDE SEWAGE PUMPOUT FACILITIES

In addition to the Chesapeake Bay locations, there is now a waterborne pumpout station that offers its service to Chesapeake boaters at no charge. The 48-foot *H. J. Elser* can be located by calling radio channel 16. During the boating season the *Elser* frequents the Annapolis, St. Michaels, Oxford, Fairlee Creek, and Solomons Island areas Thursday through Sunday. The operation is funded by Maryland's boat excise tax.

Note: Listings are subject to change, so call ahead.

Region 1. Head of Bay to Pooles Island

Facility	Location	Telephone
Schaefer's Marina	C&D Canal	410-885-2204
Chesapeake Inn Marina	C&D Canal	410-885-2040
Harbor North Marina	Elk River	410-885-5656
Locust Point Marina	Locust Point, Elk River	410-392-4994
Bohemia Bay Yacht Harbour	Bohemia River	410-885-2601
Long Point Marina	Bohemia River	410-275-8181
Two Rivers Yacht Basin	Bohemia River	410-885-2257
Losten's Marina	Bohemia River	410-275-8168
Duffy Creek Marina	Georgetown, Sassafras River	410-275-2141
Georgetown Yacht Basin	Georgetown, Sassafras River	410-648-5112
Granary Marina	Georgetown, Sassafras River	410-648-5112
Skipjack Cove Yachting Resort	Georgetown, Sassafras River	410-275-2122
Sassafras Boat Co.	Georgetown, Sassafras River	410-648-5355
Gregg Neck Boat Yard	Georgetown, Sassafras River	410-648-5360
Green Point Marina	Worton Creek	410-778-1615
The Wharf, Handy's Point	Worton Creek	410-778-4363
Worton Creek Marina	Worton Creek	410-778-3282
Mears Great Oak Landing	Fairlee Creek	410-788-5007
Northeast River Yacht Club	Northeast River	410-287-6333
Charlestown Marina	Northeast River	410-287-8125
Riverside Ponderosa Pines	Northeast River	410-642-3431
Anchor Boats & Marina	Northeast River	410-287-6000
Pat's Marina	Northeast River	410-287-5298
Tidewater Marina	Havre de Grace, Susquehanna River	410-939-0950
Havre de Grace Marina	Havre de Grace, Susquehanna River	410-939-2161
Owens Marina	Susquehanna River	410-642-6646
Perryville Yacht Club	Perryville, Susquehanna River	410-642-6364
City Park Marina	Susquehanna River	410-939-9448
Bush River Boat Works	Bush River	410-272-1882
Gunpowder Cove Marina	Gunpowder River	410-679-5454

Region 2. Pooles Island to Bay Bridges

Facility	Location	Telephone
Tolchester Marina	Main Bay	410-778-1400
Gratitude Marina	Swan Creek	410-639-7011
Haven Harbour	Swan Creek	410-778-6697
Pelorus Marine, Inc	Rock Hall Harbor	410-639-2224
Sailing Emporium	Rock Hall Harbor	410-778-1342
North Point Marina	Rock Hall Harbor	410-639-2907
Osprey Point Marina	Rock Hall Harbor	410-639-2663
Rock Hall Landing Marina	Rock Hall Harbor	410-639-2224
Spring Cove Marina	Rock Hall Harbor	410-639-2110
Castle Harbour Marina	Kent Island, Chester River	410-643-5599
Angler's Restaurant & Marina	Kent Narrows	410-827-6717
Lippincott Marine	Kent Narrows	410-827-9300

FACILITY	LOCATION	TELEPHONE	
Mears Pointe Marina	Kent Narrows	410-827-8888	
Piney Narrows Yacht Haven	Kent Narrows	410-643-6600	
Scott Marine Sales & Service	Kent Narrows	410-827-8150	
Kent Island Yacht Club	Kent Narrows	410-643-4101	
Long Cove Marina	Langford Creek, Chester River	410-778-6777	
Lankford Bay Marina	Davis Creek, Langford Creek, Chester River	410-778-1414	
Rolph's Wharf Marina	Chester River	410-778-6347	
Kiblers Marina	Chestertown, Chester River	410-778-3616	
Gunpowder Cove Marina	Gunpowder River, Taylors Creek	410-679-5454	
Baltimore Yacht Club	Sue Creek, Middle River	410-682-2310	
Boating Center of Baltimore	Sue Creek, Middle River	410-687-2000	
Porters Seneca Marina	Seneca Creek, Middle River	410-335-6563	
Norman Creek Marina	Norman Creek, Middle River	410-686-9343	
Essex Marina Boat Yard	Hopkins Creek, Middle River	410-687-6149	
Riverwatch Restaurant & Marina	Hopkins Creek, Middle River	410-687-1422	
Chesapeake Yachting Center	Frogmortar Creek, Middle River	410-335-5390	
Key Yacht Club	Back River	410-477-2578	
Riverside Marine	Back River	410-686-1500	
West Shore Yacht Center	Muddy Gut, Back River	410-686-6998	
Ventnor Marine Service	Bodkin Creek, Patapsco River	410-255-4100	
Maryland Yacht Club	Rock Creek, Patapsco River	410-255-4444	
White Rocks Marina	Rock Creek, Patapsco River	410-255-3800	
Oak Harbor Marina	Rock Creek, Patapsco River	410-255-4070	
Pasadena Yacht Yard	Rock Creek, Patapsco River	410-255-1771	
Stony Creek Bridge Marina	Stony Creek, Patapsco River	410-255-5566	
Maurgate Marina	Stony Creek, Patapsco River	410-255-0402	
Anchor Bay East Marine	Bear Creek, Patapsco River	410-284-1044	
Middle Branch Moorings	Middle Branch, Patapsco River	410-539-2628	
Lighthouse Point Marina	Northwest Harbor, Baltimore	410-522-1881	
Harbor View Marina	Inner Harbor, Baltimore	410-752-1122	
Inner Harbor Marina of Baltimore	Inner Harbor	410-837-5339	
Hamilton Harbor Marina	Magothy River	410-647-0733	
Magothy Marina	Magothy River	410-647-2356	
Pleasure Cove Yacht Club	Sandy Point	410-757-8000	
Sandy Point Marina	Sandy Point State Park	410-974-0772	

Region 3. Bay Bridges to Little Choptank River

Bay Bridge Marina	Kent Island, by Bay Bridges	410-643-3162	
Miles River Yacht Club	Long Haul Creek, Miles River	410-745-9511	
Chesapeake Bay Maritime Museum	St. Michaels, Miles River	410-745-2916	
St. Michaels Town Dock Marina	St. Michaels, Miles River	410-745-2400	
St. Michaels Harbour Inn & Marina	St. Michaels, Miles River	410-745-9001	
Knapps Narrows Marina	Knapps Narrows	410-866-2720	
Gateway Marina	Choptank River	410-476-3304	
Bachelor Point Harbor	Tred Avon River (mouth)	410-226-5592	

FACILITY	LOCATION	TELEPHONE
Crockett Bros. Boatyard	Town Creek, Tred Avon River	410-226-5115
Oxford Boatyard	Town Creek, Tred Avon River	410-226-5101
Easton Point Marina	Dixon Creek, Tred Avon River	410-822-1201
Dickerson Marine Services	La Trappe Creek, Choptank River	410-822-8556
Cambridge Municipal Yacht Basin	Cambridge, Choptank River	410-228-4031
Yacht Maintenance Co.	Cambridge Creek, Choptank River	410-228-8878
Gateway Marina & Ship's Store	Rt. 50 Bridge, Choptank River	410-476-3304
Annapolis Landing Marina	Back Creek, Severn River	410-263-0090
Bert Jabin's Yacht Yard	Back Creek, Severn River	410-268-9067
Mears Marina	Back Creek, Severn River	410-268-8282
Port Annapolis Marina	Back Creek, Severn River	410-269-1990
Annapolis City Marina	Spa Creek, Severn River	410-268-0660
City of Annapolis Pumpout Boat	Spa Creek, Severn River	410-263-7973
Annapolis Harbor Boat Yard	Spa Creek, Severn River	410-267-9050
Holiday Point Marina	Selby Bay, South River	410-956-2208
South River Marina	Selby Bay, South River	410-798-6060
Selby Bay Yacht Basin	Selby Bay, South River	410-798-0232
Pier 7 Marina	South River	410-956-2288
Londontowne Marina	Londontowne, South River	410-956-5077
Liberty Yacht Club	Rt. 2 Bridge, South River	410-266-5633
Backyard Boats	Parrish Creek, West River	410-867-3119
Parrish Creek Marine & Boatyard	Parrish Creek, West River	410-261-9662
Cadle Creek Marina	Cadle Creek, Rhode River	410-798-1915
Holiday Inn Marina	Bear Neck Creek, Rhode River	410-268-9454
Rhode River Marina	Rhode River	410-798-1658
Pirates Cove Marina	West River	410-867-2300
Herrington Harbor North	Rockhold Creek, Herring Bay	410-867-4343
Shipwright Harbor	Rockhold Creek, Herring Bay	410-867-7686
Herrington Harbor South	Herring Bay	410-741-5100

Region 4. Little Choptank River to Potomac River

Sea & Sea Marine	Madison Bay, Little Choptank River	410-228-4111
Wicomico Yacht Club	Wicomico Creek, Wicomico River	410-749-9856
White Haven Marina	Wicomico River	410-873-2662
Port of Salisbury Marina	Salisbury, Wicomico River	410-548-3176
Somers Cove Marina	Crisfield, Little Annemessex River	410-968-0925
Breezy Point Marina	Breezy Point, Main Bay	410-535-4356
Flag Harbor Yacht Haven	Flag Harbor, Main Bay	410-586-1915
Bowen's Inn & Marina	Solomons, Patuxent River	410-326-2214
Town Center Marina	Solomons, Patuxent River	410-326-2401
Calvert Marina	Solomons, Patuxent River	410-326-4251
Spring Cove Marina	Solomons, Patuxent River	410-326-2161
Zahniser's Sailing Center	Solomons, Patuxent River	410-326-2166
Comfort Inn/Beacon Marina	Solomons, Patuxent River	410-326-6303
Boatel California	Town Creek, Patuxent River	410-737-1401
Weeks Marina	Cuckhold Creek, Patuxent River	410-373-5124

FACILITY	LOCATION	TELEPHONE
Vera's White Sands Marina	St. Leonard Creek, Patuxent River	410-586-1182
Broomes Island Marina	Island Creek, Patuxent River	410-586-0304
Cape St. Marys Marina	Cat Creek, Patuxent River	410-373-2001

Region 5. Potomac River

Point Lookout State Park	Point Lookout	301-872-5688
Point Lookout Marina	Smith Creek	301-872-5145
Dennis Point Marina	Carthagena Creek, St. Marys River	301-994-2288
Tall Timbers Marina	Herring Creek	301-994-1508
Lewisetta Marina	Coan River	804-529-7299
Coan Marina	Coan River	804-529-2032
Sandy Point Marina	Shannon Branch, Yecomico River	804-472-3237
White Point Marina	Shannon Branch, Yecomico River	804-472-2977
Yeocomico Marina	West Yeocomico River	804-472-2971
Kinsale Harbor Marina	West Yeocomico River	804-472-2514
Olverson's Lodge Creek Marina	South Yeocomico River	804-529-6341
Cather Marine, Inc.	St. Patrick Creek	301-769-3335
Kopel's Marina	St. Patrick Creek	301-769-3121
Combs Creek Marina	Combs Creek, Breton Bay	301-475-2017
Harbor View Marina	Combs Creek, Breton Bay	301-475-3030
Capt. John's Crabhouse	Neale Sound	301-259-2315
Cobb Island Marina	Neale Sound	301-259-2032
Saunders Marina	Neale Sound	301-934-9266
Shymansky's Restaurant & Marina	Neale Sound	301-259-2221
Ragged Point Marina	Ragged Point, near Lower Machodoc Creek	301-472-3955
Port Tobacco Marina	Port Tobacco River	301-932-1407
Outdoor World Harbor View	Mattox Creek	804-224-8164
Stanford's Marine Railway	Monroe Creek	804-224-7644
Sweden Point Marina	Mattawoman Creek	301-743-7336
Fairview Beach Yacht Club	South of Potomac Creek	703-775-5971
Waugh Point Marina	Potomac Creek	703-775-7121
Willow Landing Marina	Aquia Creek	703-659-2653
E-Z Cruz	Neabsco Creek	703-670-8115
Tyme 'N' Tyde, Inc.	Occoquan Bay	703-491-5116
Capt. John S. Beach Marina	Occoquan River	703-339-9650
Hoffmasters Marina	Occoquan River	703-494-7161
Ft. Washington Marina	Piscataway Creek	301-292-7700
Tantallon Yacht Club	Swan Creek	301-292-3349
Belle Haven Marina	Hunting Creek, Alexandria	703-768-0018
Alexandria City Marina	Alexandria	703-838-4265
Washington Sailing Marina	Alexandria	703-546-9027
James Creek Marina	Anacostia River	202-554-8844
Port of Bladensburg	Anacostia River	301-779-4133
Gangplank Marina	Washington Channel	202-554-5000
Columbia Island Marina	Columbia Island (Pentagon)	202-347-0173

Region 6. Potomac River to Wolf Trap Light

FACILITY	LOCATION	TELEPHONE
Ocean Pines Marina	Isle of Wight Bay	410-641-7447
Shad Landing Area Marina	Shad Landing, Pocomoke River	410-632-2566
Onancock Wharf	Onancock Creek	804-787-7911
Leroy's Marina	Little Wicomico River	804-453-6806
Smith Point Marina	Little Wicomico River	804-453-4077
Ingram Bay Marina	Ingram Bay, Great Wicomico River	804-580-7292
Tiffany Yachts/Marine	Headwaters, Great Wicomico River	804-453-3464
Windmill Point Marine Resorts	Windmill Point, Rappahannock River	804-435-1166
Chesapeake Cove Marina	Broad Creek, Rappahannock River	804-776-6855
Deltaville Dockside Inn	Broad Creek, Rappahannock River	804-776-9224
Greens Marina & Boatyard.	Broad Creek, Rappahannock River	804-776-9645
J&M Marina	Broad Ceek., Rappahannock River	804-776-9860
Norview Marina	Broad Creek, Rappahannock River	804-776-6463
Waldens Marina	Broad Creek, Rappahannock River	804-776-9440
W&E Marine	Broad Creek, Rappahannock River	804-776-9592
Tides Inn	Carter Creek, Rappahannock River	804-438-5000
Irvington Marina	Carter Creek, Rappahannock River	804-438-5113
Regent Point Marina	Locklies Creek, Rappahannock River	804-758-4457
Yankee Point Marina	Corrotoman R., Rappahannock River	804-462-7018
Urbanna Yacht Sales, Inc.	Urbanna Creek, Rappahannock River	804-758-2342
Urbanna Bridge Marina	Urbanna Creek, Rappahannock River	804-758-5124
Locklies Marina	Robinson Creek, Rappahannock River	804-758-2871
Regent Point Marina	Robinson Creek, Rappahannock River	804-758-4457
Greenvale Creek Marina	Greenvale Creek, Rappahannock River	804-462-7350
Whelan's Marina & Campground	Tarply Point, Rappahannock River	804-394-9500
Deltaville Marina	Jackson Creek, Piankatank River	804-776-9633
The Narrows Marina	Milford Haven, Piankatank River	804-725-2151
Club on Fishing Bay	Fishing Bay, Piankatank River	804-776-6911

Region 7. Wolf Trap Light to Cape Henry

FACILITY	LOCATION	TELEPHONE
Northampton Marine	Cape Charles Inlet	757-331-4400
Horn Harbor Marina	Horn Harbor	804-725-3223
Mobjack Bay Marina	Blackwater Creek, North River	804-725-7245
Shelter Harbor Marina	Severn River	804-642-2800
Holiday Marina	Southwest Branch, Severn River	804-642-2528
Cook's Landing	Perrin River, York River	804-642-6177
Jordan Marine Service	Sarah Creek, York River	804-642-4360
York River Yacht Haven	Sarah Creek, York River	804-642-2156
Wormley Creek Marina	Wormley Creek, York River	804-898-5060
Chisman Creek Marina	Chisman Creek, Poquoson River	757-898-3000
Poquoson Marina	Bennett Creek, Poquoson River	757-868-6171
Marina Cove Boat Basin	Harris River, Back River	757-851-0511
Customs House	Southwest Branch, Back River	757-723-8959
Rebel Marine Sevice	Willoughby Bay	757-588-6022

APPENDICES

FACILITY	LOCATION	TELEPHONE
Willoughby Harbor Marina	Willoughby Bay	757-583-4150
Bluewater Yacht Sales	Hampton River	757-723-0795
Hampton Roads Marina	Hampton River	757-723-6774
Lee's Yachting Center	Western Branch, Elizabeth River	757-484-2652
VA Boat & Yacht Club	Western Branch, Elizabeth River	757-484-0308
Western Branch Diesel	Western Branch, Elizabeth River	757-484-6230
Tidewater Yacht Agency	Portsmouth, Elizabeth River	757-393-2525
City Marina, Waterside	Norfolk, Elizabeth River	757-441-2222
Brady's Marina	Nasemond River	757-539-8221
Menchville Marine Supply	Deep Creek, James River	757-877-0207
Pagan River Marina	Pagan River, James River	757-357-7405
Rescue Yacht Basin	James Creek, James River	757-357-4621
Kingsmill Marina	Kingsmill, James River	757-253-3919
Jamestown Yacht Basin	Jamestown, James River	757-229-8309
Eagle's Point Marina	Grays Creek, James River	757-294-3050
Jordan Point Yacht Haven	Jordan Point, James River	757-458-3398
Kingsland Reach Marina	Hatcher Island, James River	757-796-1213
Little Creek Dry Storage Marina	Little Creek	757-583-3600
Cobb's Marina	Little Creek	757-588-5401
Taylors Landing Marina	Little Creek	757-587-3480
Marina at Marina Shores	Lynnhaven Inlet	757-496-7000
Lynnhaven Yacht Marina	Lynnhaven Inlet	757-481-6909

Region 8. City Island to Sandy Hook

FACILITY	LOCATION	TELEPHONE
Sailmake R Marina	City Harbor, City Island	718-885-2700
Boathaven Marineland	City Harbor, City Island	718-885-2000
Locust Point Marina	Throgs Neck	718-822-7974
Whitestone Marina	Whitestone Point, East River	718-767-7800
World's Fair Marina	Flushing Bay, East River	718-478-0480
Liberty Landing Marina	Jersey City, Hudson River	201-985-8000
Liberty Harbor Marina	Jersey City, Hudson River	201-451-1000
Newport Marina	Jersey City, Hudson River	201-626-5550
Lincoln Harbor Marina	Union City, Hudson River	800-205-6987
Port Imperial Marina	Union City, Hudson River	201-902-8787
79th Street Boat Basin	Manhattan, Hudson River	212-496-2105
Marine Basin Marina	Gravesend Bay, Hudson River	718-372-5700
Atlantis Marina	Great Kills, Staten Island	718-966-9700
Captain's Marina	Great Kills, Staten Island.	718-984-3346
Atlantic Highlands Municipal Marina	Atlantic Highlands, Sandy Hook Bay	732-291-1100
Leonardo State Marina	Leonardo, Sandy Hook Bay	732-291-1333
Monmouoth Cove Marina	Port Monmouth, Sandy Hook Bay	732-455-4440
Channel Club Marina	Shrewsbury River	732-222-7717
Fairhaven Yacht Works	Navisink River	732-747-3010
Oceanport Landing	Navisink River	732-229-4466
Oceanic Marina	Runson, Navisink River	732-842-1194
Irwins Marina	Red Bank, Navisink River	732-741-0023

| Molly Pitcher Marina | Red Bank, Navisink River | 732-747-2500 |

Region 9. Sandy Hook to Cape May

Belmar Marina	Shark River	732-681-2266
Total Marina at Seaview	Shark River	732-775-7842
Manasquan Marina	Watson Creek, Manasquan River	732-223-4277
Hoffman's Marina	Crabtown Creek, Manasquan River	732-528-6160
Brielle Marine Basin	Manasquan River	732-528-6200
Brielle Yacht Club	Manasquan River	732-528-6250
Garden State Marina	Manasquan River	732-892-4222
Crystal Point Yacht Club	Upper Manasquan River	732-892-2300
High Bar Harbor Yacht Club	Barnegat Inlet	609-494-8801
Morrisons Beach Haven Marina	Beach Haven Inlet	609-492-2150
Shelter Harbor Marina	Beach Haven Inlet	609-492-8645
Sportsman's Marina	Beach Haven Inlet	609-492-7931
Historic Gardner's Basin	Atlantic City, Absecon Inlet	609-348-2880
Sen. Farley State Marina	Atlantic City, Absecon Inlet	800-876-4386
Cape Island Marina	Ship Channel, Ocean City, Great Egg Inlet	609-927-8886
Capt. Andy's Fishing Center	Ship Channel, Ocean City, Great Egg Inlet	609-822-0916
Harbour Cove Marina	Ship Channel, Ocean City, Great Egg Inlet	609-927-6513
Avalon Point Marina	Townsends Inlet	609-967-4100
Two Mile Marina & Restaurant	Cape May Inlet	609-522-1341
Harbor View Marina	Cape May Harbor	609-884-0808
Canyon Club Resort Marina	Canal Entrance, Cape May Harbor	609-884-0199
Utsch's Marina	Canal Entrance, Cape May Harbor	609-884-2051
South Jersey Marina	Shellenger Creek, Cape May Harbor	609-884-2400
Roseman's Boat Yard	Cape Island Creek, Cape May Harbor	609-884-0262
Cape May Marine	Cape Island Creek, Cape May Harbor	609-884-3351

Region 10. Delaware Bay & Delaware River

Long Reach Marina	Maurice River, Delaware Bay	609-785-1818
Greenwich Boat Works	Cohansey River, Delaware Bay	609-451-1777
Penn Salem Marina	Salem River, Delaware River	609-935-BOAT
Delaware City Marina	Delaware City, Delaware River	302-834-4172
Philadelphia Marine Center	Philadelphia, Delaware River	215-931-1000
Baum's Cove Marina	Tullytown PA, Delaware River	215-949-2100

Region 11. Delmarva Peninsula

River Inlet Marina	Indian River Inlet	302-227-3071
Bayside Marina	W. Ocean City, Ocean City Inlet	410-213-2277
Advanced Marina	Ocean City, Ocean City Inlet	410-723-2124
Wachapreague Marina	Wachapreague Inlet	757-787-2105

6. BIBLIOGRAPHY

Blackistone, Mick. *Sunup to Sundown: Watermen of the Chesapeake*. Annapolis MD: Blue Crab Press, 1991.

Blair, Carvel, and W. D. Ansel. *Chesapeake Bay: Notes and Sketches*. Centreville MD: Tidewater, 1970.

Boating Almanac, vol. 4, *Chesapeake Bay, Delaware, Maryland, D.C., Virginia*. Severna Park MD: Boating Almanac, 1986.

Calvert Marine Museum. *Working the Water: The Commercial Fisheries of Maryland's Patuxent River*. Ed. Paula J. Johnson. Charlottesville: University Press of Virginia, 1988.

Chapman, Charles F. *Piloting, Seamanship, and Small Boat Handling*. 51st ed. New York: Motor Boating & Sailing, 1975.

de Gast, Robert. *The Oystermen of the Chesapeake*. Camden ME: International Marine, 1970.

Ellis, William S. "Hampton Roads: Where Rivers End." *National Geographic*. Washington DC: National Geographic Society, July 1985: 72–107.

Hays, Anne, and Harriet Hazleton. *Chesapeake Kaleidoscope*. Cambridge MD: Tidewater, 1975.

Hedeen, Robert A. *The Oyster: The Life and Lore of the Celebrated Bivalve*. Centreville MD: Tidewater, 1986.

Holly, David C. *Steamboat on the Chesapeake: Emma Giles and the Tolchester Line*. Centreville MD: Tidewater, 1987.

Horton, Tom. *Bay Country: Reflections on the Chesapeake*. New York: Ticknor & Fields, 1989.

Klingel, Gilbert C. *The Bay. A Naturalist Discovers a Universe of Life Above and Below the Chesapeake*. Baltimore: Johns Hopkins University Press, 1984.

Lippson, Alice Jane, and Robert L. Lippson. *Life in the Chesapeake Bay*. Baltimore: Johns Hopkins University Press, 1997.

Peffer, Randall. *Watermen*. Baltimore: Johns Hopkins University Press, 1985.

Rothrock, Joseph T., and Jane C. Rothrock. *Chesapeake Odysseys: An 1883 Cruise Revisited*. Centreville MD: Tidewater, 1984.

Schubel, J. R. *The Living Chesapeake*. Baltimore: Johns Hopkins University Press, 1981.

Shomette, Donald G. *Pirates on the Chesapeake: Being a True History of Pirates, Picaroons, and Raiders on Chesapeake Bay, 1610–1807*. Centreville MD: Tidewater, 1985.

———. *Shipwrecks on the Chesapeake: Maritime Disasters on Chesapeake Bay and Its Tributaries, 1608–1978*. Centreville MD: Tidewater, 1982.

Townsend, Sallie, and Virginia Ericson. *Boating Weather: How to Predict It, What to Do About It*. New York: McKay, 1978.

Warner, William W. *Beautiful Swimmers: Watermen, Crabs, and the Chesapeake Bay*. New York: Penguin Books, 1987.

Wennersten, John R. *The Oyster Wars of Chesapeake Bay*. Centreville MD: Tidewater, 1981.

Whitehead, John H., III. *The Watermen of the Chesapeake Bay*. Centreville MD: Tidewater, 1987.

INDEX